The Oedipus
Casebook

STUDIES IN VIOLENCE, MIMESIS, AND CULTURE

The Oedipus Casebook

Reading Sophocles' *Oedipus the King*

Edited by Mark R. Anspach

with a new translation of *Oedipus Tyrannus* by Wm. Blake Tyrrell

Michigan State University Press · *East Lansing*

Michigan State University Press
East Lansing, Michigan 48823-5245

LIBRARY OF CONGRESS CATALOGING-IN-PUBLICATION DATA
Names: Anspach, Mark Rogin, 1959- editor. | Tyrrell, William Blake, translator.
| Sophocles. Oedipus Rex. English. 2019.
Title: The Oedipus Casebook : Reading Sophocles' Oedipus the King
/ edited by Mark R. Anspach ; with a new translation of Oedipus Tyrannus by Wm. Blake Tyrrell.
Other titles: Studies in violence, mimesis, and culture.
Description: East Lansing : Michigan State University Press, 2019.
| Series: Studies in violence, mimesis, and culture
Identifiers: LCCN 2018059547| ISBN 9781611863390 (pbk. : alk. paper)
| ISBN 9781609176150 (pdf) | ISBN 9781628953787 (epub) | ISBN 9781628963793 (kindle)
Subjects: LCSH: Sophocles. Oedipus Rex. | Greek drama (Tragedy)—History and criticism.
| Violence in literature. | Murder in literature.
Classification: LCC PA4417 .O33 2019 | DDC 882/.01—dc23
LC record available at https://lccn.loc.gov/2018059547

Book design by Charlie Sharp, Sharp Des!gns, East Lansing, MI
Cover design by David Drummond, Salamander Design, www.salamanderhill.com.
Cover art: Bartolomeo Pinelli, *Edipo Uccide Laio Suo Padre Senza Conoscerlo*, 1830.
Rome, Istituto Centrale per la Grafica. Used by kind permission
of the Ministero per i Beni e le Attività Culturali.

Visit Michigan State University Press at *www.msupress.org*

Contents

Preface

Mark R. Anspach

The Great Age of Greek Enlightenment was also, like our own time, an Age of Persecution.

—E. R. Dodds, *The Greeks and the Irrational*

Who killed Laius? At its most literal level, *Oedipus Tyrannus* is a murder mystery. "But no one who sees or reads the play can rest content with its literal coherence," notes Francis Fergusson. "Questions as to its meaning arise at once: Is Oedipus really guilty, or simply a victim of the gods, of his famous complex, of fate, of original sin?"[1] Or is he, like the Oedipal protagonist of Philip Roth's novel *The Human Stain*, a victim of collective persecution: a scapegoat?

In *The Idea of a Theater* (1949), Fergusson describes Oedipus as "the diagrammatic royal scapegoat, a marked man, from the first."[2] A half-century later, in reflections on "the idea of the tragic" reprinted here, Terry Eagleton remarks that tragedy "means 'goat song,' but it might perhaps be better translated as 'scapegoat song.'" We are all familiar with scapegoating, but the ritual context in which Sophocles created his play has long since become strange and exotic. Yet something about it still speaks to us today. When, in his tale of a respected dean and classics professor hounded out of fictional Athena College, Roth invokes "the great cathartic cycle" enacted annually in "an outdoor theater sacred to Dionysus," the reference strikes a chord.[3] This is so even if we have never heard the poignant notes of a song sung at the sacrifice of a goat—to cite Walter Burkert's reconstruction here of the meaning of *tragōidia*.

The opening casebook readings approach the ritual background to Sophocles' play from three different angles: the birth of tragedy in the festival of Dionysus; the ritual expulsion of the *pharmakos* in times of danger or during the festival for Apollo; and the Greek custom of abandoning babies with congenital defects to die of exposure. A deformed foot could mark Oedipus for expulsion even if he were simply born that way. When a plague struck Thebes, his lameness and marginal status as a foreign ruler might make him an ideal candidate to cast out in hopes of propitiating the gods. And the willingness of Oedipus to sacrifice himself for the good of his city may be likened to the way an animal victim bows its head in consent.

The studies in Part One prepare the way for the parallels between Oedipus and ritual victims developed in Part Two. It is important to emphasize that comparing Oedipus to a sacrificial victim or *pharmakos* does not mean he is either of these things. Oedipus is not literally sacrificed, nor is he formally designated as a *pharmakos*. In fact, the play ends before the decision to expel him has even been made, a point explored here by Helene Foley. One cannot fully understand *Oedipus* without some grasp of its religious backdrop, but it would be a mistake to construe it or any tragedy as deriving straightforwardly from a particular ritual. "No ritual need be seen as the source," observes Wm. Blake Tyrrell.[4] The playwright draws freely on a common store of related ideas present in the culture.

"It is evident that the Oedipus myth is intimately associated with rites analogous to those involving the pharmakos, but," René Girard cautions, "we must take care not to confuse the myth and ritual, on the one hand, with the essentially antimythical and antiritualist inspiration of the drama on the other."[5] Girard is the author who has thought most systematically and influentially about the relationship of tragedy to sacrifice. Terry Eagleton has called him "without doubt the most eminent theorist of sacrifice of modern times," while also voicing a number of objections.[6] One is directly relevant here: "Tragedy, scapegoating and sacrifice are too hastily conflated."[7]

This assertion is somewhat surprising. Far from conflating Greek tragedy with sacrifice, Girard interprets it as testifying to a historic breakdown in the very institution of sacrifice—what he terms a "sacrificial crisis." Greek tragedy belongs to a time of transition between an archaic religious order and the emergence of a more "modern" order based on state power and a judicial system.[8] The old religious order was founded on sacrifice and presupposed a distinction between sacrificial and nonsacrificial violence. Because sacrificial violence is sanctioned by the entire community, it does not provoke reprisals. For Girard, the ultimate purpose of sacrifice and religion as a whole "is to prevent the recurrence of reciprocal violence."[9] It follows that the decay of the sacrificial system favors the emergence of reciprocal violence.[10] Greek tragedy is rife with such violence. Reciprocity and symmetry characterize the relationship between tragic antagonists. Any distinguishing traits they may initially possess tend to disappear in the course of the conflict.[11] The sacrificial crisis can thus also be defined as a "crisis of distinctions—that is, a crisis affecting the cultural order" founded on sacrifice.[12]

The chorus in *Oedipus* associates the failure to respect the authority of the oracles with a more general decline of traditional religion: "Apollo is no longer honored with splendor anywhere; the worship of the gods is on the wane."[13] In an early essay on the play, Girard suggested that Oedipus unwittingly sets himself up for the victim's role by not resting content with traditional religious procedures. He could have ordered "a nice expiatory ceremony" featuring an animal sacrifice. But Oedipus "abstains from sacrificing. And he ends up taking the place of the unsacrificed goat."[14] In other words, Oedipus is not a ritual victim; he is a victim of the kind of spontaneous scapegoating that breaks out in the midst of a sacrificial crisis, when the cathartic function of ritual sacrifice has been lost.[15]

Seeing Oedipus as a scapegoat leads to a new question: did he really commit the deeds of which he is accused? Our preconceived ideas about the play may cause us to overlook the exculpatory evidence that, as Kurt Fosso has written elsewhere, is "hidden in plain view."[16] The selections in Part Three reexamine the trial of Oedipus. For, as Michel Foucault shows here, the play can be said to unfold in "the form of a trial. It is not, of course, a total and exhaustive representation of a trial, yet there is a perfectly clear judicial paradigm organized around the question of how to discover the guilty party whose crime has been established, but whose identity remains unknown."[17]

Foucault and the two authors who follow accept the conventional assumption that Oedipus must be the guilty party despite the notable discrepancies in the testimony against him. The last three texts argue cogently but more controversially that Sophocles would not have introduced those discrepancies and left them unresolved if he wished the guilt of his protagonist to be established unequivocally.

In the end, we cannot know what Sophocles thought. He "remains elusive," Girard comments here. The aim of the closing section is not to reach a final verdict, but simply to encourage readers to look at the play with fresh eyes. The empirical question of who killed Laius is, Sandor Goodhart writes, "less important than the universal matrix of scapegoat politics" concealed behind it. Guilty or not, one man cannot be the sole cause of his city's ills. Clearly, more is at work in the downfall of Oedipus. Helene Foley recognizes in him "the kind of leader a democracy would both love and desire to ostracize." Perhaps that is why the cathartic cycle enacted in the theater of Dionysus still speaks to our own enlightened age. It continues to play out around us.

"Practically no feature of ancient religion is so alien," notes Walter Burkert, as the kind of animal sacrifice whose memory "stands in the center of the Dionysiac performance." We no longer practice ritual sacrifice, but we do resort to other means of catharsis. There is nothing alien in the spectacle of an individual first raised to the loftiest heights, then stigmatized as the lowliest filth, an *agos* or smirch on the community—in Philip Roth's rendering, a *human stain*.

"It was strange to think," remarks Roth's narrator as he surveys the maligned protagonist's colleagues, "that people so well educated and professionally civil should have fallen so willingly for the venerable human dream of a situation in which one man can embody evil. Yet there is this need, and it is undying and it is profound."[18]

———

If the story of Oedipus is unsettling, the language with which Sophocles tells it can be, too. Looking at the tragedy with fresh eyes requires a translation that captures the power of Sophocles' words as they were written. Staying as close as possible to the original Greek, distinguished classics scholar Wm. B. Tyrrell has rendered each line or group of five lines with corresponding lines in English. The facing Greek text is the version established by Hugh Lloyd-Jones and Nigel G. Wilson for the Oxford Classical Text of Sophocles.

The present critical edition of *Oedipus the King* was the brainchild of Bill Johnsen. He asked me to compile the casebook readings, encouraging me to bring together many of the authors I had cited in my introductory essay to *Oedipus Unbound* (and insisting that at least part of that essay also be included here). I am grateful to Bill for everything he did along the way to facilitate this project and see it through to completion. He and Bill Tyrrell graciously took on the task of verifying the Greek, not only in the text of the play, but in the numerous quotations scattered throughout the book. Special thanks are due to the editorial staff of Michigan State University Press for their cooperation with the particular challenges entailed in a project of this nature. The publication of this book was made possible by support from the Imitatio program of the Thiel Foundation.

NOTES

1. Francis Fergusson, *The Idea of a Theater* (1949; repr., Princeton, NJ: Princeton University Press, 1968), 16.

2. Ibid., 118.

3. Philip Roth, *The Human Stain* (New York: Vintage, 2001), 314.

4. Wm. Blake Tyrrell, *The Sacrifice of Socrates: Athens, Plato, Girard* (East Lansing: Michigan State University Press, 2012), 57.

5. René Girard, *Violence and the Sacred*, trans. Patrick Gregory (Baltimore: Johns Hopkins University Press, 1977), 95.

6. Terry Eagleton, *Radical Sacrifice* (New Haven: Yale University Press, 2018), 58.

7. Ibid., 56.

8. Girard, *Violence and the Sacred*, 42.

9. Ibid., 55.

10. Ibid., 43.

11. Ibid., 46–47.

12. Ibid., 49.

13. See "Symmetry and Dissymmetry in the Myth of Oedipus," trans. Mark R. Anspach, in René Girard, *Oedipus Unbound: Selected Writings on Rivalry and Desire* (Stanford, CA: Stanford University Press, 2004), 76.

14. "*Oedipus* Analyzed," trans. Mark R. Anspach, in Girard, *Oedipus Unbound*, 47.

15. See Girard, *Violence and the Sacred*, 93.

16. Kurt Fosso, "Oedipus Crux: Reasonable Doubt in *Oedipus the King*," *College Literature* 39, no. 3 (Summer 2012): 26–60.

17. See also R. G. Lewis, "The Procedural Basis of Sophocles' *Oedipus Tyrannus*," *Greek, Roman, and Byzantine Studies* 30, no. 1 (1989): 41–66. Lewis argues that the model for the play's action may be less the trial itself than the preliminary inquiry by a commission charged with "gathering information that would identify the criminals and lead to their prosecution" (ibid., 50).

18. Roth, *The Human Stain*, 306–7.

Acknowledgments

Hugh Lloyd Jones and N. G. Wilson, *Sophocles: Fabulae*. Oxford: Oxford University Press, 1990.

Walter Burkert, "Greek Tragedy and Sacrificial Ritual." *Greek, Roman, and Byzantine Studies* 7, no. 2 (1966): 87–121.

Jan Bremmer, "Scapegoat Rituals in Ancient Greece," *Harvard Studies in Classical Philology*, volume 87, edited by D. R. Shackleton Bailey. Cambridge, Mass.: Harvard University Press. Copyright © 1983 by the President and Fellows of Harvard.

Marie Delcourt, "L'enfant exposé." From *Œdipe ou la légende du conquérant* (Droz, 1944; Les Belles Lettres, 1981). Copyright © 1985, Les Belles Lettres, Paris.

Mark R. Anspach, "Editor's Introduction: Imitating Oedipus." In René Girard, *Oedipus Unbound*, ed. Mark R. Anspach (Stanford University Press, 2004), vii–xxvi.

Girard, René. Patrick Gregory (trans.). *Violence and the Sacred*, 68–86 © 1972 Editions Bernard Grasset. English translation © 1977 The Johns Hopkins University Press. Reprinted with Permission of Johns Hopkins University Press.

René Girard, "Oedipus and the Surrogate Victim." *Violence and the Sacred*. Bloomsbury Revelations, 2013. Bloomsbury Academic, an imprint of Bloomsbury Publishing Plc.

"Thomas Mann's Hedgehog." Republished with permission of John Wiley and Sons, Inc., from *Sweet Violence: The Idea of the Tragic*, by Terry Eagleton. Copyright © 2003. Permission conveyed through Copyright Clearance Center, Inc.

Vernant, Jean-Pierre, and Page duBois (trans.). "Ambiguity and Reversal: On the Enigmatic Structure of *Oedipus Rex*." *New Literary History* 9, no. 3 (1978): 475–501. © 1978 *New Literary History*, The University of Virginia. Reprinted with permission of Johns Hopkins University Press.

Helene Peet Foley, "Oedipus as *Pharmakos*." In *Nomodeiktes: Greek Studies in Honor of Martin Ostwald*, ed. Ralph M. Rosen and Joseph Farrell. © University of Michigan Press, 1993.

Michel Foucault, Second Lecture in *Wrong-Doing, Truth-Telling: The Function of Avowal in Justice,* ed. Fabienne Brion and Bernard E. Harcourt, trans. Stephen W. Sawyer. © 2014 The University of Chicago Press.

Greene, William Chase, "The Murderers of Laius." *Transactions of the American Philological Association* 60 (1929), 75–86. © 1929 American Philological Association. Reprinted with permission of Johns Hopkins University Press.

Newton, Rick M. "The Murderers of Laius, Again (Soph. *OT* 106–7)." *Classical World*, 72, no. 4 (1978): 231–34. ©1978 The Classical Association of the Atlantic States, Inc. Reprinted with permission of Johns Hopkins University.

Karl Harshbarger, "Who Killed Laius?" TDR/*Tulane Drama Review* 9, no. 4 (Summer 1965): 120–31. © 1965 by New York University, reprinted by permission of the MIT Press.

Goodhart Sandor, "Ληστάς Εφασχε: Oedipus and Laius' Many Murderers." *diacritics* 8, no. 1 (1978), 55–71. © 1978 Cornell University. Reprinted with permission of Johns Hopkins University Press.

"An Anonymous Namer." From *Sophocles' Oedipus: Evidence and Self-Conviction* by Frederick Ahl. Copyright © 1991 Frederick Ahl. Used by permission of the publisher, Cornell University Press.

Sophocles, *Oedipus Tyrannus*

Greek text edited and annotated by H. Lloyd-Jones and N. G. Wilson

Translated into English by Wm. Blake Tyrrell

The stage building represents the house of Oedipus, tyrant of Thebes. Before its central door stands an altar. Other altars are nearby. One gangway, traditionally the one to the spectators' left, leads to the country. The other leads to the city of Thebes.

Oedipus comes out of his house to find an old man and youth approaching him quickly. He speaks to them as they are arriving and arranging about his altars (16) their suppliant branches of olive festooned with woolen fillets and taking their seats on the steps of his altars (31). By line 10, they have settled themselves.

ΟΙΔΙΠΟΥΣ

ἘΩ τέκνα, Κάδμου τοῦ πάλαι νέα τροφή,
τίνας ποθ' ἕδρας τάσδε μοι θοάζετε
ἱκτηρίοις κλάδοισιν ἐξεστεμμένοι;
πόλις δ' ὁμοῦ μὲν θυμιαμάτων γέμει,
ὁμοῦ δὲ παιάνων τε καὶ στεναγμάτων·   5
ἀγὼ δικαιῶν μὴ παρ' ἀγγέλων, τέκνα,
ἄλλων ἀκούειν αὐτὸς ὧδ' ἐλήλυθα,
ὁ πᾶσι κλεινὸς Οἰδίπους καλούμενος.
ἀλλ', ὦ γεραιέ, φράζ', ἐπεὶ πρέπων ἔφυς
πρὸ τῶνδε φωνεῖν, τίνι τρόπῳ καθέστατε,   10
δείσαντες ἢ στέρξαντες; ὡς θέλοντος ἂν
ἐμοῦ προσαρκεῖν πᾶν· δυσάλγητος γὰρ ἂν
εἴην τοιάνδε μὴ οὐ κατοικτίρων ἕδραν.

ΙΕΡΕΥΣ

ἀλλ', ὦ κρατύνων Οἰδίπους χώρας ἐμῆς,
ὁρᾷς μὲν ἡμᾶς ἡλίκοι προσήμεθα   15
βωμοῖσι τοῖς σοῖς, οἱ μὲν οὐδέπω μακρὰν
πτέσθαι σθένοντες, οἱ δὲ σὺν γήρᾳ βαρεῖς·
ἱερεὺς ἐγὼ μὲν Ζηνός, οἵδε τ' ἠθέων
λεκτοί· τὸ δ' ἄλλο φῦλον ἐξεστεμμένον
ἀγοραῖσι θακεῖ, πρός τε Παλλάδος διπλοῖς   20
ναοῖς, ἐπ' Ἰσμηνοῦ τε μαντείᾳ σποδῷ.
πόλις γάρ, ὥσπερ καὐτὸς εἰσορᾷς, ἄγαν

5 παιάνων] fortasse παιώνων scribendum, cf. 186   7 ἄλλων]
ἐμῶν Meineke (cf. Tr. 391)   8 fortasse om. P.Oxy. 2180: del.
Wunder   11 στέρξαντες Lrp: στέξαντες at: στέργοντες Dawe
(1982)   18 ἱερεὺς Bentley: -εῖς codd.   οἵδε τ' Erfurdt: οἱ δέ τ'
codd. plerique: οἱ δ' KpZr   21 ἐπ' Ἰσμηνοῦ] ἐφ' Ἰ- Dawe
dubitanter

OEDIPUS

    O children, newest of ancient Cadmus'[1] brood,
    why do you hasten to sit here before me,
    garlanded and holding branches of suppliants?
    Everywhere the city is filled with the smell of burnt incense,   5
    everywhere with songs of healing and cries of misery.
    I didn't think it right, children, to hear of this from messengers,
    from others, so I have come myself,
    Oedipus, called renowned in the estimation of all.
  Come, agéd sir, tell me, since you are fitted by birth
    to speak for these, why have you settled here?   10
    Are you stricken with fear or moved by desire? Be assured,
    I willingly offer every support, for I would be hard-hearted
    if I didn't pity such suppliants sitting before me.

PRIEST

    Well, Oedipus, ruler of my country,
    you see what years we have who sit here   15
    at your altars. Some do not yet have the strength
    of far flight, and others are heavy with old age,
    I, priest of Zeus, and these, the chosen of unmarried
    young men. The rest of the people sit garlanded
    in the marketplaces and before the two temples of Pallas,   20
    and at the prophetic ashes of Ismenos.[2]
    The city, as you see for yourself, is already

ἤδη cαλεύει κἀνακουφίcαι κάρα
βυθῶν ἔτ᾽ οὐχ οἷά τε φοινίου cάλου,
φθίνουcα μὲν κάλυξιν ἐγκάρποιc χθονόc,   25
φθίνουcα δ᾽ ἀγέλαιc βουνόμοιc, τόκοιcί τε
ἀγόνοιc γυναικῶν· ἐν δ᾽ ὁ πυρφόροc θεὸc
cκήψαc ἐλαύνει, λοιμὸc ἔχθιcτοc, πόλιν,
ὑφ᾽ οὗ κενοῦται δῶμα Καδμεῖον· μέλαc δ᾽
Ἅιδηc cτεναγμοῖc καὶ γόοιc πλουτίζεται.   30
θεοῖcι μέν νυν οὐκ ἰcούμενόν c᾽ ἐγὼ
οὐδ᾽ οἵδε παῖδεc ἑζόμεcθ᾽ ἐφέcτιοι,
ἀνδρῶν δὲ πρῶτον ἔν τε cυμφοραῖc βίου
κρίνοντεc ἔν τε δαιμόνων cυναλλαγαῖc·
ὅc γ᾽ ἐξέλυcαc ἄcτυ Καδμεῖον μολὼν   35
cκληρᾶc ἀοιδοῦ δαcμὸν ὃν παρείχομεν,
καὶ ταῦθ᾽ ὑφ᾽ ἡμῶν οὐδὲν ἐξειδὼc πλέον
οὐδ᾽ ἐκδιδαχθείc, ἀλλὰ προcθήκῃ θεοῦ
λέγῃ νομίζῃ θ᾽ ἡμὶν ὀρθῶcαι βίον.
νῦν δ᾽, ὦ κράτιcτον πᾶcιν Οἰδίπου κάρα,   40
ἱκετεύομέν cε πάντεc οἵδε πρόcτροποι
ἀλκήν τιν᾽ εὑρεῖν ἡμίν, εἴτε του θεῶν
φήμην ἀκούcαc εἴτ᾽ ἀπ᾽ ἀνδρὸc οἶcθά που·
ὡc τοῖcιν ἐμπείροιcι καὶ τὰc ξυμφορὰc
ζώcαc ὁρῶ μάλιcτα τῶν βουλευμάτων.   45
ἴθ᾽, ὦ βροτῶν ἄριcτ᾽, ἀνόρθωcον πόλιν·
ἴθ᾽, εὐλαβήθηθ᾽· ὡc cὲ νῦν μὲν ἥδε γῆ
cωτῆρα κλῄζει τῆc πάροc προθυμίαc,

29 Καδμεῖον LrpZrt: -είων pa   31 ἰcούμενον] -οc Stanley:
-οι Musgrave   35 Καδμεῖον Lp: -είων rpa   36 ὅν] ἥ
Herwerden   37 ὑφ᾽] ἀφ᾽ Blaydes   40 δ᾽ r: τ᾽ cett.
42 εὑρεῖν ἡμὶν at: ἡμὶν εὑρεῖν lrp   43 που Gᵃᶜpat: του Lrp
44–5 καὶ τὰc ξυμφορὰc et τῶν βουλευμάτων permutavit Toup
post v. 44 vel 45 lacunam statuendam censet Dawe; si tradita sana sunt,
locum similem invenias ap. A. Pers. 528   48 πάροc L s.l.,
rpat: πάλαι Lp   προθυμίαc] προμηθίαc Gγρ: προμηθείαc
Rp

reeling, no longer able to lift its head
from the depths of the bloody surge,
wasting in the earth's fruits encased in pods,   25
wasting in grazing herds and in the barren birthing
of its women. And more. The fever-bearing god,
a plague most hated, falls upon and strikes the city.
By him is the house of Cadmus emptied, and dark
Hades grows wealthy in wailing and lamentation.   30
I and these children sit at the hearth in supplication,
not because we judge you to be equal to the gods
but foremost among men in the vicissitudes of life
and in dealings with the daimons,[3]
since you came to the city of Cadmus and set us free   35
of that harsh singer's tribute we were paying,
this, too, without further knowledge or instruction from us
but with the aid of a god. For this you are said
and considered to have restored our lives to us.
Now, head of Oedipus most powerful in the estimation of all,   40
we, all these who sit as suppliants, we beseech you
to find succor for us either from hearing the voice
of one of the gods or something you know from a man.
I have seen that for men of experience the outcome
of their counsels also proves especially alive.   45
Come, best of mortals, restore the city again.
Come, take care. Since this land now calls
you savior because of your past zeal on its behalf,

ἀρχῆς δὲ τῆς σῆς μηδαμῶς μεμνήμεθα
στάντες τ᾽ ἐς ὀρθὸν καὶ πεσόντες ὕστερον.   50
ἀλλ᾽ ἀσφαλείᾳ τήνδ᾽ ἀνόρθωσον πόλιν.
ὄρνιθι γὰρ καὶ τὴν τότ᾽ αἰσίῳ τύχην
παρέσχες ἡμῖν, καὶ τανῦν ἴσος γενοῦ.
ὡς εἴπερ ἄρξεις τῆσδε γῆς, ὥσπερ κρατεῖς,
ξὺν ἀνδράσιν κάλλιον ἢ κενῆς κρατεῖν·   55
ὡς οὐδέν ἐστιν οὔτε πύργος οὔτε ναῦς
ἐρῆμος ἀνδρῶν μὴ ξυνοικούντων ἔσω.
Οι.   ὦ παῖδες οἰκτροί, γνωτὰ κοὐκ ἄγνωτά μοι
προσήλθεθ᾽ ἱμείροντες, εὖ γὰρ οἶδ᾽ ὅτι
νοσεῖτε πάντες· καὶ νοσοῦντες, ὡς ἐγὼ   60
οὐκ ἔστιν ὑμῶν ὅστις ἐξ ἴσου νοσεῖ.
τὸ μὲν γὰρ ὑμῶν ἄλγος εἰς ἕν᾽ ἔρχεται
μόνον καθ᾽ αὑτόν, κοὐδέν᾽ ἄλλον, ἡ δ᾽ ἐμὴ
ψυχὴ πόλιν τε κἀμὲ καὶ σ᾽ ὁμοῦ στένει.
ὥστ᾽ οὐχ ὕπνῳ γ᾽ εὕδοντά μ᾽ ἐξεγείρετε,   65
ἀλλ᾽ ἴστε πολλὰ μέν με δακρύσαντα δή,
πολλὰς δ᾽ ὁδοὺς ἐλθόντα φροντίδος πλάνοις.
ἣν δ᾽ εὖ σκοπῶν ηὕρισκον ἴασιν μόνην,
ταύτην ἔπραξα· παῖδα γὰρ Μενοικέως
Κρέοντ᾽, ἐμαυτοῦ γαμβρόν, ἐς τὰ Πυθικὰ   70
ἔπεμψα Φοίβου δώμαθ᾽, ὡς πύθοιθ᾽ ὅ τι
δρῶν ἢ τί φωνῶν τήνδ᾽ ἐρυσαίμην πόλιν.
καί μ᾽ ἦμαρ ἤδη ξυμμετρούμενον χρόνῳ
λυπεῖ τί πράσσει· τοῦ γὰρ εἰκότος πέρα

---

49 μεμνήμεθα Herwerden et Nauck: -ήμεθα p: -ώμεθα Lrat:
-ώμεθα Eustathius 1305. 48 et 1332. 18   50 τ᾽ a: γ᾽ t: om. LrpXs
54 ὡς] ἀλλ᾽ Suda s.v. κενόν   ὥσπερ] ἤσπερ Blaydes   54–7 del.
van Deventer, 56–7 Reeve   57 ἔσω] πόλιν Stobaeus 4. 7. 2
59–60 sic interpunxit Barrett   63–4 vv. in unum conflat Stobaeus
loc. cit.   65 ὕπνῳ γ᾽] ὕπνων r   εὕδοντα] ἐνδόντα Badham
post Reiske   67 πλάνοις LᵖᶜKΛrpt: -αις Lᵃᶜpa, T s.l.
72 ἐρυσαίμην LᵖᶜPaᵃᶜV: ἐρυσάμην l: ῥυσαίμην rpat: ῥυσοίμην Linwood   73–5 del. L. Dindorf   74 πέρα] πέρᾳ Porson, v. 75
deleto

       let us not at all remember your rule
       as the time when we stood upright and later fell,   50
       but, rather, restore this city on steadfast foundation.
       With auspicious omen, you gave us good fortune
       back then. Now in these times, prove yourself your equal.
       If you will rule this land, since you hold the power,
       more beautiful is it to hold power with men than over an empty land. 55
       Neither tower nor ship is anything
       bereft of men dwelling within together.

Oe   Pitiable sons, you have come yearning for things
       known to me, not unknown, for I know well that
       all of you are sick, and yet, though you are sick,   60
       there is none among you who is as sick as I.[4]
       Your pain comes to each of you,
       alone and by himself, and no other, but my spirit
       aches for the city, for myself, and for you together.
       So, as it is, you do not arouse me from sound sleep.   65
       Know, rather, that I have shed many tears and
       traversed many avenues in the wanderings of my thought.
       I thought well, and the only remedy I could find
       I have acted upon. The son of Menoeceus,
       Creon, my brother-in-law, I sent to Phoebus'   70
       Pythian house[5] so that he may inquire
       by what deed or word I could rescue this city.
       Already the day measured against time gone by
       distresses me over how he fares. He has been gone

ἄπεστι, πλείω τοῦ καθήκοντος χρόνου. 75
ὅταν δ' ἵκηται, τηνικαῦτ' ἐγὼ κακὸς
μὴ δρῶν ἂν εἴην πάνθ' ὅς' ἂν δηλοῖ θεός.

Ἰε. ἀλλ' ἐς καλὸν σύ τ' εἶπας, οἵδε τ' ἀρτίως
Κρέοντα προσστείχοντα σημαίνουσί μοι.

Οι. ὦναξ Ἄπολλον, εἰ γὰρ ἐν τύχῃ γέ τῳ 80
σωτῆρι βαίη λαμπρὸς ὥσπερ ὄμμα τι.

Ἰε. ἀλλ' εἰκάσαι μέν, ἡδύς· οὐ γὰρ ἂν κάρα
πολυστεφὴς ὧδ' εἷρπε παγκάρπου δάφνης.

Οι. τάχ' εἰσόμεσθα· ξύμμετρος γὰρ ὡς κλύειν.
ἄναξ, ἐμὸν κήδευμα, παῖ Μενοικέως, 85
τίν' ἡμὶν ἥκεις τοῦ θεοῦ φήμην φέρων;

ΚΡΕΩΝ
ἐσθλήν· λέγω γὰρ καὶ τὰ δύσφορ', εἰ τύχοι
κατ' ὀρθὸν ἐξιόντα, πάντ' ἂν εὐτυχεῖν.

Οι. ἔστιν δὲ ποῖον τοὔπος; οὔτε γὰρ θρασὺς
οὔτ' οὖν προδείσας εἰμὶ τῷ γε νῦν λόγῳ. 90

Κρ. εἰ τῶνδε χρῄζεις πλησιαζόντων κλύειν,
ἕτοιμος εἰπεῖν, εἴτε καὶ στείχειν ἔσω.

Οι. ἐς πάντας αὔδα. τῶνδε γὰρ πλέον φέρω
τὸ πένθος ἢ καὶ τῆς ἐμῆς ψυχῆς πέρι.

Κρ. λέγοιμ' ἂν οἷ' ἤκουσα τοῦ θεοῦ πάρα. 95
ἄνωγεν ἡμᾶς Φοῖβος ἐμφανῶς, ἄναξ,
μίασμα χώρας, ὡς τεθραμμένον χθονὶ
ἐν τῇδ', ἐλαύνειν μηδ' ἀνήκεστον τρέφειν.

Οι. ποίῳ καθαρμῷ; τίς ὁ τρόπος τῆς ξυμφορᾶς;

75 χρόνου] -ον V, coni. Purgold   77 ὅς' ἂν Cat: ὅσα lrp
78 σύ Lᵖᶜ**pat**: εὔ **lp**: cὺ εὔ **r**   79 προσστείχοντα R, et voluit C,
coni. Erfurdt: προστ- cett.   81 ὥσπερ] ὡς ἐν r**H**   λαμπρὸς]
φαιδρὸς Nauck   ὄμμα τι Wex: ὄμματι codd.   82 εἰκάσαι μέν]
εἰκάσαιμ' ἂν **r**   86 φήμην] φάτιν Zc   87 δύσφορ']
δύσθρο' Heimsoeth   88 ἐξιόντα Suda s.v. δύσφορα: ἐξελθόντα
codd.   εὐτυχεῖν] εὐ τυχεῖν Blaydes   96 v. sic interpunxit Firn-
haber   97 ὡς τεθραμμένον] ἐντεθραμμένον Blaydes
98 ἐν τῇδ'] ἐκ τῆςδ' **rC**   99 ξυμφορᾶς (ξυμ- L**rpat**: cυμ- **pa**,
T s.l.)] fortasse προσφορᾶς

beyond what is reasonable, more than the usual time.   75
Whenever he does arrive, I would be evil
if I do not accomplish all that the god reveals.

[*Those present with the priest attract his attention.*]

Pr You spoke opportunely. These just now
point out to me that Creon is approaching.
Oe O lord Apollo, may he come to us as brilliant   80
with some saving fortune as is his eye.
Pr Well, to guess, it is welcome news. Otherwise, he would not go
about like this with his head garlanded in laurel laden with fruit.

[*Creon enters by the gangway from the country. He wears a laurel
wreath (83).*]

Oe We shall soon know, for he is within hearing distance.
Lord, my kinsman, son of Menoeceus,   85
what message have you come bringing from the god?
Creon
Good news. I also say[6] things hard to bear. But if they turn out
aright, everything will be fortunate.
Oe What sort of response is this? I am neither cheered
nor frightened by what you're saying now.   90
Cr If you want to hear with these people close by,
I am ready to say it to you or else to go inside.
Oe Speak before everyone. I bear grief for them
more than even for my own life.[7]
Cr Then let me tell you what I heard from the god.   95
Phoebus clearly commands us, lord, to drive
from the country miasma that has been nourished
in this land and not to nourish it until it is past healing.
Oe By what sort of purification? What kind of misfortune?

Κρ.   ἀνδρηλατοῦντας, ἢ φόνῳ φόνον πάλιν   100
      λύοντας, ὡς τόδ᾽ αἷμα χειμάζον πόλιν.
Οι.   ποίου γὰρ ἀνδρὸς τήνδε μηνύει τύχην;
Κρ.   ἦν ἡμίν, ὦναξ, Λάιός ποθ᾽ ἡγεμὼν
      γῆς τῆσδε, πρὶν σὲ τήνδ᾽ ἀπευθύνειν πόλιν.
Οι.   ἔξοιδ᾽ ἀκούων· οὐ γὰρ εἰσεῖδόν γέ πω.   105
Κρ.   τούτου θανόντος νῦν ἐπιστέλλει σαφῶς
      τοὺς αὐτοέντας χειρὶ τιμωρεῖν τινας.
Οι.   οἱ δ᾽ εἰσὶ ποῦ γῆς; ποῦ τόδ᾽ εὑρεθήσεται
      ἴχνος παλαιᾶς δυστέκμαρτον αἰτίας;
Κρ.   ἐν τῇδ᾽ ἔφασκε γῇ. τὸ δὲ ζητούμενον   110
      ἁλωτόν, ἐκφεύγει δὲ τἀμελούμενον.
Οι.   πότερα δ᾽ ἐν οἴκοις, ἢ 'ν ἀγροῖς ὁ Λάιος,
      ἢ γῆς ἐπ᾽ ἄλλης τῷδε συμπίπτει φόνῳ;
Κρ.   θεωρός, ὡς ἔφασκεν, ἐκδημῶν πάλιν
      πρὸς οἶκον οὐκέθ᾽ ἵκεθ᾽, ὡς ἀπεστάλη.   115
Οι.   οὐδ᾽ ἄγγελός τις οὐδὲ συμπράκτωρ ὁδοῦ
      κατεῖδ᾽, ὅτου τις ἐκμαθὼν ἐχρήσατ᾽ ἄν;
Κρ.   θνῄσκουσι γάρ, πλὴν εἷς τις, ὃς φόβῳ φυγὼν
      ὧν εἶδε πλὴν ἓν οὐδὲν εἶχ᾽ εἰδὼς φράσαι.
Οι.   τὸ ποῖον; ἓν γὰρ πόλλ᾽ ἂν ἐξεύροι μαθεῖν,   120
      ἀρχὴν βραχεῖαν εἰ λάβοιμεν ἐλπίδος.
Κρ.   λῃστὰς ἔφασκε συντυχόντας οὐ μιᾷ
      ῥώμῃ κτανεῖν νιν, ἀλλὰ σὺν πλήθει χερῶν.

101 χειμάζον L in linea Gpat: -ει L s.l. Rp, Xr s.l.
102 τήνδε Rpat: τῇδε lG   105 γέ πω] γ᾽ ἐγώ Hartung
106 σαφῶς] θεός Nauck   107 τινας fere codd. (vel τινάς, ut
LᵃᶜK): τινα Aᵖᶜ, quam lectionem iam ex ed. Mediolanensi Sudae s.v.
ἐπιστέλλει cognitam probauerunt multi inde a Schaefer: θεός Heimsoeth
111 ἐκφεύγει] -ειν Valckenaer   114 ἔφασκεν] -ον Kousis: -ετ᾽
Blaydes   117 κατεῖδ᾽ P.Oxy. 2180, at: -δεν lrp
120 ἐξεύροι μαθεῖν codd.:]υροιμαθ[P.Oxy. 2180: ἐξεύροι μαθών
Herwerden: an ἐξεύροις μαθών?   121 λάβοιμεν ἐλπίδος
codd.:] . . μ . [ita praebet P.Oxy. 2180 ut potius υμυ – quam οιμx – ∪ –
habuisse videatur: λάβοι τις ἐλπίδος Herwerden: an εἰ λάβοις
προθυμίας?

Cr   By banishing one or more men or again redeeming murder
            for murder,[8]   100
     since this blood unleashes the cold storms of winter upon the city.
Oe   What man's misfortune does the god reveal?[9]
Cr   Once we had Laïos as the leader of this land,
     lord, before you began to steer this city aright.[10]
Oe   I know. I've heard of him, but I never saw him.   105
Cr   The god clearly enjoins us to take vengeance by force of hand
     on the murderers of this dead man—whoever they are.[11]
Oe   Where on earth are they? Where will be found
     this footprint, hard to discern, of an old guilt?
Cr   Apollo kept saying in this land. That which is sought   110
     is caught, but what is neglected escapes.
Oe   In his house or the fields or in another land
     did Laïos encounter this murder?
Cr   "Away to consult the oracle," Laïos kept saying.
     He did not arrive again home after he set off.   115
Oe   Did no messenger arrive or fellow traveler on the journey have
            knowledge
     from whom, if one learned it, he could put it to use?
Cr   No, they are dead except for one who fled in panic and had
            nothing
     to say with certain knowledge of what he had seen except one
            thing.
Oe   What was it? One thing might uncover ways to learn many,   120
     if we could get a small beginning of hope.
Cr   Bandits, he kept saying, bandits happened upon and slew him[12]
     not with the strength of one but with a throng of hands.

Οι. πῶς οὖν ὁ λῃστής, εἴ τι μὴ ξὺν ἀργύρῳ
     ἐπράσσετ' ἐνθένδ', ἐς τόδ' ἂν τόλμης ἔβη;   125
Κρ. δοκοῦντα ταῦτ' ἦν· Λαΐου δ' ὀλωλότος
     οὐδεὶς ἀρωγὸς ἐν κακοῖς ἐγίγνετο.
Οι. κακὸν δὲ ποῖον ἐμποδὼν τυραννίδος
     οὕτω πεσούσης εἶργε τοῦτ' ἐξειδέναι;
Κρ. ἡ ποικιλῳδὸς Σφὶγξ τὸ πρὸς ποςὶ σκοπεῖν   130
     μεθέντας ἡμᾶς τἀφανῆ προσήγετο.
Οι. ἀλλ' ἐξ ὑπαρχῆς αὖθις αὔτ' ἐγὼ φανῶ.
     ἐπαξίως γὰρ Φοῖβος, ἀξίως δὲ cù
     πρὸ τοῦ θανόντος τήνδ' ἔθεσθ' ἐπιστροφήν·
     ὥστ' ἐνδίκως ὄψεσθε κἀμὲ σύμμαχον,   135
     γῇ τῇδε τιμωροῦντα τῷ θεῷ θ' ἅμα.
     ὑπὲρ γὰρ οὐχὶ τῶν ἀπωτέρω φίλων
     ἀλλ' αὐτὸς αὑτοῦ τοῦτ' ἀποσκεδῶ μύcoc.
     ὅcτιc γὰρ ἦν ἐκεῖνον ὁ κτανὼν τάχ' ἂν
     κἄμ' ἂν τοιαύτῃ χειρὶ τιμωρεῖν θέλοι.   140
     κείνῳ προσαρκῶν οὖν ἐμαυτὸν ὠφελῶ.
     ἀλλ' ὡς τάχιστα, παῖδες, ὑμεῖς μὲν βάθρων
     ἵcταcθε, τούcδ' ἄραντες ἱκτῆρας κλάδους,
     ἄλλος δὲ Κάδμου λαὸν ὧδ' ἀθροιζέτω,
     ὡς πᾶν ἐμοῦ δράσοντος. ἢ γὰρ εὐτυχεῖς   145
     cὺν τῷ θεῷ φανούμεθ', ἢ πεπτωκότες.
Ιε. ὦ παῖδες, ἱcτώμεcθα· τῶνδε γὰρ χάριν
     καὶ δεῦρ' ἔβημεν ὧν ὅδ' ἐξαγγέλλεται.
     Φοῖβος δ' ὁ πέμψας τάσδε μαντείας ἅμα
     cωτήρ θ' ἵκοιτο καὶ νόcου παυστήριος.   150

---

127 ἐγίγνετο] ἐφαίνετο Nauck   129 εἶργε LRpat: εἴ-
Gpa   130 τὸ Lrpt: τὰ Ha   134 πρὸ LᵖᶜCat: πρὸς
LᵃᶜKrp   τήνδ' . . . ἐπιστροφήν] τήνδε θεσπίζει γραφήν Lγρ
138 αὑτοῦ LᵃᶜKrpa: αὑ- LᵖᶜPaa   139 ἐκεῖνον rpat: -oc
Lp Suda s.v. ἀπωτέρω   141 om. Lᵃᶜ   145 πᾶν] πάντ' t
δράcοντος codd. plerique: -αντος Lᵃᶜ(?), Kp

Oe	How could a bandit, unless he were acting with silver	
	from here, reach such lengths of boldness?	125
Cr	Those were our thoughts at the time, but with Laïos dead,	
	no champion appeared amid our troubles.	
Oe	After the tyranny had fallen like this, what trouble	
	impeded and prevented knowing this thoroughly?[13]	
Cr	The riddle-singing Sphinx induced us to look to	130
	what was here at our feet, and let go what lay hidden.	
Oe	Well, I shall make this clear again from the beginning.	
	How very rightly Phoebus and how rightly you, Creon,	
	have imposed this attention on behalf of the dead.	
	Thus, as is just, you will see me also an ally	135
	in taking vengeance for this land and the god together.	
	Not for the sake of far-distant friends	
	but for me myself shall I myself dispel this abomination.	
	Whoever it was who slew that man may perhaps want to	
	take vengeance upon me with similar force.	140
	Therefore, by aiding him, I am helping myself.[14]	
	Come now, as quickly as you can, sons, stand up	
	from the steps, and pick up your suppliant branches.	
	Let another gather here the host of Cadmus' people.	
	I shall do everything. Either we shall be seen	145
	to be prosperous with the god's help or fallen.	

[*Since Creon does not hear the exchange between Oedipus and Tiresias, he must exit now.*]

Pr	Sons, let us stand up. We came here	
	for what he proclaims he will do.	
	May Phoebus who sent these oracles	
	come, our savior and allayer of sickness.	150

ΧΟΡΟΣ

ὦ Διὸς ἁδυεπὲς φάτι, τίς ποτε τᾶς
    πολυχρύσου   στρ. α'
Πυθῶνος ἀγλαὰς ἔβας
Θήβας; ἐκτέταμαι φοβερὰν φρένα δείματι
    πάλλων,
ἰήιε Δάλιε Παιάν,
ἀμφὶ coì ἁζόμενος· τί μοι ἢ νέον   155
ἢ περιτελλομέναις ὥραις πάλιν ἐξανύσεις χρέος;
εἰπέ μοι, ὦ χρυσέας τέκνον Ἐλπίδος, ἄμβροτε
    Φάμα.

πρῶτα σὲ κεκλόμενος, θύγατερ Διός, ἄμβροτ'
    Ἀθάνα,   ἀντ. α'
γαιάοχόν τ' ἀδελφεὰν   160
Ἄρτεμιν, ἃ κυκλόεντ' ἀγορᾶς θρόνον εὐκλέα
    θάccει,
καὶ Φοῖβον ἑκαβόλον αἰτῶ,
τριccοὶ ἀλεξίμοροι προφάνητέ μοι·
εἴ ποτε καὶ προτέρας ἄτας ὑπερορνυμένας
    πόλει   165
ἠνύcατ' ἐκτοπίαν φλόγα πήματος, ἔλθετε καὶ νῦν.

ὦ πόποι, ἀνάριθμα γὰρ φέρω   στρ. β'
πήματα· νοcεῖ δέ μοι πρόπας
στόλος, οὐδ' ἔνι φροντίδος ἔγχος   170
ᾧ τις ἀλέξεται· οὔτε γὰρ ἔκγονα
κλυτᾶς χθονὸς αὔξεται οὔτε τόκοισιν
ἰηίων καμάτων ἀνέχουσι γυναῖκες.

151 ἁδυεπὲς LP: ἡδυ- vel -επὴς cett.   153 πάλλων]
πολλῷ Lγρ   154 Παιάν] fortasse Παιών   157 Φάμα]
Φήμα P, probat Dawe; cf. 475   159 πρῶτα cὲ Wunder: πρῶτά
cε codd. plerique: de Lᵃᶜ non liquet (πρώτην cε K): πρώταν γε Lγρ
κεκλόμενος Lrpat: -ομένῳ a: κέκλομαι ὦ Blaydes   ἄμβροτ']
ὄβριμ' Herwerden   162 εὐκλέα Lpt: -εᾶ rpa: Εὔκλεα Elmsley
163 αἰτῶ Blaydes: ἰὼ ἰὼ fere codd.: ἰὼ Heath   165 ὑπερορνυμένας Musgrave: ὕπερ ὀρνυμένας codd.

[*The priest and the others remove their wreaths from the altar's steps and exit. Nothing is said of Oedipus, so he presumably remains during the Chorus' entrance song. In line 216, he indicates that he has heard their prayers.*]

CHORUS OF THEBAN OLD MEN [*enters, singing and dancing.*]
O message from Zeus sweetly spoken, who ever are you
who have come from Pytho
rich in gold to glorious
Thebes? I am wracked, my breast fearful,
aquiver with terror,
iê, iê, Delian Healer,[15]
in awe before you. What debt will you exact from me,   155
whether new or returning in the rounds of seasons?
Tell me, O child of golden Hope, immortal
     Oracle.

Calling first upon you, daughter of Zeus,
     immortal Athena,
and upon my land's protector, your sister   160
Artemis, who sits upon her famed circular
throne in the agora,
and upon Apollo Far-Darter, I beg you,
three defenders against death, appear to me.
If ever when past devastation rose up
     over the city,   165
you banished the flame of pain to outside places, come now also.

Ah the sufferings, I bear pains beyond numbering.
The whole company is sick on me,
and there is no spear conceived by thought   170
for someone to use in our defense. The bounty
of this renowned land grows not, nor do its women
rise from wailing pains with the birthing of children.

ἄλλον δ' ἂν ἄλλα προσίδοις ἅπερ εὔπτερον
ὄρνιν   175
κρεῖσσον ἀμαιμακέτου πυρὸς ὅρμενον
ἀκτὰν πρὸς ἑσπέρου θεοῦ·

ὧν πόλις ἀνάριθμος ὄλλυται·   ἀντ. β'
νηλέα δὲ γένεθλα πρὸς πέδῳ   180
θαναταφόρα κεῖται ἀνοίκτως·
ἐν δ' ἄλοχοι πολιαί τ' ἔπι ματέρες
ἀκτὰν πάρα βώμιον ἄλλοθεν ἄλλαι
λυγρῶν πόνων ἱκτῆρες ἐπιστενάχουσιν.   185
παιὼν δὲ λάμπει στονόεσσά τε γῆρυς ὅμαυλος·
τῶν ὕπερ, ὦ χρυσέα θύγατερ Διός,
εὐῶπα πέμψον ἀλκάν.

Ἀρεά τε τὸν μαλερόν, ὃς   στρ. γ'
νῦν ἄχαλκος ἀσπίδων   191
φλέγει με περιβόητος ἀντιάζων,
παλίσσυτον δράμημα νωτίσαι πάτρας,
ἔπουρον εἴτ' ἐς μέγαν
θάλαμον Ἀμφιτρίτας   195
εἴτ' ἐς τὸν ἀπόξενον ὅρμων
Θρῄκιον κλύδωνα·
τελεῖν γάρ, εἴ τι νὺξ ἀφῇ,

175 ἄλλα Dobree: ἄλλῳ codd.   ἅπερ **rpZrt**: ἅπερ LPa
180 δὲ γένεθλα PSI 1192, **rpa**: δὲ γενέθλα pZr: δ' ἁ γενέθλα LD
181 θαναταφόρα PSI 1192, Kp: de L non liquet: -οφόρῳ **r**: -ηφόρῳ
at: -οφόρα **p**   182 ἔπι Lrpa: ἐπὶ pa (de t non liquet)
184 ἀκτὰν] ἀχὰν Nauck   πάρα (παρὰ) βώμιον **pat**: παρα-
βώμιον Lrpa, quod recepit Nauck   185 ἱκτῆρες] ἱκετῆρες O,
probat Dawe   ἐπιστενάχουσι Krp: ἐπιστο- Lpat   186 παιὼν
PSI 1192, L^ac et lm. sch., **Kt**: παιὰν cett.   188 τῶν habuit PSI 1192
(τω]ν), coni. B. H. Kennedy (1885): ὧν cett.   192 περιβόητος]
-ατος Elmsley   ἀντιάζων] -ῳ Hermann   193 δράμημα
Lpat: δρό- **rp**   194 ἔπουρον LRpt: ἀπ- Gγρ **pa**: ἄπορον GF
196 ὅρμων Doederlein: ὅρμον codd.   198 τελεῖν Hermann:
τέλει codd.: τελεῖ Kayser, qui post γάρ interpunxit   forsitan lateat
gravior corruptela

One on another, as if a well-feathered bird, you could see   175
speeding faster than indomitable fire
to the shore of the western god.

The city is perishing; its dead defy counting.
Its young litter the ground unpitied,   180
spreading pestilence and death, bereft of laments and burial due.
And more. Wives and, besides, gray-haired mothers
along the altar's edge, some here, some there,
wail, suppliants for woeful sufferings.   185
A Healer shines forth. A mournful voice attends.
For this, O golden daughter of Zeus,
send glad-faced succor.

Make it so that Ares the Rager who,   190
unclad in bronze shields of the war god,
now consumes me in his flames, attacking amid cries,
reverses his course, carried by fair winds
from my fatherland to either the great
chamber of Amphitrite's Atlantic   195
or the haven harsh on guests,
the turbulent waters of Thracian Euxine.
Whatever the night omits,

τοῦτ᾽ ἐπ᾽ ἦμαρ ἔρχεται·
τόν, ὦ τᾶν πυρφόρων   200
ἀστραπᾶν κράτη νέμων,
ὦ Ζεῦ πάτερ, ὑπὸ cῷ φθίcον κεραυνῷ.

Λύκει᾽ ἄναξ, τά τε cὰ χρυ-   ἀντ. γ΄
cοcτρόφων ἀπ᾽ ἀγκυλᾶν
βέλεα θέλοιμ᾽ ἂν ἀδάματ᾽ ἐνδατεῖcθαι   205
ἀρωγὰ προcταθέντα, τάc τε πυρφόρουc
Ἀρτέμιδοc αἴγλαc, ξὺν αἷc
Λύκι᾽ ὄρεα διᾴccει·
τὸν χρυcομίτραν τε κικλήcκω,
τᾶcδ᾽ ἐπώνυμον γᾶc,   210
οἰνῶπα Βάκχον, εὔιον
Μαινάδων ὁμόcτολον,
πελαcθῆναι φλέγοντ᾽
ἀγλαῶπι ⟨– ∪ –⟩
πεύκᾳ ᾽πὶ τὸν ἀπότιμον ἐν θεοῖc θεόν.   215

Οι.   αἰτεῖc· ἃ δ᾽ αἰτεῖc, τἄμ᾽ ἐὰν θέλῃc ἔπη
κλύων δέχεcθαι τῇ νόcῳ θ᾽ ὑπηρετεῖν,
ἀλκὴν λάβοιc ἂν κἀνακούφιcιν κακῶν·
ἀγὼ ξένοc μὲν τοῦ λόγου τοῦδ᾽ ἐξερῶ,
ξένοc δὲ τοῦ πραχθέντοc· οὐ γὰρ ἂν μακρὰν   220
ἴχνευον αὐτό, μὴ οὐκ ἔχων τι cύμβολον.
νῦν δ᾽, ὕcτεροc γὰρ ἀcτὸc εἰc ἀcτοὺc τελῶ,
ὑμῖν προφωνῶ πᾶcι Καδμείοιc τάδε·
ὅcτιc ποθ᾽ ὑμῶν Λάιον τὸν Λαβδάκου

200 τόν, ὦ τᾶν Hermann: τὸν ὦ P.Oxy. 2180, Lpat: τᾶν ὦ r
204 ἀγκυλᾶν Elmsley: -ῶν r: ἀγκύλων cett.   205 ἀδάματ᾽
Erfurdt: ἀδάμαcτ᾽ codd.   208 Λύκι᾽ Lpt: Λύκει᾽ rpa
212 ὁμόcτολον LypPaXs: μονόcτολον cett.   214 ⟨cύμμαχον⟩
G. Wolff, ⟨νυκτέρῳ⟩ J. H. H. Schmidt   220 οὐ γὰρ ἄν] ὥcτ᾽
οὐκ ἄν Blaydes   221 αὐτὸ lGypp: αὐτόc rpat   οὐκ ἔχων]
οὐ κιχὼν Headlam   μὴ οὐκ ἔχων τι cύμβολον = nisi vobiscum
aliquo modo coniunctus essem   222 ὕcτεροc] -ον Zr, coni. Blaydes
ἀcτὸc Lrpat: αὐτὸc pa, coni. Elmsley   τελῶ Lrpat: τελῶν p

day comes afterward to bring to the end.
O Zeus father, you who hold sway   200
over the power of fire-bearing lightning,
wither Ares beneath your thunderbolt.

Lycean lord Apollo, I would rather shafts indomitable
from your bowstring spun of gold be spread abroad   205
to be our champions on guard before me and Artemis'
fiery torches in whose company
she tears across the mountains of Lycia.
I call upon him of the golden headband,
bound by name to this land,   210
Bacchus of flushed cheeks, evoked with cries of *euie*,
roving companion of Maenads,
to come near, blazing with the fires
of his flashing . . . [16]
pine torch against the god without honor among gods. [17]   215

[*Oedipus comes forward to the center of the orchestra and addresses
the Chorus.*]

Oe   You are praying. As for what you pray, if you listen and consent
     to heed my words and take up an oar against this sickness,
     you would gain support and relief from your troubles.
     What I shall say I say as a stranger to the story,
     stranger to what was done. I would not be long on the hunt   220
     if I didn't have some link binding me to you.
     As it is now, since I was enrolled as a citizen among citizens
          after these events,
     I declare publicly to all the people of Cadmus the following:
     whoever of you who knows by what man

κάτοιδεν ἀνδρὸς ἐκ τίνος διώλετο,   225
τοῦτον κελεύω πάντα cημαίνειν ἐμοί·
κεἰ μὲν φοβεῖται τοὐπίκλημ' ὑπεξελὼν

.   .   .   .   .

αὐτὸς κατ' αὐτοῦ·—πείcεται γὰρ ἄλλο μὲν
ἀcτεργὲc οὐδέν, γῆc δ' ἄπειcιν ἀβλαβήc—
εἰ δ' αὖ τιc ἄλλον οἶδεν ἢ 'ξ ἄλληc χθονὸc   230
τὸν αὐτόχειρα, μὴ cιωπάτω· τὸ γὰρ
κέρδοc τελῶ 'γὼ χἠ χάριc προcκείcεται.
εἰ δ' αὖ cιωπήcεcθε, καί τιc ἢ φίλου
δείcαc ἀπώcει τοὔποc ἢ χαυτοῦ τόδε,
ἃκ τῶνδε δράcω, ταῦτα χρὴ κλυεῖν ἐμοῦ.   235
τὸν ἄνδρ' ἀπαυδῶ τοῦτον, ὅcτιc ἐcτί, γῆc
τῆcδ', ἧc ἐγὼ κράτη τε καὶ θρόνουc νέμω,
μήτ' ἐcδέχεcθαι μήτε προcφωνεῖν τινά,
μήτ' ἐν θεῶν εὐχαῖcι μήτε θύμαcιν
κοινὸν ποεῖcθαι, μήτε χέρνιβοc νέμειν·   240
ὠθεῖν δ' ἀπ' οἴκων πάνταc, ὡc μιάcματοc
τοῦδ' ἡμὶν ὄντοc, ὡc τὸ Πυθικὸν θεοῦ
μαντεῖον ἐξέφηνεν ἀρτίωc ἐμοί.
ἐγὼ μὲν οὖν τοιόcδε τῷ τε δαίμονι
τῷ τ' ἀνδρὶ τῷ θανόντι cύμμαχοc πέλω.   245
[κατεύχομαι δὲ τὸν δεδρακότ', εἴτε τιc
εἷc ὢν λέληθεν εἴτε πλειόνων μέτα,
κακὸν κακῶc νιν ἄμορον ἐκτρῖψαι βίον.

227 κεἰ μὲν φοβεῖται] καὶ μὴ φοβείcθω Blaydes et Heimsoeth
ὑπεξελὼν] -ελεῖν Blaydes et Halm: -έλοι Rauchenstein   post hunc v.
lacunam statuit P. Groeneboom: possis ex. gr. ⟨πόλεωc (vel ἄλλων)
ἐπιcπᾶν θαναcίμουc φόνου δίκαc⟩   228 κατ' αὐτοῦ Bergk:
καθ' αὐτοῦ codd.   229 ἀβλαβήc pat: ἀcφαλήc lrp   230 ἄλλον]
ἀcτὸν Vauvilliers: ἀμῆc Tournier   οἶδεν Lrpa: εἶδεν pt   ἢ 'ξ
Vauvilliers: ἐξ codd.   ἄλληc] ἀμῆc Seyffert   235 κλυεῖν
West: κλύειν codd.   239 μήτε Lrpat: μήτ' ἐν pZr: μηδὲ Elmsley   θύμαcιν LpZrt: -cι rpa   240 χέρνιβοc LN: -ac cett.
244–51 et 269–72 permutavit Dawe: 246–51 post 272 traiecit amicus viri
docti Dobree, del. Wecklein   248 ἄμορον Porson: ἄμοιρον codd.

Laïos, son of Labdacus, was slain   225
I order this man to declare everything to me.
And if he is afraid, after removing the accusation[18]

     .   .   .   .   .

against himself by his own doing—for he will suffer
nothing else hateful and will leave the land unharmed.
Further, if someone knows another or someone from another land 230
to be the murderer, let him not remain silent, for I shall pay
his reward, and my gratitude will be added besides.
Further, if you remain silent, and someone from fear
for a kinsman or himself shall reject this proclamation,
what I shall do in that case he should hear from me.   235
This man, whoever he is, I forbid anyone
of this land whose powers and thrones I wield
from either receiving him into any company or addressing him
or allowing him to join in the prayers and sacrifices
of the gods or dispensing lustral waters to him.   240
I order that all thrust him from their homes,
since he is the pollution upon us, as the Pythian oracle
of the god recently has revealed to me.
Such an ally then am I for the daimon
and for the man who is dead.   245
[I lay this curse upon the perpetrator,
whether he escapes detection alone or with accomplices,
that he, a bad man, wear away a miserable life badly.

ἐπεύχομαι δ᾽, οἴκοισιν εἰ ξυνέστιος
ἐν τοῖς ἐμοῖς γένοιτ᾽ ἐμοῦ ξυνειδότος,   250
παθεῖν ἅπερ τοῖςδ᾽ ἀρτίως ἠρασάμην.]
ὑμῖν δὲ ταῦτα πάντ᾽ ἐπισκήπτω τελεῖν,
ὑπέρ τ᾽ ἐμαυτοῦ, τοῦ θεοῦ τε, τῆςδέ τε
γῆς ὧδ᾽ ἀκάρπως κἀθέως ἐφθαρμένης.
οὐδ᾽ εἰ γὰρ ἦν τὸ πρᾶγμα μὴ θεήλατον,   255
ἀκάθαρτον ὑμᾶς εἰκὸς ἦν οὕτως ἐᾶν,
ἀνδρός γ᾽ ἀρίστου βασιλέως τ᾽ ὀλωλότος,
ἀλλ᾽ ἐξερευνᾶν· νῦν δ᾽ ἐπεὶ κυρῶ τ᾽ ἐγὼ
ἔχων μὲν ἀρχάς, ἃς ἐκεῖνος εἶχε πρίν,
ἔχων δὲ λέκτρα καὶ γυναῖχ᾽ ὁμόσπορον,   260
κοινῶν τε παίδων κοίν᾽ ἄν, εἰ κείνῳ γένος
μὴ ᾽δυστύχησεν, ἦν ἂν ἐκπεφυκότα—
νῦν δ᾽ ἐς τὸ κείνου κρᾶτ᾽ ἐνήλαθ᾽ ἡ τύχη·
ἀνθ᾽ ὧν ἐγὼ τάδ᾽, ὡσπερεὶ τοὐμοῦ πατρός,
ὑπερμαχοῦμαι κἀπὶ πάντ᾽ ἀφίξομαι   265
ζητῶν τὸν αὐτόχειρα τοῦ φόνου λαβεῖν
τῷ Λαβδακείῳ παιδὶ Πολυδώρου τε καὶ
τοῦ πρόςθε Κάδμου τοῦ πάλαι τ᾽ Ἀγήνορος.
καὶ ταῦτα τοῖς μὴ δρῶσιν εὔχομαι θεοὺς
μήτ᾽ ἄροτον αὐτοῖς γῆς ἀνιέναι τινὰ   270
μήτ᾽ οὖν γυναικῶν παῖδας, ἀλλὰ τῷ πότμῳ
τῷ νῦν φθερεῖσθαι κἄτι τοῦδ᾽ ἐχθίονι.
ὑμῖν δὲ τοῖς ἄλλοισι Καδμείοις, ὅσοις
τάδ᾽ ἔστ᾽ ἀρέσκονθ᾽, ἥ τε σύμμαχος Δίκη
χοἰ πάντες εὖ ξυνεῖεν εἰσαεὶ θεοί.   275
Χο.   ὥσπερ μ᾽ ἀραῖον ἔλαβες, ὧδ᾽, ἄναξ, ἐρῶ.

250 post γένοιτ᾽ add. ἄν **lrp**Zr: corr. **a** (etiam in L, ut vid., del. librarius cod. A)   ξυνειδότος **Lrpt**: ϲυν- **a**   257 τ᾽ R**pat**: om. L**pc**KGpD   258 ἐπεὶ κυρῶ Laur. CS 66, coni. Burton: ἐπικυρῶ cett.   τ᾽] γ᾽ Benedict   261 τε LR**pat**: δὲ Gp   264 τάδ᾽] τοῦδ᾽ Mudge   269 θεούς] θεοῖς pXs**ac**   270 ἄροτον] -òν P**ac** et Zc   γῆς Vauvilliers: γὴν codd.   273 ὑμῖν R**pat**: ἡμῖν LGp   τοῖς ⟨τ᾽⟩ Naber   Καδμείοις ⟨θ᾽⟩ F. W. Schmidt   276 ἔλαβες] εἷλες Eustathius 1809. 14

I invoke upon myself, should he prove to share
my hearth among my own with my knowledge, 250
that I suffer the curses I have just pronounced upon those.][19]
I impose upon you to fulfill all that I have said
for my sake and for the sake of the god and this
land brought so to ruin in dearth of fruits and gods.
Even were this matter not urged by gods, 255
it would be wrong to let it go uncleansed this way,
seeing that a man of birth and quality as well as your king is dead,
and not conduct an investigation. As it is, since I hold
the sovereignty that that man held before,
and I have his bed and wife as a common sowing ground 260
and common bonds of children, had his stock
not proved unfortunate, would have been begotten,
but as it is, misfortune has leapt upon his head;
in the face of this, I, as if for my father,
shall fight for him, and I shall resort to every means 265
in my search to get the perpetrator of the murder
for the son of Labdacus, son of Polydorus,
son of Cadmus before, son of Agenor of old.
And for whoever do not do as I say, I pray
that the gods send neither harvests from their land 270
nor children from their women but that they perish
by the lot now theirs and one more hateful.
For you other men of Cadmus who approve
what I say, may Justice, our ally,
and all the gods attend you in kindly beneficence always. 275

CORYPHAEUS[20]

As you have put me under curse, lord, so I will speak.

οὔτ' ἔκτανον γὰρ οὔτε τὸν κτανόντ' ἔχω
δεῖξαι. τὸ δὲ ζήτημα τοῦ πέμψαντος ἦν
Φοίβου τόδ' εἰπεῖν ὅστις εἴργασταί ποτε.

Οι.   δίκαι' ἔλεξας· ἀλλ' ἀναγκάσαι θεοὺς   280
     ἂν μὴ θέλωσιν οὐδ' ⟨ἂν⟩ εἷς δύναιτ' ἀνήρ.
Χο.   τὰ δεύτερ' ἐκ τῶνδ' ἂν λέγοιμ' ἁμοὶ δοκεῖ.
Οι.   εἰ καὶ τρίτ' ἐστί, μὴ παρῇς τὸ μὴ οὐ φράσαι.
Χο.   ἄνακτ' ἄνακτι ταῦθ' ὁρῶντ' ἐπίσταμαι
     μάλιστα Φοίβῳ Τειρεσίαν, παρ' οὗ τις ἂν   285
     σκοπῶν τάδ', ὦναξ, ἐκμάθοι σαφέστατα.
Οι.   ἀλλ' οὐκ ἐν ἀργοῖς οὐδὲ τοῦτ' ἐπραξάμεν.
     ἔπεμψα γὰρ Κρέοντος εἰπόντος διπλοῦς
     πομπούς· πάλαι δὲ μὴ παρὼν θαυμάζεται.
Χο.   καὶ μὴν τά γ' ἄλλα κωφὰ καὶ παλαί' ἔπη.   290
Οι.   τὰ ποῖα ταῦτα; πάντα γὰρ σκοπῶ λόγον.
Χο.   θανεῖν ἐλέχθη πρός τινων ὁδοιπόρων.
Οι.   ἤκουσα κἀγώ· τὸν δὲ δρῶντ' οὐδεὶς ὁρᾷ.
Χο.   ἀλλ' εἴ τι μὲν δὴ δείματός γ' ἔχει μέρος
     τὰς σὰς ἀκούων οὐ μενεῖ τοιάσδ' ἀράς.   295
Οι.   ᾧ μή 'στι δρῶντι τάρβος, οὐδ' ἔπος φοβεῖ.
Χο.   ἀλλ' οὑξελέγξων νιν πάρεστιν· οἵδε γὰρ
     τὸν θεῖον ἤδη μάντιν ὧδ' ἄγουσιν, ᾧ
     τἀληθὲς ἐμπέφυκεν ἀνθρώπων μόνῳ.
Οι.   ὦ πάντα νωμῶν Τειρεσία, διδακτά τε   300
     ἄρρητά τ' οὐράνιά τε καὶ χθονοστιβῆ,
     πόλιν μέν, εἰ καὶ μὴ βλέπεις, φρονεῖς δ' ὅμως

281 ἂν Xr, coni. Stephanus: ἀν cett.   ⟨ἂν⟩ Burton: om. codd. nostri
(suppl. 'rec' teste Pearson)   δύναιτ' Paat: δύναται L^{ac}Krp
284 ταῦθ' Xrγρ: ταῦθ' codd.   287 ἐπράξαμεν Shilleto: -άμην
codd.¹   290 παλαί'] μάται' WaZg, coni. Halbertsma
293 δρῶντ' anon. ap. Burton (1779): ἰδόντ' codd.   294 γ' P.Oxy.
2180 ut videtur, coni. Turnebus: τ' codd.: del. Hartung, qui δειμάτων
coniecit   ἔχει] τρέφει Wunder   295 post σὰς add. δ' rH,
unde ⟨γ'⟩ olim Dawe   297 οὑξελέγξων P.Oxy. 2180, a (unde in L
s.l. litteram ξ add. librarius cod. A): -έγχων cett.   νιν πάρεστιν
Heimsoeth: αὐτὸν ἔστιν codd.

Neither did I kill him, nor am I able to point
to who killed him. As for the seeking, it belongs to Apollo who
    launched it
to say this—who has done the deed.

Oe Yes, you're right, but to compel the gods   280
to what they do not wish, no one can do that.

Co Second best after this, I might say what seems best to me.

Oe If there is a third, do not let it go unsaid.

Co I know that lord Tiresias most often sees the same things
as lord Apollo. From him someone examining   285
these matters, lord, could learn very clearly.

Oe I have not acted slothfully, but I have attended to this.
At Creon's suggestion, I sent two men to escort him here.
He surprises me that he hasn't arrived long before this.

Co Yes. There are the other rumors, faint and old.   290

Oe What are they? I examine every story.

Co Laïos was said to have died at the hands of some travelers.

Oe I too heard that. No one saw the man who did this.[21]

Co Yet, even so, if he has even a particle of fear,
on hearing your curses such as they are, he will not remain.   295

Oe Whoever has no terror at doing the deed doesn't fear a word.[22]

[*Tiresias enters, led by a boy slave (444) and escorted by at least two
of Oedipus' men (298).*]

Co Well, here is someone who will cross-examine and refute him.[23]
These men are already leading the godlike seer
to whom alone of men truth is inborn.[24]

Oe O Tiresias who surveys all, what may be taught and what   300
must remain unsaid, things of the heavens and trodden earth,
the city, even if you don't see, you realize nonetheless

οἷα νόςῳ ςύνεςτιν· ἧς ςὲ προςτάτην
ςωτῆρά τ᾽, ὦναξ, μοῦνον ἐξευρίςκομεν.
Φοῖβος γάρ, εἰ καὶ μὴ κλύεις τῶν ἀγγέλων,   305
πέμψαςιν ἡμῖν ἀντέπεμψεν, ἔκλυςιν
μόνην ἂν ἐλθεῖν τοῦδε τοῦ νοςήματος,
εἰ τοὺς κτανόντας Λάιον μαθόντες εὖ
κτείναιμεν, ἢ γῆς φυγάδας ἐκπεμψαίμεθα.
ςὺ δ᾽ οὖν φθονήςας μήτ᾽ ἀπ᾽ οἰωνῶν φάτιν   310
μήτ᾽ εἴ τιν᾽ ἄλλην μαντικῆς ἔχεις ὁδόν,
ῥῦςαι ςεαυτὸν καὶ πόλιν, ῥῦςαι δ᾽ ἐμέ,
ῥῦςαι δὲ πᾶν μίαςμα τοῦ τεθνηκότος.
ἐν ςοὶ γὰρ ἐςμέν· ἄνδρα δ᾽ ὠφελεῖν ἀφ᾽ ὧν
ἔχοι τε καὶ δύναιτο κάλλιςτος πόνων.   315

ΤΕΙΡΕΣΙΑΣ

φεῦ φεῦ, φρονεῖν ὡς δεινὸν ἔνθα μὴ τέλη
λύῃ φρονοῦντι. ταῦτα γὰρ καλῶς ἐγὼ
εἰδὼς διώλες᾽· οὐ γὰρ ἂν δεῦρ᾽ ἱκόμην.
Οι.   τί δ᾽ ἔςτιν; ὡς ἄθυμος εἰςελήλυθας.
Τε.   ἄφες μ᾽ ἐς οἴκους· ῥᾷςτα γὰρ τὸ ςόν τε ςὺ   320
κἀγὼ διοίςω τοὐμόν, ἢν ἐμοὶ πίθῃ.
Οι.   οὔτ᾽ ἔννομ᾽ εἶπας οὔτε προςφιλῆ πόλει
τῇδ᾽, ἥ ς᾽ ἔθρεψε, τήνδ᾽ ἀποςτερῶν φάτιν.
Τε.   ὁρῶ γὰρ οὐδὲ ςοὶ τὸ ςὸν φώνημ᾽ ἰὸν
πρὸς καιρόν· ὡς οὖν μηδ᾽ ἐγὼ ταὐτὸν
παθω—   325
Οι.   μὴ πρὸς θεῶν φρονῶν γ᾽ ἀποςτραφῇς, ἐπεὶ
πάντες ςε προςκυνοῦμεν οἵδ᾽ ἱκτήριοι.
Τε.   πάντες γὰρ οὐ φρονεῖτ᾽. ἐγὼ δ᾽ οὐ μή ποτε
τἄμ᾽, ὡς ἂν εἴπω μὴ τὰ ς᾽, ἐκφήνω κακά.
Οι.   τί φής; ξυνειδὼς οὐ φράςεις, ἀλλ᾽ ἐννοεῖς   330

305 καί] τι L. Stephani   307 τοῦδε] τήνδε Blaydes
315 πόνων in linea vel s.l. LKpa: πόνος pat   317 λύῃ lrp: λύει
pat   322 ἔννομ᾽ lat: ἔννομον Krp   εἶπας rpa: εἶπες lpt
προςφιλῆ L in linea, P: -ὲς lrpa   324 φώνημ᾽] φρόνημ᾽ r, coni.
Naber   325 sententiam interrumpi censuit Wunder

with what sickness it is beset. Lord, we find you to be
its sole champion and savior, lord.
Phoebus, in case you did not hear the messengers,   305
has sent back his reply to us, who sent to him, that release
from this sickness would come only
if we learn well the slayers of Laïos
and slay them or send them as exiles from the land.
Accordingly, do not begrudge us an utterance from birds   310
or any other avenue of prophetic skill you may have.
Protect yourself and your city. Protect me.
Keep us from all pollution of the dead man.
We are in your hands. That a man lends aid
from whatever resources and abilities he has is a most beautiful
     labor.[25]   315

TIRESIAS

Oh how terrible it is to possess wisdom where it profits not
the one who is wise. I knew very well,
but I let it slip my mind, for otherwise, I would not have come here.

Oe   What's this? How lacking in spirit have you come.

Ti   Send me home. That way you'll endure your situation   320
to the end, and I mine, most easily if you obey me.[26]

Oe   What you said is not in keeping with the law or friendly to this city
that nourished you, when you deprive it of your words.

Ti   I see that what you say is not going toward the mark.
So that I not make the same error—   325

[*Tiresias turns to leave. Oedipus interrupts.*]

Oe   Don't, by the gods, don't turn away if you possess wisdom,
when all of us prostrate ourselves before you as your suppliants.

Ti   All of you lack wisdom. I will never reveal
my evils so that I not tell yours.

Oe   What are you saying? You know something and won't speak?   330 ἡμᾶς προδοῦναι καὶ καταφθεῖραι πόλιν;

Τε. ἐγὼ οὔτ' ἐμαυτὸν οὔτε c' ἀλγυνῶ. τί ταῦτ'
ἄλλως ἐλέγχεις; οὐ γὰρ ἂν πύθοιό μου.

Οι. οὐκ, ὦ κακῶν κάκιcτε, καὶ γὰρ ἂν πέτρου
φύcιν cύ γ' ὀργάνειας, ἐξερεῖς ποτέ,   335
ἀλλ' ὧδ' ἄτεγκτος κἀτελεύτητος φανῇ;

Τε. ὀργὴν ἐμέμψω τὴν ἐμήν, τὴν cὴν δ' ὁμοῦ
ναίουcαν οὐ κατεῖδες, ἀλλ' ἐμὲ ψέγεις.

Οι. τίς γὰρ τοιαῦτ' ἂν οὐκ ἂν ὀργίζοιτ' ἔπη
κλύων, ἃ νῦν cὺ τήνδ' ἀτιμάζεις πόλιν;   340

Τε. ἥξει γὰρ αὐτά, κἂν ἐγὼ cιγῇ cτέγω.

Οι. οὔκουν ἅ γ' ἥξει καὶ cὲ χρὴ λέγειν ἐμοί;

Τε. οὐκ ἂν πέρα φράcαιμι. πρὸς τάδ', εἰ θέλεις,
θυμοῦ δι' ὀργῆς ἥτις ἀγριωτάτη.

Οι. καὶ μὴν παρήcω γ' οὐδέν, ὡς ὀργῆς ἔχω,   345
ἅπερ ξυνίημ'. ἴσθι γὰρ δοκῶν ἐμοὶ
καὶ ξυμφυτεῦcαι τοὔργον, εἰργάcθαι θ', ὅcον
μὴ χερcὶ καίνων· εἰ δ' ἐτύγχανες βλέπων,
καὶ τοὔργον ἂν cοῦ τοῦτ' ἔφην εἶναι μόνου.

Τε. ἄληθες; ἐννέπω cὲ τῷ κηρύγματι   350
ᾧπερ προεῖπας ἐμμένειν, κἀφ' ἡμέρας
τῆς νῦν προcαυδᾶν μήτε τούcδε μήτ' ἐμέ,
ὡς ὄντι γῆς τῆcδ' ἀνοcίῳ μιάcτορι.

Οι. οὕτως ἀναιδῶς ἐξεκίνηcας τόδε
τὸ ῥῆμα; καὶ ποῦ τοῦτο φεύξεcθαι δοκεῖς;   355

Τε. πέφευγα· τἀληθὲς γὰρ ἰcχῦον τρέφω.

Οι. πρὸς τοῦ διδαχθείς; οὐ γὰρ ἔκ γε τῆς τέχνης.

Τε. πρὸς cοῦ· cὺ γάρ μ' ἄκοντα προὐτρέψω λέγειν.

332 ἐγὼ οὔτ' voluerunt **rN**: ἔγωγ' οὔτ' **p**: ἐγώ τ' codd. plerique
336 κἀτελεύτητος] κἀπαραίτητος Sehrwald   φανῇ] φανείς Suda
s.v. ἄτεγκτος   342 οὔκουν Herwerden: οὐκοῦν codd.
345 ἔχω codd. plerique: ἔχων **p**   346 ἅπερ] ὥνπερ Blaydes
347 θ' **pat**: δ' **Lrp**   349 εἶναι **rpat**: om. **lp**, unde μόνου
βροτῶν Schneidewin   μόνου] μόνον **Kp**   351 προεῖπας
Brunck: προc- codd.   355 ποῦ] ποῦ Brunck   356 ἰcχῦον]
ἰcχυρὸν Stobaeus 3. 13. 18

	Do you intend to betray us and ruin the city?	
Ti	I will not cause myself pain or you. Why do you keep	
	cross-examining me to no purpose? You will not learn from me.	
Oe	O foul thing, foulest of the foul—Oh, you would enrage	
	a stone—couldn't you speak out	335
	and not appear so obdurate and unwilling to end this?[27]	
Ti	You blamed my temper, but you did not see	
	your own dwelling within you, yet you find fault with me.[28]	
Oe	Yes, who would not be angry on hearing such	
	words you are saying now in disrespect of the city?	340
Ti	Things will come out on their own, though I would cover them	
	with silence.	
Oe	Well, if they will come out, then don't you have to tell me?	
Ti	I would speak no further. That said, if you wish,	
	rage on with that very fierce anger of yours.	
Oe	I won't leave anything out of what I understand	345
	so angry am I. Know that you appear to me	
	to have begotten this deed and carried out	
	as much of it short of killing by hands, but if you were seeing,	
	I'd say that this deed is yours alone.	
Ti	Is that true? I tell you to abide by the proclamation	350
	you spoke publicly and from this day present	
	address neither these men here nor me,	
	since you are the unholy miasma of this land.	
Oe	And so shamelessly you flushed out this word?[29]	
	And where do you think you'll escape what you said?	355
Ti	I have escaped. I hold the truth as my strength.	
Oe	Taught by whom? Surely it is not from your craft.	
Ti	By you, for you urged me to speak against my will.[30]	

Οι.   ποῖον λόγον; λέγ' αὖθις, ὡς μᾶλλον μάθω.
Τε.   οὐχὶ ξυνῆκας πρόσθεν; ἢ 'κπειρᾷ λέγειν;   360
Οι.   οὐχ ὥστε γ' εἰπεῖν γνωστόν· ἀλλ' αὖθις φράσον.
Τε.   φονέα σέ φημι τἀνδρὸς οὗ ζητεῖς κυρεῖν.
Οι.   ἀλλ' οὔ τι χαίρων δίς γε πημονὰς ἐρεῖς.
Τε.   εἴπω τι δῆτα κἄλλ', ἵν' ὀργίζῃ πλέον;
Οι.   ὅσον γε χρῄζεις· ὡς μάτην εἰρήσεται.   365
Τε.   λεληθέναι σέ φημι σὺν τοῖς φιλτάτοις
       αἴσχισθ' ὁμιλοῦντ', οὐδ' ὁρᾶν ἵν' εἶ κακοῦ.
Οι.   ἦ καὶ γεγηθὼς ταῦτ' ἀεὶ λέξειν δοκεῖς;
Τε.   εἴπερ τί γ' ἐστὶ τῆς ἀληθείας σθένος.
Οι.   ἀλλ' ἔστι, πλὴν σοί· σοὶ δὲ τοῦτ' οὐκ ἔστ', ἐπεὶ   370
       τυφλὸς τά τ' ὦτα τόν τε νοῦν τά τ' ὄμματ' εἶ.
Τε.   σὺ δ' ἄθλιός γε ταῦτ' ὀνειδίζων, ἃ σοὶ
       οὐδεὶς ὃς οὐχὶ τῶνδ' ὀνειδιεῖ τάχα.
Οι.   μιᾶς τρέφῃ πρὸς νυκτός, ὥστε μήτ' ἐμὲ
       μήτ' ἄλλον, ὅστις φῶς ὁρᾷ, βλάψαι ποτ' ἄν.   375
Τε.   οὐ γάρ σε μοῖρα πρός γ' ἐμοῦ πεσεῖν, ἐπεὶ
       ἱκανὸς Ἀπόλλων, ᾧ τάδ' ἐκπρᾶξαι μέλει.
Οι.   Κρέοντος, ἢ τοῦ ταῦτα τἀξευρήματα;
Τε.   Κρέων δέ σοι πῆμ' οὐδέν, ἀλλ' αὐτὸς σὺ σοί.
Οι.   ὦ πλοῦτε καὶ τυραννὶ καὶ τέχνη τέχνης   380
       ὑπερφέρουσα τῷ πολυζήλῳ βίῳ,
       ὅσος παρ' ὑμῖν ὁ φθόνος φυλάσσεται,
       εἰ τῆσδέ γ' ἀρχῆς οὕνεχ', ἣν ἐμοὶ πόλις
       δωρητόν, οὐκ αἰτητόν, εἰσεχείρισεν,
       ταύτης Κρέων ὁ πιστός, οὑξ ἀρχῆς φίλος,   385

360 ξυνῆκας **rpat**: cυν- Lp   ἢ nos: ἦ codd.   λέγειν]
λόγου (?) A ap. L s.l.: λόγων Brunck: τί μου Blaydes: cύ μου S. J. Harrison: alii alia   361 γνωστόν] γνωτόν Livinei 'V'   368 ταῦτ']
ταῦτ' Schneidewin   374 μιᾶς] μόνης Blaydes   375 βλάψαι
L^pcG s.l. **pat**: βλέψαι P.Oxy. 22, K in linea, **rp**D   376 ce . . . γ'
ἐμοῦ Brunck: με . . . γε cοῦ P.Oxy. 22 et codd.   378 του (sine
accentu) P.Oxy. 22^ac: cοῦ P.Oxy. 22^pc et codd.   379 δὲ] γε Brunck
380 τυραννὶ LVat (πυρανὶ P.Oxy. 22): -ὶc **rp** et Stobaeus 4. 8. 10
382 ὑμῖν Lpa: ἡμῖν **rp**: utrumque novit **t**

Oe   What did you say? Tell me again so I may learn more.

Ti   You did not understand before? Or are you trying to get me
          to speak?[31]   360

Oe   No, not enough to know. Well, tell me again.

Ti   I say that you happen to be the murderer of the man whose
          murderer you are seeking.

Oe   You won't utter such miseries twice and get away free.

Ti   Am I to tell you the rest so you can rage even more?

Oe   However much you need. Whatever you say won't matter.   365

Ti   I say that you are living in utter shame with those closest to you
          and do not know it. I say that you do not see in what foulness
              you are.

Oe   Do you actually suppose you'll talk like this forever with a smile?

Ti   Yes, I do, if there is any strength in the truth.

Oe   Well, there is, except for you. There's none for you, since   370
       you are blind in your ears, in your mind, and in your eyes.

Ti   You are wretched in taunting me with this abuse with which
          there is no one of these here who will not soon be taunting you.

Oe   You are held by one night so you couldn't hurt   375
       me or anyone who sees the light of day.

Ti   No, your lot is not to fall at my hands, since
          Apollo is sufficient. His concern it is to accomplish this.

Oe   Are these Creon's inventions or yours?[32]

Ti   No, Creon is no pain to you, but you yourself to yourself.

Oe   O wealth, tyranny, and skill surpassing   380
       skill in a life fraught with jealousy,
       how great is the envy stored within you,
       if for the sake of this rule, a thing the city
       put into my hands as a gift, not something I requested,
       from this rule Creon the faithful, friend from the beginning,   385

λάθρα μ' ὑπελθὼν ἐκβαλεῖν ἱμείρεται,
ὑφεὶς μάγον τοιόνδε μηχανορράφον,
δόλιον ἀγύρτην, ὅστις ἐν τοῖς κέρδεσιν
μόνον δέδορκε, τὴν τέχνην δ' ἔφυ τυφλός.
ἐπεὶ φέρ' εἰπέ, ποῦ σὺ μάντις εἶ σαφής;   390
πῶς οὐχ, ὅθ' ἡ ῥαψῳδὸς ἐνθάδ' ἦν κύων,
ηὔδας τι τοῖσδ' ἀστοῖσιν ἐκλυτήριον;
καίτοι τό γ' αἴνιγμ' οὐχὶ τοὐπιόντος ἦν
ἀνδρὸς διειπεῖν, ἀλλὰ μαντείας ἔδει·
ἣν οὔτ' ἀπ' οἰωνῶν σὺ προύφάνης ἔχων   395
οὔτ' ἐκ θεῶν του γνωτόν· ἀλλ' ἐγὼ μολών,
ὁ μηδὲν εἰδὼς Οἰδίπους, ἔπαυσά νιν,
γνώμῃ κυρήσας οὐδ' ἀπ' οἰωνῶν μαθών·
ὃν δὴ σὺ πειρᾷς ἐκβαλεῖν, δοκῶν θρόνοις
παραστατήσειν τοῖς Κρεοντείοις πέλας.   400
κλαίων δοκεῖς μοι καὶ σὺ χὠ συνθεὶς τάδε
ἀγηλατήσειν· εἰ δὲ μὴ 'δόκεις γέρων
εἶναι, παθὼν ἔγνως ἂν οἷά περ φρονεῖς.
Χο.   ἡμῖν μὲν εἰκάζουσι καὶ τὰ τοῦδ' ἔπη
ὀργῇ λελέχθαι καὶ τὰ σ', Οἰδίπου, δοκεῖ.   405
δεῖ δ' οὐ τοιούτων, ἀλλ' ὅπως τὰ τοῦ θεοῦ
μαντεῖ' ἄριστα λύσομεν, τόδε σκοπεῖν.
Τε.   εἰ καὶ τυραννεῖς, ἐξισωτέον τὸ γοῦν
ἴσ' ἀντιλέξαι· τοῦδε γὰρ κἀγὼ κρατῶ.
οὐ γάρ τι σοὶ ζῶ δοῦλος, ἀλλὰ Λοξίᾳ·   410
ὥστ' οὐ Κρέοντος προστάτου γεγράψομαι.
λέγω δ', ἐπειδὴ καὶ τυφλόν μ' ὠνείδισας·
σὺ καὶ δέδορκας κοὐ βλέπεις ἵν' εἶ κακοῦ,
οὐδ' ἔνθα ναίεις, οὐδ' ὅτων οἰκεῖς μέτα—

388 κέρδεσιν LNZrt: -σι **rpa**   396 γνωτόν codd. plerique:
γνωστόν **p**   398 γνώμῃ L^{pc}**Krpat**: -ης L^{ac}**p**   401 συνθεὶς]
ξυν- P.Oxy. 2180   402 ἀγηλατήσειν **rpat**: ἀγη- Lp
404-7 post 428 traiecit Enger   405 Οἰδίπου] -ους
Elmsley   413 δέδορκας κοὐ] δεδορκὼς οὐ post Reiske Brunck
414-15 οὐδ' ὅτων . . . εἶ del. West

creeping surreptitiously upon me, desires to expel me,
suborning a scheming charlatan like this one,
cunning beggar who has his sight only
on profits but who was born blind in his craft.
It's so! Come now, tell me, on what occasion were you an
      unerring prophet?   390
How did you not, when the rhapsode bitch was here,
proclaim to these townsmen some means of deliverance.
And yet the riddle was not a matter for anybody
who comes along to explain. There was need for divination,
skill *you* were shown not to possess from birds   395
or knowing from one of the gods. *I* came,
Oedipus who knew nothing, *I* stopped her,
hitting upon the solution with my wit, not learned from birds.
Now *you* are trying to expel me, thinking
you will stand near a Creontic throne.   400
I think that to your sorrow, you and the one who contrived
      these plots,
will drive me out as pollution. And if you weren't so visibly old,
you would learn by suffering just what is this wisdom you have.

Co   To us when we consider it, his words and yours,
     Oedipus, seem to have been said in anger.[33]   405
     We have no need for such words, but we need to scrutinize
     how best we will resolve the god's prophecies.

Ti   At any rate, even if you do wield the tyranny, nevertheless, the
      opportunity
     to say as much in reply must be granted equally, for I, too, have
      this power.
     I do not live as a slave to you but to Loxias.[34]   410
     Thus, I will not be registered as a foreign resident with Creon as
      my patron.
     I say the following since you actually taunted me for being blind.
     You look, and you do not see what foulness you are in
     or where you dwell or with whom you live.

ἆρ' οἶσθ' ἀφ' ὧν εἶ; καὶ λέληθας ἐχθρὸς ὢν   415
τοῖς σοῖσιν αὐτοῦ νέρθε κἀπὶ γῆς ἄνω,
καί σ' ἀμφιπλὴξ μητρός τε κἀπὸ τοῦ πατρὸς
ἐλᾷ ποτ' ἐκ γῆς τῆσδε δεινόπους ἀρά,
βλέποντα νῦν μὲν ὄρθ', ἔπειτα δὲ σκότον.
βοῆς δὲ τῆς σῆς ποῖος οὐκ ἔσται λιμήν,   420
ποῖος Κιθαιρὼν οὐχὶ σύμφωνος τάχα,
ὅταν καταίσθῃ τὸν ὑμέναιον, ὃν δόμοις
ἄνορμον εἰσέπλευσας, εὐπλοίας τυχών;
ἄλλων δὲ πλῆθος οὐκ ἐπαισθάνῃ κακῶν,
ἅ γ' ἐξαϊστώσει σε σὺν τοῖς σοῖς τέκνοις.   425
πρὸς ταῦτα καὶ Κρέοντα καὶ τοὐμὸν στόμα
προπηλάκιζε. σοῦ γὰρ οὐκ ἔστιν βροτῶν
κάκιον ὅστις ἐκτριβήσεταί ποτε.

Οι.   ἦ ταῦτα δῆτ' ἀνεκτὰ πρὸς τούτου κλύειν;
       οὐκ εἰς ὄλεθρον; οὐχὶ θᾶσσον αὖ πάλιν   430
       ἄψορρος οἴκων τῶνδ' ἀποστραφεὶς ἄπει;
Τε.   οὐδ' ἱκόμην ἔγωγ' ἄν, εἰ σὺ μὴ 'κάλεις.
Οι.   οὐ γὰρ τί σ' ᾔδη μῶρα φωνήσοντ', ἐπεὶ
       σχολῇ σ' ἂν οἴκους τοὺς ἐμοὺς ἐστειλάμην.
Τε.   ἡμεῖς τοιοίδ' ἔφυμεν, ὡς μὲν σοὶ δοκεῖ,   435
       μῶροι, γονεῦσι δ', οἵ σ' ἔφυσαν, ἔμφρονες.
Οι.   ποίοισι; μεῖνον. τίς δέ μ' ἐκφύει βροτῶν;
Τε.   ἥδ' ἡμέρα φύσει σε καὶ διαφθερεῖ.
Οι.   ὡς πάντ' ἄγαν αἰνικτὰ κἀσαφῆ λέγεις.

415 καὶ] χὡς P. Groeneboom: κοὐ Bothe   417 κἀπὸ τοῦ
P.Oxy. 2180ᵖᶜ: καὶ τοῦ σοῦ codd.   420 ἔσται λιμήν] ἔσται
Ἑλικών Blaydes   421 del. West   422 post hunc v.
lacunam statuit Dawe   425 ἅ γ' ἐξαϊστώσει σε σὺν Bergk: ἅ σ'
ἐξισώσει σοί τε καὶ codd.   429 πρὸς τούτου] προσπόλου R
κλύειν West: κλύειν codd.   430 αὖ P.Oxy. 22 in linea, coni.
G. Wolff: οὐ codd. et P.Oxy. 2180   433 ᾔδη P.Oxy. 2180 in
margine: ᾔδει(ν) codd.   434 σχολῇ σ' fere codd.: σχολῇ γ' H, lm.
Sudae s.v. σχολῇ γ' ἄν, P.Oxy. 22, ubi varia lectio est   ἐμούς ⟨σ'⟩
Porson   435 μὲν σοί] σοί μὲν Schaefer   436 ἔμφρονες
LRpa: εὔφρονες Gpt   439 κἀσαφῆ] κοὐ σαφῆ r

      Do you know from whom you came? You have gone unnoticed   415
      while being an enemy to your kinsmen, both those below and
          above upon this land.
      And the double-biting curse of your mother and your father,
      dread-footed in pursuit, will drive you from this land,
      seeing keenly now but then in darkness.
      What harbor will not receive your cry?   420
      What Cithaeron[35] will not join soon in concert
      when you realize your marriage in the house you sailed to
      after encountering fair winds offers no haven?
      There is that throng of other evils you do not realize
      that will destroy you along with your children.[36]   425
      This said, sling your mud upon both Creon
      and my mouth. There is no one of mortals
      who will ever be rubbed out more wretchedly than you.

Oe   Is this bearable to hear from him?
      Won't you perish utterly? Quickly! Back again!
      Leave! Go from my house. Go away, won't you?   430

Ti   I would not have come here had you not called me.

Oe   Yes, but I didn't know you'd talk foolishness. Otherwise,
      I would have taken my time in summoning you to my house.

Ti   I was born this way, as it seems to you, a fool,   435
      but to the ones who begot you, sensible.

Oe   To whom? Wait! Who of men sired me?

Ti   This day will sire you, and it will destroy you.

Oe   How is it that everything you say is too riddling and unclear?

Τε.   οὔκουν cὺ ταῦτ' ἄριcτοc εὑρίcκειν ἔφυc;   440
Οἱ.   τοιαῦτ' ὀνείδιζ' οἷc ἔμ' εὑρήcειc μέγαν.
Τε.   αὕτη γε μέντοι c' ἡ τύχη διώλεcεν.
Οἱ.   ἀλλ' εἰ πόλιν τήνδ' ἐξέcωc', οὔ μοι μέλει.
Τε.   ἄπειμι τοίνυν· καὶ cύ, παῖ, κόμιζέ με.
Οἱ.   κομιζέτω δῆθ'· ὡc παρὼν cύ γ' ἐμποδὼν   445
        ὀχλεῖc, cυθείc τ' ἂν οὐκ ἂν ἀλγύναιc πλέον.
Τε.   εἰπὼν ἄπειμ' ὧν οὕνεκ' ἦλθον, οὐ τὸ cὸν
        δείcαc πρόcωπον· οὐ γὰρ ἔcθ' ὅπου μ' ὀλεῖc.
        λέγω δέ cοι· τὸν ἄνδρα τοῦτον, ὃν πάλαι
        ζητεῖc ἀπειλῶν κἀνακηρύccων φόνον   450
        τὸν Λαΐειον, οὗτόc ἐcτιν ἐνθάδε,
        ξένοc λόγῳ μέτοικοc· εἶτα δ' ἐγγενὴc
        φανήcεται Θηβαῖοc, οὐδ' ἡcθήcεται
        τῇ ξυμφορᾷ· τυφλὸc γὰρ ἐκ δεδορκότοc
        καὶ πτωχὸc ἀντὶ πλουcίου ξένην ἔπι   455
        cκήπτρῳ προδεικνὺc γαῖαν ἐμπορεύcεται.
        φανήcεται δὲ παιcὶ τοῖc αὑτοῦ ξυνὼν
        ἀδελφὸc αὐτὸc καὶ πατήρ, κἀξ ἧc ἔφυ
        γυναικὸc υἱὸc καὶ πόcιc, καὶ τοῦ πατρὸc
        ὁμόcποróc τε καὶ φονεύc. καὶ ταῦτ' ἰὼν   460
        εἴcω λογίζου· κἂν λάβῃc ἐψευcμένον,
        φάcκειν ἔμ' ἤδη μαντικῇ μηδὲν φρονεῖν.

Χο.   τίc ὅντιν' ἁ θεcπιέπει-   cτρ. α'
        α Δελφὶc ἦδε πέτρα
        ἄρρητ' ἀρρήτων τελέcαν-   465
        τα φοινίαιcι χερcίν;

442 τύχη] τέχνη Bentley   445 cύ γ' K et codd. plerique (de L
non liquet): τά γ' Pa et Zc   446 ἀλγύναιc] -οιc N, coni. Elmsley
449 cοι] τοι P   456 ἐμπορεύcεται] ἐκ- Zrt
458 αὐτὸc Xs^pc, coni. Erfurdt: αὑτὸc cett.   461 post λάβῃc add.
μ' P.Oxy. 2180, codd. praeter L   ἐψευcμένον] -μένα Wilamowitz
464 ἦδε J. E. Powell: εἶδε K (non legitur L^ac) G et fortasse novit sch. L,
coni. Gitlbauer: εἶπε cett.: οἶδε dubitanter Herwerden

| Ti | If that were so, were you not born best at finding out riddles? | 440 |

Oe   Taunt me where you will find me great.

Ti   Surely this luck has destroyed you.

Oe   But if I saved this city, it matters not to me.

Ti   Then I will go. You, boy, lead me off.

Oe   Yes, let the boy lead you away. While you're here, you're trouble   445
underfoot. So if you hurry off, you won't cause more pain.

Ti   I will go after I have said what I came for with no fear
of your countenance, for there is no way you will destroy me.

[*At some point after line 448, Oedipus begins to withdraw to the
house. The sound of the doors (460) alerts Tiresias of his exit.*]

I say to you: this man whom for a long time
you have been seeking amid threats and proclamations
of a search into the murder of Laïos, this man is here,   450
a foreign immigrant in word, but then he will be revealed
a native Theban, and he will not be pleased
with the outcome, for, from one who saw now blinded,
and a beggar instead of a man of wealth,
he will make his way to a foreign land,   455
pointing the ground before him with a staff.
He will be revealed living with his children,
at once their brother and father, son and husband
of the woman from whom he was born, seeding
the same furrow as his father and his father's murderer.
Go inside, and ponder this. And should you find me out a liar,   460
then say that I possess no mantic wisdom.

[*Tiresias, led by the boy, exits, perhaps by the gangway to the city.
According to Pausanias (Geography of Greece 9.16.1), he had his bird
observatory on the acropolis of Thebes.*]

Chorus of Theban old men
Who is the man who, Delphi's
prophetic rock has sung,
committed unspeakable deeds   465
with murderous hands?

ὦρα νιν ἀελλάδων
ἵππων cθεναρώτερον
φυγᾷ πόδα νωμᾶν.
ἔνοπλος γὰρ ἐπ' αὐτὸν ἐπενθρῴcκει
πυρὶ καὶ cτεροπαῖc ὁ Διὸc γενέταc,   470
δειναὶ δ' ἅμ' ἕπονται
Κῆρεc ἀναπλάκητοι.

ἔλαμψε γὰρ τοῦ νιφόεν-   ἀντ. α'
τοc ἀρτίωc φανεῖcα
φήμα Παρνασοῦ τὸν ἄδη-   475
λον ἄνδρα πάντ' ἰχνεύειν.
φοιτᾷ γὰρ ὑπ' ἀγρίαν
ὕλαν ἀνά τ' ἄντρα καὶ
πετραῖοc ὁ ταῦροc,
μέλεοc μελέῳ ποδὶ χηρεύων,
τὰ μεcόμφαλα γᾶc ἀπονοcφίζων   480
μαντεῖα· τὰ δ' ἀεὶ
ζῶντα περιποτᾶται.

δεινά με νῦν, δεινὰ ταράccει   cτρ. β'
cοφὸc οἰωνοθέταc,
οὔτε δοκοῦντ' οὔτ' ἀποφάcκονθ',   485
ὅ τι λέξω δ' ἀπορῶ.
πέτομαι δ' ἐλπίcιν οὔτ' ἐνθάδ' ὁρῶν οὔτ' ὀπίcω.
τί γὰρ ἢ Λαβδακίδαιc
ἢ τῷ Πολύβου νεῖ-   490
κοc ἔκειτ' οὔτε πάροιθέν

467 ἀελλάδων Hesychius: ἀελλοπόδων codd.   470 cτεροπαῖc ὁ] cτεροπαῖcι t   472 ἀναπλάκητοι LPDt: ἀναμπλ- rpa
475 φήμα Lrpa: φάμα pZrt   Παρνασοῦ] -αccοῦ Xr, coni. Hermann   478 πετραῖοc ὁ fortasse L^ac sed non iam legitur: πετραῖοc
ὡc KRV: πέτραιc ὡc Gp: πέτραc ὡc pat: πέτραc ἅτε D'Orville
481 ἀεὶ] αἰεὶ t   483 με νῦν Bergk: μὲν οὖν codd.: με νοῦν
Nauck   490 ἢ] καὶ Blaydes

Time has come for him to ply
in flight a foot stronger
than storm-swift horses.
Armed with his father's fiery bolts,
Apollo, son of Zeus, is leaping after him   470
and with the god follow dreadful
Furies,[37] unfailing in pursuit.

There flashed recently
from snow-capped Parnassus[38]
an oracle: track down
by all means the unseen man.   475
He ranges under the wild
woodlands and up through the caves,
like a bull amid rocks,
bereaved and wretched with wretched foot,
trying to stay away from the prophecies   480
of the earth's navel.[39] Yet ever alive,
they flutter about him.

Dreadfully, dreadfully the skillful
augur confounds me.
I cannot accept. I do not deny.   485
I am at a loss what to say.
I hover, suspended on hopes and forebodings,
seeing neither the here and now nor what will happen.
What quarrel lies with the children of Labdacus
or with the son of Polybus   490
in the past or the present,
I know not, starting from which

ποτ' ἔγωγ' οὔτε τανῦν πως
ἔμαθον, πρὸς ὅτου δὴ
βαcάνῳ ⟨– ∪∪ –⟩
ἐπὶ τὰν ἐπίδαμον   495
φάτιν εἶμ' Οἰδιπόδα Λαβδακίδαις
ἐπίκουροc ἀδήλων θανάτων.

ἀλλ' ὁ μὲν οὖν Ζεὺς ὅ τ' Ἀπόλλων   ἀντ. β'
ξυνετοὶ καὶ τὰ βροτῶν
εἰδότεc· ἀνδρῶν δ' ὅτι μάντιc
πλέον ἢ 'γὼ φέρεται,   500
κρίcιc οὐκ ἔcτιν ἀληθήc·
cοφίᾳ δ' ἂν cοφίαν
παραμείψειεν ἀνήρ.
ἀλλ' οὔποτ' ἔγωγ' ἄν,
πρὶν ἴδοιμ' ὀρθὸν ἔποc, μεμ-   505
φομένων ἂν καταφαίην.
φανερὰ γὰρ ἐπ' αὐτῷ
πτερόεcc' ἦλθε κόρα
ποτέ, καὶ cοφὸc ὤφθη
βαcάνῳ θ' ἡδύπολιc· τὼc ἀπ' ἐμᾶc   510
φρενὸc οὔποτ' ὀφλήcει κακίαν.

Κρ.   ἄνδρεc πολῖται, δείν' ἔπη πεπυcμένοc
κατηγορεῖν μου τὸν τύραννον Οἰδίπουν
πάρειμ' ἀτλητῶν. εἰ γὰρ ἐν ταῖc ξυμφοραῖc   515
ταῖc νῦν δοκεῖ τι πρόc γ' ἐμοῦ πεπονθέναι

492 πωc nos: πω codd.   494 ubi lacuna statuenda sit incertum
est: post ἔμαθον Campbell, post ὅτου Brunck, post δὴ Hermann,
post βαcάνῳ Ritter: ⟨χρηcάμενοc⟩ Brunck: ⟨πίcτιν ἔχων⟩ G. Wolff
499 τὰ βροτῶν Lpat: τὰν βροτοῖc Krp   507 γὰρ ἐπ' αὐτῷ
om. t metri causa   509 ποτέ] τότε Blaydes   510 θ'
Λpat: δ' LᵃᶜKrp   ἡδύπολιc] ἀδύ- Erfurdt   τὼc Lloyd-Jones: τῷ
K (de Lᵃᶜ non liquet) rap: τῷδ' t: των P.Oxy. 2180   ἀπ'] πρὸc Elmsley: παρ' G. Wolff   516 δοκεῖ τι Blaydes: νομίζει codd.   γ'
ἐμοῦ pXrT: τ' ἐμοῦ KrpaTa et P.Oxy. 2180 ut videtur: de L non liquet: τί
τ' ἐμοῦ O: τί μου Hartung (τι ut gl. praebent aT)

as proof ... .[40]
in alliance with the Labdacids,
could I assail Oedipus' reputation among the people   495
because of unseen murders.

Yes, Zeus and Apollo are wise
and knowing in the ways
of mortals, but that a seer from among men
carries off a greater prize than I—   500
no true benchmark exists for that.
A man might surpass
skill with his skill.
Yet, until I see the straight story,
never would I assent when blame   505
falls upon Oedipus,
for once the winged maiden
came upon him in plain sight,
and he was seen skilled and
pleasing by the test to the city. Therefore in my mind   510
he will never be guilty of any evil.[41]

[*Enter Creon from the city.*]

Cr   Men, citizens, I have learned of terrible accusations
     that the tyrant, Oedipus, has leveled against me, and,
     unable to endure them, I have come. If in the present calamity   515
     he thinks that he has suffered something from me

λόγοιςιν εἴτ' ἔργοιςιν ἐς βλάβην φέρον,
οὗτοι βίου μοι τοῦ μακραίωνος πόθος,
φέροντι τήνδε βάξιν. οὐ γὰρ εἰς ἁπλοῦν
ἡ ζημία μοι τοῦ λόγου τούτου φέρει,   520
ἀλλ' ἐς μέγιςτον, εἰ κακὸς μὲν ἐν πόλει,
κακὸς δὲ πρὸς coῦ καὶ φίλων κεκλήςομαι.
Χο. ἀλλ' ἦλθε μὲν δὴ τοῦτο τοὔνειδος, τάχ' ἂν δ'
ὀργῇ βιαςθὲν μᾶλλον ἢ γνώμῃ φρενῶν.
Κρ. τοὔπος δ' ἐφάνθη ταῖς ἐμαῖς γνώμαις ὅτι   525
πειςθεὶς ὁ μάντις τοὺς λόγους ψευδεῖς λέγοι;
Χο. ηὐδᾶτο μὲν τάδ', οἶδα δ' οὐ γνώμῃ τίνι.
Κρ. ἐξ ὀμμάτων δ' ὀρθῶν τε κἀπ' ὀρθῆς φρενὸς
κατηγορεῖτο τοὐπίκλημα τοῦτό μου;
Χο. οὐκ οἶδ'· ἃ γὰρ δρῶς' οἱ κρατοῦντες οὐχ
ὁρῶ.   530
[αὐτὸς δ' ὅδ' ἤδη δωμάτων ἔξω περᾷ.]
Οι. οὗτος cύ, πῶς δεῦρ' ἦλθες; ἦ τοςόνδ' ἔχεις
τόλμης πρόςωπον ὥςτε τὰς ἐμὰς ςτέγας
ἵκου, φονεὺς ὢν τοῦδε τἀνδρὸς ἐμφανῶς
λῃςτής τ' ἐναργὴς τῆς ἐμῆς τυραννίδος;   535
φέρ' εἰπὲ πρὸς θεῶν, δειλίαν ἢ μωρίαν
ἰδών τιν' ἔν μοι ταῦτ' ἐβουλεύςω ποεῖν;
ἢ τοὔργον ὡς οὐ γνωριοῖμί ςου τόδε
δόλῳ προςέρπον κοὐκ ἀλεξοίμην μαθών;
ἆρ' οὐχὶ μῶρόν ἐςτι τοὐγχείρημά ςου,   540
ἄνευ τε πλούτου καὶ φίλων τυραννίδα

521 ἐς LRpat: εἰς Gpa 523 δ' P.Oxy. 2180, coni. M. Schmidt: om. codd. 524 βιαςθὲν] 'κβιαςθὲν P. Groeneboom 525 τοὔπος P.Oxy. 2180, Kr, coni. Heimsoeth: τοῦ πρὸς Lp: πρὸς τοῦ at 526 λέγοι Lrpa: λέγει CAt 528 δ' P.Oxy. 2180, rp et Suda s.v. ὀρθῆς: om. Lpa τε LPaZrt: δὲ rpa κἀπ' P.Oxy. 2180: κἀξ codd. 531 om. P.Oxy. 2180, del. H. J. Rose 535 ἐναργὴς] -ὼς C, coni. Blaydes 537 ἔν μοι Reisig: ἐν ἐμοὶ codd. ποεῖν Lrp: ποιεῖν pat 538 ἢ] ἦ Schaefer γνωριοῖμί Elmsley: -ίςοιμί codd. 539 κοὐκ] ἢ οὐκ A. Spengel 541 πλούτου anon. (1803): πλήθους codd.

in words or deeds that bears him harm,
I have no desire for a long life, bearing
such a reputation. The punishment for what has been said does
    not bear
upon me in a single aspect of my life but to the greatest degree,   520
if I shall be called evil in the city and evil by you and my friends.

Co   Well, this insult came, but perhaps it was forced out by anger
rather than being said with considered judgment.

Cr   This statement was made public, was it not, that the seer
spoke falsely because he was persuaded by my intrigues?   525

Co   He said those things. I do not know with what judgment.

Cr   With steady eyes and mind steady
was the accusation brought against me?

[*Oedipus enters from the house. Hence Creon is likely to have entered
from the city, where he heard the rumor of Oedipus' accusations.*]

Co   I do not know. What those in power do I do not see.   530
[But here is Oedipus himself approaching from the house.]

Oe   You there, how did you come here? Do you have
a face so bold that you arrive at my house,
certainly the murderer of this man[42] and red-handed bandit after
    my tyranny.   535
Come, by the gods, tell me, seeing what cowardice, what foolishness
    in me,
did you plot to carry out these schemes?
Did you believe that I wouldn't detect this move
creeping stealthily upon me and, once aware of it, I wouldn't defend
    myself?
Is yours not a fool's undertaking, hunting   540
without wealth and friends for a tyranny,

θηρᾶν, ὃ πλήθει χρήμασίν θ' ἁλίcκεται;
Κρ.   οἶcθ' ὡc πόηcον; ἀντὶ τῶν εἰρημένων
     ἴc' ἀντάκουcον, κᾷτα κρῖν' αὐτὸc μαθών.
Οι.   λέγειν cὺ δεινόc, μανθάνειν δ' ἐγὼ κακὸc   545
     cοῦ· δυcμενῆ γὰρ καὶ βαρύν c' ηὕρηκ' ἐμοί.
Κρ.   τοῦτ' αὐτὸ νῦν μου πρῶτ' ἄκουcον ὡc ἐρῶ.
Οι.   τοῦτ' αὐτὸ μή μοι φράζ', ὅπωc οὐκ εἶ κακόc.
Κρ.   εἴ τοι νομίζειc κτῆμα τὴν αὐθαδίαν
     εἶναί τι τοῦ νοῦ χωρίc, οὐκ ὀρθῶc φρονεῖc.   550
Οι.   εἴ τοι νομίζειc ἄνδρα cυγγενῆ κακῶc
     δρῶν οὐχ ὑφέξειν τὴν δίκην, οὐκ εὖ φρονεῖc.
Κρ.   ξύμφημί cοι ταῦτ' ἔνδικ' εἰρῆcθαι· τὸ δὲ
     πάθημ' ὁποῖον φὴc παθεῖν δίδαcκέ με.
Οι.   ἔπειθεc, ἢ οὐκ ἔπειθεc, ὡc χρείη μ' ἐπὶ   555
     τὸν cεμνόμαντιν ἄνδρα πέμψαcθαί τινα;
Κρ.   καὶ νῦν ἔθ' αὐτόc εἰμι τῷ βουλεύματι.
Οι.   πόcον τιν' ἤδη δῆθ' ὁ Λάιοc χρόνον—
Κρ.   δέδρακε ποῖον ἔργον; οὐ γὰρ ἐννοῶ.
Οι.   ἄφαντοc ἔρρει θαναcίμῳ χειρώματι;   560
Κρ.   μακροὶ παλαιοί τ' ἂν μετρηθεῖεν χρόνοι.
Οι.   τότ' οὖν ὁ μάντιc οὗτοc ἦν ἐν τῇ τέχνῃ;
Κρ.   cοφόc γ' ὁμοίωc κἀξ ἴcου τιμώμενοc.
Οι.   ἐμνήcατ' οὖν ἐμοῦ τι τῷ τότ' ἐν χρόνῳ;
Κρ.   οὔκουν ἐμοῦ γ' ἑcτῶτοc οὐδαμοῦ πέλαc.   565
Οι.   ἀλλ' οὐκ ἔρευναν τοῦ κανόντοc ἔcχετε;
Κρ.   παρέcχομεν, πῶc δ' οὐχί; κοὐκ ἠκούcαμεν.
Οι.   πῶc οὖν τόθ' οὗτοc ὁ cοφὸc οὐκ ηὔδα τάδε;

542 θηρᾶν LGpa: ζητῶν Rp   ὃ Lpa: ἢ rp   543 πόηcον
Lᵃᶜ: ποίηcον Pa: ποήcων vel ποιήcων K et cett.   ἀντὶ Lpat: κἀντὶ
Kr   545 κακὸc] an βραδύc? cf. 548   549 τὴν at Suda s.v.
εἴ τοι νομίζειc κτλ.: τήνδ' Lrp   555 χρείη p: χρεῖ' ἢ codd.
plerique   557 νῦν ⟨γ'⟩ Blaydes   ἔθ' L in margine, F: ἔτ' cett.
566 κανόντοc Herwerden: θανόντοc codd.: κτανόντοc Meineke
567 παρέcχομεν] ἀλλ' ἔcχομεν Schneidewin   κοὐκ ἠκούcαμεν]
κοὐκ ἠγρεύcαμεν Broadhead   568 τόθ' post οὗτοc
praebet l

a thing which is caught with the backing of a throng and money?

Cr Do you know what you should do? Instead of talking,
listen as much, and learn, and then decide for yourself.

Oe You're clever at speaking, but I'm bad at learning   545
from you. I have found you out to be hostile and burdensome.

Cr Now first listen to me. I will explain that very point.

Oe Don't talk to me about this very point—how you're not evil.

Cr If you believe that willfulness devoid of sense
is worth possessing, you are not thinking straight.   550

Oe If you believe that you can so mistreat a kinsman and
not account for that behavior, you're not thinking right.

Cr I agree that you speak justly. But teach me
what injury you say you suffered from me.

Oe Were you urging me, or were you not urging me, that I should send 555
someone to fetch the revered seer?

Cr Yes, and I am still of that opinion.

Oe How long has it been now that Laïos—

Cr Did what? I do not understand.

Oe has been gone, vanished, beneath deadly violence?   560

Cr A long time in the past would be measured.

Oe Was this seer practicing his craft at that time?

Cr Yes, as skilled as now and equally honored.

Oe Did he mention me in any way back then?

Cr No, not at all when I was standing nearby.   565

Oe You all did not mount a search for the murderer?

Cr We did, of course, yet we did not hear—

Oe How was it that this wise one did not speak out then?

Κρ. οὐκ οἶδ'· ἐφ' οἷς γὰρ μὴ φρονῶ σιγᾶν φιλῶ.
Οι. τοσόνδε γ' οἶσθα καὶ λέγοις ἂν εὖ φρονῶν—   570
Κρ. ποῖον τόδ'; εἰ γὰρ οἶδά γ', οὐκ ἀρνήσομαι.
Οι. ὁθούνεκ', εἰ μὴ σοὶ ξυνῆλθε, τὰς ἐμὰς
     οὐκ ἄν ποτ' εἶπε Λαΐου διαφθοράς.
Κρ. εἰ μὲν λέγει τάδ', αὐτὸς οἶσθ'· ἐγὼ δέ σου
     μαθεῖν δικαιῶ ταῦθ' ἅπερ κἀμοῦ σὺ νῦν.   575
Οι. ἐκμάνθαν'· οὐ γὰρ δὴ φονεὺς ἁλώσομαι.
Κρ. τί δῆτ'; ἀδελφὴν τὴν ἐμὴν γήμας ἔχεις;
Οι. ἄρνησις οὐκ ἔνεστιν ὧν ἀνιστορεῖς.
Κρ. ἄρχεις δ' ἐκείνῃ ταὐτὰ γῆς ἴσον νέμων;
Οι. ἂν ᾗ θέλουσα πάντ' ἐμοῦ κομίζεται.   580
Κρ. οὔκουν ἰσοῦμαι σφῷν ἐγὼ δυοῖν τρίτος;
Οι. ἐνταῦθα γὰρ δὴ καὶ κακὸς φαίνῃ φίλος.
Κρ. οὔκ, εἰ διδοίης γ' ὡς ἐγὼ σαυτῷ λόγον.
     σκέψαι δὲ τοῦτο πρῶτον, εἴ τιν' ἂν δοκεῖς
     ἄρχειν ἑλέσθαι ξὺν φόβοισι μᾶλλον ἢ   585
     ἄτρεστον εὕδοντ', εἰ τά γ' αὔθ' ἕξει κράτη.
     ἐγὼ μὲν οὖν οὔτ' αὐτὸς ἱμείρων ἔφυν
     τύραννος εἶναι μᾶλλον ἢ τύραννα δρᾶν,
     οὔτ' ἄλλος ὅστις σωφρονεῖν ἐπίσταται.
     νῦν μὲν γὰρ ἐκ σοῦ πάντ' ἄνευ φόβου φέρω,   590
     εἰ δ' αὐτὸς ἦρχον, πολλὰ κἂν ἄκων ἔδρων.
     πῶς δῆτ' ἐμοὶ τυραννὶς ἡδίων ἔχειν
     ἀρχῆς ἀλύπου καὶ δυναστείας ἔφυ;
     οὔπω τοσοῦτον ἠπατημένος κυρῶ
     ὥστ' ἄλλα χρῄζειν ἢ τὰ σὺν κέρδει καλά.   595
     νῦν πᾶσι χαίρω, νῦν με πᾶς ἀσπάζεται,

570 τοσόνδε codd. plerique (fortasse etiam Lᵖᶜ): τὸ σὸν δέ LᵃᶜKp,
coni. Brunck   572 τὰς] τάσδ' Doederlein   575 ταῦθ'
Brunck: ταυθ' codd.   576 φονεύς ⟨γ'⟩ Blaydes
579 ταὐτὰ γῆς] τῆς ταγῆς C. Otto   580 ἂν Paᵖᶜat: ἂν LrpXs
583 ἐγώ] ἔχω Heimsoeth   586 εἰ τά γ' αὔθ'] εἴ γε ταῦθ'
Broadhead   587 ἱμείρων] ἱμείρειν Herwerden   590 φόβου]
φθόνου Blaydes

Cr	I do not know, and in that case, I prefer to keep silent.
Oe	This much you know and could say if you're loyal of mind. 570
Cr	What is it? If I know, I will not refuse to tell you.
Oe	That if he hadn't been in league with you, he would not
	have spoken about my destruction of Laïos.
Cr	If he says this, you yourself know. But I judge it fair
	that I learn from you as you learned from me just now. 575
Oe	Learn away. Yet, understand this: I'll not be caught a murderer.[43]
Cr	Well, then? You married my sister and have her as your wife?
Oe	There is no denying what you are asking.
Cr	You rule the land with her on the same terms, sharing equally?
Oe	Everything she wants she gets from me. 580
Cr	Am I not a third, equal to the two of you?
Oe	Yes, it's precisely there you are shown to be an evil friend.
Cr	No, not if you think about it the way I do.
	Consider this first: do you suppose anyone
	would choose rule with its fears rather than 585
	to sleep untroubled if he has the same powers?
	No, he would not. I am not by nature the sort to desire
	to be tyrant rather than to do what a tyrant does.
	Neither would anyone else who knows how to be sensible.
	Now, as it is, I get everything from you without fear. 590
	But if I were ruling myself, I'd be doing many things I'd rather not.
	How could a tyranny be sweeter for me to have
	than rule without pain and with high station?
	Not ever have I been so self-deceived
	that I wanted anything except good things with returns. 595
	Now I delight in everybody, now everyone greets me,

νῦν οἱ ϲέθεν χρῄζοντεϲ ἐκκαλοῦϲί με·
τὸ γὰρ τυχεῖν αὐτοῖϲι πᾶν ἐνταῦθ᾽ ἔνι.
πῶϲ δῆτ᾽ ἐγὼ κεῖν᾽ ἂν λάβοιμ᾽ ἀφεὶϲ τάδε;
[οὐκ ἂν γένοιτο νοῦϲ κακὸϲ καλῶϲ φρονῶν.]   600
ἀλλ᾽ οὔτ᾽ ἐραϲτὴϲ τῆϲδε τῆϲ γνώμηϲ ἔφυν
οὔτ᾽ ἂν μετ᾽ ἄλλου δρῶντοϲ ἂν τλαίην ποτέ.
καὶ τῶνδ᾽ ἔλεγχον τοῦτο μὲν Πυθώδ᾽ ἰὼν
πεύθου τὰ χρηϲθέντ᾽, εἰ ϲαφῶϲ ἤγγειλά ϲοι·
τοῦτ᾽ ἀλλ᾽, ἐάν με τῷ τεραϲκόπῳ λάβῃϲ   605
κοινῇ τι βουλεύϲαντα, μή μ᾽ ἁπλῇ κτάνῃϲ
ψήφῳ, διπλῇ δέ, τῇ τ᾽ ἐμῇ καὶ ϲῇ, λαβών,
γνώμῃ δ᾽ ἀδήλῳ μή με χωρὶϲ αἰτιῶ.
οὐ γὰρ δίκαιον οὔτε τοὺϲ κακοὺϲ μάτην
χρηϲτοὺϲ νομίζειν οὔτε τοὺϲ χρηϲτοὺϲ
    κακούϲ.   610
[φίλον γὰρ ἐϲθλὸν ἐκβαλεῖν ἴϲον λέγω
καὶ τὸν παρ᾽ αὑτῷ βίοτον, ὃν πλεῖϲτον φιλεῖ.]
ἀλλ᾽ ἐν χρόνῳ γνώϲῃ τάδ᾽ ἀϲφαλῶϲ, ἐπεὶ
χρόνοϲ δίκαιον ἄνδρα δείκνυϲιν μόνοϲ,
κακὸν δὲ κἂν ἐν ἡμέρᾳ γνοίηϲ μιᾷ.   615
Χο.   καλῶϲ ἔλεξεν εὐλαβουμένῳ πεϲεῖν,
      ἄναξ· φρονεῖν γὰρ οἱ ταχεῖϲ οὐκ ἀϲφαλεῖϲ.
Οι.   ὅταν ταχύϲ τιϲ οὑπιβουλεύων λάθρᾳ
      χωρῇ, ταχὺν δεῖ κἀμὲ βουλεύειν πάλιν.
      εἰ δ᾽ ἡϲυχάζων προϲμενῶ, τὰ τοῦδε μὲν   620
      πεπραγμέν᾽ ἔϲται, τἀμὰ δ᾽ ἡμαρτημένα.
Κρ.   τί δῆτα χρῄζειϲ; ἦ με γῆϲ ἔξω βαλεῖν;

597 ἐκκαλοῦϲι] αἰκάλλουϲι diffidenter Musgrave   με] ἐμέ
Meineke   598 del. Wecklein   αὐτοῖϲι **r**: αὐτοῖϲ Lᵖᶜ**pat**:
αὐτοὺϲ Lᵃᶜ**p**Zr: 'fort. αἰτοῦϲι' Pearson   πᾶν **r**C: ἄπαν Lp: ἅπαντ᾽
pat   600 del. G. Wolff   κακὸϲ post ἂν transp. Herwerden   604 πεύθου Lᵖᶜ**pat**: πείθου ΛΚV: πύθου **rp**: πυθοῦ
Nauck   605 τοῦτ᾽ Lrpa: ταῦτ᾽ pZrt   611–12 delevimus
(611–15 del. iam van Deventer)   612 αὑτῷ vel αὐτῷ codd.
plerique: αὐτοῦ **p**   618 οὑπιβουλεύων Lrpa: -εύϲων **pat**
621 ἔϲται Lrpat: ἔϲτι **p**

now those who seek some boon from you call me aside,
since success for them lies here.
How could I let this go and take that?
[A mind thinking sensibly could not become bad.]   600
No, I was not born a lover of such a purpose,
nor would I be so bold as to help someone acting on it.
   And as for proof for this, go to Pytho, and inquire
   about the oracles, whether I reported them to you accurately.
   And this, too: if you catch me hatching plots   605
   with the diviner, arrest and kill me
   not with a single vote but with a double one, mine and yours.
   Do not charge me on your own from an unclear judgment.
   It is not right to believe without proof that bad men
   are good or that good men are bad.   610
   [To throw away a good friend and kinsman, I say, is
   the same as throwing away his life which he holds very dear.]
   You will know about this for sure in time, since
   time alone shows a man to be just,
   but you could recognize a bad man in one day.   615

Co He has spoken well to someone on guard against falling,
   lord, for those quick to make up their minds are not steady.

Oe Whenever someone who plots against me in secret advances
   quickly, I must be quick in turn to form my plans.
   If I remain at rest, his undertaking will have   620
   been accomplished, and mine gone awry.

Cr What then do you want? To banish me from the land?

Οι.   ἥκιστα· θνῄσκειν, οὐ φυγεῖν σε βούλομαι.

      ·   ·   ·   ·   ·

Κρ.   ὅταν προδείξῃς οἷόν ἐστι τὸ φθονεῖν

      ·   ·   ·   ·   ·

Οι.   ὡς οὐχ ὑπείξων οὐδὲ πιστεύςων λέγεις;   625
Κρ.   οὐ γὰρ φρονοῦντά ς' εὖ βλέπω.   Οι. τὸ γοῦν
      ἐμόν.
Κρ.   ἀλλ' ἐξ ἴσου δεῖ κἀμόν.   Οι. ἀλλ' ἔφυς κακός.
Κρ.   εἰ δὲ ξυνίῃς μηδέν;   Οι. ἀρκτέον γ' ὅμως.
Κρ.   οὔτοι κακῶς γ' ἄρχοντος.   Οι. ὦ πόλις πόλις.
Κρ.   κἀμοὶ πόλεως μέτεστιν, οὐχὶ σοὶ μόνῳ.   630
Χο.   παύσασθ', ἄνακτες· καιρίαν δ' ὑμῖν ὁρῶ
      τήνδ' ἐκ δόμων στείχουσαν Ἰοκάστην, μεθ' ἧς
      τὸ νῦν παρεστὸς νεῖκος εὖ θέσθαι χρεών.

IOKACTH
      τί τὴν ἄβουλον, ὦ ταλαίπωροι, στάσιν
      γλώσσης ἐπήρασθ'; οὐδ' ἐπαισχύνεσθε γῆς   635
      οὕτω νοσούσης ἴδια κινοῦντες κακά;
      οὐκ εἶ σύ τ' οἴκους σύ τε, Κρέον, τὰς σὰς στέγας,
      καὶ μὴ τὸ μηδὲν ἄλγος ἐς μέγ' οἴσετε;
Κρ.   ὅμαιμε, δεινά μ' Οἰδίπους ὁ σὸς πόσις
      δρᾶσαι δικαιοῖ δυοῖν ἀποκρίνας κακοῖν,   640
      ἢ γῆς ἀπῶσαι πατρίδος, ἢ κτεῖναι λαβών.
Οι.   ξύμφημι· δρῶντα γάρ νιν, ὦ γύναι, κακῶς

623–5 lacunas statuit Bruhn (cf. 641): alii aliter locum restituere conati
sunt   624 ὅταν] ὦ τᾶν M. Schmidt: ὡς ἂν Kvičala, Seyffert   προ-
δείξῃς] -εις M. Schmidt   627 κἀμόν] τοὐμόν Herwerden
628 ξυνίῃς pat: -ίεις Lrpa   γ'] δ' O, probat West   630 μέτεστιν t: μέτεστι τῆσδ' fere reliqui   οὐχὶ] οὐ DZr, coni. Brunck
631 καιρίαν at: κυρίαν LᵖᶜKrpXr   ὑμῖν Lrpa: ἡμῖν pXrt
633 παρεστὸς GH et fortasse L: -εστὼς cett.   634 τὴν] τήνδ'
Doederlein   635 ἐπήρασθ' LᵃᶜKrpt: ἐπήρατ' pa   637 post σύ τ'
add. εἰς Zrt, ἐς Lrp: corr. a   Κρέον pXr: -ων codd. plerique   τὰς
σὰς Meineke: κατὰ Lrpa: om. Zrt   640 δυοῖν ἀποκρίνας]
θάτερον δυοῖν Dindorf: τοῖνδ' ἐν ἀποκρίνας Hermann

Oe Not at all. I want you to die, not to go into banishment.

. . . . .

Cr Since you illustrate what it is to envy

. . . . 44

Oe You speak as if you will not yield or trust me.   625

Cr Yes, I see that you are not thinking well.

Oe Right enough at any rate for my own interests.

Cr You should think equally about mine.

Oe No, you were born evil.

Cr And if you understand nothing?

Oe Still, I must rule.

Cr Not if you're ruling badly.

Oe O city, city.

Cr I have a share in the city. It is not yours alone.[45]   630

[*Enter Jocasta from the house.*]

Co Stop, lords, I see Jocasta coming out of the house
just in time. This quarrel must be settled with her help.

JOCASTA
You two, really! Why have you stirred up
this discord of tongues? Aren't you ashamed, with   635
the city so sick, to be stirring up private troubles?
Won't you go inside, and you, Creon, go home,
don't work something that is nothing into a big pain.

Cr Sister of the same blood, your husband, Oedipus, claims the right
to mistreat me dreadfully, choosing from two bad choices,   640
either to drive me from my fatherland or arrest and kill me.

Oe I agree. I have caught him, wife, trying to do my person εἴληφα τοὐμὸν cῶμα cὺν τέχνῃ κακῇ.

Κρ.   μή νυν ὀναίμην, ἀλλ᾽ ἀραῖος, εἴ cέ τι
       δέδρακ᾽, ὀλοίμην, ὧν ἐπαιτιᾷ με δρᾶν.   645

Ιο.   ὦ πρὸς θεῶν πίcτευcον, Οἰδίπους, τάδε,
       μάλιcτα μὲν τόνδ᾽ ὅρκον αἰδεcθεὶc θεῶν,
       ἔπειτα κἀμὲ τούcδε θ᾽ οἳ πάρειcί coι.

Χο.   πιθοῦ θελήcαc φρονή-   cτρ.
       cαc τ᾽, ἄναξ, λίccομαι—   650

Οι.   τί coι θέλειc δῆτ᾽ εἰκάθω;

Χο.   τὸν οὔτε πρὶν νήπιον
       νῦν τ᾽ ἐν ὅρκῳ μέγαν καταίδεcαι.

Οι.   οἶcθ᾽ οὖν ἃ χρῄζειc; Χο. οἶδα. Οι. φράζε
       δή· τί φῄc;

Χο.   τὸν ἐναγῆ φίλον μήποτέ c᾽ αἰτίᾳ   656
       cὺν ἀφανεῖ λόγων ἄτιμον βαλεῖν.

Οι.   εὖ νυν ἐπίcτω, ταῦθ᾽ ὅταν ζητῇc, ἐμοὶ
       ζητῶν ὄλεθρον ἢ φυγὴν ἐκ τῆcδε γῆc.

Χο.   οὐ τὸν πάντων θεῶν θεὸν πρόμον   660
       Ἅλιον· ἐπεὶ ἄθεος ἄφιλος ὅ τι πύματον
       ὀλοίμαν, φρόνηcιν εἰ τάνδ᾽ ἔχω.
       ἀλλὰ μοι δυcμόρῳ γᾶ φθίνου-   665
       cα τρύχει καρδίαν, τάδ᾽ εἰ κακοῖc
       προcάψει τοῖc πάλαι τὰ πρὸς cφῷν.

Οι.   ὁ δ᾽ οὖν ἴτω, κεἰ χρή με παντελῶc θανεῖν,
       ἢ γῆc ἄτιμον τῆcδ᾽ ἀπωcθῆναι βίᾳ.   670

656 ἐναγῆ] ἀναγῆ Musgrave   φίλον codd. plerique: φίλων p et
Suda s.v. ἐναγῆ φίλων   μήποτέ c᾽ Nauck: μήποτ᾽ ἐν codd.
657 cύν ⟨γ᾽⟩ t   λόγων Krp: λόγῳ pa: λόγον L   λόγῳ ⟨c᾽⟩ Hermann   βαλεῖν t et Suda: ἐκβαλεῖν cett.   658 ζητῇc] χρῄζῃc
r, coni. Meineke   659 φυγὴν Lᵖᶜpat: φυγεῖν rpXr
660 post οὐ add. μὰ rp   θεῶν θεὸν Lᵃᶜrpt: θεὸν p: θεῶν Na
666 καρδίαν Hermann: ψυχὰν καὶ codd.: λῆμα καὶ Pearson   post
κακοῖc add. κακὰ codd.: del. Brandscheid   667 προcάψει] -εις
Linwood

	physical harm, evilly with his evil scheming.	
Cr	May I not prosper. May I perish cursed if ever I have done	645
	to you any of the things you charge me with doing.	

Cr   May I not prosper. May I perish cursed if ever I have done   645
      to you any of the things you charge me with doing.
Jo   By the gods, Oedipus, believe what he says.
      Respect first this oath by the gods
      and then both me and these men present here with you.
Co   Consent, think, yield, lord, I beg of you.   650
Oe   What do you want me to yield to you?
Co   Respect him. He was no fool before, and now respect him as
          someone large in his oath.
Oe   Do you know what you desire?
Co   I know.
Oe   Tell me. What are you saying?   655
Co   I say for you never on the basis of an unclear story to hold guilty
      and dishonored a friend bound by a sacred oath.
Oe   Know well that when you seek this you are seeking
      for me death or exile from this land.[46]
Co   Not by the foremost god of all the gods,   660
      Helios. May I perish without god or friend
      in the worst way possible, if I have this thought.
      Yet the withering earth wears my heart away   665
      in misery, if this trouble from you two
      will compound the old ones.
Oe   Then let him go, even if I must perish utterly
      or be driven from this land by force and deprived of honor.   670

τὸ γὰρ σόν, οὐ τὸ τοῦδ', ἐποικτίρω στόμα
ἐλεινόν· οὗτος δ' ἔνθ' ἂν ᾖ στυγήσεται.

Κρ.   στυγνὸς μὲν εἴκων δῆλος εἶ, βαρὺς δ' ὅταν
θυμοῦ περάσῃς. αἱ δὲ τοιαῦται φύσεις
αὑταῖς δικαίως εἰσὶν ἄλγισται φέρειν.   675

Οι.   οὔκουν μ' ἐάσεις κἀκτὸς εἶ; Κρ. πορεύσομαι,
σοῦ μὲν τυχὼν ἀγνῶτος, ἐν δὲ τοῖσδε σῶς.

Χο.   γύναι, τί μέλλεις κομί-   ἀντ.
ζειν δόμων τόνδ' ἔσω;

Ιο.   μαθοῦσά γ' ἥτις ἡ τύχη.   680

Χο.   δόκησις ἀγνὼς λόγων
ἦλθε, δάπτει δὲ καὶ τὸ μὴ 'νδικον.

Ιο.   ἀμφοῖν ἀπ' αὐτοῖν; Χο. ναίχι. Ιο. καὶ τίς ἦν
λόγος;

Χο.   ἅλις ἔμοιγ', ἅλις, γᾶς προνοουμένῳ   685
φαίνεται, ἔνθ' ἔληξεν, αὐτοῦ μένειν.

Οι.   ὁρᾷς ἵν' ἥκεις, ἀγαθὸς ὢν γνώμην ἀνήρ,
τοὐμὸν παριεὶς καὶ καταμβλύνων κέαρ;

Χο.   ὦναξ, εἶπον μὲν οὐχ ἅπαξ μόνον,   690
ἴσθι δὲ παραφρόνιμον, ἄπορον ἐπὶ φρόνιμα
πεφάνθαι μ' ἄν, εἴ σ' ἐνοσφιζόμαν,
ὅς γ' ἐμὰν γᾶν φίλαν ἐν πόνοις
ἀλύουσαν κατ' ὀρθὸν οὔρισας,   695
τανῦν δ' εὔπομπος αὖ γένοιο.

Ιο.   πρὸς θεῶν δίδαξον κἄμ', ἄναξ, ὅτου ποτὲ
μῆνιν τοσήνδε πράγματος στήσας ἔχεις.

672 ἐλεινόν Porson: ἐλεεινόν codd.   673 στυγνὸς] -ὼς G,
F s.l.   677 σῶς nos: ἴσως rpa: ἴσος Lpat: ἴσων Blaydes
684 ἦν Lpt: ἦν ὁ rpa   685 προνοουμένῳ V, coni. Blaydes:
προπονουμένῳ rp: προπονουμένας Lpat   690 ὦναξ t: ἄναξ
cett.   692 σ' ἐνοσφιζόμαν Hermann: σε νοσφίζομαι codd.
694 γ' p, coni. Turnebus: τ' Lrpat   695 ἀλύουσαν] σαλεύ-
ουσαν Dobree   οὔρισας P.Oxy. 1369, r, Eustathius 661. 45, 1282. 17:
οὔρησας Lpat   696 δ' K (de L non liquet) rpZrt: τ' a   αὖ
γένοιο Blaydes: εἰ δύναιο codd.: εἰ γένοιο Bergk

I am moved by your words, piteous as they are,
not by his. This man, wherever he is, will be hated.

Cr   You clearly yield with bad grace, but whenever
you go beyond the pale in your anger, you are heavy to bear.
Natures like yours are most painful for themselves to endure and
rightfully so.   675

Oe   Won't you go away and leave me alone?

Cr   I'm going. I have found you lacking every understanding of me,
but I am safe and sound, thanks to these men.

[*Exit Creon.*]

Co   My lady, why do you delay in taking him inside the house?

Jo   I will, but not until I have learned what happened here.   680

Co   Unconfirmed suspicions bandied in words . . . also the sting of
injustice.

Jo   From both of them?

Co   Yes, from both.

Jo   And what is it they quarreled about?

Co   Enough, enough. It seems best to me in thinking   685
for the land that things be left where they ended.[47]

Oe   You see where you have come, though a man of good judgment,
by trying to temper and blunt my spleen?

Co   Lord, not once alone have I said this.   690
Rest assured that I would appear out of my mind,
at a loss for sensible thought, if I abandoned you.
My beloved land was awash in troubles,
and you set her aright on course.   695
May you again prove to be fair escort.

Jo   By the gods, tell me as well, lord, over what matter
have you cause to rouse such great wrath.

Οι. ἐρῶ· cὲ γὰρ τῶνδ' ἐc πλέον, γύναι, cέβω·   700
     Κρέοντος, οἵά μοι βεβουλευκὼς ἔχει.
Ιο. λέγ', εἰ cαφῶc τὸ νεῖκος ἐγκαλῶν ἐρεῖc.
Οι. φονέα με φηcὶ Λαΐου καθεcτάναι.
Ιο. αὐτὸς ξυνειδώc, ἢ μαθὼν ἄλλου πάρα;
Οι. μάντιν μὲν οὖν κακοῦργον ἐcπέμψαc, ἐπεὶ   705
     τό γ' εἰc ἑαυτὸν πᾶν ἐλευθεροῖ cτόμα.
Ιο. cύ νυν, ἀφεὶc cεαυτὸν ὧν λέγειc πέρι,
     ἐμοῦ 'πάκουcον καὶ μάθ' οὕνεκ' ἔcτι cοι
     βρότειον οὐδὲν μαντικῆc ἔχον τέχνηc.
     φανῶ δέ cοι cημεῖα τῶνδε cύντομα.   710
     χρηcμὸc γὰρ ἦλθε Λαΐῳ ποτ', οὐκ ἐρῶ
     Φοίβου γ' ἀπ' αὐτοῦ, τῶν δ' ὑπηρετῶν ἄπο,
     ὡc αὐτὸν ἥξοι μοῖρα πρὸc παιδὸc θανεῖν,
     ὅcτιc γένοιτ' ἐμοῦ τε κἀκείνου πάρα.
     καὶ τὸν μέν, ὥcπερ γ' ἡ φάτιc, ξένοι ποτὲ   715
     λῃcταὶ φονεύουc' ἐν τριπλαῖc ἁμαξιτοῖc·
     παιδὸc δὲ βλάcταc οὐ διέcχον ἡμέραι
     τρεῖc, καί νιν ἄρθρα κεῖνοc ἐνζεύξαc ποδοῖν
     ἔρριψεν ἄλλων χερcὶν εἰc ἄβατον ὄροc.
     κἀνταῦθ' Ἀπόλλων οὔτ' ἐκεῖνον ἤνυcεν   720
     φονέα γενέcθαι πατρὸc οὔτε Λάιον
     τὸ δεινὸν οὐφοβεῖτο πρὸc παιδὸc παθεῖν.
     τοιαῦτα φῆμαι μαντικαὶ διώριcαν,
     ὧν ἐντρέπου cὺ μηδέν· ὧν γὰρ ἂν θεὸc
     χρείαν ἐρευνᾷ ῥᾳδίωc αὐτὸc φανεῖ.   725
Οι. οἷόν μ' ἀκούcαντ' ἀρτίωc ἔχει, γύναι,
     ψυχῆc πλάνημα κἀνακίνηcιc φρενῶν.
Ιο. ποίαc μερίμνηc τοῦθ' ὑποcτραφεὶc λέγειc;

706 πᾶν . . . cτόμα suspicionem movent   709 ἔχον suspectum:
alii alia   713 ἥξοι Lp: ἥξει rpat: ἕξει Canter: ἕξοι Halm
716 τριπλαῖc LGpaTa: διπλαῖc RaT (cf. ad 730)   719 εἰc post
ἄβατον traiecit Musgrave   722 παθεῖν Cγραγρ: θανεῖν codd.
724 ὧν] ἦν Brunck et Musgrave   728 ὑποcτραφεὶc] ἐπι-
Blaydes (cave credas K supra lineam ἐπ praebere)

Oe   I will tell you, for I revere you, wife, more than these men.   700
      Creon's the matter, considering the plots he has devised against me.⁴⁸

Jo   Say it, if you will tell me clearly about the quarrel amid your
        accusations.

Oe   Creon says that I am the murderer of Laïos.

Jo   He speaks from his own knowledge or did he learn from another?

Oe   No, rather, he sent his miscreant of a prophet against me.   705
      As for himself, he keeps his mouth absolutely free.

Jo   Now, be at ease over everything you have been talking about,
      and listen to me. Learn and take comfort.
      Nothing mortal has any part of the art of prophecy.
      I will show you concise proofs of this.   710
   An oracle once came to Laïos—I will not say
      from Phoebus himself but from his servants—that
      his destiny would come that he die by a son
      who would be born from me and him,
      Yet, as the story goes at least, foreign   715
      bandits murdered Laïos at the three wagon roads.
      Three days had not elapsed from the child's birth when
      Laïos yoked his feet and cast him
      by the hands of others onto a trackless mountain.
      In this case, Apollo brought it about that he did not become   720
      his father's murderer, and Laïos did not suffer
      at his son's hands, an outcome he most dreaded.
   Such stuff did the prophetic oracles define.
      Do not pay them heed at all. Whatever a god sees
      the need of, he himself will readily reveal.   725

Oe   What wandering of my spirit, reeling of my mind
      grip me, wife, on listening to you just now.

Jo   What anxiety has upset you so that you say this?

Οι. ἔδοξ᾽ ἀκοῦσαι coῦ τόδ᾽, ὡς ὁ Λάιος
     κατασφαγείη πρὸς τριπλαῖς ἁμαξιτοῖς.   730
Ιο. ηὐδᾶτο γὰρ ταῦτ᾽ οὐδέ πω λήξαντ᾽ ἔχει.
Οι. καὶ ποῦ ᾽cθ᾽ ὁ χῶρος οὗτος οὗ τόδ᾽ ἦν πάθος;
Ιο. Φωκὶς μὲν ἡ γῆ κλήζεται, cχιcτὴ δ᾽ ὁδὸc
     ἐc ταὐτὸ Δελφῶν κἀπὸ Δαυλίας ἄγει.
Οι. καὶ τίς χρόνος τοῖcδ᾽ ἐcτὶν οὑξεληλυθώς;   735
Ιο. cχεδόν τι πρόcθεν ἢ cὺ τῆcδ᾽ ἔχων χθονὸc
     ἀρχὴν ἐφαίνου τοῦτ᾽ ἐκηρύχθη πόλει.
Οι. ὦ Ζεῦ, τί μου δρᾶcαι βεβούλευcαι πέρι;
Ιο. τί δ᾽ ἐcτί coι τοῦτ᾽, Οἰδίπους, ἐνθύμιον;
Οι. μήπω μ᾽ ἐρώτα· τὸν δὲ Λάιον φύcιν   740
     τίν᾽ εἷρπε φράζε, τίνα δ᾽ ἀκμὴν ἥβης ἔχων.
Ιο. μέλας, χνοάζων ἄρτι λευκανθὲς κάρα.
     μορφῆς δὲ τῆς cῆς οὐκ ἀπεcτάτει πολύ.
Οι. οἴμοι τάλας· ἔοικ᾽ ἐμαυτὸν εἰς ἀρὰς
     δεινὰς προβάλλων ἀρτίως οὐκ εἰδέναι.   745
Ιο. πῶς φής; ὀκνῶ τοι πρὸς c᾽ ἀποσκοποῦc᾽, ἄναξ.
Οι. δεινῶς ἀθυμῶ μὴ βλέπων ὁ μάντις ᾖ.
     δείξεις δὲ μᾶλλον, ἢν ἓν ἐξείπῃς ἔτι.
Ιο. καὶ μὴν ὀκνῶ μέν, ἃ δ᾽ ἂν ἔρῃ μαθοῦc᾽ ἐρῶ.
Οι. πότερον ἐχώρει βαιός, ἢ πολλοὺς ἔχων   750
     ἄνδρας λοχίτας, οἷ᾽ ἀνὴρ ἀρχηγέτης;
Ιο. πέντ᾽ ἦσαν οἱ ξύμπαντες, ἐν δ᾽ αὐτοῖcιν ἦν
     κῆρυξ· ἀπήνη δ᾽ ἦγε Λάιον μία.
Οι. αἰαῖ, τάδ᾽ ἤδη διαφανῆ. τίς ἦν ποτε
     ὁ τούcδε λέξας τοὺς λόγους ὑμῖν, γύναι;   755
Ιο. οἰκεύς τις, ὅcπερ ἵκετ᾽ ἐκcωθεὶς μόνος.
Οι. ἦ κἀν δόμοιcι τυγχάνει τανῦν παρών;

730 τριπλαῖc **pat**: διπλαῖc **Lrpa**, T s.l.   734 ἐc **Lpat**: εἰc **rD**
κἀπὸ **Lrpat**: κἀπὶ **p**   741 εἷρπε Schneidewin: εἶχε **codd.**:
ἔτυχε Hartung   742 μέλας **rp**: μέγας **Lpat**   λευκανθὲc
LRpat: -εὶc **Gp**   747 ᾖ] ἦν Campe   749 ἃ δ᾽ ἂν **codd.**
plerique: ἂν δ᾽ Dresdensis D. 183 et Laudianus gr. 54   752 δ᾽ post
αὐτοῖcι praebent **Lrp**

Oe	I thought I heard you say that Laïos
	was slaughtered near the three wagon roads. 730
Jo	Yes, that was the rumor, and it has not stopped yet.
Oe	And where is the place where this incident occurred?
Jo	The country is called Phocis. The split road leads
	from Delphi and Daulia to the same place.
Oe	What is the time that has gone by since these events happened? 735
Jo	Just before you came into power
	over this land, it was announced to the city.
Oe	O Zeus, what have you planned to do with me?
Jo	Why does this weigh upon you, Oedipus?
Oe	Don't ask yet. Laïos, tell me about him. 740
	His build? What peak of youth?
Jo	Dark complexion.⁴⁹ His head sprinkled with a sheen of gray.
	A build not much different from yours.
Oe	O wretched me, it seems I did not know what I was doing just
	now
	when I hurled myself into dreadful curses. 745
Jo	What are you saying? I shrink with fear when I look at you, lord.
Oe	I have fearful misgivings that the seer had sight.
	You will reveal more if you tell me one thing more.
Jo	I shrink with fear also, but whatever you ask, if I know, I will
	tell you.
Oe	Was he traveling with a few, or had he many 750
	armed guards as befit a man in command?
Jo	Altogether, there were five, and among them was
	a herald. A single four-wheeled wagon carried Laïos.
Oe	Alas, everything now is crystal clear.
	Who was it who told you about this, wife? 755
Jo	A house slave who alone escaped and returned.
Oe	Does he happen to be here now, in the house?

Ιο.   οὐ δῆτ'· ἀφ' οὗ γὰρ κεῖθεν ἦλθε καὶ κράτη
      σέ τ' εἶδ' ἔχοντα Λάιόν τ' ὀλωλότα,
      ἐξικέτευσε τῆς ἐμῆς χειρὸς θιγὼν   760
      ἀγρούς σφε πέμψαι κἀπὶ ποιμνίων νομάς,
      ὡς πλεῖστον εἴη τοῦδ' ἄποπτος ἄστεως.
      κἄπεμψ' ἐγώ νιν· ἄξιος γάρ, οἷ' ἀνὴρ
      δοῦλος, φέρειν ἦν τῆσδε καὶ μείζω χάριν.
Οι.   πῶς ἂν μόλοι δῆθ' ἡμὶν ἐν τάχει πάλιν;   765
Ιο.   πάρεστιν. ἀλλὰ πρὸς τί τοῦτ' ἐφίεσαι;
Οι.   δέδοικ' ἐμαυτόν, ὦ γύναι, μὴ πόλλ' ἄγαν
      εἰρημέν' ᾖ μοι δι' ἅ νιν εἰσιδεῖν θέλω.
Ιο.   ἀλλ' ἵξεται μέν· ἀξία δέ που μαθεῖν
      κἀγὼ τά γ' ἐν σοὶ δυσφόρως ἔχοντ', ἄναξ.   770
Οι.   κοὐ μὴ στερηθῇς γ' ἐς τοσοῦτον ἐλπίδων
      ἐμοῦ βεβῶτος. τῷ γὰρ ἂν καὶ κρείσσονι
      λέξαιμ' ἂν ἢ σοὶ διὰ τύχης τοιᾶσδ' ἰών;
      ἐμοὶ πατὴρ μὲν Πόλυβος ἦν Κορίνθιος,
      μήτηρ δὲ Μερόπη Δωρίς. ἠγόμην δ' ἀνὴρ   775
      ἀστῶν μέγιστος τῶν ἐκεῖ, πρίν μοι τύχη
      τοιάδ' ἐπέστη, θαυμάσαι μὲν ἀξία,
      σπουδῆς γε μέντοι τῆς ἐμῆς οὐκ ἀξία.
      ἀνὴρ γὰρ ἐν δείπνοις μ' ὑπερπλησθεὶς μέθης
      καλεῖ παρ' οἴνῳ πλαστὸς ὡς εἴην πατρί.   780
      κἀγὼ βαρυνθεὶς τὴν μὲν οὖσαν ἡμέραν
      μόλις κατέσχον, θἠτέρᾳ δ' ἰὼν πέλας
      μητρὸς πατρός τ' ἤλεγχον· οἱ δὲ δυσφόρως
      τοὔνειδος ἦγον τῷ μεθέντι τὸν λόγον.
      κἀγὼ τὰ μὲν κείνοιν ἐτερπόμην, ὅμως δ'   785

762 ἄστεως L: -oc cett.   763 οἷ' Hermann: ὅ γ' LP: ὅδ' Κrpa:
ὧδ' O: ὅδε γε at: ὡς γ' Musgrave   766 τοῦτ'] τοῦ δ' Vᵖᶜ, coni.
Blaydes   772 καὶ κρείσσονι Blaydes: καὶ μείζονι codd. (etiam K;
de L non liquet)   773 λέξαιμ' pa: λέξοιμ' Lrpt
774 ἐμοὶ πατὴρ ἦν Πόλυβος Arist. Rhet. 1415ᵃ20   778 om.
P.Oxy. 1369   779 μέθης pat: μέθῃ Lrp   782 θἠτέρᾳ
Lrp: θἀτέρᾳ pat

Jo   No, he is not. As soon as he came from there and saw
       that you had power and Laïos was dead,
       he touched my hand and pleaded   760
       for me to send him to the fields and pastures of the flocks
       so he might be very far out of sight of this town.
       And I sent him. As slaves go, he was worthy
       to receive a favor even greater than this.

Oe   Might he could come back to us quickly?   765

Jo   It is possible, yes, but why do you order this?

Oe   I fear, wife, that I have said too much
       already, which is why I want to see him.

Jo   He will come, but surely I deserve to learn
       what is so hard for you to bear, lord.   770

Oe   You won't be deprived, since I have come
       so far into foreboding. What person more important
       could I talk to about this tale of chance that I am traversing
           than you?
   My father was Polybus of Corinth,
       and my mother, Merope, a Dorian. I was accounted   775
       a very important man among the townsmen there before
       something happened to me by chance. It's worth
       wondering about but hardly worth the seriousness I gave it.
       There was a man at dinner. He was far gone in drink.
       And in his wine, he cried out that I was a suppositious son for
           my father.   780
       Although deeply upset, I restrained myself with difficulty
       the rest of that day, but on the next, I went
       to my mother and father and questioned them closely.
       They were angry at the insult and at the man who let the word fly.
       I was comforted by what they said, but nevertheless   785

ἔκνιζέ μ' ἀεὶ τοῦθ'· ὑφεῖρπε γὰρ πολύ.
λάθρᾳ δὲ μητρὸς καὶ πατρὸς πορεύομαι
Πυθώδε, καί μ' ὁ Φοῖβος ὧν μὲν ἱκόμην
ἄτιμον ἐξέπεμψεν, ἄλλα δ' ἀθλίῳ
καὶ δεινὰ καὶ δύστηνα προὔφάνη λέγων,   790
ὡς μητρὶ μὲν χρείη με μειχθῆναι, γένος δ'
ἄτλητον ἀνθρώποισι δηλώσοιμ' ὁρᾶν,
φονεὺς δ' ἐσοίμην τοῦ φυτεύσαντος πατρός.
κἀγὼ 'πακούσας ταῦτα τὴν Κορινθίαν
ἄστροις τὸ λοιπὸν τεκμαρούμενος χθόνα   795
ἔφευγον, ἔνθα μήποτ' ὀψοίμην κακῶν
χρησμῶν ὀνείδη τῶν ἐμῶν τελούμενα.
στείχων δ' ἱκνοῦμαι τούσδε τοὺς χώρους ἐν οἷς
σὺ τὸν τύραννον τοῦτον ὄλλυσθαι λέγεις.
καί σοι, γύναι, τἀληθὲς ἐξερῶ. τριπλῆς   800
ὅτ' ἦ κελεύθου τῆσδ' ὁδοιπορῶν πέλας,
ἐνταῦθά μοι κῆρύξ τε κἀπὶ πωλικῆς
ἀνὴρ ἀπήνης ἐμβεβώς, οἷον σὺ φής,
ξυνηντίαζον· κἀξ ὁδοῦ μ' ὅ θ' ἡγεμὼν
αὐτός θ' ὁ πρέσβυς πρὸς βίαν ἠλαυνέτην.   805
κἀγὼ τὸν ἐκτρέποντα, τὸν τροχηλάτην,
παίω δι' ὀργῆς· καί μ' ὁ πρέσβυς, ὡς ὁρᾷ,
ὄχους παραστείχοντα τηρήσας, μέσον
κάρα διπλοῖς κέντροισί μου καθίκετο.
οὐ μὴν ἴσην γ' ἔτεισεν, ἀλλὰ συντόμως   810
σκήπτρῳ τυπεὶς ἐκ τῆσδε χειρὸς ὕπτιος

786 ἀεὶ Lrpa: αἰεὶ pAt   788 μ' ὁ] με Herwerden
789 ἀθλίῳ Herwerden: -ια codd. (etiam K; de Lᵃᶜ non liquet)
790 προὔφάνη] προὔφηνεν Hermann dubitanter   791 χρείη
Paᴾᶜ, coni. Dawes: χρεῖ' ἤ vel sim. cett.   δ'] τ' Elmsley
792 δηλώσοιμ' Lrpt: -αιμ' Oᴾᶜa, T s.l.   794 τὴν] γῆν Seyffert
795 τεκμαρούμενος Nauck: ἐκμετρούμενος codd.   797 post
χρησμῶν add. γ' Krpa   800 om. l   801 ἤ Elmsley: ἦν
codd.   807–8 sic interpunxit R. Kassel   808 ὄχους
Doederlein: ὄχου codd.: ὄχον H. Stephanus   810 συντόμως]
συντόνως Dobree

what the man said grated on me, for it was creeping far and wide.
Unbeknown to my mother and father, I set out
for Delphi. Phoebus sent me away without honoring me with a
    response
to what I had come for, but to poor me
he openly declared dreadful, awful things, saying   790
that I must lie with my mother and show forth to men
a generation unbearable to see, and that
I would be the murderer of the father who sired me.
After I heard this, I fled, henceforth intending
    to judge the land of Corinth by the stars,   795
    to a place where I would never see
    the disgrace of the prophecies about me fulfilled.
    As I was walking, I approached this place
    where you say this tyrant was slain.
    And to you, wife, I will tell the truth. Making my way along,   800
    I came upon the three crossroads.
    There a herald and a man sitting
    on a wagon drawn by horses, just as you describe,
    confronted me. The guide and the older man himself,
    tried to drive me from the road by force.   805
    The one who was trying to push me aside, the driver,
    I struck out of anger. And the older man, seeing what was happening,
    watched as I walked by his wagon and came down on me
    in the middle of my head with his two-pronged goad.
    He did not repay equally, but in a flash,   810
    I struck him with a scepter in this hand, he rolled out

μέσης ἀπήνης εὐθὺς ἐκκυλίνδεται·
κτείνω δὲ τοὺς ξύμπαντας. εἰ δὲ τῷ ξένῳ
τούτῳ προσήκει Λαΐῳ τι συγγενές,
τίς τοῦδέ γ᾽ ἀνδρὸς νῦν ἂν ἀθλιώτερος,   815
τίς ἐχθροδαίμων μᾶλλον ἂν γένοιτ᾽ ἀνήρ,
ὃν μὴ ξένων ἔξεστι μηδ᾽ ἀστῶν τινι
δόμοις δέχεσθαι, μηδὲ προσφωνεῖν τινα,
ὠθεῖν δ᾽ ἀπ᾽ οἴκων; καὶ τάδ᾽ οὔτις ἄλλος ἦν
ἢ ᾽γὼ ᾽π᾽ ἐμαυτῷ τάσδ᾽ ἀρὰς ὁ προστιθείς.   820
λέχη δὲ τοῦ θανόντος ἐν χεροῖν ἐμαῖν
χραίνω, δι᾽ ὧνπερ ὤλετ᾽. ἆρ᾽ ἔφυν κακός;
ἆρ᾽ οὐχὶ πᾶς ἄναγνος; εἴ με χρὴ φυγεῖν,
καί μοι φυγόντι μἤστι τοὺς ἐμοὺς ἰδεῖν
μηδ᾽ ἐμβατεῦσαι πατρίδος, ἢ γάμοις με δεῖ   825
μητρὸς ζυγῆναι καὶ πατέρα κατακτανεῖν
Πόλυβον, ὃς ἐξέθρεψε κἀξέφυσέ με.
ἆρ᾽ οὐκ ἀπ᾽ ὠμοῦ ταῦτα δαίμονός τις ἂν
κρίνων ἐπ᾽ ἀνδρὶ τῷδ᾽ ἂν ὀρθοίη λόγον;
μὴ δῆτα μὴ δῆτ᾽, ὦ θεῶν ἁγνὸν σέβας,   830
ἴδοιμι ταύτην ἡμέραν, ἀλλ᾽ ἐκ βροτῶν
βαίην ἄφαντος πρόσθεν ἢ τοιάνδ᾽ ἰδεῖν
κηλῖδ᾽ ἐμαυτῷ συμφορᾶς ἀφιγμένην.

Χο.   ἡμῖν μέν, ὦναξ, ταῦτ᾽ ὀκνήρ᾽· ἕως δ᾽ ἂν οὖν
πρὸς τοῦ παρόντος ἐκμάθῃς, ἔχ᾽ ἐλπίδα.   835

Οι.   καὶ μὴν τοσοῦτόν γ᾽ ἐστί μοι τῆς ἐλπίδος,

814 Λαΐῳ] Λαΐου Bothe   815 del. Dindorf   νῦν Lrp: om.
Oat   ἂν Bergk: ἔστ᾽ Lrp: ἔστιν at   817 ὃν Schaefer: ᾧ
codd.   τινι Dindorf: τινα codd.   818 τινα] ἔτι Blaydes: ἐμέ
Nauck   822 ὧνπερ] ἧνπερ P.Oxy. 1369 in linea: αἶνπερ C, coni.
Blaydes   823 εἶ Lrpat: ἦ pXr   824 μἤστι voluerunt Lr et
Tγρ: μήτε pat   825 μηδ᾽ Dindorf: μή μ᾽ Krp: μήτ᾽ Lᵖᶜpa
ἐμβατεῦσαι P.Oxy. 1369: ἐμβατεύειν codd.   ἢ Lrpat: εἰ p
827 del. Wunder   ἐξέθρεψε κἀξέφυσέ P.Oxy. 1369, pZr: ἐξέφυσε
κἀξέθρεψε Lrpat   829 ἂν ὀρθοίη p, coni. Schaefer: ἀνορθοίη
Lrpat   833 συμφορᾶς Lrpat: ξυμ- p   836 γ᾽ pat: om.
Lrp

instantly from the middle of the wagon onto his back.
I killed them all. If some kinship
pertains to Laïos with this stranger,
who now is more wretched than this man? 815
What man could be more hateful to the gods
whom neither stranger nor townsman is allowed
to receive into his house or anyone to address
but must thrust him from their houses? And what's more, no one
other than I myself imposed these curses upon me. 820
I'm defiling the bed of the dead man with the hands
by which he perished. Was I born evil?
Am I not utterly tainted? If I must be banished,
once I am banished, I cannot see my own people
or tread the soil of my fatherland. Otherwise, I am bound 825
to be yoked in marriage with my mother and slay my father,
Polybus, who raised and sired me.
Would not someone have the tale correct
if he judged that this comes on this man from a savage daimon?
May I never see, never see, O holy majesty of gods, 830
this day, but I would depart from men unseen
before I see a stain of such misfortune come over me.

Co   We too are frightened, lord, but until you learn everything
      from the one who was there, have hope. 835

Oe   I have only this much hope alone,

τὸν ἄνδρα τὸν βοτῆρα προσμεῖναι μόνον.
Ιο. πεφασμένου· δὲ τίς ποθ᾽ ἡ προθυμία;
Οι. ἐγὼ διδάξω ς᾽· ἦν γὰρ εὑρεθῇ λέγων
coὶ ταῦτ᾽, ἔγωγ᾽ ἂν ἐκπεφευγοίην πάθος.   840
Ιο. ποῖον δέ μου περισσὸν ἤκουσας λόγον;
Οι. λῃστὰς ἔφασκες αὐτὸν ἄνδρας ἐννέπειν
ὥς νιν κατακτείνειαν. εἰ μὲν οὖν ἔτι
λέξει τὸν αὐτὸν ἀριθμόν, οὐκ ἐγὼ 'κτανον·
οὐ γὰρ γένοιτ᾽ ἂν εἷς γε τοῖς πολλοῖς ἴσος·   845
εἰ δ᾽ ἄνδρ᾽ ἕν᾽ οἰόζωνον αὐδήcει caφῶς,
τοῦτ᾽ ἐστὶν ἤδη τοὔργον εἰς ἐμὲ ῥέπον.
Ιο. ἀλλ᾽ ὡς φανέν γε τοὔπος ὧδ᾽ ἐπίcταco,
κοὐκ ἔστιν αὐτῷ τοῦτό γ᾽ ἐκβαλεῖν πάλιν·
πόλις γὰρ ἤκους᾽, οὐκ ἐγὼ μόνη, τάδε.   850
εἰ δ᾽ οὖν τι κἀκτρέποιτο τοῦ πρόcθεν λόγου,
οὔτοι ποτ᾽, ὦναξ, τόν γε Λαΐου φόνον
φανεῖ δικαίως ὀρθόν, ὅν γε Λοξίας
διεῖπε χρῆναι παιδὸς ἐξ ἐμοῦ θανεῖν.
καίτοι νιν οὐ κεῖνός γ᾽ ὁ δύςτηνός ποτε   855
κατέκταν᾽, ἀλλ᾽ αὐτὸς πάροιθεν ὤλετο.
ὥcτ᾽ οὐχὶ μαντείας γ᾽ ἂν οὔτε τῇδ᾽ ἐγὼ
βλέψαιμ᾽ ἂν οὔνεκ᾽ οὔτε τῇδ᾽ ἂν ὕcτερον.
Οι. καλῶς νομίζεις. ἀλλ᾽ ὅμως τὸν ἐργάτην
πέμψον τινὰ cτελοῦντα μηδὲ τοῦτ᾽ ἀφῇς.   860
Ιο. πέμψω ταχύνας᾽· ἀλλ᾽ ἴωμεν ἐς δόμους.
οὐδὲν γὰρ ἂν πράξαιμ᾽ ἂν ὧν οὐ coὶ φίλον.

837 προcμεῖναι Lrpat: -βῆναι p   840 ταῦτ᾽ LGpat: ταῦτ᾽
Rpa   841 μου] μοι t   843 κατακτείνειαν pZrt: -αιεν
LᵖᶜKRpa: -ειεν Gp   845 del. Naber   τοῖς] τις Brunck
846 ante caφῶς interpungunt fere editores, sed perperam: recte Kennedy
847 εἰς] ὡς r   ἐμὲ Lpa: ἐμοὶ r: ἡμᾶς t   849 αὐτῷ Lpat:
αὐτὸ rpZr   852 τόν γε] τόνδε r   φόνον] φόβον Schubert
852-3 Λαΐου ... Λοξίας] Λοξίου φανεῖ χρηcμὸν δικαίως ὀρθόν,
ὅς γε Λάιον Nauck   859 ἐργάτην] ἀγρότην Nauck
861 ἐς Lpat: εἰς rPaD   862 οὐ coί] οὔ coι LᵃᶜC

	to wait for the man, the herdsman.	
Jo	And once he has appeared, what is your interest in him?	
Oe	I'll tell you, for if he should be found saying	
	the same story as you, I would have escaped this disaster.	840
Jo	What in particular did you hear me say?	
Oe	"Bandits." You kept saying he reported	
	that bandits killed him. If he still says	
	the same number, I did not kill Laïos,	
	for *one* would not be equal to the *many*.	845
	If he says clearly one man traveling alone,	
	this deed is already descending toward me.	
Jo	Well, know that the account was made public in this way.	
	It is not possible for him to throw it out,	
	since the city heard it, not just I.	850
	Yet if he strays somehow from his earlier story,	
	still he will not reveal, lord, the murder of Laïos	
	with proper exactitude, seeing that Loxias	
	specifically stated that he must die as the result of my son.	
	And yet that poor wretch never killed him	855
	but perished himself a long time ago.	
	Thus I would not look as far as oracles are concerned	
	either this way or that in the future.	
Oe	You're right in your thinking. But still send someone	
	to fetch the worker, and do not neglect it.	860
Jo	I will hurry and send someone. But let's go inside.	
	I would not do anything that you would not like.	

Χο. εἴ μοι ξυνείη φέροντι μοῖρα τὰν   cτρ. α'
     εὔcεπτον ἁγνείαν λόγων
     ἔργων τε πάντων, ὧν νόμοι πρόκεινται   865
     ὑψίποδες, οὐρανίᾳ 'ν
     αἰθέρι τεκνωθέντες, ὧν Ὄλυμπος
     πατὴρ μόνος, οὐδέ νιν
     θνατὰ φύcιc ἀνέρων
     ἔτικτεν, οὐδὲ μήποτε λά-   870
     θα κατακοιμάcῃ·
     μέγας ἐν τούτοις θεόc, οὐδὲ γηράcκει.

     ὕβρις φυτεύει τύραννον· ὕβρις, εἰ   ἀντ. α'
     πολλῶν ὑπερπληcθῇ μάταν,
     ἃ μὴ 'πίκαιρα μηδὲ cυμφέροντα,   875
     ἀκρότατα γεῖc' ἀναβάc'
     ἀπότομον ὤρουcεν εἰς ἀνάγκαν
     ἔνθ' οὐ ποδὶ χρηcίμῳ
     χρῆται. τὸ καλῶc δ' ἔχον
     πόλει πάλαιcμα μήποτε λῦ-   880
     cαι θεὸν αἰτοῦμαι.
     θεὸν οὐ λήξω ποτὲ προcτάταν ἴcχων.

     εἰ δέ τις ὑπέροπτα χερcὶν   cτρ. β'
     ἢ λόγῳ πορεύεται,
     Δίκας ἀφόβητος, οὐδὲ   885

863 φέροντι] τρέφοντι Soutendam   866 post ὑψίποδέc add.
γ' t   866-7 οὐρανίᾳ 'ν αἰθέρι Enger: οὐρανίαν δι' αἰθέρα
codd., nisi quod variam lectionem vel interpretationem οὐρανίαc/-ου
αἰθέροc praebent AXr (cave credas haec in L ab ipso librario addita esse)
869 θνατὰ a: θνατὴ pt: θνητὴ Lrp   870 μήποτε Paris. gr.
2884, coni. Elmsley: μίν ποτε rC: μήν ποτε cett.   λάθα Gᵖᶜpat:
λάθρα LᵃᶜKr   κατακοιμάcῃ Lp: -άcει rpat   873 ὕβρις . . .
τύραννον] ὕβριν . . . τυραννίc Blaydes   τύραννον· ὕβρις] τύραννον ὕβριν· Fraenkel   876 ἀκρότατα γεῖc' ἀναβάc' G. Wolff:
ἀκροτάταν εἰcαναβάc' codd.   877 ἀπότομον Lpat: ἀπότιμον
r: ἄποτμον a   ὤρουcεν] ἀνώρουcεν t   883 ὑπέροπτα]
-οπλα Cᵃᶜ, coni. Dobree

[Oedipus and Jocasta exit to the house.]

CHORUS OF THEBAN OLD MEN
May destiny ever attend me
as I carry off the prize of reverent purity
of all words and deeds for which laws are enshrined,   865
high-footed, born
throughout the high ether of heaven, whose father
is Olympus alone. Them no
mortal nature of men
birthed. Never will   870
forgetfulness lull them to sleep.
Great is the god within. He ages not.

Arrogance begets a tyrant. Arrogance, if
rashly filled to excess with everything
that, unseasonable and without use,   875
once ascended the wall to the high coping,
plunges into headlong doom
where its foot is of
no use. I beg the god never to abolish
the wrestling that benefits the city.   880
Never will I cease to hold the god as my protector.

If a man walks haughty
of stride in deeds or word,
without fear of Justice, without   885

δαιμόνων ἔδη cέβων,
κακά νιν ἕλοιτο μοῖρα,
δυcπότμου χάριν χλιδᾶc,
εἰ μὴ τὸ κέρδοc κερδανεῖ δικαίωc
καὶ τῶν ἀcέπτων ἔρξεται,   890
ἢ τῶν ἀθίκτων θίξεται ματάζων.
τίc ἔτι ποτ᾽ ἐν τοῖcδ᾽ ἀνὴρ θυμοῦ βέλη
τεύξεται ψυχᾶc ἀμύνων;
εἰ γὰρ αἱ τοιαίδε πράξειc τίμιαι,   895
τί δεῖ με χορεύειν;

οὐκέτι τὸν ἄθικτον εἶμι   ἀντ. β′
γᾶc ἐπ᾽ ὀμφαλὸν cέβων,
οὐδ᾽ ἐc τὸν Ἀβαῖcι ναόν,   900
οὐδὲ τὰν Ὀλυμπίαν,
εἰ μὴ τάδε χειρόδεικτα
πᾶcιν ἁρμόcει βροτοῖc.
ἀλλ᾽, ὦ κρατύνων, εἴπερ ὄρθ᾽ ἀκούειc,
Ζεῦ, πάντ᾽ ἀνάccων, μὴ λάθοι
cὲ τάν τε càν ἀθάνατον αἰὲν ἀρχάν.   905
φθίνοντα γὰρ ⟨– ∪ – ×⟩ Λαΐου
θέcφατ᾽ ἐξαιροῦcιν ἤδη,
κοὐδαμοῦ τιμαῖc Ἀπόλλων ἐμφανήc·
ἔρρει δὲ τὰ θεῖα.   910

890 ἔρξεται LGCa: ἔρ- Rpa   891 ἤ] καὶ Suda s.v.
κέρδοc   θίξεται Blaydes, qui etiam ἄψεται coniecit: ἔξεται codd.
892 τοῖcδ᾽ Lrpa: τούτοιc pZrt   θυμοῦ pa: θυμῷ Lrpa:
θυμῶν Schneidewin: θεῶν Hermann (βέλη θεῶν B. H. Kennedy)
894 τεύξεται Hölscher: ἔρξεται (vel ἔρ-) codd.: εὔξεται Musgrave
ἀμύνων Erfurdt: -νειν codd.   896 post χορεύειν add. πονεῖν ἤ
τοῖc θεοῖc IP   903 ὄρθ᾽ rpat: ὀρθὸν lV   904 πάντ᾽
ἀνάccων] παντανάccων Hartung   906 lacunam alii aliter
suppleverunt: ⟨πυθόχρηcτα⟩ Schneidewin: ⟨τοι παλαιὰ⟩ Hermann: ⟨τοι
πάλαι τὰ⟩ J. F. Martin: an ⟨καὶ πάλαι τὰ⟩?   Λαΐου Lrp: Λαΐου
παλαιὰ a: παλαιὰ Λαΐου pa: πάλαι Λαΐου p: παλαιὰ post
θέcφατα (907) praebet K: v. ita refinxit t: φθίνοντα δ᾽ ὡc ἐμοὶ δοκεῖ τὰ
Λαΐου

reverence for the images of the gods,
may an evil destiny overtake him,
in return for his ill-starred insolence,
if he shall not draw profits righteously
and refrain from unholy acts   890
or, playing the fool, touches what he ought not.
What man ever amid such happenings shall succeed
in keeping the shafts of the gods from his life?
For if such actions are held in honor,   895
why should I dance?

No longer shall I go to the sacred
navel of earth in reverence,
or to Apollo's temple at Abae,   900
or to Olympia,
unless these oracles will fit,
conspicuous for all mortals to point to.
O you who wield the power, if you are rightly so called,
Zeus, ruler of all, let it not escape
you and your sovereignty immortal, everlasting.   905
Already they disdain the withering prophecies . . . [50]
spoken about Laïos.
Nowhere is Apollo conspicuous in honors.
Things divine fall into ruin.   910

Ιο.   χώρας ἄνακτες, δόξα μοι παρεστάθη
ναοὺς ἱκέσθαι δαιμόνων, τάδ' ἐν χεροῖν
στέφη λαβούσῃ κἀπιθυμιάματα.
ὑψοῦ γὰρ αἴρει θυμὸν Οἰδίπους ἄγαν
λύπαισι παντοίαισιν· οὐδ' ὁποῖ' ἀνὴρ   915
ἔννους τὰ καινὰ τοῖς πάλαι τεκμαίρεται,
ἀλλ' ἐστὶ τοῦ λέγοντος, ἢν φόβους λέγῃ.
ὅτ' οὖν παραινοῦς' οὐδὲν ἐς πλέον ποῶ,
πρὸς σ', ὦ Λύκει' Ἄπολλον, ἄγχιστος γὰρ εἶ,
ἱκέτις ἀφῖγμαι τοῖσδε σὺν κατεύγμασιν,   920
ὅπως λύσιν τιν' ἡμὶν εὐαγῆ πόρῃς·
ὡς νῦν ὀκνοῦμεν πάντες ἐκπεπληγμένον
κεῖνον βλέποντες ὡς κυβερνήτην νεώς.

ΑΓΓΕΛΟΣ

   ἆρ' ἂν παρ' ὑμῶν, ὦ ξένοι, μάθοιμ' ὅπου
τὰ τοῦ τυράννου δώματ' ἐστὶν Οἰδίπου;   925
μάλιστα δ' αὐτὸν εἴπατ' εἰ κάτισθ' ὅπου.
Χο.   στέγαι μὲν αἵδε, καὐτὸς ἔνδον, ὦ ξένε·
γυνὴ δὲ μήτηρ θ' ἥδε τῶν κείνου τέκνων.
Αγ.   ἀλλ' ὀλβία τε καὶ ξὺν ὀλβίοις ἀεὶ
γένοιτ', ἐκείνου γ' οὖσα παντελὴς δάμαρ.   930
Ιο.   αὔτως δὲ καὶ σύ γ', ὦ ξέν'· ἄξιος γὰρ εἶ
τῆς εὐεπείας οὕνεκ'. ἀλλὰ φράζ' ὅτου
χρῄζων ἀφῖξαι χὤτι σημῆναι θέλων.
Αγ.   ἀγαθὰ δόμοις τε καὶ πόσει τῷ σῷ, γύναι.
Ιο.   τὰ ποῖα ταῦτα; παρὰ τίνος δ' ἀφιγμένος;   935
Αγ.   ἐκ τῆς Κορίνθου. τὸ δ' ἔπος οὐξερῶ—τάχα

913 λαβούσῃ] -οῦσαν Elmsley   914 ἄγαν] ἄναξ t
917 ἢν LᵖᶜKpa: εἰ rt   λέγῃ LᵖᶜKpa: -οι rpt   918 ἐς] εὔ L
ποῶ Lrp: ποιῶ pat   920 ἱκέτις LᵖᶜKrpat: -έτης pXs
κατεύγμασιν] κατάργμασιν Wunder, cf. E. IT 244   921 πόρῃς]
πόροις p   926 κάτισθ' Nᵖᶜat: κάτοισθ' LrpD   928 θ'
noverunt sch. L et Syrianus in Hermogenem (Rabe i. 37. 9): om. codd.
930 γένοιτ'] γένοι' Wecklein   931 αὔτως C: αὔ- cett.
935 παρὰ LrpZr: πρὸς at   936 sic interpunximus   τάχ'⟨ἂν⟩
Brunck

[Jocasta, attended by at least one servant (945), enters from the house.
She carries suppliant boughs and incense (912–13).]

Jo   Lords of the country, the thought occurred to me
     to visit the temples of the gods holding in my hands
     garlands and offerings of incense.
     Oedipus raises his spirits too high
     at trouble of any sort and does not judge,   915
     like a sensible man, these strange new things by the old.
     He belongs to whoever speaks to him and tells of fears.
     When I try to advise him, I get nowhere in helping him.
     I have come to you, Apollo Lykeios, for you are nearest,
     as your suppliant with this prayer: 920
     grant us clear release from this defilement.
     Now, as it is, we all shrink from fear at the sight of him
     struck out of his wits as we would at seeing our ship's helmsman.

[As Jocasta prays, an old man (1009) enters by a gangway from
the country, the one not taken before. He is usually designated as
a messenger, but he comes from Corinth on his own recognizance
(934–40) and motivations (1002–5) with rumor (939–40).[51]*]*

CORINTHIAN
     Might I learn from you, strangers, where
     the house of the tyrant, Oedipus, is?   925
     Better yet, tell me if you know where he is.
Co   This is his house, and he is inside, stranger.
     The woman here is his wife and mother of his children.   930
Cn   May she always be happy and those
     with her, since she is his wife in every way.
Jo   And likewise to you, stranger. You deserve the same
     for your words of good omen. Tell us what
     you came here needing, and what you want to tell us.
Cn   Good news for the house and for your husband, lady.
Jo   And what would that be? From whom have you come?   935
Cn   From Corinth. As for what I will say,

ἥδοιο μέν, πῶς δ' οὐκ ἄν; ἀσχάλλοις δ' ἴσως.

Ιο. τί δ' ἔστι; ποίαν δύναμιν ὧδ' ἔχει διπλῆν;

Αγ. τύραννον αὐτὸν οὑπιχώριοι χθονὸς
τῆς Ἰσθμίας στήσουσιν, ὡς ηὐδᾶτ' ἐκεῖ.   940

Ιο. τί δ'; οὐχ ὁ πρέσβυς Πόλυβος ἐγκρατὴς ἔτι;

Αγ. οὐ δῆτ', ἐπεί νιν θάνατος ἐν τάφοις ἔχει.

Ιο. πῶς εἶπας; ἢ τέθνηκε⟨ν Οἰδίπου πατήρ⟩;

Αγ. εἰ μὴ λέγω τἀληθές, ἀξιῶ θανεῖν.

Ιο. ὦ πρόσπολ', οὐχὶ δεσπότῃ τάδ' ὡς τάχος   945
μολοῦσα λέξεις; ὦ θεῶν μαντεύματα,
ἵν' ἐστέ. τοῦτον Οἰδίπους πάλαι τρέμων
τὸν ἄνδρ' ἔφευγε μὴ κτάνοι· καὶ νῦν ὅδε
πρὸς τῆς τύχης ὄλωλεν οὐδὲ τοῦδ' ὕπο.

Οι. ὦ φίλτατον γυναικὸς Ἰοκάστης κάρα,   950
τί μ' ἐξεπέμψω δεῦρο τῶνδε δωμάτων;

Ιο. ἄκουε τἀνδρὸς τοῦδε, καὶ σκόπει κλύων
τὰ σέμν' ἵν' ἥκει τοῦ θεοῦ μαντεύματα.

Οι. οὗτος δὲ τίς ποτ' ἐστὶ καὶ τί μοι λέγει;

Ιο. ἐκ τῆς Κορίνθου, πατέρα τὸν σὸν ἀγγελῶν   955
ὡς οὐκέτ' ὄντα Πόλυβον, ἀλλ' ὀλωλότα.

Οι. τί φής, ξέν'; αὐτός μοι σὺ σημήνας γενοῦ.

Αγ. εἰ τοῦτο πρῶτον δεῖ μ' ἀπαγγεῖλαι σαφῶς,
εὖ ἴσθ' ἐκεῖνον θανάσιμον βεβηκότα.

Οι. πότερα δόλοισιν, ἢ νόσου ξυναλλαγῇ;   960

Αγ. σμικρὰ παλαιὰ σώματ' εὐνάζει ῥοπή.

Οι. νόσοις ὁ τλήμων, ὡς ἔοικεν, ἔφθιτο.

Αγ. καὶ τῷ μακρῷ γε συμμετρούμενος χρόνῳ.

Οι. φεῦ φεῦ, τί δῆτ' ἄν, ὦ γύναι, σκοποῖτό τις

---

942 τάφοις] δόμοις **p**   943 τέθνηκεν Οἰδίπου πατήρ;
Nauck: τέθνηκε Πόλυβος Lrpa: τέθνηκέ που Πόλυβος γέρων Zrt:
τέθνηκε Πόλυβος ὦ γέρον; Bothe: τέθνηκεν, ἢ κλέπτεις λόγῳ;
West   944 μὴ rZrt: δὲ μὴ cett.   λέγω rZrt: λέγω 'γὼ vel
λέγω γ' ἐγὼ cett.   948 κτάνοι] -ῃ **a**   954 τίς ποτ']
ποδαπός M. Schmidt   957 σημήνας LrPa: σημάντωρ K**pat** et
γρ in L et G   962-3 del. L. Dindorf

you would soon be pleased. How could you not? Perhaps
    saddened.

Jo   What is this? What has such a double effect?

Cn   The people who live there will establish him
    as the tyrant of their Isthmian land. So was the rumor there.   940

Jo   What? Is the aged Polybus no longer in power?

Cn   No, since death has him in a grave.

Jo   What are you saying? Oedipus' father has died?

Cn   If I do not say the truth, I am ready to die.

Jo   You, servant, won't you go quickly as you can and tell this   945
    to your master. Oracles of the gods,
    see where you are! Oedipus, long afraid of this man,
    stayed away in exile so as not to kill him. Now he has
    perished in the way of things and not by Oedipus' hand.

[*Enter Oedipus from the house.*]

Oe   O dearest head of my wife, Jocasta,   950
    why did you send for me to come here from the house?

Jo   Hear this man. Listen to him and consider
    where the august oracles of the god have come.

Oe   Who is this man? What does he have to tell me?

Jo   From Corinth, to announce to you that your father,   955
    Polybus, is no longer but has perished.

Oe   What are you saying, stranger? Tell me this yourself in your
    own words.

Cn   If I must announce this clearly first,
    know well that he is dead and gone.

Oe   By treachery or by the intervention of disease?   960

Cn   A slight tipping of the scale lulls old bodies to sleep.

Oe   The poor man perished from disease, it seems.

Cn   Yes, that, and because he measured out his life over a long span.

Oe   Oh! Why ever, wife, would anybody consider

τὴν Πυθόμαντιν ἑστίαν, ἢ τοὺς ἄνω   965
κλάζοντας ὄρνεις, ὧν ὑφ᾽ ἡγητῶν ἐγὼ
κτανεῖν ἔμελλον πατέρα τὸν ἐμόν; ὁ δὲ θανὼν
κεύθει κάτω δὴ γῆς· ἐγὼ δ᾽ ὅδ᾽ ἐνθάδε
ἄψαυστος ἔγχους, εἴ τι μὴ τὠμῷ πόθῳ
κατέφθιθ᾽· οὕτω δ᾽ ἂν θανὼν εἴη ᾽ξ ἐμοῦ.   970
τὰ δ᾽ οὖν παρόντα συλλαβὼν θεσπίσματα
κεῖται παρ᾽ Ἅιδῃ Πόλυβος ἄξι᾽ οὐδενός.

Ιο. οὔκουν ἐγώ σοι ταῦτα προὔλεγον πάλαι;
Οι. ηὔδας· ἐγὼ δὲ τῷ φόβῳ παρηγόμην.
Ιο. μή νυν ἔτ᾽ αὐτῶν μηδὲν ἐς θυμὸν βάλῃς.   975
Οι. καὶ πῶς τὸ μητρὸς λέκτρον οὐκ ὀκνεῖν με δεῖ;
Ιο. τί δ᾽ ἂν φοβοῖτ᾽ ἄνθρωπος ᾧ τὰ τῆς τύχης
κρατεῖ, πρόνοια δ᾽ ἐστὶν οὐδενὸς σαφής;
εἰκῇ κράτιστον ζῆν, ὅπως δύναιτό τις.
σὺ δ᾽ ἐς τὰ μητρὸς μὴ φοβοῦ νυμφεύματα·   980
πολλοὶ γὰρ ἤδη κἀν ὀνείρασιν βροτῶν
μητρὶ ξυνηυνάσθησαν. ἀλλὰ ταῦθ᾽ ὅτῳ
παρ᾽ οὐδέν ἐστι, ῥᾷστα τὸν βίον φέρει.
Οι. καλῶς ἅπαντα ταῦτ᾽ ἂν ἐξείρητό σοι,
εἰ μὴ ᾽κύρει ζῶσ᾽ ἡ τεκοῦσα· νῦν δ᾽ ἐπεὶ   985
ζῇ, πᾶσ᾽ ἀνάγκη, κεἰ καλῶς λέγεις, ὀκνεῖν.
Ιο. καὶ μὴν μέγας ⟨γ᾽⟩ ὀφθαλμὸς οἱ πατρὸς τάφοι.
Οι. μέγας, ξυνίημ᾽· ἀλλὰ τῆς ζώσης φόβος.
Αγ. ποίας δὲ καὶ γυναικὸς ἐκφοβεῖσθ᾽ ὕπερ;
Οι. Μερόπης, γεραιέ, Πόλυβος ἧς ᾤκει μέτα.   990
Αγ. τί δ᾽ ἔστ᾽ ἐκείνης ὑμὶν ἐς φόβον φέρον;
Οι. θεήλατον μάντευμα δεινόν, ὦ ξένε.

966 ὑφ᾽ ἡγητῶν HXrT: ὑφηγητῶν cett.; cf. 1260, OC 1588
ἐγὼ Paat: δ᾽ ἐγὼ cett.   967 κτανεῖν Lrpat: κτενεῖν a: κανεῖν
ut vid. Pᵃᶜ   968 δὴ Lpat: om. rpa   970 δ᾽] γ᾽ Blaydes
975 ἐς Lpa: εἰς rpZrt   976 λέκτρον L s.l., pat: λέχος LrpZr
981 κἀν] τοῖς γ᾽ Dawe dubitanter: ᾽ν τοῖς Blaydes   985 ᾽κύρει
pat: κύρει Lpa: κυρῇ r   987 ⟨γ᾽⟩ suppl. anon. in adnott. ed.
Londiniensis a. 1746   ὀφθαλμὸς] οἰωνὸς Blaydes, G. Wolff
989 ἐκφοβεῖσθ᾽ Lrpat: εὐλαβεῖσθ᾽ p

the hearth of the Pythian prophet or the birds 965
screaming above our heads? With them as my guides,
I was going to kill my father. But he is dead
and hides beneath the ground. I am here,
without touching a weapon unless he wasted away
from longing for me. In that case, he would have died at my
      doing. 970
The issue of oracles aside, these particular ones are worthless.
Polybus packed them up and lies with them in Hades.[52]

Jo   Did I not keep telling you this for a long time now?
Oe   You said so, but I was led astray by my fear.
Jo   No longer take any of these things to heart. 975
Oe   How am I not bound to shrink in fear before my mother's bed?
Jo   Why should a man fear over whom the vagaries of chance
      exert power and who has clear foresight of nothing?
      Best to live at random, however one can.
      As for you, do not be fearful over marriage with your mother, 980
      for many men in their dreams have bedded
      with their mother. But whoever holds this
      to be nothing bears his life most easily.
Oe   All would be spoken well and fine by you,
      if the woman who bore me were not living. Now seeing that 985
      she does live, there is every need, even if you speak correctly, to
          shrink in fear.
Jo   And yet your father's grave is surely a big bright spot.
Oe   Big, I know, but fear of the woman still living abides.
CM   You both are afraid because of a woman? What woman?
Oe   Merope, old man, with whom Polybus lived. 990
Cn   What is it about her that makes you fear?
Oe   A dread oracle sent by god, stranger.

Αγ. ἡ ῥητόν; ἢ οὐ θεμιστὸν ἄλλον εἰδέναι;
Οι. μάλιστά γ'· εἶπε γάρ με Λοξίας ποτὲ
    χρῆναι μιγῆναι μητρὶ τἠμαυτοῦ, τό τε   995
    πατρῷον αἷμα χερσὶ ταῖς ἐμαῖς ἑλεῖν.
    ὧν οὕνεχ' ἡ Κόρινθος ἐξ ἐμοῦ πάλαι
    μακρὰν ἀπῳκεῖτ'· εὐτυχῶς μέν, ἀλλ' ὅμως
    τὰ τῶν τεκόντων ὄμμαθ' ἥδιστον βλέπειν.
Αγ. ἦ γὰρ τάδ' ὀκνῶν κεῖθεν ἦσθ' ἀπόπτολις;   1000
Οι. πατρός γε χρῄζων μὴ φονεὺς εἶναι, γέρον.
Αγ. τί δῆτ' ἐγὼ οὐχὶ τοῦδε τοῦ φόβου σ', ἄναξ,
    ἐπείπερ εὔνους ἦλθον, ἐξελυσάμην;
Οι. καὶ μὴν χάριν γ' ἂν ἀξίαν λάβοις ἐμοῦ.
Αγ. καὶ μὴν μάλιστα τοῦτ' ἀφικόμην, ὅπως   1005
    σοῦ πρὸς δόμους ἐλθόντος εὖ πράξαιμί τι.
Οι. ἀλλ' οὔποτ' εἶμι τοῖς φυτεύσασίν γ' ὁμοῦ.
Αγ. ὦ παῖ, καλῶς εἶ δῆλος οὐκ εἰδὼς τί δρᾷς.
Οι. πῶς, ὦ γεραιέ; πρὸς θεῶν δίδασκέ με.
Αγ. εἰ τῶνδε φεύγεις οὕνεκ' εἰς οἴκους μολεῖν.   1010
Οι. ταρβῶν γε μή μοι Φοῖβος ἐξέλθῃ σαφής.
Αγ. ἦ μὴ μίασμα τῶν φυτευσάντων λάβῃς;
Οι. τοῦτ' αὐτό, πρέσβυ, τοῦτό μ' εἰσαεὶ φοβεῖ.
Αγ. ἆρ' οἶσθα δῆτα πρὸς δίκης οὐδὲν τρέμων;
Οι. πῶς δ' οὐχί, παῖς γ' εἰ τῶνδε γεννητῶν ἔφυν; 1015
Αγ. ὁθούνεκ' ἦν σοι Πόλυβος οὐδὲν ἐν γένει.
Οι. πῶς εἶπας; οὐ γὰρ Πόλυβος ἐξέφυσέ με;
Αγ. οὐ μᾶλλον οὐδὲν τοῦδε τἀνδρός, ἀλλ' ἴσον.
Οι. καὶ πῶς ὁ φύσας ἐξ ἴσου τῷ μηδενί;
Αγ. ἀλλ' οὔ σ' ἐγείνατ' οὔτ' ἐκεῖνος οὔτ' ἐγώ.   1020
Οι. ἀλλ' ἀντὶ τοῦ δὴ παῖδά μ' ὠνομάζετο;
Αγ. δῶρόν ποτ', ἴσθι, τῶν ἐμῶν χειρῶν λαβών.

993 οὐ θεμιστὸν Johnson: οὐ θεμιτὸν codd.: οὐχὶ θεμιτὸν Brunck
994 ποτὲ] πάλαι Tᵃᶜ, Ta   1001 γε p, coni. Hermann: τε codd.
plerique   1002 ἐγὼ οὐχὶ Livineius ('p'): ἔγωγ' οὐχὶ Lᵃᶜrpa:
ἔγωγ' οὐ LᵖᶜFat   1011 ταρβῶν UY: ταρβῶ cett.   ἐξέλθῃ
pat: -οι LrpZr   1018 τἀνδρός] γ' ἀνδρός Dawe

Cn	May it be spoken? or is it unlawful for another to know?
Oe	Yes, certainly. Loxias once said that I must
	have intercourse with my own mother and 995
	take my father's blood with my hands.
	For that reason, Corinth was inhabited
	far from me this long time. It proved fortunate, but still
	it is very sweet to look upon the eyes of parents.
Cn	You have shrunk from your city from fear of this? 1000
Oe	Yes, not wanting to be my father's murderer, old man.
Cn	Why then have I not freed you from this fear, lord,
	since I came here in good will?
Oe	And truly, you would receive the thanks you deserve.
Cn	And truly, I came for this very reason that,
	when you came home, I would benefit somehow. 1005
Oe	But I will never come near those who begot me.
Cn	O my son, you clearly do not know what you are doing.
Oe	How so, old man? By the gods, tell me.
Cn	If for these reasons you flee going home? 1010
Oe	Yes, fearing that Phoebus would prove right in my case.
Cn	Fearing that you would acquire pollution from your parents?
Oe	This very possibility, elder, has always terrified me.
Cn	Do you know that, as concerns justice, you are afraid of nothing?
Oe	How can that be, if I was born the son of these parents? 1015
Cn	Because Polybus was nothing to you in kinship.
Oe	How did you mean that? Polybus did not beget me?
Cn	No more than this man before you but as much.
Oe	And how is the man who begot me equal to someone of no
	relation?
Cn	Well, because neither he nor I begat you. 1020
Oe	Well, if so, why did he call me his son?
Cn	Know that he took you as a gift from my hands.

Οι.   κᾆθ᾽ ὧδ᾽ ἀπ᾽ ἄλλης χειρὸς ἔστερξεν μέγα;
Αγ.   ἡ γὰρ πρὶν αὐτὸν ἐξέπεις᾽ ἀπαιδία.
Οι.   cὺ δ᾽ ἐμπολήcαc ἢ τυχών μ᾽ αὐτῷ δίδωc;   1025
Αγ.   εὑρὼν ναπαίαιc ἐν Κιθαιρῶνος πτυχαῖc.
Οι.   ὡδοιπόρειc δὲ πρὸc τί τούcδε τοὺc τόπουc;
Αγ.   ἐνταῦθ᾽ ὀρείοιc ποιμνίοιc ἐπεcτάτουν.
Οι.   ποιμὴν γὰρ ἦcθα κἀπὶ θητείᾳ πλάνηc;
Αγ.   cοῦ δ᾽, ὦ τέκνον, cωτήρ γε τῷ τότ᾽ ἐν χρόνῳ.   1030
Οι.   τί δ᾽ ἄλγοc ἴcχοντ᾽ ἐν χεροῖν με λαμβάνειc;
Αγ.   ποδῶν ἂν ἄρθρα μαρτυρήcειεν τὰ cά.
Οι.   οἴμοι, τί τοῦτ᾽ ἀρχαῖον ἐννέπειc κακόν;
Αγ.   λύω c᾽ ἔχοντα διατόρουc ποδοῖν ἀκμάc.
Οι.   δεινόν γ᾽ ὄνειδοc cπαργάνων ἀνειλόμην.   1035
Αγ.   ὥcτ᾽ ὠνομάcθηc ἐκ τύχηc ταύτηc ὃc εἶ.
Οι.   ὦ πρὸc θεῶν, πρὸc μητρόc, ἦ πατρόc; φράcον.
Αγ.   οὐκ οἶδ᾽· ὁ δοὺc δὲ ταῦτ᾽ ἐμοῦ λῷον φρονεῖ.
Οι.   ἦ γὰρ παρ᾽ ἄλλου μ᾽ ἔλαβεc οὐδ᾽ αὐτὸc τυχών;
Αγ.   οὔκ, ἀλλὰ ποιμὴν ἄλλοc ἐκδίδωcί μοι.   1040
Οι.   τίc οὗτοc; ἦ κάτοιcθα δηλῶcαι λόγῳ;
Αγ.   τῶν Λαΐου δήπου τιc ὠνομάζετο.
Οι.   ἦ τοῦ τυράννου τῆcδε γῆc πάλαι ποτέ;
Αγ.   μάλιcτα· τούτου τἀνδρὸc οὗτοc ἦν βοτήρ.
Οι.   ἦ κἄcτ᾽ ἔτι ζῶν οὗτοc, ὥcτ᾽ ἰδεῖν ἐμέ;   1045
Αγ.   ὑμεῖc γ᾽ ἄριcτ᾽ εἰδεῖτ᾽ ἂν οὑπιχώριοι.
Οι.   ἔcτιν τιc ὑμῶν τῶν παρεcτώτων πέλαc,
      ὅcτιc κάτοιδε τὸν βοτῆρ᾽, ὃν ἐννέπει,
      εἴτ᾽ οὖν ἐπ᾽ ἀγρῶν εἴτε κἀνθάδ᾽ εἰcιδών;
      cημήναθ᾽, ὡc ὁ καιρὸc ηὑρῆcθαι τάδε.   1050
Χο.   οἶμαι μὲν οὐδέν᾽ ἄλλον ἢ τὸν ἐξ ἀγρῶν,

1025 τυχών Bothe (cf. 1039): τεκών codd.: κιχών Heimsoeth
1030 δ᾽ G: γ᾽ cett.: τ᾽ olim Hermann   1031 ἐν χεροῖν Fγρ, coni.
M. Schmidt, W. W. Walker: ἐν καιροῖc LP: ἐν κακοῖc cett.   με **rpat**:
om. **Lp**   1035 δεινόν] καλόν Eustathius 88. 16, 1097. 25
1038 φρονεῖ] φράcει vel φανεῖ Nauck   1040 ποιμήν ⟨c᾽⟩ Herwerden   1046 γ᾽ a: γὰρ LrpZr: om. t

Oe	And yet, although from another hand, he loved me very much?
Cn	Yes, his previous childlessness convinced him.
Oe	Did you give me to him after buying or coming upon me?	1025
Cn	I found you in the wooded folds of Cithaeron.
Oe	Why were you traveling in those places?
Cn	I was in charge of the flocks on the mountain.
Oe	You are saying you were a shepherd, a vagabond for hire?
Cn	Yes, child, and your savior at the time back then.	1030
Oe	When you took me in your hands, what pain was I in?
Cn	Your feet would bear witness to that.
Oe	O me! What old wound are you speaking of?
Cn	I loosened your feet. They had been pierced.
Oe	I received an appalling shame from my swaddling clothes.	1035
Cn	Such that you were named who you are from this misfortune.
Oe	In god's name, tell me, by my mother or father.
Cn	I do not know. The one who gave you knows better than me.
Oe	You say you got me from another. You didn't come upon me yourself?
Cn	No. Another shepherd gave you to me.	1040
Oe	Who is he? Do you know how to point him out in words?
Cn	He was called, I think, one of Laïos' people.
Oe	You mean the tyrant of this land back then?
Cn	Yes, he was this man's herdsman.
Oe	And is he still living so I could see him?	1045
Cn	You who live here would best know that.
Oe	Is there any among you standing here who knows the herdsman whom he speaks of, whether actually seeing him in the fields or even here in town? Make yourself known since the time has come for this to be revealed.	1050
Co	I think that he is none other than the man from the fields

ὃν κἀμάτευες πρόςθεν εἰςιδεῖν· ἀτὰρ
ἥδ᾽ ἂν τάδ᾽ οὐχ ἥκιςτ᾽ ἂν Ἰοκάςτη λέγοι.

Οι.   γύναι, νοεῖς ἐκεῖνον, ὅντιν᾽ ἀρτίως
μολεῖν ἐφιέμεςθα; τόνδ᾽ οὗτος λέγει;   1055

Ιο.   τί δ᾽ ὅντιν᾽ εἶπε; μηδὲν ἐντραπῇς. μάτην
ῥηθέντα βούλου μηδὲ μεμνῆςθαι τάδε.

Οι.   οὐκ ἂν γένοιτο τοῦθ᾽, ὅπως ἐγὼ λαβὼν
ςημεῖα τοιαῦτ᾽ οὐ φανῶ τοὐμὸν γένος.

Ιο.   μὴ πρὸς θεῶν, εἴπερ τι τοῦ ςαυτοῦ βίου   1060
κήδῃ, ματεύςῃς τοῦθ᾽· ἅλις νοςοῦς᾽ ἐγώ.

Οι.   θάρςει· ςὺ μὲν γὰρ οὐδ᾽ ἐὰν τρίτης ἐγὼ
μητρὸς φανῶ τρίδουλος, ἐκφανῇ κακή.

Ιο.   ὅμως πιθοῦ μοι, λίccομαι· μὴ δρᾶ τάδε.

Οι.   οὐκ ἂν πιθοίμην μὴ οὐ τάδ᾽ ἐκμαθεῖν ςαφῶς.   1065

Ιο.   καὶ μὴν φρονοῦcά γ᾽ εὖ τὰ λῷςτά coι λέγω.

Οι.   τὰ λῷςτα τοίνυν ταῦτά μ᾽ ἀλγύνει πάλαι.

Ιο.   ὦ δύςποτμ᾽, εἴθε μήποτε γνοίης ὃc εἶ.

Οι.   ἄξει τις ἐλθὼν δεῦρο τὸν βοτῆρά μοι;
ταύτην δ᾽ ἐᾶτε πλουςίῳ χαίρειν γένει.   1070

Ιο.   ἰοὺ ἰού, δύςτηνε· τοῦτο γάρ ς᾽ ἔχω
μόνον προςειπεῖν, ἄλλο δ᾽ οὔποθ᾽ ὕςτερον.

Χο.   τί ποτε βέβηκεν, Οἰδίπους, ὑπ᾽ ἀγρίας
ᾄξαςα λύπης ἡ γυνή; δέδοιχ᾽ ὅπως
μὴ ᾽κ τῆς ςιωπῆς τῆςδ᾽ ἀναρρήξει κακά.   1075

Οι.   ὁποῖα χρῄζει ῥηγνύτω· τοὐμὸν δ᾽ ἐγώ,
κεἰ ςμικρόν ἐςτι, ςπέρμ᾽ ἰδεῖν βουλήςομαι.
αὕτη δ᾽ ἴςως, φρονεῖ γὰρ ὡς γυνὴ μέγα,
τὴν δυςγένειαν τὴν ἐμὴν αἰςχύνεται.

1052 κἀμάτευες edd.: καὶ ᾽μάτευες XrZrt: καὶ μάτευες cett.: καὶ
ματεύεις Elmsley   1055 τόνδ᾽ p: τόν θ᾽ Lrpat   1056 τί
LpA: τίς rpat   1056–7 μάτην . . . τάδε A. Y. Campbell: τὰ δὲ
. . . μάτην codd.   1061 ἐγώ rPa, sch. L: ἔχω L, Rγρ, pat
1062 θάρςει Brunck: θάρρει codd.   ἐὰν Hermann: ἂν ἐκ codd.
1064 δρᾶ LrpZr: δρᾶν at   1075 ἀναρρήξει pXs: -ῃ Lrpat
1078 αὕτη p, coni. Hermann: αὐτή Lrpat   1079 ἐμὴν
LᵖᶜKrpat: ἐμὴν δ᾽ pZr, unde ἐμήν γ᾽ Dawe

	whom you sought before to see. But Jocasta here	
	could tell you best.	
Oe	Wife, do you know that man, the one we just now	
	ordered to come here? Does he mean this man?	1055
Jo	Why ask about the man he is talking about? Pay it no heed.	
	Do not even desire to remember what was said. It comes to nothing.	
Oe	It could not possibly happen that I get	
	such clues and not reveal my birth.	
Jo	Do not, by the gods, if you care anything for your life,	1060
	keep seeking this. What I am suffering is enough.	
Oe	Don't worry. Not even if I shall be exposed as the thrice-born slave	
	of a mother three times over a slave, will you be revealed base born.	
Jo	Even so, obey me, I beg you. Do not keep doing this.	
Oe	I couldn't be persuaded from knowing this clearly.	1065
Jo	And yet, I am thinking correctly and speak to your best interests.	
Oe	This "what is best" has afflicted me for a long time.	
Jo	Ill-fated Oedipus, may you never discover who you are.	
Oe	Won't someone go and bring the herdsman to me?	
	Let her rejoice in her family of wealth.	1070
Jo	Alas, poor thing. I have only this	
	to address you, and no other ever.	

[*Jocasta exits to the house.*]

Co	Why has the woman left and gone, Oedipus, dashing	
	away under savage agony? I fear that	
	bad things will burst from this silence.	1075
Oe	Let whatever must burst out. Even if it is humble,	
	I desire to see my seed.	
	Perhaps she, for she is a woman and keeps high thoughts,	
	is ashamed of my lowly birth.	

ἐγὼ δ' ἐμαυτὸν παῖδα τῆς Τύχης νέμων   1080
τῆς εὖ διδούςης οὐκ ἀτιμαςθήςομαι.
τῆς γὰρ πέφυκα μητρός· οἱ δὲ ςυγγενεῖς
μῆνές με μικρὸν καὶ μέγαν διώριςαν.
τοιόςδε δ' ἐκφὺς οὐκ ἂν ἐξέλθοιμ' ἔτι
ποτ' ἄλλος, ὥςτε μὴ 'κμαθεῖν τοὐμὸν γένος.   1085

Χο.   εἴπερ ἐγὼ μάντις εἰ-   ςτρ.
μι καὶ κατὰ γνώμαν ἴδρις,
οὐ τὸν Ὄλυμπον ἀπείρων,
ὦ Κιθαιρών, οὐκ ἔςῃ τὰν αὔριον
πανςέληνον μὴ οὐ ςέ γε τὸν πατριώταν
     Οἰδίπου   1090
καὶ τροφὸν καὶ ματέρ' αὔξειν,
καὶ χορεύεςθαι πρὸς ἡ-
μῶν ὡς ἐπίηρα φέροντα
τοῖς ἐμοῖς τυράννοις.   1095
ἰήιε Φοῖβε, coὶ δὲ
ταῦτ' ἀρέςτ' εἴη.

τίς ςε, τέκνον, τίς ς' ἔτι-   ἀντ.
κτε τᾶν μακραιώνων ἄρα
Πανὸς ὀρεςςιβάτα πα-   1100
τρὸς πελαςθεῖς'; ἢ ςέ γ' εὐνάτειρά τις
Λοξίου; τῷ γὰρ πλάκες ἀγρόνομοι πᾶςαι
     φίλαι·

1084 τοιόςδε] τοιᾶςδε Platt   δ' KVa: γ' t: om. Lrpa
1085 ποτ' ἄλλος] ἄτιμος Nauck: ἀλλοῖος Dindorf   1087 γνώμαν
Kp: -ην Lrpat   1088 οὐ τὸν LGγρpat: μὰ τὸν rC: οὐ μὰ τὸν
Zr   1090 τὸν Wilamowitz: καὶ codd.   1091 ματέρ'
Dindorf: μητέρ' codd.   1093 ἐπίηρα] ἐπὶ ἦρα Jebb
1099 τᾶν Heimsoeth: τῶν codd.   ἄρα KRp: ἀρα LGpat: κορᾶν
Blaydes   1100 ὀρεςςιβάτα LFat: ὀρεςι- rpa   1101 πατρὸς
πελαςθεῖς' Lachmann: προςπελαςθεῖς' codd.: de λέκτροις πελαςθεῖς' cogitavit Jebb   ςέ γ' εὐνάτειρά τις Arndt: ςέ γε θυγάτηρ Lp:
ςέ γέ τις θυγάτηρ rpat   1103 ἀγρόνομοι Zrt: -νόμοι cett.: an
ἀγρονόμων?

I consider myself the child of Chance 1080
who gives good things, and I'll not be dishonored.
I am born from Chance, my mother. My kinsmen,
the months, have defined me as small and as great.
Born as I am from them, I would not emerge so
unlike myself that I not learn my birth. 1085

CHORUS OF THEBAN OLD MEN
If I am a seer
and skilled in judgment,
by Olympus, you shall not remain unaware,
Cithaeron, that tomorrow's full moon shall praise
you as the compatriot and nurse and mother
     of Oedipus, 1090
and you will be extolled
by our dancing,
for bringing good to my tyrants. 1095
Healer Apollo, be pleased with what I say.

Who birthed you, child?
Who of the long-livéd
Nymphs who lie with Pan, your mountain-roving
father? Or was your mother some bedfellow 1100
of Loxias to whom all the ranging pastures are
     dear?

εἴθ' ὁ Κυλλάνας ἀνάccων,
εἴθ' ὁ Βακχεῖος θεὸς   1105
ναίων ἐπ' ἄκρων ὀρέων ⟨ς'⟩ εὕ-
ρημα δέξατ' ἔκ του
Νυμφᾶν ἑλικωπίδων, αἷς
πλεῖcτα cυμπαίζει.

Οι.   εἰ χρή τι κἀμὲ μὴ cυναλλάξαντά πω,   1110
πρέcβεις, cταθμᾶcθαι, τὸν βοτῆρ' ὁρᾶν δοκῶ,
ὅνπερ πάλαι ζητοῦμεν. ἔν τε γὰρ μακρῷ
γήρᾳ ξυνᾴδει τῷδε τἀνδρὶ cύμμετρος,
ἄλλως τε τοὺς ἄγοντας ὥσπερ οἰκέτας
ἔγνωκ' ἐμαυτοῦ· τῇ δ' ἐπιcτήμῃ cύ μου   1115
προὔχοις τάχ' ἄν που, τὸν βοτῆρ' ἰδὼν πάρος.
Χο.   ἔγνωκα γάρ, cάφ' ἴcθι· Λαΐου γὰρ ἦν
εἴπερ τις ἄλλος πιcτὸς ὡς νομεὺς ἀνήρ.
Οι.   cὲ πρῶτ' ἐρωτῶ, τὸν Κορίνθιον ξένον,
ἢ τόνδε φράζεις;   Αγ. τοῦτον, ὅνπερ
εἰcορᾷς.   1120
Οι.   οὗτος cύ, πρέcβυ, δεῦρό μοι φώνει βλέπων
ὅc' ἄν c' ἐρωτῶ. Λαΐου ποτ' ἦcθα cύ;

ΘΕΡΑΠΩΝ
ἦ, δοῦλος οὐκ ὠνητός, ἀλλ' οἴκοι τραφείς.
Οι.   ἔργον μεριμνῶν ποῖον ἢ βίον τίνα;
Θε.   ποίμναις τὰ πλεῖcτα τοῦ βίου cυνειπόμην.   1125
Οι.   χώροις μάλιcτα πρὸς τίcι ξύναυλος ὤν;
Θε.   ἦν μὲν Κιθαιρών, ἦν δὲ πρόcχωρος τόπος.
Οι.   τὸν ἄνδρα τόνδ' οὖν οἶcθα τῇδέ που μαθών;

1106 ⟨ς'⟩ suppl. Dindorf   1108 ἑλικωπίδων Wilamowitz:
Ἑλικωνιάδων codd.: Ἑλικωνίδων Aᵃᶜ, coni. Porson   1110 cυναλ-
λάξαντα Lpat: ξυν- ra   1111 πρέcβεις p: -ει Lᵖᶜpa: -υ p: -υν
rat: de Lᵃᶜ et K non liquet   1113 cύμμετρος Ct: ξυμ- cett.
1114 ὥσπερ] ὄντας Nauck   1115–16 μου et που permutavit
Blaydes   1117 alterum γάρ] μὲν r   1123 ἢ Porphyrius ap.
sch. E 533, θ 186: ἦν codd.   οἴκοι τραφείς] οἰκοτραφής Porphyrius
priore loco   1125 cυνειπόμην LrpZr: ξυν- at

Or was it Hermes, lord of Cyllene?
Or Dionysus, god of the Bacchae,   1105
who dwells on mountain peaks
and received you as a happy find
from one of his brown-eyed nymphs
with whom he most frolics?

[*An old man (1147) enters by the gangway leading from the country.*
He is escorted by Oedipus' servants (1114).]

Oe I've never met the man, but if I had to guess,   1110
elders, I think I'm seeing the herdsman
we've sought this long time. He agrees with
the man we want, being of advanced age.
Besides, the men who are bringing him I recognize
as my servants. You would perhaps have the better   1115
of me in knowledge, since you have seen the herdsman before.
Co Yes, I know him. Rest assured. He belonged to Laïos
and is reliable as shepherds go.
Oe I ask you first, Corinthian stranger,
is this the man you mean?
Cn This man whom you see before you. Yes.   1120
Oe You there, elder, look this way, at me,
and answer my questions. Did you ever belong to Laïos?
HERDSMAN
Yes, not a bought slave but raised in his house.
Oe What did you do? What life did you lead?
He For most of my life I followed the flocks.   1125
Oe In what places particularly were you with your sheep?
He It was Cithaeron, and it was the nearby area.
Oe Are you aware of meeting this man anywhere there?

Θε. τί χρῆμα δρῶντα; ποῖον ἄνδρα καὶ λέγεις;
Οι. τόνδ' ὃς πάρεστιν· ἢ ξυνήλλαξας τί πω; 1130
Θε. οὐχ ὥστε γ' εἰπεῖν ἐν τάχει μνήμης ὕπο.
Αγ. κοὐδέν γε θαῦμα, δέσποτ'. ἀλλ' ἐγὼ cαφῶc
     ἀγνῶτ' ἀναμνήcω νιν. εὖ γὰρ οἶδ' ὅτι
     κάτοιδεν ἦμος τὸν Κιθαιρῶνος τόπον
     ὁ μὲν διπλοῖσι ποιμνίοις, ἐγὼ δ' ἑνὶ 1135

     ἐπλησίαζον τῷδε τἀνδρὶ τρεῖς ὅλους
     ἐξ ἦρος εἰς ἀρκτοῦρον ἐκμήνους χρόνους·
     χειμῶνι δ' ἤδη τἀμά τ' εἰς ἔπαυλ' ἐγὼ
     ἤλαυνον οὗτός τ' ἐς τὰ Λαΐου σταθμά.
     λέγω τι τούτων, ἢ οὐ λέγω πεπραγμένον; 1140
Θε. λέγεις ἀληθῆ, καίπερ ἐκ μακροῦ χρόνου.
Αγ. φέρ' εἰπέ νυν, τότ' οἶσθα παῖδά μοί τινα
     δούς, ὡς ἐμαυτῷ θρέμμα θρεψαίμην ἐγώ;
Θε. τί δ' ἔστι; πρὸς τί τοῦτο τοὖπος ἱστορεῖς;
Αγ. ὅδ' ἐστίν, ὦ τᾶν, κεῖνος ὃς τότ' ἦν νέος· 1145
Θε. οὐκ εἰς ὄλεθρον; οὐ σιωπήσας ἔσῃ;
Οι. ἆ, μὴ κόλαζε, πρέσβυ, τόνδ', ἐπεὶ τὰ σὰ
     δεῖται κολαστοῦ μᾶλλον ἢ τὰ τοῦδ' ἔπη.
Θε. τί δ', ὦ φέριστε δεσποτῶν, ἁμαρτάνω;
Οι. οὐκ ἐννέπων τὸν παῖδ' ὃν οὗτος ἱστορεῖ. 1150
Θε. λέγει γὰρ εἰδὼς οὐδέν, ἀλλ' ἄλλως πονεῖ.
Οι. cὺ πρὸς χάριν μὲν οὐκ ἐρεῖς, κλαίων δ' ἐρεῖς.

1130 ἢ LRpa: ἦ GpZr: utrumque novit t   ξυνήλλαξάς (vel cυν-)
ΛVΑ: ξυναλλάξας codd. plerique   1131 ὕπο] ἄπο Reiske
1135 post hunc v. lacunam statuit Reiske (post 1134 Kennedy): ex. gr.
⟨ἐπιστατοῦντες εἴχομεν· τότ' οὖν ἐγὼ⟩ Lloyd-Jones   'νομεὺς
διπλοῖσι ποιμνίοις ἐπιστατῶν exspectes' Nauck   1137 ἐκμήνους
Eustathius 451. 1, Porson, fortasse e cod. Cantab. Trin. Coll. R. 3. 31:
ἐμμήνους codd. nostri   1138 χειμῶνι rpa: -α LpZr: utrumque
novit t   1142 νυν t, coni. Blaydes: νῦν codd.   1144 τοῦτο
τοὖπος ἱστορεῖς Lpat: τοὖπος ἱστορεῖς τόδε rO   1151 εἰδὼς
οὐδέν rpat: οὐδὲν εἰδώς lpZr

He	Doing what? And what man do you mean?
Oe	This one standing here. Do you remember ever having dealings
	with him? 1130
He	Not so I can say offhand from memory, at least.
Cn	No wonder, master, but I will remind him.
	He clearly does not know. I know well
	that he remembers when across the area of Cithaeron
	he with two flocks, and I with one 1135

. . . . .

	kept company with this man for three six-month
	seasons from spring until fall and the arrival of Arcturus.
	Then in winter, I drove my flock
	to the fold, and he to Laïos' barns.
	Am I saying this right—what happened—or not? 1140
He	You speak truly, although from a long time ago.
Cn	All right now, tell me. Do you remember at that time
	giving me a child so I could raise him as my own?
He	What is this? Why are you telling this story?
Cn	Here he is, sir, that one who was a baby then. 1145
He	To perdition with you! Keep quiet, won't you?
Oe	Stop! Don't rebuke him, old man, since what
	you say is more in need of rebuke than his words.
He	How am I doing wrong, best of masters?
Oe	By refusing to speak of the child he asks about. 1150
He	He speaks from ignorance and causes pain to no purpose.
Oe	You won't speak to please me. Then you'll speak in pain.

Θε.   μὴ δῆτα, πρὸς θεῶν, τὸν γέροντά μ' αἰκίσῃ.
Οι.   οὐχ ὡς τάχος τις τοῦδ' ἀποστρέψει χέρας;
Θε.   δύστηνος, ἀντὶ τοῦ; τί προσχρῄζεις μαθεῖν;   1155
Οι.   τὸν παῖδ' ἔδωκας τῷδ' ὃν οὗτος ἱστορεῖ;
Θε.   ἔδωκ'· ὀλέσθαι δ' ὤφελον τῇδ' ἡμέρᾳ.
Οι.   ἀλλ' ἐς τόδ' ἥξεις μὴ λέγων γε τοὔνδικον.
Θε.   πολλῷ γε μᾶλλον, ἢν φράσω, διόλλυμαι.
Οι.   ἀνὴρ ὅδ', ὡς ἔοικεν, εἰς τριβὰς ἐλᾷ.   1160
Θε.   οὐ δῆτ' ἔγωγ', ἀλλ' εἶπον ὡς δοίην πάλαι.
Οι.   πόθεν λαβών; οἰκεῖον, ἢ 'ξ ἄλλου τινός;
Θε.   ἐμὸν μὲν οὐκ ἔγωγ', ἐδεξάμην δέ του.
Οι.   τίνος πολιτῶν τῶνδε κἀκ ποίας στέγης;
Θε.   μὴ πρὸς θεῶν, μή, δέσποθ', ἱστόρει πλέον.   1165
Οι.   ὄλωλας, εἴ σε ταῦτ' ἐρήσομαι πάλιν.
Θε.   τῶν Λαΐου τοίνυν τις ἦν †γεννημάτων†.
Οι.   ἦ δοῦλος, ἢ κείνου τις ἐγγενὴς γεγώς;
Θε.   οἴμοι, πρὸς αὐτῷ γ' εἰμὶ τῷ δεινῷ λέγειν.
Οι.   κἄγωγ' ἀκούειν· ἀλλ' ὅμως ἀκουστέον.   1170
Θε.   κείνου γέ τοι δὴ παῖς ἐκλῄζεθ'· ἡ δ' ἔσω
        κάλλιστ' ἂν εἴποι σὴ γυνὴ τάδ' ὡς ἔχει.
Οι.   ἦ γὰρ δίδωσιν ἥδε σοι;   Θε. μάλιστ', ἄναξ.
Οι.   ὡς πρὸς τί χρείας;   Θε. ὡς ἀναλώσαιμί νιν.
Οι.   τεκοῦσα τλήμων;   Θε. θεσφάτων γ' ὄκνῳ
        κακῶν.   1175
Οι.   ποίων;   Θε. κτενεῖν νιν τοὺς τεκόντας ἦν λόγος.
Οι.   πῶς δῆτ' ἀφῆκας τῷ γέροντι τῷδε σύ;
Θε.   κατοικτίσας, ὦ δέσποθ', ὡς ἄλλην χθόνα

1153 μ'] γ' P, coni. Blaydes   1155 προσχρῄζεις Blaydes:
προσχρῄζων codd.   1157 τῇδ' Zrt: τῇδ' ἐν cett.
1160 ἀνὴρ Hermann: ἀ- codd.   εἰς rpat: ἐς LP   1166 ταῦτ']
ταῦτ' Schaefer   1167 γεννημάτων] βλάστῃ δόμων ex. gr. W. S.
Barrett: ἐκ δωμάτων Herwerden   1169 λέγειν] -ων O
1170 ἀκούειν Plut. Mor. 522c, 1093b: -ων Lrpat   1171 γε
KGpa: de L et t non liquet: δὲ p   1172 κάλλιστ' Lrpat: μάλιστ'
p, coni. Nauck   1175 γ' ὄκνῳ κακῶν Lpa: ὄκνῳ κακῶν t:
κακῶν ὄκνῳ rZr   1178 ὡς Lrpa: εἰς Ct: ἔς τ' Blaydes

He   Do not, by the gods, mistreat the old man, me.

Oe   Quick now. Someone twist back his arms.

He   Poor me, for what? What do you want to learn?   1155

Oe   Did you give him the child he is asking about?

He   Yes, I gave him. O how I wish that I had died on that day.

Oe   You'll come to that if you don't say the truth.

He   Yes, and I will die much worse if I do.

Oe   This man, as it seems, will draw this out.   1160

He   No, not I. I admit I gave him a long time ago.

Oe   Where did you get him from? The house or from some other?

He   I did not give out a child of mine. I got him from someone.

Oe   From one of the citizens or from what household?

He   By the gods, master, do not ask more questions. Do not.   1165

Oe   You're dead if I ask you about this again.

He   Then, he was one of the household of Laïos.

Oe   A slave or one born kin of that one?

He   Ah me, I am close on saying something horrible.

Oe   And I to hear, but still, it must be heard.   1170

He   He was called the child of that one, Laïos. She inside,
       your wife, could tell you best how things are.

Oe   She gives him to you?

He   Yes, lord.

Oe   To what purpose?

He   For me to kill him.

Oe   Stressed after giving birth?   1175

He   Yes, from fear of monstrous oracles.

Oe   What sort of oracles?

He   The word was that he would kill those who bore him.

Oe   How is it you let him go to this old man?

SERVANT

       Out of pity, master, thinking he would take

δοκῶν ἀποίcειν, αὐτὸc ἔνθεν ἦν· ὁ δὲ
κάκ' ἐc μέγιcτ' ἔcωcεν. εἰ γὰρ αὐτὸc εἶ   1180
ὃν φηcιν οὗτοc, ἴcθι δύcποτμοc γεγώc.
Οι. ἰοὺ ἰού· τὰ πάντ' ἂν ἐξήκοι cαφῆ.
ὢ φῶc, τελευταῖόν cε προcβλέψαιμι νῦν,
ὅcτιc πέφαcμαι φύc τ' ἀφ' ὧν οὐ χρῆν, ξὺν οἷc τ'
οὐ χρῆν ὁμιλῶν, οὕc τέ μ' οὐκ ἔδει κτανών.   1185
Χο. ἰὼ γενεαὶ βροτῶν,   cτρ. α'
ὡc ὑμᾶc ἴcα καὶ τὸ μη-
δὲν ζώcαc ἐναριθμῶ.
τίc γάρ, τίc ἀνὴρ πλέον
τᾶc εὐδαιμονίαc φέρει   1190
ἢ τοcοῦτον ὅcον δοκεῖν
καὶ δόξαντ' ἀποκλῖναι;
τὸν cόν τοι παράδειγμ' ἔχων,
τὸν cὸν δαίμονα, τὸν cόν, ὢ
τλᾶμον Οἰδιπόδα, βροτῶν   1195
οὐδὲν μακαρίζω·
ὅcτιc καθ' ὑπερβολὰν   ἀντ. α'
τοξεύcαc ἐκράτηcαc οὐ
πάντ' εὐδαίμονοc ὄλβου,
ὢ Ζεῦ, κατὰ μὲν φθίcαc
τὰν γαμψώνυχα παρθένον
χρηcμῳδόν, θανάτων δ' ἐμᾷ   1200
χώρᾳ πύργοc ἀνέcταc·
ἐξ οὗ καὶ βαcιλεὺc καλῇ

1179 δοκῶν ⟨cφ'⟩ Blaydes   1180 αὐτὸc Heimsoeth: οὗτοc
codd.   1182 ἐξήκοι GXr: -ίκοι codd. plerique   1185 χρῆν
LrpZrt: χρῆν μ' a   1186 ἰὼ semel Gpa, bis KRpD: ὢ lpt
1189 τίc γάρ, τίc] τί γάρ τιc Elmsley   1189–90 an πλέον et
φέρει permutanda sunt?   1193 τὸν Camerarius: τὸ codd.
1195 οὐδὲν Hermann et fort. Cᵃᶜ: οὐδένα codd.   1197 ἐκράτηcαc
οὐ Reisig: ἐκράτηcαc τοῦ codd.: ἐκράτηcε τοῦ Ambrosianus L. 39 sup.,
coni. Hermann   1201 ἀνέcταc rpat: ἀνέcτα LPa: ἀναcτάc
Elmsley   1202–3 καλῇ ἐμὸc] ἐμὸc καλῇ Elmsley: καλῇ τ'
ἐμὸc Blaydes: κλύειc ἐμὸc Heimsoeth

the child to another land, since he was from there.
He preserved the child for the greatest evils. If you are the very   1180
one of whom he speaks, know that you were born to an ill fate.
Oe   Alas, alas, all of this comes out clear.
O light, I would look upon you for the last time now,
since I'm revealed born of those whom I ought not,
living with those I ought not, and killing those I must not.   1185

[*Oedipus exits to the house. The Corinthian and the herdsman exit
to the country.*]

Chorus of Theban old men
O generations of mortals,
how I reckon you
as passing lives of nothingness.
Who, what man wins
more happiness   1190
than seeming to be happy
and, after seeming, declines into decay?
With yours, your daimon
yours as my example,
O wretched Oedipus, I assess   1195
nothing mortal as blessed.

You let fly your arrow
inordinately and attained
a happiness not blessed in every way,
O Zeus, for you laid waste
the taloned maiden,
singer of oracles, and raised   1200
a bulwark against deaths for my land.
Thereafter you are called my king

ἐμὸς καὶ τὰ μέγιστ' ἐτι-
μάθης, ταῖς μεγάλαισιν ἐν
Θήβαισιν ἀνάccων.

τανῦν δ' ἀκούειν τίς ἀθλιώτερος,   cτρ. β'
τίς ἐν πόνοιc τίc ἄταιc ἀγρίαιc   1205
ξύνοικοc ἀλλαγᾷ βίου;
ἰὼ κλεινὸν Οἰδίπου κάρα,
ᾧ μέγαc λιμὴν
αὑτὸc ἤρκεcεν
παιδὶ καὶ πατρὶ
θαλαμηπόλῳ πεcεῖν,   1210
πῶc ποτε πῶc ποθ' αἱ πατρῷ-
αί c' ἄλοκεc φέρειν, τάλαc,
cῖγ' ἐδυνάθηcαν ἐc τοcόνδε;

ἐφηῦρέ c' ἄκονθ' ὁ πάνθ' ὁρῶν χρόνοc,   ἀντ. β'
δικάζει τὸν ἄγαμον γάμον πάλαι
τεκνοῦντα καὶ τεκνούμενον.   1215
ἰὼ Λάϊειον ⟨ὢ⟩ τέκνον,
εἴθε c' εἴθε cε
μήποτ' εἰδόμαν·
ὡc ὀδύρομαι
περίαλλ' ἰὰν χέων
ἐκ cτομάτων. τὸ δ' ὀρθὸν εἰ-   1220

1204 Θήβαισιν D: Θήβαις codd. plerique   1205 locus
nondum sanatus: τίc ἄταιc ἀγρίαιc, τίc ἐν πόνοιc Hermann: fort. τίc
ἄταιc ἀγρίαιc τόcαιc πονῶν (τόcαιc Heimsoeth, πονῶν Dawe), vel
τίc ἄταιc, τίc ἀγριωτέροιc πόνοιc   1209 αὑτὸc Brunck: αὐ-
codd.   πατρὶ] πόcει Wunder   1210 πεcεῖν] 'μπεcεῖν
Hartung   1212 ἐδυνάθηcαν Nᵖᶜ: -άcθηcαν codd. plerique
1213 ἄκονθ'] ἄκων Wilamowitz   1214 ἄγαμον γάμον]
ἀγάμῳ γάμῳ dubitanter Campbell   1216 ⟨ὢ⟩ suppl. Erfurdt
τέκνον] γένοc K   1217 alterum cε O, coni. Wunder: om. cett.
1218 εἰδόμαν t: ἰδόμην L: ἰδόμαν RVa: ἰδοίμην vel -μαν Gp   ὡc
ὀδύρομαι Kamerbeek: ὀδύρομαι γὰρ ὡc codd.   1219 ἰὰν
χέων Burges: ἰαχέων codd.

and honored magnificently,
reigning as lord
in mighty Thebes.

Now who is more wretched to hear tell of?
Who lives amid sufferings, who among savage ruins 1205
through a reversal of his life?
O renowned head of Oedipus,
for whom the same great
harbor served
for son and father
as a bed to fall into as its groom, 1210
how ever, how ever could the father's
plowed furrows endure you, wretch,
in silence for so long?

All-seeing time has found you out against your will
and brings to justice your marriage no marriage,
long producing children and produced by children. 1215
Alas, O child of Laïos,
would that I never, never,
had seen you.
How profusely I lament,
pouring my voice
from my lips. To say the truth, 1220

πεῖν, ἀνέπνευcά τ᾽ ἐκ cέθεν
καὶ κατεκοίμηcα τοὐμὸν ὄμμα.

ΕΞΑΓΓΕΛΟC

ὦ γῆc μέγιcτα τῆcδ᾽ ἀεὶ τιμώμενοι,
οἷ᾽ ἔργ᾽ ἀκούcεcθ᾽, οἷα δ᾽ εἰcόψεcθ᾽, ὅcον δ᾽
ἀρεῖcθε πένθοc, εἴπερ εὐγενῶc ἔτι   1225
τῶν Λαβδακείων ἐντρέπεcθε δωμάτων.
οἶμαι γὰρ οὔτ᾽ ἂν Ἴcτρον οὔτε Φᾶcιν ἂν
νίψαι καθαρμῷ τήνδε τὴν cτέγην, ὅcα
κεύθει, τὰ δ᾽ αὐτίκ᾽ ἐc τὸ φῶc φανεῖ κακὰ
ἑκόντα κοὐκ ἄκοντα. τῶν δὲ πημονῶν   1230
μάλιcτα λυποῦc᾽ αἳ φανῶc᾽ αὐθαίρετοι.

Χο.   λείπει μὲν οὐδ᾽ ἃ πρόcθεν ᾔδεμεν τὸ μὴ οὐ
βαρύcτον᾽ εἶναι· πρὸc δ᾽ ἐκείνοιcιν τί φῄc;

Εξ.   ὁ μὲν τάχιcτοc τῶν λόγων εἰπεῖν τε καὶ
μαθεῖν, τέθνηκε θεῖον Ἰοκάcτηc κάρα.   1235

Χο.   ὦ δυcτάλαινα, πρὸc τίνοc ποτ᾽ αἰτίαc;

Εξ.   αὐτὴ πρὸc αὑτῆc. τῶν δὲ πραχθέντων τὰ μὲν
ἄλγιcτ᾽ ἄπεcτιν· ἡ γὰρ ὄψιc οὐ πάρα.
ὅμωc δ᾽, ὅcον γε κἀν ἐμοὶ μνήμηc ἔνι,
πεύcῃ τὰ κείνηc ἀθλίαc παθήματα.   1240
ὅπωc γὰρ ὀργῇ χρωμένη παρῆλθ᾽ ἔcω
θυρῶνοc, ἵετ᾽ εὐθὺ πρὸc τὰ νυμφικὰ
λέχη, κόμην cπῶc᾽ ἀμφιδεξίοιc ἀκμαῖc·
πύλαc δ᾽, ὅπωc εἰcῆλθ᾽, ἐπιρράξαc᾽ ἔcω,
καλεῖ τὸν ἤδη Λάιον πάλαι νεκρόν,   1245
μνήμην παλαιῶν cπερμάτων ἔχουc᾽, ὑφ᾽ ὧν

1222 κατεκοίμηcα LpA: -μιcα **rpa**   1225 ἀρεῖcθε Oat: αἰ-
vel αἱ- **lrp**   εὐγενῶc Hartung: ἐγγενῶc codd.   1229 τὰ] τὸ
Elmsley   1231 αἳ Lrpt: αἳ ᾽ν a   1232 ᾔδεμεν Zc, coni.
Elmsley: ᾔδειμεν cett.   1237 αὑτῆc LrpD: αὐ- at
1240 τὰ κείνηc Xs: τἀκείνηc cett.   1242 ἵετ᾽ LRpa: ἵκετ᾽ Gpat
εὐθὺ LᵖᶜNᵖᶜa: εὐθὺc KrpZrt   πρὸc] ἐc t   1244 ἐπιρράξαc᾽
L s.l.: -ήξαc᾽ L in linea et cett.   1245 καλεῖ Ambrosianus G. 56
sup., coni. Erfurdt: κάλει codd.

I drew my breath from you, and
from you I lulled my eye to sleep.[53]

[*A servant enters from within the house. He proves to be a messenger.*]

MESSENGER
    O men always held in highest honor in this land,
what things you will hear about, what you will see,
what grief you will assume if you remain true   1225
to your birth and care for the house of Labdacus.
Neither the rivers Istros nor Phasis,[54] I think,
could cleanse this house, so many appalling deeds
does it hide, while others very soon it will disclose
to the light, all done willingly and not unwillingly.   1230
Of pains those seen to be self-inflicted hurt the most.
Co What we knew before does not fall short of deep lamentation.
What more are you saying?
Me The swiftest of tales to tell and to learn:
the godlike head of Jocasta is dead.   1235
Co O unhappy woman, from whatever cause?
Me She was the cause herself by her own hand. The most painful part
of what was done is lost. No one was there to see.
Still, as good as is the power in me to recall,
you will learn the sufferings of that wretched woman.   1240
  She was distraught when she came inside the hall.
She rushed straight to the bridal bed,
tearing at her hair with the fingers of both hands.
She went inside the bedroom and shut the doors.
She calls upon Laïos, already long dead,   1245
recalling the ancient seedings by which

θάνοι μὲν αὐτός, τὴν δὲ τίκτουσαν λίποι
τοῖς οἷσιν αὐτοῦ δύστεκνον παιδουργίαν.
γοᾶτο δ' εὐνάς, ἔνθα δύστηνος διπλῆ
ἐξ ἀνδρὸς ἄνδρα καὶ τέκν' ἐκ τέκνων τέκοι.   1250
χὤπως μὲν ἐκ τῶνδ' οὐκέτ' οἶδ' ἀπόλλυται·
βοῶν γὰρ εἰσέπαισεν Οἰδίπους, ὑφ' οὗ
οὐκ ἦν τὸ κείνης ἐκθεάσασθαι κακόν,
ἀλλ' εἰς ἐκεῖνον περιπολοῦντ' ἐλεύσσομεν.
φοιτᾷ γὰρ ἡμᾶς ἔγχος ἐξαιτῶν πορεῖν,   1255
γυναῖκά τ' οὐ γυναῖκα, μητρῷαν δ' ὅπου
κίχοι διπλῆν ἄρουραν οὗ τε καὶ τέκνων.
λυσσῶντι δ' αὐτῷ δαιμόνων δείκνυσί τις·
οὐδεὶς γὰρ ἀνδρῶν, οἳ παρῆμεν ἐγγύθεν.
δεινὸν δ' ἀύσας ὡς ὑφ' ἡγητοῦ τινος   1260
πύλαις διπλαῖς ἐνήλατ', ἐκ δὲ πυθμένων
ἔκλινε κοῖλα κλῇθρα κἀμπίπτει στέγῃ.
οὗ δὴ κρεμαστὴν τὴν γυναῖκ' εἰσείδομεν,
πλεκταῖσιν αἰώραισιν ἐμπεπλεγμένην.
ὁ δ' ὡς ὁρᾷ νιν, δεινὰ βρυχηθεὶς τάλας,   1265
χαλᾷ κρεμαστὴν ἀρτάνην. ἐπεὶ δὲ γῇ
ἔκειτο τλήμων, δεινά γ' ἦν τἀνθένδ' ὁρᾶν.
ἀποσπάσας γὰρ εἱμάτων χρυσηλάτους
περόνας ἀπ' αὐτῆς, αἷσιν ἐξεστέλλετο,

1249 διπλῆ P: -ᾶς K: -ᾶ O s.l.: -οῦς cett.   1250 ἄνδρα
LrpZrt: -ας pa   1252 εἰσέπαισεν at: εἰσέπεσεν LrpD
1253 ἐκθεάσασθαι Lrpa: ἐν- t (ἐκ- T s.l.)   1254 ἐλεύσσομεν
at: ἐλεύσομεν Lpa: ἐλεύσαμεν r: λεύσσομεν Xs   1255 φοιτᾷ
Lrpat: φοίτα p, coni. Blaydes   1260 ὑφ' ἡγητοῦ LrPa: ὑφηγη-
τοῦ pa   1262 κλῇθρα rV: κλεῖθρα cett.   1264 πλεκταῖσιν Ambrosiani G. 56 sup., L. 39 sup.: -αῖς cett.   αἰώραισιν
Ambrosianus G. 56 sup., coni. Herwerden: αἰώραις G s.l., pat: ἐώραις
Lrpa   post ἐμπεπλεγμένην add. ὁ δέ codd. nostri, quod aut delendum
aut in initio v. 1265 legendum censuit Blaydes   1265 ὁ δ' ὡς Blaydes:
ὅπως pat: ὅπως δ' Lrp, probat Herwerden   1266 ἐπεὶ Nat: ἐπὶ
Lrp   1267 ἔκειτο at (Lac non legitur): ἔκειθ' ἡ pXr: ἔκειθ' ὁ
Krp   γ' D, T s.l.: δ' cett.

he perished himself and left behind the mother,
and the ill-begetting of children for his own children.
She lamented the beds where the poor woman bore in duplicate
husband from husband, children from children. 1250
What happened next, how she died, I do not know further.
Oedipus burst in, shouting, and made it impossible
to see the woman's misery to its end.
We were looking at him running around.
He darted about, demanding that we give him a sword 1255
and asking where he would find his wife no wife
but a twice-plowed maternal field for himself and his children.
In his frenzy, some one of the daimons showed him the way.
No one of us men who were close by showed him.
He cried out and lunged at the double doors 1260
as if someone was guiding him. He bent
the doors inward from their framework and surged into the room
where we saw the woman hanging,
entangled in braided nooses, still swinging.
When he saw her, letting go a shriek laden with pain, 1265
he loosened the rope hanging her. When the poor woman
lay on the ground, what came next was awful to see.
He ripped the golden brooches from her clothes
with which she was dressed. He lifted them high

ἄρας ἔπαιςεν ἄρθρα τῶν αὑτοῦ κύκλων,   1270
αὐδῶν τοιαῦθ᾽, ὁθούνεκ᾽ οὐκ ὄψοιντό νιν
οὔθ᾽ οἷ᾽ ἔπασχεν οὔθ᾽ ὁποῖ᾽ ἔδρα κακά,
ἀλλ᾽ ἐν σκότῳ τὸ λοιπὸν οὓς μὲν οὐκ ἔδει
ὀψοίαθ᾽, οὓς δ᾽ ἔχρῃζεν οὐ γνωςοίατο.
τοιαῦτ᾽ ἐφυμνῶν πολλάκις τε κοὐχ ἅπαξ   1275
ἤραςς᾽ ἐπαίρων βλέφαρα. φοίνιαι δ᾽ ὁμοῦ
γλῆναι γένει᾽ ἔτεγγον, οὐδ᾽ ἀνίεςαν.
[φόνου μυδώςας ςταγόνας, ἀλλ᾽ ὁμοῦ μέλας
ὄμβρος †χαλάζης αἵματος† ἐτέγγετο.]
τάδ᾽ ἐκ δυοῖν ἔρρωγεν οὐ μόνου κακά   1280
ἀλλ᾽ ἀνδρὶ καὶ γυναικὶ ςυμμιγῆ κακά.
ὁ πρὶν παλαιὸς δ᾽ ὄλβος ἦν πάροιθε μὲν
ὄλβος δικαίως, νῦν δὲ τῇδε θἠμέρᾳ
ςτεναγμός, ἄτη, θάνατος, αἰσχύνη, κακῶν
ὅς᾽ ἐςτὶ πάντων ὀνόματ᾽, οὐδέν ἐςτ᾽ ἀπόν.   1285
Χο. νῦν δ᾽ ἔςθ᾽ ὁ τλήμων ἔν τινι ςχολῇ κακοῦ;
Εξ. βοᾷ διοίγειν κλῇθρα καὶ δηλοῦν τινα
τοῖς πᾶςι Καδμείοιςι τὸν πατροκτόνον,
τὸν μητρός, αὐδῶν ἀνόςι᾽ οὐδὲ ῥητά μοι,
ὡς ἐκ χθονὸς ῥίψων ἑαυτόν, οὐδ᾽ ἔτι   1290
μενῶν δόμοις ἀραῖος, ὡς ἠράςατο.
ῥώμης γε μέντοι καὶ προηγητοῦ τινος
δεῖται· τὸ γὰρ νόςημα μεῖζον ἢ φέρειν.
δείξει δὲ καὶ ςοί. κλῇθρα γὰρ πυλῶν τάδε

1270 αὑτοῦ a: αὐ- codd. plerique   1271 ὄψοιντο Cat: -οιτο
Lrpa   1276 ἐπαίρων] cf. Senecae *Oed.* 962 sq.: πείρων Nauck
1278–9 del. West   1279 χαλάζης αἵματος] ἄλαζά θ᾽ αἵμα-
τοῦςς᾽ Porson: alii alia (αἵματός ⟨θ᾽⟩ Zr^pct)   1280–1 del. Dindorf
1280 ἐκ] ἐς (. . . κάρα) Pearson   οὐ μόνου κακά] οὐ μόνου κάτα
C. Otto: οὐχ ἑνὸς μόνου Porson: alii alia   1284 ἄτη Rpat: ἄται Gp:
ἄτε l   1286 τινι Mudge et Elmsley, teste Hermann: τίνι codd.
1287 κλῇθρα Lpa: κλεῖθρα rpat   1291 μενῶν Lat: μένων rp
δόμοις ἀραῖος ὡς] δόμοιςιν ἔνοχος οἷς Nauck   1294 δείξει]
δόξει Xr, coni. Reiske   κλῇθρα L, P s.l., a: κλεῖθρα rpat   γὰρ
rpat: γε lp

and drove their pins into the orbs of his eyes, 1270
crying out that they will not see him or
what he suffers or what monstrous deeds he committed,
but forever in darkness, they will see those whom they ought not
and not recognize those whom he so desired to see.
Chanting such imprecations, he lifted his eyes and 1275
struck many times, not once. Blood
from his eyes kept wetting his chin and did not let off.
[Blood flowed not in wet drops of gore,
but a black flood like a hailstorm soaked him.]
These evils broke forth two, not one alone, 1280
but evils mingled for husband and for wife.
Happiness of olden days before was genuine
happiness. Now, on this day
mourning, ruin, death, and every sorrow
that bears a name. Nothing was lacking. 1285

Co Is the poor man now at some rest from his suffering?

Me He cries for someone to open the doors and show
to the people of Cadmus the father-killer,
his mother's—I cannot repeat his impure language—
that he will hurl himself from the land and remain 1290
no longer a curse on the house since he cursed himself.
Yet he lacks the strength and someone to guide him,
for his sickness is too severe to bear.
He will show you, too. The doors of the entrance

διοίγεται· θέαμα δ' εἰςόψῃ τάχα   1295
τοιοῦτον οἷον καὶ ςτυγοῦντ' ἐποικτίςαι.

Χο.   ὢ δεινὸν ἰδεῖν πάθος ἀνθρώποις,
ὢ δεινότατον πάντων ὅς' ἐγὼ
προςέκυρς' ἤδη. τίς ς', ὦ τλῆμον,
προςέβη μανία; τίς ὁ πηδήςας   1300
μείζονα δαίμων τῶν μηκίςτων
πρὸς ςῇ δυςδαίμονι μοίρᾳ;
φεῦ φεῦ δύςτην', ἀλλ' οὐδ' ἐςιδεῖν
δύναμαί ς', ἐθέλων πόλλ' ἀνερέςθαι,
πολλὰ πυθέςθαι, πολλὰ δ' ἀθρῆςαι·   1305
τοίαν φρίκην παρέχεις μοι.

Οι.   αἰαῖ αἰαῖ, δύςτανος ἐγώ,
ποῖ γᾶς φέρομαι τλάμων; πᾷ μοι
φθογγὰ διαπωτᾶται φοράδαν;   1310
ἰὼ δαῖμον, ἵν' ἐξήλου.
Χο.   ἐς δεινόν, οὐδ' ἀκουστόν, οὐδ' ἐπόψιμον.

Οι.   ἰὼ ςκότου   ςτρ. α᾽
νέφος ἐμὸν ἀπότροπον, ἐπιπλόμενον ἄφατον,
ἀδάματόν τε καὶ δυςούριςτον ⟨ὄν⟩.   1315
οἴμοι,

1298 ἐγώ] ἐμοὶ Herwerden   1299 ς' at: γ' C: om. lrpa
1301 μείζονα] μάςςονα Blaydes   δαίμων ante μείζονα traiecit
t   μηκίςτων t: μακίςτων L^pcK^aca: κακίςτων ΛΚ^pcrpa
1303 δύςτην' Elmsley: δύςταν' t: δύςτανος fere cett.   1306 τοίαν
P.Oxy. 1369, Nat: οἴαν r: ποίαν Lpa   1307 αἴ vel αἲ quater
P.Oxy. 1369 rpat: ter Lpa: bis C   ante δύςτανος add. φεῦ φεῦ codd.
plerique: del. Hermann   1309 πᾷ] ποῖ C   1310 διαπωτᾶται Musgrave, et fortasse habuit P.Oxy. 1369: -πέταται Lpa:
-πέπταται rpXrt   φοράδαν Page: -ην codd.   1311 ἐξήλου
Lrpat: -ήλω PaXr: -ήλλου C et coni. Hermann   1312 ἐς] ὡς H,
coni. Herwerden   prius οὐδ' Lpat: οὐκ KRp   1314 ἐπιπλόμενον
pa: -ώμενον lrpat   1315 ἀδάματον Hermann: -αςτον codd.
⟨ὄν⟩ Hermann: possis etiam δυςούριςτ' ἰόν (Jebb) vel δυςεξούριςτον
(Blaydes)

are opening. You will soon see a sight   1295
such that even someone who hates him would pity.

Co O suffering dreadful for men to behold,
most dreadful of all that I have encountered. What madness,
poor man, came over you? Who is the daimon that has leapt
farther   1300
than the longest leap upon your ill-starred destiny?
Alas, alas, poor thing, I cannot look upon you, though I desire
to ask many questions, to learn much,
to gaze long upon you.   1305
Such shivers you send through me.

Oe Aiai, aiai, wretched me,
where, poor me, in the land am I borne? Where
does my voice dart in speeding flight?   1310
O daimon, where have you leapt?

Co Into a place of dread not to be heard of, not to be seen.

Oe Oh cloud of darkness
of mine, repellant, advancing unspeakable,
invincible, driven by ill winds too far.   1315
Woe is me.

οἴμοι μάλ᾽ αὖθις· οἷον εἰςέδυ μ᾽ ἅμα
κέντρων τε τῶνδ᾽ οἴςτρημα καὶ μνήμη κακῶν.

Χο. καὶ θαῦμά γ᾽ οὐδὲν ἐν τοςοῖςδε πήμαςιν
διπλᾶ ςε πενθεῖν καὶ διπλᾶ θροεῖν κακά.   1320

Οι. ἰὼ φίλος,   ἀντ. α΄
cὺ μὲν ἐμὸς ἐπίπολος ἔτι μόνιμος· ἔτι γὰρ
ὑπομένεις με τὸν τυφλὸν κηδεύων.
φεῦ φεῦ·
οὐ γάρ με λήθεις, ἀλλὰ γιγνώσκω ςαφῶς,   1325
καίπερ ςκοτεινός, τήν γε ςὴν αὐδὴν ὅμως.

Χο. ὦ δεινὰ δράςας, πῶς ἔτλης τοιαῦτα ςὰς
ὄψεις μαρᾶναι; τίς ς᾽ ἐπῆρε δαιμόνων;

Οι. Ἀπόλλων τάδ᾽ ἦν, Ἀπόλλων, φίλοι,   στρ. β΄
ὁ κακὰ κακὰ τελῶν ἐμὰ τάδ᾽ ἐμὰ πάθεα.   1330
ἔπαιςε δ᾽ αὐτόχειρ νιν οὔ-
τις, ἀλλ᾽ ἐγὼ τλάμων.
τί γὰρ ἔδει μ᾽ ὁρᾶν,
ὅτῳ γ᾽ ὁρῶντι μηδὲν ἦν ἰδεῖν γλυκύ;   1335

Χο. ἦν τᾷδ᾽ ὅπωσπερ καὶ cὺ φής.

Οι. τί δῆτ᾽ ἐμοὶ βλεπτὸν ἢ
στερκτόν, ἢ προςήγορον
ἔτ᾽ ἔςτ᾽ ἀκούειν ἡδονᾷ, φίλοι;
ἀπάγετ᾽ ἐκτόπιον ὅτι τάχιστά με,   1340
ἀπάγετ᾽, ὦ φίλοι, τὸν μέγ᾽ ὀλέθριον,
τὸν καταρατότατον, ἔτι δὲ καὶ θεοῖς   1345

1320 θροεῖν Nauck: φορεῖν Lrpa: φρονεῖν a, coni. Bergk
1322 ἐμὸς ἐπίπολος] ἐμοῖς ἐπὶ πόνοις Lγρ   1323 με τὸν
Erfurdt: ἐμὲ τὸν Lrpa: τόν γε t   κηδεύων] κηδεμών Ebner
1329 φίλοι LpZrt: ὦ φίλοι rpa   1330 κακὰ bis rNa: semel
lpat   prius ἐμὰ rpa: om. lpat   1336 τᾷδ᾽ Nauck: τάδ᾽ Lp:
ταῦθ᾽ rpat   1337 δῆτ᾽ rpDᵃᶜt: δήποτ᾽ Lpa   ἦ] ἦν Wilamowitz
βλεπτὸν et στερκτὸν traiecit Bruhn (1897)   1339 ἔτ᾽] τί δ᾽ Herwerden   ἡδονᾷ] ἀδονᾷ Dindorf: ⟨cὺν⟩ ἀδονᾷ Heimsoeth, cf. 1359
1343 μέγ᾽ ὀλέθριον Erfurdt: ὀλέθριον μέγα pXrt, ὀλέθριον μέγαν
Lrpa: ὄλεθρόν με γᾶς Bergk

Woe is me, again. How the piercing pains of those pins
and memory of those awful deeds entered me together.

Co No wonder amid so many agonies,
you lament sorrows double and cry out a double calamity. 1320

Oe O friend,
you are my steadfast companion. Still you remain
with me, caring for the blind.
Alas, alas,
you don't elude me in my blindness. I recognize your voice 1325
clearly, although I am in the dark.

Co O you who have done dreadful things, how did you dare to
quench
the sight of your eyes in this way? Who of daimons impelled
you?

Oe This was Apollo, friends, Apollo,
who fulfilled ills, ills, these my sufferings of mine. 1330
But no one struck my sights with his own hand but my
wretched self.
What need did I have of seeing,
for when I was seeing, nothing was sweet to see. 1335

Co It was thus as you say.

Oe What can be seen or
loved by me or still heard when addressed
with pleasure, friends?
Lead me away from this place as quickly as you can. 1340
Lead me away, friends, someone utterly destroyed,
most accursed and besides to the gods 1345

ἐχθρότατον βροτῶν.
Χο. δείλαιε τοῦ νοῦ τῆς τε cυμφορᾶc ἴcον,
      ὡc c᾽ ἠθέληcα μηδαμὰ γνῶναί ποτ᾽ ἄν.

Οι. ὄλοιθ᾽ ὅcτιc ἦν ὃc ἀγρίαc πέδαc   ἀντ. β΄
      νομὰc ἐπιποδίαc μ᾽ ἔλαβ᾽ ἀπό τε φόνου ⟨μ᾽⟩   1350
      ἔρυτο κἀνέcωcεν, οὐ-
      δὲν ἐc χάριν πράccων.
      τότε γὰρ ἂν θανὼν
      οὐκ ἦ φίλοιcιν οὐδ᾽ ἐμοὶ τοcόνδ᾽ ἄχοc.   1355
Χο. θέλοντι κἀμοὶ τοῦτ᾽ ἂν ἦν.
Οι. οὔκουν πατρόc γ᾽ ἂν φονεὺc
      ἦλθον, οὐδὲ νυμφίοc
      βροτοῖc ἐκλήθην ὧν ἔφυν ἄπο.
      νῦν δ᾽ ἄθεοc μέν εἰμ᾽, ἀνοcίων δὲ παῖc,   1360
      ὁμογενὴc δ᾽ ἀφ᾽ ὧν αὐτὸc ἔφυν τάλαc.
      εἰ δέ τι πρεcβύτερον ἔτι κακοῦ κακόν,   1365
      τοῦτ᾽ ἔλαχ᾽ Οἰδίπουc.
Χο. οὐκ οἶδ᾽ ὅπωc cε φῶ βεβουλεῦcθαι καλῶc.
      κρείccων γὰρ ἦcθα μηκέτ᾽ ὢν ἢ ζῶν τυφλόc.

Οι. ὡc μὲν τάδ᾽ οὐχ ὧδ᾽ ἔcτ᾽ ἄριcτ᾽ εἰργαcμένα,
      μή μ᾽ ἐκδίδαcκε, μηδὲ cυμβούλευ᾽ ἔτι.   1370
      ἐγὼ γὰρ οὐκ οἶδ᾽ ὄμμαcιν ποίοιc βλέπων
      πατέρα ποτ᾽ ἂν προcεῖδον εἰc Ἅιδου μολών,
      οὐδ᾽ αὖ τάλαιναν μητέρ᾽, οἷν ἐμοὶ δυοῖν
      ἔργ᾽ ἐcτὶ κρείccον᾽ ἀγχόνηc εἰργαcμένα.

1348 μηδαμὰ γνῶναι Dobree: μηδ᾽ ἀναγνῶναι codd.: μηδέ c᾽ ἂν
Neue   ἂν LrpZrt: om. a   1349 ὃc t: ὃc ἀπ᾽ fere cett.
1350 νομὰc Hartung: νομάδοc codd.   μ᾽ ἔλαβ᾽ Kamerbeek post
Elmsley: ἔλαβέ μ᾽ V (fortasse e sch.): de Lac non constat: ἔλυcέ μ᾽ Krp:
ἔλυcεν a   ⟨μ᾽⟩ B. H. Kennedy   1352 ἔρυτο p: ἔρρ- Lrpat
1355 ἦ Dindorf: ἦν codd.   ἄχοc pat, fortasse P.Oxy. 1369: ἄχθοc
LrpD   1359 ⟨ἂν⟩ ὧν Heimsoeth, cf. 1339   1360 ἄθεοc
Erfurdt et Elmsley: ἄθλιοc codd.   1361 ὁμογενὴc] ὁ μονο-
γενὴc G in linea, a: ὁμολεχὴc Meineke   1365 ἔτι Hermann:
ἔφυ rpat: ἔφυι ut videtur L   1368 ἦcθ᾽ ⟨ἂν⟩ Porson et Purgold

the most hateful of mortals.

Co Equally unhappy for your intelligence and for your misfortune,
how I wish I had never known you.

Oe May he perish, whoever the wanderer was,
who took me from the cruel fetters upon my feet   1350
and delivered me from slaughter and saved my life.
He did me no favor.
Had I died then,
I would not have been so great an affliction upon my kinsmen
and myself.   1355

Co This would be my wish, too.

Oe I would not have come
to be my father's murderer and known
among men as the husband of her from whom I was born.
Now, abandoned by gods, I am the child of unholy parents,   1360
having common offspring with those from which I was sired
myself.
If there ever was any infamy graver than this infamy,   1365
it fell to the lot of Oedipus.

Co I do not know how I could say you thought this out well,
for you were better off not being alive than living in blindness.

Oe Do not try to teach me or counsel me further
that these actions were not done in the best possible way.   1370
I do not know, if I were seeing, with what eyes
I could have looked upon my father, when I arrived in Hades,
and my poor mother. I have committed acts against them both
that call for punishment worse than hanging.

ἀλλ' ἡ τέκνων δῆτ' ὄψις ἦν ἐφίμερος,   1375
βλαστοῦς· ὅπως ἔβλαστε, προσλεύσσειν ἐμοί;
οὐ δῆτα τοῖς γ' ἐμοῖσιν ὀφθαλμοῖς ποτε·
οὐδ' ἄστυ γ', οὐδὲ πύργος, οὐδὲ δαιμόνων
ἀγάλμαθ' ἱερά, τῶν ὁ παντλήμων ἐγὼ
κάλλιστ' ἀνὴρ εἷς ἔν γε ταῖς Θήβαις
τραφεὶς   1380
ἀπεστέρησ' ἐμαυτόν, αὐτὸς ἐννέπων
ὠθεῖν ἅπαντας τὸν ἀσεβῆ, τὸν ἐκ θεῶν
φανέντ' ἄναγνον καὶ γένους τοῦ Λαΐου.
τοιάνδ' ἐγὼ κηλῖδα μηνύσας ἐμὴν
ὀρθοῖς ἔμελλον ὄμμασιν τούτους ὁρᾶν;   1385
ἥκιστά γ'· ἀλλ' εἰ τῆς ἀκουούσης ἔτ' ἦν
πηγῆς δι' ὤτων φραγμός, οὐκ ἂν ἐσχόμην
τὸ μὴ ἀποκλῇσαι τοὐμὸν ἄθλιον δέμας,
ἵν' ἦ τυφλός τε καὶ κλύων μηδέν· τὸ γὰρ
τὴν φροντίδ' ἔξω τῶν κακῶν οἰκεῖν γλυκύ.   1390
ἰὼ Κιθαιρών, τί μ' ἐδέχου; τί μ' οὐ λαβὼν
ἔκτεινας εὐθύς, ὡς ἔδειξα μήποτε
ἐμαυτὸν ἀνθρώποισιν ἔνθεν ἦ γεγώς;
ὦ Πόλυβε καὶ Κόρινθε καὶ τὰ πάτρια
λόγῳ παλαιὰ δώμαθ', οἷον ἀρά με   1395
κάλλος κακῶν ὕπουλον ἐξεθρέψατε.
νῦν γὰρ κακός τ' ὢν κἀκ κακῶν εὑρίσκομαι.
ὦ τρεῖς κέλευθοι καὶ κεκρυμμένη νάπη
δρυμός τε καὶ στενωπὸς ἐν τριπλαῖς ὁδοῖς,
αἳ τοὐμὸν αἷμα τῶν ἐμῶν χειρῶν ἄπο   1400

1376 βλαστοῦς] βλαστόνθ' Hartung   προσλεύσσειν]
προσβλέπειν K   1379 ἱερά, τῶν] ἱερά θ', ὧν Nauck
1380 del. van Deventer   1383 γένους] γένος Laur. CS 41, quo
recepto τὸν pro τοῦ Blaydes   1385 τούτους Lpa: τούτοις rpZrt
1387 φραγμός] φαρυγμός Dindorf   ἂν ἐσχόμην edd. post Heath
(cave Jebb credas hanc lectionem in A extare): ἀνεσχόμην codd.
1388 τὸ μὴ Lrpat: τοῦ μὴ p   ἀποκλῇσαι Elmsley: -εῖσαι codd.
1389 ἦ Dac: ἦν cett.   1393 ἦ Elmsley: ἦν codd.   1395 μ'
⟨ἐς⟩ Zieliński

Was the sight of my children, born as they were born,   1375
   a source of delight to me to see?
   Never with these eyes of mine at any rate.
   The city, its tower, the sacred images
   of its gods, of all these this utterly wretched person that I am,
   nurtured in Thebes as no other,   1380
   deprived myself when, with my own voice, I proclaimed
   that all expel the unholy man revealed by the gods
   to be unclean and part of the family of Laïos.
After declaring such stain to be mine,
   was I going to look upon them with steady eyes?   1385
   No, not at all. But were there a way to dam the spring of hearing
   through my ears, I would not have held back
   from shutting off my miserable body
   so that I would be blind and hear nothing, for it would be sweet
   for my thoughts to dwell apart from miseries.   1390
O Cithaeron, why did you receive me? Why did you not take me
   and kill me at once so I never showed men whence I was born?
   O Polybus and Corinth and ancient abodes
   of my reputed fathers, the beauty   1395
   you reared in me is festering beneath the scar with ugliness.
   Now I am discovered a base thing from base parents.
   O three roads and hidden glen,
   copse of oaks and narrow way at the crossroads,
   you who drank my father's blood   1400

ἐπίετε πατρός, ἀρά μου μέμνησθ᾽ ἔτι
οἷ᾽ ἔργα δράσας ὑμὶν εἶτα δεῦρ᾽ ἰὼν
ὁποῖ᾽ ἔπρασσον αὖθις; ὦ γάμοι γάμοι,
ἐφύσαθ᾽ ἡμᾶς, καὶ φυτεύσαντες πάλιν
ἀνεῖτε ταὐτὸν σπέρμα, κἀπεδείξατε   1405
πατέρας ἀδελφούς, παῖδας αἷμ᾽ ἐμφύλιον,
νύμφας γυναῖκας μητέρας τε, χὠπόσα
αἴσχιστ᾽ ἐν ἀνθρώποισιν ἔργα γίγνεται.
ἀλλ᾽, οὐ γὰρ αὐδᾶν ἔσθ᾽ ἃ μηδὲ δρᾶν καλόν,
ὅπως τάχιστα πρὸς θεῶν ἔξω μέ που   1410
καλύψατ᾽, ἢ φονεύσατ᾽, ἢ θαλάσσιον
ἐκρίψατ᾽, ἔνθα μήποτ᾽ εἰσόψεσθ᾽ ἔτι.
ἴτ᾽, ἀξιώσατ᾽ ἀνδρὸς ἀθλίου θιγεῖν·
πίθεσθε, μὴ δείσητε· τἀμὰ γὰρ κακὰ
οὐδεὶς οἷός τε πλὴν ἐμοῦ φέρειν βροτῶν.   1415
Χο.   ἀλλ᾽ ὧν ἐπαιτεῖς ἐς δέον πάρεσθ᾽ ὅδε
Κρέων τὸ πράσσειν καὶ τὸ βουλεύειν, ἐπεὶ
χώρας λέλειπται μοῦνος ἀντὶ σοῦ φύλαξ.
Οι.   οἴμοι, τί δῆτα λέξομεν πρὸς τόνδ᾽ ἔπος;
τίς μοι φανεῖται πίστις ἔνδικος; τὰ γὰρ   1420
πάρος πρὸς αὐτὸν πάντ᾽ ἐφηύρημαι κακός.
Κρ.   οὐχ ὡς γελαστής, Οἰδίπους, ἐλήλυθα,
οὐδ᾽ ὡς ὀνειδιῶν τι τῶν πάρος κακῶν.
ἀλλ᾽ εἰ τὰ θνητῶν μὴ καταισχύνεσθ᾽ ἔτι
γένεθλα, τὴν γοῦν πάντα βόσκουσαν φλόγα   1425
αἰδεῖσθ᾽ ἄνακτος Ἡλίου, τοιόνδ᾽ ἄγος

1401 ἀρά μου] ἀρ᾽ ἐμοῦ Brunck   ἔτι a: ὅταν lγρ, r: ὅτι l, G in
lin., pat: τι Elmsley   1405 ταὐτὸν] ταὐτὸ 'Longinus', Subl. 23:
ταὐτοῦ Jebb   1406 sic interpunxit C. W. Macleod
1409 μηδὲ δρᾶν] μηδ᾽ ὁρᾶν Nauck   καλόν] καλά Stobaeus
3. 17. 4   1410 που] ποι Meineke   1411 del. Meineke
1411–12 καλύψατ᾽ et ἐκρίψατ᾽ permutavit Burges   1414 πίθεσθε
Elmsley: πεί- codd.   1415 post πλὴν add. γ᾽ VZr
1422 οὐχ a: οὔτ᾽ Lac: οὔθ᾽ KrpZrt Suda s.v. γελαστής   1423 οὐδ᾽
a et fortasse Lac: οὔθ᾽ ΛKrpZrt Suda   1424 καταισχύνεσθ᾽ ἔτι]
-εσθέ τι Elmsley

from my hands, do you remember me still,
what things I did to you, and coming here,
what I continued to do? O marriage, marriage
you gave me birth, and, giving birth,
you sent forth the same seed and showed   1405
fathers to be brothers, children to be bloodshed of kin,
brides to be wives, mothers,[55] and as many
acts of deepest shame as have occurred among men.
Yet it is ignoble to say what is ignoble to do: 1410
quickly as you can, by the gods, hide me somewhere
away from here, or kill me, or hurl me into the sea
where you will never see me again.

[*Enter Creon, accompanied by at least two servants (1429).*]

Come, let yourself touch me, a wretched man.
Trust me, and do not fear. My ills, my misfortunes,
no man except me can bear.   1415

Co   Well, as for what you ask, here is Creon
when needed for acting and taking counsel, since
he alone has been left as guardian of the land in your stead.

Oe   O me! What word indeed will I say to him?
What will serve as guarantee of truthfulness?   1420
I was wrong before in everything about him.

Cr   I have not come to mock you, Oedipus,
or taunt you for any of the terrible things you said,
but if you no longer feel shame before
the children of men, at least respect the flame   1425
of Lord Sun that feeds us all and do not display in this way

ἀκάλυπτον οὕτω δεικνύναι, τὸ μήτε γῆ
μήτ᾽ ὄμβρος ἱερὸς μήτε φῶς προσδέξεται.
ἀλλ᾽ ὡς τάχιστ᾽ ἐς οἶκον ἐσκομίζετε·
τοῖς ἐν γένει γὰρ τἀγγενῆ μόνοις θ᾽ ὁρᾶν   1430
μόνοις τ᾽ ἀκούειν εὐσεβῶς ἔχει κακά.
Οι.   πρὸς θεῶν, ἐπείπερ ἐλπίδος μ᾽ ἀπέσπασας,
ἄριστος ἐλθὼν πρὸς κάκιστον ἄνδρ᾽ ἐμέ,
πιθοῦ τί μοι· πρὸς σοῦ γάρ, οὐδ᾽ ἐμοῦ, φράσω.
Κρ.   καὶ τοῦ με χρείας ὧδε λιπαρεῖς τυχεῖν;   1435
Οι.   ῥῖψόν με γῆς ἐκ τῆσδ᾽ ὅσον τάχισθ᾽, ὅπου
θνητῶν φανοῦμαι μηδενὸς προσήγορος.
Κρ.   ἔδρασ᾽ ἂν εὖ τοῦτ᾽ ἴσθ᾽ ἄν, εἰ μὴ τοῦ θεοῦ
πρώτιστ᾽ ἔχρῃζον ἐκμαθεῖν τί πρακτέον.
Οι.   ἀλλ᾽ ἦ γ᾽ ἐκείνου πᾶς᾽ ἐδηλώθη φάτις,   1440
τὸν πατροφόντην, τὸν ἀσεβῆ μ᾽ ἀπολλύναι.
Κρ.   οὕτως ἐλέχθη ταῦθ᾽· ὅμως δ᾽ ἵν᾽ ἕσταμεν
χρείας ἄμεινον ἐκμαθεῖν τί δραστέον.
Οι.   οὕτως ἄρ᾽ ἀνδρὸς ἀθλίου πεύσεσθ᾽ ὕπερ;
Κρ.   καὶ γὰρ σὺ νῦν γ᾽ ἂν τῷ θεῷ πίστιν φέροις.   1445
Οι.   καὶ σοί γ᾽ ἐπισκήπτω τε καὶ προτρέψομαι,
τῆς μὲν κατ᾽ οἴκους αὐτὸς ὃν θέλεις τάφον
θοῦ—καὶ γὰρ ὀρθῶς τῶν γε σῶν τελεῖς ὕπερ—
ἐμοῦ δὲ μήποτ᾽ ἀξιωθήτω τόδε
πατρῷον ἄστυ ζῶντος οἰκητοῦ τυχεῖν,   1450
ἀλλ᾽ ἔα με ναίειν ὄρεσιν, ἔνθα κλῄζεται
οὑμὸς Κιθαιρὼν οὗτος, ὃν μήτηρ τέ μοι
πατήρ τ᾽ ἐθέσθην ζῶντε κύριον τάφον,
ἵν᾽ ἐξ ἐκείνων, οἵ μ᾽ ἀπωλλύτην, θάνω.

1428 προσδέξεται] προσδέρξεται Korais   1429 ἐσκομί-
ζετε Lpat: εἰσ- rC   1430 μόνοις θ᾽ Pflugk (μόνοις iam Dobree):
μάλισθ᾽ codd.   1437 φανοῦμαι] θανοῦμαι Meineke
1445 γ᾽ ἂν Kr: τἂν Lpat   1446 τε a: γε LrpZrt   προτρέψομαι rat: προστρέψομαι LpZr   1453 ζῶντε] -τι Pa, coni.
Toup   1454 ἀπωλλύτην at et fortasse L: ἀπο- rpD

such pollution uncovered that neither the earth
nor the sacred rain nor the light will welcome.

[*To servants.*]

    Quickly as you can, take him inside the house.
    It accords best with piety that those in the family alone   1430
    see and alone hear troubles of the family.
Oe By the gods, since you have torn me from what I expected,
    you, the best, come to me, the worst man,
    obey me in this, for I shall speak for your benefit, not mine.
Cr What do you want that you are eager to get from me?   1435
Oe Cast me from this land as quickly as you can,
    where I will be addressed by no one mortal.
Cr I would have done that, know well, but for the fact that first
    I must learn from the god what must be done.
Oe No, his oracle was revealed in full—   1440
    kill the father-slayer, unholy man, me.
Cr That was the way it was said. Still, in our present need
    it is better to learn what must be done.
Oe You will ask of the god about me, a wretched man?
Cr Yes, even you now would grant faith in the god?   1445
Oe Yes. I charge you, I will appeal to you as your suppliant:
    arrange burial for her inside the house as you yourself
    decide, for you will perform properly the rites for your own.
    Never let this city of my fathers be reckoned worthy
    of having me as an inhabitant while I'm alive.   1450
    Let me dwell in the mountains
    where Cithaeron is now called mine. My mother
    and father when alive arranged it as my proper tomb
    so I may die at the hands of those who sought to kill me.

καίτοι τοσοῦτόν γ' οἶδα, μήτε μ' ἂν νόσον   1455
μήτ' ἄλλο πέρσαι μηδέν· οὐ γὰρ ἄν ποτε
θνῄσκων ἐσώθην, μὴ 'πί τῳ δεινῷ κακῷ.
ἀλλ' ἡ μὲν ἡμῶν μοῖρ', ὅποιπερ εἶς', ἴτω·
παίδων δὲ τῶν μὲν ἀρσένων μή μοι, Κρέον,
προσθῇ μέριμναν· ἄνδρες εἰσίν, ὥστε μὴ   1460
σπάνιν ποτὲ σχεῖν, ἔνθ' ἂν ὦσι, τοῦ βίου·
ταῖν δ' ἀθλίαιν οἰκτραῖν τε παρθένοιν ἐμαῖν,
αἷν οὔποθ' †ἡμὴ† χωρὶς ἐστάθη βορᾶς
τράπεζ' ἄνευ τοῦδ' ἀνδρός, ἀλλ' ὅσων ἐγὼ
ψαύοιμι, πάντων τώδ' ἀεὶ μετειχέτην·   1465
αἷν μοι μέλεσθαι· καὶ μάλιστα μὲν χεροῖν
ψαῦσαί μ' ἔασον κἀποκλαύσασθαι κακά.
ἴθ' ὦναξ,
ἴθ' ὦ γονῇ γενναῖε. χερσί τᾶν θιγὼν
δοκοῖμ' ἔχειν σφας, ὥσπερ ἡνίκ' ἔβλεπον.   1470
τί φημι;
οὐ δὴ κλύω που πρὸς θεῶν τοῖν μοι φίλοιν
δακρυρροούντοιν, καί μ' ἐποικτίρας Κρέων
ἔπεμψέ μοι τὰ φίλτατ' ἐκγόνοιν ἐμοῖν;
λέγω τι;   1475

Κρ.   λέγεις· ἐγὼ γάρ εἰμ' ὁ πορσύνας τάδε,
γνοὺς τὴν παροῦσαν τέρψιν ἥ σ' εἶχεν πάλαι.

Οι.   ἀλλ' εὐτυχοίης, καί σε τῆσδε τῆς ὁδοῦ
δαίμων ἄμεινον ἢ 'μὲ φρουρήσας τύχοι.
ὦ τέκνα, ποῦ ποτ' ἐστέ; δεῦρ' ἴτ', ἔλθετε   1480

1455 μ' Lrpat: ἔμ' a   1458 ὅποιπερ lpat: ὅπηπερ a: ὅπως
G: ὅπερ R   1460 προσθῇ Ka: πρόσθη Lpat: πρόσθου rp:
προθῇ Elmsley   1461 ποτὲ σχεῖν] ποτ' ἴσχειν Blaydes
1463-4 obscuri   1463 οὔποθ' ἡμὴ] οὔποτ' ἀμῆς B. H.
Kennedy: alii alia   1465 τώδ' Schneidewin: τῶνδ' codd.
1466 αἷν] ταῖν Zr, coni. Heath   1469 γονῇ] γονὴν Musgrave
τᾶν rpa: δ' ἂν lVZrt   1474 ἐκγόνοιν Zn et Marc. gr. 472 teste
Jebb: ἐκγόνων Gγρ: ἐγγόνοιν cett.   1477 ἥ σ' εἶχεν Lᵃᶜt:
ἣν εἶχες Lᵖᶜra: ἥ σ' εἶχε p: ἥ σ' ἔχει Zg, coni. olim Wunder
1480 ἴτ' rpat: om. lp

And yet this much I do know. Neither sickness nor anything 1455
   will destroy me, for, as I was dying,
   I would not have been saved except for some dire evil.
   Well, let it go, my fate, wherever it goes.
   As for my male children, Creon,
   do not concern yourself. They are men so that, 1460
   wherever they are, they will not lack a livelihood.
   But my two wretched and pitiful daughters,
   apart from whom my table of food was never set
   without this man who always shared
   with them everything I touched, 1465
   take care of them. Most of all, permit me
   to embrace them with my hands and lament my troubles.

[*Antigone and Ismene enter from the house, weeping and probably escorted.*]

Come, lord,
   come, O true noble by birth. If I could touch them,
   I would seem to have them as when I saw. 1470
   What am I saying?
   Do I not hear, by the gods, my two darlings
   weeping? Did Creon have pity for me?
   Did he send to me my most beloved children?
   Am I right? 1475

Cr Yes, you are. I am the one who arranged this,
   knowing the joy you feel now as it held you in the past.

Oe May you prosper, and may the daimon watch over you
   for coming to me better than he did me.
   Children, where are you? Come here, come 1480

ὡς τὰς ἀδελφὰς τάσδε τὰς ἐμὰς χέρας,
αἵ τοῦ φυτουργοῦ πατρὸς ὑμὶν ὧδ' ὁρᾶν
τὰ πρόσθε λαμπρὰ προὐξένησαν ὄμματα·
ὃς ὑμίν, ὦ τέκν', οὔθ' ὁρῶν οὔθ' ἱστορῶν
πατὴρ ἐφάνθην ἔνθεν αὐτὸς ἠρόθην.   1485
καὶ σφὼ δακρύω· προσβλέπειν γὰρ οὐ σθένω·
νοούμενος τὰ πικρὰ τοῦ λοιποῦ βίου,
οἷον βιῶναι σφὼ πρὸς ἀνθρώπων χρεών.
ποίας γὰρ ἀστῶν ἥξετ' εἰς ὁμιλίας,
ποίας δ' ἑορτάς, ἔνθεν οὐ κεκλαυμέναι   1490
πρὸς οἶκον ἵξεσθ' ἀντὶ τῆς θεωρίας;
ἀλλ' ἡνίκ' ἂν δὴ πρὸς γάμων ἥκητ' ἀκμάς,
τίς οὗτος ἔσται, τίς παραρρίψει, τέκνα,
τοιαῦτ' ὀνείδη λαμβάνειν, ἃ τοῖς ἐμοῖς
γονεῦσιν ἔσται σφῷν θ' ὁμοῦ δηλήματα;   1495
τί γὰρ κακῶν ἄπεστι; τὸν πατέρα πατὴρ
ὑμῶν ἔπεφνε· τὴν τεκοῦσαν ἤροσεν,
ὅθεν περ αὐτὸς ἐσπάρη, κἀκ τῶν ἴσων
ἐκτήσαθ' ὑμᾶς, ὧνπερ αὐτὸς ἐξέφυ.
τοιαῦτ' ὀνειδιεῖσθε. κᾆτα τίς γαμεῖ;   1500
οὐκ ἔστιν οὐδείς, ὦ τέκν', ἀλλὰ δηλαδὴ
χέρσους φθαρῆναι κἀγάμους ὑμᾶς χρεών.
ὦ παῖ Μενοικέως, ἀλλ' ἐπεὶ μόνος πατὴρ
ταύταιν λέλειψαι, νὼ γάρ, ὣ 'φυτεύσαμεν,
ὀλώλαμεν δύ' ὄντε, μή σφε, πάτερ, ἴδῃς   1505
πτωχὰς ἀνάνδρους ἐγγενεῖς ἀλωμένας,
μηδ' ἐξισώσῃς τάσδε τοῖς ἐμοῖς κακοῖς.
ἀλλ' οἴκτισόν σφας, ὧδε τηλικάσδ' ὁρῶν

1481 ὡς] εἰς Elmsley   1483 προὐξένησαν] προὐσέλησαν
Th. Gomperz   1485 πατὴρ] ἀροτὴρ Herwerden   1487 πικρὰ
. . . λοιποῦ Kp: λοιπὰ . . . πικροῦ Lrpat   1491 ἵξεσθ' fere
codd.: ἥξεθ' L   1492 ἥκητ' Lrpa: ἵκητ' Oat   1493 ἔσται,
τίς] ἔστιν ὃς Elmsley   1494 τοῖς ἐμοῖς] τοῖσί τε Herwerden: alii
alia   1495 θ' Lpa: δ' rpt   1502 χέρσους] χήρους r
1504 ταύταιν] τούτοιν Zg   1505 πάτερ, ἴδῃς Jackson:
παρίδῃς codd.: περιίδῃς Dawes   1506 ἐγγενεῖς ⟨γ'⟩ Meineke

to these my hands as well as the hands of a brother
which have contrived for you that the once-bright eyes
of the father who begot you see in this fashion.
Neither seeing nor inquiring, I was revealed
to be your father from where I myself was sown. 1485
I weep for you, since I cannot see you,
  when I ponder the bitterness that will be the rest of your lives,
  how you must live among men.
To what gatherings of townspeople will you go,
  what festivals from which you will not return home 1490
  in tears instead of watching the spectacle?
When you arrive at the flowering of marriage,
  who will he be? Who will risk, children,
  acquiring such reproaches that will be ruin
for my[56] parents and yourselves? 1495
What cutting words will you not hear? Your father slew
his father, he sowed his mother
where he himself was sown, and got you
from the same ones from whom he himself was born.
You will be the object of such censure. Then who will marry
  you? 1500
There is no one, children, but clearly,
  you must wither away barren and without husbands.
Son of Menoeceus, since you have been left the sole father
  of these two girls, for we who gave them birth
  are destroyed, do not look upon them, your relatives, father, 1505
  as beggars wandering bereft of husbands
  or equate them with my evils.
But pity them, seeing that at their tender age they lack

πάντων ἐρήμους, πλὴν ὅσον τὸ còν μέρος.

ξύννευcον, ὦ γενναῖε, cῇ ψαύcαc χερί.　　　　1510

cφῷν δ᾽, ὦ τέκν᾽, εἰ μὲν εἰχέτην ἤδη φρέναc,

πόλλ᾽ ἂν παρήνουν· νῦν δὲ τοῦτ᾽ εὔχεcθέ μοι,

οὗ καιρὸς ἐᾷ ζῆν, τοῦ βίου δὲ λῴονος

ὑμᾶc κυρῆcαι τοῦ φυτεύcαντοc πατρόc.

Κρ. 　ἅλιc ἵν᾽ ἐξήκειc δακρύων· ἀλλ᾽ ἴθι cτέγηc

　　　ἔcω.　　　　1515

Οι. 　πειcτέον, κεἰ μηδὲν ἡδύ. Κρ. πάντα γὰρ

　　　καιρῷ καλά.

Οι. 　οἶcθ᾽ ἐφ᾽ οἷc οὖν εἰμι; Κρ. λέξειc, καὶ τότ᾽ εἴcομαι

　　　κλυών.

Οι. 　γῆc μ᾽ ὅπωc πέμψειc ἄποικον. Κρ. τοῦ θεοῦ μ᾽

　　　αἰτεῖc δόcιν.

Οι. 　ἀλλὰ θεοῖc γ᾽ ἔχθιcτοc ἥκω. Κρ. τοιγαροῦν

　　　τεύξῃ τάχα.

Οι. 　φὴc τάδ᾽ οὖν; Κρ. ἃ μὴ φρονῶ γὰρ οὐ φιλῶ

　　　λέγειν μάτην.　　　　1520

Οι. 　ἄπαγέ νύν μ᾽ ἐντεῦθεν ἤδη. Κρ. cτεῖχέ νυν,

　　　τέκνων δ᾽ ἀφοῦ.

Οι. 　μηδαμῶc ταύταc γ᾽ ἔλῃ μου. Κρ. πάντα μὴ

　　　βούλου κρατεῖν·

　　　καὶ γὰρ ἀκράτηcαc οὔ cοι τῷ βίῳ ξυνέcπετο.

Χο. 　ὦ πάτραc Θήβηc ἔνοικοι, λεύccετ᾽, Οἰδίπουc

　　　ὅδε,

　　　ὃc τὰ κλείν᾽ αἰνίγματ᾽ ᾔδει καὶ κράτιcτοc ἦν

　　　ἀνήρ,　　　　1525

1512 μοι codd. plerique (etiam Λ): με a: ἐμέ, puncto ante posito, van
Deventer　　1513 ἐᾷ Dindorf: ἀεὶ codd.: ἢ Meineke　　τοῦ βίου
Lrpat: βίου p　　1513–30 del. Teuffel　　1517 οὖν] νῦν ed.
Londiniensis a. 1747　　εἶμι Brunck: εἰμί codd.　　κλυών West:
κλύων codd.　　1518 πέμψειc Lpa: -ηc rpat　　ἄποικον Paαγρ,
t: ἀπ᾽ οἴκων Lrpa　　1519 γ᾽ Lpa: om. rpat　　1522 μου]
με Elmsley　　1524–30 Sophoclem scripsisse negant Ritter aliique,
scholio freti　　1524 λεύccετ᾽ at: λεύcετ᾽ Lrpa　　1525 ᾔδει]
ἤδη L in linea, GP

every support except for what you will do for them.

Touch me with your hand, noble sir, and nod your head in
    agreement.   1510

Children, if you already attained maturity of mind,

I would give you much advice, but now I bid you offer this prayer:

wherever opportunity allows you to live,

that you have a better life than the father who bore you.

Cr   This has gone on long enough. No more tears. Come into the
      house.   1515

Oe   I must obey, even if it is no sweet thing.

Cr   All is beautiful at the right time.

Oe   Do you know on what terms I shall go?

Cr   You will tell me, and then I will know from hearing.

Oe   That you send me abroad, away from here.

Cr   You are asking me for a gift that can come only from the god.

Oe   But I have come to be most hateful to the gods.

Cr   Therefore, you will receive your gift quickly.

Oe   And so you agree?

Cr   I am not in the habit of prattling on about what I do not mean. 1520

Oe   Lead me away from here now.

Cr   Come, now. Let go of the children.

Oe   Do not take them from me.

Cr   Do not will to have power over all things.

What you did have power over failed to follow you throughout
    your life.

[*Oedipus, Creon, servant, Antigone, and Ismene exit to the house.*]

Chorus of Theban old Men

O inhabitants of our fatherland Thebes, behold: this is Oedipus

who knew renowned riddles and was a most powerful man, 1525

οὔ τίς οὐ ζήλῳ πολιτῶν ταῖς τύχαις ἐπέβλεπεν,
εἰς ὅσον κλύδωνα δεινῆς cυμφορᾶς ἐλήλυθεν.
ὥστε θνητὸν ὄντ᾽ ἐκείνην τὴν τελευταίαν ἔδει
ἡμέραν ἐπιcκοποῦντα μηδέν᾽ ὀλβίζειν, πρὶν ἂν
τέρμα τοῦ βίου περάcῃ μηδὲν ἀλγεινὸν
        παθών.   1530

1526 οὔ τίc Martin: ὅcτιc codd.   ταῖc Canter: καὶ codd.   ἐπέβλεπεν Musgrave: ἐπιβλέπων codd.   1528 ἔδει Stanley: ἰδεῖν
codd.   1529 μηδέν᾽ . . . ἂν] πάντα προcδοκᾶν ἕωc ἂν lγρ

whose fortunes no citizen looked upon free of envy.
Into such a flood of appalling misfortunes he has come.
Thus a man in his mortality, reflecting upon that final day,
must count no one happy until he passes the end
of life without suffering pain.   1530

NOTES

1. Cadmus is the mythical founder of Thebes; his name is often used synonymously for the city itself.

2. The two temples may be those of Athena Onka and Athena Cadmeia, while "prophetic ashes" refers to the temple of Apollo Ismenos, near the Ismenus River, whose altar was made of ashes from sacrifice.

3. "*Daimon* is occult power, a force that drives man forward where no agent can be named. . . . *Daimon* is the veiled countenance of divine activity. There is no image of a daimon, and there is no cult" (Walter Burkert, *Greek Religion*, trans. John Raffan [Cambridge, MA: Harvard University Press, 1985], 180).

4. Lines 60–61: Sophocles' word for sickness, *nosos*, and its verb *noseô* are also used of the plague and have connotations of political and military strife. Oedipus points out that, although everyone else is sick on his own, he is sick for the city, himself, and all Thebans (62–64). He is predisposed by his character to act as a *pharmakos* to cleanse the city of pollution.

5. The oracle in the temple of Pythian Apollo at Delphi.

6. Line 87: In reporting the oracle, Creon does not give the words of the priestess who received them from the god. Instead, he says *lego*, "I say," so that he becomes the authority for what the oracle says, not the god or his priestess. He reports in his own words what Apollo's oracle said and is hence responsible throughout what follows for its content and meaning. Oedipus never requests the exact words of the oracle.

7. Lines 93–94: By allowing discussion to take place before the elders and by granting Creon the initiative, Oedipus loses control of the search and the direction it will take. At the same time, he reaffirms his willingness to suffer for all, culminating in his victimization.

8. Line 100: Creon's participle *andrêlatoûntas*, "banishing one or more men," consists of the word elements *andr-* "man" or "men" and *lat-* "to drive out." The participle itself is plural because it modifies an unexpressed *hêmas*, "us," but leaves as ambiguous the number of men to be driven out.

9. Line 102: "What man's (*andros*) misfortune?" Oedipus flattens the ambiguity of Apollo's words and sets his sights from the outset on finding one man. Creon, on the other hand, allows Oedipus' misunderstanding of the oracle as he reports it.

10. Lines 103–4: Creon directs Oedipus' attention to the disappearance of Laïos on the road to the oracle. Creon reports (114–15) that Laïos kept saying that he was bound for the oracle without specifying that that oracle is Apollo's at Delphi.

11. Line 107: In the phrase *tous autoentas*, "the murderers," *tous*, the definite article modifying *autoentas*, implies that the murderers are human, while *autoentas* indicates through its element

aut- "-self" that murders occurred within the family. For a detailed discussion of the use of the word *autoentas* in this line, see the article by Rick M. Newton "The Murderers of Laius, Again (Soph. *OT* 106–7)" in the present volume.

12. Line 122: Creon reports that the sole surviving witness to Laïos' murder reported that *léistas*, "bandits" or "robbers," killed him with the force of many hands. Nevertheless, in line 124 with *léistês*, "bandit," Oedipus remains focused on finding one man. On the question of one or many murderers, see the articles by William Chase Greene, Rick M. Newton, Karl Harshbarger, and Sandor Goodhart in the present volume.

13. Line 129: "Impede," etymologically "to be on the foot," reproduces the Greek *empodôn* (line 128) which, in turn, leads to Creon's describing the Sphinx as "at their (Thebans') feet." *Pous*, foot, appears in several forms as allusions to Oedipus' name, *Oidipous*, "he of the swollen foot" from *oidêma*, swelling, or "I know foot" from *oida*, I know.

14. Lines 133–41: What began as an inquiry to the oracle about the plague has turned, through Creon's interpretation of the oracle's words, into a search for the murderer of Laïos, and from a religious inquiry into a political one as Oedipus suspects that an attempt on the tyrant's (128) life would not have been possible without support from inside Thebes.

15. "Delian Healer" is an epithet of Apollo, born on the island of Delos.

16. A three-syllable word has been lost.

17. Line 215: The elders of the Chorus have responded to Oedipus' call for the people of Thebes to gather around him (144). The elders' opening song expresses everyman's piety in their belief that the gods will respond to their cries and clear away the plague and war that have beset their land. Since the Thebans are not at war, Sophocles may have had in mind the Athenians' war with the Lacedaemonians and their allies that afflicts his country. The Chorus seeks salvation from their leaders whose efforts they observe. They maintain support for Oedipus until that support begins to drive a wedge between his safety and that of their country.

18. The translation reproduces the unanimous reading of the manuscripts. Hugh Lloyd-Jones and N. G. Wilson accept that a line has been omitted (*Sophoclis Fabulae* [Oxford: Oxford University Press, 1990]; *Sophoclea: Studies on the Text of Sophocles* [Oxford: Clarendon Press, 1990], 85). Lines 227–29 have defied the efforts of editors.

19. The brackets indicate that Lloyd-Jones and Wilson regard lines 246–51 as an interpolation.

20. The Coryphaeus, or leader of the Chorus, was marked by his more brightly decorated robes and by his place in the middle of the front rank of choristers. He addressed the actors in dialogue on behalf of the others and joined them in singing the songs.

21. Line 293: Again Oedipus insists on one culprit.

22. Line 296: Oedipus has no clue as to the culprit or culprits and realizes that his imprecation and threat will have little or no effect on their behavior.

23. Line 297: Since there is no one to cross-examine and refute, *exelegxôn* is often translated "expose" or "convict." Yet Sophocles may be thinking of Tiresias' treatment of Oedipus and refutation of his charges.

24. Line 299: The following scenes between Oedipus and Tiresias and Creon are in essence contests over who best can deflect identification as the miasma causing the plague from himself and attach it to his antagonist. Oedipus has on his side his destruction of the Sphinx, but he also knows

that he slew several men at the crossroads in Phocis. Tiresias has his authority as the god Apollo's prophet, the truth of whose words the Thebans of the Chorus accept.

25. Lines 300–315: Such lavish praise undermines Oedipus' later accusations of Tiresias as a charlatan in cahoots with Creon.

26. Lines 320–38: Girard notes that "in a series of replies Tiresias warns Oedipus of the purely reciprocal nature of the approaching tragedy; that is, of the blows that each will inflict on the other. . . . The very rhythm of the [sentences], their symmetrical effects, anticipate and provoke the tragic debate. We see here violent reciprocity in action, canceling all distinctions between the two men." See René Girard, *Violence and the Sacred*, trans. Patrick Gregory (Baltimore: Johns Hopkins University Press, 1977), 71. The quoted analysis will be found in the selection from Girard's book reprinted in the present volume.

27. R. D. Dawe, ed., *Oedipus Rex* (Cambridge: Cambridge University Press, 1982), 104, deems *kàteleutêtos*, "not brought to an end, without end or purpose," to be "doubtless corrupt." Translation is tentative.

28. Thebans face the threat of continued plague unless they can ascertain, and banish or execute, the man or men who killed Laïos. Tiresias enters under the aura of truth which the Thebans of the Chorus announce for him. Oedipus also testifies to Tiresias' knowledge and closeness to Apollo. When Tiresias refuses to inform Oedipus, although he has led him to believe he has knowledge, Oedipus becomes enraged. The search for the perpetrator is frustrated, lost in the building wrath. Tiresias observes that Oedipus sees the anger in him but not in himself (337: *orgén*). What is happening amounts to a loss of differences; prophet and tyrant are disappearing, leaving only two identical angry men, while the trust that Thebans have invested in the institutions that they represent is undermined.

29. The word is *miastôr*, "he who is polluted with miasma."

30. Line 358: "If we take Tiresias's reply literally, the terrible charges of patricide and incest that he has just leveled at Oedipus did not stem from any supernatural source of information. The accusation is simply an act of reprisal arising from the hostile exchange of a tragic debate. Oedipus unintentionally initiates the process by forcing Tiresias to speak. He accuses Tiresias of having had a part in the murder of Laius; he prods Tiresias into reprisal, into hurling the accusation back at him" (Girard, *Violence and the Sacred*, 71). The quoted analysis will be found in the selection from Girard's book reprinted in the present volume.

31. Gray text indicates that Lloyd-Jones and Wilson, *Sophoclis Fabulae*, deem the word irreparable. Translation is at best tentative. In this instance, the Greek word may be omitted without significant loss of meaning.

32. Lloyd-Jones and Wilson, *Sophoclis Fabulae*, 134, print *toû* (whose) from papyrus Oxy.22^{ac}. All eighteen manuscripts have *soû* (yours).

33. Line 404–5: The Chorus considers Oedipus' accusations and Tiresias' the words of angry men that do not forward the search for the cause of the plague.

34. Loxias is an epithet of Apollo.

35. Mt. Cithaeron marks the border between Boeotia to the north and Attica to the south.

36. Richard C. Jebb, *Sophocles: The Plays and Fragments, Part I: The Oedipus Tyrannus*, 2nd ed. (Cambridge: Cambridge University Press, 1887), 66, translates the manuscript as reading "which will equalize you to yourself and to your children," which Lloyd-Jones and Wilson, *Sophoclea*, 90, deem "surely intolerably complicated." Jean-Pierre Vernant interprets the line to mean that incest,

by making Oedipus equal to his own children, will make him "equal to himself" in the sense of being a creature apart, "without equality with other men" (see Vernant's article "Ambiguity and Reversal: On the Enigmatic Structure of *Oedipus Rex*" in the present volume).

37. Furies are avenging spirits.

38. Mt. Parnassus was sacred to Dionysus, the Muses, and Apollo. At its foot lay the Delphic oracle.

39. The "earth's navel" refers to Delphi, considered to be the center of the world.

40. A word or words amounting to four syllables have been lost.

41. Line 511: Tiresias has in effect won the contest, but his awful charges brought against Oedipus have confounded the Chorus in their belief that Tiresias utters only the truth (299). They fall back upon the cliché of divine certainty versus human fallibility, but their loyalty to Oedipus has been shaken.

42. Oedipus speaks of himself as "this man" at 815, 829, and 1464, Jocasta refers to Polybus as "this man" at 947, and the Corinthian speaks of himself as "this man" at 1018.

43. Line 576: Oedipus realizes the nature of the exchange with Creon, namely, that Creon is the last person who may be culpable and if he escapes, Oedipus himself will be left to take the blame for the plague.

44. In the lacunae before and after line 624, Oedipus is thought to have commuted Creon's sentence from death to exile. Hence several lines may have been lost (Lloyd-Jones and Wilson, *Sophoclea*, 93–94).

45. Line 630: The clash between Creon and Oedipus has ended with a loss of leadership at Thebes.

46. Lines 658–59: "Oedipus's imminent fall has nothing to do with any heinous sin; rather, it should be regarded as the outcome of a tragic encounter in which Oedipus has met defeat" (Girard, *Violence and the Sacred*, 73; see the selection from Girard's book reprinted in the present volume). Oedipus realizes that absolving Creon will leave him to be victimized himself (cf. lines 669–70).

47. Lines 685–86: As from the beginning, the members of the Chorus are focused upon a solution to the plague and regard the bickering between their leaders as counterproductive. This attitude explains their ready acceptance of Oedipus as its source later in the play.

48. Lines 700ff.: It must be borne in mind that although Oedipus and Jocasta are engaged in an intimate discussion, the men of the Chorus are listening.

49. The manuscripts read both *melas* (black) and *megas* (big).

50. Comparison with its companion line (892) in the strophe indicates that the antistrophe has lost four syllables from this line.

51. For more on the Corinthian's problematic status, see Frederick Ahl's analyses in the present volume.

52. Translation follows that of J. D. Denniston, "Varia," *The Classical Review* 47 (1933): 165.

53. Lines 1186–222: The Thebans of the Chorus deem Oedipus' efforts to escape the prediction of Apollo's oracle an act of arrogance associated with a tyrant in that such a man survives only by his own wits, resources, and power and lives in fear of reprisals, treachery, and overthrow. Their support of Oedipus has been shaken as they cling to the gods as the source of salvation. For if Oedipus can succeed in escaping the oracle, they ask what is the sense of worshipping the gods. They turn from Oedipus as they accept Tiresias' and Creon's version of the story, and the process

of mythmaking that will shape Oedipus as different and unique and as responsible for the plague begins.

54. Istros is the Danube River, and Phasis is the Rion, the main river of Georgia, originating in the Caucasus Mountains. Both rivers empty into the Black Sea.

55. Translation of lines 1406–7 follows that of Colin Macleod, *Collected Essays* (Oxford: Clarendon Press, 1983).

56. The reading of the manuscripts indicates that harm would come to Laïos and Jocasta, to which Lloyd-Jones and Wilson, *Sophoclea*, 113, comment, "Oedipus' parents can hardly be in question." Yet there are two allusions in the play (416, 1355) to the effects of Oedipus' actions upon the dead.

PART ONE

The Ritual Background

Greek Tragedy
and Sacrificial Ritual

Walter Burkert

The proliferation of theses and hypotheses, of reconstructions and con-
structions on the subject of the origin of tragedy leads to reflection on
a basic problem of philological statements.[1] Evidently we ought not to
expect that we can reduce so complex a phenomenon as Greek tragedy to one
single formula of origin. Every statement is necessarily one-sided. When we
are dealing with an evolution, with *pollai metabolai* (numerous transformations; Aristotle *Poetics* 1449a14), there will be in each case persistence as well
as differentiation, yet it is difficult to describe both pertinently at the same
time. So, following his own inclination, a scholar will be apt either to praise
the creative achievement of a unique poet, be it Thespis or Aeschylus, or to
insist on the primeval elements, with the ritual still preserved. We may collect
exact information or formulate precise hypotheses as to the external organization of the Dionysia in the Polis Athens in the sixth century B.C.: temple and
theater, chorus of citizens and choregos, *poietes* (poet), *didaskalos* (director),
hupokritēs (actor), masks and actors' dress, musical instruments, figures of
dancing, musical and literary technique in the tradition of choral lyric and the
iambos. But whoever tries to grasp the unique *kairos*, that "critical moment"

First published in *Greek, Roman, and Byzantine Studies* 7, no. 2 (1966).

in the history of the human mind which brought forth tragedy, to understand
the intellectual, psychological, and social motives involved, enters a field of
basic ambiguity. On the precarious balance and the conflict of tradition and
emancipation, individual and society, religion and the profane, myth and
reason, not even Thespis himself could have given final elucidation. It is left
to us to attempt again and again to form a comprehensive picture of man and
his world out of the testimonies of the past. In each individual case, we shall
not be able to grasp more than some of the possible aspects, a few strands in
a complicated pattern. But we ought to keep in mind just this to avoid the
danger that traditional or contemporary prejudices may unduly narrow the
possibilities of approach.

It is a single aspect that shall be considered here, the question why
tragedy is called *tragōidia*—a word that seems to impose the animal on the
development of high human civilization, the primitive and grotesque on
sublime literary creations. If we seek an explanation of the word, we cannot
avoid going back to earlier strata, to the religious basis of tragedy and indeed
to Greek cult in general. Whether this has any bearing on fully developed
Attic tragedy cannot be determined in advance. The theory most prevalent
today, going back to Welcker and owing its popularity to Wilamowitz, who
claimed Aristotle's authority for it, understands *tragōidia* to mean "song of
goats," sc., of dancers dressed as goats. Scholars more concerned with the
history of religion, however, still uphold the ancient etymology, "song at
the sacrifice of a goat."[2] It will be necessary to establish first that philological criticism of the sources does not lead to a decision. When, however, the
essence of sacrificial ritual is studied, a new perspective seems to emerge in
which, eventually, even plays of Aeschylus, Sophocles, and Euripides may
reveal a ritual background.

I.

There are so many learned, subtle, and exhaustive discussions of Wilamowitz's theory of the origin of tragedy that it may suffice here to point out the
well-known difficulties involved. The only ancient evidence is a gloss in the
Etymologicum Magnum, s.v. tragōidia (764.5), which says, after three other
explanations, ἢ ὅτι τὰ πολλὰ οἱ χοροὶ ἐκ σατύρων συνίσταντο, οὓς ἐκάλουν

τράγους (because the choruses mostly were composed of satyrs, whom they called goats). The statement that tragic choruses "mostly" consisted of satyrs is clearly wrong. Yet modern scholars have combined this with a passing remark of Aristotle's that tragedy developed *ek saturikou* (*Poetics* 1449a20, cf. 22); this may mean that tragedy originated "from the satyr play," as Chamaeleon, one of Aristotle's pupils, explained *expressis verbis*.[3] The notice in the *Etymologicum Magnum* has therefore been regarded as a somewhat corrupt reproduction of the "Peripatetic theory of the origin of tragedy": that the proto-tragedy was the satyr-play—or, since Aristotle derives tragedy from the dithyramb, a "satyrdithyrambos"—and this was called "song of the goats." The first difficulty arises from the tradition that names Pratinas of Phlius, the slightly older contemporary of Aeschylus, as the inventor of the satyr-play. This piece of information is supported in a remarkable way by the pictorial tradition: scenes that undoubtedly come from satyr-plays begin to appear in vase paintings after about 520 B.C., considerably after the first production of tragedy by Thespis. The scholar who has done the most fundamental work on the pictorial representations of satyr-plays, Frank Brommer, therefore concluded as long ago as 1937 that the satyr-play was "keine Vorform der Tragödie, sondern eine neue Erfindung" (no primitive form of tragedy, but a new invention).[4] So in order to save the theory it becomes necessary to postulate a proto-satyr-play existing before Pratinas; this turns Pratinas' achievement into a mere reform of satyr-play. Insofar as the type of the satyr undoubtedly existed long before Pratinas, this is a possible way out of the difficulty; whether the Peripatetics could know anything about this proto-satyr-play is another question.

The other difficulty is more disturbing. The satyrs of the satyr-play and the even earlier satyrs that we know from vase paintings and sculpture are not "goats," but wild men with animal ears and horses' tails; only in the Hellenistic period did they acquire horns. A satyr may on occasion be called *tragos*, and when on vase paintings satyrs and goats are depicted together, their physiognomy becomes remarkably similar;[5] but still they are not *tragoi* themselves, as a satyr-play never could be called *tragōidia*. The theory necessitates a further step backwards. It is argued that the home of the proto-satyr-play, or rather goat-play, was not Athens, but the Peloponnese; Pan belongs to Arcadia, and in Corinth, about 600 B.C., Arion developed the dithyramb that Aristotle connects with tragedy. Wilamowitz unhesitatingly assumed that Arion's chorus consisted of *tragoi* (86). Now Corinthian vases of this period offer countless variations on the retinue of Dionysus, but no singing goats. Most frequently one finds the grotesque padded dancers; it is possible that they were called *saturoi*, but surely they are much less *tragoi* than the satyrs of Attic satyr-play. There also appear shaggy creatures with hairy bodies, but they lack any characteristic that would allow us to assign them to a definite species. Only someone who is determined to produce *tragoi* at all costs for the sake of *tragōidia* will call them "goats."[6] The expression *mallōtos chitōn* (coat of fleece) would rather suggest sheepskins. Only the same fixed prejudice in favor of goats explains why the *tragikoi choroi* in the cult of Adrastus at Sicyon (Herodotus 5.67) have so often been understood to be "choruses of goats."[7]

There remains what has been thought to be the supreme piece of evidence for the singing goats, an archaic bronze from Methydrion in the Peloponnese, more than a century earlier than Arion. It is so primitive that experts doubted whether the four dancing figures were goats or rams until recently when Roland Hampe, referring to similar bronzes found at Olympia, established that neither goats nor rams are represented but quite simply men. What had been taken to be horns are a primitive attempt at ears.[8] There are, of course, goatlike demons even beside Pan. Terracotta statuettes, mostly from Boeotia, represent an ithyphallic goatman with a cornucopia. His name is unknown,[9] whereas the horned dancers on the so-called Anodos-scenes may with some probability be identified as *Panes* [Pan-like deities]; they seem to be confined to this special occasion.[10]

So still there is no evidence for choruses of singing goats from which *tragōidia* could have derived its name. And at any rate there would remain the deeper question—whatever could be the relation between satyr-like gaiety and the high seriousness of tragedy? Did *tragōidia* originally lack the "tragic" element (so Wilamowitz 93)?

We also have to consider a simple but decisive linguistic fact: the primary word formation is not *tragōidia* at all, but *tragōidoi*, or rather *tragōidos*. This word is used in official inscriptions as well as in colloquial speech until well into the fourth century, where we should expect to find *tragōidia: en tois tragōidois* (among the *tragōidoi*), *theasasthai tragōidous* (watch the *tragōidoi*), *nikān tragōidois* (to win a victory with *tragōidoi*). *Tragōidoi*—that is, the chorus with its strange masks and splendid robes, as it stood before the eyes of the Athenians.[11] Now the laws of Greek word formation show that *tragōidos* cannot mean "singing goat"; nor indeed does the word *kōmōdoi* imply "singing *kōmoi*" (revels), but "singers on occasion of the *kōmos*."[12] To be exact, we are dealing with a determinative compound, in which regularly the first part determines in some way the area of operation of the second. It can be either purely nominal, like *aulōidos, kitharōidos*: the "singer" who has something to do with a "goat," "flute," "cithara"; or *-ōidos* can be verbal, "he who sings the goat," like *linōidos* (who sings the Linus song), *melōidos* (who sings the song), *thrēnōidos* (who sings the lament). At any rate, *tragōidoi* are "singers," one particular group out of different kinds of singers. There is at least one exact parallel: Dionysios of Argos, fourth or third century B.C., has preserved what he states to be an earlier name for rhapsodes, *arnōidos*, explaining the word unhesitatingly *tou de athlou tois nikōsin arnos apodedeigmenou* (from the prize offered the victors: a ram, *arnos*).[13]

To this corresponds the explanation of the name *tragōidia*—the only one current in antiquity—as "song for the prize of a goat" or "song at the sacrifice of a goat"; the two interpretations are identical, for naturally the goat won as a prize was sacrificed to Dionysos. The earliest evidence for the *tragos* (goat) as *athlon* (prize) in the tragic agon is the Parian Marble, then an epigram of Dioskorides; Eratosthenes, in his *Erigone*, certainly treated Icarius' sacrifice of a goat as the *aition* of *tragōidia: Ikarioi tothi prōta peri tragon ōrchēsanto* (tragedy: the Ikarians then first danced for a goat). The most familiar descriptions are those in the Augustan poets. Particularly detailed are the accounts given in two late Latin writers, Diomedes—whose source is supposed to be Suetonius—and Euanthius; both use the same Greek material, which may come from Didymos, *Peri poiētōn* (On the poets). The same tradition survived in the Scholia to Dionysius Thrax, in the Johannes Diaconus published by Rabe, and in Tzetzes; the intermediate source appears to be the *Chrestomathy* of Proclus.[14] A great deal was written in the Hellenistic period on matters of literary history, and what survives is absurdly scanty. Kaibel was nevertheless able to show in the case of the rather fuller literature *peri kōmōidias* (on comedy) that even in the Byzantine excerptors there are traces of a theory of the fourth century B.C., a theory that did not know the comedy of Menander. Even the latest sources may preserve excellent tradition. It is worth noting that some fragments of Aristotle, from the *Peri poiētōn*, have survived in this way.[15]

Among modern scholars the derivation of *tragōidia* from the sacrifice of a goat has not enjoyed much success. "Spielend ersonnene αἴτια," "Konstruktionen, keine Überlieferung" (strikes the note of playing *aitia*, a fabrication, not a tradition)—this was the judgment of Wilamowitz (63), who maintained that the whole thing was a fabrication of Eratosthenes; incidentally, he had overlooked the Parian Marble. Pohlenz tried to correct this oversight while retaining the result: he argued that the theory was earlier than Eratosthenes, but still post-Aristotelian, early Alexandrian. The secondary fabrication, according to him, gives itself away by its bias: while Aristotle's evidence about dithyramb and *saturikon* points toward the Peloponnese, the autochthonous origin of tragedy in Attica is here defended. Pohlenz's argument has found wide acceptance.[16] Yet it evidently depends on two assumptions: that Attic local patriotism did not start to consider tragedy until after Aristotle, and that it could contribute nothing but invention, no facts of any sort. But the Atthidographers were at work before Aristotle: Cleidemus wrote ca. 350, Phanodemus about a decade later. They were keenly interested in the Attic cults. A fragment of Cleidemus on the lesser Dionysia is extant (*FGrHist* 323 F 27). Phanodemus displays a marked Athenian bias (325 F 14, F 27). Are we to suppose that the earlier Atthidographers wrote nothing about the Great Dionysia? This festival was certainly treated by Philochorus (328 F 171; cf. F 5, F 206), who took special interest in sacrificial rites (F 178, F 194) and gave an explanation of the word *rhapsōidos* (F 212). In view of the general inflexibility of Greek cults, it is hard to maintain that even a post-Aristotelian Atthidographer would present sheer invention in matters of sacrifice.

Aristotle, however, says quite explicitly that the dispute between Athenians and Dorians for the glory of the "invention" of tragedy and comedy had been going on for some time: διὸ καὶ ἀντιποιοῦνται τῆς τε τραγῳδίας καὶ τῆς κωμῳδίας οἱ Δωριεῖς . . . ποιούμενοι τὰ ὀνόματα σημεῖον. αὐτοὶ μὲν γὰρ κώμας τὰς περιοικίδας καλεῖν φασιν, Ἀθηναίους δὲ δήμους, ὡς κωμῳδοὺς οὐκ ἀπὸ τοῦ κωμάζειν λεχθέντας ἀλλὰ τῇ κατὰ κώμας πλάνῃ ἀτιμαζομένους ἐκ τοῦ ἄστεως . . . (This is how the Dorians lay claim to tragedy and comedy . . . taking the names of these for evidence. They assert that they use the name *kōmai* for outlying villages, whereas the Athenians call them *dēmoi* with the implication that they are not called *komōdoi*, "comedians," from their reveling [*kōmazein*] but from their wanderings about to the villages [*kōmai*] because they were held in low esteem by the city (*astu*) . . . *Poet.* 1448a29 ff.). This presupposes two things: a derivation of *kōmōidia* from *kōmē* (village) in the form of an anecdote—some people, for lack of appreciation, leave the city and wander around in the villages; the song that they sing is the *kōmōidia*—and an inference from this derivation: the word *kōmē* is Doric, therefore *kōmōidia* itself must be of Doric, not Attic, origin. Now it is unlikely that both, etymology and inference from it, were produced at the same time. The word *antipoiountai* (make an opposing claim) presupposes two parties to the dispute, and therefore Athenian counter-claims. Polemic is most effective when it can take the arguments of an opponent and turn them against him. The derivation of *kōmōidia* from *kōmē* is so far-fetched, that from *kōmos* (revel) so obvious, that it would have been quite idiotic for the Doric partisans to introduce the *kōmē*-argument into the debate if it had not already been accepted by the Athenians themselves. This means that the etymology, together with the *kōmē*-anecdote, was first advanced at Athens; this is supported by the specifically Attic word *astu*; and indeed *kōmē* is an Attic word, too.[17] So Aristotle's statement presupposes at least two stages in the discussion about the origin of comedy: an Attic etymology based on a "village" custom, and a counter-attack by the Dorian party.

The Attic etymology that Aristotle rejects lived on in Greek literature; though the anecdote varies, the derivation of comedy from *kōmē* is the prevailing explanation of the name in Diomedes and Euanthius, in the treatises *Peri kōmōidias* (On comedy), in the Scholia to Dionysius Thrax and in Tzetzes[18]—in fact, in precisely those authors who offer "song over the goat" as the etymology of *tragōidia*. Thus in the case of *kōmōidia* we are dealing with a pre-Aristotelian Attic etymology that survives in the later tradition. If we may assume something analogous for *tragōidia*, this squares very well with the tradition about the *tragos*-prize. And whether this tradition really is contradicted by and incompatible with Aristotle's testimony is by no means certain.[19] So it is quite possible, though it cannot be proved, that the tradition of the goat-sacrifice is pre-Aristotelian. Even this possibility, however, is enough to destroy Pohlenz's argument: he has not succeeded in proving by *recensio* of the evidence that the tradition of the goat-sacrifice is secondary and therefore to be rejected. The *recentiores* are not necessarily the *deteriores*. Before rejecting it, we ought to try at least to make sense of the tradition.

Was a goat sacrificed in connection with the *tragōidoi* performances at the Great Dionysia? Oddly enough, this question is seldom clearly put.

Ziegler (p. 1926) thought that the answer is definitely no; in all extant tragedies and comedies, there is "nie mit einem Sterbenswort von einem Bock als
Preis die Rede."[20] This clearly is an *argumentum ex silentio*, which is contradicted by the literary-historical sources, beginning with the Parian Marble.
The evidence of the Latin sources is most detailed: Diomedes—*hircus prae-
mium cantus proponebatur, qui Liberalibus die festo Libero patri ob hoc ipsum
immolabatur, quia, ut Varro ait, depascunt vitem*;[21] Euanthius—*incensis iam
altaribus et admoto hirco id genus carminis quod sacer chorus reddebat Libero
patri tragoedia dicebatur*. In view of this testimony, the burden of proof lies
with those who deny that a goat was sacrificed at the Great Dionysia.

The sacrificial victim as prize in an agon occurs as early as the *Iliad*
(22.159).[22] Most important was the bull as prize and sacrificial victim in
connection with the dithyramb. By chance we have unimpeachable early evidence in this case: Pindar (*O.* 13.19) speaks of the *boēlatas dithurambos* (bull-
driving dithyramb) that originated in Corinth; the Scholia explain, as if it
were a matter of course, "because a bull was *epathlon* (prize) for the winner."
This is confirmed by an epigram of Simonides (79 D.), who boasts that he has
won "56 bulls and tripods." *Boēlatas dithurambos*—the bull was led along in
solemn procession; vase paintings show the bull, adorned by the victorious
Phyle and ready for sacrifice, beside the tripod.[23] Why should we not suppose
that the goat was similarly connected with tragedy? Plutarch sets the two, the
prize of bull and goat, victory with dithyramb and tragedy, in vivid proximity
when, in his essay *De gloria Atheniensium*, he describes the triumphal procession of the poets: he has the Nikai themselves, the "Victories," march up,
boun epathlon helkousas ē tragon (leading an ox as prize or a goat; 349c). This
is allegory, influenced by the pictorial tradition (n. 23), but the experience
of Greek sacrificial festivals lies behind it. In the church of Aghios Elefthe-
rios, the "Little Mitropolis" at Athens, there is an ancient frieze depicting
the months of the Attic year. Elaphebolion is represented by the figure of a
comic actor pulling along a goat: comedy and tragedy as the epitome of the
Great Dionysia, the main festival in Elaphebolion.[24] Are we to suppose that
this representation, too, owes its existence to early Hellenistic speculation
based on a stupid etymology? No one denies that the *tragos*-sacrifice played
a special part in the cult of Dionysus. The earliest evidence are vase paintings
of the sixth century, especially Attic black-figure vases: they show again and
again the he-goat together with Dionysus or satyrs, sometimes *ductus cornu*

(Verg. *Georg.* 2.395).[25] To which of the Dionysus festivals the *tragos* belongs can be seen from Plutarch (*De cupid. div.* 527D): ἡ πάτριος τῶν Διονυσίων ἑορτὴ τὸ παλαιὸν ἐπέμπετο δημοτικῶς καὶ ἱλαρῶς, ἀμφορεὺς οἴνου καὶ κληματίς, εἶτα τράγον τις εἷλκεν, ἄλλος ἰσχάδων ἄρριχον ἠκολούθει κομίζων, ἐπὶ πᾶσι δ᾽ ὁ φαλλός (The ancestral festival of the Dionysia was a simple and cheerful procession. There was a large jar of wine with vines; then someone led a goat, and another followed carrying a basket of figs, the whole thing completed by the phallus). On account of the word *patrios* (ancestral), this description is usually connected with the *Dionusia kat᾽ agrous* (rural Dionysia).[26] The combination of fig-basket and goat recurs, however, in the Parian Marble (A 39; 43) and Dioskorides (*AP* 7.410) with reference to comedy and tragedy, performed together at the Great Dionysia; so it is probably that Plutarch's source is referring to the same festival. Indeed a sixth-century institution was *patrios* (ancestral) already in the fifth century. Nevertheless it is usually assumed that the *Dionusia en astei* (city Dionysia) were modeled on the Dionysia *kat᾽ agrous*; so the *tragos* will not have been missing in either of the festivals, any more than the phallus.

The sacrifice of a *tragos* is quite an unusual event;[27] one finds only one *tragos* in a herd, perhaps in a village; he is the *dux pecoris*, Tibullus (2.1.58) says. Nor is the appetizing smell of roast meat the idea primarily associated with the *tragos*; a kid, an *eriphos* (young goat) would be better; *tragos*, that implies lewdness and foul smell.[28] Nevertheless the *tragos* is sacrificed—because his procreative power is coming to an end. A five-year-old *tragos* is no longer fit for use, Columella (7.6.3) tells us. So at least every four years the old he-goat must be removed. To get rid of the old and risk a fresh start may have been an exciting course for the farmer and goatherd. Now there follows the *ocheia* (impregnating) of the she-goats in late autumn, that the kids may be born in spring (Varro *RR* 2.3.8; Columella 7.6.6); then the *tragos* has done his duty. It is still necessary to wait for a little while until it is certain that the she-goats are pregnant—then we come to January-February, the month *Posideōn*, the month of the *Dionusia kat᾽ agrous*.[29] These simple facts of husbandry are, however, embedded in very ancient religious customs by no means confined to Greece.[30] But to follow them up seems to lead from *obscurum* to *obscurius*.

One piece of evidence, however, is unambiguous: characteristic of the Dionysiac orchestra, perhaps the very center of the circle, is the *thumelē* (altar). Already Pratinas makes the chorus conquer *Dionusiada polupataga thumelan* (the tumultuous Dionysiac *thumulē*).[31] What exactly the *thumelē* was like, was a matter of dispute even in antiquity: *eite bēme ti eite bōmos* (either some kind of rostrum or altar).[32] Most probably it was a kind of platform or flat table, as it is depicted on vase paintings amid Dionysiac scenes: perhaps it was used as an altar when this was required in the play. But *thumelē* cannot be separated from *thuein* (to sacrifice). Is it in origin the block or bench on which the victim was slaughtered and divided up? The memory of sacrifice stands in the center of the Dionysiac performance. And since the *boēlatas dithurambos* was introduced in Athens later than tragedy,[33] there remains for the original festival in the precinct of *Dionusos Eleuthereus* just the sacrifice of the *tragos*; and the *tragōidoi*.

II.

In fact, it was not critical caution in the face of late testimony or unprejudiced *recensio* of the tradition that has nearly expelled from modern discussions the explanation of the name *tragōidia* most favored in antiquity, but the seeming triviality and pointlessness of the etymology. What has the *vilis hircus* to do with tragedy? What would be the point of the sacrifice of a goat? But this is in fact the fundamental question: what is the sense of animal sacrifice, and, in particular, of a goat sacrifice in the cult of Dionysus? The slaughter of animals for sacrifice ceased in the West with the victory of Christianity (cf., however, n. 37); practically no feature of ancient religion is so alien to us as the *thusia* (burnt offering), which for the ancients was the sacred experience par excellence: *hieron, hiereus, hiereion, hiereuein* (sacrificial victim, priest, sacrificial offering, to sacrifice). Perhaps this is the reason why we find it so difficult to accept the explanation of the word *tragōidia* that seemed almost self-evident in antiquity.

Greek sacrificial practice[34] is of course a complex phenomenon; different elements may have been amalgamated in the course of time. We can still observe a change in terminology. As Aristarchus rightly observed,[35] in Homer *thuein* still means, in accordance with its etymology, "to burn so as to provide smoke"; later it is the technical term for "sacrificial slaughter," for which Homer uses *hiereuein* and *rhezein*. *Thuein* in a narrower sense is quite often contrasted with *enagizein*, the term appropriate to hero-cults; in accordance with this it is customary to distinguish as the two basic forms of Greek sacrifice the "Olympian feast-sacrifice" and the "chthonic holocaust." This convenient dichotomy must, however, not be overestimated; it is by no means all-pervasive, there are more and other differences of equal importance.[36] But as the words *hiereon, hiereuein* and, in the classical period, *thuein* cover all forms of sacrifice, we ought to keep the whole complex in view.

We are best informed on the "Olympian" feast-sacrifice.[37] It seemed puzzling as early as Hesiod. The thighbones, the tail, the fat, and the gall-bladder are burnt for the god in whose honor the sacrifice is held; the pious congregation appropriates almost all the rest. The phrase *en thusiēisi te kai eupatheiēisi* (in sacrifices and merriment) in Herodotus (8.99) is revealing. Hesiod can only explain this as the result of a trick by Prometheus. This amounts to an admission that these sacrifices could not be understood as a gift to the divinity, at any rate not as the gift of a meal. But the theory adopted by Wilamowitz and Nilsson, following Robertson Smith, that the sacrifice was a common meal of men and gods,[38] also is impossible in view of the "Promethean" division. Certainly, there were *theoxenia* (feasting of the gods)—in which the menu was largely vegetarian, corresponding to the normal diet—and there were, as in the Orient, *trapezai* (tables) for the gods. But the sacral center of the *thusia* is the *mēria kaiein*, the "burning of the thighbones." When Nilsson supposes that some pieces of meat were sent to the gods by fire and the inedible parts were immediately consumed by the same "convenient medium" (*Griech. Rel.*[2] I.144f.), he supplies his own *reductio ad absurdum*: homage and garbage-disposal combined?

It was Karl Meuli's article "Griechische Opferbräuche" that provided a decisive advance.[39] He pointed out the evident connection with the "Schädel- und Langknochenopfer" practiced by Siberian hunting peoples and attested as early as the Paleolithic period. When an animal is caught and slaughtered, the skull and the bones, above all the thighbones are presented to the god; they may be buried, or hung on a sacred tree, or set up in a sanctuary. Meuli also offered an explanation: the hunter wishes to save from complete destruction the animal he has killed, his source of food. The thighbones, as it were the marrow of its existence, remain preserved. In mythical terms, the life of the animal is restored to the lord of life. "If we should not do this, we would never catch animals again," the hunters explained. Meuli is right in interpreting this concern about the continuity of life as a deep-rooted human respect for life as such, which prevents man from utterly destroying other beings in an autocratic way. In the situation of killing, man feels guilty, and he has to overcome this reluctance by means of a complicated ritual pattern, which Meuli pertinently calls "comedy of innocence" (*Unschuldskomödie*), though we must not forget that this "comedy" has a very serious basis. At the center of the sacrifice stands neither the gift to the gods nor fellowship with them, but the killing of the animal,[40] and man as its killer. As Meuli puts it: "the Olympian sacrifice is simply ritual slaughter" ("nichts anderes als ein rituelles Schlachten," 223). The definition must be expanded only a little to cover all kinds of sacrifices involving bloodshed: sacrifice is ritual killing.[41] In the sacrificial ritual man causes and experiences death.

Thus in the sacrificial feast the joy of the festival and the horror of death interpenetrate. The Greek sacrificial rites represent in vivid detail human aversion to killing and the feelings of guilt and remorse caused by a shedding of blood. Adorned for the festival, garlanded like the celebrants, sometimes with gilded horns,[42] the animal was led along. Many legends tell how the victims have pressed forward voluntarily to the sacrifice, *theēlatou boos dikēn* (just like an ox led to the god; A. *Ag.* 1297).[43] The beginning of the rite was emphatically harmless: a vessel containing water and the basket with the sacrificial barley, brought to the place by a virgin, were carried round the altar; a line is drawn that separates the sacred from the profane.[44] Then the participants wash their hands—their first common action—and the victim has its share, too: it is sprinkled with water; *seiou* (sprinkle!), Trygaois explains (Ar. *Pax* 960): the animal was supposed to express its consent by bowing its head, *hekousion kataneuei*.[45] The meaning of the *oulai* (barleycorns) has been much discussed,[46] though the Greek expression is quite clear: *cherniba t' oulochutas te katarchesthai* (to make a start with the basket and strewing of barley)—it is the act of beginning. The participants take the barley out of the basket as if they were to prepare for a vegetarian meal; but beneath in the basket there is a knife, which is now uncovered. There is a prayer, a moment of silence and concentration; then all participants throw the *oulai* "forward" at the victim and the altar. Throwing together at a common object is the primeval gesture of aggression: lapidation, transformed into something harmless, as in the *phullobolia* (throwing of leaves). Indeed, instead of the barley, leaves can be used and, at least in one instance, stones. Everyone takes part, is guilty and innocent at the same time. There is still a last delay: the *hiereus* cuts off a few hairs from the victim's forehead and throws them in the fire. With extraordinary obstinacy, scholars have looked for daemons who demanded hair,[47] though the Greek expression again is both clear and simple: this, too, is *archesthai*, the "beginning." This first cut does no harm, does not yet draw blood, but the victim is no longer physically inviolate. This step is irreversible. Now the fatal stroke follows. At this moment, the women scream, *ololuzousin* (*Od.* 3.450); this is the *Hellēnikon nomisma thustados boēs* (the peculiar Greek custom of the sacrificial cry; A. *Septem* 269);[48] this marks the emotional climax of the *thusia*; this is *rhezein* (sacrificing). The blood is caught in a vessel and poured out at the altar:[49] the most appalling element is set first of all within the divinely appointed order. Then the thighbones are cut out, and small pieces of meat from each limb laid with them on the altar—ōmothetein,[50] and they are burnt. Wine is poured over the flames, the music of the flute and song accompany the action. Along with the burning of *mēria* (thighbones), the *splangchna*—heart, lungs, liver, kidneys—are roasted on the altar and eaten at once.[51] The slightly uncanny "vitals," the internal organs that come to light only now and may seem to contain the "life," which sometimes cause disgust and sometimes are regarded as rather a delicacy, must be disposed of first of all. No wonder that *susplangchneuein* (sharing the vitals) is the firmest foundation of fellowship. The shudder dies away in a feeling of physical well-being. When the *splangchna* have been eaten and the fire has died down, the preparation begins for the main meal, which was generally of a quite secular character.[52]

We see, then, that the ritual of a Greek sacrifice is designed to display the destruction of life as the sacral center of the action. The many complicated preparations stress how unnatural and shocking this is. There are some special cases in which the representation of the feelings of guilt, the "comedy of innocence" seems quite excessive. Above all, the Buphonia at Athens: the ox must himself be responsible for his own death; he is induced to eat barley cakes from the altar of Zeus, and then punished for sacrilege with the axe. But the sacrificing priest immediately throws the axe away and flees, a trial follows the sacrificial meal, in which the responsibility is passed from one to another, until finally a knife is pronounced guilty and thrown into the sea. But the ox is stuffed and harnessed to a plough—he is, as it were, resurrected.[53] The goat-sacrifice to Dionysus is in fact another example of making the victim responsible for its own death: the goat, it is said, has gnawed the vine and must therefore die. In Corinth, at the festival of Hera Akraia, the she-goat was made to dig up for herself the knife with which she is slaughtered (n. 71).

Most characteristic of all these rites is the ambivalence of feeling displayed in the ceremony. Man, sacrificing according to the will of the god, still has to overcome or even to outwit his reluctance to kill. Expressing his feelings of guilt and remorse, man shows his deeply rooted respect for life. Prevalent, however, is a higher necessity, which commands him to kill.

"Das Opfer ist die älteste Form der religiösen Handlung" (sacrifice is the oldest form of religious action; Kühn, *Das Problem des Urmonotheismus*, 17). From this fact, the inference has been drawn that there was some kind of "urmonotheismus," a primordial revelation of the idea of God. The "Promethean" division and the horrible fascination of bloodshed are perhaps less comforting. It could seem advisable to resign completely, considering the fact that we are led back well into Paleolithic times. We shall never have direct evidence for religious belief in this period; and even if we had, as modern ethnologists were in a position to ask hunters living under similar conditions about their motives, it would still be a question whether primitive man could give a more lucid explanation of his ritual than the Greeks, who are so often said to have misunderstood their own cults completely. But we must not overestimate the importance of beliefs and explanations in religion. Down to the beginnings of Christianity and even farther on, the justification of religion is tradition. Rites are performed *kata ta patria* (according to ancestral custom), and this is the reason why so little change took place in these rites between Paleolithic times and the Greeks, during tens of thousands of years. So the essential matter cannot have been what a hypothetical *heuretēs* (inventor) came to feel or believe, owing to his private experience or associations, but rather it was the effect of the rite on society according to the structure of the human psyche. Instead of asking which incident could bring forth some special form of religion, we should ask why it succeeded and was preserved. The answer can be seen in its function in human society. We may still speak of "ideas" inherent in the rites, but we must discard the rationalistic preconception as if there had been, first, a concept or belief, which led in a second step to action. Behavior is primary, but its form is correlated to typical human situations and, therefore, understandable. In this respect, rites may make sense. To some extent, even biology can contribute to understanding; animals, too, have their rites that control mutual recognition and cooperation. The contrast of man and animal will emerge immediately.

Indeed carnivorous animals show no sign of ambivalent feeling when eating their animal of prey; the cat has neither reluctance nor repentance while killing the mouse. But even in animals there are psychological antagonisms as regards their behavior toward animals of the same species. Here the impulses of intraspecific aggression come to work, the impulses to fight. Konrad Lorenz[54] has brilliantly shown the social importance of this instinct. But it is inhibited and controlled by contrary impulses, fear above all, but often also by a special reluctance to kill, especially important in dangerous animals. Man, by his physical endowment, is neither carnivorous nor particularly dangerous; the other primates are rather innocent creatures. Man, however, starting from the earliest times came to be a hunter, a hunter even of big animals. This presupposes the use of tools, of weapons, and social cooperation. So it is safe to say: in the center of the earliest human society, the earliest "Männerbund," there is common killing, killing the prey. The very problem of human civilization arose at the same time: his instincts will not tell man what he has to do with his weapons; instead of killing the bear or bison he can as well slay a man; it is even easier. No wonder cannibalism is attested in the oldest strata of human civilization; and man has continued killing man to an extent that no carnivorous animal has done. In the Bible there is at the very beginning of human civilization the story of the sacrifice combined with the murder of Abel; man is the descendant of Cain. Sigmund Freud[55] went still farther with his hypothesis that human society arose with the brothers killing and eating their father; since then, they are compelled to repeat again and again this primordial crime in the sacrificial slaughter. I think Freud is basically right in describing the psychic impulses underlying sacrifice, though he is wrong in assuming that this crime must have occurred as one historical fact. Generally man has been living on animals; but the hunter is always at the same time a warrior, animated by the impulses of aggression. Human sacrifice, therefore, is a possibility that, as a horrible threat, stands behind every sacrifice. This is the reason why sacrificial ritual has this complicated pattern, the "comedy of innocence."

On the other hand, more sympathetic forces too have been developing in man's psyche; the respect for life has grown universal. The hunter may imagine the animal that he is going to kill as his "brother";[56] he recognizes

death in all its manifestations. So the feelings of guilt and remorse crystal-
ize into symbolic acts through which man tries to restore the equilibrium
disturbed, to stress the continuity of life through death. Man alone among
living beings buries his dead. In a similar way, he restores at least the remains
of the animals he had to kill to some superhuman order, on which in fact the
continuity of his own civilization depends.

Society is built on the impulses of aggression controlled by ritual, as Konrad Lorenz has shown. So precisely in communities familiar with agriculture,
in which meat is of secondary importance as a source of food, rites involving
bloodshed become the center of religion. They stir the depths of the soul,
the fear of death, the frenzy of killing. *Hierōn metechein* (participation in the
sacra)—the community is knit together in the common experience of shock
and guilt. All participate, but one stands at their head, the sacrificer, *thutēr*,
the *pater familias* or the king. To him belongs the *vitae necisque potestas*, and
he demonstrates this power of his in the sacrifice. In reality, of course, there
is only a *necis potestas*, but by exercising it the *thutēr* claims and seems to reestablish *e contrario* his *vitae potestas*. There is a curious ambivalence in *thues-
thai*, which is already Indo-European: the same expression means "to sacrifice on one's own behalf" and "to be sacrificed."[57] Sacrificer and victim are so
correlated as to be nearly identified. Self-asserting life presupposes death. So
sacrificial festivals are the traditional means to overcome all sorts of social
crisis. Extraordinary situations of emergency, famine, disease may again and
again lead to human sacrifice. More firmly established are the customs that
deal with the recurrent crises of society, the succession of the young to the
old: no initiation without sacrifice. The continuous renewal of the year, too,
is given dramatic accents by sacrifices, which celebrate the destruction of the
old for the sake of the new.

The myths, too, are concerned with sacrificial ritual. They clearly tell of
the mutual substitution of man and animal: the animal dies instead of the
man,[58] be it Isaac or Iphigeneia. The equivalence of man and animal may also
lead to successive interchange, as in the cult legend of Artemis of Munichia:
to atone for the killing of a bear belonging to the goddess, a girl is supposed
to be sacrificed, but a she-goat is substituted—man for animal and animal
for man. Greek mythology also knows the horrible converse, the sacrificial
slaughter of a human instead of an animal; at the *Hestia* (altar) at Delphi,
Neoptolemus was cut up with sacrificial knives. Such scenes are not mere

phantasy. Phainias of Eresus (fr. 25 Wehrli) gives an account of the preparations for the battle of Salamis which seems intrinsically probable: in full
view of the enemy, the *sphagia* (victims) are slaughtered, blood is flowing,
the altars are burning with fire. In this moment, by chance, three captured
Persians are led along. The fire blazes up, and suddenly the seer and then the
whole crowd of warriors, greedy of blood and death, demand that these three
enemies be killed as *sphagia*; and they were. On one occasion, even Caesar
sacrificed insurgents.[59] The Catilinarians were supposed to have sealed their
conspiracy by eating human *splangchna*.[60] Classical Rome betrays an almost
Paleolithic imagination.

III.

Perhaps the larger context has made clearer what the significance of the sacrifice of a *tragos* at the *thumelē* may be. The rites of sacrifice touch the roots
of human existence. In the ambivalence of the intoxication of blood and the
horror of killing, in the twofold aspect of life and death, they hold something
fundamentally uncanny, we might almost say tragic. Our information about
the goat-sacrifice to Dionysus is scanty. Whether we are entitled to see in the
goat Dionysus himself impersonated, or to understand both goat and Dionysus as representing an "eniautos-daimon" or even the dying king, is difficult
to assess.[61] The ancient texts call the goat the enemy of Dionysus, making his
death a triumph of aggression. When Domitian tried to restrict viticulture,
the epigram of Euenus (*AP* 9.75) was turned against him as an almost deadly
weapon (Suet. *Dom.* 14.2): people readily associated the dying goat with the
emperor they hated. On the other hand, there is the "comedy of innocence,"
making the vine-gnawing goat responsible for his own death. And perhaps
there was even a kind of mock resurrection, analogous to the Buphonia: the
tragōidoi are said to have received a wineskin full of wine[62]—*askoi* (wineskins)
were made of goatskin. So we are reduced again to the basic ambivalence of
sacrifice, and perhaps this ambivalence is the most essential feature.

It is possible to establish, though by conjecture only, some striking
connections between the situation of sacrifice and tragedy. One form of
the "comedy of innocence" is lament at the sacrifice. There seem to be no
immediate parallels in the Greek world for lamentation over the victim, but

the practice is found elsewhere, e.g., in Egypt.[63] In the center of the developed tragedy (*akmēn pros autēn ērmenēs tragōidias*, Tz. *De trag.* 63) stands the kommos. Sacrifice was usually accompanied by the music of the flute, and while the cithara is the normal instrument for choral lyric otherwise, the aulos is used predominantly in tragedy.[64] There is a more important point: there is a form of the "comedy of innocence" in which masked, disguised men have to kill the animal.[65] The *tragōidoi* too hide their identity; no tragedy without masks. By preference, the choruses of tragedy wear the masks of foreigners or of women; if they represent Athenians, they can only be very old men (S. *OC* 112), hardly ever the young citizens of Athens they really are. And whereas the Greeks were so fond of names that they even made catalogues a form of poetry, no member of the tragic chorus ever seems to be called by an individual name (cf. Freud, *Totem und Tabu*, 187).

All this would fit the following hypothesis: the *tragōidoi* are originally a troop of masked men who have to perform the sacrifice of the *tragos* that falls due in spring; they perform with lamentation, song, and mumming, and in the end they may feast on the goat. It is possible that the custom was at home in Icaria; seriousness and "satyr-like" fun may have interpenetrated in a curious way. Rudiments of an agon, competition between several groups could arise at an early date. The transformation to a high level of literature, the adaptation of the heroic myth remains, of course, a unique achievement. Nevertheless, it is based on pre-existing elements: the use of masks, song, and dance at the *thumelē*, lamentation, the music of the flute, the name *tragōidia*, all combined in the basic situation of sacrifice: man face to face with death.

We may ask why it was *tragōidia* in particular which became tragedy, not a hypothetical *booidia* (song at ox sacrifice) or *kriōidia* (song at ram sacrifice). By comparison with the ox and the ram, the goat is the least attractive. But this may be just the reason. The victim has only a representative function: he is used for the fulfilment and discharge of an inevitable threat in the human soul which is really directed against man. In the sacrifice of the goat, these psychological forces are least absorbed by the symbol on which they concentrate; matter and form are never perfectly adjusted, and thus there arises the continual need for new forms of expression. The sacrifice of the bull especially had long ago become an official, civic affair; it was an immutable and established part of the ritual of the *polis*. But in the sacrifice of the goat, village-custom still allowed an element of *autoschediazesthai* (improvisation); there were changes and additions. Because it was not too serious, the mummers' play could evolve. The *thumelē* provoked what would have been impossible at an ordinary altar. This was the reason why *tragōidia* could come to depict the "tragic" *condition humaine*.

Tragōidia emancipated itself from the *tragos*. And yet the essence of the sacrifice still pervades tragedy even in its maturity. In Aeschylus, Sophocles, and Euripides, there still stands in the background, if not in the center, the pattern of the sacrifice, the ritual slaying, *thuein*. A few instances may suffice. I deliberately pass over those tragedies in which the whole plot is concerned with human sacrifice—*Iphigeneia at Aulis, Iphigeneia in Tauris, Bacchae*; Sophocles wrote a *Polyxena*, Aeschylus a *Pentheus*. Euripides used the motif of human sacrifice in many variations—*Heracleidae, Hecuba, Phoenissae, Erechtheus, Phrixus*. He made even Alcestis' death a sacrifice, Thanatos a sacrificial priest, *hiereus thanontōn* (25), whereas Aegisthus is slain by Orestes with the sacrificial knife at the sacrifice.[66] What is more general and more important: any sort of killing in tragedy may be termed *thuein* as early as Aeschylus, and the intoxication of killing is called *bakcheuein*, a word for Dionysiac frenzy.[67] In earlier choral lyric, these metaphors do not occur. This imagery, however, is not something superficial: if tragedy draws on heroic myth, every hero has his cults, i.e., his sacrifices.[68] The situation of the sacrifice may be just the point where heroic myth and Dionysiac *tragōidia* meet each other.

Three examples will illustrate these interrelations. First, Sophocles' *Trachiniae*. Herakles must sacrifice before returning (287); so Deianeira sends him the garment of Nessus with express instructions to put it on for the first time when he is sacrificing a bull to Zeus, *hēmerai taurosphagōi* (609); he shall present himself to the gods, a "sacrificer, new in a new garment" (613, cf. 659). So it happens: Herakles is sacrificing to Zeus at Cape Cenaeum in Euboea (750ff.), he stands there in his new garment, he slaughters the bulls. But "when the bloody flame of the solemn rites blazed up," *hopōs de semnōn orgiōn edaieto phlox haimatēra* (765f.), at that moment the garment of Nessus too begins to burn and destroys Herakles. Priest and victims, Herakles and the bulls suffer the same fate in the same *orgia* (ritual). The myth of the death of Herakles is based on a sacrifice, a holocaust offered on Mount Oeta; the site of the *pura* (pyre/altar) has been excavated. Nilsson interprets the custom as an annual fire ("Jahresfeuer"), although the literary evidence on this festival states that it was penteteric.[69] It is not the nature-symbolism that is primary, but human actions and passions. Fascinated by their own fire-controlling power, men celebrate the destruction of the old, originally perhaps the old king's death. The myth elucidates the sacrificial rite, which still pervades tragedy.

Second, Euripides' *Medea*: at the climax of the famous soliloquy is an echo of the language of sacrificial ritual (1053ff.):[70]

ὅτῳ δὲ μὴ
θέμις παρεῖναι τοῖς ἐμοῖσι θύμασιν,
αὐτῷ μελήσει . . .

[Whomsoever the law
Forbids to be present at my sacrifice,
Let him look to it.]

So this killing of the children is a secret sacrifice, an *aporrhētos thusia*. Mere metaphor? Vase paintings constantly show Medea killing her children at an altar. By chance we are fairly well informed about the ritual in the temple of Hera Akraia at Corinth, which underlies the Corinthian saga of Medea: seven Corinthian boys and seven girls were interned for a year in the sanctuary of Hera, where the tombs of Medea's children were shown. They wore black clothes. The climax and conclusion of their service was a sacrifice at the festival of Akraia, the sacrifice of a black she-goat. It was a holocaust, an *enagizein*, and it was combined with that special form of the "comedy of innocence" which was already mentioned: the goat had to dig up for itself a knife or sword, *machaira*, with which it was killed. Then the sword was buried again, as it was said until next year.[71] Once a year the instrument of destruction emerged from the darkness of the earth, to remain buried there and almost forgotten for the rest of the year. It is clear that the black she-goat died as a substitute for the black-clad children; they were then free from their obligation. The myth told that the children of the Corinthians suffered this penalty to atone for the children of Medea, who had died and were buried there in the temenos of Hera Akraia. The mysterious sword, which year by year was dug up and then reburied, was said to be the very sword with which Medea killed her children. We need not here go into the question of how far the ritual along with the myth is to be understood as an initiation ceremony.

At all events, the metaphor of the *thuma* (sacrifice) at the climax of Euripides' play leads back to a sacrificial ritual that comprises the mystery of death.

Lastly, the *Agamemnon* of Aeschylus: through it the language of sacrificial ritual runs like a leitmotiv. The choral song begins with the portent of the two eagles tearing in pieces the pregnant hare, *thuomenoi* (sacrificing; 137); to this corresponds the goddess' "demand for another sacrifice," *speudomena thusian heteran* (151). So Agamemnon becomes the "sacrificer" of his own daughter, ἔτλα δ᾽ οὖν θυτὴρ γενέσθαι θυγατρός (224, cf. 215), and now one evil generates another. When the news comes of Agamemnon's victory and imminent return, Clytaemestra prepares a great sacrifice (83f., 261ff., 587ff.); does the sacrificial fire burn on the altar in the orchestra? In the palace herds of sheep stand ready *pros sphagas* (for slaughter, 1056f.). Yet instead of the smell of sacrifice, Cassandra scents murder (1309f.). She calls for *ololugē* (a sacrificial cry) (1118) at the unprecedented *thuma* that is going to happen here: he who commits it deserves lapidation.[72] Later Clytaemestra boasts that she has slain her husband "for Ate and Erinys," that is, as a sacrifice (1433, cf. 1415ff.). Then she tries to disclaim responsibility: the Alastor of Atreus himself has killed, or rather sacrificed, Agamemnon, has slain him as the full-grown victim after the young animals, *teleon nearais epithusas* (adding a perfect sacrifice to the young ones, 1504). Even so, at the great sacrificial festivals, first the lesser, then the full-grown victims fell. Cassandra is another sacrifice. With full knowledge she goes to her destruction, "like a heifer driven on by a god, you go unafraid to the altar" (1297f.). One sacrifice leads to another: finally Orestes is the victim of the Erinyes—ἐπὶ δὲ τῷ τεθυμένῳ τόδε μέλος (this song is sung over the sacrificial victim, *Eu.* 329ff., cf. 305) runs the binding-song.

This again is more than a mere metaphor, a stylistic ornament. Agamemnon dies ὥς τίς τε κατέκτανε βοῦν ἐπὶ φάτνῃ (as one would kill a bull at the manger, *Od.* 4.535, 11.411); to be more exact, Clytaemestra throws a net over him and strikes him down with the axe, *pelekus, bouplēx*. This is in fact how a bull was killed; the famous gold cup from Vaphio shows the bull struggling in the net—the table decoration of some Mycenaean prince who had himself celebrated as a victor over the bull. So Cassandra in her vision sees Agamemnon as the *tauros* (bull), caught in the "black-horned device," the net.[73] A *lebēs* (basin) receives his blood (1129, cf. 1540)—even this is a feature of the ritual.

We have very little information about the Argive cults. But it is not mere fancy to conjecture that the myth of the death of Agamemnon was connected with a sacrificial ritual, a bull-sacrifice—*bouphonia*—in a similar way as the myth of the death of Medea's children was connected with the Corinthian sacrifice of a goat at the Akraia festival. The bull as a symbol of the king must have played a very important part in the Mycenaean-Minoan world, and this bull-symbolism concentrates on the major sanctuary of the Argive plain, the Heraion that was called Argos itself. Here we have herds of sacred cows, Zeus as a bull, Io as a cow, Epaphos, their common son, again as a bull, Cleobis and Biton drawing the sacred chariot as substitutes for oxen. Most remarkable is Argos Panoptēs, slain by Hermes, apparently the eponym of sanctuary and city. Argos was clad in bull's hide, having conquered the bull, and was in his turn killed by Hermes, the *bouphonos* (bull slayer). As was seen long ago, the epithet Panoptēs makes him a duplicate of Zeus himself; and how the community of Argos arose and got its name from the primordial crime of Argos' death may now be understandable. It was a *thusia leusimos* (a sacrifice worthy of stoning). Incidentally, Pausanias mentions *aporrhētoi thusiai* (forbidden sacrifices, 2.17.1) at the Heraion.[74] They may have preceded the main festival of Heraia, as in Athens the Buphonia are due in the last month of the year, to be followed by the new year festival, the Panathenaia.

Not all the problems can be solved. It was not the intention of this paper to show *the* origin of tragedy, but only to investigate the clue offered by the word *tragōidia*. It has emerged that the tradition of a goat-sacrifice deserves to be taken seriously; it leads back to the depths of prehistoric human development, as well as into the center of tragedy. This will do no damage to the originality of the Greeks. Indeed the uniqueness of their achievement emerges most clearly when we compare what in other civilizations sprang from similar roots: ceremonial hunting and warfare, human sacrifice, gladiators, bullfights. It may be that the sublimation and transformation performed by the Greek poets are so fundamental as to reduce to nothingness any crude "origins." Or do the greatest poets only provide sublime expression for what already existed at the most primitive stages of human development? Human existence face to face with death—that is the kernel of *tragōidia*.

NOTES

1. I had the opportunity to discuss this paper at the Oxford Philological Society and at the University Seminar in Classical Civilization at Columbia University, New York, and I wish to thank all participants for their suggestions and criticism. I am especially indebted to Mrs. Stephanie West, Oxford, for most of the translation. Of course I am fully responsible for any defects in style or contents.

2. The derivation of τραγῳδία from σάτυροι = τράγοι was advanced by Friedrich Gottlieb Welcker, *Nachtrag zu der Schrift über die Aeschylische Trilogie nebst einer Abhandlung über das Satyrspiel* (Frankfurt am Main: H. L. Brönner, 1826), 240; cf. Ulrich von Wilamowitz-Moellendorff [hereafter, Wilamowitz], *Euripides Herakles*, vol. 1 (Berlin: Weidmannsche Buchhandlung, 1889, repr. Darmstadt: Wissenschaftliche Buchgesellschaft, 1959), with different pagination: *Einleitung in die griechische Tragödie* (Berlin: Weidmann, 1907), 82ff.; *Kleine Schriften*, vol. 1 (Berlin: Weidmann, 1935), 372; Konrat Ziegler, in *RE* VI A (1937), 1917ff. (hereafter, Ziegler); Max Pohlenz, *Die griechische Tragödie*, 2nd ed., 2 vols. (Göttingen: Vandenhoeck & Ruprecht, 1954), 1:18ff.; A. Lesky, *Die tragische Dichtung der Hellenen*, 2nd ed. (Göttingen: Vandenhoeck & Ruprecht, 1964), 15ff. H. Patzer, *Die Anfänge der griechischen Tragödie* (Weisbaden: F. Steiner, 1962), 131f., upholds the same etymology, though rejecting any connection with the dithyramb and differentiating satyrs from goats (52ff.). The theory of the goat-prize was defended by E. Reisch, "Zur Vorgeschichte der attischen Tragödie," in *Festschrift Theodor Gomperz* (Vienna: Alfred Hölder, 1902), 466ff.; Roy C. Flickinger, *The Greek Theater and Its Drama* (Chicago: University of Chicago Press, 1918; 4th ed., 1936), 1ff.; Wilhelm Schmid, *Geschichte der griechischen Literatur*, part 1, vol. 2 (Munich: C. H. Beck, 1934), 46ff.; Arthur Wallace Pickard-Cambridge, *Dithyramb, Tragedy and Comedy* (Oxford: Clarendon Press, 1927), 164ff., whereas T. B. L. Webster in the rev. ed. of this book (Webster's additions are hereafter quoted as Webster only) (Oxford: Clarendon Press, 1962), 123f. is inclined to follow Welcker and Wilamowitz. Gerald F. Else thinks the word τραγῳδός, while deriving from the goat-prize, to be "clearly jocose or sarcastic," i.e., devoid of significance: *Hermes* 85 (1957), 42, cf. *The Origin and Early Form of Greek Tragedy* (Cambridge, MA: Harvard University Press, 1965), 69f. Martin P. Nilsson, *Neue Jahrbücher für das klassische Altertum* 27 (1911): 609ff. = *Opuscula*, vol. 1 (Lund: C. W. K. Gleerup, 1951), 61ff., combined goat-sacrifice and singers dressed as goats, cf. *infra* n. 61. Arthur B. Cook, *Zeus*, 3 vols. (Cambridge: University Press, 1914–40), 1:665ff. assumed the sacrifice to have been a σπαραγμός performed at the Lenaea; the τραγῳδοί, however, belong to the Dionysia, not the Lenaea. Further comments on the goat-sacrifice: Fernand Robert, in *Mélanges d'archéologie et d'histoire offerts à Charles Picard*, vol. 2 (Paris: Presses universitaires de France, 1949), 872–80; Karl Kerényi, *Streifzüge eines Hellenisten* (Zurich: Rhein-Verlag, 1960), 40ff.; Reinhold Merkelbach, "Die *Erigone* des Eratosthenes," in *Miscellanea di Studi Alessandrini in memoria di A. Rostagni* (Turin: Bottega d'Erasmo, 1963), 496ff.

3. Fr. 38 Wehrli, together with Plut. Q. *Conv.* 615a. There was an extensive Peripatetic literature on the history of tragedy; cf., besides Chamaeleon, Heracleides fr. 179 W., Aristoxenus fr. 113ff., Hieronymus fr. 29ff. W. On account of the Arabic translation, Gudeman, followed by Lesky, *Die tragische Dichtung der Hellenen*, 16, emended Arist. *Poet.* 1449a20 ἐκ (τοῦ)σατυρικοῦ; the emendation is not accepted by R. Kassel (OCT, 1965), cf. Patzer, *Die Anfänge der griechischen Tragödie*, 53. Gerald F. Else, *Aristotle's Poetics: The Argument* (Cambridge, MA: Harvard University Press, 1957), 164ff., thinks a19 ἔτι–a21 ἀπεσεμνύνθη to be an interpolation, but hesitates himself (*Origin*, 16) to draw conclusions from this hypothesis. A vase painting from the fifth century represents ΤΡΑΓΩΙΔΙΑ being awakened by satyrs: Chous Oxford 534 = J. D. Beazley, *Attic Red-Figure Vase-Painters*, 2nd ed. [hereafter, *ARV*²] (Oxford: Clarendon Press,

1963), 1258, 1; cf. bell-crater Compiègne 1025 = *ARV*² 1055, 76; chous Leipzig T 527 = *ARV*²
1258, 2; H. Herter, *RE* VI$_A$ (1937), 1897. Dionysus, satyrs, tragedy still belong together.

4. Frank Brommer, *Satyroi* (Würzburg: K. Triltsch, 1937), 36, cf. Brommer, *Satyrspiele*, 2nd ed.
(Berlin: de Gruyter, 1959); Patzer, *Die Anfänge der griechischen Tragödie*, 128ff. Pratinas as
inventor of satyr-play: Suda *s.v.* Pratinas, Ps.-Acr. *in* Hor. *AP* 216 (*Cratini* Cd., *Pratinae* Pohlenz),
cf. Dioskorides, *AP* 7.37, 707; Max Pohlenz, *Das Satyrspiel und Pratinas von Phleius* (*Nachrichten
von der Gesellschaft der Wissenschaften zu Göttingen*, 1927), 298–321 = *Kleine Schriften*, vol. 2
(Hildescheim, 1965), 473–96.

5. On satyrs, goats, and horses, cf. Adolf Furtwängler, *Kleine Schriften*, vol. 1 (Munich: Beck, 1912),
134ff., 190ff.; Wilamowitz, 83f.; Ziegler, 1920ff.; Lesky, *Die tragische Dichtung der Hellenen*,
23ff.; Patzer, *Die Anfänge der griechischen Tragödie*, 57ff.; Else, *Origin*, 15ff. Satyrs sometimes
wear goatskins (E. *Cyc.* 80), but Pollux (4.118) also mentions νεβρίς, παρδαλῆ, θήραιον, χλανὶς
ἀνθινή as satyr's dress, whereas girls wore goatskins in some Dionysiac ritual, Hsch. τραγηφόροι.
More important are A. fr. 207 Nauck = 455 Mette, *S. Ichneutai* 357f., Hsch. τράγους σατύρους
. . . (where the accusative shows that the lemma comes from a quotation); together with the vase
paintings (n. 25), these texts show that satyr and goat formed a current association, whereas there
seems to be no evidence for a satyr called ἵππος. Webster, 301 no. 6, affirms that the ΣΙΑΕΝΟΙ on
the François Vase (Florence 4209) have legs of goats; on the reproduction (Adolf Furtwängler and
Karl Reichhold, *Griechische Vasenmalerei* [Munich: F. Bruckmann A.-G., 1904–32], pl. 11/12) I
am unable to see any difference between the silens' and the mule's legs.

6. Webster, 114, arguing that these dancers surely are not horses. Μαλλωτὸς χιτών of silens: D.H.
7.72.10. On the subject of the Corinthian dancers, cf. Webster, 100f., 113ff., 169ff.; Lennart
Breitholz, *Die dorische Farce im Griechischen Mutterland vor dem 5.Jh.* (Göteborg: Almquist &
Wilksell, 1960); Patzer, *Die Anfänge der griechischen Tragödie*, 114ff., who, following Buschor,
calls them σάτυροι. One Corinthian vase has a τράγος amidst the Dionysiac revelers, Webster, no.
37, cf. n. 25.

7. E.g., Wilamowitz, 84, Pohlenz, *Die griechische Tragödie*, 2:10, Ziegler, 1919f.; *contra*, Nilsson,
Opuscula, 1.93f.; C. del Grande, *ΤΡΑΓΩΙΔΙΑ*, 2nd ed. (Milan, 1962), 40ff.; Else, *Origin*, 17f.;
Patzer, *Die Anfänge der griechischen Tragödie*, 19f., 59f. The only natural way to express "chorus
of goats" in Greek would be τράγων χορός. A sufficient reason for Herodotus or his source
to call these choruses "tragic" could have been that they wore masks and sang on πάθη; but a
goat-sacrifice is entirely possible (Flickinger, *Greek Theater and Its Drama*, 13ff., combining the
date given by Eusebius' and Jerome's *Chron.* Ol. 47, 2). One ought to take seriously the tradition
about Epigenes of Sicyon (the evidence: *RE* VI [1909], 64), considering the fact that there was a
relatively old Σικυωνίων ἀναγραφή (*FGrHist* 550) dealing especially with the history of literature
and music.

8. The bronze of Methydrion, Athens Nat.Mus. 13789, was found and published in 1911 by F.
Hiller von Gaertringen and H. Lattermann, *AbhBerl* 1911, 4, pl. 13; "vier widderartige aufrechte
Gestalten," 24; "rams" Pohlenz, *Die griechische Tragödie*, 1:18, Martin P. Nilsson, *Geschichte
der griechischen Religion*, 2nd ed., vol. 1 (Munich: Beck, 1955), pl. 50, 2; identified as "goats"
by Brommer, *Satyroi*, 10, cf. Patzer, *Die Anfänge der griechischen Tragödie*, 64f., 124. *Contra*, R.
Hampe, *Gymnasium* 72 (1965): 77ff. Lead figurines from the sanctuary of Artemis Orthia in
Sparta represent standing he-goats; Brommer, *Satyroi*, concluded they were "mythische Wesen
oder deren menschliche Nachahmer," cf. Patzer, *Die Anfänge der griechischen Tragödie*, 65. The
standing goat, however, is an iconographic type since Sumerian times, cf. n. 30 below.

9. Franz Winter, *Die Typen der figürlichen Terrakotten*, vol. 1 (Berlin: W. Spemann, 1903), 220; P.

Baur, *AJA* 9 (1905): 157ff.; Cook, *Zeus*, 1:704f. Webster, no. 73 refers to a bronze statuette of similar type, as it seems, from Samos.

10. Reisch, "Zur Vorgeschichte der attischen Tragödie," 456ff.; Patzer, *Die Anfänge der griechischen Tragödie*, 62ff.

11. Τραγῳδοί in the Attic *Fasti*, A. W. Pickard-Cambridge, *The Dramatic Festivals of Athens* (Oxford: Clarendon Press, 1953), 104; ἐν τοισι τραγῳδοῖς Ar. *Av.* 512, cf. *Pax* 531; *IG* II/III² 956, 34; Aeschin. 3.41, 45; D. 21.10; ἐνίκα τραγῳδοῖς *IG* II/III² 3091; cf. And. 4.42; τραγῳδοῖς χορηγεῖν Lys. 21.1, cf. 19.29, 24.9; Is. 5.36; τεθέασαι τραγῳδούς Men. *Epit.* 149. In light of these well-established usages of τραγῳδοί, it is very improbable that the word should be "Rückbildung" (Lesky, *Die tragische Dichtung der Hellenen*, 22 n. 3), secondary to τραγῳδία, cf. Ziegler, Else, *Origin* 25f. Else, however, holds that τραγῳδός was the actor-poet (*Hermes* 85 [1957] 20ff.). In this case it would be difficult to account for the constant plural νικᾶν, χορηγεῖν τραγῳδοῖς; χορηγῶν ἐνίκα τραγῳδοῖς *IG* II/III² 3091: there is only one poet for each χορηγός. The parallelism ἀνδρῶν—παίδων—κωμῳδῶν—τραγῳδῶν in *IG* II/III2 2318 is revealing, too. Whereas "no one of the ὑποκριταί ever danced" (Περὶ τραγῳδίας ed. R. Browning, *ΓΕΡΑΣ: Studies Presented to George Thomson* [Prague: Charles University, 1963], 70 line 74), dancing is characteristic of the τραγῳδός, Ar. V. 1476ff. Τραγῳδοί and ὑποκριτής are contrasted in the vita of Aeschines, *P. Oxy.* 1800 fr. 3 col. II 47ff.: ἐτριταγωνίστει τραγῳδοῖς ὑποκρινόμενος.

12. The first to stress this fact was Reisch, "Zur Vorgeschichte der attischen Tragödie," 467, followed by Pickard-Cambridge, *Dithyramb, Tragedy and Comedy*, 164f. They could not apply the more exact rules of word-formation developed by linguistics since then; cf. Ernst Risch, *Wortbildung der homerischen Sprache* (Heidelberg: de Gruyter, 1937); *IGForsch* 59 (1944/9) 1ff., 245ff.; Eduard Schwyzer, *Griechische Grammatik*, vol. 1 (Munich: Beck, 1950), 428ff.; W. H. Willis in *Studies Presented to D. M. Robinson*, vol. 2 (Saint Louis, MO: Washington University Press, 1953), 553ff.; I am indebted to A. Heubeck (Erlangen) for advice. There are very few exceptions among the determinative compounds where the second part determines the first, e.g., ἱπποπόταμος, αἴγαγρος. In an attempt to refute Pickard-Cambridge, Patzer (*Die Anfänge der griechischen Tragödie*, 132) adduces, besides κωμῳδός, χορῳδός and μονῳδός; this word, however, is found only in Tzetzes, χορῳδός seems not to be attested at all. Lesky (*Die tragische Dichtung der Hellenen*, 22 n. 3) refers to E. Kalinka, *Commentationes Aenopontanae* 10 (1924): 31, who, however, shows his unawareness of Greek word-formation by referring to ῥοδδάκτυλος: this, the *bahuvrihi*-type, is exocentric, i.e., used as adjective, Schwyzer 429, 454; ῥαψῳδός belongs still to another, the τεψίμβροτος-type. Del Grande, *ΤΡΑΓΩΙΔΙΑ*, 56ff., 354ff., thinks τραγῳδός has nothing at all to do with τράγος, "goat." If, however, a goat was sacrificed at the Dionysia in the time of Thespis, it is difficult to believe that the Athenians would keep τραγῳδοί and τράγος apart.

13. *FGrHist* 308 F 2 = Schol. *in* Pi. *N.* 2.1; Eust. p. 6.25; *EM*, Hsch. *s.v.* ἀρνῳδός, Phot. *s.v.* ῥαψῳδός. The *Lex sacra* of Coresus, *SIG*³ 958.36 assigns κρεῶν μερίδα to the rhapsode. So there is no reason to look for another etymology of ἀρνῳδός as Welcker, *Nachtrag zu der Schrift über die Aeschylische Trilogie*, 241, did.

14. Marm.Par. *FGrHist* 239 A 43, cf. Euseb./Hieron. *Chron.* Ol. 47,2; Dioskorides, *AP* 7.410, cf. 411, Ἐratosth. fr. 22 Powell – Hygin. *Astr.* p. 35.4ff. Bunte, cf. Friedrich Solmsen, "Eratosthenes' Erigone: A Reconstruction," *Transactions of the American Philological Association* 78 (1947): 270ff.; Karl Meuli, "Altrömischer Maskenbrauch," *Museum Helveticum* 12 (1955): 226f.; Merkelbach, "Die *Erigone* des Eratosthenes," 496ff. Patzer (*Die Anfänge der griechischen Tragödie*, 33f.) thinks Eratosthenes is referring to the ἀσκώλια rather than to tragedy, though admitting that περὶ τράγον ὀρχεῖσθαι does not suit the jumping on the goatskin. Eratosthenes' theory, however, seems to have been that both tragedy and comedy sprang from the same root, the τρυγῳδία

understood as "vintage-song," to which the ἀσκώλια too are said to have belonged, cf. Paus. *Gr.*
Ed. Erbse α 161 = Eust. p. 1769.45ff. (Erbse is not right in leaving out the phrases on κωμῳδεῖν
and τραγῳδοί; the word κωμῆται in Paus. Gr. clearly points to κωμῳδία, cf. Meuli, "Altrömischer
Maskenbrauch," 226 n. 4); other texts gathered by Meuli, "Altrömischer Maskenbrauch." It seems
impossible to accept Eratosthenes' theory in this respect, because the Dionysia was not a vintage-
festival; but the falsity of the combination does not invalidate the single pieces of information
Eratosthenes could use, e.g., on τραγῳδοί and τράγος. Verg. *Georg.* 2.380ff. with Serv. Auct.
383, Prob. 380/4, Schol. Bern.; Hor. *AP* 220 with Ps.-Acr.; Tib. 2.157f. Diomedes, *Grammatici
Latini* I.487 = Suetonius p. 5.16ff. Reifferscheid (cf. *infra* n. 21); Euanthius in *Aeli Donati q.f.
commentum Terenti* ed. P. Wessner, vol. 1 (Leipzig: Teubner, 1902), 13 = *CGF* p. 62. Diomedes
and Euanthius present nearly the same material in different arrangement; Euanthius does not use
Diomedes (-Suetonius), since he has some more Greek material (*Apollo* Νόμιος, Ἀγυαῖος p. 13.16
Wessner), but—except the obvious reference to Vergil—not the Latin quotations (Varro, Lucilius)
found in Diomedes (-Suetonius). Didymos, Περὶ ποιητῶν, is quoted by Orion p. 58.7ff. Sturz for
an etymology of ἔλεγος which recurs in Diomedes p. 484 K. and Procl. *Chr.* 319$_B$6ff. Proclus in his
Chrestomathy must have dealt with tragedy and comedy, but nothing is extant in the excerpts of
Photios; from Proclus, however, seem to be derived the excerpts of Iohannes Diakonos ed. Rabe,
RhM. 63 (1908), 150, Schol. *in* Dionys. Thr. p. 18.3ff.; 172.20, 306.27, 475.3 Hilgard; Tz. *ad*
Lyc. p. 2.21, 3.1 Scheer; Tz. *Diff. Poet.* 100, 124 (*CGF* pp. 37f.). Cf. G. Kaibel, *Die Prolegomena*
ΠΕΡΙ ΚΩΜΩΙΔΙΑΣ (*AbhGött.* II.4 1898), a study of basic importance for the evaluation of the
later sources. Else, *Origin*, 17, declaring Iohannes Diakonos "worthless," ignores these affiliations.
Patzer, affirming that the explanation "τραγῳδία = 'Gesang beim Bocksopfer'" was "in der Antike
nirgends als Namensdeutung versucht" (*Die Anfänge der griechischen Tragödie*, 34 n. 1), is
overlooking Vergil and Euanthius. Vergil and Euanthius agree with the tradition of the goat as a
prize as to the fact that the τραγῳδοί sang while the goat was still alive; cf. *infra* n. 68 at the end.

15. Fr. 676 Rose = Schol.Bob. *in* Cic. *Pro Arch.* p. 358 Orelli, on elegists; fr. 677 = Procl. *Chr.* 320$_A$31,
on Arion; Rose included both fragments among the *dubia*, conjecturing Ἀριστοκλῆς instead of
Ἀριστοτέλης. He could not yet know Iohannes Diakonos p. 150 Rabe (*infra* n. 19) and Schol. *in*
Dionys. Thr. p. 306.9 Hilgard, on Susarion.

16. Pohlenz, *Das Satyrspiel*, cf. Pohlenz, *Die griechische Tragödie*, 2:8ff., accepted by Ziegler, 1925,
Lesky, *Die tragische Dichtung der Hellenen*, 20ff., Patzer, *Die Anfänge der griechischen Tragödie*,
24. Pohlenz, referring to Jacoby, stated the source of the Parian Marble to be an early third-
century Atthis. Surely Eratosthenes in his *Erigone* was drawing on the Atthidographers, as did
Callimachus in his *Hecale*. Jacoby, however, thought of Ephorus, Περὶ εὑρημάτων, too, as a possible
source for the Parian Marble, *FGrHist* II D 668, cf. II C 42. It is the merit of Solmsen, Meuli,
Merkelbach (*supra* n. 14) to have revived the interest in the "Eratosthenian" theory of the drama.

17. Else, *Aristotle's Poetics*, pointed out the Attic setting of the anecdote and the Attic word ἄστυ
(121 n. 101). He thinks the pro-Dorian party to consist of Aristotle's own pupils, Dicaearchus
and Aristoxenus (123); "the whole idea of a competition between Dorian and Athenian claims
to the origination of the drama could only have arisen in the fourth century and in the context of
Aristotle's school" (Else, *Origin*, 23)—as if the question of the εὑρετής were not already present
in Pi. *O.* 13.18, Hdt. 1.23, cf. Jacoby, *FGrHist* II C p. 42.25 on Ephorus Περὶ εὑρμάτων. On κώμη,
Swoboda in *RE* Suppl. IV (1924), 951.

18. Diom. p. 488 quoting Varro; Euanthius p. 13f. Wessner; Donatus p. 23.1ff. Wessner; *CGF* p. 6, p.
14 col. B 39; Schol. *in* Dionys. Thr. p. 18.15ff., 172.26, 306.16, 450.30 Hilgard; *EM* p. 764.13ff.;
Tz. *ad* Lyc. p. 2.32 Scheer; Iohannes Diakonos p. 149f. Rabe; Schol. *in* Pl. *Remp.* 394c.

19. Aristotle had little interest in etymology: φύσει τῶν ὀνομάτων οὐδέν ἐστιν (*Int.* 16a27); therefore

it is quite doubtful whether in his remarks on σατυρικόν he was thinking of the word τραγῳδία and hypothetical Peloponnesian τράγοι. Of course, even satyrs could sacrifice a goat, cf. the vase paintings (*infra* n. 25, esp. no. 17). The Iohannes Diakonos passage p. 150 Rabe contains, together with the much-discussed testimony of Solon on Arion as inventor of tragedy, the statement ἄμφω δὲ (i.e., tragedy and comedy) παρ᾽ Ἀθηναίοις ἐφεύρηνται, καθάπερ Ἀριστοτέλης φησίν. There is no methodological reason why we should accept the testimony of Solon and reject the testimony of Aristotle. Aristotle, however, knew and quoted Solon's elegies (cf. e.g., *Ath.* 5, 12); so he will not have overlooked so ancient an authority on tragedy, and still he is said to have maintained its Attic origin. So the question comes up again what Solon really said. There is a well-established tradition that Arion "invented" the dithyramb (Hellanikos, *FGrHist* 4 F 86; Hdt. 1.23; Arist. in Procl. *Chr.* 320₍Λ₎31; Dicaearchus fr. 75 Wehrli; Schol. *in* Pi. *O.* 13.26 b; Schol. *in* Pl. *Remp.* 394₍C₎; Tz. *ad* Lyc. p. 2.15 Scheer; alluded to in Pindar, *O.* 13.18). Aristotle thought dithyramb to be the ἀρχή of tragedy (*Poet.* 1449a9ff.); whatever he meant by this statement and whether or not he was right, it must be noted that ἀρχή in his terminology implies that dithyramb was itself not tragedy, but an "ontologically" earlier step. His followers and epitomators, however, would not always keep to these subtle distinctions. The result was some confusion between dithyramb and tragedy. As Philoxenus is said to have been διθυραμβοποιὸς ἢ τραγῳδοδιάσκαλος (Schol. *in* Ar. *Pl.* 290), *a fortiori* Arion came to be considered the first tragic poet (Suda *s.v.* Arion, Tz. *ad* Lyc. p. 3.7 Scheer). If Solon only spoke of Arion's κύκλιος χορός (κύκλιον ἤγαγε χορόν—a somewhat unusual word order—Schol. *in* Pi. [*supra*], cf. Procl., Tz. [*supra*]), this could develop into the statement of Iohannes Diakonos: the author's name and the title of his work are preserved, but instead of the text we have a questionable interpretation. So the quotation of Solon in Iohannes Diakonos may be similar to the quotation of Hesiod in Diog. Laer. 8.48: Hesiod there is said to have taught the sphericity of the earth, because Zenon (*SVF* I no. 276) read it into his text.

20. "In Ikaria und bei vielen anderen Dionysosfesten" there were goat-sacrifices, according to Ziegler, 1926, but not at the Dionysia when tragedy was performed. Even so it would be less far-fetched to derive τραγῳδοί from Icaria than from hypothetical Peloponnesian τράγοι. Patzer (*Die Anfänge der griechischen Tragödie*, 24) thinks the goat-prize to be a mere "inference" from the wrong etymology. Lesky (*Die tragische Dichtung der Hellenen*, 20) is more circumspect: "Man berief sich dabei gewiss auf alten attischen Dorfbrauch."

21. Diomedes—who is quoting Varro (*De scaenicis originibus* fr. 304 Funaioli) only for the *quia* phrase, as the change in number seems to indicate—explicitly refers to the Attic Dionysia, p. 488: *Liberalibus apud Atticos, die festo Liberi patris, vinum cantatoribus pro corollario dabatur* (cf. Philochoros, *FGrHist* 328 F 171); Serv. Auct. *in Georg.* 2.383 states that the Dionysiac goat-sacrifice originated at the Attic Dionysia. For the myth of Icarius and the first goat-sacrifice, there is no incontrovertible evidence prior to Eratosthenes. Attic black-figure vases represent a man receiving Dionysus (amphora BM B 149 = J. D. Beazley, *Attic Black-Figure Vase Painters*, hereafter, *ABV* [Oxford: Clarendon Press, 1956], 245,60 and B 153 = *ABV* 243,45); the man is traditionally called Icarius, but Amphiction and Semachus, too, are possible names. The story of Icarius in Porph. *Abst.* 2.10 was reluctantly attributed to Theophrastus by Jacob Bernays, *Theophrastos' Schrift über Frömmigkeit* (Berlin: W. Hertz, 1866), 61, and, with less hesitation, by Walter Pötscher, *Theophrastos ΠΕΡΙ ΕΥΣΕΒΕΙΑΣ* (Leiden: Brill, 1964), 22ff. This, however, can be refuted: according to Theophrastus, the sanguinary sacrifice was caused by λιμὸς ἤ τινος ἄλλης δυστυχίας περίστασις (Porph. *Abst.* 2.9 first sentence)—which is neither "unglücklicher Zufall" nor "Missgeschick" (Pötscher, 16, 153), but something like "inescapable impact of calamity" (cf. Theophrastus' definition of tragedy as ἡρωικῆς τύχης περίστασις Diom. p. 487). Introduced by αὐτίκα τῶν κατὰ μέρος ... there follow in Porphyry the Attic anecdotes about the first sacrifice of a pig, a goat, a bull, which make ἢ ἀγνοίας ἢ ὀργὰς ἢ φόβους the origin of sacrifice; this is not δυστυχίας περίστασις. In the middle of chapter 10 (p. 141.3 Nauck; fr. 6 Pötscher), the κατὰ

μέρος-examples come to an end, and suddenly the motive of λιμός reappears: this is Theophrastus again, the stories before are ἐμβεβλημένοι μῦθοι of Porphyry (*Abst.* 2.32). Nevertheless, the non-Theophrastean anecdotes may still be very old popular tradition, perhaps again preserved by Atthidographers. Later testimonies on the Dionysiac goat-sacrifice: Varro, *RR* 1.2.19; Ov. *Met.* 15.111ff.; *Fast.* 1.349ff.; Serv. *in Aen.* 3.118; Prob. *in Georg.* 2.380/4; above all Leonidas of Tarentum, *AP* 9.99, and Euenus of Ascalon, *AP* 9.75, an epigram that is also inscribed on a Pompeian wall-painting, *MonInst.* 10 (1876) T.36. Hellenistic and Roman representations of the goat-sacrifice are collected by O. Brendel, *RömMitt.* 48 (1933): 153ff. A choragus paid 30 minas for one tragic agon (Lys. 21.1), the price of a goat in Erchia (*SEG* 21 [1965] no. 541) is 10 to 12 drachmas, i.e., less than ½ percent—*vilis hircus* indeed.

22. Cf. the foundation of Kritolaos in Amorgos, *IG* XII 7, 515.80: the meat of a sacrificed ram is to be used as ἔπαθλα for the victors in an athletic agon. Cf. also Schol. *in* Theocr. 7.106/8d.

23. On these "dithyrambic vases" cf. G. E. Rizzo, *RivFC* 30 (1902): 471ff.; Ernst Pfuhl, *Malerei und Zeichnung*, vol. 2 (Munich: F. Bruckmann, 1923), §617; esp. the neck-amphora BM E 298 = *ARV*² 1581, 20, *CVA* pl. 51, 1, with the inscription ΑΚΑΜΑΝΤΙΣ ΕΝΙΚΑ ΦΥΛΕ; the calyx-crater Bologna PU 286 = *ARV*² 1158, with Dionysus, seated, expecting the sacrifice of the bull led by Nike. On later representations of bull-sacrifices, O. Brendel, *RömMitt.* 45 (1930): 196ff. Further testimonies on the dithyrambic bull-sacrifice: Chamaeleon fr. 34 Wehrli explaining Simonides fr. 69 Diehl; Dionysus ταυοφάγος, S. fr. 607 Nauck = 668 Pearson; Schol. *in* Pl. *Remp.* 394c; the expression θύσων διθύραμβον Pi. fr. 86a.

24. Ludwig Deubner, *Attische Feste* (Berlin: H. Keller, 1932), 252 and pl. 38.

25. Surprisingly little attention has been paid to these unimpeachable τράγοι in the retinue of Dionysus. My collection (surely incomplete):

    1. Amphora BM B 168 = *ABV* 142,3 (satyr riding on goat)
    2. Amphora New York, Metr. Mus. 06.1021.68 = *ABV* 289 (Dionysus, satyr, goat)
    3. Amphora Oxford 213 = *ABV* 340,1 (maenad and satyr, Dionysus, maenad and goat)
    4. Amphora Eduard Gerhard, *Auserlesene Vasenbilder* (Berlin: G. Reimer, 1840–58), pl. 54 = *ABV* 370,127 (Dionysus and Ariadne in a chariot drawn by goats)
    5. Amphora ibid. pl. 32 = *ABV* 372,155 (satyr, Dionysus with goat, satyr)
    6. Oinochoe Cambridge 162 = *ABV* 385,28 (man, maenad, winejug, man riding on a goat, amphora, dancing man)
    7. Stamnos Bruxelles R 251 = *ABV* 388,2 (on the neck: man between goats, goat between men; main picture: chariot race and dancing men, surrounded by vines and grapes)
    8. Pelike Oxford 563 = *ABV* 396,21 (satyrs with goat)
    9. Amphora BM B 178 = *ABV* 396,27 (Dionysus with goat, two satyrs)
    10. Amphora BM B 258 = *ABV* 402,9 (Ariadne with panther, Apollo with cithara, Dionysus with cantharus and goat)
    11. Oinochoe *ABV* 431,11 (maenad riding on goat)
    12. Lekythos Berlin = *ABV* 518,3 (goats, satyrs, a goat with human face, caught at the horn by a satyr)
    13. Skyphos Agora P 1544 = *ABV* 518,47 (procession with flute-player, youth carrying a wine-amphora, old man with ivy-wreath, other comasts, goat)
    14. Skyphos Agora P 1547 = *ABV* 518,49 (procession with flute-player, man catching a goat at the horn)
    15. Skyphos Bruxelles R 283 = *ABV* 627,2 (youth holding goat at horn; vines with grapes)
    16. Amphora BM B 265 = *CVA* pl. 66 (Great Britain 211) 1 (return of Hephaestus, goat beside the mule)

17. Amphora Gerhard *supra* pl. 37 (Dionysus with goat)
18. Skyphos Bologna C 44 = *CVA* 2 pl. 42 (Italia 341) (goat, satyr, Hermes; suspended, a knapsack containing the head of a goat)
19. Skyphos Baltimore, *CVA* 1 pl. 22 (USA 155) (Dionysus in a chariot, goat, man)
20. Skyphos Athens 820 *bis*, A. Frickenhaus, *Lenaeenvasen*, Winckelmannsprogramm 72 (Berlin, 1912), no. 2 (Dionysus-idol with women; under the handle, goat)
21. Amphora Warsaw 199184 = *CVA* 4 pl. 17 (Pologne 146) 2/3 (Dionysus with goat)
22. Amphora Philadelphia L 64.259 = *ABV* 285,6 (satyr and maenad, Dionysus with goat, satyr)
23. Oinochoe Paris, Cab. des Méd. 276, A. de Ridder, *Catalogue des vases peints de la Bibliothèque Nationale* (Paris: Ernest Leroux, 1902), fig. 28 (silen with flute, goat, wineskin)

A goat is depicted on the altar of Dionysus on the cup of Makron, Acr. 325 = *ARV*² 460,20, Frickenhaus, *Lenaeenvasen*, 22. There is also a goat on a Boeotian cotyle in the British Museum, *JHS* 31 (1911): 4ff. (together with satyr) and on one Corinthian kothon, Würzburg no. 118 (Webster, no. 37). Similar representations recur in Attic red-figure, e.g., the cup of Gorgos, Agora P 24113 = *ARV*² 213,242. It seems the vase painters felt some equivalence of he-goat and satyr (nos. 3, 12) and an intimate connexion of Dionysus and τράγος (nos. 5, 9, 10, 15). The sacrifice of an ἔριφος is represented on a South Italian vase (Naples H 2411, Lewis R. Farnell, *The Cults of the Greek States*, vol. 5 [Oxford: Clarendon Press, 1909], pl. 41); otherwise, the act of sacrifice to Dionysus is not represented in classical vase-painting (Henri Metzger, *Recherches sur l'imagerie athénienne* [Paris: E. de Boccard, 1965], 113).

26. Deubner, *Attische Feste*, 136; Pickard-Cambridge, *Dramatic Festivals of Athens*, 41; Else, *Hermes* 85 (1957): 18 n. 3: "in any case not the Greater Dionysia"; Patzer, *Die Anfänge der griechischen Tragödie*, 36: "ohne jede Rücksicht auf die Tragödie." Pohlenz, however, pointed out the connection with the Parian Marble and Dioskorides, in *Das Satyrspiel*, 304 n. 1.

27. The *Leges Sacrae* make a distinction between the sacrifice of an ἔριφος and a τράγος, cf. F. Sokolowski, *Lois sacrées de l'Asie Mineure* (Paris: E. de Boccard, 1955), no. 67ᴮ3, 10; Sokolowski, *Lois sacrées des cités grecques* (Paris: E. de Boccard, 1962), no. 104: Διονύσῳ ῥάγον . . . The Erchia-inscription (*SEG* 21 [1965] no. 541) distinguishes οἷς from κριός (E 52); it has 11 times the sacrifice of an αἴξ, no τράγος (cf. also S. Dow, *BCH* 89 [1955]: 199ff.).

28. Hor. *Epod.* 10.23; Mart. 3.24 (cf. *infra* n. 62).

29. The αἴτιον of the goat gnawing the vine, however, fits Elaphebolion, the month of the Greater Dionysia: the goat "invented" the pruning of the vine (Hygin. *Fab.* 274.1), which takes place ὑπ᾽ αὐτὴν τὴν βλάστησιν (Thphr. *CP* 3.13.1), i.e., about April.

30. The goat eating from a tree, endangered by carnivorous beasts, is an iconographic type down from Sumerian times; cf. the gold-silver-statuettes from Ur, James B. Pritchard, *The Ancient Near East in Pictures* [hereafter *ANEP*] (Princeton, NJ: Princeton University Press, 1954), nos. 667/668; a seal from Uruk, Berlin VA 10537, *ANEP* no. 672; Henri Frankfort, *Cylinder Seals* (London: Macmillan, 1939), 21f., pl. 3a (cf. pl. 3b, 4j, 17c): a man, standing beside a block (altar?), feeding goats (or a kind of sheep?) with a (stylized) twig; he is probably to be called Dumuzi-Tammuz: Anton Moortgat, *Tammuz* (Berlin: de Gruyter, 1949), 3ff., 29f.; a relief from Assur, first half of second mill. B.C., *ANEP* no. 528: a god with grapes, on each side a goat gnawing the grape-vine; a relief-vase, W. Andrae, *Kultrelief aus dem Brunnen des Assurtempels zu Assur* (Berlin: J. C. Hinrichs, 1931), 10. Pl. 7d: goat gnawing grapes, threatened by beastlike demons. Some connection of Dionysus-cult and Tammuz-cult is entirely possible, considering esp. the equation βάκχον᾽ κλαυθμόν. Φοίνικες (Hsch.) and Ἰκάριος—Accadian *ikkaru* "farmer, planter" (Michael C. Astour, *Hellenosemitica* [Leiden: E. J. Brill, 1965], 174f.; 194 n. 6).

31. Fr. 708 Page; cf. Pohlenz, *Das Satyrspiel*, and Ervin Roos, *Die tragische Orchestik im Zerrbild der altattischen Komödie* (Lund: C. W. K. Gleerup, 1951), 209ff.

32. Pollux 4.123. To make the problem more complicated, the Tholos in Epidaurus was called θυμέλα (*IG* IV.1² 103), a Delian inscription mentions τὴν θυμέλην τοῦ ωμοῦ (*IG* XI.2 161ᴀ95), whereas Pherecrates (*CAF* I.204, fr. 214) is said to have used the word instead of θυηλαί. The tragic poets use θυμέλη as a kind of equivalent to ἑστία, A. S. F. Gow, *JHS* 32 (1912): 213ff., Fernand Robert, *Thymélè* (Paris: E. de Boccard, 1939), 259ff., Hsch. *s.v.* θυμέλη . . . οἱ δὲ τὸ ἐπίπυρον; E. *Supp.* 64 δεξίπυροι θυμέλαι—but E. *Ion* 114 θυμέλαν = δάπεδον 121; therefore Pickard-Cambridge concluded that there was an altar in the center of the orchestra, the upper part of which was the θυμέλη (*Dithyramb, Tragedy and Comedy*, 175, 177; *The Theatre of Dionysus in Athens* [Oxford: Clarendon Press, 1946], 9f.). Metzger, *Recherches sur l'imagerie athénienne*, 101f., calls the round altar amid the Dionysiac thiasos on a vase painting θυμέλη (calyx crater Athens 12255 = *ARV²* 1435, Metzger pl. 44). C. Robert had vigorously contested that there could have been an altar in the orchestra (*Hermes* 32 [1897] 438ff., followed by F. Schmidt, *De supplicum ad aras confugientium partibus scenicis* [Diss. Königsberg, 1911]); his derivation of θυμέλη from the root θη-, θεμέλιον must however be discarded on linguistic grounds; on the suffix -μελ-, H. Frisk, *Eranos* 41 (1943): 51, and *Griechisches etymologisches Wörterbuch* (Heidelberg: C. Winter, 1960), *s.v.* θυω 2. Other testimonies point to θυμέλη = βῆμά τι: Orion p. 72.8 Sturz (~*Et. Gen., EM* 458.32ff.) *s.v.* θυμέλη: τράπεζα δὲ ἦν . . . ἐφ ἧς ἑστῶτες ἐν τοῖς ἀγροῖς ἧδον, μήπω τάξιν λαβούσης τραγωδίας (cf. Pollux 4.123 on ἐλεός); *EM* 743.35 μετὰ δὲ τὴν ὄρχηστραν (meaning "stage" here) βωμὸς ἦν τοῦ Διονύσου, τετράγωνον οἰοδόμημα κενὸν ἐπὶ τοῦ μέσου, ὃ καλεῖται θυμέλη. This rectangular platform was discovered by G. Löschcke (in E. Bethe, *Prolegomena zur Geschichte des Theaters im Alterthum* [Leipzig: S. Hirzel, 1896], 76f.; cf. A. Frickenhaus, *Die altgriechische Bühne* [Strassburg: K.J. Trübner, 1917], 83ff.; Margarete Bieber, *Denkmäler zum Theaterwesen im Altertum* [Berlin: Vereinigung wissenschaftlicher verleger, 1920], 8ff.; Bieber, *History of the Greek and Roman Theater*, 2nd ed. [Princeton, NJ: Princeton University Press, 1961], 55, fig. 48) on the Brygos-cup BM E 65 = *ARV²* 370,13, in a scene of a satyr-play; the same platform on calyx crater Bologna 329 = *ARV²* 1410,21, in a Dionysiac scene. Musicians are often represented performing on similar platforms, so the later concept of θυμελικοὶ ἀγῶνες (J. Frei, *De certaminibus thymelicis* [Diss. Basel, 1900]) is easy to explain (Bieber, *Denkmäler*). Pollux 4.123 mentions an altar ἐπὶ τῆς σκηνῆς. In the theater of Priene, there is an altar at the rim of the orchestra opposite the stage, accessible from the orchestra (Martin Schede, *Die Ruinen von Priene*, 2nd ed. [Berlin: de Gruyter, 1964] 70ff.); a similar altar in a theater on Cos (*Enciclopedia dell'arte antica*, vol. 2 [1959], 799). That the choreuts (of dithyramb and tragedy?) in strophe and antistrophe were dancing round the altar is stated by the Hellenistic scholar Ptolemaios (*RE* XXIII [1959] 1862–63 *s.v.* no. 78) in Schol. *in* Pi. III p. 311 Drachmann, cf. *EM* 690.44ff., Byz. Schol. *in* E. *Hec.* 647 (ed. Dindorf; not in Schwartz), cf. Robert, in *Mélanges d'archéologie et d'histoire*, 874ff.; Lillian B. Lawler, *The Dance of the Ancient Greek Theater* (Iowa City: University of Iowa Press, 1964), 11ff.

33. 510/508 B.C. according to Marm. Par. A 46; Pickard-Cambridge, *Dithyramb, Tragedy and Comedy*, 15, 22f.; it was organized by Lasos of Hermione, who therefore was sometimes called "inventor" of dithyramb. There is no reason to assume earlier performances of dithyrambs in Athens at the time of Peisistratos, as, e.g., Patzer (*Die Anfänge der griechischen Tragödie*, 93) does.

34. Only sanguinary sacrifices are studied here, not σπονδαί, ἀπαρχαί, etc. One of the most important contributions to the question is still W. Robertson Smith, *Lectures on the Religion of the Semites*, 2nd ed. (London: Adam and Charles Black, 1894), though his theory of totemism has been abandoned. He vitally influenced Sigmund Freud, *Totem und Tabu* (Vienna: Hugo Heller, 1913) = four essays in *Imago* 1–2 (1912–13) = *Gesammelte Schriften* 10 (Leipzig: Internationaler Psychoanalytischer Verlag, 1924). There is the sociological approach: Henri

Hubert and Marcel Mauss, "Essai sur la nature et la function du sacrifice," *Année sociologique* 2 (1898): 29ff., Engl. transl.: *Sacrifice, Its Nature and Function* (Chicago: University of Chicago Press, 1964); their definition: "sacrifice is a religious act which, through the consecration of a victim, modifies the condition of the moral person who accomplishes it . . ." (13)—which leaves the question open why such advantage is gained by the destruction of life. They also define sacrifice as "establishing a means of communication between the sacred and the profane worlds through the mediation of a victim" (97)—basically the same definition as in E. O. James, *Sacrifice and Sacrament* (London: Thames & Hudson, 1962), who gives a convenient survey of the material and literature. An original attempt at explanation: Adolf E. Jensen, "Über das Töten als kulturgeschichtliche Erscheinung," *Paideuma* 4 (1950): 23ff. ~ *Mythos und Kult bei Naturvölkern* (Wiesbaden: Franz Steiner Verlag, 1951), 197ff. (*infra* n. 55). On Greek sacrifice: Paul Stengel, *Die Opferbräuche der Griechen* (Leipzig: Teubner, 1910); Stengel, *Die griechischen Kultusaltertümer*, 3rd ed. (Munich: C. H. Beck, 1920); Samson Eitrem, *Opferritus und Voropfer der Griechen und Römer* (Kristiania: J. Dybwad, 1915); Friedrich Schwenn, *Gebet und Opfer* (Heidelberg: C. Winter, 1927); L. Ziehen, *RE* XVIII (1939), 579ff. *s.v.* Opfer, *RE* III$_A$ (1929), 1669ff. *s.v.* σφάγια. Of special importance are: A. Thomsen, "Der Trug des Prometheus," *ArchRW* 12 (1909): 460ff.; A. D. Nock, "The Cult of Heroes," *HthR* 37 (1944): 141ff.; above all Karl Meuli, "Griechische Opferbräuche," in *Phyllobolia: Festschrift für P. von der Mühll* (Basel: Schwabe, 1946), 185ff., who established the connection of the Olympian sacrifice with the "Schädel- und Langknochenopfer," on which cf. Anton Vorbichler, *Das Opfer auf den heute noch erreichbaren ältesten Stufen der Menschheitsgeschichte* (Mödling: St.-Gabriel-Verlag, 1956), and Herbert Kühn, *Das Problem des Urmonotheismus* (*AbhMainz.*, 1950), 22. Unfortunately there is no exhaustive study of interrelations of Greek and ancient Near Eastern sacrificial rites (on which cf. B. Meissner, *Babylonien und Assyrien*, vol. 2 [Heidelberg: C. Winter, 1925], 73ff.; Giuseppe Furlani, "Il sacrificio nella religione dei Semiti di Babilonia e Assiria," *MemLinc*. VI, 4 [1932]: 103–370; Friedrich Blome, *Die Opfermaterie in Babylonien und Israel* [Rome: Pontifical Biblical Institute, 1934]; Kurt Galling, *Der Altar in den Kulturen des alten Orients* [Berlin: K. Curtius, 1925]; Yvonne Rosengarten, *Le Régime des offrandes dans la société sumérienne d'après les textes présargoniques de Lagaš* [Paris: E. de Boccard, 1960]; on the still very frustrating Ugaritic evidence, A. de Guglielmo, *CathBiblQuart.* 17 [1955]: 196ff.). It seems to be well established that, on the one hand, the Minoans and Mycenaeans had quite different sacrificial rites, because they had no altars of the Greek type (Constantine G. Yavis, *Greek Altars* [Saint Louis: Saint Louis University Press, 1949]), and, on the other hand, that the nearest relatives of Greek altars are to be found in Assur, 13th cent. (Galling, *Der Altar*, 46ff.; *ANEP* nos. 576/577), and that Semitic (Phoenician and Hebrew) sacrificial rites offer the closest parallels to Greek ritual (Royden Keith Yerkes, *Sacrifice in Greek and Roman Religions and Early Judaism* [New York: Scribner, 1952]). It is one of the paradoxes of our discipline that neither Nilsson nor Meuli, in their expositions of Greek sacrificial ritual, refers to the Old Testament, which contains the largest extant collection of ancient sacrificial rites.

35. Schol. A. *in Il.* 9.219 = K. Lehrs, *De Aristarchi studiis Homericis*, 3rd ed. (Leipzig: S. Hirzel, 1882), 82ff.; Schol. *in Od* 14.446; Eust. p. 641.61; Frisk, *GriechEtymWörterb.* 1:699. The more comprehensive use of θύειν is to be seen in the gloss Hsch. *s.v.* θῦμα· ἱερεῖον σφάγιον ὁλοκαύτωμα.

36. On "Olympic" and "chthonic" sacrifice, cf. Stengel, *Die griechischen Kultusaltertümer*, 105ff.; Ziehen (*supra* n. 34); Meuli, "Griechische Opferbräuche," 201ff.; the evidence for the contrast ἐναγίζειν—θύειν is most fully collected by Friedrich Pfister, *Der Reliquienkult im Altertum*, vol. 2 (Giessen: A. Töpelmann, 1912), 466ff. In slaughtering, the throat of the animal was sometimes turned to the sky, sometimes pressed to the earth (H. v. Fritze *Jdl.* 18 [1904]: 58ff.; Schol *in* Ap. Rh. 1. 587; *Et. Gen.* p. 115 Miller = *EM s.v.* ἔντομα). There are, besides the high "Olympian" altars, altars low and large for holocausts, but there are also ἐσχάραι just on the earth and βόθροι

dug out (Yavis, *Greek Altars*, 91ff.; Schol. *in* E. *Ph.* 274; Porph. *Antr.* 6; Serv. *in* Verg. *Buc.* 5.66 etc.). In fact ὁλοκαυτώματα were not very frequent, either in the cult of heroes or of the gods whom the Greeks called χθόνιοι (the evidence: Ziehen, *RE* IIIA [1929], 1674ff.), and they occur also in cults of "Olympians" (cf. Meuli, "Griechische Opferbräuche," 209ff.); the Erchia-inscription has Διὶ ᾽Επωπετεῖ χοῖρος ὁλόκαυτος (*SEG* XXI [1965] no. 541 Γ 23), i.e., for the god whose name seemed to designate the sky-god "looking down from above" (L. Preller and C. Robert, *Griechische Mythologie*, 4th ed., vol. 1 [Berlin: Weidmann, 1894], 117 n. 2). On the other hand, the sacrificial feast is quite common in the cult of heroes and χθόνιοι (Nock, "The Cult of Heroes," with 11 examples; the ram sacrificed to Pelops in Olympia was eaten, too, but not by participants in the festival, Paus. 5.13.2f.). People even ate from καθάρσια, cf. οἱ σπλαγχνεύοντες Ath. 9.410B; only Porphyry's θεολόγοι tried to eliminate this custom (*Abst.* 2.44). At the oath-sacrifices, however, the victim was not eaten (*Il.* 19.266, Schol. *in Il.* 3.310, Paus. 5.24.10, 3.20.9), nor were, of course, the σφάγια proper, slain on the battlefield under the eyes of the enemy. The holocausts themselves usually have their place as a preliminary rite in a larger context: first the burnt sacrifice—χοῖρος or ἀρήν—for the hero, then the sacrificial feast—mostly βοῦς—in honor of the god: inscription from Cos, *SIG*³ 1027 (Herakles); Paus. 3.19.3 (Hyacinthus-Apollon); Paus. 2.11.7 (Alexanor-Euamerion). This goes along with the rhythm night-day in Greek time-reckoning: the new "day" begins at sunset, cf. Pi. *I.* 4.67ff. *c.* Schol. In an analogous way, the "normal" sacrifice consists, first, in the burning of sacred parts; second, in the meal. In one case, the same animal was half burnt, half eaten (Paus. 2.10.1, Sicyon). There are many other special provisions in sacrificial ritual, each of which has its own function and meaning, e.g., about εὐνουχίζειν (*infra* n. 62), or οὐ φορά, i.e., the victim must be consumed at the spot: 22 times in the Erchia-inscription (*SEG* XXI no. 541); S. Dow, *BCH* 89 (1965): 210, thinks this to be a "purely secular matter," but cf. Ar. *Pl.* 1138 *c.* Schol.; Theopompus fr. 70 (*CAF* I.751); *SIG*³ 1004, 1024, 1025, 1026, 1041, Sokolowski, *Lois sacrées de l'Asie Mineure*, no. 34; L. Ziehen, *Leges Graecorum sacrae e titulis collectae* (Leipzig: Teubner, 1906), no. 125; Paus. 2.27.1, 10.4.10, 10.38.8, 8.38.8; the same rule from the Old Testament (Ex. 12.8, Passover; cf. 29.31, 34) through Rome (Cato *Agr.* 83; *CIL* VI 1, 576) up to Alaska (A. Gahs, in *Festschrift P. W. Schmidt*, ed. W Koppers [Vienna: Mechitharisten-Congregations-Buchdr., 1928], 251). The rite of drowning a victim in a spring or lake (D. S. 5.4: Cyane) is also attested as early as the Paleolithic period (Kühn, *Das Problem des Urmonotheismus*, 22).

37. The most elaborate descriptions of sacrifice are in Homer *Il.* 1.447ff., 2.410ff., *Od.* 3.429ff., 14.414ff.; Hes. *Th.* 535ff.; most detailed is Pherecrates, fr. 23 (*CAF* I.151): people burn τὼ μηρώ, τὴν ὀσφὺν κομιδῇ ψιλήν, τὸν σπόνδυλον. Menander mentions ὀσφὺν ἄκραν and χολήν *Dysc.* 447ff., cf. fr. 264 Koerte. The comedians used to make fun of this ritual, cf. also Eubulus fr. 95 (*CAF* II.197) and 130 (*CAF* II.210), Adesp. fr. 1205 (*CAF* III.606). An interesting description of a sacrificial meal is given by Harmodios, *FGrHist* 319 F 1. Vase paintings containing sacrificial scenes are collected by G. Rizza, *ASAtene*. 37–38 (1959–60): 321ff. and Metzger, *Recherches sur l'imagerie athénienne*, 107ff.; they usually represent the altar with the fire and the tail of the victim, the σπλαγχνόπτης, wine-libations, flute-player. The cup of Brygos (*supra* n. 32) shows Iris, who came to fetch from the altar ὀφσὺν καὶ σπόνδυλον, attacked by satyrs. Most surprising survivals of sacrificial ritual were found until recent times among the Greeks of Pharasa, Cappadocia: there is a stone in the chapel opposite the altar, on which incense is burnt; it is called θάλι (< λιθάρι); the victim is led three times around the θάλι, pelted with leaves and flowers, slaughtered in the chapel so that the θάλι may receive its blood; the minister (παπᾶς) receives the right thigh, the hide, head, and feet of the victim: G. A. Megas, ᾽Ελληνικαὶ ἔθιμα τῆς λαϊῆς λατρείας (Athens, 1956), 15f.; he also refers to similar customs in Thrace (17: the victim is slaughtered εἰς βόθρον in the churchyard) and at Lesbos (17f.). Cf. also Cook, *Zeus*, 3:1168ff.

38. ἡγοῦντο γὰρ ὥσπερ συσσιτεῖσθαι τοῖς θεοῖς Schol. AT *in Il.* 3.310; Ulrich von

Wilamowitz-Moellendorff, *Der Glaube der Hellenen*, vol. 1 (Berlin: Weidmann, 1931), 287; Nilsson, *Geschichte der griechischen Religion*, 144f.; *contra*, Nock, "The Cult of Heroes," 150ff., 156: "there was a conscious fellowship of the worshippers with one another, rather than of the worshippers with the deity honored." Wilamowitz thought the Promethean division was an "early" depravation of the original common meal; he could not know that this would lead back to times earlier than the Paleolithic age. That μηρία really means "thighbones" is proved by Meuli, "Griechische Opferbräuche," 215ff.

39. Nilsson, *Geschichte der griechischen Religion*, objects to Meuli, stressing that "nur gezähmte Tiere, fast nie wilde geopfert warden"; but this, far from being a "durchschlagender Einwand," merely means that the Neolithic farmers took over and transformed for their kind of civilization the rites of the Paleolithic hunters. Another change took place when the Greeks (like the Western Semites) began to burn the sacred parts, establishing as it were fire as a means of communication with the divine, cf. n. 34. Whether the sacrificial rites presuppose from the start some kind of belief in god, even an "Urmonotheismus," is a question difficult to answer. Meuli wrote: "diese Jagdriten sind weder deistisch noch prädeistisch und sagen über Götterglauben überhaupt nichts aus . . . in der Beziehung von Mensch und Tier gehen sie vollständig auf " ("Griechische Opferbräuche," 249); *contra*, Kühn, *Das Problem des Urmonotheismus*, and esp. Vorbichler, *Das Opfer*; curiously enough, Freud's theory in this case comes to the same result as does P. W. Schmidt.

40. The Greeks were fully aware of this: ζωῆς δὲ διὰ θυσιῶν ἀπαρχόμεθα Sallust 16.1. Iamblichus turns the same idea into magic: by destruction (ἀνάλυσις) sacrifice provokes to action the higher principles (*Myst.* 5.24). In a very crude form, the same concept returns in a modern definition of sacrifice: "Mobilmachung von Kraftstoff zu Gunsten des Opfernden," A. Bertholet, *Der Sinn des kultischen Opfers* (*AbhBerl.* no. 2, 1942), 10.

41. As a reverse, every slaughter is sacrifice. The Mosaic law was very outspoken about this, Lev. 17.2ff. (Yerkes, *Sacrifice in Greek and Roman Religions*, 147), but Josiah, concentrating the cult in Jerusalem, had to allow profane slaughter (Deut. 12.15), which had been common in the civilizations of Egypt and Mesopotamia. The Arabs still perform every slaughter "in the name of Allah" (*Die Religion in Geschichte und Gegenwart*, 3rd ed., vol. 4 [Tübingen, 1956ff.], 1640); for the Siberian čukčes, every slaughter of a reindeer is a sacrifice (A. Gahs, in *Festschrift P. W. Schmidt*, 253); and in India, some temples still are slaughter-houses (H. Zimmern, *Eranos-Jb* 6 [1938]: 180).

42. *Od.* 3.432ff.; this was preserved in German and Slavic folk-custom down to modern times: a "Pfingstochse" with gilded horns led along through the streets of the town, to be slaughtered afterward; each family would buy part of his meat: Ulrich Jahn, *Die deutschen Opferbräuche bei Ackerbau und Viehzucht* (Breslau: Wilhelm Koebner, 1884), 137ff., 315ff.; a striking example in a festival at Lesbos: Megas, Ἑλληνικαὶ ἔθιμα τῆς λαϊκῆς λατρείας, 17.

43. Cf. Ael. *NA* 10.50 (Eryx), 11.4 (Hermione); Apollon. *Mir.* 13 (Halicarnassus); Arist. *Mir.* 844a35 (Pedasia); Plut. *Pel.* 21 (Leuktra), *Luc.* 24.6f. (Persian Artemis = Anahita); Porph. *Abst.* 1.25 (Gadeira, Cyzicus); Philostr. *Her.* 17, p. 329 Kayser (Leuke), 8 p. 294 (Rhesus); Plin. *NH* 32.17 (Atargatis); the same is required for human sacrifice, Neanthes, *FGrHist* 84 F 16 (Epimenides), Serv. *in Aen.* 3.57 (Massalia), cf. Euripides' tragedies. Cf. also the lore of the haruspices, Serv. Auct. *in Georg.* 2.395, Macr. *Sat.* 3.5.8, and Lucan 7.165, D.C. 41.61; for India, cf. Hubert and Mauss, "Essai sur la nature et la function du sacrifice," 30. At the sacrifice of Poseidon Helikonios, on the contrary, the bull was expected to bellow fiercely, Schol. B. *in Il.* 20.404. Cf. Paus. 4.32.3.

44. Cf., e.g., Ar. *Pax* 956ff., E. *IA* 1568ff.; Eitrem, *Opferritus und Voropfer*, 7ff.; *supra* n. 37.

45. Delphic oracle in Porph. *Abst.* 2.9 = no. 537 in H. W. Parke and D. E. W. Wormell, *The Delphic*

Oracle, vol. 2 (Oxford: Blackwell, 1956), cf. Meuli, "Griechische Opferbräuche," 254ff., 266f.; Schol. *in* Ar. *Pax* 960; Schol. *in* Ap. Rh. 1.425; Plut. *QConv.* 729f., *DefOrac.* 435$_{BC}$, 437$_A$; *SIG*³ 1025.20 (Cos): θύεται δὲ (ὁ βοῦς), αἰ μέγ κα ὑπο [κύψ] ει τᾶι Ἰστίαι; an Arabian parallel in Eitrem, *Opferritus und Voropfer*, 7 n. 1. Cf. the stamnos Munich 2412 = *ARV*² 1036, 5: the dithyrambic bull (*supra* n. 23) bowing to drink water poured by Nike; Italiote Calpis Altenburg, *CVA* pl. 84 (Germany 869): bull kneeling down to be adorned by a woman (the Phyle). A modern survival in Megas, Ἑλληνικαὶ ἔθιμα τῆς λαϊῆς λατρείας, 18 (Lesbos): λένε ὅτι τότε γονατίζει τὸ ζῶο . . .

46. "Dunkel" according to Meuli, "Griechische Opferbräuche," 265. Stengel concluded from the word προβάλοντο that the οὐλοχύται "originally" were thrown at the earth, *ergo* it was a gift to the earth-goddess (*Die griechischen Kultusaltertümer*, 110); Ziehen used the term "cathartic," *Hermes* 37 (1902): 391ff., *RE* XVIII (1939), 626f.; Eitrem, *Opferritus und Voropfer*, 262, saw the equivalence to the καταχύσμαα but, following Ernst Samter, *Familienfeste der Griechen und Römer* (Berlin: G. Reimer, 1901), 1ff., he thought them to be a gift to ancestor-ghosts or demons. Χέρνιβά τ᾿ οὐλοχύτας τε κατάρχετο *Od.* 3.445, cf. E. *IA* 955, 1568ff.; Ar. *Pax* 956ff., *Av.* 850. That the knife is hidden (cf. Scandinavian customs of slaughter, E. Klein *ArchRW.* 28 [1930]: 167) in the basket, is stated at Pl. Com. fr. 91 (*CAF* I.626), Ar. *Pax* 948 c. Schol., E. *El.* 810, *IA* 1565f., Philostr. *VA* 1.1, Juv. 12.84. The barley is thrown at the victim, according to Schol. A *in Il.* 1.449, Schol. *in Od.* 3.441, Schol *in* Ar. *Nu.* 260, D.H. 7.72.15; at the altar, according to E. *IA* 1112, *El.* 804, Schol. *in* Ap. Rh. 1.409, Eust. p. 132.25. Theophrastus thought the οὐλαί to be a relic of an "old way of life." Porph. *Abst.* 2.6, Schol. A *in Il.* 1.449, cf. Eust. (*supra*), Schol. *in Od.* 3.441; he seems to have taken as a real religious rite the φλλοβολία *Od.* 12.357f.: Eust. p. 132.39f. In Pharasa the victim is pelted with χορτάρια καί λουλούδια, Megas, Ἑλληνικαὶ ἔθιμα τῆς λαϊῆς λατρείας, 16. Ψηφῖδες instead of οὐλαί Paus. 1.41.9, at the sacrifice to Tereus in Megara, cf. Schol. *in* Ar. *Nu.* 260.

47. Eitrem, *Opferritus und Voropfer*, 344ff., takes it to be "eine selbständige Opfergabe," for the souls of the dead, of course (413). Meuli, ("Griechische Opferbräuche," 265f.), who adduces a parallel from Mexico, refrains from giving an explanation. This ἀπάρχεσθαι is mentioned, e.g., *Od.* 3.446, 14.422; E. *Alc.* 74ff., *El.* 811. Ernest Hemingway, *For Whom the Bell Tolls*, describes the cutting of the hair as ἄρχεσθαι in another situation of violence.

48. Cf. Schol. *ad loc.*, A. *Ag.* 595, 1118; Hdt. 4.189. Ludwig Deubner, *Ololyge und Verwandtes* (*AbhBerl.* 1941, 1). An inscription from Pergamon mentions αὐλητρίς and ὀλολύκτρια as belonging to the sanctuary, *SIG*³ 982.25.

49. The altars depicted on vase paintings clearly show the traces of the αἱμάσσειν τοὺς βωμούς; cf., e.g., B. 11.111, Poll. 1.27, Eust. p. 1476, 41; ἀμνίον *Il.* 3.4444; σφαγεῖον Pol. 10.65.

50. Cf. Meuli, "Griechische Opferbräuche," 218, 256f., 262; D.H. 7.72.15ff. That there was some rule how to place the pieces on the altar is implied in εὐθετίσας Hes. *Th.* 541. The flute-player is often seen on vase paintings (*supra* n. 37); cf. Hdt. 1.132; Apollod. 3.15.7.4; παιωνίζειν, Sokolowski, *Lois sacrées de l'Asie Mineure*, no. 24 A.34 (Erythrai); the Paian of Iphigeneia, E. *IA* 1468ff. Flutes play the Καστόρειον μέλος when the Spartans slaughter the σφάγια before battle, *Xen. Lac. Pol.* 13.8, *HG* 4.2.20; Plut. *Lyc.* 22.2.

51. Cf. Meuli, "Griechische Opferbräuche," 246f., 268ff. That the σπλάγχνα were roasted on the altar is shown by the name σπλαγχνόπτης (Plin. *NH* 22.44, 34.81) together with the pictorial tradition (Rizza [*supra* n. 37]). On συσπλαγχνεύειν cf. Ar. *Pax* 1115, Eup. fr. 108 (*CAF* I.286), Ath. 9.410b; σπλάγχνων μετουσία D.H. 1.40.4; D.C. 37.30.3.

52. Cato *Agr.* 50: *ubi daps profanata comestaque erit*; καθαγισάντων δὲ ταῦτα . . . Ath. 149c; on the exception, οὐ φορά, *supra* n. 36.

53. Cf. Deubner, *Attische Feste*, 158ff. I cannot discuss here his somewhat hypercritical treatment of Porph. *Abst.* 2.29f.; Meuli, "Griechische Opferbräuche," 275f.

54. Konrad Lorenz, *Das sogenannte Böse: Zur Naturgeschichte der Aggression* (Vienna: G. Borotha-Schoeler, 1963).

55. See Freud, *Totem und Tabu.* He immediately saw the connection with tragedy, *Gesammelte Schriften*, 10:187f. Alfred Winterstein, *Der Ursprung der Tragödie* (Leipzig: Internationaler Psychoanalytischer Verlag, 1925) was too dependent on Freud on the one hand, on the philologists on the other, to bring progress. On man "aping" beasts of prey, Robert Eisler, *Man into Wolf* (New York: Philosophical Library, 1951). A. E. Jensen, "Über das Töten als kulturgeschichtliche Erscheinung," tries to understand the rites of killing as an expression of a "mythical perception" ("mythische Erkenntnis") of a fundamental law of life: man cannot exist without destroying other living beings for food. In this respect, however, a symbolic way of expression ought to be sufficient, and Jensen is forced to assume that actual bloodshed is a depravation of a more sublime form of religion.

56. Cf. Meuli, "Griechische Opferbräuche," 225f., 250f.

57. ἐπὶ δὲ τῷ τεθυένῳ τόδε μέλος A. *Eu.* 328f., τεθυμένος ἐτύγχανεν Xen. *HG.* 5.1.18.

58. Theophrastus (Porp. *Abst.* 2.27 = fr. 13 Pötscher) already assumed, like some modern anthropologists (Edwin M. Loeb, *The Blood Sacrifice Complex* [*Mem. Anthropol. Assn.* 30, Menasha, WI, 1923]), that sacrifice arose out of cannibalism. Pythagoreans sacrificed animals ἀνθ᾽ ἑαυτῶν Porph. *Abst.* 2.28, cf. *FGrHist* 752 F 1. On Abraham sacrificing Isaac (Gen. 22.13, cf. Lev. 17.11), see Robertson Smith, *Lectures on the Religion of the Semites*, 309ff. Munichia: Zen. Athous 1.8 p. 350 Miller, Eust. p. 331.25 = Paus. *Gr.* ed. Erbse ε 35. Luc. *SyrD.* 58 tells how people sacrificed children in Bambyke, shouting "they are calves"; Athamas kills Learchos "as a deer," Apollod. 3.4.3. The rite described at Ael. *NA* 12.34 explains sufficiently why Palaimon of Tenedos could be called βρεφοκτόνος Lyc. 229. At Salamis (Cyprus), the human sacrifices were replaced by βουθυσία Porph. *Abst.* 2.54, as among the Carthaginians at least temporarily, G. Charles-Picard, *Les religions de l'Afrique antique* (Paris, 1954), 491. Cf. *infra* nn. 59 and 66.

59. D. C. 43.24.4, connected with the *equus-October*-sacrifice by Georg Wissowa, *Religion und Kultus der Römer*, 2nd ed. (Munich: C. H. Beck, 1912), 421 n. 2. Bacchides, general of Antiochus IV, is said to have "sacrificed" prisoners, ἔθυσεν ἰς φρέαρ LXX 1 Macc. 7.19. On the analogies of capital punishment and sacrifice, K. v. Amira, *Die germanischen Todesstrafen* (*AbhMünchen*. 1922).

60. Sallust *Cat.* 22; D. C. 37.30.3.

61. That Dionysus is killed as a goat is a theory advanced esp. by Cook, *Zeus*, and Nilsson, *Opuscula*. Dionysus is called Ἔριφος in Sparta (Hsch. εἰραφιώτης); in myth he was transformed into an ἔριφος (Apollod. 3.4.3); but ἔριφος is not τράγος (*supra* n. 27). The theory of the Eniautos-Daimon was developed by J. Harrison in cooperation with F. M. Cornford and G. Murray, in *Themis*, 2nd ed. (Cambridge: Cambridge University Press, 1927), 331ff., 341ff. It is accepted, with modifications, by Webster (128f.; *BullInstClassStud.* 5 [1958] 43ff.); criticism in Pickard-Cambridge, *Dithyramb, Tragedy and Comedy*, 185ff.; Else, *Origin*, 27f. The oriental texts are interpreted according to the "seasonal pattern" by Theodor Gaster, *Thespis*, 2nd ed. (New York: Anchor Books, 1961). In fact, ἐνιαυτός is rather seldom personified and never called δαίμων (cf. *RE* V [1905], 2568f.); what is more important, the "seasonal" festivals seem to be a secondary interpretation, indeed the most harmless designation of older ritual. The exceptional fires lit in times of emergency ("Notfeuer," Jahn, *Die deutschen Opferbräuche bei Ackerbau und Viehzucht*, 34f.) are more primitive than the annual fires; and the fires as well as the combat rites can take place in any time of the year: the rites are independent of the seasons. Of course man has always

been apt to project his feelings into surrounding nature, and the invention of agriculture and the establishment of an annual calendar of festivals were to stress this interpretation. Still, the main problem for man is not winter, but man.

62. *Uter musti plenus* Euanthius p. 13.10 Wessner; Serv.Auct. *in Georg.* 2.380; Diom. p. 488. Another possibility of mock resurrection would be that one of the participants dresses in the skin of the victim and begins to dance. There is abundant evidence for such customs elsewhere (Meuli, "Griechische Opferbräuche," 242 n. 2), and it would be tempting to see the interrelation goat-satyr in this way, but there is no Greek evidence to support it. Martial explicitly states that the he-goat was castrated in the moment of slaughter, 3.24; in a similar way, the *equus October* had its tail torn off (cf. H. Wagenvoort, *Serta philologica Aenopontana* [Innsbruck, 1962] 273ff.). Whether this rite was always connected with the Dionysiac goat-sacrifice, we do not know.

63. Hdt. 2.39f., 42; Tibullus 1.2.28; cf. Robertson Smith, *Lectures on the Religion of the Semites*, 299ff., 430ff. In Siebenbürgen (Rumania), there was, down to the nineteenth century, a ceremony of pig-slaughter called "pig-memorial" (Schweinegedenkmal: Heinrich von Wlislocki, *Aus dem Volksleben der Magyaren* [Munich: M. Huttler, 1893], 30), in which "sich der jüngste Ehemann auf den Fussboden und zwar auf den Bauch gekehrt und ausgestreckt niederlegt. Er darf kein Glied rühren ... während die Hausfrau auf einem grossen Teller den gesottenen oder gebratenen, mit Tannengezweig und Immergrün umwundenen Schweinskopf ihm auf das Hinterhaupt setzt, worauf die Gesellschaft ihn wild stampfend und jubelnd umtanzt. Fällt der Teller dabei von seinem Haupte, so gibt dem daliegenden Genossen jeder der Gäste einige Hiebe"; cf. Ἰκάριοι τόθι πρῶτα περὶ τράγον ὠρχήσαντο. On the kommos in tragedy, cf. esp. Nilsson, *Opuscula*, 75ff.

64. H. Huchzermeyer, *Aulos und Kithara in der griechischen Musik* (diss., Münster, 1930), 54ff.

65. Meuli, "Griechische Opferbräuche," 228: "Die Jäger des Kreises Turudansk bemalen sich das Gesicht mit Russ, dann kennt sie der Bär nicht." In Württemberg (Germany), pigs are slaughtered on Shrove Tuesday, and mummers break into the house and fetch their share of the freshly killed meat: *Handwörterbuch des deutschen Aberglaubens*, vol. 7 (1935–36), 1083.

66. E. *El.* 785ff., 816, 838. Clytaemestra, too, arrives for sacrifice, 1125; 1132, 1142; afterward Orestes says: κατηρξάμαν (1222); cf. Murray in Harrison, *Themis*, 356. Neoptolemus in Delphi is killed when sacrificing, E. *Andr.* 1112ff.; Pi. *N.* 7.42, *Pae.* 6.116ff. Polyphontes in Euripides, *Kresphontes* is killed on occasion of a sacrifice (Hygin. *Fab.* 137). Cf. the saga of Titus Tatius, D.H. 2.52.3. Perhaps it is no coincidence that the Scholion on Harmodios and Aristogeiton expressly states that their deed occurred Ἀθηναίης ἐν θυσίαις (*Carm.Pop.* 895 Page).

67. Cf. E. *HF* 451 (with Wilamowitz, *ad loc.*): Megara, returning toward the altar that failed to protect her, asks for the ἱερεύς, the σφαγεύς. Herakles himself is to accomplish the sacrifice (922ff.; θῦμα 995), cf. *infra* n. 69. S. *El.* 1422f.: φοινία δὲ χεὶρ στάζει θυηλῆς Ἄρεος ... The metaphorical use of θύειν is found once in Pindar, fr. 78, never in the earlier lyrics; it is common then in Timotheus (*Pers.* 29; cf. fr. 783 Page) and Philoxenus (fr. 823 Page), cf. Schol. A. *in Il.* 9.219. On βακχεύειν see A. *Septem* 498, E. *Hec.* 1077, *HF* 1119, *Or.* 1493. Orestes as *gravis sacerdos*, Accius *Erigone* fr. 55 Ribbeck.

68. This is completely overlooked by Else, who writes (*Origin*, 63): "The regular source of tragic material is heroic epic, not religious cult." Of course the tragic poets drew on the epic, Stesichorus et al., but they saw them through the medium of their experience of Greek religious life, in which a hero was not a purely literary figure. It would lead too far, though it would not be impossible, to investigate the ritual of destruction in the case of Eteocles and Polyneices, of Aias, Antigone, or King Oedipus. It is significant, however, that even those plays of Euripides which seem to foreshadow Menander have as their climax a sacrifice: *Hel.* 1554ff., *Ion* 1124ff. R. Merkelbach

drew my attention to the only surviving drama of the Maya: *Der Mann von Rabinal, oder Der Tod des Gefangenen, Tanzspiel der Maya-Quiché*, trans. and intr. by E. W. Palm (Frankfurt am Main: Suhrkamp, 1961): here the whole play is an ἄρχεσθαι for the human sacrifice that forms its conclusion.

69. On the site of Mount Oeta, Martin P. Nilsson, *Archiv für Religionswissenschaft* 21 (1922): 310ff. = *Opscula*, 348ff.; Yves Béquignon, *La vallée du Spercheios* (Paris: E. de Boccard, 1937), 204ff.; the main testimony: Schol. T. *in Il*. 22.159 καὶ νῦν Οἰταῖοι ῾Ηρακλεῖ πεντετήριον ἀγῶνα ποιοῦντες βύρσας διδόασιν (to the victorious athletes); βύρσα usually is "oxhide" (the passage in Homer has βοείην), which presupposes βουθυσία. On Cape Cenaeum there was an altar of Zeus said to be founded by Herakles, S. *Tr.* 752f., Apollod. 2.7.7.7. On earlier testimonies for the myth, cf. Stylianos G. Kapsomenos, *Sophokles' Trachinierinnen und ihr Vorbild* (Athens, 1963), 1ff. Many vase paintings show Herakles as a θυτήρ, cf. Rizza (*supra* n. 37); sometimes he is represented in a "new garment," not in the lion-skin, holding a cantharus (e.g., Berlin 3232 = *ARV*² 117,2), but the presence of a satyr makes it difficult to find here the event of Cape Cenaeum. In Sophocles, Hyllos is forced to sacrifice his father (1192); the Theban myth presents the reversal of the situation, Herakles burning his sons (Pherecydes, *FGrHist* 3 F 14, Apollod. 2.4.12). Pindar describes the pyre of the corresponding festival, "blazing up to the sky throughout the night" (*I.* 4.67ff.).

70. Cf. sacrificial regulations as γυναικὶ οὐ θέμις, ξένῳ οὐ θέμις *SIG*³ 1024.9,27; Sokolowski, *Lois sacrées des cités grecques*, nos. 63, 66; E. *IT* 1226ff. Pohlenz, *Die griechische Tragödie*, (1:256, 2:105) failed to understand the ritual language of Medea 1053ff.; cf. the commentary of D. L. Page (Oxford, 1938), *ad loc.*, who, however, thinks the words to be "simply a macabre metaphor." The three vase paintings (Paris Cab.d.Méd. 876; Louvre K 300; Munich 3296; see Frank Brommer, *Vasenlisten zur griechischen Heldensage*, 2nd ed. [Marburg: N.G. Elwert, 1960], 349) are reproduced in Louis Séchan, *Etudes sur la tragédie grecque dans ses rapports avec la céramique* (Paris: Champion, 1926), 403f. and pl. 8.

71. On the Corinthian rite see Martin P. Nilsson, *Griechische Feste von religiöser Bedeutung* (Leipzig: B. G. Teubner, 1906), 58, who, however, does not quote the most important sources: Phot. ed. Reitzenstein, *s.v.* αἴγος τρόπον, Zen.Athous 2.30 p. 361.12ff. Miller (abridged in *App.Prov.* 4.16; by mistake, Zenobius and *Appendix Proverbiorum* have οἴς instead of αἴξ); Markellos in Eus. *Adv.Marc.* 1.3 (ed. Klostermann [Berlin, 1906] fr. 125). Markellos says: φασὶν γὰρ Μήδειαν ἐν Κορίνθῳ τὰ τέκνα ἀποκτείνασαν κατακρύψαι τὴν μάχαιραν αὐτόθι· τοὺς δὲ Κορινθίους κατὰ χρησμὸν αὐτοῖς δοθέντα αἴγα μέλαιναν ἐναγίζοντας ἀπορεῖν μαχαίρας· τὴν δὲ αἴγα σκάλλουσαν τῷ ποδὶ τὴν Μηδείας ἀνευρεῖν μάχαιραν. Zenobios has substantially the same, but is more explicit on the rite: ... οἱ δὲ Κορίνθιοι θύοντες ἀνὰ πᾶν ἔτος διὰ ζ᾽ ἠιθέων καὶ παρθένων ὡσαύτως ζ᾽ κρύπτουσι τὸ ξίφος ἐν τῷ ἱερῷ· τοῦ δὲ ἔτους περιελθόντος οἱ κληρωθέντες νέοι θύουσιν, ἡ δὲ οἷς ... ἀνιχνεύει τὸ ξίφος. The "comedy of innocence" is particularly apparent in Photios: οἱ τὴν παροχὴν μεμισθωμένοι γῇ κρύψαντες τὴν μάχαιραν ἐσκήπτοντο ἐπιλελῆσθαι.... (= Paus. *Gr.* ed. Erbse η 2) ... μετὰ τὸ ἐναγίσαι τὴν μάχαιραν ἀποκρύπτουσι, τῷ δὲ ἑξῆς ἔτει τὸ μέλλον πάλιν ἐναγίζεσθαι ἱερεῖον ... (= Paus. *Gr.* ed. Erbse α 42; cf. Zen. *Par.* 1.27, Hsch. *s.v.* αἴξ αἴγα, Suda αι 235 etc.). It is not quite clear whether the knife was left in the soil for the whole year or removed and rehidden in secret, but this does not make any difference for the meaning of the rite. The fate of the goat was proverbial, Com. adesp. fr. 47 Demianczuk, Klearchos fr. 83a Wehrli; the anecdote was even transmitted to Arabs and Indians, S. Fraenkel, *ZDMG* 46 (1892): 737ff.; R. Pischel, *ZDMG* 47 (1893): 86ff. Besides the paroemiographers, the main testimony on the Corinthian rite is Parmeniskos in Schol. *in* E. *Med* 264; black garments: Paus. 2.3.7. That Medea, though inadvertently, killed her own children in the temple of Hera Akraia was already in Eumelos (Paus. 2.3.11); as it seemed strange that the Corinthians should atone for Medea's crime, the myth was altered to make the Corinthians the

murderers of the children. On the connection with initiation rites, A. Brelich, *Studi e materiali di storia delle religioni* 30 (1959): 227ff. Cf. also G. Dobesch, *Wst.* 75 (1962): 83–89.

72. On θῦμα λεύσιμον see E. Fraenkel (Oxford, 1950), *ad loc.*; but he does not quote the decisive parallel from sacrificial ritual, the sacrifice to Dionysus in Tenedus, Ael. *NA* 12.34: ὅ γε μὴν πατάξας αὐτὸ (the calf) τῷ τελέκει λίθοις βάλλεται τῇ ὁσίᾳ καὶ ἔστε ἐπὶ τὴν θάλατταν φεύγει. Cf. the *aition* for the bull-sacrifice in Lindos, Philostr. *Im.* 2.24; the rite of mummification, D.S. 1.91; *infra* n. 74.

73. Aeschylus associates the net with fishing, 1382, 1432, but ἄγρευμα θηρός *Ch.* 998; the crater Boston 63.1246 (E. Vermeule *AJA* 70 [1966]: 1ff., pl. 1–3) depicts it as a kind of Coan garment. On Aesch. *Ag.* 1127 cf. Fraenkel's discussion.

74. On the cults performed in the Heraion, see Charles Waldstein, *The Argive Heraeum*, vol. 1 (Boston: Houghton Mifflin, 1902), 1ff.; Nilsson, *Griechische Feste*, 42ff. The myths were told at least in four different ways already in the old epics—Danais, Phoronis, Aigimios, Hesiodean Catalogues; cf. Eduard Meyer, *Forschungen zur alten Geschichte*, vol. 1 (Halle: M. Niemeyer, 1892), 67ff. The connection with Egypt may, however, be much older than Meyer argued, cf. Astour, *Hellenosemitica*, 80ff., and T. T. Duke *CJ* 61 (1965): 134. "Euboia," Paus. 2.17.1; sacred cowherds, Schol. *in* Pi. *N.* pp. 3f. Drachmann; Argos and Io in the sanctuary, Apollod. 2.1.3; Zeus transformed into a bull, A. *Supp.* 301; Epaphos = Apis, Hdt. 2.153, Meyer, *Forschungen zur alten Geschichte*, 78; = Apopi "Bull," Duke (*supra*); Argos clad in oxskin, Apollod. 2.1.2, Schol. *in* E. *Ph.* 1116, vase paintings, e.g., *ABV* 148,2 = Cook, *Zeus*, 3:632, *ARV²* 579,84 = Cook, *Zeus*, 3:633, *ARV²* 1409,9 = Cook, *Zeus*, 1:460. Genealogists contrasted Argos the king to Argos Panoptes, though they differed considerably as to the relationship of the two Argoi (Hes. in Apollod. 2.1.3.3; Pherekydes, *FGrHist* 3 F 66/67 with Jacoby's commentary). Argos the king clearly is the secondary figure (cf. Meyer, *Forschungen zur alten Geschichte*, 90). The cult devoted to Argos (Varro in Aug. *Civ.* 18.6) must therefore originally have dealt with the Panoptes. Ζεὺς πανόπτης A. *Eu.* 1045, cf. Preller and Robert, *Griechische Mythologie*, 396 n. 1. Meyer thought there was no answer to the question "wie soll man es erklären, dass er (Argos), also ursprünglich Zeus, von Hermes erschlagen wird?" (*supra* 72 n. 1). On the death of the aboriginal king, cf. *Historia* 11 (1962): 365ff. Hermes is called βουφόνος *Hymn.Merc.* 436. The symbolic lapidation of Hermes for slaying Argos: Xanthos, *FGrHist* 765 F 29, Antikleides, *FGrHist* 140 F 19, Eust. p. 1809.38ff. Varro (Aug. *Civ.* 18.6, from *De gente populi Romani*; Varro, *RR* 2.5.4) mentions an Argive hero "Homogyros" (changed to "bomagiros" by Wilamowitz in the edition of Varro, *RR* by G. Goetz [Leipzig, 1912], but he overlooked the parallel passage in Augustine), equivalent to the Athenian Buzyges, slain by the thunderbolt. Could his name mean "he who leads the bull round the altar" (cf. *supra*, nn. 37 and 44) in an Argive Buphonia-ritual?

Scapegoat Rituals
in Ancient Greece

Jan Bremmer

1. Problem

In the Old Testament a curious purification ritual occurs of which the final ceremony is described as follows: "And Aaron shall lay both his hands upon the head of the live goat and confess over him all the iniquities of the children of Israel, and all their transgressions in all their sins, putting them upon the head of the goat, and shall send him away by the hand of a fit man into the wilderness: And the goat shall bear upon him all their iniquities unto a land not inhabited: and he shall let go the goat in the wilderness" (*Leviticus* 16, 21f.). It is this ceremony which has given its name to a certain ritual complex: the (e)scapegoat ritual.[1] Similar rituals can be found among the Greeks,[2] Romans,[3] Hittites (§ 3), in India,[4] and even in mountainous Tibet (§ 7). In our study we will restrict ourselves to an analysis of the Greek rituals, although we will not leave the others completely out of consideration.

The Greek scapegoat rituals have often been discussed. The so-called Cambridge school in particular, with its lively and morbid interest in everything strange and cruel, paid much attention to it.[5] Our own time too has

First published in *Harvard Studies in Classical Philology* 87 (1983).

become fascinated once again by these enigmatic rituals: I only need mention here René Girard's *Violence and the Sacred*, which has already reached a fourth printing in two years.[6] Gradually, too, the meaning of these rituals is becoming clearer. Where earlier generations, still influenced by Mannhardt, often detected traces of a fertility ritual in the scapegoat complex, Burkert has rightly pointed out that in these rituals the community sacrifices one of its members to save its own skin.[7] Although the general meaning is clear, many details are still in need of clarification. For that reason I shall analyze the ritual complex in a more detailed way, paying special attention to its structure. First, however, I shall present a general survey of the evidence.

2. Evidence

Our fullest evidence comes from the sixth-century poet Hipponax of Kolophon (fr. 5–11 West), who wishes that his enemies be treated as *pharmakoi* or "scapegoats." This evidently implies that they will be fed with figs, barley cake, and cheese. Then, in inclement weather, they will be hit on the genitals with the squill and with twigs of the wild fig tree and other wild plants.[8] Tzetzes (*Chil.* 5. 737–39), our source for the fragments of Hipponax, adds that the *pharmakós* was finally burned on "wild" wood and his ashes strewn into the sea. However, despite this detailed description Hipponax's information should be used with the utmost care. Invective played an important role in ancient poetry and it is typical of this kind of poetry to disregard the conventions of real life by exaggerating the point the poet wants to make.[9] Thus the mention of inclement weather already shows that Hipponax is not describing the real ritual, since the Thargelia took place in early summer, but conjures up a fate even worse than that experienced at the actual scapegoat ritual.[10] Neither does it seem very probable that the scapegoat was hit on the genitals, since this is not mentioned in our sources for any of the other comparable ceremonies. This too looks much like a product of Hipponax's malicious imagination, even though the scapegoat will have been expelled with the squill and twigs of the wild fig tree, just as the slave in Chaeronea (see below) was chased out with twigs of the agnus castus.

As regards Athens, our sources are divided. One group states that in exceptional times, such as a drought or a famine, certain ugly people were selected and sacrificed.[11] Another group states that at the Thargelia, a festival for Apollo, a man with white figs around his neck was expelled from the city as a purification for the men, and another man with black figs for the women.[12] In Abdera, a poor man was feasted once, led around the walls of the city and finally chased over the borders with stones.[13] In Massilia another poor devil offered himself during a plague. He was feasted for a year and then cast out of the city.[14] In Leukas a criminal was cast off a rock into the sea for the sake of averting evil during a festival of Apollo.[15] Another notice reports that every year a young man was cast into the sea with the words "be thou our off-scouring." [16]

From this survey it appears that the ritual was performed during the Thargelia, a festival peculiar to the Ionians, in normal times, but evidently also during extraordinary circumstances such as plague, famine, and drought (events which can of course hardly be separated).[17] With these rituals scholars usually connect a notice of Plutarch that in his home town of Chaeronea every year a ceremony was performed in which *Boúlimos*, or "Famine," represented by a slave, was chased out of the city with rods of the agnus castus, a willow-like plant.[18] Finally, it is related in the romance of Iamboulos (Diod. Sic. 2.55) that the Aethiopians, in order to purify themselves, put two men into boats and sent them away over the sea, never to return again.

With these rituals in which the elimination of one or two members saves the whole of the community we may compare those stories in which the death of one or two people saves the city from destruction. This is a motif which we frequently find in ancient Greece. During a war of Thebes with Orchomenos two girls sacrificed themselves, as an oracle required, in order that Thebes should win the war (Paus. 9.17.1). When a plague had struck Orchomenos the daughters of Orion sacrificed themselves in order to stop the plague.[19] When Eumolpos threatened to conquer Athens, the daughters of Erechtheus sacrificed themselves.[20] Just as noble was the behavior of the daughters of Leōs when Athens was struck by a plague or a famine.[21] However, not only girls sacrificed themselves. When Zeus Idaios caused a cleft in the earth, Anchuros, the son of the king, rode into it and, subsequently, the cleft closed up.[22] Even more interesting is the case of the Athenian king Kodros, which will be discussed below (§ 3).[23] The close connection of these mythical tales with the historical rituals appears also from the fact that on the island of Naxos the girl Polykrite was honored with sacrifices during the

Thargelia festival, because, as was told, she had died after saving the city from destruction.[24]

3. Scapegoats

After this general survey of the evidence I will now proceed to a more detailed discussion, starting with the scapegoats themselves. Who was chosen as a scapegoat, and why these particular people? Some victims were clearly lower class, the poor devils of Abdera and Massilia, for instance, and the *Boúlimos* in Chaeronea who was represented by a slave. The Athenian *pharmakoí*, too, are described as "of low origin and useless" (Schol. Ar. *Eq.* 1136) and "common and maltreated by nature" (Schol. Ar. *Ra.* 733). The Leucadians even went so far as to choose a criminal. According to Tzetzes, too, the ugliest person was selected.[25] But in the fictional romance of Iamboulos the scapegoats are strangers, and in the aetiological myth of the Athenian Thargelia they are young men.[26] Finally, we encounter young women and a king.

Now the question naturally arises whether these categories—criminals, slaves, ugly persons, strangers, young men and women, and a king—have something in common (however *bien étonnés de se trouver ensemble!*). Or, to put this question in different terms: do these different *signifiers* perhaps possess the same *signified*? It seems to me that we can give an affirmative answer to this question, since all these categories have in common that they are situated at the margin of Greek society. For the first categories this is obvious enough. Criminals put themselves outside the community, and strangers naturally do not belong to it.[27] Slaves, poor and ugly persons did not count in ancient Greece. As for young men and women, it has recently been shown that their place was not inside but at the margin of society.[28] The king distinguished himself from the rest of the population in that he alone could claim contact with the divine. *Diotrephés*, or "raised by Zeus," is a stock epithet of kings in Homer.[29] Where criminals are marginals at the bottom of society, the king is the lonely marginal at the top.[30] The myth shows, however, that high and low are interchangeable: the Athenian king Kodros who saved the Athenian community by his death was killed dressed up as a woodworker.[31]

When we now survey our material, we are struck by a curious dichotomy. On the one hand we find the poor, the ugly, and criminals, who only occur in the historical rites. This must have been such a recurrent feature of the scapegoat rituals that the words used to denote the scapegoat—*pharmakós*,[32] kátharma,[33] *perikátharma*,[34] *perípsema*[35]—soon became terms of abuse.[36] On the other hand there are the attractive, aristocratic, and royal figures, who are found only in the mythical and unhistorical tales.[37]

We can explain this dichotomy as follows. When a catastrophe can be averted from the community by the death of one of its members, such a member must naturally be a very valuable one. This is continually stressed in the mythical tales. The oracle, for example, asks for the death either of the person with the most famous ancestors (Paus. 9.17.1), or of the daughters of the king, as in the case of Leōs (Ael. *VH.* 12.28) and Erechtheus (Lyc. *Leoc.* 98f.), or for the most precious possession, as in the case of Anchuros. In other cases the beauty of the scapegoat is stressed. The youth who sacrificed himself in Athens is described by the aetiological myth as a "handsome lad,"[38] and Polykrite, the name of the girl who saved Naxos, means "she who has been chosen by many."[39]

In real life, during the annual scapegoat ritual, there was of course little chance that the king (if any) would sacrifice himself or his children. Here, society chose one of its marginals. Nevertheless the people realized that they could not save their own skin by sacrificing the scum of the polis. For that reason the scapegoat was always treated as a very important person. In Massilia he was kept by the state—a treatment usually reserved for very important people—for one year and then chased from the city, dressed in holy clothes.[40] In Abdera (Call. fr. 90 Pf.) he was treated to an excellent dinner before being chased away. In Athens (Schol. Ar. *Eq.* 1136), too, he was kept by the state, and in the end led out of the city in fine clothes (Suid. *kátharma*).

In Kolophon the *pharmakós* received in his hand figs, barley cake, and cheese.[41] Hipponax mocks the simplicity of the food, but the ritual is older than his time, and we find a striking parallel in a Hittite scapegoat ritual, which we quote in full:

> When evening comes, whoever the army commanders are, each of them
> prepares a ram—whether it is a white ram or a black ram does not matter
> at all. Then I twine a cord of white wool, red wool, and green wool, and the
> officer twists it together, and I bring a necklace, a ring, and a chalcedony
> stone and I hang them on the ram's neck and horns, and at night they tie

them in front of the tents and say: "Whatever deity is prowling about (?),
whatever deity has caused this pestilence, now I have tied up these rams for
you, be appeased!" And in the morning I drive them out to the plain, and
with each ram they take 1 jug of beer, 1 loaf, and 1 cup of milk (?). Then
in front of the king's tent he makes a finely dressed woman sit and puts
with her a jar of beer and 3 loaves. Then the officers lay their hands on the
rams and say: "Whatever deity has caused this pestilence, now see! These
rams are standing here and they are very fat in liver, heart, and loins. Let
human flesh be hateful to him, let him be appeased by these rams." And
the officers point at the rams and the king points at the decorated woman,
and the rams and the woman carry the loaves and the beer through the
army and they chase them out to the plain. And they go running on to the
enemy's frontier without coming to any place of ours, and the people say:
"Look! Whatever illness there was among men, oxen, sheep, horses, mules,
and donkeys in this camp, these rams and this woman have carried it away
from the camp. And the country that finds them shall take over this evil
pestilence."[42]

In this ritual the scapegoats evidently also receive food which we would
not term particularly exquisite; nevertheless it is clearly considered as something special. In this prescription of a certain Ashkella we are also struck by
the adornment of the scapegoats. This must have been a recurrent feature
of the Hittite scapegoats, since in the prescription of Uhhamuwa a *crowned*
ram has to be sent away, and in the one of Pulisa the god has to be content
with a "lusty, decorated bull with earring."[43] We find a similar adornment
in Israel where a crimson thread was bound around the horns of the goat,
the least valuable of the domestic animals.[44] In all these cases a woman or a
cheap or relatively superfluous animal—for the continuation of the herds
only few male animals need be kept from the many that are born—is sent
away after being made more attractive than it originally was. This structural
similarity with our Greek material is a welcome corroboration of our interpretation.

Summing up, we conclude that in historical reality the community sacrificed the least valuable members of the polis, who were represented, however,
as very valuable persons. In the mythical tales one could pass this stage and
in the myths we always find beautiful or important persons, although even

then these scapegoats remain marginal figures: young men and women, and a king.

4. Voluntariness

According to Petronius (fr. 1) the scapegoat offered himself spontaneously in Massilia. Such behavior is the rule in our mythical examples, where the victims always sacrifice themselves voluntarily.[45] Thus Origen (*c. Cels.* 1.31) can compare these mythical examples with Jesus:[46]

> They [the apostles] not only dared to show to the Jews from the words of the prophets that he was the prophesied one, but also to the other people that he, who had been recently crucified, voluntarily died for mankind, like those who died for their fatherland, to avert plague epidemics, famines, and shipwreck.[47]

However, according to another source the scapegoat in Massilia was lured by "rewards,"[48] and in Abdera (Call. fr. 90 Pf.) he had to be bought for money. These reports must surely be nearer the historical truth; yet the mythical tales, as so often, give a valuable insight into Greek sacrificial ideology. In Greece, as Karl Meuli has brilliantly demonstrated, sacrifice had to be conducted on a basis of voluntariness.[49] People pretended the victim went up to the altar of its own accord, and even asked for its consent. Whenever the animal did not shake its head in agreement, wine or milk was poured over its head. When, subsequently, the animal tried to shake this off its head, this was interpreted as a sign of its consent! In myth or legend such a trick was not necessary and it was often said that animals went up to the altar voluntarily. Sometimes it was pretended that the animal had committed a crime, but in that case its death was its own fault! We meet this line of reasoning in the aition of a scapegoat ritual in an unknown Ionian city. Here it was related that a man, whose very name was Pharmakos, was stoned (§ 6) by the companions of Achilles for stealing holy cups belonging to Apollo.[50] We find a similar line of reasoning in the legend of Aesopus who is pictured as a *pharmakós* and who is thrown over a cliff (cf. the case of Leukas in § 2) after having been accused of stealing a golden cup.[51]

5. Plants

According to Tzetzes (*Chil.* 5.736f.) the *pharmakós* was whipped with squills, twigs of the wild fig tree, and other wild plants, and finally burned on a fire made of "wild" wood. Why this insistence on wild plants, and what is the connection between these wild plants, on the one hand, and, on the other hand, the squill and the agnus castus, which was used in the Chaeronean ritual? For the discussion of this problem we will take our point of departure in Rome, where the point we want to make is rather more obvious.

In Rome a distinction was made between the fruit-bearing tree, *arbor felix*, and the unproductive one, *arbor infelix*. The latter category comprised not only the unproductive trees—although they constituted its main part— but also those trees which were thorny, had black fruit, or blood red twigs.[52] It was on an *arbor infelix* that the traitor was hung and scourged to death; monstrosities and prodigies were burned on its wood.[53] The idea seems clear.[54] Trees useful for the community could not be used for persons and animals which had situated themselves outside the community. For the modern city dweller such a distinction has probably lost most of its significance, but in the Middle Ages it was still of great importance, since the unproductive trees, called *mort-bois*, were free to be taken away from the woods.[55]

We meet the same idea in Greece. Monstrosities like the snakes who had tried to strangle Heracles were burnt on "wild" wood.[56] Theocritus (24.89f.) mentions that the wood had to be of thorny material which in Rome too was considered as an *arbor infelix*, and even in the Middle Ages was thought to be *mort-bois*.[57] Whenever one of the Locrian Maidens—girls who lived in a state of marginality—died, she had to be burned on "wild" wood.[58] A connection between death and a wild tree also seems to follow from a fragment of Euripides' *Sciron* (fr. 679 N²) where there is a reference to impaling on the branches of the wild fig tree. Unfortunately, we do not know for whom this unpleasant treatment was meant. It will now hardly be surprising that the *pharmakós* too was reported to have been burnt on "wild" wood. Ancient Greece evidently made the same connection as ancient Rome between wild trees and persons who had to be removed from the community.

Hipponax tells us that the *pharmakós* was hit on the genitals with the squill.[59] Even though this particular anatomical target seems unlikely (§ 2), the hitting of the body with squills does not seem improbable, since the

Arcadians, when returning home from an unsuccessful hunt, used squills to whip the statue of Pan, the god closely associated with the hunt.[60] It seems that the squill was chosen because this plant too was an unproductive one. The status of the squill was very low, as appears from the words of Theognis (537f.) to the effect that a free child will never be born from a slave, just as neither a rose nor a hyacinth will be born from a squill. The plant had the effect of a stinging nettle,[61] and Artemidorus (3.50) informs us that the plant was inedible, as is also illustrated by an anecdote from the life of the Palestinian monk Kyriakos (Cyr. Alex. *Kyr.* 227). When Kyriakos had withdrawn into the desert and one day could not find his customary food, the roots of wild plants, he prayed to God to make the squill edible, because, as he argued, God can turn bitterness into sweetness. The Suda (s.v. *skilla*) even calls the plant "death-bringing." Now, when we see that in Rome the parricide was whipped with the red twigs of the cornel tree, an *arbor infelix*, the conclusion seems evident.[62] Not only for the execution of criminals but also for whipping them wood was chosen which belonged to the category of the unproductive trees.

The squill was also used for fighting. We know that in Sicily and Priene the ephebes fought with squills.[63] This probably meant that they pelted each other with the bulbs, although a fight with the leaves cannot be excluded. The connection of the ephebes with the squill will hardly be fortuitous. Just like the *pharmakós* the ephebes too are marginal persons (§ 3).

The distinction between fruit-bearing and unproductive trees also helps throw light on the chasing away of Famine with rods of agnus castus in Chaeronea. The willow is already called "fruit-destroying" by Homer (*Od.* 15.510) because the willow was thought to lose its fruit before ripening. During the Thesmophoria the Athenian women slept on twigs of the lygos or agnus castus—a tree usually identified with the lygos—because the plant was thought to promote infertility.[64] Pliny, too, mentions the plant as a means to induce infertility.[65] For the early Christian writers the tree has even become the symbol of chastity.[66]

This *arbor infelix* aspect of the lygos will help us understand its role in some other Greek myths and rituals. In Sparta Artemis was worshiped under the epithet Lygodesma, or "willow-bound," because her statue was reputed to have been found in a thicket of willows, and a willow supported her statue (Paus. 3.16.11). The statue was a dangerous one, as appears from the fact that

Astrabakos and Alopekos became crazy when they found it (Paus. 3.16.9). In Samos Hera was said to have been born near a lygos tree in her Heraion (Paus. 7.4.4).[67] The local historian Menedotus (*FGrH* 541 F 1) even tells a complete aition of Hera's connection with the lygos tree. From this tale it appears that her statue was fastened onto a mat made of willow. The lygos also occurs in mythical tales. In the story of Dionysos' kidnapping by pirates the god is bound with twigs of the lygos (*h. Bacch.* 7), as was Hermes by Apollo (*h. Merc.* 410).[68]

All these gods—Artemis, Hera, Dionysos, and Hermes—have in common that myths and rituals of reversal play a role in their cults. The late Karl Meuli, to whom we owe a first analysis of this aspect of these gods, even called them "die gefesselten Götter," because their statues were often fettered and sometimes only untied once a year.[69] A connection of precisely these gods with an *arbor infelix* like the lygos seems therefore completely understandable.

We are, however, not yet finished with the lygos. It was a plant from which wreaths were made. What kind of people wore such wreaths? From our analysis so far we may expect that a lygos wreath was worn by marginal people. This is indeed what we find. In the cult of Hera of Samos it was the Carians, that is to say non-Greeks, who had to wear a lygos wreath (Menedotus, *loc. cit.*).

According to myth, Prometheus, too, had to wear a lygos wreath, and Prometheus was a kind of culture hero, a being always situated at the margin of society.[70] Our last example is less clear. We have a fragment of Anacreon which says: "the friendly Megistes has already been wearing a lygos wreath for ten months and is drinking honeysweet new wine." Unfortunately, this is all the fragment says, but it seems to us that Gow and Page rightly conclude that Anacreon describes the behavior of Megistes as being odd.[71] Given this dubious status of the lygos it can hardly be chance that the inhabitants of Magnesia reserved a spot for their cow dung in a place full of willows.[72]

Finally, our classification of the lygos as an *arbor infelix* does not mean that the tree should be considered a useless one. On the contrary, we know that the tree was used for all kinds of basketry. It does mean that the early Greeks in their struggle for survival distinguished primarily between fruit-bearing trees and unproductive ones.

However, we have not yet discussed all the relevant plants. In Athens the *pharmakoi* were led out of the city, one man with black figs around his neck, the other with white ones. Burkert has rightly pointed to the "marginal" quality of the fig.[73] The fruit has obscene connotations and is in opposition to the fruits of cereal agriculture. We find this symbolic quality again in the rites involving Athenian girls. Aristophanes in his *Lysistrata* (641–45) describes their "career" as follows:

> At the age of seven I immediately became an *arrephóros*.
> Then, at ten, I was an *aletrís* for the presiding goddess;
> then I was a bear at the Brauronia with the saffron-robe;
> and, being a beautiful girl, I carried the basket with a necklace of dried
>   figs.[74]

We do not have many details about this necklace or about the girls who carried the basket (*kanephóroi*), but a fragment of the Athenian comedian Hermippos (fr. 26 Kock) speaks of "*kanephóroi* covered with white flour."[75] This white flour cannot be separated from the mythical tales of young girls covered with scurvy, as Burkert has demonstrated.[76] Where myth spoke of a real illness, ritual characteristically (§ 7) required only white flour. We infer from this fragment that the carrying of a basket was a duty for girls in a state of marginality and the figs will have signified this state, as the squills did in the case of the ephebes.

The reader may, however, object that the fig tree is a useful and fruit-bearing tree. This is certainly true, and I would therefore add to Burkert's explanation that the black fig came from a *wild* fig tree (Theophr. *HP.* 2.2.8; Plin. *NH.* 17.256), as did the white one (Athenaeus 3.76 cde). This means that these fruits, too, fit into the pattern we have explored: marginal persons are connected with marginal plants.

6. Leaving the City

The elimination of a citizen from the polis was a serious matter. How exactly did it happen? The Greek scholar Keramopoullos has persuasively argued that the *pharmakós* was led out of the city in a procession.[77] In Chaeronea this procession started from the public hearth, as Plutarch (*M.* 693 e) informs us. This hearth was situated in the prytaneion, the Greek town hall. Since people who were kept by the state, as happened with the scapegoats in Athens and Massilia, were also entertained in the prytaneion,[78] the conclusion seems reasonable that normally the procession started from the prytaneion. Elimination from the community started from the heart of that community.

While the procession left the city, flutes played a special melody which was called the "melody of the wild fig."[79] We do not know anything more about that melody, but the analogy with folk music does perhaps suggest something about the nature of the music. It has recently been pointed out that music in traditional rites can be divided into harmonious and unharmonious.[80] The latter kind of music was played especially during the removal of persons from the community, as in the case of a charivari. Now Hipponax (fr. 153 West) tells us that his fellow poet Mimnermus (T 5 Gentili/Prato) played this melody. Given the malicious nature of Hipponax he will hardly have meant this as a compliment. It seems therefore not unreasonable to assume that in this case too the music will not have been particularly harmonious.

Plutarch (M. 518b) tells us that cities had special gates for those condemned to death, and for purgations and purificatory offerings. Similarly, the public prison in Athens had a special gate, the gate of Charon, for those condemned to death.[81] The scapegoats, too, will have left the city by a special gate, since at least for Abdera we hear of such a gate, the Prauridian gate (Call. fr. 90 Pf.).

After the passage through the special gate the scapegoat was led around the city in a procession. This is certain for Massilia and Abdera, and probable for Athens. The Cynic Diogenes too alluded to this custom. He was supposed to have said during a visit to the Isthmian games: "One should lead around those potbellies (the athletes!) and purify (the place) all around, and then chase them over the border" (Dio Chr. 8.14). Deubner denied the circumambulation and thought that the procession only touched upon as many points as possible within the city.[82] However, he had overlooked the text from Dio and, moreover, the two types of procession—going around and staying within the city—are not mutually exclusive, since both rites were performed during medieval and more recent plague epidemics.[83] A circumambulation is a ritual which can be performed in different contexts: apotropaic, cathartic, and as rite of aggregation.[84] In the scapegoat ritual the cathartic aspect was most prominent, since the ritual was called *perikathaírein*, or "to purify around," and the scapegoat *perikátharma*.

Finally, the *pharmakós* was chased over the border. In Athens and Massilia this happened by means of pelting with stones, and the aetiological myth of the killing of Pharmakos and the story of Polykrite also presuppose a stoning. In a most interesting discussion of this horrific ritual D. Fehling has pointed out that stoning was not always meant to kill; it was often only a kind of *Imponier* behavior.[85] Whether this was the case with the scapegoat we will discuss in our next section.

It was typical of stoning that everybody present took part in it, and Fehling has suggested that this participation of all people involved was necessary, because those who kept themselves aloof could still think of the expelled person as one of the group; such a thought could become responsible for heavy conflicts within the community.[86] This suggestion is highly persuasive, but there is another aspect too to be considered. The involvement of all persons in the expulsion of one member of the group helps reconstitute that group, and this fits in well with the general meaning of the Thargelia festival.

After chasing the scapegoats over the border people probably returned without looking back, as was the rule in the case of purificatory offerings.[87] A prohibition on looking back is typical for the moment of separation: as with the wife of Lot from Sodom, and in modern Greek folklore the bride when leaving the parental home.[88] The person who is looking back still has a tie with what is lying behind him; the prohibition therefore is a radical cut with all connections with the past. It is, to use the terminology of Van Gennep, a typical rite of separation. By not looking back the citizens definitely cut through all connections with the scapegoat.

7. Death?

The final fate of the *pharmakós* has, understandably, fascinated (and divided) scholarly opinion. According to some they were killed, according to others not, and Nilsson even stated that this was a matter of indifference, since in both cases the goal—the expulsion from the community—was reached. This is of course true, but does not solve the problem. We will therefore once again look at the evidence in a systematic way.

We start with Abdera. Till 1934 it was commonly believed that in this city the scapegoat was stoned to death, since this was reported by our only source, Ovid (*Ibis* 467f. and scholion *ad loc.*). In 1934, however, a papyrus with a fragment of Callimachus (fr. 90 Pf.) was published, which stated unequivocally that the scapegoat was chased over the border with stones but certainly not killed.

We meet a similar discrepancy in Massilia where the scapegoat was expelled from the city according to Petronius (fr. 1),[89] but according to later scholia (on Statius *Theb.* 10.793) was stoned to death. In Leukas the criminal was, it is true, thrown from a rock, but birds and feathers were fastened to him to soften his fall and in the sea boats were waiting for him to pick him up and transport him over the border. The other source which reports the hurling from a rock speaks of a sacrifice. In Athens the scapegoats were expelled over the border in historical times, but in the aetiological myth the scapegoat was killed. Finally, the scapegoats in the romance of Iamboulos were put into boats, of which it is explicitly said that they were seaworthy (Diod. Sic. 2.55.3).

When we discount the death of the scapegoats in the myths, since it is now generally accepted that the myths are not always an exact reflection of the ritual, we are left with two cases. In Philostratus' *Life of Apollonius of Tyana* (4.10) it is described how during a plague in Ephesus Apollonius pointed to a squalid beggar and ordered him to be killed, since he was an enemy of the gods. Burkert considers the possibility of a historical background for this tale, and Apollonius is indeed often connected with plague epidemics;[90] yet the passage looks rather novelistic.[91] The eyes of the beggar are full of fire and after his death his body has disappeared. In its place a dog is found as big as the biggest lion. Although this story follows the scapegoat pattern—this is clear and has often been recognized—the event can hardly be considered historical.

The only case left to be discussed is the death of the scapegoat in Hipponax. This death has been much debated, even though our evidence points to a clear solution. Wherever we have a good picture of the historical events, as in Abdera, Athens, Leukas, and Massilia, it appears certain that the scapegoat was not killed but expelled. But in the aetiological and later versions the scapegoat was often killed. When we confront this conclusion with Hipponax, our inference can hardly be otherwise than that Hipponax also has derived his description of the end of the scapegoat from an aetiological myth or a legendary version, if it is not his own invention—a possibility which is not at all improbable. An alternative solution, however, is also not completely improbable. The burning of the scapegoat on "wild" wood, which is not mentioned in any of the Hipponax fragments, may also be Tzetzes' own invention.[92] Should this be the case, the burning probably derived from the ritual of the Locrian maidens, since a description of this ritual immediately follows the one of the *pharmakós* (Chil. 5.738ff.). But whichever solution we choose, in either case our conclusion must be that the *pharmakós* stayed alive.

The Greeks then expelled a living scapegoat as did, e.g., the Hittites. For this expulsion we also have a hitherto neglected parallel from Tibet which shows a striking resemblance with the Greek ritual—the occasion of the performance around New Year, the selection of a lower-class person who is treated as very special,[93] the unharmonious music, the stoning—as appears from the following description:

> At Gyanese, the person selected to act as the scapegoat is fed and clothed at State expense for a year previous to the ceremony. On the appointed day (just before New Year) with a bloody sheepskin bound round his head, yak's entrails hung round his neck, but otherwise naked, he takes his position in the local Jong, or Fort. In his right hand he carries a fresh sheep's liver, his left being empty. After blasts from long trumpets, beating of drums, clashing of cymbals, and incantations by the officiating lamas, the scapegoat scratches the ground with a stick, to indicate that the season of ploughing and sowing is at hand, flings the sheep's liver among the crowd, and rushes down the hill on to the plain below. The people fling after him stones and dirt, taking, however, great care not to wound him severely, or prevent him from reaching the open country. Should the scapegoat not succeed in making good his escape, the devils would remain in the place. Shots from the prong guns fired into the air increase the pandemonium that accompanies his flight, in the midst, once he has reached the plain, the lamas perform a solemn dance of triumph, concluding by burning *torma* offerings.[94]

If, however, the scapegoat was only expelled in historical reality—why do the mythical tales often speak of a killing? In our analysis we have repeatedly shown that the myth clarified the meaning of the ritual. Symbolic acts in the ritual became reality in the myth.[95] This will also have been the case with the scapegoats. The expulsion of the scapegoats in practice amounted to a killing, since, like the dead, they disappeared from the community, never to return. In a way, therefore, Nilsson was right in considering death and expulsion as having the same effect. However, we may wonder whether the historical scapegoats will have shared his academic indifference as regards choosing between these two modes!

8. Thargelia

We will finally consider the place of the scapegoat ritual in the Greek religious calendar. The scapegoats were expelled on the sixth of the month Thargelion, the first day of the two-day festival of the Thargelia. It is rather surprising to note that on the same day that the scapegoats were expelled the Greeks also celebrated the fall of Troy,[96] the victories at Marathon and Plataea, and even the victory of Alexander the Great over Darius (Ael. *VH* 2.25). Evidently the expulsion of evil was felt so intensely that this seemed to be the appropriate day to celebrate these victories.

On the second day of the Thargelia a first-fruit sacrifice was celebrated and a kind of May tree, the *eiresióne*, was carried around.[97] Choirs of men and boys competed in singing hymns and we know of the Thargelia in Miletus that large amounts of undiluted wine and expensive food were consumed. The *eiresióne* and the first-fruit sacrifice are typical signs of seasonal renewal: the first signs of coming prosperity after the scarceness of the winter period.[98] There is a large amount of ethnological material showing that the beginning of a new year—which often coincides with a first-fruit festival—or the arrival of a period of plenty is often celebrated with an *orgia alimentare*: people take an advance on the new harvest.[99] From a psychological point of view the "orgy" is a kind of collective relaxation by the community, which for a while need not worry any more about the often precarious food situation. In Greece the exceptional character of the meal was stressed by the drinking of undiluted wine, for in normal circumstances wine was always diluted with water.[100]

Since the Thargelia was a festival for Apollo we may expect that the god also shows a connection with seasonal renewal. Such a connection seems indeed to exist. In a hitherto neglected text Athenaeus (10.424f.) informs us that the Thargelia in Athens was the festival of Apollo Delius. Although the epithet was most likely added after the Athenians concerned themselves with Delos in 425 BC (Thuc. 3.104), it seems reasonable to assume that they must have seen a connection between Apollo Delius and the Apollo of the Thargelia. The main festival of Apollo Delius, the Delia, was a festival of *renouvellement saisonnier* and was connected with the growth of the adolescents.[101] This coincides to a large degree with the festival of the Thargelia where, as we have seen, seasonal renewal and the boys also played an important role. Apollo Delius will thus have been chosen because of the similarity of the Delia and the Thargelia.

This study has thus shown that the expulsion of the scapegoat in the religious calendar preceded a day of seasonal renewal. A similar structure could also be found in Tibet (§ 7) and in Rome where the ancient New Year (the first of March) was preceded by a month full of purificatory rituals. The same alternation could still be found in the carnival rites of Western Europe where at the beginning of the year society expelled all kinds of evil.[102] The pattern is fully understandable: no new beginning before a complete *kátharsis* of the old situation. This applies of course to the fixed date of the Thargelia as well as to special occasions when a new beginning had to be established after the disturbance of the seasonal and cosmic order through drought or plague. However, it remains enigmatic why the Greeks had to use a human being, whereas the Hittites sometimes and the Israelites always found an animal sufficient. Evidently, to be more civilized does not always mean to be more humane.[103]

NOTES

1. Roland de Vaux, *Les sacrifices de l'Ancien Testament* (Paris: Gabalda, 1964), 86f. (with older bibliography); Edmund R. Leach, *Culture and Communication* (Cambridge: Cambridge University Press, 1976), 92f.; Douglas Davies, "An Interpretation of Sacrifice in Leviticus," *Zs. f. Altt. Wiss.* 89 (1977): 387–99; Hayim Tawil, "Azazel the Prince of the Steppe: A Comparative Study," *Zs. f. Altt. Wiss.* 92 (1980): 43–59.

2. Viktor Gebhard, *Die Pharmakoi in Ionien und die Sybakchoi in Athen*, diss. Munich 1926 (with older bibliography) and *RE* V A (1934), 1290–1304 (with additions and changes which are not always improvements); Martin P. Nilsson, *Geschichte der griechischen Religion*, 3rd ed., vol. 1 (Munich: Beck, 1967), 107–10; Jean-Pierre Vernant, "Ambiguïté et renversement: Sur la structure énigmatique d'*Œdipe roi*" [translation reprinted in the present volume] in Jean-Pierre Vernant and Pierre Vidal-Naquet, *Mythe et tragédie en Grèce ancienne* (Paris: F. Maspero, 1972), 99–131 = *Tragedy and Myth in Ancient Greece*, trans. Janet Lloyd (Brighton: Harvester Press, 1981),

87–119; Henk S. Versnel, "Polycrates and His Ring: Two Neglected Aspects," *SSR* 1 (1977, 17–46): 37–43; Walter Burkert, *Griechische Religion der archaischen und klassischen Epoche* (Stuttgart: Kohlhammer, 1977), 139–42 and *Structure and History in Greek Mythology and Ritual* (Berkeley: University of California Press, 1979), 59–77, 168–76; see also the extensive apparatus to the relevant fragments in the forthcoming [1983] Teubner edition of Hipponax by Enzo Degani.

3. Burkert, *Structure and History*, 63f., 170 (with older bibliography); M. A. Cavallaro, "Duride, i *Fasti Cap.* e la tradizione storiografica sulle *Devotiones* dei Decii," *ASAA* 54 (1976 [1979]): 261–316; Henk S. Versnel, "Self-Sacrifice, Compensation, Anonymous Gods," in *Entretiens Fondation Hardt* [*Le sacrifice dans l'antiquité*] 27 (1981): 135–94; L. F. Janssen, "Some Unexplored Aspects of the Decian *devotio*," *Mnemosyne* IV, 34 (1981): 357–81.

4. Burkert, *Structure and History*, 60.

5. Jane Ellen Harrison, *Prolegomena to the Study of Greek Religion* (Cambridge: University Press, 1903), 95–119; Lewis Richard Farnell, *The Cults of the Greek States*, vol. 4 (Oxford: Clarendon Press, 1907), 268–84; Gilbert Murray, *The Rise of the Greek Epic* (Oxford: Clarendon Press, 1907), 13–16, 253–58; James G. Frazer, *The Golden Bough*, 3rd ed., vol. 9 (London: Macmillan, 1913), 252–74.

6. René Girard, *La violence et le sacré* (Paris: Grasset, 1972) = *Violence and the Sacred*, trans. Patrick Gregory (Baltimore: Johns Hopkins University Press, 1977). An excerpt from this work appears in the present volume.

7. Burkert, *Griechische Religion*, 141 and *Structure and History*, 70.

8. For a convincing defense of the transmitted θυμῷ (fr. 10) instead of Schmidt's θύμῳ which is accepted by West, see Enzo Degani, "Note ipponattee," in *Studi classici in onore di Quintino Cataudella*, vol. 1 (Catania: Università di Catania, 1972), 97–103. L. Koenen, *ZPE* 31 (1978): 86 compares the flogging of Encolpius' penis in Petronius (c. 138). This is highly persuasive, since Petronius evidently was interested in the scapegoat ritual. He is our main source for Massilia (fr. 1) and the only Latin author to use the word *pharmacus* (c. 107).

9. Gregory Nagy, *The Best of the Achaeans* (Baltimore: Johns Hopkins University Press, 1979), 222–42.

10. For a convincing defense of the transmitted χειμῶνι (fr. 6), see Albert Henrichs, "Riper than a Pear: Parian Invective in Theokritos," *ZPE* 39 (1980): 7–27, esp. 26f.

11. Schol. Ar. *Eq.* 1136; Suid. s. v. κάθαρμα and φαρμακός.

12. Harpoc. s. v. φαρμακός; Helladios *apud* Photius *Bibl.* 534a Henry. Hesych. s. v. φαρμακός wrongly states that the pair consisted of a man and a woman, see Gebhard *RE* V A (1934), 1291.

13. Call fr. 90 Pf.; Ov. *Ibis* 467f. and schol.

14. Petronius fr. 1; Lactantius on Statius *Theb.* 15.793; Schol. Luc. 10.334.

15. Strabo 10.2.9; Ampelius 8.

16. Photius and Suida s. v. περίψημα. The two are connected by Nilsson, *Geschichte*, 109f.

17. For the close connection of λιμός and λοιμός, see Louis Robert, *Hellenica* 4 (1948): 128; M. L. West on Hes. *Op.* 243; R. Nisbet and M. Hubbard on Hor. *C.* 1.21.13.

18. Plut. *M.* 693f., see Henk S. Versnel, *Triumphus* (Leiden: Brill, 1970), 160f.; Jean-Pierre Vernant, *Mythe et pensée chez les Grecs*, 6th ed., vol. 1 (Paris: F. Maspero, 1981), 164f.; V. Rotolo, "Il rito

della βουλίμου ἐξέλασις," in *Miscellanea di studi classici in onore di Eugenio Manni*, vol. 6 (Rome: Giorgio Bretschneider, 1980), 1947–61. For the chasing of Hunger cf. the late epigram of Termessos (*TAM* III, 103) in which a certain Honoratus is honored because "he chased hunger to the sea" (δίωξε γὰρ εἰς ἅλα λιμόν).

19. Anton. Lib. 25; Ov. *Met.* 13.685.

20. Colin Austin, *Nova fragmenta Euripidea in papyris reperta* (Berlin: de Gruyter, 1968), 22–40; Uta Kron, *Die zehn attischen Phylenheroen* (Berlin: Gebr. Mann, 1976), 196f.; P. Carrara, *Euripide: Eretteo* (Florence: Gonnelli, 1977), 18–27.

21. Kock, *RE* XII (1925), 2000–2001; Kron, *Die zehn attischen Phylenheroen*, 195–98.

22. Ps. Call. *FGrH* 124 F 56, see A. Reinach, *Klio* 14 (1915): 326f. This case has to be added to Versnel's ("Self-Sacrifice," 152–56) dossier of people riding into the Underworld. For this motif, see also A. H. Krappe, "La poursuite du Gilla Dacher et les dioscures celtiques," *Rev. Celt.* 49 (1932): 96–108; Joseph F. Nagy, "Shamanic Aspects of the *Bruidhean* Tale," *History of Religions* 20 (1981): 308f. Versnel ("Self-Sacrifice," 154 n. 3) wrongly compares the fact that boys and girls are called πῶλοι, see Claude Calame, *Les chœurs de jeunes filles en Grèce archaïque*, vol. 1 (Rome: Edizioni dell'Ateneo & Bizzarri, 1977), 374f.

23. For other possible examples of kings, see Versnel, "Self-Sacrifice," 144 n. 2.

24. G. Radke, *RE* XXI (1951), 1753–59; Burkert, *Structure and History,* 72f.

25. Tzetzes *Chil.* 5.732; Schol. Aesch. *Sept.* 680.

26. Neanthes *FGrH* 84 F 16; Diog. Laert. 1.110.

27. A. Dorsingfung-Smets, "Les étrangers dans la société primitive," *Recueil Jean Bodin* 9 (1958): 59–73; Emile Benveniste, *Le vocabulaire des institutions indo-européennes* (Paris: Éditions de Minuit, 1969), 1:355–61; Ph. Gautier, "Notes sur l'étranger et l'hospitalité en Grèce et à Rome," *Ancient Society* 4 (1973): 1–21; Julian Pitt-Rivers, *The Fate of Shechem* (Cambridge: Cambridge University Press, 1977), 94–112, 179–81; O. Hiltbrunner, "Hostis und ξένος," in *Festschrift F. K. Dörner*, vol. 1, *EPRO* 66 (Leiden: Brill, 1978), 424–45.

28. Young men: Bremmer, "Heroes, Rituals and the Trojan War," *SSR* 2 (1978): 5–38; Pierre Vidal-Naquet, *Le chasseur noir* (Paris: Maspero, 1981), 151–207. Girls: Calame, *Les chœurs de jeunes filles*, passim; F. Graf, "Die lokrischen Mädchen," *SSR* 2 (1978): 61–79.

29. *Il.* I.176, II.98, etc.

30. Girard, *Violence and the Sacred*, 12; see also Geo Widengren, *Religionsphänomenologie* (Berlin: de Gruyter, 1969), 360–93; Charles Segal, *Tragedy and Civilization* (Cambridge, MA: Harvard University Press, 1981), 43ff.

31. Scherling, *RE* XI (1922), 984–94; Burkert, *Structure and History*, 62f. There existed a monument picturing Kodros' death, cf. *IG* II² 4258 with the comments by A. Wilhelm, *AAWW* 87 (1950): 366–70. The name Kodros already occurs in the Linear-B tablets, cf. C. A. Mastrelli, "Il nome di Codro," in *Atti e Memorie VII Congr. Intern. di Scienze Onomast.* (Florence, 1963), 3:207–17.

32. Ar. *Eq.* 1405; Lys. 6.53; Petr. *c.* 107.

33. Johan Wettstein, *Novum Testamentum Graecum*, vol. 2 (Amsterdam: *Ex Officina Dommeriana*, 1752), 114f. who could not yet know Men. *Sam.* 481.

34. F. Hauck, *Theologisches Wörterbuch zum Neuen Testament*, vol. 3 (1938), 434.

35. G. Stählin, *Theologisches Wörterbuch zum Neuen Testament*, vol. 6 (1959), 83–92; Ceslas Spicq, *Notes de lexicographie néo-testamentaire*, vol. 2 (Göttingen: Vandenhoeck & Ruprecht, 1978), 681f.

36. As was already shown by Hermann Usener, *Kleine Schriften*, vol. 4 (Leipzig: Teubner, 1913), 258; see also Gebhard, *Pharmakoi*, 22–24.

37. We find a similar dichotomy in Rome, although this has not yet been recognized. According to Macrobius (*Sat.* 3.9.9) *dictators imperatoresque soli possunt devovere*, but he does not give a single historical instance of such a *devotio*. Similarly, all the examples adduced by Versnel, "Self-Sacrifice"—Curtius, Decius, and the *seniores* at the Celtic invasion of 390 BC—belong to the world of legend, as Versnel (142f.) himself recognizes. Livy (8.10.11), however, explicitly says *licere consuli dictatorique et praetori, cum legiones hostium devoveat, non utique se, sed quem velit ex legione Romana scripta civem devovere*. We may safely assume that the members of the Roman élite rather sacrificed a common *legionarius* than themselves. For the Greek inspiration of the Decius legend, see now Cavallaro, "Duride."

38. Neanthes FGrH 84 F 16 μειράκιον εὔμορφον.

39. Burkert, *Structure and History*, 73. Versnel, "Self-Sacrifice," 144f., appropriately compares the Roman examples of Curtius (Liv. 7.6.2) and St. Caesarius (*Acta Sanctorum*, Nov. 1, 106f.). Note that J. Toutain, *Annuaire de l'Ecole des Hautes Etudes* 1916–17, 1ff., which is quoted by Versnel, 145 n. 2, has been reprinted in Toutain, *Nouvelles études de mythologie et d'histoire des religions antiques* (Paris: Jouve, 1935), 126–48; also add to Versnel's bibliography on St. Caesarius: *Bibliotheca Sanctorum*, vol. 3 (Rome: Città Nuova, 1963), 1154f.

40. Petr. fr. I; Schol. Statius *Theb.* 10.793.

41. Hipp. fr. 8 West, cf. Tzetzes *Chil.* 5.734. Barley was considered to be slave's bread: Hipp. fr. 26.6, 115.8 West; Aesch. *Ag.* 1041; Wettstein, *Novum Testamentum Graecum*, 1:876f.; Bremmer, *ZPE* 39 (1980): 32.

42. Oliver Robert Gurney, *Some Aspects of Hittite Religion* (Oxford: Oxford University Press, 1977), 49.

43. Uhhamuwa: Gurney, *Some Aspects of Hittite Religion*, 48. Pulisa: Gurney, 48 = Hans M. Kümmel, *Ersatzrituale für den hethitischen König* (Wiesbaden: O. Harrassowitz, 1967), 111ff.

44. Thread: Burkert, *Structure and History*, 64. Value: Gustaf Dalman, *Arbeit und Sitte*, vol. 6 (Gütersloh: C. Bertelsmann, 1939), 99.

45. Johanna Schmitt, *Freiwilliger Opfertod bei Euripides* (Giessen: A. Töpelman, 1921); P. Roussel, "Le thème du sacrifice volontaire dans la tragédie d'Euripide," *RBPhH* (1922): 225–40; Versnel, "Self-Sacrifice," 179–85 with an interesting discussion.

46. It is interesting, as Charles Segal points out to me, that Eur. *Bacch.* 963 μόνος σὺ πόλεως τῆσδ' ὑπερκάμνεις, μόνος, which Dionysos says to Pentheus and in which Dodds (*ad. loc.*) rightly sees an allusion to the scapegoat ritual, in the *Christus Patiens* (1525) is said of Jesus: μόνος σὺ φύσεως ὑπερκάμνεις βροτῶν. See also Sam K. Williams, *Jesus' Death as Saving Event: The Background and Origin of a Concept* (Missoula, MT: Scholars Press, 1975); Martin Hengel, *The Atonement: A Study of the Origins of the Doctrine in the New Testament* (London: SCM, 1981).

47. For human sacrifice at sea, see L. Röhrich, "Die Volksballade von 'Herrn Peters Seefahrt' und die Menschenopfer-Sagen," in *Märchen, Mythos, Dichtung: Festschrift F. von der Leyen*, ed. Hugo Kuhn (Munich: Beck, 1963), 177–212; H. Henningsen, "Jonas, profet og ulykkesfugl," *Handels- og Søfartsmuseets Årbog* (Helsinki, 1966), 105–22.

48. Schol. Statius *Theb.* 10.793 *proliciebatur praemiis.*

49. Karl Meuli, *Gesammelte Schriften*, vol. 2 (Basel: Schwabe, 1975), 993–96; see also Walter Burkert, *Homo Necans* (New York: de Gruyter, 1972), passim. For examples outside Greece, see, besides Meuli and Burkert, I. Tolstoi, *Ostrov Belyi i Tavrika na Jevskinskom Ponte* (Leningrad, 1918), 35 n. 2; F. Cumont, "L'archevêche de Prédachtoé et le sacrifice du faon," *Byzantion* 6 (1931): 521–33; Saul Lieberman, *Hellenism in Jewish Palestine*, 2nd ed. (New York: Jewish Theological Seminary of America, 1962), 158–60; Felix J. Oinas, *Studies in Finnic-Slavic Folklore Relations* (Helsinki: Soumalainen Tiedeakatemia, 1969), 193–201 ("Legends of the voluntary appearance of sacrificial victims"); Alfonso Maria di Nola, *Anthropologia religiosa* (Florence: Vallecchi, 1974), 201–62.

50. Istros *FGrH* 334 F 50 and Jacoby *ad loc.*

51. Cf. Anton Wiechers, *Aesop in Delphi* (Meisenheim: A. Hain, 1961), 31–36; F. R. Adrados, "The 'Life of Aesop,'" *QUCC* 30 (1979): 93–112; Nagy, *Best of the Achaeans*, 279–82.

52. Most important evidence: Macr. *Sat.* 3.20.3, cf. J. André, "Arbor felix, arbor infelix," *Hommages à Jean Bayet*, ed. Marcel Renard and Robert Schilling (Brussels: Latomus, 1964), 35–46; A. Dihle, *RhM* 108 (1965): 179–83; Jean Bayet, *Croyances et rites dans la Rome antique* (Paris: Payot, 1971), 9–43; Th. Köves-Zulauf, *ANRW* II.16.1 (1978), 262f.

53. Traitor: Liv. 1.26.6 and Ogilvie *ad loc.*; Cic. *Rab. perd.* 13. Monstrosities: Luc. 1.590f.; Macr. *Sat.* 3.20.3.

54. Graf, "Die lokrischen Mädchen," 70.

55. Georg Rabuse, "Mort Bois und Bois Mort," in *Verba et vocabula: Ernst Gamillschegg zum 80. Geburtstag*, ed. Helmut Stimm and Julius Wilhelm (Munich: W. Fink, 1968), 429–47.

56. Phryn. *PS.* p. 15.12; *AB* 10.26.

57. Rome: André, "Arbor felix, arbor infelix," 40f.; Kurt Lembach, *Die Pflanzen bei Theokrit* (Heidelberg: C. Winter, 1970), 75f. Middle Ages: Rabuse, "Mort Bois und Bois Mort," 442–44.

58. Lyc. 1157 and schol.; see also Graf, "Die lokrischen Mädchen," 67–72.

59. For the squill, cf. Steier *RE* A III (1929), 522–26; Lembach, *Die Pflanzen bei Theokrit*, 63–65.

60. Schol. Theoc. 7.108, cf. Philippe Borgeaud, *Recherches sur le dieu Pan* (Rome: Institut suisse de Rome, 1979), 107–14; for a medieval parallel, see Jacob de Voragine, *Legenda Aurea* 3.8.

61. Arist. fr. 223 Rose; Nic. *Alex.* 254.

62. Mod. *Dig.* 48 tit. 9.1 prooem. *virgis sanguineis verberatus*, cf. Bayet, *Croyances et rites*, 36.

63. Sicily: Schol. Theoc. 7.106 / 8d τῶν ἐφήβων ἐν Σικελίᾳ γίνεται ἀγὼν ἐν σκίλλαις. The reading ἐν Σικελίᾳ is unnecessarily doubted by Wilamowitz *apud* C. Wendel, *Scholia in Theocritum vetera* (Leipzig: Teubner, 1914), 104. Priene: *I. Priene* 112.91, 95 ἀγῶνα τε σκιλλομαχίας.

64. Thesmophoria: All sources (although repeatedly misinterpreted): Eugen Fehrle, *Die kultische Keuschheit im Altertum* (Giessen: A. Töpelmann, 1910), 139–41; see also Marcel Detienne, *The Gardens of Adonis*, trans. Janet Lloyd, 2nd ed. (Princeton, NJ: Princeton University Press, 1994), 79–81. Lygos/agnus castus: Plin. *N.H.* 24.9.38; Eustath. p. 834.34; Fehrle, 152; D. Page, *Sappho and Alcaeus* (Oxford: Clarendon Press, 1955), 202; Louis Robert, "Les Kordakia de Nicée, le combustible de Synnada et les poissons-scies," *Journal des Savants* (1961): 134; G. J. de Vries on Plato *Phdr.* 230b.

65. Plin *N.H.* 16.26.110. This aspect of the plant was taken up by medieval medicine and still in our

day by homeopathy which prescribes the plant to promote libido, although scientific tests (as perhaps could have been expected) do not indicate great effectiveness, cf. Otto Leeser, *Lehrbuch der Homöopathie*, vol. 2 (Heidelberg, 1971), 585–96.

66. Cf. Hugo Rahner, "Die Weide als Symbol der Keuschheit," *Zs. f. Kath. Theol.* 56 (1932): 231–53 and *Griechische Mythen in christlicher Deutung* (Zurich: Rhein-verlag, 1945), 361–413. In the Middle Ages the tree became the symbol for infertility and the "world" as opposed to the Christian way of life. Cf. Wilhelm Fraenger, *Hieronymus Bosch* (Gütersloh: Verlag der Kunst, 1975), index s. v. *Weide*; M. Bambeck, "Weidenbaum und Welt," *Zs. f. franz. Sprache und Lit.* 88 (1978): 195–212.

67. For the Samian Hera, see Robert Fleischer, *Artemis von Ephesos und verwandte Kultstatuen aus Anatolien und Syrien, EPRO* 35 (Leiden: Brill, 1973), 202–23; Meuli, *Gesammelte Schriften*, vol. 2, 1059–64; Hans Walter, *Das Heraion von Samos* (Munich: Piper, 1976); Fleischer, *Festschrift F. K. Dörner*, vol. 1, 343f.; Burkert, *Structure and History*, 129f.

68. Dionysos: S. Eitrem, "Heroen der Seefahrer," *SO* 14 (1935): 53–67; Burkert, *Homo Necans*, 222f.; U. Heimberg, *JDAI* 91 (1976): 260–65; Laurence Kahn, *Hermès passe* (Paris: F. Maspero, 1978), 113–17; H. Herter, "Die Delphine des Dionysos," *Archaiognosia* 1 (1980): 101–34. Hermes: Kahn, 75–117. Ludwig Radermacher, *Der homerische Hermeshymnus* (Leipzig: Hölder-Pichler-Tempsky, 1931), 145f., already connected this binding with Artemis Lygodesma and Hera of Samos. S. Eitrem, *RhM* 64 (1909): 333–35 also explained the epithet Polygios of Hermes in Trozen as Poly-lygios, or "with much willow," which is not impossible.

69. Meuli, *Gesammelte Schriften*, vol. 2, 1035–81, and the critical observations by F. Graf, *Gnomon* 51 (1979): 209–16.

70. A. Brelich, "La corona di Prometheus," in *Hommages à Marie Delcourt* (Brussels: Latomus, 1970), 234–42; Marcel Detienne and Jean-Pierre Vernant, *Les ruses de l'intelligence*, 2nd ed. (Paris: Flammarion, 1978), 95f.; Bremmer in M. J. Vermaseren, ed., *Studies in Hellenistic Religions* (Leiden: Brill, 1979), 14.

71. Anacr. fr. 352, 496 Page; A. S. F. Gow and D. L. Page, *The Greek Anthology: The Hellenistic Epigrams* (Cambridge: University Press, 1965), 2:421.

72. *I. Magnesia* 122 fr. e, 12 ἐν χω(ρίῳ) Λυγωίῳ, cf. Robert, "Les Kordakia de Nicée," 135–37.

73. Burkert, *Griechische Religion*, 140.

74. The exact text is disputed, see C. Sourvinou-Inwood, *CQ* 65 (1971): 339–42; T. C. W. Stinton, *CQ* 70 (1976): 11–13; G. T. W. Hooker, *JHS* 98 (1978): 191.

75. For the *kanephóroi*, see Angel Brelich, *Paides e parthenoi* (Rome: Edizioni dell'Ateneo, 1969), 274–90.

76. Burkert, *Homo Necans*, 189–91 (with all sources); see also Calame, *Les chœurs de jeunes filles*, vol. 1, 214–18.

77. Antonios D. Keramopoullos, Ὁ Ἀποτυμπανισμός (Athens: Estia, 1923), 116–19, who compares Aesch. *Cho.* 98; Plato *Crat.* 396e and Schol. *Leg.* 9.877; Lys. 6.53.

78. F. Gschnitzer, *RE* suppl. XIII (1973), 805; Stephen G. Miller, *The Prytaneion* (Berkeley: University of California Press, 1978), 13f.; M. J. Osborne, "Entertainment in the Prytaneion at Athens," *ZPE* 41 (1981): 153–70.

79. Hipp. fr. 153 West; Hesych. s. v. κραδίης νόμος.

80. C. Marcel-Dubois, "Musiques cérémonielles et sociétés rurales," *Proceedings of the 8th International Congress of Anthropological and Ethnographical Sciences* (Tokyo: Japan Science Council, 1968), 2:340, and "Fêtes villageoises et vacarmes cérémoniels," in Jean Jacquot and Elie Konigson, *Les fêtes de la Renaissance*, vol. 3 (Paris: Centre national de la recherche scientifique, 1975), 603–15.

81. Poll. 8.102; Zen. 6.41; H. Lloyd-Jones, *ZPE* 41 (1981): 28.

82. Ludwig Deubner, *Attische Feste* (Berlin: H. Keller, 1932), 181.

83. Jean Delumeau, *La peur en Occident* (Paris: Fayard, 1978), 139f.

84. Cf. V. Hillebrandt, "Circumambulatio," *Mitt. Schles. Gesells. f. Vkd.* 13 / 4 (1911): 3–8; Samson Eitrem, *Opferritus und Voropfer der Griechen und Römer* (Kristiania: J. Dybwad, 1915), 6–29; E. F. Knuchel, *Die Umwandlung in Kult, Magie und Rechtsbrauch* (Basel: G. Krebs, 1919); Weinkopf, *Handwörterbuch des Deutschen Aberglaubens*, vol. 8 (1936–37), 1315–46; W. Pax, "Circumambulatio," *RAC* 3 (1957): 143–52; Henk S. Versnel, "Sacrificium lustrale: The Death of Mettius Fufetius (Livy I.28)," *Mededelingen van het Nederlands Instituut te Rome* 37 (1975): 97–115.

85. Detlev Fehling, *Ethologische Überlegungen auf dem Gebiet der Altertumskunde* (Munich: Beck, 1974), 59–82.

86. Fehling, *Ethologische Überlegungen*, 72f.

87. Aesch. *Cho.* 98; cf. Keramopoullos, Ὁ Ἀποτυμπανισμός, 116.

88. For the prohibition on looking back, see Ernst Samter, *Geburt, Hochzeit, Tod* (Leipzig: Teubner, 1911), 147–50; Theodor Gaster, *Myth, Legend and Custom in the Old Testament* (New York: Harper and Row, 1969), 159f. (Lot's wife); A. S. Pease on Cic. *Div.* 1.49; A. F. Gow on Theoc. 24.96; F. Bömer on Ov. *Fa.* 5.439; John K. Campbell, *Honour, Family and Patronage: A Study of Institutions and Moral Values in a Greek Mountain Community* (Oxford: Clarendon Press, 1964), 136 (modern Greece).

89. Petr. fr. 1 *et sic proiciebatur*. Thus all the manuscripts, but Stephanus (who has frequently been followed), on the basis of Schol. Statius *Theb.* 10.793, emended *proiciebatur* into *praecipitabatur* "was hurled from a height." James G. Frazer, *The Scapegoat*, 3rd ed. (London: Macmillan, 1913), 253 n. 2, however, already noted that this change was not supported by the textual tradition, and the recent editions of Servius, our source for Petronius' fragment, and Petronius have both returned to *proiciebatur*. For *proicio* "cast out of a city," cf. Cic. *Cat.* 2.2 *quod (urbs) tantam pestem evomuerit forasque proiecerit*; Ov. *Met.* 15.504 *immeritumque pater proiecit ab urbe*.

90. Burkert, *Structure and History*, 70. For plague epidemics and Apollonius, see E. L. Bowie, "Apollonius of Tyana: Tradition and Reality," *ANRW* II 16.2 (1978): 1652–99, esp. 1687.

91. Cf. Gerd Petzke, *Die Traditionen über Apollonius von Tyana und das Neue Testament* (Leiden: Brill, 1970), 126f.; Dietmar Esser, *Formgeschichtliche Studien zur hellenistischen und zur frühchristlichen Literatur unter besonderer Berücksichtigung der Vita Apollonii des Philostrat und der Evangelien* diss. Bonn (1969), 59, suggests an "aetiologischer Lokallegende."

92. Cf. W. J. W. Koster on Tzetzes Ar. *Ra.* 733a who notes Tzetzes' careless handling of the sources in this specific case; Gebhard, *Pharmakoi*, 3ff.; Deubner, *Attische Feste*, 184.

93. The person selected is often a beggar: Giuseppe Tucci and Walther Heissig, *Die Religionen Tibets und der Mongolei* (Stuttgart: Kohlhammer, 1970), 197.

94. David Macdonald, *The Land of the Lama* (London: Seeley, Service, 1929), 213f.

95. Cf. Graf, "Die lokrischen Mädchen," 66, on a similar discrepancy: "Der Mythos stellte das Ritual weniger abgemildert dar, extrapolierte sozusagen vom tatsächlichen Geschehen zum Verständnis dieses Geschehens in den Augen der Praktizierenden."

96. Damastes *FGrH* 5 F 7; Hellanikos *FGrH* 4 F 152a.

97. For the Thargelia, see Martin P. Nilsson, *Griechische Feste von religiöser Bedeutung* (Leipzig: B. G. Teubner, 1906), 105–15; Deubner, *Attische Feste*, 179–98; Herbert W. Parke, *Festivals of the Athenians* (London: Thames and Hudson, 1977), 146–49; Willem den Boer, *Private Morality in Greece and Rome* (Leiden: Brill, 1979), 129–32.

98. For the *eiresióne*, see Burkert, *Structure and History*, 134 (sources and bibliography); add W. Klinger, "L'irésione grecque et ses transformations postérieures," *Eos* 29 (1926): 157–74 (with interesting Caucasian material); S. Follet, *RPh* 48 (1974): 30–32 (epigraphical examples).

99. Vittorio Lanternari, *La grande festa: Vita rituale e sistemi di produzione nelle società tradizionali*, 2nd ed. (Bari: Dedalo, 1976), passim. Add Greg. Tur. *VP.* 6.2.

100. For the opposition of mixed and neat wine, see F. Graf, "Milch, Honig und Wein," in G. Piccaluga, ed., *Perennitas: Studi in onore di Angelo Brelich* (Rome: Ateneo, 1980), 209–21; add Bremmer, *Arethusa* 13 (1980): 295 n. 49 and *ZPE* 39 (1980): 32f.

101. Calame, *Les chœurs de jeunes filles*, vol. 1, 202.

102. Emmanuel Le Roy Ladurie, *Le Carnaval de Romans* (Paris: Gallimard, 1979), 342–44.

103. This article is a version of a lecture which I had the pleasure of presenting at Princeton and Harvard during the year 1980–81. For helpful comments I am especially indebted to Richard Buxton, Fritz Graf, Albert Henrichs, Theo Korteweg, Robert Parker, and Zeph Stewart.

The Exposed Infant

Marie Delcourt

Translated by Malcolm DeBevoise

I n an earlier work I tried to show that Oedipus is one of those malefic new-born children whom ancient communities did away with because their deformity was a proof of divine wrath.[1] I did not sufficiently insist there on the fact that the exposed infants were *emissary* (or surrogate) *victims*. Their sacralization, in the event they were rescued, had the effect of bringing about a reversal of values, so that what had been seen as evil was now considered to be good. Similarly, a divine judgment, involving a trial from which the child emerges alive, ended not in an acquittal pure and simple, but in the *preferment* of the accused and the *punishment* of the accuser. And every exposure entailed a divine judgment.

Nevertheless it would be a mistake to reduce all tales of exposed infants to a single type. In most of them the evil character does not appear at all, or else is introduced belatedly when a psychological explanation is wanted for each of the acts that make up such tales. This leads us to recognize, alongside the theme of the *misshapen child*, which has its origin in a known rite meant to ward off barrenness, the themes of *submersion in water* and *rearing in the*

These excerpts from chapter 1 of *Œdipe ou la légende du conquérant* (Droz, 1944; Paris: Les Belles Lettres, 1981) have been translated for the present volume.

mountains, which must go back to ancient rituals of initiation, tests whose usual purpose was to induct a young man into the class of adult males. It may be that the most painful tests corresponded to the highest investitures; this is in any case implied in the event that they come to be transposed into legend.

Indeed, as paradoxical as it may seem, the two ritual orders discernible in the theme of the exposed infant—the judgment of malefic newborns, on the one hand, and the testing of youths on the other—end up producing synonymous legends: the abnormal infant who is rescued and the youth who survives initiation are both destined to a brilliant future. There can be no doubt that, as legendary narratives gradually took shape, this idea was more clearly brought out by secondary influences whose operation has yet to be fully understood.

Oedipus was exposed as an infant. The poets of classical Greece tell us why: Laius and Jocasta were warned by the oracle of Apollo [at Delphi] that their issue would bring misfortune upon Thebes. Aeschylus and Euripides place the warning before the conception of Oedipus; Sophocles, after his birth. Sophocles considers the prohibition pronounced by Delphi to be groundless. Euripides justifies it by Laius's shameful love for Chrysippus, son of Pelops; and while he seems not to have invented this reason, he did place it in a new context. He interpreted the will of the gods more strictly than Sophocles did, and found it difficult to accept that their decisions might be arbitrary.

Let us emphasize first the reason for the exposure, namely, the *sanction* announced by the oracle in case of disobedience. Thebes as a whole was liable to suffer if a child born of Laius and Jocasta were allowed to grow up. This theme is exceptional in tales of exposed newborn children, which suggests that Aeschylus may have found it in an early version of the legend. Subsequently, once the sentimental elements of the legend had supplanted the political elements, the oracle also announced parricide and incest. These were late additions borrowed from analogous but somewhat different accounts, in which a newborn is persecuted by someone who fears he will grow up to be an enemy one day. The persecutor is generally the mother's father. The baby is miraculously saved through the intervention of a god, of whom he is the son. Oedipus, son of a mortal father, is the only child (along with Paris) to have been exposed at birth by his own parents, obliged to choose between their son and the city to which they owe allegiance. Atalanta was also exposed by her father, Iasos, but this because he was disappointed at having no sons. Additionally, there was later added to the legend of Iasos an oracle warning that his life would be threatened by his daughter and by her descendants—a detail that was to figure in every legend of this type once it had become commonplace. Yet there are no synonymous legends in Greek folklore. If one goes to the trouble to compare all those having a common theme, one realizes that the theme reflects a particular context in each case, with the result that it takes on a unique meaning. It will be useful, then, to begin by methodically classifying the tales of exposed infants.

These tales have been collected by several authors, but never in their entirety. Usener, studying the myth of Deucalion, a sort of Greek Noah, rightly suspects that he was an exposed infant to begin with. This leads him to perceive similarities with other such adventures. He attaches too much importance to the detail of the floating chest, however, which he takes to be the equivalent of a theophoric boat or fish. Seeing exposures of divine offspring as a mythical transcription of the epiphany of a sun god, he arbitrarily neglects the theme of exposure in the mountains, though it figures in several legends (Dionysus, Oedipus, Telephus) as a variant of exposure on the water in a chest. These alternate motifs need to be studied in tandem. Usener also neglects semihistorical accounts, such as those involving Cypselus, Cyrus, and Ptolemy Soter. Glotz detects in all these legends a transposition of ordeals of legitimation, and he closely studies those that bring an accusation of unchaste behavior against the mother (Danaë, Auge, Semele, Rhea Silvia). Sir James Frazer, who does not cite Glotz, arrives at the same conclusion after systematically analyzing almost all the parallels of the story of Moses. . . . [2]

Usener's reading of this series of legends is well known. The character inside the chest, he says, is always a god, or the descendant of a god, who crosses the sea and arrives safely in a foreign land. The legend, in other words, is a romantic transposition of a divine epiphany. To the same race of heroes belong Oedipus and Deucalion, whose name Δευκαλίων (or Δεύκαλος) means "little Zeus," "son of Zeus."

Glotz and Frazer adopted Usener's grouping of the legends and gave them another common denominator: the undergoing of an ordeal. Here we are in the domain of material facts. Glotz shows very clearly that there were several kinds of ordeals. This is why the tales, while they resemble one another, do not coincide in every detail. An explanation of this sort shows little interest in the specifically religious element of the myth of the exposed infant, however, and it wholly ignores a detail to which Usener rightly drew attention, namely, the hero's deportation from his native land. As a result of the persecution of which he is a victim, and of the ordeal to which he is then subjected, an innocent child is removed away from the country of his birth: either he comes back to it later (Oedipus, Perseus) or he goes on to conquer other lands and to found cities (Tenes, Telephus, Anius); but in any case he grows up far away from the place where normally he would have been raised. In what follows I shall try to cast some light on this obscure motif. But first it will be necessary to consider a few more legends, pointing out their distinctive features as well as the difficulties they present. The most curious is certainly the legend of Deucalion. No critic has made a study of it that amounts to anything more than a collection of local Greek traditions concerning a flood, a saved man, and the place where he came ashore.[3]

Deucalion escapes the flood in a λάρναξ or in a κιβωτός, which is to say in a square chest. Whichever word is used, there can be no question that it refers to the instrument of the actual ordeals that shaped—if they did not in fact give birth to—the myth of the exposed innocent. It must have been a closed crate, just large enough for the child's survival to be improbable, but not impossible. "Confinement in a chest was retained throughout [ancient] Greek history in the penal law concerning the family," Glotz says, "and this punishment with suspensive effect always seemed to be an invitation for the gods to intervene. . . . Moreover, in Italy, the *arca* was always used as a punishment for slaves."[4] This amounts to saying that Deucalion was saved under conditions in which, normally, he ought to have perished. The difference between his story and that of Noah, in the state in which the two tales have come down to us, is that Noah escapes the flood *because* he has taken refuge in a boat, whereas Deucalion survives *in spite of* having been placed in an object that was supremely unsuited for ensuring his safety over the course of a long and difficult journey by sea. Yahweh, in Genesis, does all that can be done to save Noah. Zeus, by contrast, is indifferent to Deucalion's fate at the outset; Deucalion is saved, not by Zeus's counsels, but by those of Prometheus (according to Apollodorus) or thanks to an idea that came to him (according to Ovid). Following the child's rescue, Zeus begins to look favorably upon him. Thereafter everything happens as if Zeus had wished, not to *spare* him, but first and foremost to *test* him. This would indicate that the god was able to appeal to a jurisdiction higher than himself, which is not at all surprising since, to the ancient Greek mind, pure elements [water among them] had a force capable of immediately punishing anyone who is guilty.[5] The story of Noah is coherent. The story of Deucalion is absurd, if it must be accepted that Prometheus had put him (or that Deucalion had put himself) in the chest in order to assure his safety. . . .

Those who have studied the theme of the ordeal have nevertheless neglected one aspect of it. They are solely interested in the fate of the accused, never the fate of the accuser. Now, the legends that have come down to us prove that, to the Greek mind, one does not appeal to the justice of the gods without putting oneself in danger. Readers of Glotz's book might suppose that a divine judgment absolves or condemns only that person who is explicitly subject to it. Not at all. The trial always ends in an acquittal or a conviction. If the accused is found innocent, his adversary, even if he has acted in good faith, pays for his error. Acrisius dies at the hand of Perseus, Aleus loses his sons because of Telephus, Cycnus is at least placed in danger by Tenes. The flood myth, which certainly implies an ordeal (even if the myth signifies something else as well), concludes with the salvation of the one who has been tested and the death of everyone else. Later we will speak about the murder of Laius.

The expiation of the accuser, as it is described in the legends, has two constant features:

1. The parricide is presented as involuntary or nearly so. Perseus kills his grandfather inadvertently; Tenes cuts the mooring ropes of his father's boat in a fit of anger; Oedipus, in the versions that we have, has many excuses for having killed Laius. The saved infant is a sympathetic figure, merely an instrument of the divine wrath aroused by the suspicions of his persecutor.

2. Eventually it came to be forgotten that punishment of the accuser automatically follows acquittal of the accused. On the other hand, the structure of the legends prevented the punishment from being represented as an act of vengeance performed through the rescued

child. The child acts solely as an intermediary between those on high who are responsible for the administration of earthly justice and the person who unwisely appealed to them, in vain. Because error is no longer imagined to reside in the accuser, his misfortune is represented instead as the fulfillment of an oracle. It is owing to a dream, or to a divine threat, that a man persecutes his offspring—a useless precaution that in the end is turned against him. That the theme of the oracle was a late addition to legends of this kind becomes clear on closer inspection. It is absent from very old accounts that have been discovered through other versions, for example the tale of Semele's exposure; and absent as well from accounts that have never, or only seldom, received literary treatment, for example the tale of Rhoeo and Anius. By contrast, it is found in the story of Cypselus and, later, in the legend of Cyrus, which was elaborated over a quite brief period whose extent is exactly known, since Cyrus died in 529 [BCE] and Herodotus must have prepared the first book [of the *Histories*] about 450. Sometime around the end of the sixth century, then, the legend of a child chosen by the gods must have arisen from the idea of a threat of divine origin. As a motif [of tragic drama], this idea was all the more convenient as it allowed the elements of the plot to be closely connected with one another, and made it possible to foreshadow the denouement in the prologue and to establish the innocence of all the actors of the drama, the convicted persecutor no less than the persecuted chosen one. It must have been a motif of late invention as well, for the oracles themselves are not very old.[6]

It remains to discover how, in the absence of an oracle, another motif could explain the sequence of events. Danaë, Auge, and Semele may have been persecuted, like Tyro and Melanippe, because they had become mothers without having married, and indeed Glotz sees the exposed infant essentially as a bastard who emerges victorious from a legitimation ordeal. Apollodorus attributes to Auge yet another misdeed: she hid her infant son in a precinct sacred to Athena, which brought a great scourge upon the land [so that it remained barren].[7] In the legends of Cypselus and of Cyrus, the oracle is indispensable in imparting narrative consistency to an account constructed from folkloric materials that are roughly consistent with historical fact.

Cyrus could not be given a god for a father, since everyone knew he was the son of Cambyses, nor could he be made Astyages's murderer, since everyone knew he had treated his grandfather rather generously.[8] The hostility shown by Astyages towards the son of Mandane could therefore be explained only by a threat issuing from a god.

And if Laius had received no divine warning, the exposure of Oedipus would have no readily apparent explanation. We therefore find ourselves back where we started. Let us pause here to consider the points on which the story of Oedipus differs from the stories we have just examined.

Oedipus's existence in no way threatened the lives of either his grandfather or his maternal uncles. We know of no archaic version that mentions an oracle. The oldest one that has come down to us, [Aeschylus's] *Seven against Thebes*, says simply that, should Laius die without issue, he will save Thebes.[9] In [Sophocles's] *Oedipus the King*, the oracle announces—after the birth of the child, and so too late for calamity to be averted—that the newborn will kill his father (lines 713, 1176). In [Euripides's] *Phoenician Women*, the announcement is placed, as in Aeschylus, before the birth; the oracle predicts the death of the father and the quarrel of the sons, which is to say the civil war for control over Thebes. Here Euripides's skillfulness in exploiting the innovations of his predecessors is manifest. The prediction never involves marriage with the mother, except in the version due to Nicolaus of Damascus (fragment 15): "The god says to Laius that he will sire a son who will kill him and who will marry his own mother"; and in [John] Malalas, who mentions only the marriage with the mother and not the murder of the father (*Chronographia* 2.59.0 [ed. L. Dindorf (Bonn, 1831), p. 50]). The sources from which Nicolaus of Damascus and Malalas draw are unknown, and probably no longer extant. Both authors refer to the legend as they recollected it from memory, neglecting to distinguish between the first response of the oracle, at Delphi, given to Laius in connection with the birth of his son, and the response given twenty years later to Oedipus when he came to Corinth to submit to the god his doubts concerning his birth.[10] If the mythographers confused the two warnings it is because, between Aeschylus's time and theirs, the legend had evolved: political in its beginnings, it became more and more *sentimental*, and the theme of incest steadily gained in importance; in Aeschylus, political motives were still predominant. Let us therefore take as our point of departure the oracle's response as it is formulated in *Seven against Thebes.* This way of proceeding is recommended additionally by the fact that the threat conveyed by the oracle in this case is not the same as the one that frightens Acrisius, Aleus, or Astages. It does not express the familiar prediction that the newborn will grow up to be the murderer of his grandfather or of his uncles—an adventitious detail that ultimately was to enter into all the legends of this type. It expresses a motif that is peculiar to the legend of Oedipus. I therefore think that, while it is foreign to the primitive myth, it nonetheless has to have appeared at a much earlier time than the one in which all tales of an exposed infant came to be stereotyped on the story of Perseus.

The idea that a child must be sacrificed because, if he lives, he will bring misfortune to an entire community is encountered, so far as I am aware, in only three legends, those of Oedipus, Paris, and Cypselus. I leave to one side that of Romulus, which is closely related to them, but whose independence— or lack of independence, as one may well be inclined to suspect—cannot be argued here.

The exposure of Alexander (Alexandros) is known to us solely through texts in which one detects the influence of tales concerning Oedipus and Cyrus.[11] In Homer, Alexander, like the other Trojan princes, herds his father's flocks to graze on Mount Ida. There is no mention of his having either been exposed or raised in the mountains. A fragment of Pindar speaks of a frightening dream in which Hecuba is warned of the misfortune that will befall Troy if Paris survives.[12] In the [lost] plays entitled *Alexandros* by Sophocles and Euripides the legend is found in its complete form, though we are unable to determine to what extent it had already been worked out before them. The infant is exposed on Ida, nursed by a she-bear, and raised by a shepherd who names him Paris. He soon surpasses all the companions of his childhood in strength and beauty, and vanquishes all who attempt to raid his flocks, as a result of which he is called Alexandros ["protector of men"]. His parents organize games at Troy in honor of their exposed son, whom they believe to have died long ago. Paris returns and emerges victorious in competition with his brothers, notably Hector and Deiphobus, who threatens to kill him.

To be sure, it is difficult to say which part of this account is likely to be old. Hecuba's dream could be a replica of Astyages's dream: the Trojan prince distinguishes himself in competition with his rivals exactly as the Persian child does. Nevertheless it must be recognized that the Greek playwrights, in elaborating the legend, preserved not only the religious coloring of each episode but also what might be called its archaic efficaciousness, as I will attempt to show in a moment.

Cypselus's childhood is known to us through Herodotus, who seems to have been determined to drive later historians to despair, so carefully does he obscure the religious content of his narratives. Deciding how much archaic reality lies concealed in a tale reported by Pausanias or Apollodorus is not especially difficult, for they frankly reproduce details they no longer understand. Herodotus rationalizes everything he touches, covering over authentic traditions, as well as the links he establishes between them in order to make them more acceptable, with a varnish of bourgeois plausibility. Let us therefore make due allowance for a certain folkloric element implicit in what he says of Cypselus.[13]

The Bacchiadae reign at Corinth. They have a daughter named Labda, who is afflicted with lameness. None of the men of the family wishes to take her as a wife. Finally she is wed to Eëtion, son of Echecrates, from the township [deme] of Petra. Echecrates himself is descended from Caeneus, a Lapith. Time goes by. Eëtion and his wife are still unable to conceive. Eëtion consults the oracle, which answers: "Eëtion, none esteem you though you are worthy of many honors. Labda is pregnant; she will give birth to a round boulder [ὀλοοίτροχος]. It will fall among royal men; it will punish the Corinthians."

The oracle is reported to the Bacchiadae. It reminds them of another, much more enigmatic one that they had long known without having ever been able to interpret it: "A fertile eagle among the rocks; it will bring forth a strong lion that will break the knees of many men. Mind you well, Corinthians, who live near lovely Peirene and haughty Corinth."

The Bacchiadae perceive that the two predictions concern the same child. When Cypselus is born, ten men from the Bacchiad clan are sent at once to the deme where Eëtion lives (ἐσ τὸν δῆμον, ἐν τῷ κατοίκητο ὁ Ἀετίων) with orders to seize the newborn and kill him. But the infant smiles, disarming the envoys; and after each one had passed him to the next in the hope that one of them would finally have the courage to "smash [him] against the stone threshold" [the Greek verb, προσουδίσαι, literally means to dash against the ground], in keeping with the plan they had agreed upon, they gave him back to his mother. Labda heard them reproaching one another, understood the danger, and hid the infant in a round chest—a *cypséle* [κυψέλη], hence the name later given to her son—where, on their return, they did not think to look for him.

This story, like that of Cyrus, is influenced by the tale of Perseus, whose popularity must have been great in preclassical Greece. The child is a menace to his maternal relatives; warned by an oracle, they seek to make him die. It is awkward to leave the prophecy of an oracle unfulfilled, however, and Nicolaus of Damascus was later to relate that Cypselus, in order to seize power, kills a Bacchiad, whom the manuscripts first identify as Hippoclides, then as Patroclides. On the other hand, the folkloric spirit that suffuses this legend bears the trace of earlier beliefs that caused malefic infants to be exposed. Exposure is always described as the action of an entire community.[14] This is why the ten Bacchiad envoys presented themselves to the local authorities before entering Eëtion's home. What they were demanding was a sort of right of extradition, for in antiquity, apart from precisely this case of *apothesis*, the father as paterfamilias had absolute authority over his offspring. The envoys obtained the permission they sought because the Bacchiadae had been shrewd enough to identify their cause with that of Corinth as a whole. The father on his return rescued the infant, hidden in a chest used for measuring out grain, and brought him to Olympia as a supplicant of the god.[15]

The laws relating to *apothesis* all say that the infant must be exposed immediately following birth. The head of the house of the Bacchiadae sends his messengers the moment Labda has delivered her child (ὡς δὲ ἔτεκε ἡ γυνὴ τάκιστα). But he made their mission a dangerous one by charging them, not with exposing the infant, but with killing it on the spot. An ancient Greek had few scruples about sending a guilty person to a certain death; he had many more when it was a matter of shedding blood, particularly that of someone who, in dying before his time, was liable to become a particularly dreaded ghost. None of the Bacchiad envoys wished to bring upon himself the stain of such a murder, or run the risk that would result from it. This is why, Herodotus says, they decided between them that the one to whom the mother handed over the infant would be responsible for smashing it on the ground. When the moment came, no one had the courage to carry out the plan. Herodotus, always ready to rationalize, would have us believe that the reason was not *fear*, but *pity*, and in order to make the envoys' reaction more plausible he adds that the infant smiled—without realizing that this embellishment is incompatible with the exact instruction[16] he had quoted earlier, namely, that the execution take place at the moment of birth, for a newborn baby does not smile. . . .

The village of Petra near Corinth is unknown to us. The name was probably inferred—perhaps by Herodotus himself—from the oracle, which says that the Eagle will inseminate among rocks. One may wonder whether ἐν πέτρῃσι κύει does not simply mean to fertilize unproductive land, that is, *to sow on stony ground.* The issue of Eëtion and Labda (which must be smashed against the ground [a "stone threshold"]) will be fatal in the manner of a "round boulder that a stream swollen by the storm has thrown down from the rock that it crowned." It is to the fall of one such boulder that the *Iliad* compares charging Hector (13.136–39). One must not try to read too much into images selected by an oracle that couches very simple realities in enigmatic terms. The oracle can only mean that Cypselus, son of an eagle inseminating stony ground, will be hard for Corinth, just as his mother was. His mother's name, Labda, poses several problems, however.

Since what period, and in what parts of Greece, were *labda* and *lambda* understood to signify a particular disability, that is, lameness? The entry for βλαισός in the *Etymologicum Magnum* says: "Knock-kneed, paralyzed, someone whose feet are turned outward like the letter λ. It is for this reason that Eëtion's wife, mother of the tyrant Cypselus, was called Lambda."[17] *Labda*, which is not an adjective, is known as a proper name only through the passage in Herodotus. The phrasing of the *Etymologicum Magnum* proves that its author did not know, any more than we do, the least thing about the word's literary use outside of Corinthian history. But as a nickname it has all the characteristics of a piece of slang, and may very well have been current in the popular tongue.[18] If the word, in the fifth century [BCE], designated someone who is lame, Herodotus, encountering the story of a woman named Labda, could have interpreted it as a nickname and inferred from it what he says about the young woman's infirmity. But in that case how are we to explain the strange parallelism of this tale with that of Oedipus, whose grandfather is called Labdacus? Labdacus is a grandfather, Labda the mother, of a newborn [Oedipus, Cypselus] who is declared before his birth to be evil and who is destined to die. None of these characters has a proper name. They have nicknames, taken in the case of the ascendants from an infirmity, and in the case of the descendants from an episode in which their lives were saved. At least this is how the Greeks understood, how they interpreted, the words *Oidipous* and *Cypselos.*

The two tales cannot have had any influence on each other. Both are recent and [may be at least roughly] dated. The names of Labda and Labdacus could have acquired the meaning indicated by the *Etymologicum Magnum* only after the introduction of the Phoenician alphabet. At Thebes, so far as we know, the letter *lambda* was written not ⅂, but ﹂.[19] Labdakos, a character without any accompanying legend, must have been a late interpolation between Polydorus and Laius in the line of Theban kings. Cypselus reigned in the mid-seventh century. The mythopoetic imagination that created his legend was constrained, as in the case of Cyrus as well, by the need to take into account historical facts that had not yet completely faded from memory.

The legend of Oedipus, like that of Cypselus, was, I believe, transcribed from an actual practice, the habit of exposing deformed newborn children from birth. But Cypselus and Oedipus are both victorious, and the ancients could not accept that their heroes might have been physically defective; the maleficent infirmity was therefore attributed to a forebear, a grandfather or a mother—mere personifications of the illness that is at the very root of the legendary creation. . . .

———————

The ancients were familiar with two versions of the exposure of Oedipus.

1. Sometimes he is placed in a chest and cast into the sea. It washes up ashore at Sicyon or at Corinth. The scholiast and the mythographer to whom we owe this information do not tell us the names of whoever it was who recounted this version of the story, but it had to have been current because it was treated by ceramists.[20] The arrival at Corinth or Sicyon is explained by the rival claims of several cities—claims either grounded in local traditions or merely authorized by a poetic text.

2. Or else he is abandoned on [Mt.] Cithaeron.

The two methods alternately occur in legends relating the legitimation of a divine *parthénios.* Both are also encountered in attested customs concerning the exposure of evil offspring. With regard to this latter point, however, it is necessary to distinguish between times and between places.

In Sparta, evil offspring are relegated to a place called the Repository, "located near [Mt.] Taygetus, full of holes," as Plutarch puts it in his account of Spartan laws. In Athens, they are hidden in a mysterious and unknown place according to Plato, who describes a custom that by his time had fallen into disuse. In Rome, under the Republic, they are brought to the sea in a chest and dumped into the sea far off the coast, without ever having touched the ground. If their deformity is such that they are no longer recognizably human, they are burned and their ashes thrown into the sea—the fate reserved for monstrous animals.[21] It seems therefore that the extermination of evil offspring by drowning is peculiar to Rome and not attested in Greece. The extreme aversion expressed by Greek authors must nonetheless be taken into account, as well as the physical aspect of such monsters and the treatment that they were made to undergo. Livy, who is not ashamed of national superstitions, is more explicit. Finally, we know nothing whatever about the "holes" [mentioned by Plutarch], the mysterious places where the exposures were carried out. Perhaps they were channels carved out by torrential mountain streams.

However that may be, we arrive at the following conclusion: in Hellenic *legend*, predestined bastard children are exposed [at birth], either on water or in the mountains; in the archaic *customs* of Greece and Italy, malefic newborns suffer the same fate, exposed in the mountains in Greece, on water in Italy.

Strange as it may seem, both kinds of infant were treated similarly. It will be necessary to come back to this parallclism later and try to explain it. First, however, let us consider the two versions of Oedipus's exposure. Which one is likely to be the older of the two? One is tempted to reply: exposure on water. First, because it is not mentioned by any of the poets whose works have come down to us, and cannot serve to explain the name given to the infant who is rescued. Exposure on [Mt.] Cithaeron would presumably have been invented, and then preferred, so that the detail of the pierced feet could be inserted, which had the dual advantage of giving a sign that could be recognized later and also of furnishing an *aition* for the name. At this juncture, however, a few observations will be in order.

The detail of the pierced feet is absurd under any construction that may be placed upon it. A newborn infant abandoned in the countryside or on water risks death whether or not his feet are bound. Several ancient grammarians were well aware of the difficulty and sought to resolve it. One scholiast, commenting on line 26 of [Euripides's] *Phoenician Women*, says that the parents mutilated Oedipus to prevent him from being rescued and raised to adulthood. It is true that in the historical period, on finding exposed infants, people who otherwise had not the least humanitarian feeling gave shelter to boys who showed promise of growing up to be robust and to girls who were likely to be pretty. Another scholiast commenting on the same verse, as well as Nicolaus of Damascus (in fragment 15), thought to dispose of this vexing detail simply by saying that Oedipus's feet had become swollen on account of his swaddling clothes.

The scars [left by Oedipus's wounds] do not assist recognition in any of the [primary] works that have come down to us, only in two summaries and then without any indication of sources. The first is fable 230 of the Second Vatican Mythographer, who says that "one day, as Oedipus was putting on his sandals, his mother saw his scars, and, recognizing her son, wept and moaned miserably." It is probable that this passage summarizes a partially lost commentary on the beginning of Statius's *Thebaid*, a hypothesis formulated by Keseling and accepted by Robert. The second is fable 67 of Hyginus: "Menoetes, the old man who had exposed Oedipus, recognized him as the son of Laius by the scars on his feet and his ankles." It has been supposed that old Menoetes had to have been a character in the [lost] *Oedipus* by Euripides. In any case, he had to belong to a mythopoeia influenced by *Oedipus the King*, for it was Sophocles who had the idea of ascribing the recognition of the identifying signs to secondary characters, the Corinthian shepherd and the Theban shepherd.[22] . . .

In the poems that have been preserved, Oedipus is never identified by the scars on his ankles. In the *Odyssey*, the gods reveal to Jocasta the identity of her husband; we do not know which signs could have served them as an instrument, perhaps the weapons taken from Laius. In Pisander's summary, Jocasta first recognizes the *murderer*, from Laius's weapons, then her formerly exposed *son*, by the swaddling clothes and the clasps still in the possession of the stableman from Sicyon who rescued the infant Oedipus.[23] It is obvious that if the signs (whatever they may have been) were there for Jocasta to see, then, on pain of implausibility, the moment of recognition must have immediately followed her marriage [to Oedipus]. Some poets tried to postpone the recognition until after the birth of their four children; but this meant having to deprive Jocasta of everything that could have enlightened her. In *Oedipus the King*, Sophocles makes her ignorant in the presence of two shepherds who, between them, can give a complete account of the exposure and rescue of the infant. I am inclined to believe that this episode was suggested to the poet by Herodotus's account of Cyrus's childhood. In the Sophoclean mythopoeia, Jocasta does not know that Oedipus's feet had been pierced. The wound was inflicted on the infant by the Theban shepherd, who points to the scars as proof of his own assertions—a useless proof since Jocasta, on the one hand, and the Corinthian shepherd, on the other, were witnesses to the beginning and the end of the story. The old man does not say why he pierced the infant's feet. No one questions him about this inexplicable and unexplained act.

Nor would anyone watching Sophocles's play have noticed that the detail of the pierced feet was incongruous. And yet when so great an artist, so skillful a dramatist keeps an episode that is at once superfluous and absurd, it is because this episode was imposed upon him by a prior mythopoeia. Since the wound appears not to have served any purpose in bringing about recognition, unless perhaps in later accounts, it must have been invented in order to explain the name.

Here it is impossible not to think of the hero Melampus, whose name, related to that of Oedipus, was explained in the same way, by a clumsily contrived episode that no poet was able to link up with the rest of the story. He has a black foot because his mother neglected to protect it against the rays of the sun. The story of Melampus exhibits several features analogous to that of Oedipus.[24] Why one is called "Tanned Foot," the other "Swollen Foot," is not understood. In each case the name must be older than the tale that purports to justify it.

Did *Oidipous* primitively signify "Swollen Foot" (or "Feet")? For once, linguists accept the etymology proposed by the ancients, and, for once as well, a Greek hero bears a transparent name, as meaningful as one could wish, wholly similar to the descriptive names that the heroes of folktales bear.[25] But the translation, however certain it may be, creates more problems than it clears up. Let us weigh the following two hypotheses:

1. There was a hero named Swollen Foot (that is, Misshapen Foot), who was the mythic personification of the old Greek custom of exposing

deformed newborn infants. This one miraculously survived. His destiny was at once glorious and terrible, for he avenged himself more or less voluntarily on those who had condemned him to death. Later, because on the one hand what is related about him is incompatible with the loss of strength implied by an infirmity, and because on the other hand illness, physical suffering (unless it results from a wound or from some mysterious cause), and natural death are unknown to Greek legend, the deformity gradually faded from memory. It was replaced by a lesion sustained after birth that is capable of explaining the name. In this case, however, the exposure is no longer motivated. It will therefore be given an extrinsic cause: an oracle forbidding the parents from founding a family.

This hypothesis accounts for the names borne by Oedipus's father and grandfather:

- Labdacus (*Labdakos*, "lame") was inserted in Cadmean genealogy because the circumstance that originally motivated the exposure had not yet been wholly forgotten. The physical defect was carried back from the grandson to the grandfather.
- The name Laius (*Laios*) is equivalent to the Latin names *Publius* and *Publicola*, according to a hypothesis proposed some years ago now,[26] but still accepted. No one has been able to justify this etymology, however. Let us recall that the presence of a deformed newborn was considered to be a danger to the community as a whole; and that it is the representatives of the community who make the decision to do away with it, whether in Sparta or in Rome or Athens. Oedipus is the only infant exposed by his father. But this father [interpreting his name literally] is called "He who is of the people." Faced with so many telling facts and revealing names, I think it is difficult not to recognize in the legend of Oedipus a mythical transcription of *apothesis*.

2. The name of the hero may not originally have had the form and meaning given to it later. The content of the legend could have acted upon the word and made it mean what it needed to mean. Whether the word had been meaningful from the first, or whether it became so

only after a more or less long period of uncertainty, is scarcely of any importance. In the first case, the name and the myth were invented together; in the second, the myth sought to provide itself with a hero. The most we can say is that, as far as we are able to go back, the hero had already been found.

The moment when a custom is most likely to be transformed into a myth is when it begins to fall into disuse, or else when, while continuing still to be practiced, it ceases to be understood; for if it is no longer its own justification, if it is no longer immediately efficacious, an attempt is made to explain it by means of a distinctive story, associated with a particular character. We have no information concerning *apothesis* in the immediate vicinity of Thebes. All we know is that Aelian (*Historical Miscellany* 2.7) mentions a Boeotian law restricting the rights of the father in respect of *ekthesis*. Unfortunately, he does not say to what period this law he mentions belonged. But it is certain that it had to stand in contrast to the customs of the rest of Greece. It is therefore not impossible that *apothesis* had also disappeared in Boeotia sooner than in the rest of Greece.

The various accounts of Atalanta's early life were likewise inspired by *ekthesis*. Her father exposes her because she is a girl and he had hoped for a boy. The custom of exposing unwanted infants, especially girls, was practiced throughout historical Greece. It is therefore from a contemporary custom that the reason for the heroine's being raised in the mountains was taken. According to other versions, her father condemned her to death on the advice of an ominous oracle. The oracle is a recent invention in this legend, as in others of the same type. It is plain to see, comparing the two stories, how an archaic religious custom is transposed into a myth, whereas a utilitarian custom, intelligible to all, enters as an intruder into a legend whose incoherence requires a rational justification, and as a result transforms it into a romance.

I am prepared to believe that, in the various accounts of Oedipus's early life, the versions of exposure at sea and exposure in the mountains are equally ancient. The two are also found in the case of Telephus. What is more, the storytellers who accepted [Oedipus's] exposure in the mountains described his rescue in several different ways. The Beugnot amphora, a work in the style of Phideas, shows a young horseman carrying the infant Oedipus in his arms to King Polybus, an episode unknown to other sources. Now, an artist depicts only scenes that are familiar to his audience. Whether or not Carl Robert was right to detect in Oedipus's features an expression of physical suffering, the painter of the amphora manifestly does not indicate the faintest sign of a lesion on Oedipus's feet.[27]

Exposed infants made to undergo the trial of the chest and deformed infants who were excommunicated as portents of evil were both treated in a way that in many respects resembles the fate of *pharmakoi*. How far are we entitled to assimilate these three categories to one another? Let us begin by studying the obvious kinship between *pharmakoi* and abnormal children.

Recent researches have clarified the dual character ascribed by the Greeks to scapegoats.[28] The act by which a *pharmakos* was solemnly expelled from the community was intended both to increase the fertility of its land and to ward off evil in the person of an individual made to bear the community's transgressions. To the modern mind these two ideas are quite different, and it was a long time before the scapegoat was recognized both as a "sin-eater" [purifier], weighed down with the accumulated burden of so many individual culpabilities, and as someone related to the "spirits of vegetation" who is thrashed in order to ensure a bountiful harvest. This dual quality is nonetheless certain, with the expiatory character of the *pharmakos* probably being the more modern of the two. Little by little, it would appear, agrarian rites were transformed into "atonements."[29] This evolution will become clear if we compare scapegoats with abnormal infants who were exposed.

In both cases one encounters the same psychological components: fear in the face of the wrath of mysterious forces (to speak here of the gods is probably an anachronism); anxiety in the face of an unknown transgression that is more or less explicitly conceived as the cause of the harm [to the community]; a desire to transfer this harm to an individual who then can be excluded from the community.

Let us lay stress on the common elements, and also on a few details that until now have not been satisfactorily explained. We will see at once why a magical act meant to ensure fertility appears at the same time to be an expiatory rite.

1. *Identity of harm and remedy.* The wrath of the gods is manifested not

only by barrenness, but also by the birth of misshapen infants. Once exposed, these infants serve as a remedy by counteracting the harm of which they are the symptom and by preventing it from spreading. In Rome they figured in all collective calamities. With the outbreak of war, if the enemy threat became dire, abnormal individuals—which is to say those who had been lucky enough to have been ignored at the time of their birth—were rounded up. Instead of being exposed, they were executed at once: aversion to shedding blood gave way to fear and the need to find expiatory victims as soon as possible. The very intensity of the evil they were thought to embody made them especially well suited to become healers, so long as one knew how to make use of them in accordance with the will of the gods. Bouché-Leclercq had drawn attention earlier to the ambivalent—malign or beneficial—character of persons who have been "dedicated." Riess emphasized the identical role played in magic by *aori* [ones who have died untimely deaths]: "An early and violent death renders the soul capable of becoming a magical *paredra* [sacred consort]."[30]

Let us now turn again to the evidence regarding Greek antiquity. Unfortunately, we have nothing here as valuable as Livy's admirably simple and candid testimony [concerning the treatment of deformed newborns in Rome (*History of Rome* 27.37.5–6)]. But a [Greek] poet is credited by a [Byzantine] commentator with an observation similar to the one made by the Roman historian. Tzetzes relates that in Ionia, according to Hipponax, τῶν πάντων ἀμορφότερον ἦγον ὡς πρὸς θυσίαν [the most deformed of all they conducted as to a sacrifice]. The Greek word ἄμορφος may mean "ugly" or "deformed." The same ambiguity is found in a scholium on Aristophanes, which seems to confirm the sacrifice of "wretches and those whom nature had mistreated."[31] V. Gebhard has tried to explain the fact by the apotropaic character of caricatural ugliness.[32] But I believe that the question here is much less one of ugliness than of deformity. Note that in the passage quoted from Aristophanes one finds mentioned, among the dregs of humanity, redheads.[33] The dominant conception here is not ugliness, but strangeness. It is exactly this quality that governs the expulsion of newborns.

2. *Ordeal.* As a rule, misshapen infants are simply exposed in conditions such that they could scarcely avoid death. Similarly, *pharmakoi* were chased away under a shower of stones. This does not mean they were always killed. Harpocration (see the entry for φαρμακός) says that the expulsion of the

scapegoat in the Thargelia commemorates the execution of Pharmakos, thief of Apollo's holy cups, who was stoned by Achilles. But an *aition* is invariably more precise and more intelligible than the rite it claims to justify. Two grammarians say that the *pharmakos* was *sacrificed*.[34] In addition to the fact that θυσία and θύειν, in later writing, may refer to any religious act whatsoever, it needs to be kept in mind that they are probably employing a shorthand, in an imprecise fashion, to express the idea that death sometimes followed the brutal expulsion of the unfortunate surrogate. Nevertheless one should not too hastily reject the account reported by Tzetzes, who says that the victim, after having been beaten, "was burned on a rough-hewn pyre, and the ashes then cast into the sea, to the winds, in order to purify the stricken city, as Lycophron also recalls in connection with the Locrians" (*Chiliades* 5.735ff.). Gebhard wholly discredits this testimony, arguing that it can only be due to confusion with another rite, the postmortem cremation of the priestesses sent from Locris to Ilion to atone for the sacrilege committed by Ajax.[35] I am not so sure that the detail of the incinerated corpse comes from a foreign context. In Rome, monstrous animals were burned and their ashes cast into the sea. The same treatment is mentioned once in connection with a misshapen infant having a particularly frightening appearance.[36] The fates of scapegoats and malefic abnormal infants are so closely related that the information furnished by Tzetzes must have some basis in fact. All one can say is that the events he attests were isolated and probably rare, and that cremation can only have taken place under exceptional circumstances, perhaps when the victim, having been fatally wounded by the stones hurled at him by his pursuers, died before he left their territory. Tzetzes's information might even have its source in a layer of very archaic beliefs (while implying nothing whatsoever with regard to the era in which the event was actually witnessed), beliefs that were associated with harvest rites in which a creature is immolated in order to restore to nature the forces residing in it. Gradually these rites seem to have become charged with expiatory significance. Once this evolution was complete, the sacrificed creature having in the meantime come to be seen as a "bearer of sins," its killing was no longer necessary. Now excommunication was enough—and this all the more as it resulted from a *race* [between pursued and pursuers], which is to say from a rite that in the very remote past seems to have possessed an inherently cathartic or stimulating quality.[37]

Let us leave any unverifiable hypothesis to one side, however, along with any uncorroborated information from which no conclusions can be drawn. We may nonetheless be certain that, in the historical era, the scapegoat— exactly like the exposed infant—was handed over to the will of the gods. To avoid death by stoning he probably had to flee, and run fast enough to remove himself from the community that was chasing him from its territory. Nothing more was asked of him. This much stands out from a passage in Strabo describing the leap of *pharmakoi* who, [on the island of] Leucas, were forced to throw themselves [from a great height] into the sea during the annual sacrifice performed in honor of Apollo: "At the foot of the rocky promontory a circle of small boats waited to rescue [any who survived the leap] and, as soon as they had been taken on board, to conduct them safely outside the borders of the territory." . . .

3. *Rescue of the pharmakos*. In Strabo's time, those forced to make the ritual leap at Leucas were accused criminals, which scapegoats certainly were not, at least not at first. Moral reasoning had become more sophisticated in the interval, and a community no longer dared to saddle an innocent victim with its transgressions. Instead the community sought to reconcile its belief in the efficacy of banishment with its growing need for justice by selecting as a surrogate someone presumed to be guilty of a crime. In earlier times it is probable that some poor misshapen creature was chosen, someone who could not defend himself. The first quality has a religious value, the second a rational value. In Aristophanes, *pharmakós* is more or less equivalent to the French word *misérable*, in both of its senses [impoverished, wretched]. There is also a sense of contempt implicit in the Greek word, whose shades are so subtle that it is difficult to distinguish between a moral nuance, a social nuance, and even an aesthetic nuance. The poor and ugly *pharmakos* belongs to the scum of humanity, even if to his naturally abject condition no specific crime is added. In Marseilles, in Petronius's time, the scapegoat was a poor devil who gladly accepted the following offer: for a year he would be well fed, and after that he would take his chances.[38]

Now, with regard to those criminals [plunging into the sea] at Leucas, an attempt was made to rescue them and give them safe conduct outside the territory. This is rather curious, for all sources are agreed that they were presumed to be guilty of crimes and could justly have been abandoned to their fate, leaving the gods free to save them if they were innocent. It is tempting to explain such surprising indulgence in terms of a general softening of moral attitudes. Similarly, during the classical period in Greece, deformed newborns gradually ceased to be exposed. In Rome, Livy speaks of abnormal adults, which indicates that some children at least were spared at birth, though we know nothing about the circumstances under which they survived. Did their parents keep them, or were they exposed in such a way that their lives could be saved? I believe that it was not only on account of pity that scapegoats and deformed offspring were given the greatest possible chance of survival. All the legends that we have studied here have a common theme: one who has been consecrated, and whom the gods have chosen to save, becomes a source of good. . . .

At the moment when he rises to the surface, the scapegoat—who represents an entire community—is cleansed of all his sins and, along with him, all those who hurled him into the sea. Even more importantly, sacralization endows him with the beneficent force that we have already noticed in those who were subjected to ordeals and saved. If he survives, it is because the gods approve of his starting over again, along with the whole group he represents; of his beginning a new life, better than the one he had led until then.

NOTES

Translator's note: The English version has been made from the text of the first edition published in 1944, with reference also to the 1981 reprint issued by Les Belles Lettres, which corrects some (but by no means all) misprints in the original. As a courtesy to nonspecialist readers, I have placed a certain amount of additional information in square brackets in both the text and the notes, while also giving full bibliographic detail for all citations, silently correcting errors of attribution, and, wherever possible, indicating exact page ranges. Ellipses not within quotations indicate portions of Delcourt's French text that are not translated here.

1. See Marie Delcourt, *Stérilités mystérieuses et naissances maléfiques dans l'antiquité classique* (Paris: E. Droz, 1938).

2. See Hermann Usener, *Die Sintfluthsagen* (Bonn: F. Cohen, 1899), 80ff.; Gustave Glotz, *L'ordalie dans la Grèce primitive: Étude de droit et de mythologie* (Paris: A. Fontemoing, 1904); James George Frazer, "Moses in the Ark of Bulrushes," in *Folk-lore in the Old Testament: Studies in Comparative Religion, Legend, and Law*, 3 vols. (London: Macmillan, 1918), 2:43ff.

3. Neither Paul Weizsäcker nor Karl Tümpel gave a proper analysis, any more than Usener, Glotz, or Frazer did. See the entries on Deucalion by Weizsäcker, in W. H. Roscher, ed., *Ausführliches Lexikon der griechischen und römischen Mythologie*, 6 vols. and Supplement (Leipzig: B. G. Teubner, 1884–1937), vol. 1, cols. 994–98; and by Tümpel, in August Friedrich Pauly and Georg Wissowa, eds., *Realencyclopädie der classischen Altertumswissenschaft*, first series [A–Q] (Stuttgart: J. B. Metzler, 1894–1963), vol. 5.1, cols. 261–76.

4. See Glotz, *L'ordalie dans la Grèce primitive*, 27.

5. See Delcourt, "La pureté des éléments et l'invocation de Créuse dans 'Ion,'" *Revue belge de philologie et d'histoire* 17, nos. 1–2 (1938): 195–203.

6. "The legend of Oedipus," Robert remarks, "is certainly older than all the oracles." Carl Robert, *Oidipus: Geschichte eines poetischen Stoffs im griechischen Altertum*, 2 vols. (Berlin: Weidmann, 1915), 1:11.

7. See Apollodorus, *Library* 3.9.1, 2.7.4.

8. See Alexander Haggerty Krappe, "Le mythe de la naissance de Cyrus," *Revue des études grecques* 43, nos. 200–201 (1930): 153–59.

9. Aeschylus, *Seven against Thebes* 748: ϑνάσκοντα γέννας ἄτερ σῴζειν πόλιν.

10. See Sophocles, *Oedipus the King* 715 (first oracle); 790 (second oracle). Ask any honest person how the oracle replied to Laius and—if he does not have the text of Sophocles's play in front of him—he will answer as Nicolaus of Damascus did, the two replies being superimposed in his memory.

11. See the texts in Carl Robert, ed., *Die griechische Heldensage,* constituting the second volume of Ludwig Preller, *Griechische Mythologie,* 2 vols. (Berlin: Weidmann, 1920–26), 2:978 nn. 3, 4.

12. See Pindar, *Paeans,* no. 8 (ed. O. Schröder [Leipzig, 1908], p. 280; also *Oxyrhynchus Papyri* [*P. Oxy.*] 5.841.

13. See Herodotus, *Histories* 5.92.

14. Regarding the practice of infant exposure (ἀπόθεσις) in Sparta, Athens, and Rome, see my *Stérilités mystérieuses et naissances maléfiques,* 36ff. [The term ἔκθεσις was used by Greek authors to signify the act of exposing a newborn child, whereas ἀπόθεσις adds to this the idea of abandonment. The basic meaning of the two terms, *apothesis* and *ekthesis,* is nonetheless the same.—Trans.]

15. See Nicolaus of Damascus 7.58, in Felix Jacoby, *Die Fragmente der griechischen Historiker* [*FGrHist*] (Berlin: Weidmann, 1923–58), 1:301.

16. Historical accuracy is not at issue in the case of Cypselus, about whose infancy we are wholly ignorant. His legend nevertheless exactly transcribes a practice that, in Herodotus's time, was probably no longer observed in Athens as faithfully has it had been in earlier times.

17. The original text reads: ΒΛΑΙΣΟΣ: Παραλυτικός | . . . ὁ τοὺς πόδας ἐπὶ τὰ ἔξω διεστραμμένος, καὶ τῷ Λ στοιχείῳ ἐοικώς | Διὰ τοῦτο καὶ Λάμβδα ἐκαλεῖτο ἡ γυνὴ μὲν Ἡετίωνος, μήτηρ δὲ Κυψέλου τοῦ Κορίνθου τυράννου. See *Etymologicum Magnum* (ed. T. Gaisford [Oxford, 1848], p. 199, col. 573, ll. 23–27).

18. Like the synonym for *boîteux* [lame, limping], "cinq et trois font huit" [five and three make eight], which will perhaps disappear from French slang without leaving any written trace. "Although the authenticity of the word [*lambda*] may be doubted," Mr. [René] Fohalle tells me, "it must be kept in mind that the vowel *a,* relatively rare in Indo-European, occurs there notably in words having a popular character, particularly in names of infirmities." Cf. Antoine Meillet, *Introduction à l'étude des langues indo-européennes,* 7th ed. (Paris: Hachette, 1934), 90.

19. See Robert, *Oidipus,* 1:59.

20. See, for example, the scholium on Euripides, *Phoenician Women* 26: Οἳ δὲ εἰς θάλασσαν ἐκριφῆναι [φασὶ τὸν Οἰδίποδα] βληθέντα εἰς λάρνακα καὶ προσοκείλαντα τῇ Σικυῶνι ὑπὸ Πολυβίου ἀνατραφῆναι [They threw Oedipus into the sea (it is said), after having put him in a chest; he landed at Sicyon and was raised there]; and ibid., 28: τινὲς δὲ εν λάρνακι βληθέντα καὶ εἰς ϑάλασσαν ριφέντα τὸν παῖδα

προσπελασθῆναι τῇ Κορίνθῳ φασίν [Certain (mythographers) say that the child, put in a chest and thrown into the sea, washed up on the shore of Corinth]. Also Hyginus, *Fables* (no. 66): *Hunc* [Oedipus] *Periboea Polybi regis uxor cum vestem ad mare lavaret exposito sustulit Polybo sciente.* … [Periboea, wife of King Polybus, found Oedipus, who had been exposed, as she was washing clothes at the shore and, with Polybus's consent, raised him]. See too the Homeric bowl published by Edmond Pottier in a triennial volume (1885–88) issued in Paris by the Association pour l'encouragement des études grecques, pl. 8, p. 48; also reproduced in Carl Robert, "Homerische Becher," *Programm zum Winckelmannsfeste der Archaeologischen Gesellschaft zu Berlin*, vol. 50 (Berlin: G. Reimer, 1890), 76 c, and in Robert, ed., *Die griechische Heldensage*, 2:885.

21. The relevant passages in each case are found in Delcourt, *Stérilités mystérieuses et naissances maléfiques*, 37–66.

22. See Robert, *Oidipus*, 1:77, 1:324; and Ferdinand Keseling, *De mythographi Vaticani secundi fontibus*, inaug. diss. (Halle, 1908), 62.

23. Nicolaus Wecklein supposes, for Euripides's *Oedipus*, a mythopoeia in which the chariot taken from Laius and given to Polybus made recognition possible; see *Die kyklische Thebais, die Oedipodee, die Oedipussage und der Oedipus des Euripides* (Munich: Sitzungsberichte der Bayerischen Akademie der Wissenschaften, 1901), 671ff. [The shorthand "Pisander's summary" refers to a commentary on *Phoenician Women* 1760 (= Peisandros *FGrHist* 16 F10) by a Greek author of uncertain identity that, according to Erich Bethe, contains a summary of the *Oedipodeia* alluded to by Euripides. Bethe was fiercely attacked by Carl Robert and Ludwig Deubner; his few remaining defenders include Marie Delcourt and, more recently, Hugh Lloyd-Jones. Delcourt discusses the notorious "Pisanderscholion" in the introduction to her *Œdipe* and reproduces the Greek text on pp. xix–xx of the original edition.—Trans.]

24. See p. 166 [in the original French edition of Delcourt's book]; also the note by Paul Kretschmer in *Glotta* 12 (1923): 59, who likewise feels that the two names are prior to the etiological legends that attempt to explain them. I will not follow Kretschmer, however, in suggesting that the two heroes were ancient serpent-gods.

25. Herbert Petersson (in a comment on Martin P. Nilsson's review of Robert, *Oidipus*, in *Göttingische gelehrte Anzeigen* 184 (1922): 45) feels that the name cannot come from οἰδέω, οἰδάω [to swell, become swollen] and proposes that it be attached instead to *οδιοός (an unattested form constructed on the model of κυδρός), from the same root as the hypothetical *eitar, poison. The meaning would remain the same. Obviously it is impossible to conclude anything from guesses based on other guesses.

26. It was initially proposed, I believe, by August Friedrich Pott, "Mytho-etymologica (schlufs)," *Zeitschrift für vergleichende Sprachforschung* [*KZ* (= *Kuhns Zeitschrift*)] 7 (1858): 324. Robert attributes it to Wilamowitz, who simply adopted it—without citing Pott—in "Excurse zum Oedipus des Sophokles," *Hermes* 34 (1899): 77. "The linguist can examine the form of a word and indicate the possibilities that it suggests," Mr. Fohalle writes me in this connection, "but these possibilities are many and one of them may be overlooked, because a word of this kind is exposed to the most diverse accidents, for example to a folk etymology, precisely because the form is not supported by a stable value."

27. See Robert, *Oidipus*, 1:72–73, and figure 22 there; cf. André de Ridder, *Catalogue des vases peints de la Bibliothèque Nationale*, 2 vols. (Paris: E. Leroux, 1901–2), 2:272, no. 372.

28. All the testimonia together with a brief survey of modern interpretations may be found in Viktor Gebhard, *Die Pharmakoi in Ionien und die Sybakchoi in Athen* (Munich: Hueber, 1926).

29. Wilhelm Mannhardt was the first, I believe, in *Mythologische Forschungen* (Strassburg: K. J. Trübner, 1884), to hold that the agrarian rite was prior to the expiatory rite. His opinion was subsequently shared by Henri Hubert and Marcel Mauss, first in "Essai sur la nature et la fonction du sacrifice," *L'Année sociologique* 2 (1898): 29–138 (see esp. pages 102ff.), then in *Mélanges d'histoire des religions* (Paris: F. Alcan, 1909). Martin Nilsson, in the chapter on the Thargelia in his *Griechische Feste von religiöser Bedeutung mit Ausschluss der Attischen* (Leipzig: B. G. Teubner, 1906), 105ff., thinks that it was simply a matter of two equally old liturgies being merged together.

Georges Dumézil, in *Le festin d'immortalité: Étude de mythologie comparée indo-européenne* (Paris: P. Geuthner, 1924) sees the Thargelia, with its three main acts—expulsion of the *pharmakos*, procession of Eiresione, feast—as a festival of Ambrosia. According to Harpocration, Pharmakos stole the holy cups of Apollo and afterward was stoned by Achilles [see Istros *FGrHist* 334 F 50 = Harpocration 180, 19, s.v. *pharmakós*]. Pharmakos is the demon thief who, in other mythologies, steals ambrosia from the gods, in punishment for which he is buried under rocks.

It is necessary on this view, then, to suppose that the eponymous Pharmakos of the rite (a rite that goes beyond the Thargelia) absorbed the story of the demon thief: the thief lost his primitive name; the ritual figure in turn gained a biography; and a liturgy of complex meaning resulted from the merger of the two. It should however be noted that the superposition of an agrarian rite and an expiatory rite is rather frequent, and that it can be explained without invoking a very hypothetical festival of Ambrosia.

30. Ernst Riess, "Aberglaube," in *RE*, first series, vol. 1, col. 92. See also the article by Auguste Bouché-Leclercq, "Devotio," in Charles Daremberg and Edmond Saglio, eds., *Dictionnaire des antiquités grecques et romaines d'après les textes et les monuments*, 10 vols. (Paris: Hachette, 1877–1919), 2:113–19.

31. The scholium on Aristophanes, *Frogs* 730 reads: τοὺς φαύλους καὶ παρὰ τῆς φύσεως ἐπιβουλευομένους εἰς ἀπαλλαγὴν αὐχμοῦ ἤ ... ἔθυον [Wretches and those whom nature had mistreated they sacrificed, in order to ward off drought and famine]. In suggesting this translation to me, Mr. [Armand] Delatte advises that, in the Byzantine period, the image that previously had been conveyed by ἐπιβουλεύω was now completely eclipsed. Yet the expression seems a very mannered one from the pen of a grammarian; in place of the present ἐπιβουλευομένους (which seems corrupt, but for which I have no correction to propose) one would have expected a perfect participle. Gebhard (*Die Pharmakoi*, 30) glosses this testimony—rather than translating it, though plainly he understands it as we do—thus: "Die Aristophanesscholien berichten von Leuten niederster Herkunft, Taugennichtsen, die zu gar nicht brauchbar waren, von Krüppeln denen die Natur eine böse Stiefmutter war" [The scholia on Aristophanes refer to people of the lowest origins, to bad persons, who are good for nothing, to the crippled, to whom nature was a cruel stepmother].

32. See Gebhard, *Die Pharmakoi*, 79–80. Let me note in passing that my explanation makes it possible to see something other than a mere romantic flourish in a detail provided by Athenaeus regarding Cratinus, who voluntarily gives his life during the purification of Attica by Epimenides. Cratinus is εὔμορφος: well formed, handsome. Athenaeus, used to seeing scapegoats whose appearance was altogether different, evidently thought it useful to point out so exceptional a detail (*Sophists at Dinner* 13.602c), which Diogenes Laertius (*Lives and Opinions of Eminent Philosophers* 1.10) does not mention.

33. Redheads are placed in the same category as persons suffering constitutional defects; see Eupolis, fragment 5 of *The Golden Race* in August Meineke, ed., *Fragmenta comicorum Graecorum*, 5 vols. (Berlin: G. Reimeri, 1839–57), 2:537. Nevertheless a passage such as the one found on this subject in Adamantius's *Physiognomonica* shows that it is difficult to separate the physical notion of redheadedness from the moral ideas that, for the ancients, were associated with it; see the

[Greek] text in Richard Foerster, ed., *Scriptores physiognomonici graeci et latini*, 2 vols. (Leipzig: B. G. Teubner, 1893), 1:394 F.

34. See scholia on Aristophanes, *Frogs* 730 (ἔθυον) and *Wealth* 454 (Θυόμενοι).

35. See Juliette Davreux, *La légende de la prophétesse Cassandre d'après les textes et les monuments* (Paris: E. Droz, 1942), 53.

36. See my *Stérilités mystérieuses et naissances maléfiques*, 57. "In 1474," Krappe says, without giving any indication as to his source, "a cock was burned at Basel for having laid an egg" (Alexander Haggerty Krappe, *La genèse des mythes* [Paris: Payot, 1938], 46).

37. See Gebhard, *Pharmakoi*, 109; Nilsson, *Griechische Feste*, 113; and my further discussion at p. 169 of the present work.

38. See Aristophanes, *Frogs* 730ff., *Knights* 1405ff.; and Servius, *In Vergilii Aeneidem commentarii* [*Ad Aen.*] 3.57.

PART TWO

King and Victim

Imitating Oedipus

Mark R. Anspach

"There is none but Chu-bu."

... "There is also Sheemish."

—Lord Dunsany, "Chu-bu and Sheemish"

W hat happens when a new god is installed in the temple of Chu-bu? In Dunsany's fable,[1] Chu-bu is a small god, but a proud one. He could not but resent the worship given to that callow upstart Sheemish. One night, to Chu-bu's deep satisfaction, a bird soiled the newcomer's head. "There is dirt upon thy head, O Sheemish," exulted Chu-bu. "Dirt, dirt, dirt, upon the head of Sheemish."

Alas, the time came when a bird soiled Chu-bu's own head. This turn of events could scarcely go unremarked by Sheemish. "Dirty Chu-bu," he cried triumphantly, setting off an endless exchange of accusations between the two gods. "All night long they spake," writes Dunsany, "and all night said these words only: 'Dirty Chu-bu,' 'Dirty Sheemish.' 'Dirty Chu-bu,' 'Dirty

Excerpt from the editor's introduction to René Girard, *Oedipus Unbound: Selected Writings on Rivalry and Desire* (Stanford, CA: Stanford University Press, 2004).

Sheemish.' . . . And gradually Chu-bu came to realize that he was nothing more than the equal of Sheemish."

To Chu-bu, there may be something tragic in this hard-won realization. Yet nobody would mistake him for a tragic hero. Dunsany's protagonist lacks gravitas. His squabbling is hopelessly childish.

Children, of course, like nothing better than to trade insults. The object is to come up with a sally so devastating it cannot possibly be topped. However, the target of the sharpest barb always has a surefire retort available. All she has to do is say: *I know you are, but what am I?*

Pronounced in the mocking tones of a smug big sister, the annoyance value of this all-purpose formula is hard to beat. Like some improbable Star Wars antimissile system, it swoops down from above and intercepts oncoming insults before they land, automatically lobbing them back at the assailant without even stopping to scan their contents.

Such a mechanical response is effective because, however varied the content of insults may be, the structure of the exchange is always the same. "Who are you calling a dummy? You're the dummy!" *I know you are, but what am I?* tops all comers by operating at the meta-level of pure structure. It reduces schoolyard repartee to a mathematical equation through the principle of the dummy variable. Just plug in your rival's favorite jibe and apply it to him. "Who are you calling an (x)? You're the (x)!"

Although the structure in question may be simple, there is a paradox to it. When I hurl your own insult back at you, I mirror your behavior as precisely as possible, taking you as my model at the very moment I make you my target. I know you are worthy of insult, since you just insulted me, but, since I just insulted you . . . what am I? If I imitate you, can I be anything more than your equal?

A Plague of Doubles

The paradoxical tendency of rivalry to beget imitation—and of imitation to beget rivalry—is the point of departure for the theory of human culture that René Girard has patiently elaborated and refined over the past four decades. Of course, Girard takes on subjects more serious than schoolyard quarrels. He has tackled literary criticism and psychoanalysis, structural anthropology, comparative religion, and Continental philosophy; he has given us fresh readings of Shakespeare, Dostoyevsky, Proust, Freud, and the Bible, not to mention of primitive mythology and Greek tragedy. His range is staggering. And yet, wherever he looks, he cannot help turning up the selfsame structure of imitation and rivalry.

Take *Oedipus the King*, for example. It would be hard to think of a more serious work than this. After having solved the riddle of the Sphinx, Oedipus must confront the deepest, darkest secret of all, the secret of patricide and incest. So fearsome is this secret that even the famed seer Tiresias hesitates to reveal it. Indeed, when Oedipus asks him who killed Laius, Tiresias will only say, in effect: "That's for me to know and you to find out."

Increasingly exasperated by the other's refusal to answer, Oedipus finally accuses Tiresias of having plotted the murder himself. But as soon as Oedipus launches this accusation, his target lobs it right back at him, accusing Oedipus of having carried out the murder *himself*. And when Oedipus dares Tiresias to repeat his harsh words, Tiresias not only repeats them, he tops them off with an inflammatory insinuation involving the other's mama.

Oedipus then reacts the same way anyone might upon being called a murderous mother-lover. "Oh yeah," he says in so many words, "well, you're a blind fool!" This is a low blow because Tiresias, as it happens, *is* blind, so now he really loses his cool. "Who are you calling blind?" he demands. "You're the one who's blind, since you don't even see the truth about yourself." At this point, Girard steps in and asks whether Tiresias sees the truth about *himself*. Does Tiresias realize that he is *imitating Oedipus*? Does he understand that the more he lashes back at his adversary, the more he becomes his equal?

I know you are—but what am I? "Every man is Oedipus, the guilty party, *to the Other*," remarks Girard, "and Tiresias, the misjudged prophet, *to him-self*."[2] "Dirty Tiresias," "Dirty Oedipus." "Dirty Tiresias," "Dirty Oedipus": as the debate between the prophet and the king degenerates, the members of the chorus look on with growing dismay. Barely able to get a word in edge-wise, they do manage to admonish Oedipus that anger "inspires Tiresias's words, and yours too" (lines 404–5).

Animosity is contagious. Tiresias "'catches' Oedipus's hate the way one catches a contagious disease," writes Girard.[3] The chorus fears that, as Oedipus and Tiresias bicker, they are losing sight of what should be paramount: the need to rid Thebes of the plague. In a bold stroke, Girard ties these two threads together. Violent conflict is itself a form of plague, he observes. By virtue of its imitative nature, it can spread like a devastating contagion, and like a contagion it obliterates distinctions, turning individuals into symmetrical doubles.

Every plague is a plague of doubles. Girard has commented elsewhere on the striking similarities that mark literary and mythical treatments of plagues: "The curious thing about these similarities is that they ultimately involve the very notion of the similar. The plague is universally presented as a process of undifferentiation, a destruction of specificities."[4] Girard could have illustrated this observation by quoting the following lines from Thucydides' description of the plague that struck Athens in 430 BC: "Some of the sufferers died from want of care, others equally who were receiving the greatest attention. No single remedy could be deemed a specific; for that which did good to one did harm to another. No constitution was of itself strong enough to resist or weak enough to escape the attacks; the disease carried off all alike."[5] Thucydides' words are all the more relevant in that *Oedipus the King* is believed to have originally been produced some time between 429 and 425 BC—during or immediately following the outbreak of the Athenian plague. Since a Theban plague was not part of the earlier Oedipus tradition, Sophocles must have been inspired by the epidemic in his own city.[6]

If Girard does not dwell on the specific historical context in which the play was written, that is doubtless because he prefers to stress its universal import. In *Violence and the Sacred*, he remarks: "Even if Sophocles had in mind the famous Athenian plague of 430 BC, he clearly did not mean to limit his reference to one specific microbiotic visitation. The epidemic that interrupts all the vital functions of the city is surely not unrelated to violence and the loss of distinctions."[7] However, given Girard's avowed tendency to find similarities among all great works of literature, some readers may wonder whether he is not himself heedless of distinctions. An intruder in the temple of classical studies, he is automatically suspect. It seems only fair to ask whether his interpretation of *Oedipus* respects the specificity of the ancient Greek text.

———————

The most frequently used word for "plague" in both Sophocles' play and in Thucydides is *nosos*. According to American classics scholar Frederick Ahl:

The meaning of *nosos* may also be extended into a political metaphor. Plato describes in book 5 of the *Republic* (470C) the conflicts among the Greek states not just as civil wars but as themselves a kind of *nosos*, "sickness": "in such a situation Greece is sick." Many in Sophocles' audience may have shared Plato's view that the internecine wars among Greeks are "the ultimate sickness (*nosêma*) of the *polis*" (*Republic* 8.544C).[8]

Historically speaking, the two kinds of "sickness" coincided. The microbial plague descended on Athens while it was caught up in the Peloponnesian War, which was still raging when Sophocles wrote *Oedipus*. Moreover, Sophocles links his Theban epidemic to war in mythical terms by having the chorus blame the city's affliction on the god of war, Ares. Ahl comments: "In the chorus' thoughts, then, the plague is accompanied by a war, and it is above all the war that they want ended. The verb they use to ask Zeus to destroy Ares, *phthison* (201), is the same verb the priest uses twice to describe the destructive effects of the plague upon Thebes in lines 25–26 (*phthinousa*)."[9] The use of the same verb points to a loss of distinctions of the kind Girard associates with the contagious spread of violence. Zeus must combat the destructive power of Ares by wielding the same destructive power himself.

This pattern recurs again and again, not only in *Oedipus*, but in Sophocles' other plays as well. French classics scholar Suzanne Saïd finds a typical example in his *Electra*, where the title character plots the murder of her mother as revenge for the mother's murder of the father: "In Sophocles' tragedy as in the recent analyses of R. Girard, the avenger necessarily becomes her adversary's double. Electra, who wishes to be her father's daughter and his alone, must acknowledge that she is also the worthy daughter of her mother, since she has become, like the latter, 'ill-tempered, shrill, shameless' and has learned to commit infamy from her example."[10]

But if the adversaries are doubles, *each* learns from the other's example. Hence the heartfelt cry common to tragic antagonists and squabbling schoolchildren alike: "She started it!" Saïd draws attention to a debate between Electra and her mother in which "each of the two women denies having been the one to start": when the mother proclaims that she has never done more than "answer with harsh words the harsh words she has heard," Electra observes pointedly that the same cannot be said "this time."[11] In other words, "Who are you to accuse me of being the first to use harsh words? *You* are the first to launch a harsh accusation against me right now!" This exchange of harsh words between Electra and her mother not only follows the pattern identified by Girard in the similar exchange between Oedipus and Tiresias, it also refers to the pattern explicitly, thus confirming Sophocles' conscious interest in the symmetrical structure of such exchanges.

By zeroing in on what one critic has called the "festooning of quasi-math-ematical symmetries" in *Oedipus*,[12] Girard seeks to show that the structural equivalences between characters outweigh any distinguishing features they may seem to possess. Now, this is clearly a challenge in the case of the title character, who may be said, without exaggeration, to possess the mother of all distinguishing features. Oedipus is, after all, the only character who can claim to have possessed his mother. For Freud, of course, he has acted out a universal impulse, but one which normally lies hidden. When Oedipus con-cludes at the end of the play that his wife Jocasta was the woman who bore him, the incomparable horror of the situation prompts him to gouge his eyes out. Where is the loss of distinctions here?

Before coming to Girard's interpretation of the incest theme, let us see how far the posited equivalence between Oedipus and Tiresias will take us. The events at the end of the play are framed by the earlier dispute between the two in which Tiresias voices the first hint that Oedipus is guilty of incest and predicts that he will soon be as blind as the aged Tiresias is himself. When Oedipus ultimately accepts his guilt and puts out his own eyes, Tiresias is vindicated on both counts. Oedipus has become Tiresias's physical double, but the parallel ends there. The unique circumstances of Oedipus's blindness set him apart, or so it seems.

In reality, we cannot be sure where the parallel ends without knowing the circumstances of Tiresias's blindness. Although the play does not tell us, the story would have been familiar to Sophocles' Athenian spectators. Indeed, it was their city's namesake, the goddess Athena herself, who struck Tiresias blind when he was still a small child. Athena was bathing; Tiresias's offense—as inadvertent as Oedipus's—was to have accidentally seen her unclothed. Having misused his eyes, Tiresias was condemned to lose them. If we return now to the play, we will notice that Oedipus blinds himself with brooches torn from Jocasta's dress (1268–70)—the very brooches that failed to keep him from seeing her unclothed. Thus, Oedipus's punishment fits the crime in the same way that Tiresias's punishment fit the crime. He too loses his eyes after misusing them. Oedipus is therefore Tiresias's equal not only in his blindness but in the reason for it.

A Freudian might object that this demonstration of the loss of distinctions conveniently leaves the element of incest out of account. But it is easy enough to restore this element to the equation by assuming, in Freudian fashion, that when little Tiresias glimpsed the adult Athena bathing, he must have been filled with unconscious lust for her as a mother-figure. In fact, Roheim, who does not hesitate to equate Oedipus and Tiresias, even cites a version of the myth, in Callimachus's *Lavacrum Palladis*, in which Tiresias encounters the goddess bathing *with his mother*.[13] It follows that Tiresias's offense was "oedipal" before the fact—in which case it might be just as apt to call Oedipus's offense "tiresian." Either way, the distinction between the two is lost.

Filthy Oedipus

For Girard, the theme of incest is itself significant primarily as an extreme indicator of the loss of distinctions. By erasing the line dividing the roles of son and husband or mother and wife, an incestuous union undermines the most fundamental differences on which the social order rests. Moreover, any offspring such a union produces will necessarily suffer from the same loss of distinctions,[14] so that Oedipus laments having sired "children brothers of their father." As Greek classics scholar Maria Daraki observes, "what the king of Thebes accuses himself of in horror, is of having mixed generations. In Sophocles' tragedy, incest is not strictly speaking a *sexual* transgression; it offends the laws of a certain type of *descent*."[15] Following Sophocles' own lead, Girard emphasizes this "scandalous scrambling of kinship,"[16] which is cited repeatedly throughout the play as the monstrous consequence of incest.

In its power to confound distinctions, incest is akin to violence. Just as incest turns family members into doubles, violent conflict turns enemies into doubles. The accusation of incest gives symbolic expression to the same process of undifferentiation that unfolds before our eyes as we witness the conflict between Oedipus and Tiresias. But that is only half the story. The accusation of incest is not just a symbol, it is also a weapon used by one antagonist against the other. When Tiresias calls Oedipus a father-killing mother-lover, he is hitting him with the biggest insult he can muster. It would be hard to charge anyone with a viler crime, except perhaps raping a nun (and, as we shall see, this omission is easily repaired).

While incest destroys specificities, the *accusation* of incest has the power to destroy a specific individual: the accused. If the accusation is made to stick, the latter will be destroyed in the eyes of the community, singled out as the sole source of what may actually be a more general process of undifferentiation. In the first part of Sophocles' play, for instance, the city is already in the grip of a plague, which the Delphic oracle attributes to an act of regicide. Oedipus and Tiresias each blame the other for the initial violation of a fundamental distinction. As they defend with equal vehemence and an equal lack of evidence their equal and opposite accusations, they only deepen the preexisting crisis of differences. But once Tiresias succeeds in definitively pinning on his adversary the blame for the regicide, along with shocking new charges of patricide and incest, Oedipus stands alone as a unique embodiment of the breakdown of distinctions. "In Oedipus," observes Girard, "difference is so radically destroyed that all men shrink back in horror. And this shrinking back, this putting at a distance, is the restoration of the lost difference."[17]

Here we have reached the turning point in the dynamic of the crisis described by Girard and in Girard's own argument. At the very moment when all differences are imperiled and each antagonist seems to be nothing more than the equal of the other, a paradoxical reversal occurs: by virtue of being concentrated in a single individual, undifferentiation itself is transmuted into the basis for a new difference. Incest represents an excess of undifferentiation sufficient to make Oedipus "more equal" than—and therefore different from—everyone else: this is not merely Girard's interpretation, it is what Tiresias himself affirms through a play on words analyzed by Jean-Pierre Vernant, France's leading authority on classical Greece. In "Ambiguity and Reversal," an article on *Oedipus* published not long after Girard's "Symmetry and Dissymmetry," Vernant writes:

> The equalization of Oedipus and his sons is expressed in a series of brutal
> images. . . . But it is Tiresias who gives all its tragic weight to this vocabulary
> of equality when he addresses himself to Oedipus in these terms: there will

come evils that "will make you equal to yourself by making you equal to your children" (425). The identification of Oedipus with his own father and his own children, the assimilation in Jocasta of mother and wife, make Oedipus equal to himself, that is, they make him an *agos* ["thing of filth"], a being *apolis*, without common dimensions, without equality with other men.[18]

Tiresias stigmatizes Oedipus for his distinctive lack of distinctions. Being equal to his children makes him unequalled in his iniquity. No one is as filthy as he. "There is dirt upon thy head, O Oedipus," Tiresias proclaims. "Dirt, dirt, dirt, upon the head of Oedipus." But isn't Tiresias right? By the end of the play, everyone agrees that Oedipus killed his father and married his mother, including the accused himself. Isn't Oedipus guilty as charged?

Looking for Clues

Sophocles' *Oedipus* is often deemed the world's first mystery story, and a very sophisticated one at that. After questioning witnesses and assembling evidence, the hero deduces that he himself is the villain. This twist is so dramatic that we may lose track of what the mystery was about in the first place. The question the hero originally set out to answer was not, after all, "Who killed his father and married his mother?" It was not even, strictly speaking, "Who killed Laius?" As the story opens, no one is even thinking about Laius. His death has been forgotten amidst the generalized death and destruction caused by the plague. It is this crisis, not one man's murder, that the people of Thebes call upon their ruler to solve. And from the standpoint of the crisis, the relevant question is not so much "Who done it?" as "Who started it?" When Oedipus sends to Delphi for advice, the oracle's reply addresses the latter question.

Every good mystery story includes a red herring to throw alert readers off the track. In *Oedipus*, the oracle supplies what modern readers would ordinarily regard as an obvious red herring. According to the oracle, Thebes is harboring an unpunished killer whose festering presence is responsible for the plague. Now, this cannot be right. We know that plagues are not caused by the mere presence of miscreants, no matter how foul the deeds they may have committed. Yet Oedipus and the Thebans immediately swallow this colossal red herring hook, line, and sinker. To Girard, there is something fishy about the way they drop everything to go chasing after Laius's killer.

There is, of course, an easy explanation for their behavior: being ancient Greeks, they would presumably have shared a cultural belief in the magical potency of blood pollution. To demonstrate how "strongly this superstition worked, even in the days of the 'enlightenment,'" J. T. Sheppard quotes from a speech composed for Athenian prosecutors by the orator Antiphon as a model of "the kind of argument to which a jury will respond": "It is against your own advantage that this person, so bloodstained and so foul, should have access to the sacred precincts of your gods and should pollute their purity; should sit at the same table with yourselves, and should infect the guiltless by his presence. It is this that causes barrenness in the land. It is this that brings misfortune upon men's undertakings."[19] If one believes that contact with a person bloodstained and foul can cause pestilence, sterility, or all-around misfortune, then it is only logical, when a plague or similar calamity strikes, to go hunting for the foul individual responsible.

The extent to which enlightened Greeks of Sophocles' era still gave credence to such archaic beliefs is open to debate. In the end, however, the precise nature of their beliefs is of secondary importance here. Culturally specific beliefs cannot account for behavior which is not culturally specific, and there is little that is culturally specific about the behavior of the characters in *Oedipus*. All over the world, people of widely varying beliefs have responded to calamity by going hunting for the foul individuals responsible.

The reference to culturally specific Greek belief is therefore itself something of a red herring. It allows us to feel guiltless by making sure the holders of such bloodthirsty beliefs do not sit at our table and infect us by their presence. Yet, though we ourselves do not believe that a Theban plague could be cured by tracking down the individual responsible, we too are caught up in the thrill of the hunt.

This thrill doubtless explains in large measure the popularity of both *Oedipus* and modern crime fiction.[20] Girard quotes Northrop Frye's observation that the "growing brutality" of the mystery story comes "as close as it is normally possible for art to come to the pure self-righteousness of the lynching mob."[21] If *Oedipus* is a detective story, Girard is a meta-detective who sniffs out the evidence of mob violence hidden behind the surface details of the narrative. These details fit together like the pieces of a puzzle. On the one hand, we have a disaster threatening the community. On the other, we have a single individual who is blamed for the disaster, while at the same time being accused of unspeakable moral transgressions. Between these alleged transgressions and the general disaster, no rational causal link is possible. For that very reason, the conjunction of the two disparate types of charges is all the more striking.

This conjunction provides Girard with a vital clue, for hapless individuals have been the victims of such two-pronged accusations throughout much of Western history. "During the great medieval plague epidemics, for instance, the Jews were often the victims of these accusations, and so were the foreigners and strangers who happened to find themselves in some panic-stricken town. A century or two later, the same pattern of accusation reappears in the great epidemic of witch-hunting in the Western world."[22]

Girard identifies a further clue in the lameness of Oedipus, whose very name is an epithet meaning "swollen foot": "In a panicked community, an individual's chances of being selected as a victim are greatly increased if, in addition to being a highly visible and powerful stranger who became successful too fast, he is afflicted with some physical infirmity that the multitude regards as uncanny."[23] The inelegant manner in which Oedipus's name alludes to his infirmity is lost on non-Greek ears. Shelley remedied this problem in a parody whose inspired title, *Swellfoot the Tyrant*, conveys the meaning of the original better than more reverent versions.

When things fall apart, it doesn't take the clairvoyance of a Tiresias to figure out where to lay the blame. Any child could point a finger at the newcomer who walks funny. "Swellfoot started it! It's Swellfoot's fault." The pure self-righteousness of the accuser is contagious. Soon everyone will take up the refrain. "There is dirt upon Swellfoot's head. Dirt, dirt, dirt, upon the head of Swellfoot."

By joining together to heap abuse on a common target, the members of the community can surmount the quarrels that are bound to divide them in a time of crisis. This is especially true when, as in the case of disease or drought, little can be done to attack the real causes. "Through its recourse to arbitrary violence," writes Girard, "the helpless populace manages to forget its helplessness in the face of uncontrollable events."[24]

Naturally, the populace does not regard its violence as arbitrary. It feels fully justified in going after an individual so bloodstained and so foul. "A lynching mob must believe in the malevolence of its victim," Girard observes. "Which means that a lynching process described by the lynchers themselves must necessarily come out as something other than itself, as the Oedipus myth for instance."[25]

The myth does not present Oedipus as an arbitrary victim; it tells us that he really did commit patricide and incest and that he really did cause the plague. Now, when it comes to the plague, we know he cannot possibly be guilty as charged, but we may still hesitate to reject the accusation of patricide and incest. After all, a son of the king and queen of Thebes could conceivably be abandoned as an infant, saved by herdsmen and raised as the son of the king and queen of Corinth before chancing to kill the king of Thebes and chancing to wed his widow. It is not likely, but it *could* happen. We might therefore conclude that although the myth has arbitrarily accused this club-footed stranger of being a provoker of plagues, it has nonetheless credibly identified him as a father-killing mother-lover.

What if it further alleged that the same individual had begun by defiling hundreds of nuns? In a Russian folk variant on the Oedipus myth,[26] there is no microbial plague, but a veritable epidemic of sin sweeps through a convent when the devil inspires a stranger who had been abandoned as an infant to "defile the nuns one by one, sometimes by force, other times with love in secret." We may apply to this onslaught Thucydides' comment on the Athenian plague quoted earlier: "No constitution was of itself strong enough to resist or weak enough to escape the attacks." Indeed, only after the diabolical stranger has violated all three hundred inmates of the convent, including the Mother Superior, is he expelled by the assembled nuns. He then goes on to kill his father, marry his mother, and murder three priests for good measure—or so we are told. By this time, however, we may doubt the narrative's credibility. Although the enormities it alleges could conceivably happen, they are so unlikely we are liable to acquit the accused of all charges.

This Russian folk narrative demonstrates the vanity of treating the accusation of patricide and incest differently from the other accusations made against Oedipus and similar mythic figures. Whether we are told that they defiled their mothers and hordes of nuns or, as in further variants of the Oedipus myth, that they devoured their own baby sons,[27] these allegations do not deserve to be taken seriously any more than the allegation that Oedipus caused a plague by committing regicide.

But why should we take seriously anything that mythic narratives tell us? Aren't they just stories in the first place—pure fiction from beginning to end?

———————————

René Girard was originally trained as a medieval historian.[28] When he later turned his attention to primitive and classical myths, he was struck by their similarity to medieval accounts of persecutions written from the persecutors' viewpoint.[29] The authors of these accounts believe self-righteously in the malevolence of the victims despite the manifestly fanciful nature of the charges made against them. We may be told, for example, that in a time of plague Jews were put to death as diabolical traitors by an angry populace after being accused of devouring Christian babies and poisoning the water supply. Although we reject both of these fanciful charges, we do not dismiss the entire account as pure fiction from beginning to end. Instead, we take it seriously as evidence that, in a time of plague, Jews may well have been put to death as diabolical traitors by an angry populace after being accused of devouring Christian babies and poisoning the water supply.

Girard takes myths seriously in the same way. He sees them as evidence of real persecutions. Even when the link to particular historical events is irretrievably lost, the types of accusations we find in myths betray their origin. The more outlandish these accusations are, however, the easier it is for us to view them as harmless poetic conceits. This outlandishness gradually fades as we near the modern period. Our Russian folktale is already less fantastic than the Greek myth, since the diabolical stranger is not blamed for provoking an actual plague, but the notion that he defiled three hundred nuns is still extravagant enough to pass for an innocuous flight of fancy. But what if a century-old narrative from the American South stated that a diabolical black mother-lover had defiled, one by one, sometimes by force, other times by love in secret, a series of virginal white maidens? Surely we would then conclude, as Girard concludes of mythology, that the "conjunction of themes" displayed could not be the product of a "purely poetic imagination."[30]

A change in the identities of the characters and locations may suffice to make us treat a narrative differently. When we read an overwrought account of a Southern lynching or medieval witch-hunt written from the persecutors' viewpoint, we do not praise it as a colorful contribution to world mythology.

But when a narrative comes to us cloaked in the glorious mantle of ancient Greece, we approach it with different assumptions. In his book *The Scapegoat*, Girard proposed a "simple experiment": "I'm going to give the story of Oedipus a homely disguise; I shall remove his Greek clothing. . . . In so doing, the myth will descend several steps on the social ladder":

> Harvests are bad, the cows give birth to dead calves, no one is on good terms with anyone else. It is as if a spell had been cast on the village. Clearly, the cripple is to blame. He arrived one fine morning, no one knows from where, and made himself at home. He even took the liberty of marrying the most prominent heiress in the village and had two children by her. They say the wildest things go on in their house! The stranger is suspected of having done away with his wife's first husband, a sort of local potentate, who disappeared under mysterious circumstances and was rather too quickly replaced in both roles by the newcomer. One day the fellows in the village had had enough; they took their pitch forks and forced the disturbing character to clear out.[31]

By stripping the myth of its familiar trappings, Girard's experiment allows us to see it in a new light.

Frederick Ahl conducted a similar experiment on a more elaborate scale in the classroom, using the students in his Greek literature courses as guinea pigs. This time, the focus of the experiment was not the myth of Oedipus, but Sophocles' tragedy. Over a period of two years, Ahl gave some classes an undisguised translation of *Oedipus* and others a second version in which the names and locations were changed. Even though he presented the play identically to both groups as "the story of a man who discovered that he had killed his father and contracted an incestuous marriage," Ahl observed a "marked difference" in the students' responses:

> Those given the disguised version read the play much more carefully than those who knew from the outset that they were reading Sophocles' tragedy. And they asked far more questions and expressed a great deal more skepticism about the conventional interpretation I offered them. It became clear that those familiar with the Oedipus myth were beginning with assumptions about what the play *must* mean, and that they tended to privilege

that assumption even when the language of the play did not itself tend to support it. Thus I began to realize that there was a very special tension in *Oedipus* between the "received" myth and the structure of the drama itself.[32]

Prodded by his students' questions, Ahl undertook his own word-by-word study of the play in the original Greek, the results of which he presents in his landmark 1991 book *Sophocles' Oedipus: Evidence and Self-Conviction*. Ahl's examination of the evidence suggests that Girard may have been too cautious, if anything, in formulating his interpretation of Sophocles.

In *Violence and the Sacred*, Girard ventures a "strange and well-nigh fantastic thought": "If we eliminate the testimony brought against Oedipus in the second half of the tragedy, then the conclusion of the myth, far from seeming a sudden lightning flash of the truth, striking down the guilty party and illuminating all the mortal participants, seems nothing more than the camouflaged victory of one version of the story over the other."[33] But if Ahl is right, it should be possible to sustain Girard's interpretation without eliminating the testimony found in the play's second half, for, in reality, "no conclusive evidence is presented that Oedipus killed his father and married his mother." If we decide that he did, Ahl contends, "we are doing so on the basis of assumptions external to the arguments presented."[34]

Such assumptions may stem not only from our knowledge of the myth, but also from our understanding of the way mystery stories operate. Once the Delphic oracle launches the hunt for Laius's killer, we have a right to expect that the culprit will ultimately be identified. What kind of detective story ends with the hero fingering the wrong man? Unless we can be sure that the accused is the guilty party, we will be cheated of the catharsis so reliably delivered by modern mysteries and ancient tragedies alike. But perhaps Sophocles has concocted a mystery even more sophisticated than we thought. At the risk of lessening the satisfaction produced by a tidy ending, let us go back and ask whether Oedipus is really the man the oracle was talking about.

Phrased in this way, the question is misleading because it implies that the oracle blamed a single individual for Laius's death. In fact, as Sandor Goodhart emphasizes in a seminal essay cited by Ahl, the oracle in Creon's report "speaks distinctly of a multiplicity of murderers. 'Apollo now clearly commands us to punish with [heavy] hand his murderers, whoever they may be'" (line 107).[35] Creon goes on to add that the only member of Laius's party to escape "insisted [*ephaske*] that many brigands [*lêistas*] waylaid him: many hands, not one man's force" (122–23).[36] Indeed, the fact that the assailants were numerous was the "one thing" of which the witness was "certain." The chorus and Jocasta later confirm having heard the same thing. Some critics have opined that a witness who flees in fear might lie about the number of attackers. Perhaps, but there is no suggestion to this effect in the text. Oedipus himself affirms that, when he is able to question the witness, the apparent discrepancy as to the number of murderers will be the key point: "if he still says the same number, I was not the killer; for one cannot be equal to many" (843–45). Moreover, a similar discrepancy exists, not mentioned by Oedipus, concerning an equally crucial point: the number of victims. Since Oedipus recalls having killed an unidentified old man and "all" the members of his party, the very fact that one member of Laius's party lived to tell the tale is good evidence that Laius and his party were not the victims of Oedipus.[37] All save one cannot be equal to all.

Now, surely the ancient Greeks were capable of doing the math. It doesn't take a rocket scientist to see that, unless the interrogation of the murder witness produces dramatic new evidence regarding these points, Oedipus cannot be convicted of killing Laius. But when the witness arrives, Oedipus fails to ask him a single question about Laius's death. He is distracted by questions about his own birth raised by a visitor from Corinth who claims first to have found Oedipus as a baby, then to have received him from none other than the murder witness.[38] The latter then states he gave Jocasta's baby to the Corinthian, telling Oedipus: "If you're who he says you are, then you were born to a grim fate" (1180–81).[39]

But *is* Oedipus who the other says? Ahl maintains there is no evidence he is: "We have only the anonymous Corinthian's word for it."[40] One might object that we also have the evidence of Oedipus's feet. Since the feet of Jocasta's baby were pinned together, the Corinthian fastens on Swellfoot's infirmity to clinch his case. The argument is hardly decisive, however. If Jocasta's husband has bad feet and Jocasta's son has bad feet, it does not follow that her husband is her son. To conclude that he is, we are still obliged to rely on the anonymous Corinthian's word.

Most translators confer an aura of authority on this nameless stranger by labeling him a "messenger." In reality, as R. D. Dawe notes, he is "not an official representative, but one hoping to earn a reward on his own account by enterprisingly informing Oedipus of local gossip."[41] Having heard a rumor in Corinth that Oedipus will succeed to the throne following the death of his father, the stranger hurried to Thebes with the news, aiming to ingratiate himself with the incoming king. But Oedipus will not think of regaining his homeland as long as his mother still lives. When he explains that he has long feared fulfilling a prophecy of incest and patricide, the Corinthian asks: "why have I not yet freed you from this fear?" (1003). The following dialogue then takes place (1004–7):

> OEDIPUS: And I'd reward you well if you still could.
> CORINTHIAN: And I came here primarily for this:
> the hope that I'd do well when you came home.
> OEDIPUS: I'll never go where my begetters live.[42]

The Corinthian then proceeds to tell Oedipus the one thing he can tell him if he still wants to collect a royal recompense, namely, that Oedipus was not begotten in Corinth.

The anonymous Corinthian might be telling the truth, but Sophocles has supplied him with a good reason for lying, and Oedipus is Jocasta's son only if the Corinthian is not lying. Had Sophocles wished to place the belief in Oedipus's incest on a firm basis, he could have made its source an official envoy rather than a self-seeking gossipmonger. And yet, swept along by the momentum of a drama in which all suspicion comes to center on a single individual—Oedipus—we are not apt to stop and question the motives of other characters. "Sophocles' great achievement here," Ahl comments, "is to make us do what Oedipus does: to disregard or rationalize away everything that might demonstrate the hero's innocence."[43]

In ruling out the hero's innocence, we are following the lead of the hero himself: in a word, we are *imitating Oedipus*. When the murder witness, after telling how he disposed of Jocasta's baby, says Oedipus was born to a grim fate *if* he is who the Corinthian says (1180–81), Oedipus ignores this prudent caveat and leaps to the conclusion that he has committed both incest and patricide: "how it all could come so clear! . . . forbidden marriage and killings

I should not have carried out!" (1182, 1185). Not only does Oedipus accept without question that he has married his mother, he instantly assumes that he has murdered his father as well. But the murder witness's testimony about Jocasta's baby has brought us no closer to knowing who killed Laius. As one critic observed long ago, the fulfillment of the prophecy of patricide is not "directly established," it is "inferred" from the fulfillment of the prophecy of incest.[44]

This "inference" is not a logical deduction but a mythological one. Logically, the incest charge should have no bearing on the murder investigation. Even if Oedipus is Jocasta's son, it does not follow that he killed Laius. But an incestuous son is a transgressor of mythic proportions; as one capable of anything, he can be accused of anything. No proof is needed to blame him for further crimes, and the hunt for Laius's killer may cease on the spot, the niceties of detective work forgotten now that the taint of incest has turned Oedipus into an all-purpose culprit: a scapegoat.

Thus, what began as a mystery story stands revealed as something else, something more like the tale of a lynching. If the object were to find Laius's killer, the alleged incest would be no more than a red herring. But, as we noted at the outset, the question of who killed Laius was already a red herring with regard to the crisis brought on by the plague. Since no single individual is responsible for this general disaster, the investigation was bound to end by imputing guilt to a scapegoat. Oedipus's suitability as a scapegoat was made evident by his infirmity. Once this was used to identify him with Jocasta's baby, his conviction on all charges was a foregone conclusion. "Swellfoot is a dirty mother-lover; therefore he must be the foul individual who killed the king and caused the plague": this spurious chain of reasoning is all the more persuasive for being adopted by the interested party. "There is dirt upon my head," proclaims Swellfoot. "Dirt, dirt, dirt, upon the head of Swellfoot."

Oedipus "joins in the unanimous chorus that proclaims him to be the most abominable filth; he is repulsed by himself and beseeches the city of Thebes to repulse him literally from its midst." The cooperation of victims with their persecutors has often been observed, notes Girard: "We are told in the sixteenth century that witches themselves choose the stake; they were made to understand the horror of their misdeeds. Heretics, too, often call for the punishment merited by their abominable beliefs," a phenomenon visible in our time with the Stalinist show trials.[45] A persecution best succeeds in replacing dissension with consensus when no member of the community questions the myth of the victim's guilt: "The victim must participate if there is to be perfect unanimity. . . . The perspective of the persecutors is transformed into indisputable truth by Oedipus' final submission to the imbecilic judgement of the crowd."[46]

The pivotal role played by the crowd in Oedipus's downfall is demonstrated by the chorus's speech that immediately follows the words of Oedipus quoted above: "forbidden marriage and killings I should not have carried out!" When Oedipus speaks, he is still king; once the chorus has spoken, he is king no longer. The chorus's speech includes a line whose significance was pointed out by Michel Foucault: "He was our bastion against disaster, our honoured King" (1200–1202).[47] Foucault drew attention to the chorus's use of the past tense here, "meaning that the people of Thebes, at the same time that they recognize in Oedipus the one who had been their king . . . declare him now stripped of his kingship."[48] Oedipus is summarily deposed by collective fiat.

"The ritual expulsion demanded by Oedipus at the end of the play echoes the collective violence which constitutes the true mainspring of mythological creation," Girard affirms.[49] If we imitate Oedipus in assuming that he actually committed incest and patricide, then we join in the chorus of those who contribute to keeping the myth alive. That is why, for Goodhart, "Sophocles' play is a critique via Oedipus of us," a "critique of mythogenesis."[50] Of course, Sophocles does not tell us that Oedipus is innocent any more than the myth does. Rather, what both Goodhart and Ahl argue, in effect, is that Sophocles' play operates at two levels, just as Girard has argued that the plays of Shakespeare operate at two levels.[51] Sophocles has constructed his drama so artfully that, in Ahl's words, we "are lured into overlooking the same sort of detail that Oedipus overlooks until, at the end, we share his conviction of guilt."[52] At the same time, however, Sophocles has strewn the trail with clues indicating that there is more to the story than meets the eye.

When One Is Equal to Many

The biggest clue is the statement "one cannot be equal to many," which Goodhart's article brought to the attention of Girard. We saw that Oedipus makes this statement after hearing that the murder witness had said Laius's killers were many: "if he still says the same number, I was not the killer; for one cannot be equal to many" (843–45). In *Job: The Victim of His People*, Girard observes that this sentence echoes an earlier sentence spoken by Oedipus that implies, on the contrary, one *can* be substituted for many: "In the first scene the king said to the Thebans, who had come to beg him to cure them: 'I suffer more than any one of you, for I, your king, must suffer for everyone at once.'" It is the king's job to take upon his own head all the ills that afflict his people, even at the price of becoming the victim of his people. As king, he must be willing to sacrifice himself for the good of the kingdom. Thus, Oedipus's suitability as a scapegoat is determined not only by his infirmity but also by the lofty position he occupies. "By accepting the kingship," Girard comments, "every man runs the risk of becoming a scapegoat, and that is what Oedipus implicitly recognized in his first sentence."[53]

The two contradictory sentences spoken by Oedipus embody the dilemma he faces. In purely rational terms, he cannot be guilty, for "one" and "many" are not interchangeable. But if no culprit is found, the crisis will continue indefinitely. In the last resort, Oedipus must assume the role of culprit himself. This entails arbitrarily ignoring the witness's testimony and forsaking the rational logic in which "one" and "many" are not interchangeable for the scapegoating logic in which a single man may be made to suffer in the place of many.

"If it is I, the Singular Man, who is guilty, (let the punishment) spare the many! If it is the many who are guilty, let the (punishment) be for me, the Singular Man!" These words, which so well express the heads-you-win/tails-I-lose logic of the scapegoat, are said to have been uttered by an ancient Chinese emperor who offered himself as "victim" to end a drought.[54] Oedipus and the Chinese ruler both exemplify what is in fact an intrinsic aspect of kingship. Since any crisis affecting a kingdom is the king's responsibility, he functions by the very nature of things as an all-purpose culprit. The chorus told us that when Oedipus was their "honored King," they counted on him to be their "bastion against disaster." It is only natural that when disaster struck, they would deem it to be the bastion's fault. Like the African monarchs described by Simon Simonse, Oedipus is a "king of disaster," destined to be sacrificed when all else fails.[55]

"In Homer and Hesiod," notes Jean-Pierre Vernant, "the fecundity of the earth, of the flocks, of women depends on the person of the king, offspring of Zeus.... Thus the normal solution, when the divine scourge strikes a people, is to sacrifice the king." But less drastic remedies were also available, which involved delegating the part of the unfit king to a substitute victim:

> Such is the *pharmakos*: double of the king, but in reverse, like those carnival rulers crowned for the duration of a festival, when order is set upside down, social hierarchies reversed: sexual prohibitions are lifted, theft becomes legal, the slaves take their masters' place.... But when the festival is over, the counter-king is expelled or put to death, taking with him all the disorder which he incarnates and of which the community is purged at one blow.[56]

Once he is charged with subverting social hierarchy and sexual prohibitions through patricide and incest, Oedipus embodies all the disorder of which the community must be purged.[57] In the opening scene, he had promised the crowd of Thebans complaining of the plague that, as their king, he would take their ills upon himself; in the closing scene, the plague has been forgotten and Oedipus, king no longer, tells the Thebans to expel him, saying: "My ills are mine, no other mortal was made to bear them" (1414–15). As one critic observes, "the sense in which his downfall means his city's salvation is immediate and intimate."[58] May we conclude, then, that Oedipus is a *pharmakos*?

It would be more accurate to say that Oedipus becomes a scapegoat—a "*pharmakos* figure" in Northrop Frye's sense[59]—for want of a ritual *pharmakos* in the strict sense. It is precisely because he does not delegate the scapegoat's role to a substitute victim that Oedipus ends up becoming the victim himself. His victimhood is the outcome of a spontaneous process, not a ritual procedure. "Oedipus is a scapegoat in the fullest sense *because he is never designated as such*," Girard stresses.[60] Oedipus is not designated as a *pharmakos*, he is designated as the father-killing mother-lover who caused the plague. Sophocles' play is not the dramatization of a ritual. But it is not the dramatization of a myth, either. Sophocles never shows Oedipus killing his father or marrying his mother. Instead, he stages the process through which, in a time of crisis, everyone comes to *believe* that Oedipus killed his father and married his mother. In this sense, Sophocles' *Oedipus* is indeed "a play about the genesis of a myth."[61]

NOTES

1. "Chu-bu and Sheemish" (1912), reprinted in Lord Dunsany, *Beyond the Fields We Know*, ed. Lin Carter (London: Pan/Ballantine, 1972), 245–50.

2. "*Oedipus* Analyzed," in René Girard, *Oedipus Unbound: Selected Writings on Rivalry and Desire*, ed. Mark R. Anspach (Stanford, CA: Stanford University Press, 2004), 41.

3. Ibid., 43.

4. "The Plague in Literature and Myth," in René Girard, *"To double business bound": Essays on Literature, Mimesis, and Anthropology* (Baltimore: Johns Hopkins University Press, 1978), 136.

5. Thucydides, *The Peloponnesian War*, Book 2, excerpted in Luci Berkowitz and Theodore F. Brunner, eds., *Oedipus Tyrannus* (New York: Norton, 1970), 39. Helene P. Foley notes for her part that Thucydides analyzed the Athenian plague "in terms that suit Girard's," linking it "to the breakdown of the social and religious order"; see Helene P. Foley, *Ritual Irony: Poetry and Sacrifice in Euripides* (Ithaca, NY: Cornell University Press, 1985), 59.

6. Frederick Ahl, *Sophocles' Oedipus: Evidence and Self-Conviction* (Ithaca, NY: Cornell University Press, 1991), 35. An excerpt from this work appears in the present volume.

7. René Girard, *Violence and the Sacred*, trans. Patrick Gregory (Baltimore: Johns Hopkins University Press, 1977), 76. An excerpt from this work appears in the present volume.

8. Ahl, *Sophocles' Oedipus*, 46.

9. Ibid., 68.

10. Suzanne Saïd, "La tragédie de la vengeance," in Gérard Courtois, ed., *La vengeance*, vol. 4 (Paris: Cujas, 1984), 64.

11. Ibid., 63.

12. John Jones, *On Aristotle and Greek Tragedy* (New York: Oxford University Press, 1962), excerpted in Berkowitz and Brunner, *Oedipus Tyrannus*, 146.

13. Géza Roheim, "Teresias and Other Seers," *Psychoanalytic Review* 33 (1946): 314–34; cited in Richard S. Caldwell, "The Blindness of Oedipus," *International Review of Psycho-Analysis* 1 (1974): 209.

14. In a series of medieval variants on the Oedipus story centered on the legendary Pope Gregory, the incestuous hero is himself the product of an incestuous union. See Lowell Edmunds, *Oedipus: The Ancient Legend and Its Later Analogues* (Baltimore: Johns Hopkins University Press, 1985), 20; see also Thomas Mann's novel on the same theme, *The Holy Sinner* (*Der Erwählte*).

15. Maria Daraki, *Dionysos* (Paris: Arthaud, 1985), 135.

16. Girard, "*Oedipus* Analyzed," 44.

17. "Symmetry and Dissymmetry in the Myth of Oedipus," in Girard, *Oedipus Unbound*, 85.

18. Jean-Pierre Vernant, "Ambiguity and Reversal: On the Enigmatic Structure of *Oedipus Rex*," trans. Page duBois, *New Literary History* 9 (1978): 493. This essay is reprinted in the present volume. The translation of Tiresias's words in the quoted passage has been modified to restore the original reference to Oedipus's equality with himself; cf. Jean-Pierre Vernant, "Ambiguïté et renversement: Sur la structure énigmatique d'*Œdipe-Roi*" (1970), in Jean-Pierre Vernant and Pierre Vidal-Naquet, *Mythe et tragédie en Grèce ancienne* (Paris: Maspero, 1981), 128.

19. John Tressider Sheppard, *The Oedipus Tyrannus of Sophocles* (Cambridge: Cambridge University Press, 1920), excerpted in Berkowitz and Brunner, *Oedipus Tyrannus*, 192.

20. On this point, see Jacques-Jude Lépine, "Agatha Christie: Maîtresse du soupçon," *Stanford French Review* 16, no. 1 (1992): 95–109.

21. Northrop Frye, *Anatomy of Criticism* (Princeton, NJ: Princeton University Press, 1971), 47.

22. "The Myth of Oedipus, the Truth of Joseph," in Girard, *Oedipus Unbound*, 109–10.

23. Ibid, 110.

24. Ibid.

25. "Doubles and the *Pharmakos*," in Girard, *Oedipus Unbound*, 101.

26. "Andrej," trans. R. Pardyjak from N. Kostomarov, *Pamjatniki Starinnoj Russkoj Literatury* ("Monuments of Old Russian Literature," first published in St. Petersburg in 1860), in Edmunds, *Oedipus*, 188–92.

27. See Edmunds, *Oedipus*, 202–5. Alain Moreau has located intriguing circumstantial evidence that the original Oedipus story may once have included an episode in which he unwittingly ate his own offspring. Although the existence of such an episode cannot be proven, Moreau concludes that Oedipus's crimes must be understood within a Greek mythic context in which patricide and incest bore a "close, essential and universal" relationship to cannibalism; see Alain Moreau, "A propos d'Œdipe: La liaison entre trois crimes—parricide, inceste et cannibalisme," in Suzanne Saïd et al., *Etudes de littérature ancienne* (Paris: Presses Universitaires de l'Ecole Normale Supérieure, 1979), 120.

28. He studied at the venerable Ecole Nationale des Chartes.

29. For an extended comparative analysis of myths and medieval persecution texts, see the first four chapters of René Girard, *The Scapegoat*, trans. Yvonne Freccero (Baltimore: Johns Hopkins University Press, 1986).

30. Girard, "The Myth of Oedipus, the Truth of Joseph," 110.

31. Girard, *The Scapegoat*, 29; cf. René Girard, *Le bouc émissaire* (Paris: Grasset, 1982), 45–46 (in this and subsequent notes, the reference to the French text is provided whenever an English translation has been modified to better reflect the original meaning).

32. Ahl, *Sophocles' Oedipus*, x.

33. Girard, *Violence and the Sacred*, 73.

34. Ahl, *Sophocles' Oedipus*, x. For a detailed critique of Ahl's reasoning, see R. Drew Griffith, "Oedipus Pharmakos? Alleged Scapegoating in Sophocles' *Oedipus the King*," *Phoenix* 47, no. 2 (1993): 95–114. But note that Griffith wrongly ascribes to Ahl the thesis that "Oedipus is totally innocent of the crime" and "never laid a finger on Laius" (95). While Ahl casts doubt on the belief "that Oedipus' guilt is proved" (265), he does not claim to prove his innocence, suggesting instead that Sophocles has made Oedipus's guilt or innocence an open question.

35. Sandor Goodhart, "Ληστὰς Ἔφασχε: Oedipus and Laius' Many Murderers," *diacritics* 8, no. 1 (March 1978): 58; this essay has since been reprinted in Sandor Goodhart, *Sacrificing Commentary: Reading the End of Literature* (Baltimore: Johns Hopkins University Press, 1996), and is included in the present volume.

36. Ahl, *Sophocles' Oedipus*, 62.

37. Goodhart, "Λῃστὰς Ἔφασχε," 59–60.

38. See lines 1026, 1038–40.

39. Ahl, *Sophocles' Oedipus*, 206.

40. Ibid.

41. R. D. Dawe, *Sophocles: Oedipus Rex* (Cambridge: Cambridge University Press, 1982), 192; quoted by Ahl, *Sophocles' Oedipus*, 161.

42. Ahl, *Sophocles' Oedipus*, 171, 174. For a fuller analysis of the dialogue between Oedipus and the Corinthian, see the excerpt from Ahl's book included in the present volume.

43. Ibid., 207.

44. William Chase Greene, "The Murderers of Laius," *Transactions of the American Philological Association* 60 (1929): 81. Greene nonetheless assumes that Oedipus committed both crimes. His essay is reprinted in the present volume.

45. Girard, *The Scapegoat*, 64–65; cf. *Le bouc émissaire*, 94–95.

46. René Girard, *Job: The Victim of His People*, trans. Yvonne Freccero (Stanford, CA: Stanford University Press, 1987), 35–36.

47. Sophocles, *The Theban Plays*, trans. E. F. Watling (Harmondsworth, Middlesex: Penguin, 1947), 59.

48. Michel Foucault, "La vérité et les formes juridiques," *Chimères* 10 (Winter 1990–91): 21 (the text of a lecture originally delivered in Brazil in 1973).

49. Quoted by Goodhart, "Λῃστὰς Ἔφασχε," 70, from René Girard, "Dionysus and the Violent Genesis of the Sacred," *boundary* 2 (1977): 487–505.

50. Goodhart, "Λῃστὰς Ἔφασχε," 66, 67.

51. In "Doubles and the *Pharmakos*," Girard credits Shakespeare with devising a "two-tier arrangement," an argument fully developed in René Girard, *A Theater of Envy: William Shakespeare* (New York: Oxford University Press, 1991). In an interview originally published in the same issue of *diacritics* as Goodhart's essay, Girard expressed his own uncertainty regarding a possible parallel between Shakespeare and Sophocles: "I do not find the position of Sophocles as clear as I do that of Shakespeare, perhaps because of the greater cultural distance. I may be mistaken. Sandor Goodhart thinks that Sophocles is as fully in charge as Shakespeare. He may be right" ("An Interview with René Girard," in *"To double business bound,"* 223).

52. Ahl, *Sophocles' Oedipus*, 217.

53. Girard, *Job*, 40; cf. René Girard, *La route antique des hommes pervers* (Paris: Grasset, 1985), 62–63.

54. After he offered up his shorn hair and fingernails, the rain came, ending the drought that had followed his overthrow of the previous ruler. See Marcel Granet, *Danses et légendes de la Chine ancienne* (Paris: Presses Universitaires de France, 1959), 2:451–52; quoted in Françoise Lauwaert, "Le saint, le boiteux et l'héritier: A propos de la fonction impériale en Chine," *L'Homme* 148 (October–December 1998): 86.

55. Simon Simonse, *Kings of Disaster: Dualism, Centralism and the Scapegoat King in Southeastern Sudan* (Leiden: Brill, 1992): "When the country is hit by disaster or enemies, the King is there to receive the blame. In theory he can be killed for each failure to maintain the community's

immunity. In practice the sentence is suspended as long as there is a possibility to restore the relationship between King and people. . . . Negatively his power is defined as the capacity to allow enemies and disasters to enter the community, positively he is the community's patron against these dangers" (428). A revised edition of Simonse's book has since been published. It is available in both print (Kampala: Fountain, 2017) and electronic format (East Lansing: Michigan State University Press, 2018).

56. Vernant, "Ambiguity and Reversal," 489–90; cf. "Ambiguïté et renversement," 122–23.

57. As a *tyrannos*, a ruler exercising unrestrained power obtained outside of normal legal channels, Oedipus was already well suited to embody disorder. In *Il tiranno e l'eroe: Per un'archeologia del potere nella Grecia antica* (Milan: Bruno Mondadori, 1996), Carmine Catenacci demonstrates a systematic association between tyranny and disordered sexuality (142–70) and explores the mythic and ritual dimensions of the tyrant's typically violent and untimely end, which he compares to that of a *pharmakos* (241–55).

58. Jones, *On Aristotle and Greek Tragedy*, in Berkowitz and Brunner, *Oedipus Tyrannus*, 142.

59. See Girard, "Doubles and the *Pharmakos*."

60. Girard, "The Plague in Literature," 146.

61. Ahl, *Sophocles' Oedipus*, 264.

Oedipus and
the Surrogate Victim

René Girard

Sophocles is often praised for having created in Oedipus a highly indi-
vidualized character. Here, it is said, is a hero who is very much his own
man. And what sort of a man is he? It is traditional to note both his
"generosity," and his "impulsiveness." At the opening of the play we admire his
"noble serenity," as he dedicates himself to solving the mystery of the plague
that afflicts his subjects. But the least obstacle, delay, or provocation suffices
to upset his poise. The diagnosis seems clear: Oedipus is prone to fits of anger.
The king himself acknowledges this fault, presenting it, so it seems, as that
unique but fatal flaw without which a hero cannot attain tragic stature.

The "noble serenity" is in evidence first; the fits of anger follow. Tiresias
provokes the initial outburst, Creon the second. In Oedipus's own account
of his past life he informs us that he has frequently succumbed to this "flaw."
He admits to overreacting to hasty phrases heedlessly uttered; a drinking
companion in Corinth had blurted out some remark casting doubt on Oedipus's parentage; Oedipus reacted with an outburst of anger that precipitated
his departure from the city. And it was in a fit of anger that he struck down
at the crossroads an old man who blocked his way.

Chapter 3 of *Violence and the Sacred* (Baltimore: Johns Hopkins University Press, 1977).

The description of his character seems unambiguous, and *anger* is surely as good a word as any to use in describing the *personal* reactions of the hero. However, we cannot help asking ourselves whether these tantrums really serve to distinguish Oedipus from the other characters. In other words, can they be said to perform the differential function upon which the whole concept of "character" is based?

If we look closely at the myth we notice that "anger" crops up everywhere. It was a kind of suppressed anger that incited Oedipus's companion at Corinth to cast doubt on the hero's parentage. At the fateful crossroads it was anger that goaded Laius initially to raise a hand against his son. It was yet an earlier act of anger, preceding any actions by Oedipus, that prompted the father's decision to do away with his infant son.

It is clear that Oedipus has no monopoly on anger in the play. Whatever the author's intentions, there would be no tragic debate if the other protagonists did not become angry in turn. It is true that these outbursts only occur after a certain delay; and it is tempting to regard them as "justified reprisals," warranted by Oedipus's inexcusable and provoking displays of temper. But we have seen that Oedipus's anger is never without antecedents; it is always preceded and determined by an initial outburst. Even that initial anger is never truly the original anger. In the domain of impure violence, any search for origins leads back to myth.[1] One cannot engage in a search of this sort, much less place any credence in the ultimate success of such a search without destroying [the] violent reciprocity; without, in short, having recourse to those very mythological distinctions from which tragedy is striving to extricate itself.

Tiresias and Creon keep their tempers at the outset: their initial serenity is matched by Oedipus's own serenity in the first episode. In fact, we have to do with an alternation of calm and anger. The only distinction between Oedipus and his adversaries is that Oedipus initiates the contest, triggering the tragic plot. He thus has a certain head start on the others. But though the action does not occur simultaneously, its symmetry is absolute. Each protagonist in turn occupies the same position in regard to the same object. This object is none other than the particular tragic conflict whose association with the plague we have already noted[2] and will explore in more detail further on. At first, each of the protagonists believes that he can quell the violence; at the end each succumbs to it. All are drawn unwittingly into the structure of violent reciprocity—which they always think they are outside of, because they all initially come from the outside and mistake this positional and temporary advantage for a permanent and fundamental superiority.

The three protagonists believe themselves to be above the battle. After all, Oedipus is not from Thebes, Creon is not king, and Tiresias is soaring aloft, high amid the clouds. Creon returns from Delphi armed with the latest oracle.[3] Oedipus and especially Tiresias bring to bear their formidable divinatory skills. In this capacity they possess all the prestige of the modern "expert," whose services are reserved for exceptionally difficult cases. Each believes himself to be an impartial observer, detached from the action; each wants to assume the role of arbitrator and judge. The solemnity of the three sages rapidly gives way to fury, however, when each senses his prestige challenged, if only by the silence of the other two.

The force exerted by the three men in the struggle corresponds to each man's illusion of superiority, his hubris.[4] In other words, nobody possesses sophrosyne, and on that level, too, the differences among them are illusory or quickly effaced. The passage from calm to anger is in each case rendered inevitable. It seems arbitrary, therefore, to relegate to Oedipus, as a distinctive "character trait," an attribute shared equally by all—especially if this common attribute is drawn from the tragic context of the play and provides a more coherent interpretation than the psychological approach allows.

Far from bringing differences into sharp relief, the plunge into opposition reduces the protagonists to a uniform condition of violence; they are engulfed in the same storm of passion. A single glance at an Oedipus [already] drunk with violence and eager to engage him in "dialogue" convinces Tiresias that he has been led astray. But the knowledge comes too late: "Alas, alas, how terrible to know the truth, when this knowledge serves for naught. I was not totally ignorant of this truth, but had thrust it from my mind. Otherwise I would not have come."

Tragedy is not a matter of differing opinions. The symmetrical quality of the conflict determines the limits of the tragic inspiration.[5] In asserting that there is no difference between the antagonists in a tragedy, we are saying that ultimately there is no difference between the "true" and the "false" prophet. The statement seems ridiculous, even unthinkable, at first glance. For does not Tiresias proclaim the truth about Oedipus at the outset, while Oedipus is vilifying Tiresias with odious calumnies?

With Tiresias's entrance our quest for symmetry receives a sharp rebuff. As soon as it catches sight of this stately personage, the chorus exclaims:

> Here approaches the most inspired of prophets,
> he alone who is the keeper of hidden truth.

Clearly we are dealing here with the infallible and omniscient prophet, the sole possessor of an indubitable verity, long ripened in the keeping. For once, it seems, difference has triumphed. However, some lines further on this difference is eclipsed; we encounter a resurgence of reciprocity, more explicit than ever. Tiresias himself rejects the traditional interpretation of his role, the very one proposed by the chorus. In reply to Oedipus, who has questioned him derisively on the origins of his prophetic gifts, Tiresias denies that he possesses any truth except the truth conferred on him by Oedipus himself:

> OEDIPUS: Who taught you the truth? Was it part of your training as a
>   prophet?
> TIRESIAS: You taught me, in forcing me to speak against my will.

If we take Tiresias's reply literally, the terrible charges of patricide and incest that he has just leveled at Oedipus did not stem from any supernatural source of information. The accusation is simply an act of reprisal arising from the hostile exchange of a tragic debate. Oedipus unintentionally initiates the process by forcing Tiresias to speak. He accuses Tiresias of having had a part in the murder of Laius; he prods Tiresias into reprisal, into hurling the accusation back at him.

The only difference between the initial accusation and the counter-charge is the paradoxical quality of the latter. This quality, which could well be a weakness, in fact becomes an added strength. Tiresias, not content to answer Oedipus's "You are guilty," by echoing, "You are guilty," underlines what from his point of view is the most scandalous aspect of the accusa-tion—a guilty man is leveling the charge: "You pronounce me guilty and think yourself innocent whereas, O wondrous world, the guilty one is you. The criminal you pursue is none other than Oedipus."

To accuse the other of Laius's murder is to attribute to him sole responsibility for the sacrificial crisis;[6] but as we have seen, everybody shares equal responsibility, because everybody participates in the destruction of a cultural order. The blows exchanged by enemy brothers may not always land on their mark, but every one of them deals a staggering blow to the institutions of monarchy and religion. Each party progresses rapidly in uncovering the truth about the other, without ever recognizing the truth about himself.

Each sees in the other the usurper of a legitimacy that he thinks he is defending but that he is in fact undermining. Anything one may affirm or deny about either of the adversaries seems instantly applicable to the other. Reciprocity is busy aiding each party in his own destruction.[7] The tragic debate is clearly the verbal equivalent of the fight between such enemy brothers as Eteocles and Polyneices.

In a series of replies Tiresias warns Oedipus of the purely reciprocal nature of the approaching tragedy; that is, of the blows that each will inflict on the other. As far as I know, nobody has proposed a satisfactory interpretation of these lines. The very rhythm of the phrases, their symmetrical effects, anticipate and provoke the tragic debate. We see here violent reciprocity in action, canceling all distinctions between the two men:

Enough. Let me go home now. If you follow my advice, we will both find it easier to bear our separate destinies. . . .

Ah! I see that your own words fall wide of the mark; and I fear to have no better success with mine. . . .

I do not want to inflict pain on either of us. . . .

You reproach me for my stubbornness, but refuse to see the stubbornness that dwells within you; and therefore out of stubbornness cast blame on me. . . .

The violent elimination of differences between the antagonists, their total identity, suddenly illuminates these responses, which give perfect expression to the true nature of tragic relationships. The fact that these responses, even today, still seem obscure, confirms our lack of understanding.[8] It should be said, however, that there is good reason for this lack: one cannot persevere in bringing to light the symmetrical quality of tragedy—as we are now doing—without contradicting the fundamental implications of the myth.[9]

If the myth does not explicitly set forth the problem of differences, it nonetheless manages to resolve the problem in a manner both brutal and categorical. The solution involves patricide and incest. In the mythical version of the story the issue of reciprocity—the identity of Oedipus with the others—never arises. One can assert with total conviction that Oedipus is unique in at least one respect: he alone is guilty of patricide and incest. He is presented as a monstrous exception to the general run of mankind; he resembles nobody, and nobody resembles him.

The tragedian's version of the Oedipus story differs radically from the myth; indeed, it is impossible to do justice to this presentation without abandoning the myth altogether.[10] Interpreters of Sophocles' play invariably devise compromises that conceal the underlying contradiction between the tragedy and the myth. I shall not have recourse to these venerable compromises, nor try to invent new ones. My quest leads elsewhere; I intend to trace the tragic vein to its source, if only to see where it leads. I hope this exploration will yield something of value about the genesis of the myth.

First let us return to the issue of patricide and incest and attempt to determine whether these crimes can be attributed to one particular protagonist, and to *one alone*. As we have seen, the tragedy transforms the murder of Laius, and the patricide and incest themselves, into an exchange of mutual incriminations. Oedipus and Tiresias each attempt to place the blame for the city's plight on the other; the accusations of patricide and incest are only especially striking contributions to a conventional exchange of incivilities. At this stage of the debate there is no reason to assume that either party is more guilty of any crime than the other. Both sides seem equally matched; neither seems able to gain the upper hand. The myth breaks the deadlock, however, and does so unequivocally. We must now, in the light of our understanding of tragic reciprocity, examine on what basis and under what conditions the myth succeeds in intervening decisively in the struggle.

At this point a strange and well-nigh fantastic thought suggests itself. If we eliminate the testimony brought against Oedipus in the second half of the tragedy, then the conclusion of the myth, far from seeming a sudden lightning flash of the truth, striking down the guilty party and illuminating all the mortal participants, seems nothing more than the camouflaged victory of one version of the story over the other, the polemical version over its rival[11]—the community's formal acceptance of Tiresias's and Creon's version of the story, thereafter held to be the true and universal version, the verity behind the myth itself.

At this point the reader may well suspect that I harbor some strange illusions about the "historical" potential of these texts and about the information that one may reasonably expect to draw out of them. I hope that what follows will help to dissipate these fears. However, before proceeding I feel obliged to address myself to another type of objection that the present inquiry seems certain to attract.

Literary criticism concerns itself with tragedy; mythology is outside its proper bailiwick. Students of mythology, one the other hand, exclude tragedy from their area of concern and even display on occasion a hostile attitude toward it.

This division of labor harks back to Aristotle, who declares in the *Poetics* that the competent tragic poet will avoid manipulating the myths and limit his borrowings from them to certain "subjects." This interdict of Aristotle still stands in the way of our confronting the symmetrical quality of tragedy and the mythical concern with differences, which protects "literature" from "mythology" and also protects their respective specialists from the subversive consequences that might result from a confrontation.

It is precisely this confrontation I want to emphasize. Indeed, one cannot but wonder how attentive readers of *Oedipus the King* have managed to overlook it. At the climactic moment of the tragic struggle Sophocles has inserted into his text two replies that seem to pertain directly to our reading. Oedipus's imminent fall has nothing to do with any heinous sin; rather, it should be regarded as the outcome of a tragic encounter in which Oedipus has met defeat. Oedipus replies to the chorus, which has pleaded with him to spare Creon: "What you are asking, if the truth be told, is neither more nor less than my death or exile."

The chorus insists that Creon does not deserve punishment; he should be allowed to withdraw in peace. Oedipus yields to their request, but reluctantly, and he reminds the chorus once again of the true nature of this struggle whose outcome is still unclear. To spare an enemy brother from death or exile is to condemn oneself to death or exile: "Well, then, let him depart though his departure means my certain death, or else my ignominious expulsion from Thebes."

Should we follow tradition and attribute such responses to the "tragic illusion"? In that case the whole play and its wondrous equilibrium must also be a figment of this same illusion. We will be on safer ground, I believe, if we turn our attention from "tragic illusion" to tragic vision. I cannot help feeling that Sophocles himself is prompting us to do so.

Yet Sophocles himself remains elusive. Tragic subversion has its limits; if the playwright challenges the basis of the myth, he only dares to do so in muted and devious fashion. He does not want to compromise his own enterprise or demolish the mythological framework in which he operates.

We are left with no model or guide; we are engaged in a cultural activity that remains undefined, and we can have recourse to no known critical discipline. What we are about to do is as novel to tragedy or literary criticism as it is to psychoanalysis or ethnology.

We must return once again to the so-called crimes of the son of Laius. The act of regicide is the exact equivalent, vis-à-vis the polis, of the act of patricide vis-à-vis the family. In both cases the criminal strikes at the most fundamental, essential, and inviolable distinction within the group. He becomes, literally, the slayer of distinctions.

Patricide represents the establishment of violent reciprocity between father and son, the reduction of the paternal relationship to "fraternal" revenge. This reciprocity is explicitly indicated in the tragedy; as we have noted, Laius displays violence towards Oedipus even before his son actually attacks him.

When it has succeeded in abolishing even the traditional father-son relationship, violent reciprocity is left in sole command of the battlefield. Its victory could hardly be more complete, for in pitting father against son it has chosen as the basis of their rivalry an object solemnly consecrated as belonging to the father and formally forbidden the son: that is, the father's wife and son's mother. Incest is also a form of violence, an extreme form, and it plays in consequence an extreme role in the destruction of differences. It destroys that other crucial family distinction, that between the mother and her children. Between patricide and incest, the violent abolition of all family differences is achieved. The process that links violence to the loss of distinctions will naturally perceive incest and patricide as its ultimate goals. No possibility of difference then remains; no aspect of life is immune from the onslaught of violence.[12]

Patricide and incest will thus be defined in terms of their consequences.

Oedipus's monstrosity is contagious; it infects first of all those beings engendered by him. The essential task is to separate once more the two strains of blood whose poisonous blend is now perpetuated by the natural process of generation. Incestuous propagation leads to formless duplications, sinister repetitions, a dark mixture of unnamable things. In short, the incestuous creature exposes the community to the same danger as do twins. These are indeed the manifestations, real and transfigured, of the sacrificial crisis always referred to by primitive societies in connection with incest. Indeed, the mothers of twins are often suspected of having conceived their children in incestuous fashion.

Sophocles attributes Oedipus's incest to the influence of the god Hymen, who after all is directly implicated in the affair as the god of matrimonial laws and the regulator of family distinctions.

> Hymen, O Hymen, to whom I owe my birth, and who, having engendered me, employed the same seed in the same place to cast upon the outraged world a monstrous commingling of fathers, brothers, sons; of brides, wives, and mothers!

The Oedipus myth (note that we are not referring here to the tragedy) makes no effort to link patricide and incest to anything else, not even to Laius's abortive attempt at infanticide. They are presented as separate events, so anomalous that it is impossible to think of them as part of the tumult that rages around them, involving elements of conflicting symmetry. The dual disasters, incest and patricide, seem to be divorced from all context and visited on Oedipus alone either by pure chance or at the bidding of Destiny or some other sacred force.

Patricide and incest serve the same purpose here as do twins in many primitive religions. The crimes of Oedipus signify the abolishment of differences, but because the nondifference is attributed to a particular individual, it is transformed into a new distinction, signifying the monstrosity of Oedipus's situation. The nondifference becomes the responsibility, not of a society at large, but of a single individual.

Patricide and incest thus play the same role in the Oedipus myth as do the other mythical and ritual motifs considered previously.[13] They serve to conceal the sacrificial crisis far more effectively than they reveal it. To be sure, they manage to express both aspects of the crisis, both reciprocity and forced similarities; but they do so in a way that strikes terror into the beholder and suggests that they are the exclusive responsibility of a particular individual. We lose sight of the fact that this same reciprocity operates among every member of the community and signifies the existence of a sacrificial crisis.

Another thematic device, in addition to patricide and incest, cloaks the sacrificial crisis in parallel and inverse fashion: the motif of the plague or epidemic.

We have already referred to various epidemics as "symbols" of the sacrificial crisis.[14] Even if Sophocles had in mind the famous Athenian plague of 430 BC, he clearly did not mean to limit his reference to one specific microbiotic visitation. The epidemic that interrupts all the vital functions of the city is surely not unrelated to violence and the loss of distinctions. The oracle itself explains matters: it is the infectious presence of a *murderer* that has brought on the disaster.

The play makes it clear that the infection and the onslaught of reciprocal violence are one and the same. The process by which the three protagonists are each in turn tainted with violence corresponds to the progress of the disease, always quick to lay low those who would contain it. Without explicitly declaring the identical nature of the two strains, the text nonetheless calls attention to their parallel qualities. Begging Oedipus and Creon to end their quarrel, the chorus exclaims: "The sight of this dying country fills me with anguish. Must we now add to our misery the miseries which flow from you?"

In tragedy, and outside it as well, plague is a symbol for the sacrificial crisis; that is, it serves the same function as patricide and incest. It seems reasonable to ask why two different symbols are used when one would do, and whether these two symbols really play identical roles.

We need only compare the two themes—plague and patricide/incest— to remark how they differ and what this difference implies. Vital aspects of the sacrificial crisis are apparent in both symbolic presentations, but they are differently distributed. The plague motif illuminates but a single aspect: the collective character of the disaster, its universally contagious nature. This motif ignores violence and the nondifferential character of the crisis. With the patricide/incest motif, on the other hand, violence and nondifference are presented in magnified and highly concentrated form, but limited to a single individual. Here it is the collective element that has been ignored.

Both the patricide/incest and the plague motifs serve to disguise the presence of the sacrificial crisis, but the disguises are not the same. One complements the other, however, and when they are brought together and uniformly applied to all members of the community, the shape and substance of the crisis becomes clear. Once again it is impossible to make any affirmative or negative judgements about the participants. The responsibility for the events is evenly distributed among all.

If the crisis has dropped from sight, if universal reciprocity is eliminated, it is because of the unequal distribution of very real parts of the crisis. In fact, nothing has been truly abolished, nothing added, but everything has been *misplaced*. The whole process of mythical formulation leads to a transferal of violent undifferentiation from all the Thebans to the person of Oedipus. Oedipus becomes the repository of all the community's ills.

In the myth, the fearful transgression of a single individual is substituted for the universal onslaught of reciprocal violence. Oedipus is responsible for the ills that have befallen his people. He has become a prime example of the human scapegoat.

At the conclusion of his drama Sophocles has Oedipus address the Thebans in the terms best calculated to quell their doubts and fears. He assures them that all the evils abroad in the community are the sole responsibility of the surrogate victim, and that he alone, as that victim, must assume the consequences for these ills: "Believe me, you have nothing more to fear. My ills are mine alone, no other mortal is fit to bear them." Oedipus is the responsible party, so responsible that he frees the community from all accountability. The concept of the plague is a result of this situation. The plague is what remains of the sacrificial crisis when it has been emptied of all violence. It calls to mind the passivity of the "patient" in the modern world of medicine. Everyone is sick. Nobody owes anybody anything by way of recompense or atonement—except, of course, Oedipus.

If the community is to be freed of all responsibility for its unhappy condition and the sacrificial crisis converted into a physical disorder, a plague, the crisis must first be stripped of its violence. Or rather, this violence must be deflected to some individual—in this case, Oedipus. In the course of the tragic debate all the characters do their utmost to assist in this process. As we have seen, the inquest on Laius's death is in fact an investigation into the general subject of the sacrificial crisis; and it is clearly a matter of pinning the responsibility for the troubled state of the community on some individual, of framing a reply to the mythical question *par excellence*: "Who initiated the crisis?" Oedipus fails to fix the blame on Creon or Tiresias. Creon and Tiresias are successful in their efforts to fix the blame on him. The entire investigation is a feverish hunt for a scapegoat, which finally turns against the very man who first loosed the hounds.

Having oscillated freely among the three protagonists, the full burden of guilt finally settles on one. It might very well have settled on another, or on none. What is the mysterious mechanism that determines how the guilt shall fall?

The attribution of guilt that henceforth passes for "true" differs in no way from those attributions that will henceforth be regarded as "false," except that in the case of the "true" guilt no voice is raised to protest any aspect of the charge. A particular version of events succeeds in imposing itself; it loses its polemical nature in becoming the acknowledged basis of the myth, in becoming the myth itself. The mythical attribution can only be defined as a phenomenon of unanimity. At the point where two, three, or hundreds of symmetrical and inverted accusations meet, one alone makes itself heard and the others fall silent. The old pattern of each against another gives way to the unified antagonism of all against one.

How does it happen that the community's sense of unity, destroyed by the sacrificial crisis, is suddenly, almost miraculously, restored? Here we are in the very midst of the crisis, when all the circumstances seem to militate against any united course of action. It is impossible to find two men who agree on anything, and each member of the community seems intent on transferring the collective burden of responsibility to the shoulders of his enemy brother. Chaos reigns. No connecting thread, however tenuous, links the conflicts, antagonisms, and obsessions that beset each individual.

Yet at this very moment, when all seems lost, when the irrational runs amok amid an infinite diversity of opinions, the resolution of the dilemma is at hand. The whole community now hurls itself into the violent unanimity that is destined to liberate it.

What is the source of this mysterious unanimity? The antagonists caught up in the sacrificial crisis invariably believe themselves separated by insurmountable differences. In reality, however, these differences gradually wear away. Everywhere we now encounter the same desire, the same antagonism, the same strategies, the same illusion of rigid differentiation within a pattern of ever-expanding uniformity. As the crisis grows more acute, the community members are transformed into "twins," matching images of violence. I would be tempted to say that they are each *doubles* of the other.

In Romantic literature, in the animistic theory of primitive religious practices and in modern psychiatry, the term *double* is perceived as essentially unreal, a projection of the imagination. I mean something different here. Although *doubles*, in my use of the term, convey certain hallucinatory associations (which I shall discuss further on[15]), they are in themselves not at all imaginary—no more than the tragic symmetry of which they form the ideal expression is imaginary.

If violence is a great leveler of men and everybody becomes the double, or "twin," of his antagonist, it seems to follow that all the doubles are identical and that any one can at any given moment become the double of all the others; that is, the sole object of universal obsession and hatred. A single victim can be substituted for all the potential victims, for all the enemy brothers that each member is striving to banish from the community; he can be substituted, in fact, for each and every member of the community. Each member's hostility, caused by clashing against others, becomes converted from an individual feeling to a communal force unanimously directed against a single individual. The slightest hint, the most groundless accusation, can circulate with vertiginous speed and is transformed into irrefutable proof. The corporate sense of conviction snowballs, each member taking confidence from his neighbor by a rapid process of mimesis. The firm conviction of the group is based on no other evidence than the unshakable unanimity of its own illogic.

The universal spread of "doubles," the complete effacement of differences, heightening antagonisms but also making them interchangeable, is the prerequisite for the establishment of violent unanimity. For order to be reborn, disorder must first triumph; for myths to achieve their complete integration, they must first suffer total disintegration.

Where only shortly before a thousand individual conflicts had raged unchecked between a thousand enemy brothers, there now reappears a true community, united in its hatred for one alone of its number. All the rancors scattered at random among the different individuals, all the divergent antagonisms, now converge on an isolated and unique figure, the *surrogate victim*.

The general direction of the present hypothesis should now be abundantly clear; any community that has fallen prey to violence or has been stricken by some overwhelming catastrophe hurls itself blindly into the search for a scapegoat. Its members instinctively seek an immediate and violent cure for the onslaught of unbearable violence and strive desperately to convince themselves that all their ills are the fault of a lone individual who can be easily disposed of.

Such circumstances bring to mind the forms of violence that break out spontaneously in countries convulsed by crisis: lynching, pogroms, "summary justice," etc. It is perhaps worth noting that these forms of collective violence generally justify themselves by making accusations of an Oedipal variety: parricide, incest, infanticide, etc.

Such comparisons are of only limited value, but they shed some light. They reveal a hidden connection among certain tragedies that at first glance seem utterly foreign to one another. It is impossible to say whether Sophocles was aware of the full implications of his theme, though to judge from the passages we have cited from *Oedipus the King*, it is difficult to believe that he shared our ignorance. It could well be that the tragic inspiration was neither more nor less than the sudden inkling of the origins of certain mythological themes. This view seems to find support in other tragedies besides *Oedipus* and other tragedians besides Sophocles—in particular in the work of Euripides.

The heroine of *Andromache* is Neoptolemus's mistress; Hermione is his wife. The two women, prime examples of enemy sisters, engage in a tragic debate. The humiliated wife accuses her rival of the "typical" crimes of parricide and incest, those with which Tiresias charged Oedipus at the same crucial moment of another tragedy:

> Have you, woman, no shame at all? You do not scruple to sleep with the son of your husband's murderer [Neoptolemus's father Achilles had killed Hector] or to bear his children. Such is the way of barbarians: the father sleeps with the daughter, the son with the mother, the brother with the sister. And they think nothing of killing one another, nor does their law condemn the practice. We want no such customs here.

The "substitution" is clear. The foreigner, Andromache, is made to appear the incarnation of the sacrificial crisis that threatens the community.

She is declared capable of committing precisely those crimes that figure so predominantly in mythology and that consequently form the subject of classical tragedy. Hermione's ominous final phrase, "We want no such customs here," already hints at the collective fury and fear that might be launched against Andromache at Hermione's instigation. Already the mechanism has been put in motion for the selection of a surrogate victim.

It is difficult to believe that Euripides did not know what he was doing when he framed these passages, that he was unaware of the close relationship between the genesis of mythology and the collective mechanism he alludes to here; nor can I believe that he was not attempting to issue a warning to his public, to instill a sense of uneasiness without defining the problem precisely or confronting it directly.

We like to believe that we are well acquainted with the mechanisms of collective violence. In fact we know them only in their most degenerate forms, as pale imitations of the collective machinery that produced such mythological material as the story of Oedipus. In the following pages[16] *violent unanimity* will, I believe, reveal itself as the fundamental phenomenon of primitive religion; although wherever it plays a crucial role it is completely, or almost completely, absorbed by the mythological forms it engenders. We perceive only its marginal and bastardized manifestations, which are unproductive as far as myths and ritual are concerned.

It is generally assumed that collective violence—in particular, the pitting of all against one—is an aberration in the history of a society; a perversion more or less pathological in nature, whose study can hardly be expected to yield anything of sociological significance. Our rationalist bent (about which I will have more to say further on) leads to an innocence of outlook that refuses to concede to collective violence anything more than a limited and fleeting influence, a "cathartic" action similar, in its most extreme forms, to the catharsis of the sacrificial ritual. However, the fact that the Oedipus myth has survived over several millennia and that modern culture continues to hold it dear would suggest that the effects of collective violence are greatly underestimated.

The mechanism of reciprocal violence can be described as a vicious circle. Once a community enters the circle, it is unable to extricate itself. We can define this circle in terms of vengeance and reprisals, and we can offer diverse psychological descriptions of these reactions. As long as a working capital of accumulated hatred and suspicion exists at the center of the community, it will continue to increase no matter what men do. Each person prepares himself for the probable aggression of his neighbors and interprets his neighbor's preparations as confirmation of the latter's aggressiveness. In more general terms, the mimetic character of violence is so intense that once violence is installed in a community, it cannot burn itself out.

To escape from the circle it is first necessary to remove from the scene all those forms of violence that tend to become self-propagating and to spawn new, imitative forms.

When a community succeeds in convincing itself that one alone of its number is responsible for the violent mimesis besetting it; when it is able to view this member as the single "polluted" enemy who is contaminating the rest; and when the citizens are truly unanimous in this conviction, then the belief becomes a reality, for there will no longer exist elsewhere in the community a form of violence to be followed or opposed, which is to say, imitated and propagated. In destroying the surrogate victim, men believe that they are ridding themselves of some present ill. And indeed there *are*, for they are effectively doing away with those forms of violence that beguile the imagination and provoke emulation.

It may seem absurd to assign any practical purpose to the concept of the surrogate victim.[17] Yet we have only to substitute the word *violence*, as it is used in these pages, for the particular *ills* or *sins* that the victim is supposed to take upon himself to realize that we are indeed dealing, not simply with an illusion and a mystification, but with the most formidable and influential illusion and mystification in the whole range of human experience, one whose consequences are real and manifold.

Because modern man clings to the belief that knowledge is in itself a "good thing," he grants little or no importance to a procedure, such as the one involving the surrogate victim, that only serves to conceal the existence of man's violent impulses.[18] The optimistic falsification could well constitute the worst sort of ignorance.[19] Indeed, the formidable effectiveness of the process derives from its depriving men of knowledge: knowledge of the violence inherent in themselves with which they have never come to terms.[20]

As Oedipus and Tiresias show us, the knowledge of these violent impulses continues to expand in the course of the sacrificial crisis. However, far from restoring peace, the knowledge only increases the antagonists' awareness of the *other's* violence, thereby serving to intensify the controversy. This baleful knowledge, this lucidity that is only another manifestation of violence, is succeeded by an all-inclusive ignorance. At a single blow, collective violence wipes out all memory of the past. Now we see why the sacrificial crisis is never described in myths and ritual as it really is. There human violence is envisioned as issuing from some force exterior to man. It is one with religion, as well as with those forces that really do emanate from without human will: death, illness, natural phenomena.

Men cannot confront the naked truth of their own violence without the risk of abandoning themselves to it entirely. They have never had a very clear idea of this violence, and it is possible that the survival of all human societies of the past was dependent on this fundamental lack of understanding.

The Oedipus myth, as we have attempted to explain it in the preceding pages, follows a structural pattern that conforms to that of the surrogate victim. We will have to try to determine whether the pattern recurs in other myths. From what we have seen, it seems likely that the process of finding a surrogate victim constitutes a major means, perhaps the sole means, by which men expel from their consciousness the truth about their violent nature— the knowledge of that past violence which, if not shifted to a single "guilty" figure, would poison both the present and the future.

The Thebans—religious believers—sought a cure for their ills in a formal acceptance of the myth, in making it the indisputable version of the events that had recently convulsed the city and in making it the charter for a new cultural order—by convincing themselves, in short, that all their miseries were due exclusively to the plague. Such an attitude requires absolute faith in the guilt of the surrogate victim. And the very first results, the sudden restoration of peace, seem to confirm the identification of the guilty party and also the general correctness of the diagnosis. The crisis is seen as a mysterious illness introduced into the community by an outsider. The cure lies in ridding the community of the sole malignant element.

The curative process is not an illusion, and if we give our attention to the matter we see that no attempt has been made to conceal that process. In fact, it is constantly mentioned, but in a language and with a thematic content of its own derivation. Naturally, this process manages to encompass the oracular pronouncement reported by Creon: the cure must depend on the identification and expulsion of the individual whose presence pollutes the community. In other terms, everybody must agree on the selection of a guilty individual. The surrogate victim plays the same role on the collective level as the objects the shamans claim to extract from their patients play on the individual level—objects that are then identified as the cause of the illness.

The same forces are at work in both cases; but though similar, the two facets of the metaphor are not equivalent. The mechanism of violent unanimity is not modeled on the technique of the shamans, nor is it basically metaphorical in nature; on the other hand, there is reason to believe that the technique of the shamans is modeled on the mechanism of unanimity, interpreted in mythical fashion. Parricide and incest provide the community with exactly what it needs to represent and exorcise the effects of the sacrificial crisis. The myth is there to prove that we are dealing with a spontaneous process of collective self-mystification, the nature of which escapes not only its direct but also its indirect beneficiaries—the Freudian psychoanalyst, for instance. As far as can be ascertained the operation does not make use of vulgar dissimulation or willful manipulation of the facts concerning the sacrificial crisis. Because the violence is unanimously ordained, it effectively restores peace and order. And the false premises that it maintains acquire, in consequence, an impregnable authority. These premises serve to hide from sight the unanimous resolution as well as the sacrificial crisis. The resolution serves as the framework of the myth, invisible as long as the structure remains intact. There would be no *themes* without the structural support of the *anathema*. The anathema's true object is not Oedipus, who is only one thematic element among others, but the unanimous quality of his selection which, if it is to remain effective, must be shielded from scrutiny, protected from any outside contact or intervention. This anathema still operates today in the form of neglect, through our total indifference to the concept of collective violence and our refusal to attach any significance to the phenomenon, even when it thrusts itself upon our attention.

The structure of the myth remains unshaken even today. Transferring it intact into the realm of the imaginary only serves to strengthen it, to render it even less susceptible to analysis. No interpretation has penetrated to the core of the myth. Even Freud's famous explanation of the Oedipus story, the most brilliant and misleading of many, failed to establish the true identity of the object being "suppressed": not the desire for patricide or incest but the violence that lurked behind these all-too-visible motifs, the menace of total destruction that was diverted and concealed by means of the surrogate victim.

My hypothesis does not require that the mythological text offer a *thematic* treatment of condemnation or expulsion directly related to the underlying source of violence. Quite the contrary. The absence of this theme in certain versions of the myth by no means invalidates my theory. All traces of collective violence can, and must, be eliminated. This does not mean that the effects of the violence have been spent; in fact, they are stronger than ever. In order for the anathema to deploy its full force, it must slip from sight and from conscious memory.

It is not the absence of the anathema from tragedy, but rather its presence, that would pose a problem were it not for our belief that the tragic muse effects a partial demolition of the myth.[21] The traces of religious anathema unearthed in tragedy should be regarded not as anachronistic survivals from a primitive past but as being in the nature of an archaeological find. The *anathema* of *Oedipus the King* should be viewed as part of Sophocles' reading of the myth, a reading perhaps more radical in its implications than we originally imagined.[22] The poet puts some very revealing words in Oedipus's mouth: "Quickly, in the name of the gods! hide me somewhere far away from here. Kill me, or hurl me into the sea, where I will never be seen again."

The extent of the poet's understanding of the myth and its origins is hard to ascertain, but it does not have to be complete for tragedy to represent a progress in the direction of mythical dismantling. The mechanism that produces the surrogate victim is dependent on no one particular theme because it has engendered them all; it cannot be comprehended by means of a purely thematic or structural interpretation of the play.

Until now we have seen Oedipus only in terms of his polluted presence, as a receptacle for universal shame. And prior to the onslaught of collective violence, the hero of *Oedipus the King* is just that. Another Oedipus emerges, however, from the final operation; a "definitive" Oedipus, first glimpsed in the final tragedy of the Oedipus cycle, *Oedipus at Colonus*.

In the opening episodes we are still dealing with the original, polluted figure, whose appearance within their boundaries fills the inhabitants of Colonus with dread. As the play progresses, however, a remarkable change takes place. Oedipus is still a dangerous, even a terrifying figure, but he has also become very precious to the community. Colonus and Thebes begin to squabble over the future possession of the patricide's corpse, which is already looked upon as a valuable relic.

What has brought about this change? Initially, Oedipus was associated with the evil aspects of the crisis. He possessed no positive qualities. If his exile was a "good" thing, it was so in a purely negative sense, as the amputation of a gangrenous limb is "good" for an afflicted body. In *Oedipus at Colonus*, however, the scope of the drama has been enlarged. Having plunged the community into strife, the surrogate victim restores peace and order by his departure. Whereas all the previous acts of violence compounded the violence, the violence directed against the surrogate victim banished all trace of violence. The explanation for this extraordinary difference falls naturally within the domain of religion, whose concern with the problem is far from idle, since its solution touches on the well-being, if not the survival, of the community. Because human thought has never succeeded in grasping the mechanism of violent unanimity, it naturally turns toward the victim and seeks to determine whether he is not somehow responsible for the miraculous consequences of his own death or exile. Attention is drawn not only to the distinctive traits of the decisive act—the form of the murder, for example—but also to the victim's personality. Because the violence directed against the victim was intended to restore order and tranquility, it seems only logical to attribute the happy results to the victim himself.

At the supreme moment of the crisis, the very instant when reciprocal violence is abruptly transformed into unanimous violence, the two faces of violence seem to be juxtaposed; the extremes meet. The surrogate victim serves as catalyst in this metamorphosis. And in performing this function he seems to combine in his person the most pernicious and most beneficial aspects of violence. He becomes the incarnation, as it were, of a game men feign to ignore, one whose basic rules are indeed unknown to them: the game of their own violence.[23]

It is not enough to say that the surrogate victim "symbolizes" the change from reciprocal violence and destruction to unanimous accord and construction; after all, the victim is directly responsible for this change and is an integral part of the process. From the purely religious point of view, the surrogate victim—or, more simply, the final victim—inevitably appears as a being who submits to violence without provoking a reprisal; a supernatural being who sows violence to reap peace; a mysterious savior who visits affliction on mankind in order subsequently to restore it to good health.

To our modern way of thinking a hero cannot be "good" without ceasing to be "evil," and vice versa. Religious empiricism sees matters in a different light; in a sense, it confines itself to recording events as it sees them. Oedipus is initially an evil force and subsequently a beneficial one. It is not a question of "exonerating" him, because the question of blaming him, in the modern moralistic sense of the term, never arises. Nor for that matter does religious empiricism show any interest in initiating one of those programs of "rehabilitation" so fashionable today among thinkers who claim to have freed themselves from the shackles of morality. The claims of religious thought are too modest, too tempered by fear, for its proponents to assume such lofty attitudes. The mysterious union of the most evil and most beneficial forces is of vital concern to the community, and can neither be challenged nor ignored. Nevertheless, it is a paradox that totally escapes human comprehension; and religion humbly acknowledges its impotence. The beneficial Oedipus at Colonus supersedes the earlier, evil Oedipus, but he does not negate him. How could he negate him, since it was the expulsion of a *guilty* Oedipus that prompted the departure of violence? The peaceful outcome of his expulsion confirms the justice of the sentence passed on him, his unanimous conviction for patricide and incest. If Oedipus is indeed the savior of the community, it is because he is [perceived as] a patricidal and incestuous son.[24]

NOTES

1. [The end of this sentence is not translated correctly. The search for origins does not "lead back to myth"; it is, Girard writes, "properly mythical" in itself.]

2. [In the earlier chapters of the book from which this text is excerpted.]

3. [The original sentence reads: "Creon returns from Thebes." This is obviously a slip of the pen. Creon returns to Thebes, where the play's action takes place, from Delphi.]

4. [This sentence has been mistranslated. It should read: "The force that draws the three men into the conflict is one with their illusion of superiority."]

5. [This sentence has been mistranslated. It should read: "We must attend without fail to the conflictual symmetry, if only to make apparent the limits of the tragic inspiration." The symmetry is a product of the tragic inspiration. The limits of that inspiration are reached when symmetry gives way to illusory distinctions, such as the difference between the "true" and "false" prophet of which the next sentence speaks.]

6. [Girard elaborates the concept of "sacrificial crisis" in chapter 2 of *Violence and the Sacred*, which immediately precedes the chapter excerpted here. For a brief explanation of the term, see the preface to the present volume.]

7. [This sentence has been mistranslated. Girard writes that reciprocity incessantly "feeds on" each party's efforts to destroy "it." In other words, each party's efforts to overcome reciprocity by defeating his antagonist succeed only in reinforcing the reciprocity between them.]

8. [Here and elsewhere in the text, the French word *répliques* has been rather confusingly rendered as "replies" or "responses." In the context of a play, *répliques* simply means "lines of dialogue."]

9. [The end of this sentence has been mistranslated. One cannot persevere in following the symmetry of tragedy to its logical conclusion without contradicting, not the "implications" of the myth, but certain basic facts that the myth treats as "givens" (such as the patricide and incest supposedly committed by Oedipus).]

10. [The translation of these lines is misleading. Girard writes, "The tragic reading is radically opposed to the content of the myth. One cannot remain faithful to it without leaving the myth itself behind." The idea is once again that the emphasis on identity and reciprocity in the tragic reading of the myth is at odds with the myth's explicit content and thus subtly undermines it. No claim is made that Sophocles offers a radically different "version" or "presentation" of the surface elements of the story.]

11. [Girard refers to the victory of "a" polemical version over its rival, not of "the" polemical version— the rival versions are equally polemical.]

12. In an essay entitled "Ambiguïté et renversement: Sur la structure énigmatique d'*Oedipe Roi*" [see "Ambiguity and Reversal" in this volume], Jean-Pierre Vernant has aptly defined this loss of cultural difference. Patricide and incest, he writes, "constitute . . . a direct violation of the game of draughts in which each piece stands, in relation to the others, at a specified place on the draught board of the city." In effect, the results of the two crimes are always expressed in terms of lost distinctions: "The equalization of Oedipus and his sons is expressed in a series of brutal images: the father has sown his children in the same place where he himself was sown; Jocasta is a wife, not-wife but mother, whose furrows have yielded a double harvest of father and children; she has been sown, and from these same furrows, these 'equal' furrows, he has obtained his children. But it is left to Tiresias to endow this talk of equality with its true tragic weight when he addressed Oedipus in the following terms: Evils will befall you which 'will establish an equality between yourself and your children.'" In *Echanges et communications*, ed. Jean Pouillon and Pierre Maranda (The Hague, 1970), 2:1253–79.

13. [In the earlier chapters of the book from which this text is excerpted.]

14. [In the earlier chapters of the book from which this text is excerpted.]

15. [See *Violence and the Sacred*, 159–66.]

16. [Of the book from which this text is excerpted.]

17. [In the original French text, Girard speaks of the "efficacy" (not "practical purpose") of the surrogate victim "principle" (not "concept"). For Girard, the action of the surrogate victim principle (or mechanism) is spontaneous, not purposeful, and it does not presuppose the existence of the "concept" of the surrogate victim.]

18. [The term used by Girard here is not "procedure," but "mechanism." He writes that the surrogate victim mechanism "conceals from men the truth of their violence." He does not say that this is the

"only" thing it does (for Girard, it does considerably more than that), nor that it "serves" to do this (which would suggest purposeful action).]

19. [The meaning of the phrase "optimistic falsification" in the translation of this sentence is obscure. In the original text, the sentence begins with the words "This optimism," meaning the optimistic belief that knowledge is "always a good thing" (and hence that the scapegoat mechanism must be of scant importance because it conceals the truth and, as the next sentence puts it, "deprives men of knowledge").]

20. [In the original text, Girard says that men have "never succeeded in coexisting" with the *knowledge* of their violence. That is why he deems too optimistic the belief that "knowledge is always a good thing."]

21. [The original text speaks of our "understanding" (not "belief") that tragic insight effects a partial "deconstruction" (not "demolition") of the myth—i.e., a deconstruction that uncovers traces of the mechanism behind the myth.]

22. [The original text credits Sophocles with having produced a radical "critique" of the myth, not simply a "reading" of it.]

23. We will see further on [in chapter 6 of *Violence and the Sacred*] that this phenomenon of the transformation of secular into sacred elements is facilitated by hallucinatory effects that are basic to the primordial religious experience. However, it is not essential to have experienced these effects to grasp the main principles of primitive religious systems. The logic of such systems is now open to view.

24. [The remaining paragraphs of chapter 3 of *Violence and the Sacred* are not reprinted here.]

Excerpt from
Sweet Violence

Terry Eagleton

Most theory of tragedy is a hangover from the old days of cult, a version of antique ritual updated for modern consumption. Rather than finding the value of tragic sacrifice in ethical terms, it sees such destruction as somehow valuable in itself, thus regressing to notions of the fertilizing power released by the mutilated god. In this sense, it undoes the ethical reinterpretation of the natural which is central to the Judaic tradition. The Old Testament is among other things a record of Yahweh's unenviable struggle to persuade his people that he is not a nature god to be appeased or manipulated, but the god of freedom and justice. Ritual sacrifice continues, but its meaning has now to be grasped in this context, as the symbolic affirmation of a community in which cult takes second place to justice and liberation. And the crucial test of these values is what the Hebrew scriptures call the *anawim*, meaning the destitute and dispossessed. St. Paul refers to them rather colorfully as "the shit of the earth." The *anawim* are the dregs and refuse of society, its tragic scapegoats. They are the flotsam and jetsam of history who do not need to abandon themselves to be remade, since they are lost to themselves already. And it is with them that Yahweh identifies. He will

From chapter 10 of *Sweet Violence: The Idea of the Tragic* (Malden, MA: Blackwell, 2003).

be known for what he is, in the words of Luke 1: 53, when you see the mighty cast down and the lower orders exalted, the hungry filled with good things and the rich sent away empty. The true sacrificial figure, the one which like the burnt offering will pass from profane to powerful, loss of life to fullness of it, is the propertyless and oppressed.

The scapegoat or *pharmakos* has a long history in tragic thought. Tragedy means "goat song," but it might perhaps be better translated as "scapegoat song." It may be that Greek tragedy has some roots in animal sacrifice,[1] though the question is controversial. Pickard-Cambridge and Gerald Else think there is no evidence to suggest that the Greek theatre derives from ritual or religion, from hero cults, Eleusinian mysteries or indeed from the cult of Dionysus.[2] The origins of the art form are shadowy, and Georges Bataille describes it somewhat hyperbolically as "the least explained of all the 'mysteries.'"[3] If it is indeed a Dionysian form, it contains precious little allusion to the god. But the genetic issue aside, the figure of the scapegoat is clearly central to a certain strain of tragedy. At the annual rite of Thargelia in ancient Greece, the pollution accumulated by the city during the previous year was expelled by selecting for purification two *pharmakoi*, chosen from among the most destitute and deformed of the city, who were housed and maintained by the state and fed on certain special foods, then paraded through the streets, struck on the genitals, thrust out of town and in early times perhaps even put to death. One could be, so to speak, a professional *pharmakos*, as one cannot really be a professional martyr; but this is logical, since the whole point of the scapegoat is its anonymity, as a human being emptied of subjectivity and reduced to refuse or nothingness. When it comes to victimage, anyone will do. Or at least anyone of suitably degraded status. Because being rescued from that status would demand a universal transformation, this desolate, abandoned figure is a negative sign of social totality.

The *pharmakos* is symbolically loaded with the guilt of the community, which is why it is selected from among the lowest of the low. It is then thrust out into the wilderness, the symbol of a traumatic horror which we dare not contemplate. Yet in thus representing the community and having the power to deliver it from its trespasses, it is an inverted image of the king, who is likewise a representative figure charged with the health of the *polis*. In the figure of the scapegoat, the borders between power and weakness, sacred and profane, central and peripheral, sickness and health, poison and cure, are accordingly blurred. The scapegoat is a holy terror, a "guilty innocent"[4] like Prometheus, another outcast whose simultaneous theft and gift of fire recalls the doubleness of the *pharmakos*. As [Northrop Frye] remarks, "The *pharmakos* is neither innocent nor guilty,"[5] inhabiting like the subjectively innocent but objectively polluted Oedipus some indeterminate zone between the two. Both ruler and scapegoat are free of the laws of the city, the former by being set above them and the latter by falling below them. To be sacred is to be marked out, set apart, and thus to resemble the criminal or outsider; human *pharmakoi* were sometimes recruited from the local gaols. The criminal has come into contact with the gods, however negatively, and thus retains something of that aura. As René Girard comments: "Because the victim is sacred, it is criminal to kill him—but the victim is sacred only because he is [to be] killed."[6]

The scapegoat incarnates dirt, deformity, madness and criminality, and rather like the insane of classical antiquity, it is both shunned and regarded with respectful awe. This unclean thing is a substitute for the people, and thus stands in a metaphorical relation to them; but it also acts as a displacement for their sins, and is in that sense metonymic. In burdening it with their guilt, the people at once acknowledge their frailty and disavow it, project it violently outside themselves in the slaying of the sacrificial victim or its expulsion beyond their political frontiers. The victim is thus both themselves and not themselves, both a thing of darkness they acknowledge as their own as well as a convenient object on which to off-load and disown their criminality. Both pity and fear, identity and otherness, are at stake. The scapegoat must be neither too foreign nor too familiar; it must be in Lacan's term *extime*, different enough to dread and loathe, yet enough of a mirror-image to be a credible point of displacement for one's sins. As such, it bears an oblique relation to the Freudian notion of the uncanny, another ambiguous phenomenon caught between life and death, the strange and the familiar.[7] It is a "monstrous double,"[8] as indeed is the word "sacred" itself, which in Latin can mean both holy and accursed. The *pharmakos*, being both poison and cure,[9] symbol of both transgression and redemption, has a homeopathic doubleness rather like *catharsis*, which similarly provokes sickness in order to cure it.

Pity and fear reflect here alternative political agendas. To fear the scapegoat is to load it with whatever ails the *polis* and thrust it beyond its limits, so that the status quo may be purged and strengthened. Sacrifice in this sense is a consolidation, not a revolution. To pity the *pharmakos*, however, is to identify with it, and so to feel horror not of it but of the social order whose failure it signifies. The scapegoat, itself beyond speech and sociality, becomes a judgement on that order in its very being, embodying what it excludes, a sign of the humanity which it expels as so much poison. It is in this sense that it bears the seeds of revolutionary agency in its sheer passivity; for anything still active and engaged, however dissidently, would still be complicit with the *polis*, speaking its language and thus unable to put it into question as a whole. Only the silence of the scapegoat will do this.

Charles Segal writes that "Greek tragedy . . . operates both within and beyond the limits of the *polis*, at the borders where polarities merge, definitions become unclear, the orderly composition of human institutions becomes ambiguous."[10] The tragic hero in Segal's view demonstrates the necessity of order by infringing it, and so has a foot in both camps. And the drama itself is hybrid in this respect, releasing the forces of disorder within an artistic form which contains them. Tragedy breaks down the barriers between gods, humans and beasts; and the *pharmakos*, a human being thrust down to the depths of animal destitution yet thereby curiously sacred, combines something of all three species. The great *pharmakos* of Greek tragedy, as Segal recognizes, is Oedipus—in Adrian Poole's words, "the paradigm of doubleness, monstrous but still familiar, and the same but two and different."[11] As Francis Fergusson writes, "The figure of Oedipus himself fills all the requirements of the scapegoat, the dismembered king or god-figure."[12] But Antigone, described by Creon as derelict and abandoned, is another such incarnate ambiguity. As indeed is Philoctetes, that monstrous outcast from human society who is at once blessed and cursed, crippled and potent, fearful and pitiful. Marooned between life and death, he is a rotting human body which will nonetheless prove historically fertile.

The *pharmakos* is at once holy and terrifying, and thus has something of the dual structure of the sublime. But whereas the sublime beggars description by soaring above it, the scapegoat puts paid to speech by falling below it, slipping through the net of discourse into sheer brute ineffability. It is that which is cut off from language, about which there is absolutely nothing to be said—all those violently disfigured creatures who have strayed beyond the frontier of the human into some ghastly life-in-death limbo beyond it. Rebuffing the claims of the symbolic order, such creatures—or rather the

Abrahams, Lears, Oedipuses and Antigones who represent them—inaugurate a revolutionary ethics by their death-dealing, heroically tenacious commitment to another order of truth altogether, a truth which discloses the negativity of the subject rather than legitimating a positive regime, and which figures for Jacques Lacan as the terrifying abyss of the Thing or the Real.[13] Such figures represent a truth which the system must suppress in order to function; yet since they therefore have the least investment in it of any social group, they also have the strange, hallowed power to transform it. They incarnate the inner contradictions of the social order, and so symbolize its failure in their own. The demonic see nothing in value but shit, whereas it is in shit that the revolutionary finds value. Holy shit, as they say. Evil finds its own lack of being unbearable, and seeks to plug this gap with the plundered lives of others. Rather than confronting this frightful abyss in itself, it is prepared to will the loathsome and excremental, the mad and meaningless. The rite of the *pharmakos*, by contrast, recognizes that non-being is the only path to true identity, and that to embrace this dissolution can be life-giving rather than annihilating.

Oedipus, as Poole remarks, is a doubled subject, as indeed is humanity in general, caught contradictorily between gods and beasts. The theatre is itself an image of this dual condition, since gods there have anyway to be represented by humans. The themes of incarnation and hybridity, difference and identity, demi-gods and god-men, are built into the theatrical apparatus itself. Humanity is a riddle, definable only by paradox and aporia. It is open like the Sphinx's conundrum to conflicting readings, a question which is its own solution since it can be defined only in terms of itself. Oedipus the decipherer of enigmas is himself an enigma he cannot decipher.[14] The unknowable, the Kantian *noumenon*, is humanity itself, constituted as it is by something which is centrally missing. And this enigma in Sophocles' drama is also the riddling or garbling of incest, which scrambles or telescopes the various stages of life (youth/age, parent/child) which the Sphinx's riddle lays out in sequence. Incest erases boundaries, as does Oedipus' answer to the Sphinx's query. The human confounds categories just like the Sphinx itself, composite of bird, lion, and woman.

But Oedipus is also dual because he is both Law and transgressor, *énonciation* and *énoncé*, a split subject "spoken" by the discourse of the Other (the gods) in a way at odds with his conscious identity, receiving his true selfhood back from that oracular Other in enigmatic form. With his usual managerial efficiency, he is successful in ridding Thebes of its curse; it is just that the curse turns out to be himself. Oedipus is *tyrannos*, meaning a self-made king, proud of his self-dependence and forensic powers. Marrying your mother and becoming your own father is doubtless the nearest you can come to being entirely self-generated. Yet something quite alien acts and speaks in him, persisting as a riddling subtext within his speech, decentering his imaginary selfhood and finally destroying him.

This is the true sense in which, as Freud suggests, Oedipus is all of us, not because we are all potential parricides or aspiring mother-lovers. As with the rest of us, there is a gap between his objective location in the symbolic order and his imaginary idea of himself, between what he is for the Other and what he is for himself. He is what he is—king, husband, father—only by virtue of this separation. The truth of the ego does not coincide with the truth of the subject, divided as they are by some fatal slippage or opacity; but Oedipus will never be more estranged from himself than when these two registers merge in the terrible light of recognition. To come to selfhood is to acknowledge your self-alienation, the fact that subjectivity just is the process whereby the self constantly gives itself the slip. Oedipus is both king of Thebes and stranger to the city, both kinsman and exile. In being too intimate with the other, the wife-mother or husband-father, you are blinded to your own being, since it depends on distance and otherness for its constitution. Too much probing into the poisoned sources of your identity will put out your eyes.

Oedipus, as we have seen, is divided in his very name between knowledge and monstrosity—between *oida* ("know") and *oidieo* ("swell," "be swollen"), referring to his wounded foot. There is a fissure in his name between the enlightened subject of cognition and the obscure trauma which brings it to birth. Simon Goldhill adds other possible word-plays on his name ("I don't know," "I suppose," "Know where"), observing that "the name of the king is excessive, overdetermined in its excess."[15] When you come to self-knowledge, you confront yourself as a piece of deformity. Oedipus believed that he was equated with the gods; but the Chorus has added up the total of the life of this man so talented in working out equivalences, and finds that it amounts to zero.[16] The swollen foot is the sign of a secret history of dependency upon others;[17] but it is an acknowledgement of these lowly dependencies and material affinities which prevents you from being a monster in the literal sense of self-sufficient beast.

So it is that in casting himself out, Oedipus recognizes his own pollution and arrives at Colonus as the *pharmakos*, the reviled, unclean thing which will prove the city's salvation. Redemption lies in taking to oneself this obscene disfigurement of humanity, as Theseus welcomes the wounded king into his city. In doing so, he learns to pity what he fears. "I come to offer you a gift—my tortured body—a sorry sight," Oedipus informs him, "but there is value in it more than beauty." Something has come of nothing, as the defiled body of the parricide is transformed into a sacred totem to protect the city. As the Chorus comments: "Surely a just God's hand will raise him up again." From identifying with the besmirched and contaminated, a great power for good is bound to flow.

It is in this sense that value and tragic suffering finally converge—not that destruction is an inherent good, but that when humanity reaches its nadir it becomes a symbol of everything that cries out for transformation, and so a negative image of that renewal. "Am I made a man in this hour when I cease to be?" Oedipus wonders aloud when he arrives at Colonus. Such change can spring only from a full acknowledgement of the extremity of one's condition. If even *this* can be salvaged, then there is hope indeed; but unless the promise of redemption extends even to the flesh of those like Oedipus who are destitute and polluted, then it is ultimately worthless. In this sense, tragedy of this kind is itself a *pharmakos*, both gift and threat, power and weakness. "Through tragedy," writes Adrian Poole, "we recognize and refeel our sense of both the value and the futility of human life, or both its purposes and its emptiness."[18]

This dual vision is marked in ancient Greece, with its sense of the human as both precious and precarious, its affirmation of culture along with the dark forces which threaten it with dissolution. Perhaps it is this tenacious Greek belief in civility on the one hand and the turbulent powers which ravage it on the other which lays the foundation for tragedy, as it does in the writings of the later Freud. Certainly Plato discerns something of this scapegoat-like ambiguity in the poet himself, a representative figure who must nevertheless be driven into exile. For Nietzsche and Romanticism later, the poet is both holy and accursed because as the bearer of a dreadful knowledge he peers into the foundations and finds instead a bottomless abyss. If the power to gaze unflinchingly into that depth makes him quasi-divine, the infinite emptiness of it makes him a signifier of nothingness.

The scapegoat represents a kind of death-in-life, and so is a more positive version of the living death of evil. Evil, which reaps a sham sort of vitality from destruction, is a parody of the martyr or sacrificial victim who plucks life from death. Slavoj Žižek write of Oedipus that "he has lived the 'human condition' to the bitter end, realizing its most fundamental possibility; and for that very reason, he is in a way 'no longer human,' and turns into an inhuman monster, bound by no human laws or considerations."[19] The monster is in this sense as lordly as the monarch. To press the human all the way through is to find the other-than-human installed at its heart. Oedipus, Žižek argues, is "less than nothing, the embodiment of some unspeakable horror," one of those who like Lear have trespassed beyond the limits of humanity and entered that hellish realm of horror and psychosis which the ancient Greeks call *ate*. It is a liminal domain suspended between life and death, in which a human being "encounters the death drive as the utmost limit of human experience, and pays the price by undergoing a radical 'subjective destitution,' by being reduced to an excremental remainder."[20] In Christian terms it is Christ's descent into hell, sign of his solidarity with torment and despair. . . .

The Judaeo-Christian tradition plucks an ethico-political meaning from the cyclical cult of sacrifice and seasonal round of fertility. Rather than leaving them behind as so much benighted paganism, it reads them in a fresh light. The natural now becomes a metaphor for the ethical and historical. But in doing so one must be careful not to *over*-humanize the natural, and so hubristically overshoot it. Perhaps this is the point of the *Oresteia*'s final incorporation of the holy, horrible Furies into the democratic settlement. You must not ethicize, politicize, and historicize to the point where you forget about humanity's roots in a recalcitrant otherness which we share with stoats and asteroids. Modern-day left-historicisms have been largely deaf to this caveat. Tragedies like those of Oedipus and Lear thus retain a trace of the archaic as a kind of drag or ballast within the historical, a reminder that whatever our civilized achievements we remain an arbitrary outcropping of Nature, monstrous or amphibious animals who straddle two domains and will never be quite at home in either.

NOTES

1. See, for example, Walter Burkert, "Greek Tragedy and Sacrificial Ritual," *Greek, Roman and Byzantine Studies* 7, no. 2 (1966) [reprinted in this volume]. Francis Fergusson's *The Idea of a Theater* (Princeton, NJ: Princeton University Press, 1949), 26, assumes that tragedy has its origins in fertility cults. John Holloway traces what he sees as a pattern of ritual scapegoating in Shakespeare in *The Story of the Night* (London: Routledge and Kegan Paul, 1961).

2. See A. W. Pickard-Cambridge, *Dithyramb, Tragedy and Comedy* (Oxford: Clarendon Press, 1927) and Gerald F. Else, *The Origin and Early Form of Greek Tragedy* (Cambridge, MA: Harvard University Press, 1965). A similar case is argued by H. D. F. Kitto, *Form and Meaning in Drama* (London: Methuen, 1956), 219, and by Oliver Taplin in "Emotion and Meaning in Greek Tragedy" in Erich Segal, ed., *Oxford Readings in Greek Tragedy* (Oxford: Oxford University Press, 1983), 4. The classic case for tragedy as deriving from Dionysian ritual is famously advanced in Jane Ellen Harrison, *Themis: A Study of the Social Origins of Greek Religion* (Cambridge: Cambridge University Press, 1927), which includes a celebrated excursus by the classical scholar Gilbert Murray on supposedly ritual forms in Greek tragedy.

3. Georges Bataille, *Visions of Excess: Selected Writings, 1927–1939*, ed. Allan Stoekl (Minneapolis: University of Minnesota Press, 1985), 218.

4. The phrase is Paul Ricoeur's in *The Symbolism of Evil*, trans. Emerson Buchanan (Boston: Beacon Press, 1969), 225.

5. [Editor's note: Eagleton mistakenly attributes this statement to E. R. Dodds, citing page 41 of *The Greeks and the Irrational*. The actual source of the quotation is page 41 of Northrop Frye, *Anatomy of Criticism* (Princeton: Princeton University Press, 1971).]

6. René Girard, *Violence and the Sacred*, trans. Patrick Gregory (Baltimore: Johns Hopkins University Press, 1977), 1.

7. See "The Uncanny," in James Strachey, ed., *The Standard Edition of the Psychological Works of Sigmund Freud* (London: Hogarth Press, 1955), vol. 17.

8. Girard, *Violence and the Sacred*, 271.

9. See Jacques Derrida, "Plato's Pharmacy," *Dissemination*, trans. Barbara Johnson (London: Athlone, 1981). Derrida gives only a brief account in this essay of the scapegoat, concerned as he chiefly is with writing as ambiguously poison and cure, death and life. William Righter's essay "Fool and *pharmakon*," in Christopher Norris and Nigel Mapp, eds., *William Empson: The Critical Achievement* (Cambridge: Cambridge University Press, 1993), is concerned with both terms as examples of Empson's "complex words" but overlooks the substantive link between them.

10. Charles Segal, *Tragedy and Civilization* (Cambridge, MA: Harvard University Press, 1981), 45–46.

11. Adrian Poole, *Tragedy: Shakespeare and the Greek Example* (Oxford: Blackwell, 1987), 106.

12. Fergusson, *The Idea of a Theater*, 27.

13. For Lacan's discussion of these questions, see in particular his *Seminar VII: On the Ethics of Psychoanalysis*, ed. Jacques-Alain Miller, trans. Dennis Porter (New York: Norton, 1992).

14. For a fuller interpretation along these lines, see Jean-Pierre Vernant, "Ambiguity and Reversal: On the Enigmatic Structure of *Oedipus Rex*" [reprinted in this volume], in Segal, *Oxford Readings in Greek Tragedy*.

15. Simon Goldhill, *Reading Greek Tragedy* (Cambridge: Cambridge University Press, 1986), 217.

16. I am indebted here to the work of Bernard Knox, especially *The Heroic Temper* (Berkeley: University of California Press, 1954), and his article on Oedipus reprinted in R. P. Draper, ed., *Tragedy: Developments in Criticism* (London: Macmillan, 1980).

17. A. D. Nuttall considers that Greek poetry is obsessed with feet (personal communication).

18. Poole, *Tragedy*, 239.

19. Slavoj Žižek, *The Ticklish Subject* (London: Verso, 1999), 156.

20. Ibid., 161.

Ambiguity and Reversal

On the Enigmatic Structure of *Oedipus Rex*

Jean-Pierre Vernant

n his 1939 study of ambiguity in Greek literature, W. B. Stanford notes that from the point of view of amphibology, *Oedipus Rex* occupies a special position as a model.[1] No literary genre in antiquity, in fact, uses so abundantly as tragedy expressions of double meaning, and *Oedipus Rex* includes more than twice as many ambiguous forms as the other plays of Sophocles (fifty, according to the table that Hug drew up in 1872).[2] The problem, however, is less one of a quantitative order than of nature and function. All the Greek tragedians had recourse to ambiguity as a means of expression and as a mode of thought. But double meaning assumes quite a different role according to its place in the economy of the play and the level of language where the tragic poets situate it.

It can be a matter of ambiguity in vocabulary, corresponding to what Aristotle calls *homōnumia* (lexical ambiguity); this type of ambiguity is made possible by the vacillations or contradictions of language.[3] The playwright plays with them to translate his tragic vision of a world divided against itself, torn by contradictions. In the mouths of several characters, the same words take on different or opposed meanings, because their semantic value is not the same in the religious, legal, political, and common languages.[4]

First published in *New Literary History* 9, no. 3 (1978).

Thus, for Antigone, *nomos* designates the opposite of what Creon, in the circumstances in which he is placed, also calls *nomos*.[5] For the young girl the word means a religious rule; for Creon, an edict promulgated by the head of the state. And indeed, the semantic field of *nomos* is sufficiently extended to cover, among others, both of these meanings.[6] Ambiguity then translates the tension between certain values felt as irreconcilable in spite of their homonymy. The words exchanged in the theatrical space, instead of establishing communication and agreement between the characters, on the contrary underline the impermeability of minds, the freezing of character; they mark the barriers which separate the protagonists, and they trace the lines of conflict. Each hero, enclosed in the universe which is his own, gives a word a meaning, a single meaning. Against this unilaterality, another unilaterality clashes violently. Tragic irony may consist in showing how, in the course of the action, the hero finds himself literally "taken at his word," a word which turns itself against him in bringing him the bitter experience of the meaning which he insisted on not recognizing.[7] It is only over the heads of the characters, between the author and the spectator, that another dialogue is woven, where language recovers its property of communication and almost its transparency. But what transmits the tragic message, when it is understood, is precisely that in the words exchanged between men there exist zones of opacity and incommunicability. In the moment when, on stage, he sees the protagonists adhering exclusively to one meaning and, thus blinded, lose themselves or tear each other apart, the spectator is led to understand that there are in reality two possible meanings or more. The tragic message becomes intelligible to him to the extent that, wrested from his former certainties and limitations, he realizes the ambiguity of words, of values, of the human condition. Recognizing the universe as full of conflict, opening himself to a problematic vision of the world, he makes himself embody the tragic consciousness through the spectacle.

The *Agamemnon* of Aeschylus may provide good examples of another type of tragic ambiguity. Implications are used in a completely conscious way by certain characters in this play to conceal in the discourse which they address to their interlocutor a second discourse, contrary to the first, a discourse whose meaning is perceptible only to those persons, actors or audience, having the necessary information.[8] Welcoming Agamemnon at the threshold of his palace, Clytemnestra uses this double-keyed language:

it sounds agreeably like a token of love and of conjugal fidelity in the ears of her husband; but, already equivocal for the chorus, which has a presentiment of an obscure threat, it reveals itself as completely sinister to the spectator, who easily deciphers in it the plan for death which she has contrived against her husband.[9] The ambiguity no longer marks the conflict of values but the duplicity of a character. An almost demonic duplicity: the same discourse, the same words which entice Agamemnon into the trap by concealing danger at the same time proclaim to the world the crime about to be perpetrated. And because the queen, in the hate which she vows to her spouse, turns herself into the instrument of divine justice in the course of the play, the secret language hidden in the words of her welcome has oracular value. In speaking of the death of the king, she, like a prophet, makes it inevitable. What Agamemnon cannot understand in the words of Clytemnestra is then the very truth of what is said. Formulated aloud, this word acquires all the executive force of a curse; it inscribes into being, in advance and forever, what is enunciated by her. To the ambiguity of the discourse of the queen corresponds exactly the ambiguity of the symbolic values attached to the purple carpet spread out by her in front of the king and on which she persuades him to walk. When he enters into his palace, as Clytemnestra invites him to in terms which evoke at the same time quite another dwelling, these are indeed the doors of Hades through which, without knowing it, Agamemnon passes. When he places his bare foot on the "sumptuous fabrics" with which the ground has been strewn, the road of purple given birth beneath his steps is in no way, as he imagines it, an almost too elevated consecration of his glory, but is instead a way to deliver him over to the infernal powers, to pledge him to death without remission, that "red" death which comes to him in the same "sumptuous fabric" prepared by Clytemnestra for trapping him as in a net.[10]

The ambiguity which one finds in *Oedipus Rex* is quite different. It concerns neither an opposition of values nor duplicity on the part of the character who is leading the action and delights in playing with his victim. In the drama where he is the victim, Oedipus, and Oedipus alone, leads the "play." Nothing except his stubborn will to unmask the guilty, the lofty idea which he has of his burden, of his capacities, of his judgement (his *gnōmē*), his passionate desire to know the truth at any price—nothing obliges him to push the inquiry to its end. Teiresias, Jocasta, the Shepherd try successively to stop him. In vain. He is not a man to content himself with half measures, to accommodate himself to compromise. Oedipus goes to the end. And at the end of the road which he has traced against all opposition, Oedipus discovers that in leading the play from beginning to end it is he himself, from the beginning to end, who has been played. Thus in the moment when he knows himself responsible for making his unhappiness, he will be able to accuse the gods of having prepared all, done all.[11] The equivocation in the words of Oedipus corresponds to the ambiguous status which is conferred on him in the play and upon which the whole tragedy is constructed. When Oedipus speaks, he sometimes says another thing or the opposite of what he says. The ambiguity of his words translates not the duplicity of his character, which is all of a piece, but more profoundly the duality of his being. Oedipus is double. He constitutes by himself a riddle whose meaning he will guess only by discovering himself in every respect the opposite of what he believed himself and seemed to be. Oedipus does not hear the secret discourse which is established, without his knowing it, at the heart of his own discourse. And no witness to the drama on the stage, apart from Teiresias, is any more capable than he of perceiving it. It is the gods who send back to Oedipus, as an echo to certain of his words, his own discourse, deformed or turned around.[12] And this inverted echo, which sounds like a sinister burst of laughter, is in reality a rectification. What Oedipus says without wishing to, without understanding it, constitutes the only authentic truth of his words. The double dimension of Oedipus' language reproduces, then, in an inverted form, the double dimension of the language of the gods as it expressed in the enigmatic form of the oracle. The gods know and speak the truth, but they make it known by giving it expression in words which seem to men to say something quite different. Oedipus neither knows nor says the truth, but the words he uses to say something other than truth make this truth clear, without his knowledge, for anyone who has the gift of double hearing, as the diviner has double vision. The language of Oedipus thus appears as the place where two different discourses weave themselves and confront each other in the same language: a human discourse, a divine discourse. In the beginning, the two discourses are quite distinct, as if cut off one from the other; at the end of the play, when all is made clear, the two discourses are rejoined; the riddle is solved. On the tiers of the theater, the spectators occupy a privileged position which permits them, like the gods, to understand at the same time

the two opposed discourses and to follow their confrontation from one end
to the other, through the play.

We understand then why, from the point of view of amphibology,
Oedipus Rex has exemplary significance: Aristotle, recalling that the two
constitutive elements of tragic plot are, besides the "pathetic," recognition
(*anagnōrisis*) and *peripeteia*—that is, the reversal of the action to its opposite
(*eis to enantion tōn prattomenōn metabolē*)—notes that the recognition in
Oedipus Rex is the most beautiful because it coincides with the *peripeteia*.[13]
The recognition which Oedipus brings about in fact bears on no one but
Oedipus. And this final identification of the hero by himself constitutes a
complete reversal of the action, in the two meanings which one can give to
Aristotle's formula (which is not itself free of ambiguity): the situation of
Oedipus, by the very act of recognition, is revealed as contrary to what it
was previously; Oedipus' action ends up with the opposite result from that
aimed at. At the opening of the play, the Corinthian stranger, decipherer of
riddles, savior of Thebes, installed at the head of the city, whom the people
venerate as the equal of a god for his knowledge and his devotion to the state,
must face a new riddle, that of the death of the former king. Who killed
Laius? At the end of the investigation, the judge discovers himself identical
with the assassin. Behind the progressive elucidation of the detective riddle,
which forms the thread of the tragic action, what is being played out in fact
is the recognition by Oedipus of his identity. When he appears for the first
time, at the opening of the play, to announce to the supplicants his resolution
to discover the criminal at any cost, and his certainty of success, he expresses
himself in terms whose ambiguity underlines the presence, behind the question which he hopes to answer (who killed Laius?), of another problem
(who is Oedipus?). In going back in his turn [to the origin (of yet unknown
events)], the king declares proudly, "I will bring this to light [*egō phanō*]."[14]
The scholiast does not fail to observe that there is in this *egō phanō* something concealed, something Oedipus does not mean, but which the spectator
understands, "since all will be discovered in Oedipus himself [*epei to pan en
autō phanēsatai*]." *Egō phanō*: "it is I who will bring the criminal to light," but
also "I will discover myself criminal."

What then is Oedipus? Like his own discourse, like the word of the
oracle, Oedipus is double, enigmatic. From the beginning to the end of the
play he remains psychologically and morally the same: a man of action and of

decision, with courage nothing can beat down, with conquering intelligence, a man to whom one can impute no moral fault, no deliberate oversight of justice. But without knowing it, without having asked for or deserved it, the character of Oedipus in all his dimensions—social, religious, human—is the reverse of what he appears at the head of the city. The Corinthian stranger is in reality a native of Thebes; the decipherer of riddles, a riddle which he cannot decipher; the judge, a criminal; the clairvoyant, a blind man; the savior of the city, its damnation. Oedipus, he who for all is renowned (8), the first of men (33), noblest of men (46), the man of power, of intelligence, of honors, of wealth, finds himself the last, the most unhappy (1204–6, 1296ff., 1397), and the worst of men (1365), a sinner (1398), a festering foulness (1396), object of horror to his equals (1306), hated by the gods (1345), reduced to beggary and exile (455, 1518).

Two features underline the significance of this "reversal" of Oedipus' condition. In the first words he addresses to him, the priest of Zeus makes Oedipus in some way the equal of the gods: *isoumenos theoisi* (31). When the riddle is solved, the chorus recognizes in Oedipus the model of a human life which, through this paradigm, appears equal to nothingness: *isa kai to mēden* (1187–88). At the start Oedipus is the clairvoyant mind, the lucid intelligence which, without anyone's aid, without the help of a god or an omen, knew how to guess, by the resources of his *gnōmē* alone, the riddle of the Sphinx. He has only scorn for the blind gaze of the diviner whose eyes are closed to the light of the sun and whose life, according to his own expression, "is one long night" (374). But when the shadows are dispelled, so that all is made clear (1182), when light bears on Oedipus, it is then precisely that he sees day for the last time. As soon as Oedipus is "elucidated," found out (1213), offered to the eyes of all as a spectacle of horror (1397), it is no longer possible for him to see or to be seen. The Thebans turn their eyes away from him (1303–5), incapable of looking in the face of this evil which is a "terrible sight for men to see" (1298), this grief of which one can bear neither the telling nor the sight (1312). And if Oedipus blinds himself, it is, as he explains (1370ff.), because it has become impossible for him to suffer the gaze of another human creature among the living and the dead. If he could have, he would also have stopped his ears to wall himself in a solitude cut off from the society of men. The light which the gods projected on Oedipus is too bright for mortal eye to gaze on. It casts Oedipus out from this world, made for the light of the sun, the human glance, social contact. It restores him to the solitary world of night, where Teiresias lives, who has himself paid with his eyes for the gift of double sight, the access to the other light, the blinding and terrible light of the divine.

Considered from the point of view of men, Oedipus is the clairvoyant leader, equal to the gods; considered from the point of view of the gods, he appears blind, equal to nothing. The turning around of the action, like the ambiguity of the language, marks the duplicity of a human condition which, like a riddle, invites two opposite interpretations. Human language is inverted when the gods speak through it. No matter how great, just, happy one may be, the human condition is reversed as soon as one measures it against the gods. Oedipus had "shot his bolt beyond the others and won the prize of happiness complete" (1196–97). But in the eye of the Immortals, he who raises himself to the highest is also the lowest. Oedipus the blessed touches the bottom of unhappiness: "What man," sings the chorus, "what man on earth wins more of happiness than a seeming and after that turning away? Oedipus, you are my pattern of this, Oedipus, you and your fate! Luckless Oedipus, whom of all men I envy not at all."[15]

If such is indeed the meaning of the tragedy, as Hellenists agree, we will recognize that *Oedipus Rex* is not only centered on the theme of the riddle, but that in its presentation, its development, its denouement, the play is itself constructed as a riddle.[16] The ambiguity, the recognition, the peripeteia, homologous with each other, are equally integrated into the enigmatic structure of the work. The keystone of the tragic architecture, the model which serves as matrix to its tragic organization and to its language, is reversal, that is, that formal scheme by which positive values are inverted to negative values when one passes from one to the other of the two planes, human and divine, which tragedy unites and opposes, just as a riddle, according to Aristotle's definition, joins together irreconcilable terms.[17]

Through this logical scheme of inversion, corresponding to the ambiguous mode of thought proper to tragedy, an instruction of a particular type is proposed to the spectators: man is not a being which we can describe or define; he is a problem, a riddle whose double meanings we have never finished deciphering. The meaning of the work depends neither on psychology nor on morality; it is of a specifically tragic order.[18] Parricide and incest correspond neither to Oedipus' character, to his ēthos, nor to a moral fault, *adikia*, for which he might be responsible. If he kills his father, if he sleeps with his mother, it is not because, more or less obscurely, he hates the first or is in love with the second. For those whom he believes to be his true, his only parents, Merope and Polybus, Oedipus has feelings of filial tenderness. When he kills Laius, it is in legitimate defense against a stranger who struck him first; when he marries Jocasta, it is a marriage without affection, which the city of Thebes imposes on him with a stranger in order to permit his accession to the throne, as recompense for his exploit: "Though I did not know, Thebes married me to evil; Fate and I were joined there. . . . I thought of her as my reward. Ah, would I had never won it! Would I had never served the State that day!"[19] As Oedipus declares, in committing parricide and incest, neither his person (*sōma*) nor his acts (*erga*) are at issue; in reality, he himself has done nothing (*ouk erexa*).[20] Or rather, during his action its meaning, unknown to him and without his having anything to do with it, reversed itself. Legitimate defense became parricide; marriage, consecrating his glory, incest. Innocent and pure from the point of view of human law, he is guilty and contaminated from the religious point of view. What he accomplished, without knowing it, without evil purpose or felonious intent, is nonetheless the most terrible wrong conceivable against the sacred order which governs human life. Like those birds which eat birds' flesh, to recall the expression of Aeschylus,[21] he is twice satiated with his own flesh, first by spilling paternal blood, then by uniting himself to maternal blood. Oedipus thus finds himself, by a divine curse as gratuitous as the selection from which other heroes of legend profit, cut off from the social bond, thrown outside humanity. He is from then on *apolis*; he incarnates the figure of the excluded. In his solitude, he appears at once not yet human, a wild beast, a savage monster, and beyond the human, bearer of a formidable religious qualification, like a *daimōn*. His stain, his *agos*, is only the reverse side of the supernatural power which is concentrated in him in order to destroy him: at the same time as contaminated, he is sacred and saint, *hieros* and *eusebēs*.[22] To the city which will welcome him, to the earth which will hold his corpse, he will bring the promise of the greatest blessings.

This play of inversion is expressed by other stylistic and dramatic procedures besides that of ambiguity, in particular by what Bernard Knox calls a "reversal" in the use of the same terms in the course of the tragic action.[23] The reader is referred to his fine study of which we will recall only a few examples. A first form of this reversal consists in using, to characterize the status of

Oedipus, a vocabulary the values of which are systematically inverted when they pass from active to passive. Oedipus is presented as a hunter on the trail, tracking down and startling the wild animal (111, 221, 475ff.) which wanders on the mountain, hastened into flight by the hunt (467), hidden away far from humans (479–80). But in his hunt, the hunter at length finds himself the game: hunted by the terrible curse of his parents (417), Oedipus wanders and bellows like a wild animal (1260, 1265) before putting out his eyes and fleeing into the wild mountains of Cithairon (1451).

Oedipus leads an investigation, at the same time judiciary and scientific, which is underlined by repeated use of the verb *zētein*.[24] But the investigator is also the object of the investigation, the *zētōn* is also the *zētoumenon*,[25] just as the examiner, the questioner[26] is also the answer to the question (1180–81). Oedipus is the discoverer[27] and the object of the discovery (1026, 1213), that very one who is discovered (*heuriskomai*, 1397). He is the doctor using a medicinal vocabulary to speak of the evil from which the city is suffering, but he is also the sick man (61, 674) and the sickness (1294, 1389, 1396–97).

Another form of reversal is the following: the terms which designate Oedipus at the height of his glory detach themselves from him one by one to come to rest on the gods; the grandeur of Oedipus vanishes in proportion as—in contrast with his—that of the gods is affirmed. At line 14 the priest of Zeus, in his first words, addresses himself to Oedipus as sovereign: *kratunōn*; at 903 the chorus implores Zeus as sovereign: *ō kratunōn*. At 47 the Thebans call Oedipus savior: *sōter*; at 150 it is Apollo who is invoked as savior (*paustērios*) to put a stop to the evil, as Oedipus formerly had put a "stop" to the Sphinx (397). At line 236 Oedipus gives orders as master of the power and of the throne (*egō kratē te kai thronous nemō*); at 200 the chorus implores Zeus "the [master of the power] of lightning" (*astrapan kratē nemōn*). At 441 Oedipus recalls the exploit which made him great (*megas*); at 871 the chorus recalls that in the celestial laws resides a great (*megas*) god who does not age. That dominion (*archē*) which Oedipus prides himself in exercising (259, 380), the chorus recognizes as forever immortal between the hands of Zeus (905). That help (*alkē*) which the priest at 42 asks of Oedipus, the chorus implores Athena, at 189, to give to them. In the first line of the tragedy, Oedipus addresses himself to the suppliants as a father speaks to his children; but at 198, to destroy the pestilence of the city, it is on Zeus that the chorus confers the title of father: *ō Zeu pater*.

Even the name of Oedipus invites these effects of reversal. Ambiguous, it bears in it the same enigmatic character which marks the whole tragedy. Oedipus is the man with the swollen (*oidos*) foot, an infirmity which recalls the cursed child, rejected by his parents, exposed to die in savage nature. But as Oedipus, he is also the man who knows (*oida*) the riddle of the foot, who succeeds in deciphering, without misconstruing it,[28] the "oracle" of the sinister prophetess, of the Sphinx with the dark song (1200, 130).[29] And this knowledge enthrones in Thebes the foreign hero, establishes him in the place of the legitimate kings. The double meaning of *Oidipous* is found again at the interior of the name itself in the opposition between the first two syllables and the third. *Oida*: "I know," one of the master words in the mouth of Oedipus triumphant, Oedipus the tyrant.[30] *Pous*: "the foot"—the mark imposed since birth on him whose destiny is to finish as he began, excluded, like the savage beast which his *foot* makes flee (468), whom his *foot* isolates from humans, in the vain hope of escaping the oracles (479ff.), pursued by the curse with the terrible *foot* (417) for having transgressed the sacred laws with his lifted foot (866), and incapable from then on of extricating his foot from the evils into which he has precipitated himself by raising himself to the height of power.[31] The whole tragedy of Oedipus is thus contained in the play to which the riddle of his name lends itself. To that wise, knowing master of Thebes, whom happy omen protects, is at every point opposed the cursed infant, the Swollen Foot cast out of his fatherland. But in order for Oedipus really to know who he is, the first of the two characters which he initially assumed must be inverted until it turns into the second.

The knowledge of Oedipus, when he deciphers the riddle of the Sphinx, already bears in a certain fashion on himself. What is the being, asks the sinister songstress, who is at once *dipous, tripous, tetrapous*? For *Oi-dipous*, the mystery is only in appearance; it is about him surely, it is about man. But this answer is knowledge only in appearance; it masks the true problem: what then is man, what is Oedipus? The pseudo-response of Oedipus opens to him the gates of Thebes. But in installing him at the head of the state, this answer realizes, by hiding it from him, his true identity as parricide and committer of incest. To penetrate his own mystery is for Oedipus to recognize in the stranger who reigns in Thebes the formerly rejected child of the land. This identification, instead of definitively uniting Oedipus with his fatherland, instead of fixing him on the throne which he occupies from then on not as a foreign tyrant but as the legitimate son of the king, turns him into a monster whom it is necessary to expel forever from the city, to cut off from the human world.

Venerated as the equal of a god, uncontested master of justice, holding in his hands the health of the whole city—such, placed above other men, is the character of Oedipus the Wise, who at the end of the play is reversed, projected into an opposite figure: at the last rung of disgrace appears Oedipus-Swollen Foot, abominable contamination, concentrating in himself all the impurity of the world. The divine king, purifier and savior of his people, rejoins the contaminated criminal whom it is necessary to expel like a *pharmakos*, a scapegoat, so that the city, pure again, may be saved.

It is in fact by means of the axis occupied at the summit by the divine king, at its base by the *pharmakos*, that the series of reversals takes place which affects the figure of Oedipus and makes of the hero the "paradigm" of ambiguous man, of tragic man.

The quasi-divine aspect of the majestic figure who advances on the threshold of his palace, at the beginning of the tragedy, has not escaped the commentators. Already the ancient scholiast noted in his commentary at line 16 that the suppliants come to the altars of the royal house as to the altars of a god. The expression which the priest of Zeus uses, "You see us assembled near *your* altars," seems so heavy with meaning that Oedipus himself asks: "Why do you hold yourselves thus crouched in a ritual attitude of supplication towards me, with your boughs crowned with fillets?" This veneration towards a man whom one places higher than man because he saved the city "with God's assistance" (39), because he has been revealed by supernatural favor as the *Tuchē*, the "happy omen" (52) of the city, is maintained from one end of the play to the other. Even after the double contamination of Oedipus has been revealed, the chorus celebrates nonetheless as its savior this man whom it calls "my king," "standing a tower against death for my land" (1200–1201). At the very moment when it evokes the inexpiable crimes of the unhappy one, the chorus concludes, "To speak directly, I drew my breath from you at the first" (1222–23).[32]

But it is at the crucial moment of the play, when the fate of Oedipus rests on the razor's edge, that the polarity between the status of demigod and that of scapegoat reveals itself most clearly. What is the situation at that point? We know already that Oedipus may be the murderer of Laius; the symmetry of the oracles given on the one hand to Oedipus, on the other to Laius and Jocasta, increases the anxiety that grips the heart of the protagonists and the Theban notables. The messenger from Corinth arrives in the midst of all this. He announces that Oedipus is not the son of those whom he believes to be his parents, that he is a foundling; he has himself taken him from the hands of a shepherd on Cithairon. Jocasta, to whom all is clear by now, begs Oedipus not to push the investigation further. Oedipus refuses. The queen then addresses this last warning to him: "Unhappy one, may you never know who you are!" But once again the tyrant of Thebes is mistaken about the meaning of what Oedipus is. He thinks the queen fears that the base origin of the foundling will be disclosed and that her marriage will be revealed as a misalliance with someone less than nothing, a slave, son of a slave to the third generation (1062). It is precisely then that Oedipus draws himself up—in his battered soul, the announcement of the messenger brings forth a mad hope which the chorus shares and which it expresses joyously in its song. Oedipus proclaims himself son of *Tuchē*, of happy omen, who, reversing his situation in the course of the years from the "little" one he was, has made him "great" (*mikron kai megan*: 1083), that is to say, has transformed the deformed, foundling child into the wise master of Thebes. Irony of words: Oedipus is not the son of *Tuchē*; as Teiresias predicted, he is her victim (442), and the reversal is produced in the inverse sense, bringing the great Oedipus back to what is lowest, back from the god's equal to the equal of nothing.

However, the illusion of Oedipus and the chorus is understandable. The exposed child can be a reject which one wants to get rid of, a deformed monster or lowly slave. But he can also be a hero with an exceptional destiny. Saved from death, victor of the test imposed on him at his birth, the excluded one reveals himself elect, invested with supernatural powers.[33] Having returned triumphant to the country which excluded him, he will no longer live there as an ordinary citizen, but as absolute master, reigning over his subjects in the manner of a god among men. That is why the theme of exposure figures in almost all the Greek legends of heroes. If Oedipus was rejected at birth, cut off from his human lineage, it is doubtless, as the chorus imagines, because he is the son of some god, of the nymphs of Cithairon, of Pan or of Apollo, of Hermes or of Dionysus (1086–109).

This mythic image of the hero exposed and saved, rejected and returning as victor, continues in a transposed form, in a certain representation of the *turannos*. Like the hero, the tyrant accedes to royalty by an indirect route, outside the legitimate lineage; like him, he qualifies himself for power by his acts, his exploits. He reigns, not by virtue of his blood, but by his own virtues: he is the son of his deeds and of happy omen at the same time. The supreme power which he, outside of ordinary norms, was able to conquer places him, for good and bad, above other men, above the laws.[34] According to the just remark of Bernard Knox, the comparison of tyranny with the power of the gods (gods defined for the Greeks as "the strongest," "the most powerful") is a commonplace of the literature of the fifth and fourth centuries. Euripides and Plato agree in speaking of *turannis isotheos*, of tyranny equal to deity, inasmuch as it is absolute power to do all one wishes, to permit oneself everything.[35]

The other face of Oedipus, complementary and opposed (his appearance as scapegoat), has not been so clearly defined by the commentators. We have seen that Oedipus, at the end of the tragedy, is cast out from Thebes as one expels the *homo piacularis* in order to "ward off the contamination [*to agos elaunein*]."[36] But Louis Gernet established the relationship of the tragic theme with the Athenian ritual of the *pharmakos* in a more precise way.[37]

Thebes suffers from a *loimos* which according to the traditional schema is manifested by a drying up of the sources of fecundity; earth, flocks, women bear no more, while pestilence decimates the living. Sterility, sickness, death are experienced as the same power of contamination, a *miasma* which has disrupted the normal course of life. It is a matter then of discovering the criminal who *is* the stain of the city, its *agos*, in order to get rid of the evil through him. This is what is known to have happened in Athens, in the seventh century, when to expiate the impious murder of Kylon, the Alcameonids were expelled and declared impure and sacrilegious (*enageis kai alitērioi*).[38]

But there also exists, in Athens as in other Greek cities, an annual rite which aims at periodically expelling the contamination accumulated in the course of the past year. "It is the custom in Athens," reports Helladios of Byzantium, "to parade two *pharmakoi* for purification, one for the men, the other for the women."[39] According to the legend, the origin of the rite lay in the impious murder committed by the Athenians on the person of Androgeos the Cretan: to get rid of the *loimos* set off by the crime, the custom of a recurrent purification by the *pharmakos* was instituted. The ceremony took place on the first day of the holiday of the Thargelia, the sixth of the month *Thargeliōn*.[40] The two *pharmakoi*, wearing necklaces of dried figs (black or white according to the sex they represented), were paraded through the whole city; they were struck on the genitals with squill bulbs, figs, and other wild plants,[41] then they were expelled; perhaps, at the beginning, they were even put to death by stoning, the corpses burnt, the ashes dispersed.[42] How were the *pharmakoi* chosen? Everything leads us to believe that they were recruited from the dregs of the population, among the *kakourgoi*, jailbirds, designated by their misdeeds, their physical ugliness, their base condition, their vile and repugnant occupation, as inferior beings, degraded, *phauloi*, the rejects of society. Aristophanes, in the *Frogs*, opposes to the well-born citizens, wise, just, honest, who are like the good money of the city, the bad pieces of copper, "foreign, red-haired, beggars born from beggars," the latest arrivals, whom the city would not have accepted easily at random even as *pharmakoi*.[43] Tzetzes, citing the fragments of the poet Hipponax, notes that when a *loimos* struck a city, the most wretched of all (*amorphoteron*) was chosen as *katharmos* and *pharmakos* of the diseased city.[44] At Leucas, they took for purification a man condemned to death. At Marseilles, some wretch offered himself as "cure all." He thus gained a year of life, supported at public expense. At the end of the year he was paraded around the city with solemn curses so that the transgressions of the community would fall on him.[45] So the image of the *pharmakos* comes quite naturally to Lysias' mind when he wishes to denounce to the judges the repugnant foulness of a person like Andocides, impious, sacrilegious, informer and traitor, exiled from city to city, and seemingly marked in his miseries by the finger of god. To condemn Andocides "is to purify the city, liberate it from contamination, expel the *pharmakos*."[46]

The Athenian Thargelia included another panel. With the expulsion of the *pharmakos* is associated another ritual which took place on the seventh of the month, the day dedicated to Apollo. They dedicated to the divinity the first fruits of the earth in the form of the *Thargēlos*, a cake and a pot filled with seeds of all kinds.[47] But the central element of the holiday was the carrying of the *eiresiōnē*, a branch of olive or laurel ribboned with wool, garnished with fruits, with cakes, with little flasks of oil and wine.[48] Young boys paraded these "maypoles" across the city. They placed them at the threshold of the temple of Apollo, they hung them at the doors of private houses (*pros apotropēn limou*) to avert famine.[49] The *eiresiōnē* in Attica, at Samos, Delos, and Rhodes, the *kōpō* at Thebes, signify springtime renewal. Accompanied by songs and by an offering of gifts, their procession consecrates the end of the old season and inaugurates the young new year under the sign of the gift, of abundance, of health.[50] Society's need, by dismissing those which have faded during the year, to reinvigorate the forces of fecundity on which its life depends appears clearly in the Athenian rite. The *eiresiōnē* remains attached to the houses' doors where it fades and dries until the day of Thargelia when the new year's green one replaces it.[51]

But the renewal symbolized by the *eiresiōnē* cannot be produced unless all contaminations of the group have been cast off, unless earth and men have been made pure. As Plutarch[52] recalls, the first fruits of all kinds which decorate the *eiresiōnē* commemorate the end of the *aphoria*, the sterility which struck the soil of Attica as punishment for the murder of Androgeos, that murder which the expulsion of the *pharmakos* ought precisely to expiate. The major role of the *eiresiōnē* in the Thargelia explains what Hesychius glosses *thargēlos: hē hiketēria*, because in its form and function, the *eiresiōnē* is nothing but a suppliant's branch.[53]

These are precisely the *hiketeriai*, these suppliants' branches crowned with wool, which, at the beginning of Sophocles' play, the representatives of the Theban youth, grouped in classes by age, children and very young people, parade up to the gates of the royal palace and set down in front of the altar of Apollo to ward off the *loimos* oppressing the city. Another indication permits us to define more precisely the ritual scenario evoked by the first scene of the tragedy. Twice it is recalled that the city resounds with "groans and hymns and incense" (5, 186). The paean is normally a joyous song of victory and of thanksgiving. It is opposed to the threnody, a song of mourning, a plaintive melody. But we know from a scholiast of the *Iliad* that there exists another type of paean, that which is sung "to end evils or in order that they not occur."[54] This cathartic paean, whose memory was kept alive by the Pythagoreans in particular, also takes the form of a threnody, according to the scholiast. This is the paean mixed with sobs of which the tragedy speaks. This purifying song is used at a very precise moment of the religious calendar, at that turning of the year which spring represents, when, at the threshold of summer, the period of human undertakings begins: harvests, navigation, war.[55] Situated in May, before the beginning of the harvest, the Thargelia belong to this complex of spring holidays.

These details must have imposed on the spectators of the tragedy the comparison with the Athenian ritual so much the more easily in that Oedipus is presented implicitly as the *agos*, whose contamination it is necessary to expel.[56] From his first words he defines himself, without wishing to, in terms that evoke the figure of the scapegoat: "I know," he says to the suppliants, "you are all sick, yet there is not one of you, sick though you are, that is as sick as I myself. Your several sorrows each have single scope and touch but one of you. My spirit [*psuchē*] groans for city and myself and you at once" (59–64). And a little further on: "the grief I bear, I bear it more for these [others] than for my own heart" (93–94). Oedipus is wrong: this evil, to which Creon immediately gives its real name in calling it *miasma* (97), is precisely his own. But in being wrong he says, unknowingly, the truth. Because he is himself, as *miasma*, the *agos* of the city, Oedipus indeed carries the weight of all the unhappiness which overwhelms his fellow citizens.

Divine king—pharmakos: such are the two faces of Oedipus, which constitute him as a riddle by uniting two figures in him, as in an expression with double meaning, the one the inverse of the other. Sophocles attributes a general significance to this inversion in Oedipus' nature. The hero is the model of the human condition. But Sophocles did not have to invent the polarity between the king and the scapegoat (a polarity which the tragedy situates at the very heart of the person of Oedipus). It was inscribed in the religious practice and in the social thought of the Greeks. The poet simply lent it a new significance in making it the symbol of man and of his fundamental ambiguity. If Sophocles chose the couple *turannos-pharmakos* to illustrate what we have called the theme of reversal, it is because in their opposition these two persons appear symmetrical and in certain respects interchangeable. Both appear as *individuals* responsible for the *collective* health of the group. In Homer and Hesiod, the fecundity of the earth, of the flocks, of women depends on the person of the king, offspring of Zeus. If he shows himself irreproachable (*amumōn*) in his sovereign justice, everything prospers in his city;[57] if he errs, it is the *whole city* which pays for the fault of one man. The son of Cronos makes unhappiness fall back on all, *limos* and *loimos*, famine and plague all together: men die, women cease to give birth, the flocks no longer reproduce.[58] Thus the normal solution, when the divine scourge strikes a people, is to sacrifice the king. If he is the master of fecundity, and it dries up, it is because his power as sovereign is in some way reversed; his justice has become crime, his virtue contamination, the best (*aristos*) has become the worst (*kakistos*). The legends of Lycurgus, of Athamas, of Oinocles thus require, for the expulsion of *loimos*, the stoning of the king, his ritual sacrifice, or failing that, the sacrifice of his son. But sometimes the painful role of unworthy king, of sovereign in reverse, is delegated to a member of the community. The king unburdens himself on an individual who like an inverted image represents everything negative in his person. Such is the *pharmakos*: double of the king, but in reverse, like those sovereigns at carnival crowned at holiday time, when order is set upside down, social hierarchies reversed: sexual prohibitions are lifted, theft becomes legal, the slaves take their masters' place, the women trade their clothes with men; then the throne must be occupied by the basest, ugliest, most ridiculous, most criminal of men. But, the holiday once ended, the counter-king is expelled or put to death, carrying with him all the disorder which he incarnates and of which the community is purged at one blow.

In classical Athens, the rite of the Thargelia still makes clear certain traits, in the person of the *pharmakos*, which evoke the figure of the sovereign, master of fecundity.[59] The horrible person who must incarnate contamination is supported at the cost of the state, nourished on especially pure foods: fruits, cheese, consecrated cakes of *maza*.[60] If in the course of the procession he is decorated, like the *eiresiōnē*, with necklaces of figs and branches, and struck on the sexual parts with squill bulbs, it is because he possesses a beneficent virtue of fecundity. His contamination is a religious designation which can be used in a beneficent sense. Like that of Oedipus, his *agos* makes him a *katharmos*, a *katharsios*, a purifier. Moreover, his person's ambiguity is marked even in the etiological accounts which claim to explain the foundation of the rite. To the version of Helladios of Byzantium which we have cited is opposed that of Diogenes Laertius and of Athenaeus:[61] when Epimenides purified Athens of the *loimos* caused by the murder of Kylon, two young people, one named Cratinos, seem to have made a voluntary gift of their persons to purify the land which had nourished them. These two young people are presented, not as the refuse of society, but as the flower of Athenian youth. According to Tzetzes, as we have seen, they choose as *pharmakos* a particularly ugly being (*amorphoteros*); according to Athenaeus, Cratinos was, on the contrary, a very handsome adolescent (*meirakion eumorphon*).

The symmetry of the *pharmakos* and the legendary king, the first assuming a role below analogous to that which the second plays on high, perhaps casts light on the institution of ostracism whose character J. Carcopino has shown to be strange in many respects.[62] In the framework of the Greek city, there is no longer, as we know, a place for the person of the king, master of fecundity. When Athenian ostracism was instituted at the end of the sixth century, it is the figure of the tyrant who inherited, transposed, certain of the religious aspects belonging to the former sovereign. Ostracism aims as a rule at getting rid of that citizen who, raised too high, threatens to accede to the tyranny. But, in this completely positive form, the explanation cannot take account of certain of the institution's archaic features. It functions every year, doubtless between the sixth and the eighth prytaneion, following rules contrary to the ordinary procedures of political and legal life. Ostracism is a judgment which aims at "ridding the city" of a citizen by a temporary exile of ten years.[63] It is pronounced outside the tribunals, by the assembly, without there having been a public denunciation or even accusation against anyone. A first preliminary session decides by the raising of hands if the procedure of ostracism will take place or not for the year in progress. No name is pronounced; no debate takes place. If those voting have declared themselves favorable, the assembly is called back again in exceptional session some time later. It sits in the agora and not, as usual, on the Pynx. To proceed to the actual vote, each participant inscribes the name of his choice on a potsherd. This time no debate either: no name is proposed; there is neither accusation nor defense. The vote takes place without there being any appeal to reason, political or judicial. Everything is organized to give to the popular feeling which the Greeks call *phthonos*[64] (both envy and religious mistrust in regard to one who rises too high, succeeds too well) the occasion to manifest itself in the most spontaneous and unanimous form (it requires at least six thousand voters), outside all rule of law, all rational justification. For what is the ostracized reproached but for those same superiorities which raise him above the common and for his fortune, too great, which threatens to attract divine prosecution to the city. The fear of tyranny is mixed with a deeper apprehension, of a religious kind, in regard to someone who puts the whole group in danger. As Solon writes: "A city perishes by its overly great men [*andrōn d'ek megalōn polis ollutai*]."[65]

The commentary which Aristotle devotes to ostracism is in this regard characteristic.[66] If a being goes beyond the common level in virtue and in political capacity, he says, he cannot be accepted on a footing of equality with the other citizens: "Such a being in fact will naturally be like a god among men." That is why, Aristotle adds, the democratic states instituted ostracism. In doing so, they followed the example of the myth: the Argonauts abandoned Heracles for an analogous motive. The ship Argo refused to carry him like the other passengers because of his excessive weight. And Aristotle concludes that things are in this matter as in the arts and sciences: "A master of a chorus would not permit among his singers one whose voice would surpass in force and beauty all the rest of the chorus."

How could the city admit into its heart one who, like Oedipus, "has shot his bolt beyond the others" and has become *isotheos*? When it establishes ostracism, it creates an institution whose role is symmetrical to and the inverse of the ritual of the Thargelia. In the person of the ostracized, the city expels what in it is too elevated, what incarnates the evil which can come to it from above. In the person of the *pharmakos*, it expels what is vilest in itself, what incarnates the evil that menaces it from below.[67] By this double and complementary rejection it delimits itself: it takes the proper measure of the human in opposition on one side to the divine and heroic, on the other to the bestial and monstrous.

What the city thus realizes spontaneously in the play of its institutions Aristotle expresses in a fully conscious and deliberate way in his political theory. Man, he writes, is by nature a political animal; he then who finds himself by nature *apolis* is either *phaulos*, "a degraded being, a subman," or *kreittōn ē anthrōpos*, "above humanity, more powerful than man." Such a man, Aristotle continues, is "like an isolated piece in a checkers game [*ate per azux ōn hōsper en pettois*]." And the philosopher comes back to the same idea a little further on, when he notes that one who cannot live in a community "is not at all part of the city and finds himself by consequence either a brute beast, or a god [*ē thērion ē theos*]."[68]

It is the very status of Oedipus, in its double and contradictory aspect, which finds itself thus defined: above and below the human, hero more powerful than man, equal to god, and at the same moment brute beast rejected in the wild solitude of the mountains.

But Aristotle's remark goes further. It permits us to understand the role of parricide and incest in the reversal which makes the equal of god and the equal of nothing coincide in the person of Oedipus. These two crimes constitute in effect an attack on the fundamental rules of a checkers game where each piece is situated, by its relation to others, in a determinate place on the checkerboard of the city.[69] By making himself guilty of them, Oedipus has shuffled the cards, mixed up positions and pieces: he finds himself from then on out of the game. By his parricide, followed by incest, he installs himself in the place occupied by his father; he mingles, in Jocasta, mother and wife; he identifies himself at the same time with Laius (as Jocasta's husband) and with his own children (of whom he is at the same time father and brother), mixing together three generations of the line. Sophocles underlines this equalization, this identification of what ought to remain distinct and separate, with an insistence which has sometimes shocked moderns but which the interpreter must take fully into account. He does it with a verbal play centered on the words *homos* and *isos* (like and equal), with their compounds. Even before knowing anything of his true origin, Oedipus defines himself, in his relation to Laius, as sharing the same bed and having a *homosporon* (260) wife. In his mouth the word means that he "sows" the same wife whom Laius "sowed" before him; but at line 460 Teiresias takes up the term again to give it its true value: he announces to Oedipus that he will discover himself to be at once the murderer of his father and his *homosporos*, his cosower (1209–12). *Homosporos* ordinarily has another meaning: born from the same sowing, relative of the same stock. In fact, Oedipus, without knowing it, is of the same stock, just as much of Laius as of Jocasta. The equalization of Oedipus and his sons is expressed in a series of brutal images: the father has sown his sons where he was sown; Jocasta is a wife, not-wife but mother whose furrow produced in a double harvest both father and children; Oedipus has sown her who engendered him, from the place where he was himself sown, and from the same furrows, from these "equal" furrows, he has received his children.[70] But it is Teiresias who gives all its tragic weight to this vocabulary of equality when he addresses himself to Oedipus in these terms: there will come evils [that "will make you equal to yourself by][71] establishing a grim equality between you and your children" (425). The identification of Oedipus with his own father and his own children, the assimilation in Jocasta of mother and wife, make Oedipus equal to himself, that is, they make him an *agos*, a being *apolis*, without common dimensions, without equality with other men, and who, believing himself equal to a god, finds himself finally equal to nothing.[72] The tyrant *isotheos* no more recognizes than could a wild beast the rules of the game which are the foundation of the human city.[73] Among the gods, who form a single family, incest is not prohibited. Cronos and Zeus attacked and dethroned their father. Like them, the tyrant can believe that everything is permitted him. Plato calls him "parricide"[74] and compares him to a man who, by virtue of a magic ring, would have the freedom to infringe the most sacred rules with impunity: to kill whomever he wishes, unite with whoever pleases him, "master of any action, like a god among men."[75] Wild beasts also are not bound to respect the interdicts on which the society of men rests. They are not, like the gods, above the laws through an excess of power; they are beneath the laws, through a lack of *logos*.[76] Dio Chrysostom reports the ironic remark of Diogenes on the subject of Oedipus: "Oedipus bewails being at the same time the father and brother of his children, the husband and son of his wife; but about that cocks are not indignant, nor dogs, nor any bird."[77] Among them there is neither brother, father, husband, son, nor wife.[78] Like isolated pieces in a checkers game, they live without rules, without knowing difference or equality in the confusion of *anomia*.[79]

Out of the game, excluded from the city, rejected from the human by incest and parricide, Oedipus is revealed, at the end of the tragedy, identical to the monstrous being evoked by the riddle whose solution he thought himself to have found in his pride as "sage." What is the creature with one voice, asked the Sphinx, who has two, three, and four feet? The question presented, confused, and mixed together the three ages through which man travels successively and which he can know only one after another: child when he walks on all fours, adult when he holds himself firm on his two legs, old man helping himself with his staff. In identifying himself all at once with his young children and his old father, Oedipus, man with two feet, effaces the boundaries which ought to keep the father rigorously separated from the sons and from the grandfather, in order that each human generation occupy in the course of time and in the order of the city the place assigned to it. Last tragic reversal: it is his victory over the Sphinx which makes of Oedipus not the answer which he guessed, but the very question which was asked of him, not a man like the others, but a creature of confusion and chaos, the only one, we are told, of all those who go on the earth, in the air and the waters, to "change his nature" instead of keeping it distinct.[80] Formulated by the Sphinx, the riddle of man thus admits of a solution, but one which turns itself back against the conqueror of the monster, the decipherer of riddles, to make him appear himself as a monster, a man in the form of a riddle, a riddle this time without an answer.

From our analysis of *Oedipus Rex* we can draw some conclusions. In the first place, there is a model which the tragedy puts to work on all the levels where it deploys itself: in language, with its multiple stylistic procedures; in the structure of the dramatic account where recognition and peripeteia coincide; in the theme of Oedipus' destiny; in the very person of the hero. This model is not given somewhere in the form of an image, a notion, a complex of feelings. It is a pure operative scheme of reversal, a rule of ambiguous logic. But this form has, in the tragedy, a content. To capture the countenance of Oedipus, paradigm of the double man, of man reversed, the rule is incarnated in the reversal which transforms the divine king into a scapegoat.

Second, if the complementary opposition between the *turannos* and the *pharmakos*, on which Sophocles plays, is indeed, as it seemed to us, present in the institutions and in the political theory of the Ancients, does the tragedy do anything but reflect a structure already given in the society and in common thought? We think, on the contrary, that, far from presenting a reflection of it, the tragedy calls it into question. In social practice and theory, the polar structure of superhuman and subhuman aims at delineating in its specific features the field of human life as defined by the ensemble of *nomoi* which characterize it. The subhuman and superhuman correspond only as two lines which neatly draw the boundaries within which man finds himself enclosed. On the contrary, in Sophocles, superhuman and subhuman are joined and are mixed together in the same person. And as this person is the model of man, all limits which would permit one to delineate human life, to fix unequivocally its status, are erased. When he wishes, like Oedipus, to pursue the investigation of what he is, man discovers himself enigmatic, without stability or a domain proper to him, without fixed connection, without defined essence, oscillating between the equal of a god and the equal of nothing. His real greatness consists in the very thing which expresses his enigmatic nature: the [posing of] question[s].

Finally, the most difficult thing perhaps is not to restore, as we have tried to do, its authentic meaning to the tragedy, that meaning which it had for the Greeks of the fifth century, but to understand the counter-meanings which it has invited, or rather, how it has lent itself to so many counter-meanings. Whence comes the relative malleability of the work of art, which is also its youth and its perpetuity? If the true mainspring of the tragedy is in the last analysis this form of reversal which comes into play like a logical schema, we understand that the dramatic account remains open to diverse interpretations and that *Oedipus Rex* could be charged with a new meaning to precisely that extent that through the history of Western thought the problem of the ambiguity in man has been displaced, has changed terrain, and the riddle of human existence has been formulated in other terms than it was for the Greek tragedians.

NOTES

In a slightly modified form, this text reproduces a study published in *Échanges et Communications: Mélanges offerts à Claude Lévi-Strauss* (Paris, 1970), 2:1253–79.

1. William Bedell Stanford, *Ambiguity in Greek Literature* (Oxford: Blackwell, 1939), 163–73.

2. A. Hug, "Der Doppelsinn in Sophokles *Oedipus Köenig*," *Philologus* 31 (1872): 66–84.

3. "Nouns are finite in number, while things are infinite. So it is inevitable that a single noun has several meanings." Aristotle, *De Sophisticis Elenchis*, 1, 165a 11.

4. See Euripides, *The Phoenician Women*, 499–502: "If all men saw the fair and wise the same, men would not have debaters' double strife. But nothing is like or even among men except the name they give—which is not the fact" (trans. Elizabeth Wyckoff, in *Euripides V*, ed. David Grene and Richmond Lattimore [New York: Washington Square Press, 1968]).

5. The same ambiguity appears in the other terms which hold a major place in the texture of the work: *dikē, philos* and *philia, kerdos, timē, orgē, deinos.* Cf. Robert F. Goheen, *The Imagery of Sophocles' Antigone* (Princeton: Princeton University Press, 1951), and Charles P. Segal, "Sophocles' Praise of Man and the Conflicts of the Antigone," *Arion*, 3, no. 2 (1964): 46–66.

6. Benvéniste, in his *Noms d'agent et noms d'action en indo-européen* (Paris: Adrien-Maisonneuve, 1948), 79–80, has shown that *nemein* retains the idea of a regular attribution, of an apportionment ruled by the authority of customary law. This meaning takes account of the two great series in the semantic history of the root **nem. Nomos*, regular attribution, rule of usage, custom, religious rite, divine or civic law, contention, *nomos*, territorial attribution fixed by custom, pastureland, province. The expression *ta nomizomena* designates the whole of what is owed to the gods; *ta nomina*, the rules with religious or political value; *ta nomismata*, the customs or coinage having circulation in a city.

7. In the *Antigone*, at line 481, Creon condemns the young girl who has transgressed "the established *nomoi.*" Toward the end of the play, at 1113, disturbed by the threats of Teiresias, he swears to respect from then on "the established *nomoi.*" But from the one expression to the other, *nomos* has

changed meaning. At line 481 Creon uses it as a synonym of *kerugma*, a public edict proclaimed by the head of the city; at 1113, the word has found again, in the mouth of Creon, the meaning which Antigone gave it at the start: religious law, funeral ritual.

8. As the Watchman says: "For those who know, I speak, for those who do not know, on purpose, I hide myself (or, I forget: *lēthomai*)" (38–39). We find a good example of amphibologic dexterity at line 137: almost every word is susceptible to a double interpretation. We can understand "massacring a trembling hare with her brood before she has given birth" and also "sacrificing a poor trembling creature, his own daughter, at the front of the army."

9. Cf. Stanford, *Ambiguity in Greek Literature,* 137–62. Some examples: in her first words, Clytemnestra, recalling the sufferings she has known in the absence of her husband, declares that if Agamemnon had received as many wounds as rumor had it, "his body would have more holes than a net of mesh" (868). The expression has a sinister irony: it is exactly in this way that the king is going to die, caught in the net of death (1115), the web with no exit, the fishnet (1382) that she, with Aegisthus, stretches around him (1110). The gates, *pulai* (604), the dwellings, *domata* (911), to which she alludes several times are not those of the palace, as those who hear believe, but, according to the established expression, those of Hades (1291). When she affirms that the King regains in her *gunaika pistēn, domatōn kuna*, she says in reality the opposite of what she seems to: *gunaik' upistēn*, a faithless woman, who has behaved like a bitch (606–7). As the scholiast remarks, *kuōn* (bitch) means a woman who has more than one man. When she evokes Zeus as *Teleios*, the Zeus by whom all is completed, in order that he accomplish (*telei*) her wishes (973–74), it is not of the Zeus of the happy return that she thinks, as one might imagine, but of the funerary Zeus, master of death "who ends all."

10. We may compare lines 910, 921, 936, 946, 949 on the one hand, and 960–61, 1383, 1390 on the other, and we will note the sinister play on words *eimatōn baphas* (960), dyeing of cloths, which evokes *haimatōn baphas*, dyeing of blood. (Cf. *Choephoroi*, 1010–13.) We know that in Homer blood and death are called *porphureoi*. According to Artemidorus, *Onirocriticon*, 1, 77 (84, 2–4, Pack): "The color purple has a certain affinity with death." Cf. Louis Gernet, "Dénomination et perception des couleurs chez les Grecs," in *Problèmes de la couleur*, ed. Ignace Meyerson (Paris: S.E.V.P.E.N., 1957), 321–24.

11. Cf. R. P. Winnington-Ingram, "Tragedy and Greek Archaic Thought," in *Classical Drama and its Influence: Essays Presented to H. D. F. Kitto*, ed. Michael J. Anderson (London: Methuen, 1965), 31–50.

12. Here again we will send the reader back to the work of Stanford and to the commentaries of R. Jebb, *Oedipus Tyrannus* (1887), and of J. C. Kamerbeek, *The Plays of Sophocles: Commentaries*, Pt. 4, *The Oedipus Tyrannus* (Leiden: Brill, 1967). We will mention only a few examples. Creon has just spoken of the brigands, in the plural, who killed Laius. Oedipus responds: how would the murderer (*ho lēstēs*) have been able to commit this act without complicity? (124). The scholiast notes: "Oedipus thinks of his brother-in-law." But by this singular, Oedipus, without knowing it, condemns himself. As he will recognize a little further on (842–47), if there were murderers, he is not guilty, but if there was one single man, the crime is evidently chargeable to him. At lines 137–41, there are three ambiguities: (1) In dispelling the contamination, he does it not for faraway friends, but himself, for himself—he does not understand how well he speaks. (2) The murderer of the king could be tempted to lift his hand against him; in fact, Oedipus strikes out his own eyes. (3) In coming to help Laius, he serves his own cause—no, he will destroy himself. The whole passage 258–65, with its conclusion, "For these reasons, *as if Laius were my father*, I will fight for him," is ambiguous. The phrase "If his lineage had not aborted" also means "If his lineage had not been doomed to a destiny of unhappiness." At 551, the threat of Oedipus to Creon, "If

you believe that you will attack a relative without paying for it, you deceive yourself," turns against Oedipus himself: he will pay for the murder of his father. At 572–73, a double meaning: "He would not have claimed that I killed Laius," but also "He would not have revealed that I killed Laius." At 928, the position of *hēde*, between *mētēr* and *tōn teknōn*, brings together *gunē* and *mētēr*: his wife, who is also his mother. At 955–56: "He announces to you that your father Polybus is dead"; but also, "He announces to you that your father is not Polybus, but a dead man." At 1183, Oedipus wishes for death and cries out, "O light, would that I have seen you for the last time!" But *phōs* has two meanings in Greek: light of life, light of day. It is the meaning which Oedipus does not mean to say which will come true.

13. *Poetics*, 1452a, 32–33.

14. *Oedipus Rex*, 132. All subsequent references to the play, with line numbers included parenthetically in the body of the essay, are taken from the translation by David Grene, in *Sophocles I*, ed. David Grene and Richmond Lattimore (Chicago: University of Chicago Press, 1954).

15. Ibid., 1190–96. In this sense tragedy, since before Plato, runs counter to the point of view of Protagoras and of the "philosophy of enlightenment" developed by the Sophists of the fifth century. Far from man's being the measure of all things, it is god who is the measure of man, as of the rest. Cf. Bernard Knox, *Oedipus at Thebes: Sophocles' Tragic Hero and His Time* (New Haven: Yale University Press, 1957), 150ff., 184.

16. Cf. E. R. Dodds, "On Misunderstanding the *Oedipus Rex*," *Greece and Rome*, 2nd Series, 13 (1966): 37–49.

17. *Poetics*, 1458a, 26. We may compare this scheme of reversal with that which one finds in the thought of Heraclitus, especially fr. 88, expressed by the verb *metapiptein*. Cf. Clémence Ramnoux, *Héraclite ou L'homme entre les choses et les mots* (Paris: Les Belles Lettres, 1959), 33ff., 392.

18. Concerning this specificity of the tragic message, see Jean-Pierre Vernant, "Tensions et ambiguïtés dans la tragédie grecque," in Jean-Pierre Vernant and Pierre Vidal-Naquet, *Mythe et tragédie en Grèce ancienne* (Paris: Maspero, 1973), 23.

19. *Oedipus at Colonus*, trans. Robert Fitzgerald, in *Sophocles I*, 525, 539–40.

20. Ibid., 265ff., 521ff., 539.

21. *Suppliants*, 226.

22. *Oedipus at Colonus*, 287.

23. Knox, *Oedipus at Thebes*, 138.

24. *Oedipus Rex*, 278, 362, 450, 658–59, 1112.

25. Cf. Plutarch, *De Curiositate*, 522c, and *Oedipus Rex*, 362, 450, 658–59, 1112.

26. *Oedipus Rex, skopein*: 68, 291, 407, 564; *historien*: 1150.

27. Ibid., *heurein, heuretēs*: 68, 108, 120, 440, 1050.

28. Scholia to Euripides, *The Phoenician Women*, 45.

29. Euripides, *The Phoenician Women*, 1505–6.

30. *Oedipus Rex*, 58–59, 84, 105, 397; cf. also 43.

31. Ibid., 876. See Knox, *Oedipus at Thebes*, 182–84. Upon arrival, the messenger from Corinth asks: Do you know where Oedipus is? As Knox observes, the three lines 924–26 end on the name of Oedipus and on the interrogative adverb *hopou*, which gives: *mathoim' hopou-Oidipou-hopou*. "These violent puns," writes Knox, "suggesting a fantastic conjugation of a verb 'to know where' formed from the name of the hero who, as Teiresias told him, does not know where he is (413–14)—this is the ironic laughter of the gods whom Oedipus 'excludes' in his search for the truth."

32. [Editor's note: I have omitted the closing words of the quoted sentence as translated by David Grene ("and so now I lull my mouth to sleep with your name") because they diverge confusingly from the letter of the Greek text (translated in the present volume by William Tyrrell as "I lulled my eye to sleep"). In Vernant's concise rendering, the chorus says simply that it drew from Oedipus breath "and rest."]

33. Cf. Marie Delcourt, *Œdipe ou la légende du conquérant* (Paris: Droz, 1944), where this theme is amply developed and where its place in the Oedipus myth is well shown [see the excerpts from this book reprinted in the present volume].

34. Including the matrimonial laws recognized as the norm by the city. In "Mariages de tyrans," in *Hommage à Lucien Febvre* (1954), 41–53, Louis Gernet, recalling that the prestige of the tyrant originates in the past in many of its aspects and that his excess has models in legend, observes that "for Periander the mythical theme of incest with the mother was raked up again. This mother is called *Krateia*, which means sovereignty."

35. *The Trojan Women*, 1169; *Republic*, 568 b, 360 b-d.

36. On Oedipus *agos*, see 1426; and also 656, 921, with comments of Kamerbeek, *Plays of Sophocles*, on these passages.

37. In a course taught at the Ecole des Hautes Etudes but which has not been published; see now Jean-Pierre Guépin, *The Tragic Paradox: Myth and Ritual in Greek Tragedy* (Amsterdam: A. M. Hakkert, 1968), 89ff. Delcourt, *Œdipe*, 30–37, underlined the relations between the rite of exposure and that of the scapegoat [see the excerpts reprinted in the present volume].

38. Herodotus 5, 70–71; Thucydides 1, 126–27.

39. Photius, *Biblioteca*, 534 (Bekker), cf. Hesychius, s.v.

40. The sixth of Thargelion, birthday of Socrates, is, Diogenes Laertius tells us (2, 44), the day on which the Athenians "purify the city."

41. Photius, *Biblioteca*; Hesychius, s.v. *kradiēs nomous*; Tzetzes, *Chiliades* V. 729; Hipponax, fr. 4 and 5, Bergk.

42. Scholia to Aristophanes, *Frogs*, 730, *Knights*, 1133; Suda, s.v. *pharmakos*; Harpocration, citing Istros, s.v. *pharmakos*; Tzetzes, *Chiliades*, V. 736.

43. Aristophanes, *Frogs*, 730–34.

44. Tzetzes, *Chiliades*. The scholiast at Aristophanes, *Knights*, 1133, writes that the Athenians supported, to so serve them as *pharmakoi*, people extremely *ageneis kai achrestous*, of low origin, wrongdoers; the scholiast at *Frogs*, 703, that they sacrificed, to drive away the famine, *tous phaulous kai para tēs phuseōs epibouleuomenous*, beings degraded and deformed (literally: those who have been mistreated by nature); cf. Delcourt, *Œdipe*, 31 n. 2.

45. Leucas: Strabo, 10, 9, p. 452: Photius, s.v. *Leukatēs*. Massilia: Petronius in Servius. *ad En.*, 3, 57; Lactantius Placidus, *Comment. Stat. Theb.*, 10, 793.

46. *Against Andocides*, 108, 4: "*Tēn polin kathairein kai apodiopompeisthai kai pharmakon attopempein*." Lysias uses a religious vocabulary. On *diopompein, apodiopompeisthai, apopempein* and the rites of expulsion, the *pompaia*, cf. Eustathius, *ad Odys.*, 22, 481. In *O. R.* at 696, the choryphaeos, after the quarrel which has opposed Creon and Oedipus, wishes the latter to remain the "happy guide" of the city, *eupompos*. On this point also, the reversal will be complete; the leader will be led away, the *eupompos* will be the object of the *pompaia*, of the *apopempsis*.

47. Plutarch, *Quaest. Conv.*, 717 d; Hesychius, s.v. *Thargēlia*; Schol. to Aristophanes, *Plutus*, 1055, and *Knights*, 729; Athenaeus, 114 a; Eustathius, *ad Il.*, 9, 530.

48. On the *eiresiōnē*; cf. Eustathius, *ad. Il.* 1283, 7; Schol. to Aristophanes, *Plutus*, 1055; *Et. Magnum*, s.v. *eiresinē*; Hesychius, s.v. *Koruthalia*; Suda, s.v. *Diakonion*; Plutarch, *Life of Theseus*, 22.

49. Sch. Aristophanes, *Plutus*, 1055; Sch. Aristophanes, *Knights*, 728: *hoi men gar phasin hoti limou, hoi de hoti loimou*; Eustathius, *ad. Il.*, 1283, 7: *apostrophē limou*. In the religious calendar, the *eiresiōnē* occurs again in the month *Puanepsiōn*, at the time of the holiday of the Oschophoria. The month of *Puanepsiōn* marks the end of the summer season as the month of Thargeliōn (or the immediately preceding month, *Mounichiōn*) marks its beginning. The ritual offering of the *puanion* (Athenaeus, 648 b) on the seventh of the autumn month corresponds to the offering of the *Thargelos* on the seventh of the spring month; in both cases, it involves a *panspermia*, a porridge of all the seeds of the earth's fruit. In the same way, the springtime procession of the *eiresiōnē* corresponds in the myth to the departure of Theseus (Plutarch, *Life of Theseus*, 18, 1 and 2), its autumnal procession to the return of the same hero (ibid., 22, 5–7). Cf. Ludwig Deubner, *Attische Feste* (Berlin: H. Keller, 1932), 198–201, 224–26; Henri Jeanmarie, *Couroi et Courètes* (Lille: Bibliothèque Universitaire, 1939), 312–13, 347ff.; J. and L. Robert, *Revue des Etudes Grecques*, 62 (1949): 106.

50. Talisman of fertility, the *eiresiōnē* is sometimes called, like the *Thargelos*, *euetēria*, *hygieia*, prosperity and health. The scholiast at Aristophanes, *Knights*, 728, notes that the seasons, *hai hōrai*, are "attached to the branches." Plato, *Symposium*, 188 a, writes that when the seasons allow just measure in their ordering (relationships of dry and humid, of hot and cold), they bring to man, animals, plants *euetēria* and *hygieia*; when on the contrary there is *hubris* in their mutual relations, *loimoi* appear, numerous sicknesses, which also come over animals and plants. The *loimos* manifests a disorder of the seasons close enough to the disorder of human conduct that the latter may also bring with it the former; the rite of the *pharmakos* realizes the expulsion of human disorder; the *eiresiōnē* symbolizes the return to the good order of the seasons. In both cases, it is *anomia* which is averted.

51. Aristophanes, *Knights*, 728, and the Scholion; *Plutus*, 1054. "The least spark would set it aflame like an old *eiresiōnē*" (*Wasps*, 399). We can compare the drying out of the spring bough with the drying out of the earth and men, in the case of *limos* (*limos*, famine, is often associated with *auchmos*, dryness). Hipponax, cursing his enemy Boupalos, this *agos* whose expulsion he desires, would like to see him *xēros limō*, dried out from hunger, paraded like a *pharmakos* and like him whipped seven times on his genitals.

52. Plutarch, *Life of Theseus*, 22, 6–7. Cf. 18, 1: after the murder of Androgeos "the divinity ruined the land, striking it with sterility and sicknesses, drying up the rivers."

53. Hesychius, s.v. *Thargēlia*: "*kai tēn hiketērian ekaloun Thargēlon*," cf. also Plutarch, *Life of Theseus*, 22, 6, and 18, 1; Eustathius, *ad Il.* 1283, 6.

54. *Schol. Victor. ad Iliad.*, 10, 391: "Paean: that which one sings to end evils and in order that none occur. Primitive music was related not only to banquets and dancing but also to the threnodies. It was still honored during the time of the Pythagoreans, who called it purification (*katharsis*)."

Cf. also Aeschylus, *Agam.*, 645, *Choephoroi,* 150–51, *Seven*, 868, 915ff. Cf. Louis Delatte, "Note sur un fragment de Stésichore," *L'Antiquité Classique*, 7, no. 1 (1938): 23–29. Albert Severyns, *Recherches sur la Chrestomathie de Proclos*, vol. 2 (Paris: E. Droz, 1938), 125ff.

55. L. Delatte, "Note sur un fragment"; Stesichorus, Fr. 37, Bergk = 14 Diehl, Iamblichus, *V.P.*, 110, Deubner; Aristoxenos of Tarentum, fr. 117 Wehrli: "To the inhabitants of Locris and Rhegium who consulted the oracle to learn how to cure the madness of their women, the god answered that it was necessary to sing paeans in the spring for sixty days." On the importance of spring, which is less a season like the others than a break in time, marking at the same time the renewal of the products of the earth and the depletion of human reserves in this critical moment of "welding" of one agricultural year to the next, cf. Alcman, fr. 56 D = 137 Ed.: "The Seasons (Zeus) made them three, summer, winter, autumn as the third, and a fourth, spring, when everything flowers and grows but one cannot eat his fill."

56. *Oedipus Rex*, 1426; see note 36 above.

57. Homer, *Od.*, 19, 109ff.; Hesiod, *Works*, 225 ff.

58. Hesiod, *Works*, 238ff.

59. On this double aspect of the *pharmakos*, cf. Lewis Richard Farnell, *Cults of the Greek States*, vol. 4 (Oxford: Clarendon Press, 1907), 280–81.

60. Suda, s.v. *Pharmakous*; Hipponax, fr. 7 (Bergk); Servius, *ad Aen.*, 3, 57; Lactantius Placidus, *Comment. Stat. Theb.*, 10, 793: "*publicis sumptilbus alebatur purioribus cibis.*"

61. Diogenes Laertius, 1, 110; Athenaeus, 602 cd.

62. Jérôme Carcopino, *L'Ostracisme athénien* (Paris: F. Alcan, 1935). The principal texts are conveniently assembled in the work of Aristide Calderini, *L'Ostracismo* (Como: C. Marzorati, 1945). We owe to Gernet the idea of the comparison between the institution of ostracism and the rite of the *pharmakos*.

63. *Methistasthai tēs poléos*; cf. *Et. Magnum*, s.v. *ex ostrakismos*; Photius, s.v. *ostrakismos*.

64. We note, in *Oedipus Rex*, the presence of the theme of *phthonos*, in regard to the one who is at the head of the city; see 380ff.

65. "It is from the storm-cloud that snow and hail strike. Thunder issues from the resplendent lightning. It is from men too great that the ruin of the city comes." Solon, fr. 9–10 (Edmonds).

66. *Politics*, III, 1284 a3-b13.

67. In a lecture that he gave in February 1958, at the *Centre d'études sociologiques*, but which has not been published, Louis Gernet noted that between the two opposed poles of the *pharmakos* and the ostracized there is occasionally produced, in the play of the institution, something like a short circuit. Such was the case in the last application Athens knew of ostracism. In 417 there were two persons of the first rank whom one might expect to see designated by the vote, Nicias and Alcibiades. The two confederates acting in concert succeeded in having the ostracism fall on a third man, Hyperbolos, a demagogue of low rank, generally hated and despised. Hyperbolos was thus ostracized but, as Gernet observed, ostracism was not taken up again: horror-stricken by this "shunting error," which underlined at the same time the polarity and the symmetry of the *pharmakos* and the ostracized, the Athenians were forever disgusted with the institution.

68. *Politics*, I, 1253 a 2–7. To define the degraded being, the subman, Aristotle uses the same term, *phaulos*, that the scholiast uses to characterize the *pharmakos*. On the opposition brute beast— hero or god, cf. *Nic. Ethics*, 7, 1145 a 15ff: "As to the status opposed to bestiality, one could

doubtless not do better than to speak of superhuman virtue, heroic and divine, in short. If it is rare to find a divine man . . . bestiality is no less rare among men."

69. In the expression of Aristotle which we quoted conforming to the usual translation, "like an isolated piece in a checkers game," there is not only opposition between *azux*, an odd counter, and *pettoi* or *pessoi*, the normal pieces which the players use. Cf. J. Tréheux, "Sur le sens des adjectifs *peridzux* et *peridzugos*," *Revue de Philologie*, 32 (1958): 89. In fact, in the category of games which the Greeks designated by the verb *pesseuein*, there is one to which they gave the name *polis*. According to Suetonius, "*polis* is also a type of dice in which the adversaries took pieces from each other, placed as in checkers (*pettentikōs*) on squares marked off by crossed lines. Not without wit, they called cities (*poleis*) the squares thus marked off and dogs (*kunes*) the pieces which were opposed to each other." According to Pollux "the game where one moves many pieces is a checkerboard, provided with squares, marked off by lines. They call the board *polis*, the pieces *kunes*." Cf. Jean Taillardat, *Suetone: Des termes injurieux. Des Jeux grecs* (Paris: Les Belles Lettres, 1967), 154–55. If Aristotle, in order to define the *apolis* individual, refers to checkers, it is because, in the Greek game, the checkerboard which marks off the positions and the respective moves of the pieces is susceptible, as its name indicates, of representing the order of the *polis*.

70. Cf. 1256–57, 1485, 1496–98: *k'ak tōn isōn ektēsasth'humas, hōnper autos exephu.*

71. [Editor's note: I have restored the allusion to the equality of Oedipus with himself (omitted from the Grene translation) whose significance Vernant explains in the next sentence.]

72. On this "nonequality" of Oedipus in relation to the other Thebans, among whom some, like Teiresias and Creon, claim the right to equal status opposite him, cf. 61, 408–9, 544, 579 and 581, 630. [When Laius strikes him with his whip, Oedipus also responds "not equally" (810).] The last wish the fallen Oedipus expresses concerning his children is that Creon "not make them equal with myself in wretchedness" (1507).

73. "One cannot speak of virtue apropos God any more than of vice apropos a beast: the perfection of God has more honor than virtue and the wickedness of the beast is of another kind than vice." Aristotle, *Nic. Ethics*, 7, 1145 a 25.

74. *Republic*, 569 b.

75. Ibid., 360 c. It is in this context that it is necessary, we believe, to understand the second *stasimon* (863–911) about which very diverse interpretations have been proposed. It is the only moment when the chorus adopts a negative attitude with regard to Oedipus-tyrant; but the criticisms which they associate with the *hubris* of the tyrant appear entirely misplaced in the case of Oedipus, who would really be the last, for instance, to profit from his situation to reap "gains without justice" (889). In fact, the chorus' words concern not the person of Oedipus, but his status "apart" within the city. The feelings of quasi-religious veneration with regard to this man who is more than a man are transformed into horror as soon as Oedipus reveals himself as the one who could formerly have committed a crime, and who seems today no longer to lend credence to the divine oracles. In this case, the *isotheos* no longer appears as the guide to whom one can abandon oneself, but as a creature unbridled and lawless, a master who can venture all, permit himself all.

76. *Logos*, word and reason, is what makes man the only "political animal." The beasts have only a voice, while "discourse serves to express the useful and harmful, and, as a result, the just and the not-just: because it is the proper character of man in relation with the other animals to be the only one to have the consciousness of the just and the not-just, and other moral notions, and it is the community of these feelings which engenders family and city." Aristotle, *Politics*, I, 1253 a 10–18.

77. Dio Chrysost., 10, 29; cf. Knox, *Oedipus at Thebes*, 206; cf. also Ovid, *Metamorphoses*, 7, 386–87: "Menephron had to couple with his mother, as wild animals do!" Cf. also 10, 324–31.

78. At the beginning of the tragedy, Oedipus strives to integrate himself into the line of the Labdacids, from which, as a foreigner, he feels himself distanced (cf. 137–41, 258–68); as Knox writes, "The resounding, half-envious recital of Laius' royal genealogy emphasizes Oedipus' deep-seated feeling of inadequacy in the matter of birth . . . and he tries, in his speech, to insert himself into the honorable line of Theban kings" (56). But his unhappiness resides not in the too great difference which separates him from the legitimate line, but in his belonging to this very line. Oedipus worries also about a base origin which would make him unworthy of Jocasta. But there again his unhappiness springs not from too much distance but from too close proximity, from the complete absence of difference between the lines of the spouses. Worse than a misalliance, his marriage is incest.

79. Bestiality implies not only lack of *logos* and of *nomos*, it is also defined as a state of "confusion" where all is jumbled and mixed by chance: Aeschylus, *Prometheus Bound*, 450; Euripides, *Suppliant Women*, 201.

80. Cf. the argument of Euripides' *Phoenicians: allasei de phuēn monon.*

Oedipus as *Pharmakos*

Helene Peet Foley

The opening of *Oedipus Tyrannus* creates for its audience a powerful set of expectations. The stage is filled with suffering suppliants from a city wracked by disease. Almost immediately, Oedipus, ironically preparing the audience for the contents of the oracle that Creon brings from Delphi, equates his own sufferings with that of the city (59–61).[1] The source of the city's sufferings is the polluted killer of Laius. Apollo commands that the community (96) must either banish this source of pollution or exact blood in exchange for blood (100–101). In ignorance Oedipus reinforces the command of the oracle with an edict and a curse that condemns the criminal to exile, not death (229, 241).[2] A second set of religious sanctions is thus called down on the head of the killer. Teiresias, the representative of Apollo, then predicts that Oedipus will soon journey to another country, tapping out his path with a stick (455–56; see also 420–23). In the scenes with Teiresias and Creon, the mimetic rivalry, which René Girard has argued always precedes the sacrifice of a scapegoat, begins to color the action.[3] Here Oedipus begins to display the hybristic qualities of a typical stage tyrant, and both he and Jocasta flirt with

First published in *Nomodeiktes: Greek Studies in Honor of Martin Ostwald* (Ann Arbor: University of Michigan Press, 1993).

dismissing the words of the god. Once Oedipus begins to suspect the truth, he is horrified that he may have condemned himself to exile (813–20). Until the final scene of the play, then, we are repeatedly led to expect the banishment of Oedipus from Thebes.

Furthermore, as many scholars have pointed out, Athens itself was no stranger to the ritual expulsion of the *pharmakos*.[4] At the Thargelia it practiced annual rites in which two scapegoats were beaten and driven from the city.[5] And at a time perhaps shortly before the production of this play, the Spartans charged the preeminent leader of the democracy, Pericles, with the ancestral pollution that his maternal relatives, the Alcmaeonids, acquired from the killing of Cylon.[6] Scapegoats in myth were generally kings or young people. In ritual they were often (if not always) the lowest, even criminal members of society. Vernant has stressed how Oedipus, as the greatest king and the most terrible criminal, shares the features of the scapegoat in both myth and ritual.[7]

These extraordinarily powerful expectations are in the end frustrated, since the play closes without completing the expulsion of the scapegoat. Oedipus pleads first with the chorus, then with Creon, to complete his banishment, and/or death (1290–91, 1340–46, 1410–12, 1436–37, 1449–53, 1518). The chorus withdraws in favor of Creon, and Creon insists on returning to the oracle for further and more exact instructions (1438–43). Oedipus is still polluted in Creon's view (in the eyes of the messenger, the house is polluted, 1227–29), but his pollution now seems more domestic than civic (1424–31). His parricide and incest will damage the future of his daughters, who will have difficulty finding husbands, but it can for the moment be shut up in the house, where, as was traditionally the case, relatives, who share the criminal's pollution,[8] could look on and cope with dangers from which the outside world must be shielded.[9] In any case—even if it seems likely that Oedipus will soon depart from Thebes as Teiresias predicts and the hero desires—the source of pollution for the moment remains in the city. Indeed, the plague-ridden city has not received any explicit mention since the quarrel between Creon and Oedipus, where Jocasta and the chorus have to remind the two squabbling leaders of the sufferings of Thebes (634–36, 665–67).

In this brief chapter, I do not raise questions unfamiliar to the scholarly tradition. There has been much interest, especially of late, both in the relation of the play to larger religious issues concerning scapegoats and pollution and in the problems of the ending, although curiously the first discussion has taken place largely in isolation from the second.[10] I simply wish to emphasize that the problems raised by the play's failure to expel its *pharmakos* are even more complex than they have been considered to be and, by reviewing some of the dimensions of this problem, to reconsider the implications of the play's conclusion.

Let me emphasize further the disturbing quality of the play's ending. As Deborah Roberts has recently stressed,[11] Sophoclean endings often leave us with loose ends. At the end of *Oedipus at Colonus*, for example, we look forward to the battle between the brothers and Antigone's struggle to bury Polyneices. The *Trachiniae* does not predict the traditional apotheosis of Heracles. *Electra* perhaps concludes before the appearance of Furies who will undermine its otherwise "happy" ending. Nevertheless, these hints of a future in tension with the dramatic conclusion only cast an oblique shadow over a body of plays that by and large have been justly famous for offering us a model sense of closure. Even more important, expectations generated concerning ritual and/or oracular command are elsewhere in Sophocles explicitly fulfilled. Oedipus receives his promised cult in *Oedipus at Colonus*, Heracles' disrupted sacrifice is completed through the instructions of the hero himself, the supplication over the body of Ajax is answered with the concluding burial and hints of a future hero cult, Orestes carries out Apollo's command, Philoctetes and Neoptolemus will undertake their predestined role in Troy, and Antigone is vindicated for her devotion to the cause of the gods below, while Creon is punished for violating that cause. Yet in *Oedipus Tyrannus* the oracle's instructions concerning the polluted murderer of Laius have not been carried out at the play's conclusion. Indeed, we cannot be certain that we know what the oracle will say when Creon consults it for a second time.

Furthermore, Sophocles has gone out of his way to create trouble for himself. The plague caused by the presence of a polluted murderer was at best an obscure part of the literary tradition about Oedipus, and we cannot be certain that his banishment occurred in any of the story's literary versions known prior to Sophocles; Oedipus apparently remained in Thebes after his crime was discovered and died there.[12] Indeed, immediate banishment causes a basic complication for the traditional myth, because it leaves no room for motivating Oedipus' curse on his own sons, who failed in various ways to

show the proper filial devotion to their father. No wonder Sophocles adopted
a delay in Oedipus' banishment when he returned to the story in *Oedipus
at Colonus*. Furthermore, unlike most mythical plagues, the Theban plague
in *Oedipus Tyrannus* breaks out many years after the crime. This anomaly
perhaps betrays the uneasy position this story of Oedipus as scapegoat has in
the larger myth—however relevant it may possibly have been (depending on
the date of its performance) to the plague-stricken Athens of Pericles. Did
Sophocles choose to invent a version of the story, or to emphasize an obscure
alternative in the tradition, only to dismiss it—or at least to leave it in some
doubt—at the conclusion of his play? Would not an audience judging this
play, an audience ever alert to ingenious new interpretations of a myth, have
been taken aback by Sophocles' refusal to follow out to its conclusion his
most striking and, given the opening, visually arresting innovation?

We cannot escape from this problem by adopting Dawe's recent conclusion that lines 1524–30 are an interpolation and that we thus do not have the
original conclusion of the play.[13] Deleting these lines, or even 1515–23, as some
have proposed in a far more speculative fashion,[14] does not eliminate Creon's
insistence on returning to the oracle for further instructions, which first
occurs at 1438–44. On what dramatically effective grounds would Creon
reverse himself on the banishment, given that his position here is completely
consistent with the caution that he has displayed from his first appearance on
stage? We are unavoidably left with the vision of Oedipus struggling to carry
out the dictates of curse and oracle, in the face of a community and its new
leader that refuse to take immediate action. This means, as Howe pointed
out, that we are faced with the anomaly of a scapegoat trying to enact his own
exile/destruction, in isolation from the community that traditionally plays
that role in every other version of this story (or ritual) pattern.[15] The repeated
emphasis in earlier scenes of the play—and in the oracle itself, which asked
for communal involvement—that it is the responsibility of *all* to remove the
pollution from Thebes is ignored in the last scene (223, 463–76, 1378–83).

The final scene of the play itself makes no explicit reference to the difficulties of the city but concentrates on the problem that Oedipus poses to
his house. Indeed, any direct mention of the plague would make Creon's
cautious insistence on delay absurd and support Oedipus' sense of urgency
about the matter. But when Oedipus asks the chorus to banish him, kill him,
or cast him into the sea (1410–12; the third alternative is a form of death not

mentioned in either curse or oracle) and when Creon and Oedipus dispute over the oracle, I argue (contrary to most critics) that they bring back for consideration the issues so powerfully associated with the oracle in the earlier scenes. Although Oedipus does not name the plague, the oracle was sought to save the city from the plague. Can we in the last scene simply reduce the oracle to a problem internal to the house of Laius, or are the civic issues implicit in any mention of the oracle?[16] And when Oedipus says at 1449–50, "Let not the city (ἄστυ) of my ancestors be condemned to have me as a living inhabitant," what else comes to mind but the city's earlier troubles? Through Sophocles' clever dramaturgy, the audience may simply forget the plague in the final scene;[17] yet it is entirely possible that the failure of Oedipus and above all Creon to be concerned directly with the city's ills and the failure of the drama to fulfill the audience's expectations concerning curse and oracle condition our reaction to this scene.

In insisting on this second possibility, we must ask ourselves whether the Greek audience, given its traditions about pollution, curse, and scapegoat ritual, would be likely to forget the plague and Oedipus' curse so easily (the curse is in fact mentioned by Oedipus in the final scene at 1291 and 1345) and simply dismiss Oedipus' sense of urgency in favor of Creon's leisurely caution.[18] This is not an easy question to answer. First, critics have made a good case for the important roles that traditional story patterns have in tragedy; Strohm and Burnett in particular have shown that Greek dramatists deliberately played on the audience's expectations of these story patterns. Why should *Oedipus Tyrannus* be an exception? Second, Oedipus' curse is analogous to Draco's law on homicide, which requires the kin of a murdered man and the king archon to ban the killer from recognized practices like libations, prayer, and sacrifice.[19] Third, although it is far more difficult to size up the state of traditions about pollution and scapegoats, I think it is safe to conclude that a Greek audience would not take such matters lightly (especially in combination with other religious sanctions); and, if the play were performed during or after the plague, they would be impossible to forget.

Not only Greek law and cult[20] but tragedy regularly recognizes the threat of the pollution created by shed blood, although it sometimes finds ways around it. Whereas tragedies like Aeschylus' *Suppliants* treat the Danaids' threat to pollute the city with the utmost seriousness, Theseus in Euripides' *Heracles* chooses to ignore the hero's pollution on the grounds of friendship

(1214–34)—although he will still perform a ritual of purification for him in Athens. And in Sophocles' *Oedipus at Colonus*, Theseus does not expel Oedipus from the city (1132–34)—although he keeps his physical distance from the hero.[21] In *Oedipus Tyrannus*, Creon does recognize Oedipus' pollution as an important issue in the final scene, but he domesticates it, ignoring the plague generated by the presence of the murderer of Laius in the city.

As Parker has stressed,[22] despite rhetoric to the contrary, history does not offer certain examples of the expulsion of a citizen who was discovered to be the source of a city's afflictions. Furthermore, "no reliable instances of the dispatch of scapegoats outside the seasonal framework are anywhere recorded," although sources say they could be performed in response to a specific crisis.[23] Scapegoats of the kind *Oedipus Tyrannus* threatens to make of Oedipus belong more clearly to the realm of the mythical. Yet myths about figures like Athamas, Oenoclus, or Lycurgus, and Hesiod's insistence that an unjust ruler can destroy his populace, still make Sophocles' failure to carry out the traditional pattern surprising.[24] Of course the play only flirts with this possibility; we have every expectation that the oracle will resolve the problem—in the fashion predicted by Teiresias and demanded by Oedipus. Yet, having gone to such trouble to elicit the audience's expectations concerning serious religious issues and to stress the urgency of the problem, why does the play conclude with a frustrating delay?

If we assume that the delay is deliberate and meant to be noticed with some concern by an audience who had expected and wanted a different conclusion, what does the play gain by making the issue of the plague at best implicit in the final scene and by leaving the fate of Oedipus unresolved?[25] Above all, the last scene as we have it allows us to observe at some length a clash between Oedipus' and Creon's views about the correct action to take in the situation and to juxtapose for our consideration two different styles of leadership, the leadership of Oedipus, who is still trying to exercise his old mastery in a characteristic way, and the new leadership of Creon. The audience is forced to make a judgment over whose interpretation of the situation is preferable, the ending advocated by Oedipus or that advocated by Creon. This is emphasized by having Creon and Oedipus clash not once but twice over the issue of the banishment in the final scene, and, if we have the end of the play, by marking the final exit of Creon and Oedipus with this undecided issue. Finally, the audience is encouraged to consider how the city will be led once Oedipus is fully removed from the scene. Yet it must be stressed that only by suppressing the issue of the plague could Sophocles make the situation appear genuinely ambiguous. Creon could hardly have advocated the time-consuming journey to Delphi so blithely if the audience were reminded of the bodies of citizens dropping daily before him. In making this suggestion, I am here rather reluctantly rejecting the recent and intriguing suggestion of some critics that the play denies Oedipus' banishment in favor of once again entrapping him in the problems of his ancestral house.[26] Teiresias' predictions[27] and the terms of the oracle—unless it were to deny its original command—seem to rule out this possibility, at least for the long term. In any case, we remain uncertain as to the outcome.

Our judgment of the conflicting positions of Oedipus and Creon in the final scene depends in part on our evaluation of the attitude each displays concerning the oracle. Oedipus, as Knox in particular has emphasized,[28] has acquired by the end of the play a certain religious authority, a more than human prophetic vision about his own past and future. He is convinced that he and Apollo have acted together in the blinding (a blinding that Apollo's mouthpiece Teiresias predicted, 454–56, 1329–32). He knows that if he is banished he will not die; he has been saved for some strange evil destiny (1455–57). He sees a logic to his situation unavailable to the chorus and Creon. The banishment to Cithaeron that he envisions (1391–93, 1449–54) has, as Taplin argues, a compelling rightness of its own.[29]

The overall dramatic situation also functions to make Oedipus convincing on these points. He is no longer in a state of ignorance about his own identity and that of the murderer. The audience has ceased to view him through the veil of tragic irony. It may be significant, as Pucci has recently pointed out, that Oedipus uses the verb οἶδα at 1455; for in the earlier scene between Teiresias and Oedipus, the text gives Teiresias an exclusive claim to this verb, whereas Oedipus ironically (but correctly) characterizes himself as the one "knowing nothing" (397).[30] In the final scene, "Swellfoot" has perhaps at last fulfilled the knowledge implicit in his name. Because the oracle commanded the death or expulsion of the murderer, because Teiresias has predicted Oedipus' exile, because the entire logic of the play has prepared us for a decisive conclusion of this kind, and because the death or expulsion of the murderer has been so strongly linked with the safety of the city, Oedipus' insistence on banishment is intuitively convincing. Finally, if we are to transfer to the now blind Oedipus the association between blindness and religious insight established in the case of Teiresias, Oedipus' oracular pronouncements link him significantly with his wiser double.[31]

Creon's insistence on consulting the oracle once again incurs the dramatic disadvantage of running contrary to what the audience expects and even wants to happen. At the same time, there is some justification for his caution.[32] He has consistently advocated making decisions by consulting the gods; he goes to Delphi, he suggests to Oedipus that he consult Teiresias, and he criticizes Oedipus for his former lack of trust in Apollo (1445). Unlike Oedipus, who has great confidence in his own problem-solving ability and unconsciously condemns himself or at times carelessly modifies or ignores the words of the oracle (e.g., 1411–12, where he adds at one point an alternative not mentioned, that he should be cast in the sea), Creon is a man who is cautious in both speech and action. When he does not know something, he holds his tongue (568; see also 1520). And he does not accept Oedipus' final interpretation of the oracle.

Oedipus is optimistic about the human ability to interpret oracles and treats the oracle as he treated the riddle of the Sphinx. In advocating exile, he ultimately conflates the two alternatives offered in the oracle: *Banished* to Cithaeron, he will *die* where his parents attempted to destroy him (1436–42, 1449–55).[33] In reducing the "either/or" of the oracle to a "both" Oedipus performs the same gesture of interpretation of an oracle that we find made correctly in the *Trachiniae*, where the prediction that either Heracles will die or the labors will come to an end so that he will live in peace are found to be one and the same.[34]

Creon, on the other hand, acknowledges what the oracle said but apparently wants exact instructions on how to act. One wonders, given the nature of oracles, whether he has any right to expect such exactitude from the god, an exactitude that uncharacteristically removes any need for human initiative or interpretation altogether. And as Oedipus points out at 280–81, no one can force the gods to speak against their will.

Creon reports Apollo's words as follows:

> CREON: Lord Phoebus bid us clearly to expel the pollution nurtured in this
>   land and not to make it incurable.
> OEDIPUS: By what rite of purification? How can we escape this misfortune?[35]

CREON: Either we banish him or dissolve bloodshed with bloodshed, knowing
    that this shed blood traps the city in its storm. (96–101)

The oracle is said to be clear. Yet these words contain greater ambiguities
than the fateful *or*. What is meant by releasing φόνος with φόνος? Killing the
criminal—the interpretation adopted by Oedipus? A rite of purification
involving sacrifice? (Apollo in *Eumenides* performs such a rite for Orestes
at Delphi, but the Furies remain convinced of his guilt.) The blinding of
Oedipus, in which Oedipus sheds blood for blood?[36] The very ambiguity of
the words warranted some caution.[37]

The struggle over the expulsion of Oedipus evolves as a conflict between
two styles of leadership. Creon is represented throughout the play as the
reluctant leader.[38] He claimed earlier to be happy to have the benefits of
power without its painful responsibilities. In the final scene, he is willing to
forget his past conflict with Oedipus, and Oedipus is moved by his generosity in remembering to bring his daughters to their bereaved father (1422–23,
1473–74). But in fact Creon does little more than temporize and struggle to
assert his will against the persistent Oedipus.[39] Creon is not a decisive actor,
yet he is unlikely to be guilty of hybris, of doubting the gods, or of acting
before he knows.

Creon views Oedipus' insistence on offering repeated instructions
to himself as an inappropriate attempt to continue to rule even in defeat
(1522–23).[40] Indeed Oedipus is to the end eager to act, command, and interpret, to keep a large place for human initiative. This style of leadership, the
leadership of a man superior to others in energy and intelligence, has been
shown in the play as a whole to have both its dangerous and its positive
aspects. It is prone to misinterpretations and often threatens to collapse
into tyrannical behavior—although it should be recognized that in this
case it does not. Unlike other stage tyrants, such as Pentheus, or Creon in
Antigone, Oedipus always stops short of violence against others.[41] He does
not take action against Teiresias, due to his blindness (a nicety ignored
by Pentheus), and he pulls back at the request of Jocasta and the chorus
from acting on his anger at Creon. Oedipus leaps to conclusions before he
knows what he is facing and he has a history of compounding his own and
others' troubles when he tries to dismiss or avoid the words of the god. At
the same time, the city in the first scene is shown to be eager for the kind

of leadership that Oedipus has given and will give them, and the chorus continues to support him after his quarrel with Teiresias; they even sing an ode of joyous anticipation about Oedipus' birth, after they suspect that he is the polluted murderer of their king (1086–109). He anticipates what should be done and acts decisively; most of his misinterpretations coincide with the words of the oracle. He succeeds in his proposed aim of discovering the killer of Laius, and the only damage he deliberately causes to anyone is to himself. His love for the city is passionate, and he is willing to accept death or banishment for its sake (658–59), even before he comes to understand these alternatives as his only real choice. The second stasimon (863–910) probably obliquely reflects the concerns his leadership raises for the chorus. In this ode they reject the hybris of the tyrant; they want the oracles to retain respect; yet they value the struggle, the wrestling, of the leader, for the benefit of the city.[42]

The question of leadership, and of the value of Oedipus' leadership to the city, is central to the play—and explicit in its content—from the first scene, where the city comes to Oedipus to solve its problems because of his ability as a leader and a solver of riddles, to Creon's last words, in which he chastises Oedipus for continuing to try to rule in defeat (1522–23).[43] Let us consider (against the background of the expectations created earlier in the play) Sophocles' alternatives for disposing of Oedipus in the final scene. If the city had acceded to Oedipus' demands for banishment, Creon, and the views and style of leadership he represents, could not have served as a serious foil to the hero. The city would appear to be losing an irreplaceable savior instead of struggling with a continuing problem. Kitto would prefer this ending: "The stranger who once saved Thebes by his own intelligence must now, though Theban born, save it by leaving the city forever. How did Sophocles come to miss such a dramatic ending?"[44] If Creon or the city had acted independently to kill or banish Oedipus—an unlikely scenario, given both the character of Oedipus and the traditional mythological pattern, which requires the con- sent of the scapegoat—the conclusion would have emphasized far more deci- sively the dangerous side of the hero.[45] Yet paradoxically, if the city *had* killed or banished Oedipus by the conclusion of the play, it would have shown less need of him; the city and its new leader would have shown a capacity to act decisively in the public interest, and the vacuum left by Oedipus' destruction would have been less obvious.

In short, by not giving Oedipus his way concerning the banishment, the play leaves open the whole question Oedipus and his leadership pose for the city. Neither the inspired activism of Oedipus nor the cautious piety of Creon is at least on the surface any more than a style of trying to interpret what cannot be interpreted in a complex human environment. Both advocate in their own way obedience to the oracle. But it is hard to avoid the impression that Sophocles has deliberately chosen to make his destroyed hero the sole champion of the expectations raised by his own plot. After uncovering the murderer, Oedipus now attempts to insure the safety of a city that refuses to play the role assigned to it in all scapegoat myths and cults. The entire movement of the drama, underlined by the religious force of the curse and the scapegoat pattern itself, is likely to convince its audience that the blind Oedipus must intuitively be advocating the right position, and that under the moderate and admirable Creon, Thebes will continue to experience a form of rule that could hardly be characterized as leadership.[46]

Finally, all members of the cast, both chorus and protagonists, are distracted from the plague that grips the city by their concern with the fate of Oedipus as destroyer of his own house. This compounds the uncertainty created about the future of the city in the hands of Creon. The chorus is lost in its fascinated horror at the downfall of the great man, its fear and desire of looking at him. Oedipus, who has the excuse of suffering to explain his self-concern, nevertheless makes the one mention of the welfare of the city (1449–50). Creon finds himself in the structural position of Oedipus in the opening scene.[47] He has tried to anticipate what should be done and has determined to consult the oracle. Yet he ignores the issue of the plague and expresses no sense of urgency about taking immediate action. He is appropriately punctilious about Oedipus' pollution but views it as a family matter. Similarly, as in the first scene, where he clearly prefers to inform Oedipus about the oracle in private, Creon takes the first step toward resolving the problem of Oedipus by concealing him within (if only temporarily).

The real paradox of a figure like Oedipus is his extraordinary capacity to save and destroy through his assertive leadership. We do not have to equate Oedipus with Pericles in order to find the paradox he presents relevant to the city of Athens. As early as Solon (fr. 9.3 W) we are warned that "a city can perish from its too great men." Thucydides and Aristophanes, to give but two notable examples, are openly concerned with the problematic relation between the democracy and outstanding aristocratic leaders like Pericles or, to take a more obviously difficult case, Alcibiades. Thucydides is convinced that the democracy was at its best under the leadership of Pericles. Aristophanes is constantly urging the city to heed rather than reject the advice of its best men. The problem of Alcibiades becomes the central political question put to Euripides and Aeschylus at the close of the *Frogs*. Like Oedipus, Alcibiades is there represented as both potential savior and destroyer of the city.

Sophocles' *Oedipus Tyrannus* is about many things, and the multiplicity of interpretations it has generated testifies to its richness as a text. But its surprising ending seems designed above all to raise, in the oblique fashion typical of tragedy, a set of profound questions about political leadership, both in Thebes and, indirectly, in classical Athens. Just as the tragedy of Oedipus is left incomplete and promises new chapters in this final scene,[48] so the history of Thebes is incomplete. Thebes both still needs and must reject Oedipus. He is the kind of leader a democracy would both love and desire to ostracize. Creon, the cautious and reluctant leader, would in some respects fit admirably in a democracy. He is a man outstanding in heritage, who would never overstep his limits. He seemingly embodies the σωφροσύνη that tragedy often praises in the ideal leader:

> It is necessary to crown with garlands men who are intelligent and coura-
> geous—both whatever man provides the finest leadership for the polis,
> because he is a man of restraint (σώφρων) and justice, and whatever man
> by his speech wards off evil deeds, preventing battles and civil strife—since
> their actions are fair both for the entire city and for all the Hellenes. (Eur.
> fr. 282.23–28 Nauck)[49]

Yet how many troubled cities can wait to acquire divine knowledge before they act? Oedipus, when asked by Creon what acting in ignorance would mean to him, asserts he must rule nevertheless (628). Creon is repre-sented in this final scene as the man who refuses to speak or act in ignorance.[50] Yet, as Martin Ostwald has recently argued, "the condemnation of humanity to ignorance and to the necessity of acting in this ignorance is the tragic real-ity which *Oedipus Tyrannus* conveys to us."[51] Oedipus' final confrontation with the chorus makes vivid his dangerous, rash, incomprehensible side.

They wish they had never known him and think him better dead than living (1347–48, 1356, 1367–68). Yet by refusing to permit the expected banishment of Oedipus, Creon ironically expands the tragic authority of the man whom he is hurrying to confine in the private world of his house.[52]

NOTES

I read *Oedipus Tyrannus* for the first time with Martin Ostwald in a seminar on Greek Tragedy at Swarthmore College. Reading his own recent article on the play made me realize once again how much my own understanding of the play was, and still is, conditioned by that first experience. A preliminary version of this chapter was presented at a conference on Oedipus at Cornell in spring 1990 ["Oedipus at the Crossroads: Psychoanalysis, Philosophy, and the Classics"]. I benefited from the discussion there, and above all from conversations with Rachel Kitzinger as well as from her conference paper on the play. Richard Seaford and Suzanne Saïd also offered helpful comments. I cite from the text of R. D. Dawe, ed., Sophocles, *Oedipus Rex* (Cambridge: Cambridge University Press, 1982).

1. Jean-Pierre Vernant, "Ambiguity and Reversal: On the Enigmatic Structure of *Oedipus Rex*," in Jean-Pierre Vernant and Pierre Vidal-Naquet, *Myth and Tragedy in Ancient Greece*, trans. Janet Lloyd (New York: Zone Books, 1988), 131.

2. The fact that the oracle and the curse converge on exile increases our expectations for the first of the alternatives proposed by the oracle.

3. René Girard, *Violence and the Sacred*, trans. Patrick Gregory (Baltimore: Johns Hopkins University Press, 1977) has recently been well criticized by Pietro Pucci, "The Tragic *Pharmakos* of the *Oedipus Rex*," *Helios* 17 (1990): 41–49, who points out that the rivalry between Oedipus, Teiresias, and Creon is not marked by mimetic desire of the kind that occurs between Pentheus and Dionysus in the *Bacchae*; tensions are diffused and do not in fact serve to prepare for the expected scapegoating at the conclusion of the play. Nevertheless, the doubling that does occur, and the sense of potentially explosive tension between Oedipus, Teiresias, and Creon, may still help to reinforce the audience's expectations for the banishment of Oedipus.

4. For a discussion of scapegoat ritual and/or pollution in Sophocles' play and/or in Greek society see Jan Bremmer, "Scapegoat Rituals in Ancient Greece," *Harvard Studies in Classical Philology* 87 (1983): 299–320 [reprinted in the present volume]; Walter Burkert, *Structure and History in Greek Mythology and Ritual* (Berkeley: University of California Press, 1979), 59–77; Walter Burkert, *Greek Religion*, trans. John Raffan (Cambridge, MA: Harvard University Press, 1985), 82–84; G. Daux, "Œdipe et le Fléau (Sophocle, *Œdipe-roi*, 1–275)," *Revue des études grecques* 53 (1940): 97–122; Marie Delcourt, *Stérilités mystérieuses et naissances maléfiques dans l'antiquité classique* [1938] (Paris: Les Belles Lettres, 1986); Girard, *Violence and the Sacred*; Thalia Phillies Howe, "Taboo in the Oedipus Theme," *Transactions and Proceedings of the American Philological Association* 93 (1962): 124–43; Robert Parker, *Miasma. Pollution and Purification in Early Greek Religion* (Oxford: Clarendon Press, 1983); Pucci, "The Tragic *Pharmakos* of the *Oedipus Rex*"; Vernant, "Ambiguity and Reversal," 125–40.

5. On the connection see Vernant, "Ambiguity and Reversal," 128, 134–35, and the more skeptical discussion of Parker, *Miasma*, 269–70.

6. Plut. *Per.* 33.1–2 and Hdt. 7.71. The Spartan attempt, which pre-dated the plague, in fact

increased sympathy for Pericles. The precise date of the play and its relation to Pericles and the plague at Athens must remain uncertain.

7. Vernant, "Ambiguity and Reversal," 131–38. See also Bremmer, "Scapegoat Rituals in Ancient Greece," 303–7. Vernant's excellent discussion does not confront the incomplete scapegoat pattern of the play.

8. Parker, *Miasma*, 205, 318.

9. Creon speaks of sun, land, rain, and light of day. What threat Oedipus poses to his fellow citizens as a polluted parricide is unclear. Oedipus seems to deny his pollution when he asks the chorus to approach and touch him without fear (1413–15).

10. See n. 4 above. All those who discuss the ritual elements, except Pucci, ignore the failure to expel the *pharmakos* at the conclusion. On the ending see esp. the discussion of H. D. F. Kitto, *Poiesis: Structure and Thought* (Berkeley: University of California Press, 1966); Oliver Taplin, *Greek Tragedy in Action* (Berkeley: University of California Press, 1978) and "Sophocles in His Theatre," in *Sophocle: Sept exposés suivis de discussions*, ed. Jacqueline de Romilly, Fondation Hardt Entretiens 29 (Geneva: Fondation Hardt, 1983), 155–83; D. A. Hester, "The Banishment of Oedipus," *Antichthon* 18 (1984): 13–23; and G. H. Gellie, "The Last Scene of the *Oedipus Tyrannus*," *Ramus* 15 (1986): 35–42.

11. Deborah H. Roberts, "Sophoclean Endings: Another Story," *Arethusa* 21 (1988): 177–96; cf. her further observations on problems of dramatic closure in "The Frustrated Mourner: Strategies of Closure in Greek Tragedy," in *Nomodeiktes: Greek Studies in Honor of Martin Ostwald*, ed. Ralph M. Rosen and Joseph Farrell (Ann Arbor: University of Michigan Press, 1993), 573–90. See also the earlier remarks of Taplin, "Sophocles in His Theatre."

12. Extant sources prior to Sophocles include Homer, Hesiod, fragments of the epic cycle, the Lille papyrus, and the fragments of Aeschylus' Theban trilogy. See E. L. Kock, "The Sophoklean Oidipous and his Antecedents," *Acta Classica* 4 (1961): 7–27; Jennifer R. March, *The Creative Poet: Studies on the Treatment of Myths in Greek Poetry, Bulletin of the Institute of Classical Studies at the University of London*, suppl. 49 (London, 1987). Aeschylus had Oedipus blind himself, and March, *The Creative Poet*, 139–48, speculates that he was the first to make Oedipus' four children the product of incest and to exile the king (although, since Oedipus was buried in Thebes, he was probably not treated as a polluted scapegoat in the Sophoclean fashion). Edmunds' study of the myths and cults relating to Oedipus' exile suggest a fundamental connection between Oedipus' name and cults, his wandering and his banishment; hence it is unlikely that Sophocles invented this aspect of the myth (Lowell Edmunds, "The Cults and the Legend of Oedipus," *Harvard Studies in Classical Philology* 85 [1981]: 221–38). In Homer, murderers are not viewed as polluted; even when Oedipus is viewed as a source of pollution in the *Thebaid*, he remains in Thebes. Euripides' *Phoenissae* takes Oedipus' pollution lightly, and banishes him for purely secular reasons. If he is reflecting a pretragic (or Aeschylean) tradition in this, Sophocles' insistence on making Oedipus a polluted scapegoat seems all the more idiosyncratic.

13. R. D. Dawe, *Studies in the Text of Sophocles*, vol. 1 (Leiden: Brill, 1973), 266–73. Dawe's views have won wide acceptance, although I incline to share the more cautious evaluation of Deborah H. Roberts, "Parting Words: Final Lines in Sophocles and Euripides," *Classical Quarterly* 37 (1987): 63, Brian Arkins, "The Final Lines of Sophocles, *King Oedipus* (1524–30)," *Classical Quarterly* 38 (1988): 555–58, and H. Lloyd-Jones and N. G. Wilson, eds., *Sophoclea: Studies in the Text of Sophocles* (Oxford: Clarendon Press, 1990), 113–14.

14. D. A. Hester, "Oedipus and Jonah," *Proceedings of the Cambridge Philological Society* 203 (1977): 46, "The Banishment of Oedipus," 21–22, and March, *The Creative Poet*, 148–54, reviving the

theory of Graffunder in 1885, argue that the play originally concluded with the exile of Oedipus [see P. L. Graffunder, "Über den Ausgang des König Oedipus von Sophokles," *Neue Fahrbücher für Philologik und Paedogogik* 132 (1885): 389–408]. Both speculate that these lines were added to accommodate a production of *Oedipus Tyrannus* and *Oedipus at Colonus* together. The technical arguments for eliminating 1515–23 are hardly overwhelming. It is true, as these scholars stress, that Oedipus' speech of farewell to his daughters and his final instructions about Jocasta's burial suggest a preparation for departure, although Creon did not bring the daughters for that reason. Oedipus is fixed on exile and preparing for it. But this does not prove that the play ended with that exile. If the ending is basically authentic, his speeches simply serve to enhance the conflict between an Oedipus assertively taking all the steps necessary for his banishment and a Creon who wishes further knowledge before acting.

15. Howe, "Taboo in the Oedipus Theme," 130, 136. The scapegoat normally consents to banishment, but the community performs the act. See Bremmer, "Scapegoat Rituals in Ancient Greece," 307–8. For Howe ("Taboo in the Oedipus Theme," 139), Oedipus substitutes for the traditional pollution of the scapegoat a new sense of guilt.

16. Graham Ley, "On the Pressure of Circumstance in Greek Tragedy," *Ramus* 15 (1986): 43–51, correctly emphasizes the importance of the fate of cities to the ancient audience of Greek tragedies.

17. M. Dyson, "Oracle, Edict, and Curse in *Oedipus Tyrannus*," *Classical Quarterly* 23 (1973): 212, argues that Sophocles eliminates the plague "to leave the individual tragedy untouched by consolation." Taplin, "Sophocles in his Theatre," 172, makes a similar point: "Sophocles insists that Oedipus' paradigmatic reversal of fortune should be complete, without mitigation."

18. Howe, "Taboo in the Oedipus Theme," 130, suggests that the "function of the plague appears to be more dramaturgical than religious," and that Sophocles' audience would be too skeptical to take it seriously. Parker, *Miasma*, to be discussed shortly, gives a far more balanced and cautious evaluation of these issues.

19. See Thomas Gould, *Oedipus the King* (Englewood Cliffs, NJ: Prentice-Hall, 1988), 148. Ironically, Oedipus plays both a civic and a familial role. See also Parker, *Miasma*, chap. 6.

20. Parker, *Miasma*, chap. 4.

21. Ibid., 309–11.

22. Ibid., 25, 130, 141, 258, 271, 278, and 309. See also Bremmer, "Scapegoat Rituals in Ancient Greece." In aetiological myths the community, rather than the ruler, is more often said to be the cause of an affliction.

23. Parker, *Miasma*, 25.

24. For these and other examples see Parker, *Miasma*, 259–67; Vernant, "Ambiguity and Reversal," 132.

25. G. H. Gellie, *Sophocles: A Reading* (Melbourne: Melbourne University Press, 1972), 101, thinks that the last scene serves to show us that Oedipus can learn from his suffering and endure the truth.

26. This is an unpublished suggestion of Colin MacCleod, reported by Taplin, *Greek Tragedy in Action*, 46, and effectively criticized by M. Davies, "The End of Sophocles' *O.T.*," *Hermes* 110 (1982): 273. Gellie, "The Last Scene of the *Oedipus Tyrannus*," 39, argues that it would be bad drama to bring Oedipus back into a relation with the community in the last scene and then expel him, and that to expel Oedipus would emphasize his guilt too strongly.

27. See March, *The Creative Poet*, 148.

28. Bernard M. W. Knox, *Oedipus at Thebes* (New Haven: Yale University Press, 1957), chap. 5.

29. Taplin, *Greek Tragedy in Action*, 45–46.

30. Pucci, "The Tragic *Pharmakos* of the *Oedipus Rex*," 43, 47.

31. As Rebecca Bushnell, *Prophesying Tragedy* (Ithaca, NY: Cornell University Press, 1988), 84, notes, Oedipus is hardly a second Teiresias, for his knowledge of his own future is—in contrast to that of the dying Hector—not precise. Nevertheless, Oedipus' shift to a sense of instinctive certainty about the future is strongly marked.

32. Critics are divided on the subject of Creon's caution. Kitto, *Poiesis*, 220–22, is his staunchest defender, but he has won few adherents.

33. Bremmer, "Scapegoat Rituals in Ancient Greece," 318, makes the same point about scapegoats in general: "The expulsion of scapegoats in practice amounted to killing, since, like the dead, they disappeared from the community, never to return."

34. See D. A. Hester, "'Either . . . or' versus 'both . . . and': A Dramatic Device in Sophocles," *Antichthon* 13 (1979): 12, on the *Trachiniae* and other passages in Sophocles—although not this one.

35. This is my attempt to get the probable sense of a corrupt sentence.

36. This is the interpretation of Howe, "Taboo in the Oedipus Theme," 137.

37. In myth (especially aetiological myths) scapegoats often, but do not always, die; in cult they are normally exiled. See esp. Bremmer, "Scapegoat Rituals in Ancient Greece," 315–18. I assume here that the oracle is unlikely, as some have thought, to reverse itself and advocate keeping Oedipus at home, and that the audience could only imagine that Creon is looking to remove the ambiguity, especially the *or*, in the original oracle. At Hdt. 7.141. the Delphic oracle partially reverses itself on a second consultation, since it gives the Athenians some hope for a future after their city is destroyed by the Persians. Yet even there the basic message, that the Athenians have no choice but to abandon their city to the enemy, remains the same.

38. The symmetries with the earlier scene between Oedipus and Creon are suggestive of other possibilities. In Oedipus' argument with Creon, he threatens to kill (not banish) Creon (623), who has suggested first death, then banishment as a punishment if he is guilty (606–7, 622). Before Jocasta, Creon then restates Oedipus' threat (inaccurately) as a threat to kill *or* banish himself (640–41). In surrendering to Jocasta's plea, Oedipus goes on to insist that sparing Creon will require his own death or banishment (658–59). In the final scene the power relations are reversed. Does the text make us wonder if Creon will (or even unconsciously wishes to) discover from the oracle divine authority to inflict on Oedipus the punishment of death that the king had earlier planned for Creon himself?

39. As Gellie, *Sophocles: A Reading,* 102, puts it, "Oedipus begs with authority while Creon dictates timorously."

40. Knox, *Oedipus at Thebes*, chap. 5, Hester, "Oedipus and Jonah," 45, and Davies, "The End of Sophocles' *O.T.*," 274–75, among others correctly emphasize the unchanging ethos of the two throughout the play. G. M. Kirkwood, *A Study of Sophoclean Drama* (Ithaca, NY: Cornell University Press, 1958), 132, sees this continuity as ensuring "the continued domination (dramatic, that is) of the tragic hero."

41. See Froma I. Zeitlin, "Thebes: Theater of Self and Society in Athenian Drama," in *Greek Tragedy*

and Political Theory, ed. J. Peter Euben (Berkeley: University of California Press, 1986), 101–41, for a discussion of the characteristics typical of Theban tyrants.

42. This ode has provoked interpretations too numerous to consider here. Yet it seems reasonable to consider that it has this degree of relevance to the previous scenes. See Hester, "Oedipus and Jonah," 42–43, for a sensible review of the issue and bibliography.

43. Gellie, "The Last Scene of the *Oedipus Tyrannus*," 40–41, and Pucci, "The Tragic *Pharmakos* of the *Oedipus Rex*," 47–48, point out some of the structural parallels between his actions in the first and last scenes. The verb κρατεῖν appears in both cases (14, 1522). In both cases, Oedipus strives to protect stricken children and to mitigate disaster with compassion and courage.

44. H. D. F. Kitto, *Greek Tragedy: A Literary Study*, 3rd ed. (London: Routledge, 1961), 179.

45. See n. 15 above.

46. As M. Davies, "The End of Sophocles' *O.T.*," 276, puts it, "the accession to the throne . . . has not bestowed on him any of the Oedipodean heroism he would require to master the Sphinx should that creature raise her ugly head again."

47. See John Gould, "The Language of Oedipus," in *Sophocles' Oedipus Rex*, ed. Harold Bloom (New York: Chelsea House, 1988), 157.

48. This is Pucci's intriguing explanation of the inconclusive ending ("The Tragic *Pharmakos* of the *Oedipus Rex*," 46–48).

49. See Helen North, *Sophrosyne* (Ithaca, NY: Cornell University Press, 1966), 72–73, for the translation of the fragment and a general discussion of the issue.

50. For a similar analysis of Creon see esp. Gellie, *Sophocles: A Reading*, 88, 102.

51. Martin Ostwald, "On Interpreting Sophocles' *Oedipus Tyrannus*," in *The Verbal and the Visual: Essays in Honor of William Sebastian Heckscher*, ed. Karl-Ludwig Selig and Elizabeth Sears (New York: Italica Press, 1990), 149.

52. Here I find myself between those critics who find that Oedipus regains dignity and self-knowledge in disaster (e.g., Knox, *Oedipus at Thebes*, chap. 5) and those who see Oedipus, unchanged and having learned nothing, going down to complete defeat by Creon (e.g., Davies, "The End of Sophocles' *O.T.*"; Taplin, "Sophocles in His Theatre"). Oedipus is unable to compel others to carry out what he feels to be right. But to the degree that his position has credibility, he does not go down to utter defeat.

PART THREE

Oedipus on Trial

Excerpt from *Wrong-Doing, Truth-Telling*

Michel Foucault

Today I am going to offer what may be the millionth reflection on
Sophocles' *Oedipus Rex*.[1] For this I can offer but one excuse: that this
reflection will not be focused on that extraordinary, monstrous, and
unique thing that Oedipus did, but, to the contrary, on the very regular way (I
was even going to say ordinary way) in which this thing was brought to light by
Oedipus and for Oedipus. In other words, what I would like to present—in a
somewhat haphazard way, as a kind of textual commentary and nothing more,
so that we might discuss afterwards—are a few reflections on how Oedipus's
wrong-doing and truth-telling are tied together in Sophocles' play. In other
words, it is not so much Oedipus and his interdiction or malediction that I
would like to study,[2] but rather his veridiction.[3]

I will try to explore this question of veridiction in different forms of
either judicial practices or cultural experiences. Oedipus—I mean *Oedipus
Rex*, the play by Sophocles—is, as you know, a foundational representation
of law. Naturally, in saying this I am repeating a platitude and a truism.

Second Lecture (April 28, 1981) in a series of lectures delivered by Foucault at the Catholic University
of Louvain and published in English under the title *Wrong-Doing, Truth-Telling: The Function of Avowal
in Justice* (Chicago: University of Chicago Press, 2014). The opening remarks, which do not bear
directly on Oedipus, are not reprinted here.

Everyone knows that in Greek tragedy, the theme of representing law—of the foundational representation of law—is essential. Whether it be Aeschylus through *Prometheus* or *Oresteia*, or Sophocles with *Antigone* and *Electra*, the problem of the confrontation of rights, the confrontation between the law of the family and the law of the city, the problem of the foundation of the law, the original institution of the tribunal, or the question of vengeance—all of this constitutes a theme which, if not universal, is at least constant throughout Greek tragedy.

Moreover, it seems to me that, generally speaking, in most societies we would refer to as Indo-European, or at least from the theater of Greece to that of the sixteenth and seventeenth centuries, this question of the representation of law in theater was a constant. After all, the central problem in Shakespeare—or in the political plays among Shakespeare's works—it seems to me, is the question of the foundation of sovereign right: How ... can a sovereign succeed in legitimately exercising power that he seized through war, revolt, civil war, crime, or violating oaths? It seems to me as well that classical French theater—I am thinking especially of Corneille, of course—touches on and represents these problems of public law. It also seems to me that the question of law and of representing the foundation of law through theater was essential for Schiller as well. It could be interesting, I think, to study the entire history of theater in our societies from the perspective of this question of the representation of law. One has the impression—or at least, it seems to me this is something that would merit further study—that from the time of Greek theater up to at least the end of the eighteenth century, one of the functions, although certainly not the sole function, of theater in European societies was to be the place or a stage for debating the problem of the law. This was unlike the novel, but not, perhaps, unlike the epic or the American Western, which, after all, also presents a problem of law, of the confrontation of rights, of the confrontation of law and vengeance, of the right of conquest. It seems to me that there is an entire side to the institutions of representation—of the representative arts—in European societies that are organized around this question of the foundation of law and whose significance and meaning is to manifest, in one way or another, the fundamental problems of law. But let's leave that question under the heading of possible areas for further study.[4]

In any case, *Oedipus Rex* is clearly a representation of law since it involves a crime, a crime in the double sense of an infraction of fundamental law and a religious sullying[5]—two aspects that are inseparable in ancient Greek thought and culture. It is equally a question of discovering who is responsible for the crime and, finally, a question of how to punish the criminal—a problem that remains unresolved in the play. Let's say in very schematic terms, for example, that in the case of *Electra* or *Antigone*, the problem was that of knowing how to make room for the law of the family within the law of the city, how they should confront one another, and how they should be coordinated. In the case of *Oedipus*, a more straightforward juridical problem is posed: the question of discovering the identity of the unknown murderer. The question of what procedure to employ in order to uncover the unknown murderer was a well-known question not only in classical Greek law, but also in classical Greek philosophy. For example, while book 9 of Plato's *Laws*, section 874a, does not evoke Oedipus explicitly, it discusses precisely his general situation.[6] Plato writes of a clear case of assassination, where the murderer remains unknown in spite of the investigators' best efforts. We have, then, a very simple juridical situation which is far less complex than the case of *Electra* or *Antigone*: a crime has been committed and the perpetrator, whose name and identity remain unknown, must be found. That being said, from the very start and throughout the play, the text contains a series of technical and precise juridical terms which were completely comprehensible for a Greek audience and which reveal that the play unfolds in the form of a trial. It is not, of course, a total and exhaustive representation of a trial, yet there is a perfectly clear judicial paradigm organized around the question of how to discover the guilty party whose crime has been established, but whose identity remains unknown.

By way of orientation, I will indicate a few of the elements of this general paradigm. For example, take the very beginning of the text, when Oedipus sends Creon to ask the oracle of Delphi why Thebes has been afflicted with the plague. Creon returns with the response, and Oedipus asks him: "Now, of what murder is Apollo informing us?"[7] The Greek text uses the verb *mēnuein*, which the French translation[8] renders by suggesting that Apollo indicates the crime as the cause of the plague. In fact, the verb *mēnuein* is a technical term that designates a precise form of judicial process.[9] In classical Greek law, there were two ways of denouncing a crime: either before the council, the *boulē*, or before the assembly. One procedure, the *exangelesia*, could only be heard if the denouncer was a citizen. When the denouncer was not a citizen and could not present his denunciation in that form, he followed a different procedure called *mēnusis*—to which this denunciation corresponded. For indeed, Apollo was not a Theban, so he does not have to follow the procedure of *exangelia* as if he were a citizen. He introduces a *mēnusis*—which is the technical term employed here. So this is a case of a noncitizen who denounces a crime committed on the city's territory.[10] What is interesting is that Apollo's *mēnusis*, his denunciation, takes two forms: it takes the form of the plague, the plague that was sent in response to an impurity, as a consequence of the impurity provoked by the crime; and this denunciation, it is also the oracle that was delivered and that Creon brought back. The procedure—the judicial procedure, named by the text—is perceived as embedded within both divine action (Apollo's vengeance) and the religious ritual of prophecy (the oracle).

Oedipus responds to this *mēnusis*, to this denunciation by Apollo, as would a chief justice: "Because there has been a denunciation, I am going to start over"—I am citing the French translation—"I am going to start everything from the beginning."[11] This corresponds exactly to the procedure, which is also well defined juridically, that must follow the denunciation of the crime once it has been accepted either by the council or the assembly. Investigators, the *zētētai*,[12] are designated and charged with investigating the affair from the beginning to determine the truth of the denunciation. In order to mark the judicial character of the procedure that he has set in motion, first Oedipus promises a reward to anyone who discloses information; then he curses those who hide what they know; and third, he absolves those who would testify against interest.[13]

Naturally, through the extraordinary density and complexity of the text and the echoes that resonate throughout the play, we know well that the curse on those who hide their knowledge and the absolution of those who would testify against themselves, all of this is going to take on a dramatic meaning—or rather a tragic sense—that we know so well. But it is also important to recognize that these are not simply dramatic effects within the larger economy of the play. Oedipus's famous curse on the unknown criminal that ricochets back onto him is also a well-documented judicial procedure in classical Athenian law. For example, in the famous sacrilege trial of 415 (415 was a few years after *Oedipus*, if indeed the play was staged in 420), in this famous sacrilege trial recounted by Thucydides[14] and then Plutarch,[15] there are accounts of this type of procedure, in which a reward was promised to those who could provide information, just as impunity was ensured for those who would testify against interest. Oedipus's famous curse against the unknown criminal, who turns out to be himself, directly echoes, even in its very terms, a religious and judicial practice that was common during the period and to which Plato attests. In book 9 of the *Laws* it is written, precisely in the case of the unknown murderer: "If someone is found dead and the murderer is unknown and remains undiscovered by investigation, proclamations against the murderer must be made"—which Oedipus does—"and the herald must proclaim in the public market that the murderer, whoever he is, must not set foot in any sacred place in his own country or that of the victim."[16] Oedipus says exactly this. In such a case, "if he does this and it is discovered, may he be put to death and thrown outside the frontiers without burial."[17] This too is precisely what is discussed at the end of Sophocles' play.

So the very instruments of the inquiry are put in place. And once again this inquiry unfolds in a very recognizable juridical form. First there is Tiresias—Tiresias the seer, as you know—who comes, and comes entirely as a witness. The text states as much: "He came,"[18] *eiseléluthas—eiserchomai* means "to appear before" in the technical juridical sense of the term. "I have come," Tiresias says, "because you have called me," *kaleis*[19]—here again a juridical term. And Tiresias is going to act like a reluctant witness[20] who is under threat, while Oedipus finally puts an end to his testimony by dismissing him with another ritual saying, *aphes*—"be gone."[21] After Tiresias leaves, the chorus discusses his testimony just as a jury would discuss a witness's testimony. Creon follows Tiresias, but not as a witness. To the contrary, he comes to complain before the chorus, before the jury, that he has been the victim of Oedipus's slanderous accusations. To which Oedipus replies with another accusation. The specific term used in his accusation, *kakotechnia*,[22] is a juridical term which generally means a "deceitful maneuver" or may mean, in more specific circumstances, "subornation of a witness"—and indeed this is precisely what Oedipus accuses Creon of doing. He accuses him of having suborned the oracle as witness and having falsified the oracle's meaning. At least this is Oedipus's complaint against Creon. And finally the last scene, which leads to the revelation of the truth and to which we will return for a closer reading, is clearly a judicial scene of testimony and investigation—of interrogation, of extortion of an avowal under threat of torture, and ultimately avowal. Thus, the general framework of the play is a procedural one that is easily recognizable. Once again, it does not reproduce a trial exactly, but rather a judicial paradigm that would have been perfectly comprehensible and recognizable to a Greek audience and spectators.

So, after this slightly belabored and technical introduction, it is time to home in on the central question that I would like to pose: What exactly is being represented on this stage, in this judicial scene?

Since Aristotle, everyone knows—that is, those who are familiar with Aristotle know—that Greek tragedy traditionally rests on two elements: the peripety that reverses the good fortune of the characters and transforms happiness into misery or luck into misfortune;[23] and on the other hand, the other great technique is recognition, in which the real identity of some hitherto unknown or misknown person is revealed. Indeed, most Greek tragedies rely on these two mechanisms and, in general, the *peripeteia*[24]—that is, the reversal of the situation—allows one to recognize the truth of each. *Oedipus Rex* has the peculiarity of being among the very rare, if not the only, Greek tragedies in which the *peripeteia*—that is, the transformation of events or of the fortune of the characters—does not reveal the truth. It is the revelation of truth, the *anagnōrisis*,[25] the recognition of the character's real identity, that constitutes the peripety that leads to Oedipus's fall and turns this envied man, with what appeared a most desirable fate, into a man doomed to abomination and endless misfortune. It is thus a play built entirely on the mechanism of recognition, of *anagnōrisis*.

In fact—and here is where I would like to situate my own analysis with regard to the more common ones—it seems to me that there are two *anagnōrises*, two moments of recognition in *Oedipus Rex*. On the one hand, there is the axis stretching from Oedipus's own ignorance or lack of awareness of himself to his obligation to recognize who he is. This is the axis of individual recognition, the axis of Oedipus as the subject of an action he does not remember—or rather, for which he had neither the keys to, nor the possibility of, understanding the significance—but that is revealed at the end of the play as one that he not only committed, but committed as the son of the one he killed and the son of the one he married. So there is this individual *anagnōrisis*, the emergence of truth in the subject. And then there is another axis, and this is the one that I would prefer to focus on: the axis of establishing the truth not in the eyes of Oedipus but in the eyes of the chorus, a character that I believe to be absolutely central, as it is in all Greek plays. For if indeed Oedipus is searching for the truth, he is doing so precisely so that the chorus can recognize it—the chorus, that is, the citizens, the people in assembly, or what is constituted as the judicial body with the responsibility for discovering, establishing, and validating the truth.[26] How does Oedipus's truth establish itself in the eyes of the chorus? This is the axis I would like to study: the establishment of truth in valid and legitimate juridical terms.

There is indeed one thing that is striking in the play: that is, while it is true that until the end Oedipus is the one who does not recognize himself for who he is, nevertheless we must recognize that the truth, the truth of what he is, is known not only to the spectators before the beginning of the play—but what's more, the entire play is punctuated with elements reminding them that they know this truth. And the fact is, this truth is produced explicitly at least three times in the course of the play.

This truth that is so difficult to know and that Oedipus refuses to recognize, this truth is told entirely, completely, and exhaustively for the first time by two characters—for it is always two characters, coupled together, who produce this truth through their complementary dialogue.[27] The first couple that produces this truth is Apollo and Tiresias. Apollo indicates why there is the plague, and Tiresias states who is guilty. This is the first manifestation of truth, the first production of truth, the first veridiction, which, for a number of reasons that we will need to study, does not work, does not stick, is not accepted, is neither validated nor legitimated. Then there is a second production of truth, which is once again the work of two complementary characters, Jocasta and Oedipus. They recount their memories, providing all the necessary information to recognize Oedipus as his mother's husband and his father's assassin. This second veridiction, this second alethurgy, once again remains suspended and is not accepted; it is not validated, it remains surrounded by an element of uncertainty. It is only the third time, with the third alethurgy, when a new couple appears, that the truth is finally, not produced, because this had already happened, but this time accepted and validated, and can finally produce the judicial and dramatic effects that we expect of it. And this third couple that speaks the truth, this third couple of veridiction, this third wave of alethurgy, is presented by the messenger from Corinth and a slave, the shepherd of Cithaeron; together, once again combining the elements of their knowledge, they produce the truth. There is, then, Apollo and Tiresias on the level of the gods, Oedipus and Jocasta on the level of kings and chiefs, and the messenger and the shepherd on the level of the slaves and servants. And it is the slaves and servants who produce the veridiction that the kings and the gods were unable to produce or, in any case, were unable to produce in such a way that they could be recognized as valid by the juridical institution. Three manifestations of truth, three alethurgies, three types of veridiction—this is precisely what I would like to study.[28] How did each of these veridictions unfold? How did each of these alethurgies unfold? And why is it the third that, in some way, worked? Why is it the third that effectively produced the truth?

So, turning to the first alethurgy, the first couple: the god and the seer. You will recall what has happened. The plague is raging in Thebes, and Oedipus has sent Creon to consult Apollo. Creon has returned from the oracle, and what has the oracle said? First, the plague will be vanquished through purification. "And why is purification necessary? Purification of what?" Oedipus asks. "Purification of a murder." But what murder then requires purification? The oracle's response, brought by Creon, is: "It is the murder of Laius." But who committed this murder? "Someone who is in this very country, who is in Thebes."[29] Such is the oracle's response, and not a word more is said because—as it is stated in the text—the god only says exactly what he sees fit to say.[30] We could say that we have, in one sense, half the story with this response from the oracle, because it is simply a denunciation by the god of a murder that was committed and whose victim is known to us. We know that it was this murder and this victim that brought on the plague. What remains is the other half, which in one sense must be discovered—namely, the half which is the assassin's identity. We know the victim; now we must learn who the assassin is.

Tiresias, who was also called as a witness by Oedipus, appears at this moment. Tiresias is in one sense Apollo's double, the god's double. He is his other side: blind, while of course the god sees all. And he is the one who is capable of interpreting what the god said and completing it with a complementary discourse, of saying who is the true assassin. Tiresias is interrogated in the juridically acceptable form of a reluctant witness. And since he refuses to tell the truth he knows, we see Oedipus's threats and how he reacts to the witness's refusal to say what he knows. Oedipus first blames him for the harm that has been inflicted upon his fellow citizens by his refusal to tell the truth[31]—that is his first reproach. The second reproach is graver still: "You have insulted the city and as a result not only have you wronged your fellow citizens, but the life and very existence of your city may be compromised by your attitude."[32] And finally, third, Oedipus reverses this refusal as he turns towards Tiresias, who refuses to speak, and makes an accusation against him: he suspects him of having committed the crime because he does not want to speak, or because he is speaking in a way that prevents proper understanding of what he is saying and whom he is accusing.[33] So when the seer is faced with Oedipus's accusation, he says everything. He tells all. He says: "Who committed the crime? It is Oedipus."[34] He even goes further and adds in the course of the discussion: "Not only did you assassinate Laius, but you also married your mother—Jocasta was your mother."[35]

So the truth has been spoken—the entire truth has been spoken, and in one sense the play could end here. Or rather, the problem arises of knowing why this truth, told in this way and by no small authority (after all, it comes from the oracle and a seer, and the text has insisted that they are never mistaken and always speak the truth), why this truth may very well be said under those conditions, and yet cannot be received. Of course it is not received by Oedipus; and we may well imagine that Oedipus's conduct is justified, since he would be accused, indeed he is the one accused by both the oracle's and the seer's responses. But what is more interesting, and what I would like to focus on, is the following: it is that the choragus and the chorus itself refuse the oracle's verdict. Or, in any case, they explicitly refuse to accept Tiresias's divination. For example, when Tiresias and Oedipus confront one another during the interrogation and Oedipus refutes Tiresias's accusations, the choragus says: "Anger has gotten the best of both of you, Oedipus and Tiresias."[36] And once Tiresias retreats, the chorus says: "I cannot believe what Tiresias has said. I can neither believe it nor refute it. What can I say? I do not know."[37] That is to say that the choragus and the chorus refuse to take sides between the two. Why do they refuse to accept the words of such sacred authorities? I believe that if we look at the way these words are presented in the play, we can understand why they are unacceptable for the choragus and the chorus.

First, the word of the god and the word of the seer are words that are only pronounced if the god and the seer desire it. This is emphasized on a number of occasions: no one can force the god to speak if he does not want to do so. And when Oedipus presses Tiresias, the seer, to speak, he responds: "But you do not command me, only the god does. I am the servant of Loxias and thus I will speak if I want to."[38] The refusal to speak, legitimated by the fact that the god is the god, and by the fact that the seer is the god's servant, is entirely typical. He refuses the politico-judicial authority that could and will, as we shall see at the end of the play, legitimately extract an avowal, testimony, or declaration. Within the judicial order, one is obliged to speak. And if one has the right to say during the interrogation, "I refuse to speak because I am not forced to obey you," then at that moment the judicial machine cannot work. So first, this word is only spoken if it wants to be spoken.

Second, it is a word that has a curious or strange relationship to the truth, or that is not in any case the relationship that an ordinary witness would have with the truth. Tiresias says as much: "The force of truth resides in me."[39] And the chorus responds to the prophecy of the god by saying: "It is shining and brilliant, the word gushes forth from snowy Parnassus."[40] That is, we are dealing with a word that has authority in itself, that decides for itself to speak or not, and that carries the truth by natural right. It holds the truth in itself: truth dwells within it, or it dwells within the truth. There is a bond of belonging between the word of the god, the word of the seer, and the truth. It is for this reason that they use the verb *phēmi*—I pronounce, I affirm.[41] When it is used in the strictest, emphatic sense, *phēmi* means: "When I speak, I affirm that what I say is true." The affirmation, and the fact that I affirm it, is sufficient to constitute the law, the assurance, and the guarantee of this truth.

Third, the third aspect of this word is that it justifies itself through a seeing, but a peculiar form of seeing, naturally. First, of course, because as far as the god Apollo is concerned, he sees everything—there is, in fact, no difference between what Apollo sees and what he wants: he wants what he sees and he sees what he wants. It is sufficient that he see it for it to become effectively, sooner or later, truth and reality. On the other hand, the seer also has a peculiar relationship to what is said and what is seen—first of all because he is blind (and Oedipus does not miss the opportunity to remind him: "You are a blind man whose ears are as closed as his eyes. You live in darkness").[42] And at the same time, the seer, who sees even though he is blind, sees the future as he does the present and the past (so the seer says to Oedipus: "You do not see what misery you find yourself in at this moment. You cannot anticipate the flood of disaster that is going to ravage you and your children").[43] Which is to say, everything that humans cannot see (because it lies in the future and has not yet happened), the seer sees in an atemporality that is characteristic of his relationship to the truth.[44]

It is entirely understandable why Oedipus does not recognize himself in this word—in such a prophetic, oracular, or divine word. He cannot recognize himself in these accusatory words. And he says as much to the seer: "You speak nothing but foolishness.[45] You speak in vain."[46] The words are empty. Nor can the chorus recognize such words, or rather, it cannot recognize the validity of its own words. What I would like to emphasize, then, is that throughout this play there is a perpetual correlation between Oedipus's recognition of who he is and the chorus's recognition of the juridical validity of the truth. Oedipus will only be able to recognize himself once the chorus has recognized the validity of what is said. Oedipus cannot recognize himself in the words of the seer and the oracle of the god, and neither can the chorus recognize their validity. I believe that the chorus that is sung at this moment, after Tiresias's departure, is important because it shows the chorus's function throughout the play: the chorus is the body that tests, accepts, or refuses, and establishes the truth told. And no sooner has Tiresias left than the chorus begins its chant.

This chorus is very interesting and merits close study. There are two parts to the chorus. The first part is dedicated to the oracle and oracles in general. The chorus says the following: "Yes, the oracles tell the truth. When the oracle pronounces its word, we can be sure that what it says has happened, is happening, is going to happen. The arrow has been released, and the one who is targeted had better hurry and run quickly because the arrow is already behind him and will get to him no matter what. He runs and he should run, but he is condemned nonetheless. The arrow was released out of the flames and lightning."[47] We are in a world which is of course a world of fate, which is a world of brilliance and of light, which is therefore the world of the truth and the world of the inevitable.

And yet—this is where the second part of the chorus begins—the chorus says: "Yes, but this does not apply in my case." It isn't said exactly like that; it reads, "The arrow has been released amidst the flames and the lightning—but as for myself, my opinion drifts in the wind. I can neither believe nor deny what Tiresias has said. I see nothing, neither in front nor behind me."[48] In counterpoint and in opposition to the world of fate, atemporality, pure light, and the brilliance of the lightning that manifests the truth and guarantees destiny, the chorus asserts its right not to believe, not to know—its right to remain in the dark and only see precisely what is presented. Nothing beyond, in the realm of the future (or rather, for the Greeks, in the realm of the future, which is situated behind oneself), and nothing in the past (or what is in front of oneself).[49] It only has access to the imminent, and the chorus makes this explicit in stating: "Zeus and Apollo are clairvoyant, they are learned in the destiny of mortals, but humans? Humans?"[50] And the chorus then poses the question of Tiresias, the seer. It states: "Can the seer tell the truth?" Well, it says, "Can one truly claim that, among men, a seer possesses gifts superior to mine?"[51] And obviously, the very fact that it asks the question implies a negative response: "The seer does not have talents superior to my own," it says, "and if it is true that there are some men who know more than others, then they still must provide proof."[52]

I believe we have two important elements here. First, no one has talents superior to the chorus—that is, in the order of truth of this moment, there is no body that is superior to that of the just or of the assembly, to the power that, in the form of the tribunal, decides what is true and what is not, who is guilty and who is not. Consequently, this judicial body is superior. Second, this judicial body must function through proof, and in this context the chorus continues to speak of Oedipus, stating that he has provided proof. He has given proof of his wisdom and of his love for Thebes (of course, this is a reference to the Sphinx and to Oedipus's victory over the Sphinx). Since he has provided proof, only proof may count against him: "Before having seen," *idioimi*, says the text, "justification of the god's spoken words, I cannot approve them."[53] *Idoimi, phanera*:[54] this entire series of words suggests that we are in the order of seeing, but no longer a seeing that is of divine light, that both brings things forth and seals one's destiny. It is no longer the divine sight that cuts through time and is atemporal. What the chorus demands, and what prevents it from accepting what was so clearly spoken in the oracular veridiction, what it wants are visible elements, proof, a demonstration. The truth of seeing, seeing for oneself, seeing that constitutes proof—this is what the jury demands. This is what the chorus and the choragus seek.

And this is why the first veridiction—in spite of the fact that everything was said—is refused, is sidelined.

Thus begins—I will skip a certain number of elements, in particular the episode with Creon that we may return to in the discussion later—thus begins the second alethurgy, the second wave of veridiction. This alethurgy takes place not on the level of the god and the seer, but on that of the kings, between Jocasta and Oedipus. Following Tiresias and Creon's departure, Jocasta is the first to intervene, and she picks up precisely where the chorus ended: that is to say the problem of prophetic and divine veridiction. Jocasta affirms, "If the god wants to reveal things, he can do so perfectly well and he knows perfectly well how to do so himself."[55] As for the seer, she says, "You'll see," addressing Oedipus, "that no human creature has ever possessed the art (*technē*) of predicting."[56]

I will return in a few moments to this problem of *technē*, but I think that Jocasta's first intervention situates the problem or the question well. Can there be a *technē* of prediction? And if there is not a *technē* of prediction, can there be another technique to produce the truth? On the basis of this refusal of divine and divinatory veridiction, Jocasta says: "That the seers do not possess the art of predicting, of that I am going," Jocasta says to Oedipus, "to give you the proof."[57]

"I am going to give you the proof of this." This scene of the proof, of the demonstration that the art of prediction is unfounded, this demonstration unfolds throughout the scene by means of an intervention by Jocasta, of a dialogue with Oedipus, and finally of a monologue or account by Oedipus. There are three elements, then: Jocasta, the dialogue between Jocasta and Oedipus, and Oedipus's monologue-account.

The initial element (that of Jocasta) and the terminal one (Oedipus's monologue): these two elements correspond to one another—they are absolutely symmetrical. In her first intervention, Jocasta demonstrates that predictions do not tell the truth by explaining to Oedipus what she did to prevent her own son from killing Laius in spite of them. At the end of the scene, in continuity with the demonstration that the seers do not tell the truth, Oedipus explains how, in spite of the prediction that he was to kill Polybus—in spite of the prediction that he was going to murder his father—he succeeded in not killing the one whom he believed to be his father, namely Polybus. We have here, with these two elements, initial and final, the deployment of human processes through which, first, one escapes the seers' predictions, and second, one may thereby show that the predictions of the seers do not tell the truth.

In between these two elements is a long dialogue between Oedipus and Jocasta that unfolds, once again, in the form of questions and answers, like in testimony. Oedipus interrogates Jocasta and asks her a number of questions. He interrogates her like a witness. Based on what? Based on what she has learned about the death of Laius: what she was told, public rumors, her memories, Laius's physical bearing, the number of people who accompanied him, and whether anyone survived or not. In short, it is an entire inquiry based on what Jocasta may have known or learned. And naturally, the truth is uncovered and is practically told through this game of questions and answers. It is almost told and yet it is not accepted—neither by Oedipus nor by Jocasta, who refuse to hear truly what they are saying. They are not going to draw the final conclusions that would allow them to identify and recognize themselves in the episodes that they themselves have just told. So they escape.

How do they escape? Well, first they escape because an element is missing in this story they tell; or rather there is an ambiguous element in their story, which is the number of people who killed Laius. The reported testimonies, the public rumors, and all the information that Jocasta could gather suggest that Laius was killed by several persons. Yet Oedipus, himself, who fears and is almost certain that the person he killed was Laius, knows full well that he was alone when he killed him. So this element provides a degree of uncertainty through which they may escape this hint of this truth that they are in the process of discovering. And then, they also escape the truth they have discovered by convincing themselves that one can escape destiny and that human technique allows one to pass through the web spun by the gods. Laius could not have been killed by his son, since he took all the precautions necessary to prevent it from happening.

The truth is told, then, but it remains unacknowledged by Oedipus. It is a truth in which Oedipus does not yet recognize himself, even if he is the one who formulated it. At this point the chorus intervenes for a second time. This intervention is also of capital importance because it is both very similar—very symmetrical to the one I evoked earlier, after the first wave of veridiction—it is at once similar and symmetrical and at the same time much less clear. First of all, this intervention is a reverse image of the first. In the first, you'll remember, the chorus began by affirming the omnipotence of the gods. It made reference to the arrow of the gods that always hits its target. But in the face of this, because it could see neither into the future nor into the past, it had asked for solid proof. In the chorus that follows the discussion between Oedipus and Jocasta, things, the unfolding of the text itself, is reversed. First, the chorus opens strangely with a curse against tyranny and excess, against the arrogance of tyrants who believe they are at the height of their fortune and then fall to the deepest depths.[58] After this curse against tyranny, they speak once again of this famous question of oracles—oracles about which it was stated in the first chorus that while their declarations were true, of course, something else was necessary. Here in this second chorus, the question of the oracles comes at the end, and what is proclaimed is the necessity of respecting them. They were insufficient in the first chorus, but now they must be respected absolutely; and cursed be those who refuse to accept the lesson of these oracles, who refuse to accept what is said by the oracles.[59]

There is then something slightly enigmatic that we must try to explain. Why on the one hand do Jocasta and Oedipus speak the truth, but remain incapable of recognizing themselves in it? And how is it possible, on the other hand, that the chorus, without of course saying that it recognizes the truth of what has been said, nevertheless ceases to take Oedipus's side directly? The chorus has an ambiguous and strange attitude when it criticizes tyranny and celebrates the oracles. As in the previous situation, where it was a question of asking ourselves what was exactly this divine veridiction (what was its form, and why was it unacceptable from the point of view of justice), I believe that here too we have to examine Oedipus's veridiction. How did he speak the truth and what did he know? In other words, instead of investigating Oedipus's ignorance, as we usually do, I would like to take a quick look at what he knew and how he knew it, because he knew quite a bit. Oedipus is full of knowledge.[60]

In the course of Oedipus and Tiresias's discussion, there is a remarkable passage: it is when Tiresias pits an accusation against Oedipus that the latter believes (and truly believes) to be false. Oedipus exclaims abruptly: "*O ploute kai tyranni technē technēs*—what jealousy you incite."[61] "*O ploute tyranni technē technēs*," oh wealth, oh tyranny—power, sovereignty, "crown,"[62] in

Mazon's translation—and "*technē technēs*," supreme art. By evoking the three elements of wealth, tyranny, and supreme art, Oedipus naturally is attributing them to himself. If Tiresias is envious of him, it is because Oedipus has wealth, power, and *technē technēs*.

That power be accompanied by these two attributes seems important to me. The coupling of wealth and the exercise of power, of wealth and sovereignty, of wealth and tyranny (with all the ambiguity this last word implies), this coupling is classic and commonplace: one exercises power because one is rich, or one becomes rich because one exercises power—in any case, the joining of these two things poses no problem. On the other hand, what is this *technē technēs*, this supreme art or supreme knowledge, which constitutes the third element in the trilogy and symmetrically joins tyranny and wealth? It is rather remarkable, I think, because in the ancient texts, while power and wealth are always associated, power is never associated with the notion of *technē*. Power is never associated with the idea of technical knowledge or a particular art. On the other hand, it is a theme that is, as you know, absolutely capital and important in philosophical and political discussions of the fifth and fourth centuries. The entire discussion among the Sophists, Socrates, and Plato turns around this question: can the exercise of political power be considered a *technē*, a technique that can be learned, that can be taught, that can ensure that the political man exercise power just as it ensures an architect the ability to construct a house? This expression of *technē technēs* is important precisely because later on it becomes the traditional expression for designating government—government not only in the global general sense of a political art, but also, as you know, in the sense of the government of individuals by one another, the government of souls. The expression *technē technēs* will be used all the way up through the Christian pastoral to designate the manner—and therefore the art, the technique—that allows for the government of souls and for their guidance toward salvation.

Let's return to Oedipus's notion of *technē*. What is Oedipus's *technē*, and why is he able to evoke *technē technēs* in speaking of himself and his power? I believe that here Oedipus should be compared to two other characters who are specifically lacking in *technē* even though they exercise power.

First, with Creon—Creon who is of course his brother-in-law, the brother of Jocasta, and whom Oedipus sent to Delphi to consult the oracle. Creon returns and reports what the oracle says, and Oedipus accuses him of having falsified the oracle's response. Oedipus then accuses him of being one of Tiresias's accomplices and of trying to seize his power. Creon responds to this accusation by saying: "But you know very well that I could not be jealous of you, nor do I have the desire to take your place and exercise power in your stead, because I have a good life."[63] This line of reasoning takes the form of a defense and is typically Sophist: in order to dismiss an accusation, one shows how implausible it would be (such a technique can be found in Antiphon, for example) to do that of which one is accused.[64] Thus, "it is completely implausible that I would want to take your place because I have a good life." And what is this good life that Creon describes? Well, he says, it is "the life of a king." It is "the life of a king in which I am given gifts, I am solicited, one seeks my favor, and I am surrounded spontaneously by honors. And all of this, thanks to my birth. As a result, I have no worries. The people give me gifts and you, Oedipus, shower me with kindness."[65] In other words, Creon's own description of himself is that of someone who lives like a king without being a king, or rather, without himself governing. He has *archē*, the highest rank. He has *dynasteia*—in other words, power. And he does not have *tyrannis*, he does not have tyranny—that is, he does not individually and personally exercise power.[66] Everything comes to him from his status. Everything comes to him from his prerogatives. Everything comes to him from this precedence. Therefore, he does not need *technē*; he does not need art, knowledge, or savoir-faire to have his place or benefit from it. This is why he will be able to use a very important word in speaking about himself; he will say that he is *sōphrōn*,[67] that he is wise, that he is thoughtful, that he is tempered. As he does not exercise power and does not need *technē*, the virtue that he is going to practice is good measure. This will allow him to avoid being either arrogant or excessive with regard to others while all the same exercising his precedence and prerogatives. The fundamental virtue of these aristocratic prerogatives is to be *sōphrōn*. And thus, there is no *technē*.

As for Tiresias, can we say that he too has a *technē* like Oedipus? The word *technē*, in Sophocles' text, is mentioned three times with regard to Tiresias, but each time in an entirely ironic sense. Oedipus uses the term *technē* twice with regard to Tiresias.[68] First, when Oedipus says to him, "But, at the moment when the Sphinx was ravaging the Theban lands, were you already exercising your *technē*?" This is a way of saying, "If you, Tiresias, you had *technē*, what were you doing with it and why did you not apply it at the moment when the Sphinx was destroying Thebes? You did not have *technē* then, did you?" In the same way, a little later, Oedipus tells him: "But with all of your *technē*, or your so-called *technē*, something that could be considered a technique, you were incapable of solving the enigma." And finally, Jocasta uses the term *technē* a third time with regard to Tiresias when she says, in the passage that I brought up earlier, "No mortal has ever possessed the *mantikē technē*, the art of divination."[69] That is, the seer does not have *technē* and the idea of a *mantikē technē*, a divine art, cannot be sustained.[70]

The gods [*inaudible*] are certain; men simply have *tekmērion*—they have the sign, they have the trace, they have the mark.[71] The word *tekmērion* can also be found in Aristotle to mean proof—it is what allows for demonstration. In the text of *Oedipus Rex*, it seems to me that *tekmērion* is used above all to designate a knowledge trajectory; it allows one to go from what one doesn't know to what one does know (and to constitute oneself as a subject who knows, even though one is ignorant) through a number of trajectories that stretch from the present to the past, the past to the present, from presence to absence, or from absence to presence.[72] From the present to the past: Oedipus explains that it is necessary to uncover every moment of what happened the famous day that Laius was killed, on the basis of what we have now before our very eyes—on the basis of witnesses who still exist, for example. Inversely, *tekmērion* is also what allows us to return from the past to the present: this is what Jocasta would like to do, and what she criticizes Oedipus for not doing. Starting from what has happened—that is, from the fact that up to now it has been possible to escape the predictions of the seers and the oracles of the gods—it must be assumed that this possibility still remains open now, and that we are not subject to predictions because we have been able to escape them thus far. *Tekmērion* allows for the passage from presence to absence— that is, by hearing the witnesses who are actually present, to try to uncover what escaped and continues to escape understanding. It is a question of going from the absence of those who merely heard or know that someone saw something, to presence or witnesses who actually saw, heard, and were there.

I believe that Oedipus's *technē* is this art of discovery that uses signs, traces, and marks, that allows us to go from what we don't know to what we do know by piecing together material elements that lead from one to the other with high probability. And this art of discovery, Oedipus's art, what does it shed light on? Certainly not the decrees of the gods, because these are known to people like Tiresias in whom the power of truth dwells. Certainly not the laws, those laws that the chorus says were born on Olympus and that no mortal could bring forth. Rather, Oedipus's *technē* allows for the discovery of what he calls—he who calls himself son of *tychē*[73]—it is what allows for the discovery of the meeting, of the event, of what happens: the intersection between what happens to men—or the undertakings of men, the agitations of men—and the gods' decrees. It is an art of discovering, through clues, the events. To be more exact, we have here an art, *technē*, which is attached— and Sophocles' text explains this clearly—to two other *technai* of the same type: medicine, which is mentioned twice, and the art of navigation, which is mentioned once. Sophocles' text associates Oedipus's *technē* to these two other arts. This trilogy—the art of governing, the art of healing, the art of navigation—this trilogy, you know well, would remain absolutely essential to political thought up to the seventeenth and eighteenth centuries in the West. During Sophocles' times, this classic trilogy made an analogy between the political leader and the doctor and the pilot, demonstrating that there was a type of knowledge that was proper to the exercise of political power, and that this knowledge could not be reduced or summarized, nor could it really be based on what was said prophetically by the seers or by the gods. A knowledge that was proper to the exercise of political power—that knowledge had the technical form of a discovery of truth through material elements that are interrogated for their meaning or for their referents by means of a technique that was proper to the exercise of this knowledge.

This was of course an entirely novel idea at the time, an idea that was debated and in which one could recognize the idea that Oedipus was the man of *technē technēs*. For a Greek audience of the period, this was a perfectly contemporary discussion that was being articulated here and evoked in this way: philosophers and sophists discussed the very possibility of this new science of government, this new science that Oedipus laid claim to in connection with the exercise of political power or, more precisely, in connection with the exact form of the exercise of political power that was tyranny. Tyranny, of course, with the ambiguous meaning that it had in this period: tyranny which meant both the exercise of personal power by someone with the status of a hero and a privileged relationship with the gods that allowed him to give laws to the city; but tyranny as well—and this was the obverse side of the tyrant—as the man of excess or abuse who used his power beyond rule or measure. This in effect is what happens to Oedipus's *technē*: through his *technē*, Oedipus unleashes a series of investigations that ultimately uncover the truth by using the interplay of all the signs and signposts, all the *tekmēria*, that can be found. At the same time, though, with this same *technē* Oedipus believed he could escape the gods' decrees, and it is in this excess that he meets his doom. It is all very well that the *technē* of political power be sufficiently precise, sufficiently informed, sufficiently rational to discover the truth of things; but that one attempt to oppose the god's decrees with this *technē*, this is something that is inextricably linked to the very abuse of tyrannical power. This is how one may understand the chorus that brings the second alethurgy, the second veridiction, to a close when Oedipus and Jocasta, following the god and the seer, tell the same truth again.

The chorus may now be understood. First, the celebration of the laws, the *nomoi*, which, according to the chorus, all words and acts must obey: these *nomoi* are born on Olympus and no mortal gave birth to them. Second, in this chorus, the denunciation of the immoderation of the tyrant, who has his ups and downs and who, precisely, tries to escape what was fixed by the gods and by the laws in the exercise of his power; and a curse on those who display their pride, look only for wealth, and violate that which must not be violated. And lastly, the final point of the chorus, the elegy of the oracles that must be respected: with these tyrannical, violent, and excessive characters, who consider null and void and pretend to abolish the oracles brought to the old Laius, Apollo is deprived of all honor and, as a result, all respect for the gods disappears. The enigmatic chorus may be understood if its functions are placed in the context of the concluding scene between Oedipus and Tiresias. In that first chorus, it was a question of saying why the truth of the oracle was unsatisfactory. In the second chorus, now, after the second veridiction, it is a question of challenging Oedipus's knowledge or, rather, of picking up on the only part that conforms to *nomos* and, instead of condemning, of putting a malediction on that part of the *technē* that served to nourish the excesses of his tyrannical power.

Thus, the last alethurgy, the last production of truth, the last veridiction may begin. It is presented as being neither that of the gods (which was challenged for the reasons I mentioned) nor that of the kings (which was useful and fecund, but also had its excesses and its dark side). The veridiction that will be recognized is that of the servants. There are then two characters: the messenger from Corinth who comes to announce that Polybus is dead, and the shepherd of Cithaeron whom Oedipus, with his *technē* and in search of *tekmēria*, went to find in the depths of his woods. These two characters, the messenger who arrives spontaneously and the shepherd who is summoned, are brought face to face. And at this point, of course, the truth appears through this confrontation. The chorus, for that matter, announces it in advance. Assuming in a paradoxical, almost ironic way the position of the prophet, it says: "If I am a good prophet, if the light reveals the truth to me, yes, by Olympus"—this is an explicit reference, at the moment when the truth is going to appear in the very mouths of the servants, to the oracle of the gods and the authority of the divine word—"yes, by Olympus, as early as tomorrow, you will see that the Cithaeron has become one of Oedipus's compatriots and the truth of Oedipus's birth will be known."[74]

How does this last alethurgy unfold? Well, it unfolds—entirely and exhaustively—like a true judicial interrogatoire that follows all the procedural rules.

First, there is the interrogation of identity. When the shepherd of Cithaeron arrives, Oedipus, in his role as chief justice, poses the question: "Is this shepherd who has been brought to us truly the one who the messenger from Corinth once knew and who gave him the famous child who was to be Oedipus?" So Oedipus asks the question, and he gives a first element of response. He says: "I do not know him. I cannot even know if he is the same. But I recognize the servants that brought him and those servants are mine."[75] At this moment the choragus completes the point, saying: "I recognize the shepherd. He is indeed the one who was in the service of Laius."[76] And the Corinthian, the messenger from Corinth, brings the third element of recognition. Indeed, he says: "This man who I now see before me is indeed the one of whom I spoke[77] and who in time past gave me, handed me the child in question."[78]

After this interrogation of identity, the shepherd is questioned about what he did and what happened. The shepherd, naturally, resists sharing as much of his knowledge as possible. First, he refuses because he committed the fault of not killing Oedipus as Laius and Jocasta had asked of him, and then because he knows full well that what he is going to say will set off a catastrophe. But while the god could say at the beginning of the play, "I only speak when I wish to do so," or in any case this is what was said of the god, the god only speaks when he wants to; and while Tiresias could say, "I do not obey you, because I am not your servant. I am the servant of Loxias"; here, the shepherd will be obliged to speak. He is reminded that he must speak. And since he is still reluctant, he is threatened with torture: "Bind his hands,"[79] says Oedipus, "I will make you speak or you will be killed."[80] The threat of death punctuates the entire interrogation—this was clearly stated in classical Athenian law: that is, to obtain an avowal, torturing a slave was acceptable on the sole condition that it be authorized by his master.[81] Now this was precisely the case here: Oedipus himself, as the one who has power, who exercises power over the servant, threatens him with execution, and consequently the servant is going to be forced to tell the truth, to tell this truth, the truth of what he did. He is going to be obliged to avow. And the interrogation, in effect, unfolds around a precise point: what the witness himself did. It is no longer a question of prophetic words. It is no longer this great vision that cuts through time. It is not this light that comes from a released arrow. It is a question of what the witness himself might have done. "Do you remember that I told you this?"[82] says the servant of Corinth. "Who gave you the child? What was your intention in doing this or that?"[83] And the servant's response is grammatically very distinct. Each time the servant responds: "Yes, I myself found this child in the Valley of Cithaeron. Yes, I was keeping a herd. Yes, it was I who released your two feet."[84] "Yes, I am the one to whom Jocasta handed you."[85] "It is I who did not kill him—*autos*."[86]

I believe that we have here the very blueprint—and the introduction onto the stage—of this procedure of avowal, which is also characterized in the play by the acceptance of the chorus as being that which, as opposed to the other forms of veridiction, effectively produces an incontestable truth. For the truth to be juridically acceptable, it is not necessary that the gods speak. For the truth to be accepted, it is not necessary that it be produced by kings—because, if indeed they use the wise method of *tekmēria*, of signs, they may also use it to escape the destiny of the gods. With the slave, we have truthful speech [*une parole de vérité*], a truthful speech that does not even necessitate a consideration of the more or less probable signs that allow one to pull what one wants to know from what one doesn't know. This is a speech that is entirely true because the one who speaks may say: "Yes, I did that. Yes, I am the one, *autos*. I saw it. I heard it. I gave it. I did it."[87] And with this word, despite the fact that it emanates from the mouth of a slave who is threatened with execution, Oedipus's truth will appear. The chorus recognizes and accepts this truth. It alone ensures justice. And once this truth is effectively recognized, or rather, the very moment this truth is recognized by the chorus and by everyone—and by the spectators—at that moment, Oedipus recognizes himself. He recognizes himself as the one who did it all.

While all the elements of truth that he had already spoken, while all the predictions around him already told him, and had already told him on multiple occasions what had happened, Oedipus could only recognize himself when faced with an avowal—an avowal that, you will note, did not come from himself. Oedipus does not avow. What would he avow, in any case? Oedipus does not avow. The avowal comes from the slave. And it is when the slave produces this avowal, by means of this procedure, that Oedipus is able to say—recognizing himself and inhabiting in some sense this character that was designated by the slave's avowal—Oedipus is able to say: "In this way, all will be true in the end! I reveal myself to be the son of the one of whom I should not have been born. I reveal myself to be the husband of the one I should not have married. I reveal myself to be the murderer of the one I should not have killed."[88] In turn, Oedipus is finally able to say "I" about all his crimes.

Please excuse this somewhat long and, in any case, very partial reading of Sophocles' play. Do not think for a moment that I wanted to present anything like a global or exhaustive interpretation of *Oedipus Rex*. Nor should you think I wanted to present you with a chapter on the legal history of the emergence and establishment of avowal in Greek penal procedure. I simply wanted to show you how this procedure of avowal that was, if not recent at the moment when Sophocles wrote *Oedipus Rex*, at least a part of the judicial apparatus, part of a judicial practice that classical Athens was both proud of and celebrated but also questioned—it seems to me that it is interesting to see how avowal introduced itself with such solemnity into something as culturally and politically important as this ritual representation of law that the city of Athens gave itself.

I would like to underscore as well that Oedipus's realization advances exactly in step with the chorus's validation—or rather, what is discovered in himself, which is where most of the commentaries and analyses will end, this discovery of the self by Oedipus is fundamentally nothing more than the obverse side of the legitimate production of truth that is juridically acceptable and that is effectively accepted by the chorus. This legitimate truth is the one that is produced neither in the form of a prophecy nor in the form of a deduction through clues, but in the form of the interrogation of witnesses, the interrogation of oracular witnesses who are ultimately forced to avow what they have seen themselves, said themselves, done themselves.

Finally, what I wanted to emphasize is that, as you see, Oedipus, because he is a man of *technē*, finds himself placed between the prophetic word and the testimony of avowal. In one sense, we have Oedipus, with his *technē* and his tyranny as well, to thank for this procedure of searching out witnesses. He is the one who challenged the prophetic and oracular form of veridiction. He is the one who also wanted the interrogation of witnesses. He is the one who sent someone in search of the shepherd of Cithaeron. In this sense—and this is the good aspect of the tyrant—at this point he is still the savior of the city; he is still the one who righted the city; he is still the good pilot. And it is even thanks to this, thanks to this truth that is produced, that the city will possibly be saved. But—and this is the other side, that of tyrannical immoderation—in wanting to use the *technē* against the decrees of the gods in order to escape them, he simply tightens destiny's grip to the point of sealing the condemnation that had been spun for him.

In this sense, Oedipus was necessary for the truth to appear. He was necessary for the creation of this well-regulated form of the judicial machine that is capable of producing the truth. But he was eliminated, as a kind of "excess," now, by the very judicial machine he brought forth. And from the perspective of the foundation of law, the lesson of the tragedy is that the veridiction obtained by the correct procedure—while it did not take the same path as the word of the gods, even though one cannot dispense with it because the gods had spoken—this indispensable veridiction could do nothing but confirm, if properly done, the prophetic word of the gods. Oedipus's drama was his desire to escape the prophetic word of the gods precisely by establishing a procedure of veridiction. Once veridiction was obtained through the correct procedure—once the judicial machine functioned so well that it could extricate the most essential truth from the lips of the most unessential character (the slave)—at that moment, the truth that appeared through this purely human procedure in conformity with *nomos* and the law, this procedure only confirmed the prophetic words of the gods. This veridiction, thus developed and regulated in this way, does not obey the tyrant's excess: rather, it conforms with *nomos*, with the law, the law that comes from Olympus. And it is this law and fidelity to *nomos* that allows the truth-telling of the slave who saw to guarantee for the chorus the truth-telling of a seer who was blind. The public square that stages the judicial institutions assures, guarantees, and confirms what has been said through the flash of divine prophecy.

So this is how *Oedipus Rex* may serve not, once again, as a direct testimony of Athenian judicial procedure, nor as a direct testimony of its true history, but rather as the first dramatic representation of this relatively new judicial practice (relatively new at the time) that made avowal and all other regular procedures of avowal an essential piece of the judicial system.

NOTES

1. Foucault also analyzed *Oedipus Rex* in the following contexts: in 1971 in *Leçons sur la volonté de savoir: Cours au Collège de France, 1970–1971*, ed. Daniel Defert (Paris: Gallimard/Seuil, 2011), 177–92; in March 1972 in a lecture given at SUNY Buffalo ("Le savoir d'Oedipe"), published in *Leçons sur la volonté de savoir*, 223–53; in 1973 in "Truth and Juridical Forms," in Michel Foucault, *Power*, ed. James D. Faubion, 1–89 (New York: The New Press, 2000), 18–33; and in 1980 in *Du gouvernement des vivants: Cours au Collège de France, 1979–1980*, ed. Michel Senellart (Paris: Gallimard/Seuil, 2012), especially lectures of January 9, 16, 23, and 30, 1980. The theme of truth as the product of the confrontation of two half-truths was taken up again in the context of a comparison between *Oedipus Rex* and *Ion* in 1983. See Michel Foucault, *Le gouvernement de soi et des autres: Cours au Collège de France, 1982–1983*, ed. Frédéric Gros (Paris: Gallimard/Seuil, 2008), lectures of January 19 and 26, 1983, 71–136; English edition, Michel Foucault, *The Government of Self and Others: Lectures at the College de France, 1982–1983*, English series ed. Arnold I. Davidson, trans. Graham Burchell, 75–147. This comparison also takes up the themes of the necessary succession of moments of veridiction, a necessity that is carried over from the assumption of truth by the subject in *Wrong-Doing, Truth-Telling* to the right to speak in *Le gouvernement de soi et des autres* (French edition, 140; English edition, 152).

2. This is possibly a reference to the interpretation of the tragedy proposed by Sigmund Freud in *The Interpretation of Dreams* (1899). Foucault had contested Freud's reading as early as 1971 in his *Leçons sur la volonté de savoir*, where he referred to "Freud's error," as well as to that "of cultural theorists regarding Freud's error"—an allusion, according to Daniel Defert (in Foucault, *Leçons sur la volonté de savoir*, 193 n. 18), to Bronislaw Malinowski's book *La sexualité et sa répression dans les sociétés primitives* (Paris: Payot, 1939). For a similar reading see Jean-Pierre Vernant, "'Œdipe' sans complexe," *Raison présente* 4 (1967): 3–20 (reprinted in Jean-Pierre Vernant and Pierre Vidal-Naquet, *Œdipe et ses Mythes* [Brussels: Éditions Complexe, 2006], 1–22); see also Bernard Knox, *Oedipus at Thebes* (New Haven: Yale University Press, 1957), 4–5.

3. On this point see Louis Gernet, "Le temps dans les formes archaïques du droit," *Journal de Psychologie* 53 (July–September 1956): 379–406; English translation, "The Concept of Time in the Earliest Forms of Law," 216–39, in Louis Gernet, *The Anthropology of Ancient Greece*

(Baltimore: Johns Hopkins University Press, 1968); see also Marcel Detienne, *Les maîtres de vérité dans la Grèce archaïque* (Paris: Librairie François Maspero, 1967), 130 n. 101.

4. Foucault mentioned this theatrical question on multiple occasions. On February 25, 1976, he offered a series of remarks on Greek tragedy as "tragedy of law," and on Shakespearean tragedies as "rituals of re-memorization of problems of public law," which he extended to the tragedies of Corneille and Racine. See Michel Foucault, "*Il faut défendre la société*": *Cours au Collège de France 1975–1976*, eds. Mauro Bertani and Alessandro Fontana (Paris: Gallimard/Seuil, 1997), 155–57; English edition, Michel Foucault, *Society Must Be Defended: Lectures at the Collège de France, 1975–1976*, English series ed. Arnold I. Davidson, trans. David Macey (London: Penguin, 2004), 174–75. On March 15, 1978, Foucault offered a series of remarks on the "theatrical practices of the reason of state." Here he evoked the appearance in the classical age of a "political theater with the functioning of theater as its opposite, in the literary sense of the term, as the privileged site of political representation and particularly the representation of the coup d'état." He observed that Shakespearean theater as well as the theater of Corneille and Racine offered "many representations of *coups d'état*." Michel Foucault, *Sécurité, territoire, population: Cours au Collège de France 1977–1978*, ed. Michel Senellart (Paris: Gallimard/Seuil, 2004), 271; English edition, Michel Foucault, *Security, Territory, Population: Lectures at the Collège de France 1977–1978*, English series ed. Arnold I. Davidson, trans. Graham Burchell (New York: Picador, 2007), 265.

5. On this point, cf. Foucault, *Leçons sur la volonté de savoir*, 161–93 (lectures of March 10 and 17, 1971). On the question of religious sullying, it is possible that one of the sources Foucault consulted was Louis Moulinier, *Le pur et l'impur dans la pensée et la sensibilité des Grecs jusqu'à la fin du IVe siècle avant J.-C.* (Paris: Klincksiek, 1952), a text which is discussed by Jean-Pierre Vernant in "Le pur et l'impur," *L'Année sociologique,* 1953–54, Paris, 331–52 (reproduced in Vernant, *Mythe et Société en Grèce ancienne* [Paris: François Maspero, 1974, new edition 1982], 121–40).

6. See Plato, *Œuvres complètes. Les Lois. Livres VII–X*, trans. and ed. Auguste Diès (Paris: Les Belles Lettres, 2003); English edition, *The Laws of Plato*, trans. and ed. Thomas L. Pangle (New York: Basic Books, 1980). Two excerpts from book 9 of *The Laws* are applicable to Oedipus's situation. The first establishes the punishments that must be applied when someone kills his father or mother (book 9, 869 a–c, Diès, 121–22; Pangle trans., 263–64). The second, which Foucault presents in detail later in the same lecture, establishes the procedures to be employed when the murderer is unknown (book 9, 874 a–b, Diès, 128–29; Pangle trans., 269).

7. Sophocle, *Œdipe Roi*, verse 102, trans. P. Mazon (Paris: Les Belles Lettres, 2007), 10–11; English edition, *Oedipus the King*, ed. David Grene and Richmond Lattimore (Chicago: University of Chicago Press, 1942), 15 ("Who is this man whose fate the God pronounces?"). Note that the Greek word used here is *tychē* (fate); on the various significations of *tychē* in the text of Sophocles' tragedy, see Knox, *Oedipus at Thebes*, 176–81.

8. Daniel Defert (in Foucault, *Leçons sur la volonté de savoir*, 192 n. 1) gives as the edition of reference *Œdipe-Roi*, in Sophocle, *Œuvres*, vol. 1, ed. and trans. P. Masquenay (Paris: Les Belles Lettres, 1922). At Louvain-la-Neuve in 1981, Foucault also uses the translation by Paul Mazon without specifying the exact edition, which could therefore refer to either *Œdipe Roi*, in Sophocle, *Œuvres*, vol. 2, ed. A. Dain and trans. Paul Mazon (Paris: Les Belles Lettres, 1972), or *Œdipe Roi*, in Sophocle, *Tragédies complètes*, trans. Paul Mazon (Paris: Gallimard, coll. "Folio," 1973). The references to the French text we will henceforth use will be to Sophocle, *Œdipe Roi*, trans. Paul Mazon (Paris: Les Belles Lettres, 2007).

9. On the notions of *mēnuein* and *mēnusis*, see Knox, *Oedipus at Thebes*, 80, on which, it would appear, Foucault rests his analysis here and in the following three paragraphs.

10. Ibid., 81.

11. Sophocle, *Œdipe Roi*, verse 132; Mazon, 12–13; Grene and Lattimore, 16 ("I will bring this to light again").

12. Cf. Knox, *Oedipus at Thebes*, 80–81.

13. Sophocle, *Œdipe Roi*, verses 224–75; Mazon, 18–23; Grene and Lattimore, 19–21; cf. Knox, *Oedipus at Thebes*, 81–82; Detienne, *Les maîtres de vérité dans la Grèce archaïque*, 48–59.

14. Thucydide, *La guerre du Péloponnèse*, book 6, sections 27–29 and 60–61, trans. Louis Bodin and Jacqueline de Romilly (Paris: Les Belles Lettres, 1955), 21–22 and 44–46; English edition, Thucydides, *The Peloponnesian War*, ed. Martin Hammond and Peter John Rhodes (Oxford: Oxford University Press, 2009), 322–23 and 339–40. Cf. Knox, *Oedipus at Thebes*, 82.

15. Plutarque, *Les vies des hommes illustres: Vie d'Alcibiade*, sections 18–23, trans. Dominique Ricard (Paris: Lefèvre, 1838), 488–92; English edition, Plutarch, *Lives, Volume IV: Alcibiades and Coriolanus; Lysander and Sulla*, trans. Bernadotte Perrin (Cambridge, MA: Loeb Classical Library, 1916), chapters 18–23, pp. 47–67; cf. Knox, *Oedipus at Thebes*, 82.

16. Platon, *Œuvres complètes: Les Lois, livre IX*, 874a–b, ed. Diès, 128; trans. Pangle, 269.

17. Ibid., 874b, Diès, 128–29; Pangle, 269.

18. Sophocle, *Œdipe Roi*, verse 319; Mazon, 26–27; Grene and Lattimore, 23 ("What is this? How sad you are now you have come!"); cf. Knox, *Oedipus at Thebes*, at 84 and 226 n. 134.

19. Sophocle, *Œdipe Roi*, verse 432; Mazon, 34–35; Grene and Lattimore, 29.

20. Cf. Knox, *Oedipus at Thebes*, 83: "But when Oedipus's appeal to the prophet is followed by Tiresias's disturbing regrets that he has come, we find ourselves suddenly in a familiar ambience, the examination of a reluctant witness."

21. Oedipus dismisses Tiresias by asking him to leave (see verse 431; Mazon, 34–35; Grene and Lattimore, 29: *apostrapheis apei*), but he does not use the term *aphes*, which indeed means "be gone." Foucault is probably citing Sophocles' text from memory. According to Knox, *Oedipus at Thebes*, 84, *aphes* is the technical term, in ancient Greek penal procedure, for release, acquittal, or dismissal.

22. Sophocle, *Œdipe Roi*, verse 642–43; Mazon, 50–51; Grene and Lattimore, 38; cf. Knox, *Oedipus at Thebes*, at 90 and 229 (discussing Plato, *The Laws*, book 11, 936d).

23. According to Aristotle, histories are simple or complex depending upon whether the actions they imitate are simple or complex. An action that is "as one continuous whole, I call simple, when the change in the hero's fortunes takes place without Peripety or Discovery"; while a complex action is where the reversal takes place "when it involves one or the other, or both." Aristote, *Poétique*, X, trans. M. Magnien (Paris: Le Livre de Poche, 2008), 100; English edition, Aristotle, *Poetics*, in *The Basic Works of Aristotle*, ed. Richard McKeon (New York: Random House, 1941), 1465.

24. *Peripeteia*, a reversal. Aristotle cites Oedipus as an example: "Here the opposite state of things is produced by the Messenger, who, coming to gladden Oedipus and to remove his fears as to his mother, reveals the secret of his birth." Ibid., XI, ed. Magnien, 101; ed. McKeon, 1465.

25. Recognition or discovery (*anagnōrisis*), the other element of complex action, is the "change from ignorance to knowledge, and thus to either love or hate, in the personages marked for good or evil fortune." Ibid., XI, ed. Magnien, 101; ed. McKeon, 1465. Aristotle uses *Oedipus* twice as an illustration of tragic beauty. In chapter 11 he writes: "The finest form of Discovery is one attended

by Peripeties, like that which goes with the Discovery in *Oedipus*." Ibid., XI, ed. Magnien, 101; ed. McKeon, 1465. In chapter 16 Aristotle writes: "The best of all Discoveries, however, is that arising from the incidents themselves, when the great surprise comes about through a probable incident, like that in the *Oedipus* of Sophocles." He then makes a distinction between four different forms of recognition (by distinctive signs, imagined by the poet, brought about by memory, and based on a deduction). Ibid., XVI, ed. Magnien, 109–10; ed. McKeon, 1471–72. Cf. Jean-Pierre Vernant, "Ambiguïté et renversement: Sur la structure énigmatique d'*Oedipe-Roi*" [see "Ambiguity and Reversal" in this volume], in *Échanges et Communications: Mélanges offerts à Claude Lévi-Strauss à l'occasion de son soixantième anniversaire* (Paris: Mouton, 1970), 2: 1253–73; republished in Jean-Pierre Vernant and Pierre Vidal-Naquet, *Mythe et tragédie en Grèce ancienne* (Paris: La Découverte, 1972), 1: 99–131. Foucault refers to this study in his lecture of January 16, 1980, at the Collège de France in *Du gouvernement des vivants*; and Foucault, "Le savoir d'Œdipe," in Foucault, *Leçons sur la volonté de savoir*, 225.

26. This is possibly a reference to Marcel Detienne, *Les maîtres de vérité dans la Grèce archaïque*, 102.

27. The idea of truth being produced by two persons, in a couple, who speak in complementarity—what Foucault refers to in "Le savoir d'Œdipe" as the "law of halves" (226)—refers both to the thematic of proof (Foucault, "Le savoir d'Œdipe," 229; *Leçons sur la volonté de savoir*, 191), and to what Marcel Detienne called the "secularization of speech" in *Les maîtres de vérité dans la Grèce archaïque*, 81; see also Detienne, ibid., 100–101, and Louis Gernet, "Le temps dans les formes archaïques du droit," 1982 edition, 129–37.

28. In 1971, 1972, and 1973, Foucault analyzes Sophocles' tragedy not in terms of a succession of alethurgies, but instead as the clash of different types of knowledge [*savoirs*]. See lecture of March 17, 1971, and "Le savoir d'Œdipe," in Foucault, *Leçons sur la volonté de savoir*, 189–92 and 225–51. The differentiation of types of knowledge, as Daniel Defert notes, was theorized by Foucault in his *Archaeology of Knowledge* (1969). The theorization of the different forms of alethurgy will be further developed and completed in *Le courage de la vérité: Cours au Collège de France*, 1984, ed. Frédéric Gros (Paris: Gaillmard/Seuil, 2009), especially in the lecture of February 1, 1984; English edition, Michel Foucault, *The Courage of Truth: The Government of Self and Others II: Lectures at the Collège de France, 1983–1984*, English series ed. Arnold I. Davidson, trans. Graham Burchell (New York: Palgrave, 2011).

29. CREON: King Phoebus in plain words commanded us to drive out a pollution from our land, pollution grown ingrained within the land; drive it out, said the God, not cherish it, till it's past cure.
   OEDIPUS: What is the rite of purification? How shall it be done?
   CREON: By banishing a man, or expiation of blood by blood, since it is murder guilt which holds our city in this destroying storm.
   OEDIPUS: Who is this man whose fate the God pronounces?
   CREON: My Lord, before you piloted the state we had a king called Laius.
   OEDIPUS: I know of him by hearsay. I have not seen him.
   CREON: The God commanded clearly: let some one punish with force this dead man's murderers.
   OEDIPUS: Where are they in the world? Where would a trace of this old crime be found? It would be hard to guess where.
   CREON: The clue is in this land; that which is sought is found; the unheeded thing escapes.
      . . .
   Sophocles, *Œdipus the King*, verses 96–111; Grene and Lattimore, 14–15; Mazon, 8–11.

30. CHOIR: . . . but since Phoebus set the quest it is his part to tell who the man is.

OEDIPUS: Right; but to put compulsion on the Gods against their will—no man can do
that.

Ibid., verses 278–81; Grene and Lattimore, 21; Mazon, 22–23.

31. Ibid., verses 322–23; Mazon, 26–27; Grene and Lattimore, 23.

32. Ibid., verses 330–31; Mazon, 26–27; Grene and Lattimore, 24.

33. Ibid., verses 345–49; Mazon, 28–29; Grene and Lattimore, 25. The enigmatic character of
prophetic veridiction will become, in *The Courage of Truth*, one of the traits by means of which
Foucault will distinguish this form of truth-telling from *parrhēsia*.

34. Ibid., verses 352 and 362; Mazon, 28–29; Grene and Lattimore, 25–26.

35. Ibid., verses 366–67; Mazon, 28–29; Grene and Lattimore, 26; also ibid., verses 445–61; Mazon,
34–37; Grene and Lattimore, 30.

36. Ibid., verses 404–5; Mazon, 32–33; Grene and Lattimore, 28.

37. Ibid., verses 485–86; Mazon, 38–39; Grene and Lattimore, 31.

38. Ibid., verses 408–10; Mazon, 32–33; Grene and Lattiore, 28.

39. Ibid., verse 356; Mazon, 28–29; Grene and Lattimore, 25.

40. Ibid., verses 473–75; Mazon, 36–37; Green and Lattimore, 31.

41. See, e.g., ibid., verse 362; Mazon, 28–29; Grene and Lattimore, 26 ("I say you are the murderer of
the king whose murderer you seek").

42. Ibid., verses 370–71 and 374; Mazon, 30–31; Grene and Lattimore, 26.

43. Ibid., verse 413 and 424–25; Mazon, 32–33; Grene and Lattimore, 28.

44. According to Jean-Pierre Vernant ("Figuration de l'invisible et catégorie psychologique du double:
Le colossos," presentation at the conference on "Le signe et les systèmes de signes," Royaumont,
April 12–15, 1962, in Vernant, *Mythe et pensée chez les Grecs, II* [Paris: Maspero, 1974], 75 n.
32), the seer, like the colossus, "belongs at the same time to the world of the living and to that of
the dead. It's this ambiguity that is conveyed by the image of the 'blind person who can see.'" Cf.
Marcel Detienne, *Les maîtres de vérité dans la Grèce archaïque*, 47.

45. Sophocle, *Œdipe Roi*, verse 433; Mazon, 34–35; Grene and Lattimore, 29.

46. Ibid., verse 365; Mazon, 28–29; Grene and Lattimore, 26.

47. "Who is the man proclaimed by Delphi's prophetic rock as the bloody handed murderer, the doer
of deeds that none dare name? . . . For the child of Zeus leaps in arms upon him with fire and the
lightning bolt, and terribly close on his heels are the Fates that never miss. [*Antistrophe*] Lately
from snowy Parnassus clearly the voice flashed forth, bidding each Theban track him down, the
unknown murderer. In the savage forests he lurks and in the caverns like the mountain bull. He
is sad and lonely, and lonely his feet that carry him far from the navel of earth; but its prophecies,
ever living, flutter around his head." Ibid., verses 463–82; Grene and Lattimore, 30–31; Mazon,
36–39.

48. "The augur has spread confusion, terrible confusion; I do not approve what was said nor can I
deny it. I do not know what to say; I am in a flutter of foreboding; I never heard in the present
nor past of a quarrel between the sons of Labdacus and Polybus, that I might bring as proof in
attacking the popular fame of Oedipus, seeking to take vengeance for undiscovered death in the

line of Labdacus. [*Antistrophe*] Truly Zeus and Apollo are wise and in human things all knowing; but amongst men there is no distinct judgement, between the prophet and me—which of us is right. One man may pass another in wisdom but I would never agree with those that find fault with the king till I should see the word proved right beyond doubt." Ibid., verses 483–506; Grene and Lattimore, 31–32; Mazon, 38–39.

49. In his March 24, 1982, lecture in *The Hermeneutics of the Subject*, 445–48 of the French edition and 464–67 of the English translation, Foucault explains why, for the Greeks, one's back was turned to the future, so that one had the past in front of oneself and the future behind. This is helpful background to this intriguing passage. Thanks to Daniel Nichanian for this useful reference.

50. Sophocle, *Œdipe Roi*, verses 497–99; Mazon, 38–39; Grene and Lattimore, 31.

51. Ibid., verses 499–500; Mazon, 38–39; Grene and Lattimore, 31.

52. Ibid., verses 502–6; Mazon, 38–39; Grene and Lattimore, 31–32.

53. Ibid., verses 504–6; Mazon, 38–39; Grene and Lattimore, 32 (" . . . but I would never agree with those that find fault with the king till I should see the word proved right beyond doubt").

54. Ibid., verse 508; Mazon, 40–41; Grene and Lattimore, 32.

55. Ibid., verses 724–25; Mazon, 56–57; Grene and Lattimore, 42.

56. Ibid., verses 708–9; Mazon, 54–55; Grene and Lattimore, 41.

57. Ibid., verse 710; Mazon, 54–55; Grene and Lattimore, 41.

58. "Insolence breeds the tyrant, insolence if it is glutted with a surfeit, unseasonable, unprofitable, climbs to the roof-top and plunges sheer down to the ruin that must be, and there its feet are no service. But I pray that the God may never abolish the eager ambition that profits the state. For I shall never cease to hold the God as our protector. [*Strophe*] If a man walks with haughtiness of hand or word and gives no heed to Justice and the shrines of Gods despises—may an evil doom smite him for his ill-starred pride of heart!—if he reaps gains without justice and will not hold from impiety and his fingers itch for untouchable things. When such things are done, what man shall contrive to shield his soul from the shafts of the God? When such deeds are held in honour, why should I honour the Gods in the dance?" Ibid., verses 872–96; Grene and Lattimore, 48; Mazon, 66–67.

59. Ibid., verses 906–10; Mazon, 68–69; Grene and Lattimore, 49 ("The oracles concerning Laius are old and dim and men regard them not. Apollo is nowhere clear in honour; God's service perishes").

60. Foucault had already privileged the knowledge of Oedipus, rather than his lack of knowledge or unconscious, in "Le savoir d'Œdipe" (Foucault, *Leçons sur la volonté de savoir*, 234, 245, and 250–51). These themes concerning the will to know and Oedipus's knowledge are also developed by Vernant in his essay "Ambiguïté et renversement" [see "Ambiguity and Reversal" in this volume], and by Knox in *Oedipus at Thebes* (see especially the index entries for "Oedipus" at 276–77, including "and the scientific spirit," "intellectual progress," "as investigator," "as questioner," "as revealer," "as teacher," "as discoverer," "as physician," and "as mathematician").

61. Sophocle, *Œdipe Roi*, verses 380–82; Mazon, 30; Grene and Lattimore, 27.

62. Ibid., verses 380–81; Mazon, 31; Grene and Lattimore, 27 ("Wealth, sovereignty and skill outmatching skill for the contrivance of an envied life! Great store of jealousy fill your treasury chests . . .").

63. Ibid., verses 583–86; Mazon, 46–47; Grene and Lattimore, 36 ("Not if you will reflect on it as I do. Consider, first, if you think anyone would choose to rule and fear rather than rule and sleep untroubled by a fear if power were equal in both cases").

64. The reference here is either to Antiphon the Sophist, mentioned by Xenophon, or his contemporary, Antiphon the logographer, mentioned by Thucydides. The latter Antiphon was born around 480, and started out by devoting himself to the oratorical arts and writing defense pleas and speeches before playing a leading role in the oligarchic revolution of the Four Hundred; brought to justice after the fall of the oligarchs, he was sentenced to death and executed in 411 for having contributed to the overthrow of Athenian democracy. See Antiphon, *L'apologie d'Antiphon; ou, Logos peri metastaseos: D'après des fragments inédits sur papyrus d'Egypte*, ed. Jules Nicole (Geneva-Basel: Librairie Georg, 1907), at 12–14. The question of knowing whether Antiphon the sophist and Antiphon the logographer were the same person is discussed by, among others, Louis Gernet in his introduction to Antiphon, *Discours*, followed by *Fragments d'Antiphon le Sophiste*, ed. and trans. Louis Gernet (Paris: Les Belles Lettres, 1923), a work that Foucault probably knew, and later by Gerard Pendrick in his introduction to Antiphon, *Antiphon the Sophist: The Fragments*, ed. and trans. Gerard J. Pendrick (Cambridge: Cambridge University Press, 2002).

65. Sophocle, *Œdipe Roi*, verses 587–600; Mazon, 46–47; Grene and Lattimore, 36 ("I, at least, I was not born with such a frantic yearning to be a king—but to do what kings do. . . . As it stands now, the prizes are all mine—and without fear. But if I were the king myself, I must do much that went against the grain. . . . Now every man's my pleasure; every man greets me; now those who are your suitors fawn on me,—success for them depends upon my favour. Why should I let all this go to win that? My mind would not be traitor if it's wise . . .").

66. Foucault is possibly making reference to the following verses in which three concepts are mentioned: *archē, dynasteia,* and *tyrannis.* "Comment pourrais-je donc trouver le trône [*turannis*] préférable à un pouvoir [*arkhes*], à une autorité [*dunasteias*] qui ne m'apportent aucun souci?" Ibid., verses 592–93; Mazon, 46–47; Grene and Lattimore, 36 ("How should despotic rule seem sweeter to me than painless power and an assured authority?")

67. "Je ne suis pas né avec le désir d'être roi [*turannos einai*], mais bien avec celui de vivre comme un roi (*turanna dran*)." Ibid., verses 587–89; Mazon, 46–47; Grene and Lattimore, 36 ("I, at least, I was not born with such a frantic yearning to be a king—but to do what kings do. And so it is with every one who has learned wisdom and self-control").

68. The word *technē* appears in the dialogue between Oedipus and Tiresias in verses 357 and 389. The first time it is mentioned is in the following line: ibid., verse 357, Mazon, 28–29; Grene and Lattimore, 25 ("And who has taught you truth? Not your profession surely!"). The word appears for a second time in the passage where Oedipus, after having deplored the jealousies generated by his wealth, power, and *technē technēs*, calls upon Tiresias, who is blind to his art. Ibid., verses 389–92; Mazon, 30–31; Grene and Lattimore, 27.

69. Ibid., verses 708–9; Mazon, 54–55; Grene and Lattimore, 41.

70. There is a break here due to the tape change. The change is responsible for a lacuna that can be filled from the original typescript, deposited at the IMEC, of an audio recording that has since been lost. In the following paragraph we reproduce the entirety of the extract from the original typescript with a few small spelling corrections:

> In fact, what characterizes Tiresias's practice is not the possession of *technē*. If Tiresias tells the truth, it is because there is a natural link between what he says and the truth. The truth dwells in his words—"I have the truth within me and you know it," Tiresias says. And this possibility of truth-telling without having recourse to *technē* allows

Tiresias . . . When he speaks of what he does, he uses the word *phronein*; he thinks, he reflects, he turns inward on himself. It is within himself that, hearing the words of the god, he grasps the truth and tells it. There are then three elements, if you will: first there is the power of Creon, which is aristocratic and is exercised through the law and by the law of precedence—it is a power that implies *sōphronēma* as a virtue. There is the power of Creon, which is a power to know the truth and tell it, but which does not require any particular technique because there is a shared nature between the truth and what he says. There is the power of Tiresias, who took part in an activity and demonstrated his strength and virtue as a man through reflection on himself and through the original profundity of his thought. What does Oedipus do in relation to all this? What does Oedipus's *technē* consist of? For he has *technē* while the others do not. It consists of his ability to discover (*euriskein*). Those who speak of Oedipus make reference to this capacity for discovery. This is what characterizes his *technē*. The city called upon him so that he might relieve them (verse 27) and he announced his solution to all the people (verse 68). He accused the Thebans of not taking on the task of finding the murderer that he was going to discover (verse 258). He tries to discover the murderer himself (verse 340). He believes he has discovered the plot spun by Creon (verse 546) and then Tiresias tells him as well, does the knowledge of men . . . The gods are certain . . . (typescript, lecture of April 28, 1981, 14–15).

71. According to Knox (*Oedipus at Thebes*, 122–23), this refers to a sentence of Alcmaeon of Croton, philosopher and medical theorist of the fifth century BCE, who used the verb *tekmairesthai* in a scientific sense, "to describe human knowledge as distinguished from that of the gods: 'The gods have certainty, for men there is inference.'" Ibid., 123; see also ibid., 239 n. 55.

72. The word *tekmērion* does not appear in the text of *Oedipus Rex*. However, the form *tekmairetai*, which is built from the same radical, is mentioned once by Jocasta. Sophocle, *Œdipe Roi*, verses 914–15; Mazon, 68–69; Grene and Lattimore, 49; cf. Knox, *Oedipus at Thebes*, 123.

73. Sophocle, *Œdipe Roi*, verses 1080–81; Mazon, 82–83; Grene and Lattimore, 58 ("But I account myself a child of Fortune, beneficent Fortune, and I shall not be dishonoured "). On this identification, see Vernant, "Ambiguïté et renversement" [see "Ambiguity and Reversal" in this volume]. Note that Foucault had already cited this verse in "Le savoir d'Œdipe," where he referred to it to characterize tyrannical power (236) and knowledge (243), and in both cases associated it with Oedipus's pride.

74. Sophocle, *Œdipe Roi*, verses 1087–107; Mazon, 82–83; Grene and Lattimore, 58–59.

75. Ibid., verses 1110–16; Mazon, 84–85; Grene and Lattimore, 59 ("If some one like myself who never met him may make a guess,—I think this is the herdsman, whom we were seeking. His old age is consonant with the other. And besides, the men who bring him I recognize as my own servants. You perhaps may better me in knowledge since you've seen the man before").

76. Ibid., verses 1117–18; Mazon, 84–85; Grene and Lattimore, 59.

77. Ibid., verse 1120; Mazon, 84–85; Grene and Lattimore, 59.

78. Ibid., verses 1142–43; Mazon, 86–87; Grene and Lattimore, 60 (the messenger from Corinth asks: "Do you remember giving me a child to bring up as my foster child?").

79. Ibid., verse 1154; Mazon, 86–87; Grene and Lattimore, 61.

80. Ibid., verse 1158; Mazon, 86–87; Grene and Lattimore, 61.

81. On this point, see Louis Gernet, *Droit et société dans la Grèce ancienne* (Paris: Recueil Sirey, 1955),

153, where he writes that "torture of slaves was commonly practiced in murder cases and there are many examples." Similarly, "the consent of the master" is necessary to ensure the appearance of the slave as witness because as "owner, he has the right of opposition." However, the text explains that "the faculty of witnessing excludes the use of torture. And yet, the torture of slaves was commonly practiced in murder cases and we have multiple examples [. . . .] The law declared that a slave's testimony was acceptable. As a result, it was not forbidden to use another means of evidence. In other words, the slave would only testify if the adversary consented. The adversary could insist that the slave be tortured." See the chapter "Aspects du droit athénien de l'esclavage," 151–72; Knox, *Oedipus at Thebes*, 97–98.

82. Sophocle, *Œdipe Roi*, verses 1132–40; Mazon, 86–87; Grene and Lattimore, 60 (the messenger from Corinth says: "That is no wonder, master. But I'll make him remember what he does not know. For I know, that he well knows the country of Cithaeron, how he with two flocks, I with one kept company for three years—each year half a year—from spring till autumn time and then when winter came I drove my flocks to our fold home again and he to Laius' steadings. Well—am I right or not in what I said we did?").

83. The question is posed by Oedipus to the shepherd. Ibid., verses 1163–74; Mazon, 88–89; Grene and Lattimore, 62–63.

84. These elements are given by the messenger from Corinth:

OEDIPUS: Was I a child you bought or found when I was given to him?
MESSENGER: On Cithaeron's slopes in the twisting thickets you were found.
OEDIPUS: And why were you a traveller in those parts?
MESSENGER: I was in charge of mountain flocks. . . .
OEDIPUS: What ailed me when you took me in your arms?
MESSENGER: In that your ankles should be witnesses.
OEDIPUS: Why do you speak of that old pain?
MESSENGER: I loosed you; the tendons of your feet were pierced and fettered.

Ibid., verses 1025–28 and 1031–34; Grene and Lattimore, 54–55; Mazon, 76–79.

85. Ibid., verse 1174; Mazon, 88–89; Grene and Lattimore, 63.

86. Ibid., verse 1179; Mazon, 88–89; Grene and Lattimore, 63.

87. Foucault, in his *Leçons sur la volonté de savoir*, 179, portrays the shepherd of Cithaeron not as an avowing subject but rather as a witness, an *istōr*; and the same is true as well in "Le savoir d'Œdipe," 248. On the notion of the *istōr*, see [Foucault's] "First Lecture" [in *Wrong-Doing, Truth-Telling*], n. 29; see also Detienne, *Les maîtres de vérité dans la Grèce archaïque*, at 101; Gernet, *Droit et institutions en Grèce antique*, 152–53; and Foucault, *Leçons sur la volonté de savoir*, 77–78.

88. Sophocle, *Œdipe Roi*, verses 1182–85; Mazon, 90–91; Grene and Lattimore, 63.

The Murderers of Laius

William Chase Greene

N ear a fork in the road leading from Delphi to Thebes, Oedipus met an elderly man with his attendants; after an altercation, he slew not only the old man but, as he supposed, all the party, and went on his way. Apparently the incident almost faded from his memory,—a surprising fact, perhaps, but perhaps less surprising in the good old days of the heroic age than in our day; at any rate, when he arrived at Thebes and almost immediately became king of a distressed land, his suspicions were not aroused, if we are to believe Sophocles, when he learned the generally accepted story of the death of his predecessor King Laius. To be sure, he learned only the barest outline of the story, and had no idea from what source it emanated (*O. T.* 105; 109–13; 116–23; 292f.). And certain it is that if his suspicions had been fully aroused at once, the train of events comprising most of the antecedents and the action of the *Oedipus Tyrannus* would have been blocked from the start. As it is, Sophocles somewhat strains our credulity in this as in other matters lying "outside the action proper"; so Aristotle noted (*Poetics*, 1454b, ἔξω τῆς τραγῳδίας). Of his successors in the treatment of the story, Corneille, Dryden, and Voltaire found it difficult to account

First published in *Transactions of the American Philological Association* 60 (1929).

for this delayed suspicion, Corneille blandly ignoring it, Dryden betraying what Jebb calls "an uneasy conscience," and glossing it over by suggesting that the story of Laius' death had been forgotten "like a morning dream," Voltaire elaborating an explanation as improbable as the circumstance to be explained.[1] Now if Sophocles, too, puts a strain on our credulity at this point, it is best to admit, with Jebb, that "the true defence of this improbability consist in frankly recognizing it."[2] Nevertheless it seems to me that Sophocles, far from bungling the matter, has made a virtue of necessity. The necessity is to delay the ἀναγνώρισις [anagnōrisis, recognition] and make it coincide with the περιπέτεια [peripeteia, reversal]. The virtue consists in the choice and the manipulation of a method that heightens the tragic irony of Oedipus' position, and that also derives reasonably, as we should expect of Sophocles, from the character of one of the persons in the play.

In order to appreciate the poet's method, we must first review the passages in the play in which reference is made to the death of Laius. The earliest reference comes from Creon, who reports the command of Phoebus, enjoining on Oedipus the wreaking of vengeance on the unknown murderers of the former king:

> τούτου θανόντος νῦν ἐπιστέλλει σαφῶς
> τοὺς αὐτοέντας χειρὶ τιμωρεῖν τινας. (107f.)

We can not help noting at once the use of the plural, "murderers," in spite of the fact that we, like the Athenian audience and the gods, know full well that it was one man, Oedipus, who did the fell deed. But how does the phrase fall on his ears? τοὺς αὐτοέντας . . . τινας—a vague phrase, but enough to let him infer that Laius died a violent death at the hands of several definite human beings, as yet unidentified, but to be sought out. There is nothing yet to excite his suspicions.

It soon transpires that this story was brought to Thebes by the one survivor of Laius' party, and that he had reported but one fact,—namely, that a number of brigands had fallen on Laius.

> ληστὰς ἔφασκε συντυχόντας οὐ μιᾷ
> ῥώμῃ νιν κτανεῖν, ἀλλὰ σὺν πλήθει χερῶν. (122f.)

Any self-incriminating suspicions on the part of Oedipus are further disarmed by the emphatic position of ληστάς, given in the plural, and expanded both by the explicit denial of a single murderer's responsibility and by the suggestion of a crowd.[3] In spite of this very pointed use of the plural Oedipus immediately replies with a question in the *singular*: πῶς οὖν ὁ ληστής κτλ (124f.). "How could the *murderer* have dared the deed, unless bribed?" Jebb (note on 294) regards the reversion from plural to singular as "unconscious." That is a natural, but not complete, explanation. Oedipus is politically minded: it is not merely Laius, but the monarchy that has fallen. And, furthermore, perhaps because he, too, has once killed his man and embers of old memories are faintly fanned, he pictures in his mind an individual murderer who strikes the blow, even though he can conceive of the deed only as the result of a bribe. So, too, in the immediate sequel, he declares his intention of taking vengeance, both in behalf of the murdered man and in his own behalf, on the *murderer*, thus unconsciously by the use of the singular giving a powerful impetus to the irony of the whole passage.

ὅστις γὰρ ἦν ἐκεῖνον ὁ κτανών κτλ. (139)

Presently, in making his proclamation and curse on the unknown agency that caused the death of Laius, Oedipus again uses the singular:

ὅστις ποθ᾽ ὑμῶν Λάιον τὸν Λαβδάκου
κάτοιδεν ἀνδρὸς ἐκ τίνος διώλετο,
τοῦτον κελεύω πάντα σημαίνειν ἐμοί. (224ff.)[4]

"Whoever of you knows at what man's hands Laius perished, him I bid reveal this man to me." And Oedipus proceeds to deal with this culprit,—τὸν αὐτόχειρα (231),[5]—and his possible shielders, in such a way as again to expose himself to the arrows of irony. To be sure, he incidentally reckons with the contingency that the perpetrator of the deed may have had accomplices: he curses him whether the undetected offender be single or one of several.

κατεύχομαι δὲ τὸν δεδρακότ᾽, εἴτε τις
εἷς ὢν λέληθεν εἴτε πλειόνων μέτα, κτλ. (246f.)

But when the chorus, enjoined to assist in the man-hunt, make reply through their leader, it is to a single culprit that reference is made:

οὔτ᾽ ἔκτανον γὰρ οὔτε τὸν κτανόντ᾽ ἔχω
δεῖξαι. (276f.)

Yet before Teiresias, already summoned, enters, the leader of the chorus, referring to the current, now almost forgotten version of the story of the death of Laius, makes the remark: "He was said to have met his death at the hands of certain wayfarers" (πρός τινων ὁδοιπόρων, 292). With this version of the story, Oedipus himself immediately concurs; it is what he has heard (293). We note that it preserves the plural, the form in which the survivor brought the tale to Thebes, though substituting "wayfarers" for the "brigands" of line 122. Oedipus does not demur at the changed description,—wayfarers or brigands, it matters not; he recognizes in it what may be termed the vulgate version of the story. And that version includes several persons. But the survivor, the witness, is not yet present to be cross-examined (293). And the leader of the chorus, thinking intently of the culprit, whose fear of the curse must reveal or exile him, refers to him in the singular,—unconsciously, Jebb observes. Oedipus, however, is not so certain that the slayer's conscience will prove to be tender; a man who shrinks not from a deed fears not a word (295). Oedipus still carries in his mind the image of a single murderer, as person or as type.

Teiresias enters, and Oedipus, in charging him to reveal what he knows, uses the vulgate version, and speaks of "the murderers" (τοὺς κτανόντας, 308). Teiresias, when driven to speak out of the fullness of his knowledge, naturally denounces Oedipus in the singular as the murderer (φονέα, 362), and refers in the singular to "the man whom thou hast long sought" (449). In the ensuing *stasimon* the chorus, their ears still ringing with the amazing words of Teiresias, follow imaginatively the fortunes of the red-handed murderer, whoever he may be,—not Oedipus, they feel confident (463ff.).

Creon appears, injured dignity incarnate, and is denounced by Oedipus in a perverted form of what is becoming a conventional phrase, as φονεύς [murderer] of himself and as ληστής [robber] of his kingly power (534). Oedipus, for his part, cannot conceive that unless Teiresias has conspired with Creon he would have spoken of the slaying of Laius as his deed (572). We may note in passing the plural form of the phrase τὰς ἐμὰς . . . Λαΐου διαθοράς, significant only as reflecting Oedipus' agitated state of mind, which views a matter so nearly touching his interests and happiness as of utter importance, and therefore dignifies it with a plural.

Little should be made of the fact that Oedipus, in recounting to Jocasta his supposed grievance against Creon, says that Creon accuses him (through Teiresias) of being the murderer (φονέα) of Laius (703); in the context anything but a singular noun would be forced; the undertone of irony nevertheless gains by each repeated instance of the sort.

Jocasta, to convince Oedipus of the untrustworthiness of soothsayers, briefly recounts the story of the murder of Laius in the vulgate form, mentioning foreign brigands (ξένοι λῃσταί, 715) who slew him "where three highways met"; and she also cites the previous exposure of her child as proof that that child was not the murderer (φονέα, 721) of its father, despite Apollo's oracle. The verbal opposition of the vulgate and the true versions of the death of Laius is becoming insistent; the moment is almost ripe for it to be employed with still more telling effect.

Oedipus starts at the mention of "the place where three highways met"; he elicits from Jocasta the fuller account of the death of Laius; and, scenting a fatal connection between it and his own adventure at such a spot, he ascertains the source of the story, namely, the servant, the sole survivor of Laius' party. Incidentally he hears of the servant's subsequent career, to which we must revert presently. Oedipus asks that the servant be summoned, and Jocasta assents (769; cf. 861). But before the servant appears, Jocasta learns from Oedipus his own tale, somewhat strangely withheld from her to this moment, though the withholding, quite necessary for the plot, may be justified as falling among matters ἔξω τῆς τραγῳδίας [outside the action of the play]. Oedipus is full of apprehension; Jocasta is confident, for prophecies about Laius have already proved false. On one point, however, Oedipus rests his hopes and his fears; that is, on the discrepancy in one particular between the servant's story and his own grim adventure at the triple ways.

λῃστὰς ἔφασκες αὐτὸν ἄνδρας ἐννέπειν
ὥς νιν κατακτείναιαν. εἰ μὲν οὖν ἔτι
λέξει τὸν αὐτὸν ἀριθμόν, οὐκ ἐγὼ 'κτανον·
οὐ γὰρ γένοιτ' ἂν εἷς γε τοῖς πολλοῖς ἴσος.

εἰ δ' ἄνδρ' ἕν' οἰόζωνον αὐδήσει, σαφῶς
τοῦτ' ἐστὶν ἤδη τοὔργον εἰς ἐμέ ῥέπον. (842ff.)

Here, then, is the test; if the servant adheres to his tale of several robbers, Oedipus is acquitted; if he now speaks of but one wayfarer, Oedipus is implicated. One cannot be the same as many. Jocasta, though but half convinced,—for the apparent foiling of the earlier oracle fills her whole horizon,—assents and summons the servant.

Of the episode that follows, little need be said. The visit of the Corinthian messenger, beginning auspiciously, reveals just what is needed to identify Oedipus as the murderer of Laius, *if* the shepherd who once delivered the infant Oedipus to him proves to be the same person as the old servant who has already been summoned to give information on a different point. This identity Jocasta divines in a flash when the messenger ventures the guarded remark that the other shepherd was reputed to be one of the household of Laius (1042); and she passionately and naturally, if illogically, seeks all too late to prevent further investigation. Oedipus misunderstands her motive, and she rushes forth to her end.

The old servant of Laius, already summoned, at length enters, to be confronted by the Corinthian messenger. The two lines of evidence about the identity of Oedipus and the murderer of Laius thus converge. But although the Theban servant was summoned for the specific purpose of being asked whether one or more than one brigand had murdered Laius, it has often been noted (for example, by Voltaire, in fault-finding mood) that no question is asked on this point. But, as Jebb has urged, the omission "is better than consistent; it is natural. A more urgent question has thrust the other out of sight." It may be added that the presence of the Theban servant is required for the dovetailing of the evidence about Oedipus' babyhood, and that it is sufficiently explained by his having been summoned for a quite different reason. This pretext having served its purpose, the question of brigand or brigands quietly drops out of view, and the catastrophe is sufficiently promoted by the discovery of the origin of Oedipus. This establishes him as the son of Laius; but it does not directly carry forward his knowledge of the fact that he did on a definite occasion kill Laius beyond the strong presentiment which he felt when the triple ways were first mentioned (715; cf. 726ff.), a presentiment which needed to be confirmed or disproved by investigation about this very matter of brigands, whether one or several. In other words, his knowledge that he has indeed killed Laius is not directly established, but is inferred from the discovery of his origin and from the discovery that he has fulfilled the half of the Delphic oracle that prophesied incest; *ergo*, his inference would run, presumably the other half that foretold parricide has been fulfilled, in view of his previous strong suspicions on this score.

The dramatic usefulness of the ambiguous story of the death of Laius is now clear; it serves on the one hand, by its use of the untrue tale of brigands, to keep Oedipus plausibly in the dark as to his identity till the convenient moment for the περιπέτεια [*peripeteia*], also providing a definite test-point of the kind characteristic of the modern courtroom or detective story. On the other hand, by its use of the true version of a single murderer which Oedipus himself unconsciously or intuitively uses at times, it has served the needs of tragic irony, or as Lewis Campbell would prefer to term it, "pathetic contrast."[6]

It remains to inquire how far it was possible or natural for Greeks to speak thus ambiguously of an event, vacillating between singular and plural in an important detail. Of course the use of the plural substantive where the singular would seem more natural is a common and characteristic phase of Greek idiom, especially in poetry. The grammarians provide numerous examples.[7] Of common varieties I may mention the "plural of majesty";[8] the "allusive plural," in which an unnamed individual may be referred to in the plural, as when the shade of Clytaemnestra in the *Eumenides* speaks of what she has suffered πρὸς τῶν φιλτάτων, meaning Orestes,[9] or when in our play Teiresias in intentionally vague language alludes to Oedipus' relations with Jocasta, σὺν τοῖς φιλτάτοις αἴσχισθ᾽ ὁμιλοῦντα (366); the masculine plural used often in tragedy for the feminine singular;[10] and the so-called plural of modesty, analogous to the "editorial 'we.'"[11] With these varieties I should connect two others, neither of which has been sufficiently studied: one is the "we" used by a speaker in a Platonic dialogue, including himself and by courtesy his interlocutor, but not to be confused with the "we" that the self-conscious mouthpiece of a philosophic school might affect.[12] The other somewhat neglected use of the plural is found especially in tragedy; the use of the plural of a single event viewed emotionally as of great interest or importance to the speaker. I should describe it conveniently as the "plural of tragic importance," or the "emotional plural." I have already called attention to the phrase τὰς ἐμὰς Λαΐου διαφθοράς,[13] used by Oedipus to refer to the murder of Laius with which Teiresias charged him. Other instances in our play, some of them classified by Kühner under the plural of majesty, seem to me to be better explained as "emotional": τὰ μητρὸς νυμφεύματα (980), used by Jocasta, "marriage with thy mother"; ἀδήλων θανάτων (496), by the Chorus of "the undiscovered murderer" of Laius; τοὺς τεκόντας (1176), by the servant, of the *father* of Oedipus; τοῖς φυτεύσασιν (1007), by Oedipus, of Merope. Still more striking are the plurals that the remorseful Oedipus uses of his mother and of his father respectively at the moment of complete enlightenment, in self-accusation,

ξὺν οἷς τ'
οὐ χρῆν ὁμιλῶν, οὕς τέ μ' οὐκ ἔδει κτανών. (1185f.);

and the supreme instance occurs where the complex relationships of the household of Oedipus are held up for horror-stricken contemplation:

πατέρας, ἀδελφούς, παῖδας, αἷμ' ἐμφύλιον,
νύμφας γυναῖκας τε, κτλ. (1406f.)

Other instances could easily be multiplied from other plays; but sufficient evidence has been cited for the present purpose. "Greek writers," remarks Professor Smyth, "often shift from a particular to a general statement and *vice versa*, thus permitting a free transition from singular to plural or from plural to singular."[14]

But where, after all, did the ambiguity with regard to the story of Laius' death originate? With the untruthful story brought by the Theban servant; and it is a characteristic bit of Sophoclean art that the motive for the prevarication should be unobtrusively suggested, and should issue from the character of the servant. What do we know about him? He was a home-born slave, δοῦλος οὐκ ὠνητός, ἀλλ' οἴκοι τραφείς (1123), that is, one of the most trusted class of servants; so Jocasta distinctly says, for when he asked of her after the death of Laius that he be sent away from the town to the pastures, she readily sent him, "for he was worthy, for a slave, to win even a greater boon than that" (758–64); and the leader of the chorus later observes of him that he was indeed one of Laius' servants, and, he adds quite gratuitously, "trusty as any man, for a shepherd" (εἴπερ τις ἄλλος πιστὸς ὡς νομεὺς ἀνήρ., 1118). Furthermore, this trusty servant is prone to pity; for when he was bidden to make away with the infant Oedipus, it was in pity (κατοικτίσας, 1178) that he gave him instead to the Corinthian. That is essential for the plot, and is of course common in many other tales of children exposed in infancy and reappearing later. But it is also an indication that the trusty servant is not above practicing a deception.

Years pass; and it falls to his lot to accompany Laius on his ill-fated expedition to Delphi. He alone, of the party of Laius, escaped unperceived the murderous blows of angry Oedipus. Not an heroic escape, to be sure; he might, with greater resolution, have died fighting for his old master. What account could he, the trusty and sensitive retainer, bring back to Thebes? That Laius was dead, of course, and, to save in some degree his own good name, that the party of Laius had battled against odds,—against a band of robbers, not a single wayfarer. With such an apparently innocent deception, I take it, he tried to save his reputation. And so, indeed, the scholastic implies.[15] One is irresistibly reminded of "valiant Jack" Falstaff's "eleven men in buckram": for when he is set upon by his two friends in disguise, "Falstaff, after a blow or two, runs away," but when he comes to tell his tale, he was "at half-sword with a dozen of them two hours together," or with "two or three and fifty," and the "men in buckram" whom he vanquished grow from two to four, from seven to nine, to eleven at last. "O monstrous"! cries Prince Hal, "eleven buckram men grown out of two"![16] So with the servant of Laius, who is compelled much later to "mark now how a plain tale shall put [him] down." Most modern editors of Sophocles, including Jebb, fail to call attention to the motives that led the servant to bring a distorted story; not so E. Wunder,[17] who suggests explicitly that the story was invented by the survivor "quo magis poenam neglecti desertique regis effugeret," and that it also delays the revelation of Oedipus as the murderer. Paley argues that "the report of the attendant must be supposed to precede the arrival of Oedipus at Thebes. He can therefore have had no reason for his falsehood except the natural temptation to veil his cowardice by exaggerating the force from which he fled."

Either when the servant told his tale, or more probably shortly thereafter,—though Sophocles does not clearly preserve the indications of time at this point,[18]—he found Oedipus on the throne of Thebes. I am inclined to believe that he recognized in the new king the murderer of his old master,[19] for the interval of time was not long. Perhaps he even had begun to reflect on the old prophecies about that child of Laius who was to slay his father; for he had been familiar with them (1175), and he at least could not be sure that the infant had died. Possibly he even recognized in the form of the new king of Thebes some resemblance to Laius, as Jocasta herself recognized it (743). What an intolerable position for a trusty old servant, caught in a mesh of circumstances for which he feels no slight qualms of responsibility! No wonder that he begs to be sent away from this city of unhappy memories to the pastures. And when he is later summoned and confronted by the Corinthian, who, we note, immediately recognizes him, what wonder that he seeks as long as possible to evade the issue, to hold his tongue about matters that he has long sought to put out of mind? But it is too late; his deeds, his well-meaning version of the death of Laius, the knowledge locked in his memory, have done their worst for Oedipus, and have contributed notably to the skill with which Sophocles has wrought his drama.

NOTES

1. Cf. Richard C. Jebb, ed. and trans., *Oedipus Tyrannus*, 3rd ed. (Cambridge: Cambridge University Press, 1893), introduction, xlv-xlvii.

2. Jebb, introduction to *Oedipus Tyrannus*, xxv.

3. πλήθει χερῶν. Cf. 541f.; it is folly to attempt to win royal power from a tyrant "without numbers and friends," says Oedipus in his flyting with Creon. Cf. Dryden, act 1, scene 1.

    He said, a band of robbers watched their passage,
    Who took advantage of a narrow way
    To murder Laius and the rest; himself
    Left too for dead.

    Oedipus: A Tragedy, in *Works of John Dryden*, ed. Walter Scott, vol. 6 (London: William Miller, 1808), p. 147.

4. Cf. Dryden, act 1, scene 1, "the murderer" (in the curse).

5. Cf. also 266.

6. Jebb, introduction to *Oedipus Tyrannus*, 126–33.

7. Cf. Raphael Kühner, *Ausführliche Grammatik der Griechischen Sprache*, 3rd ed. (Hanover: Hahnsche Buchhandlung, 1890), § 348; Herbert Weir Smyth, *A Greek Grammar for Colleges* (New York: American Book Company, 1920), §§ 1000–1012.

8. θρόνοι (*Ant.* 1041); ἡμᾶς (*Alc.* 680).

9. *Eum.* 100.

10. Cf. Soph. *Ant.* 926; *El.* 399; Eur. *Alc.* 383; *I. T.* 399.

11. ἡμῖν, Xen. *Cyr.* I, 1, 1.

12. So I have argued, against Burnet, in interpreting *Phaedo*, 70 D, 75 D, "Plato's View of Poetry", *Harvard Studies in Classical Philology* 29 (1918), 5. I might call attention, in passing, to another Platonic use of the plural with delicious effect, at the beginning of the *Ion*; the pompous rhapsode reports that he has just won a first prize at Epidaurus: τὰ πρῶτα τῶν ἄθλων ἠνεγκάμεθα. "Bravo," replies Socrates, noting the plural; "See to it that 'we' win at the Panathenaic Festival, too" (*Ion* 530 B). Lindbergh's "we" was different.

13. 572; see above.

14. Smyth, *Greek Grammar for Colleges*, § 1012, citing Xen. *Hiero*, 5, 4. For Latin parallels see Oskar Weise, *Language and Character of the Roman People*, trans. H. A. Strong and A. Y. Campbell (London: Kegan Paul, Trench, Trübner & Co., 1909), p. 44: "The plural is employed instead of the singular to express emphatically and distinctly the strength of any emotion. This is particularly remarkable in the case of abstract words." (Examples are cited.)

15. ἄκρως δὲ ὑπέγραψε τὸ ἦθος τῶν δειλῶν. ἅμα μὲν γὰρ ἐξαίρουσι τὰ πεπραγμένα, ἵνα μὴ δόξωσι διὰ δειλίαν φευγεῖν, ἅμα δὲ καὶ ἐν παραφρνήσει ὄντες τὰ βραχέα μείζω δοξάζουσι (cited, in modern editions, apparently only by Bruhn, in his revision of the Schneidewin-Nauck edition [Berlin: Weidmann, 1910].)

16. Shakespeare, *Henry IV*, act 2, scenes 2 and 4. For another amusing and close analogy, see the three versions of an adventure in Spain as related by J. M. Kemble, and recorded by Frances M. Brookfield, *The Cambridge "Apostles"* (New York: Charles Scribner's Sons, 1906), 171.

17. Eduard Wunder, 4th ed., revised by Nicolaus Wecklein, 1875. Wunder was followed by T. Mitchell, 1841; W. B. Jones, 1867, citing Falstaff; similarly F. H. M. Blaydes, 1859.

18. Cf. Jebb, *ad* 736 and 758. Corneille has the servant wounded and helpless for more than a year, act 4, scene 4.

19. So Corneille's servant is made to say quite explicitly. Voltaire makes Phorbas (the servant) subject to suspicion of having murdered Laius, and has him sent away for safety by Jocasta, who trusts him (act 1, scene 3). When he confronts Oedipus, he immediately recognizes the king as the murderer of Laius (act 4, scene 2). Patin (*Études sur les Tragiques Grecs* [Paris: Hachette, 1885], 167) suggests that it was *une réserve douloureuse* that prompted the servant in Sophocles to hold his peace when he saw the murderer of Laius enthroned and married to Jocasta; but if he has already shown cowardice, is not fear a more natural explanation?

The Murderers of Laius, Again (Soph. *OT* 106–7)

Rick M. Newton

t is well known that much of the plot of Sophocles' *Oedipus Tyrannus* depends on a confusion regarding the number of Laius' murderers.[1] This confusion originates with the false assertion of the sole surviving eyewitness to the murder that "brigands" slew the old king, "not with the might of a single man but with an entire force" (122–23). This claim, which Oedipus accepts at face value, is the source of his suspicions of hired conspirators who may still be at work. Only halfway through the play (765), after the failure of his charge against Tiresias and Creon as the culprits, does he finally summon the witness in order to settle a discrepancy which has arisen: Oedipus suddenly remembers killing a man fitting Laius' description at the same triple crossroad where Laius is said to have met his fate. Oedipus, however, was traveling alone at the time and cannot therefore be the same man as the "many brigands" described by the witness. Since "one cannot be equal to many" (845), the witness must come forth to balance the equation.

The numbers problem has been studied extensively in the criticism of the play, receiving both praise and blame for its effect on the entire drama.[2] In addition to its dramaturgical aspect, the problem has also been studied for its

---

First published in *Classical World* 72, no. 4 (1978).

contribution to the meaning of the play, primarily concerning the theme of human knowledge and its limitations.[3] Oedipus, despite his fame for having solved the riddle of the Sphinx, is woefully ignorant of facts. Faced with the problem of finding Laius' murderer, he has only the testimony of the witness on which to base his investigation. But in the course of the play it becomes clear that the man simply lied about what he saw.[4] The very foundation of Oedipus' suspicions of plural murderers, therefore, is revealed to be false. His human knowledge is limited and faulty because it is ultimately based on an untruth.

But, aside from the testimony of the witness, Oedipus' suspicion of more than one man is based on another bit of evidence which has hitherto not been studied in the criticism of the play: the oracle itself leads him to look for more than a single culprit. When Creon returns from Delphi in the prologue, he relates the god's message, 106–7: "Now that Laius is dead (*toutou thanontos*), the god clearly (*saphōs*) commands us to punish by force (*cheiri*) the murderers (*tous autoentas*), whoever they are."[5] Although we can clearly understand whatever motives may have driven the witness to give his false testimony, how do we explain this bit of deception which comes from the oracle itself?[6] For oracles do not lie, least of all in this play. But they do not fully reveal, either. Heraclitus' famous statement describes the nature of oracular expression, fr. 93D: "The lord whose oracle is in Delphi neither conceals nor reveals; rather, he gives a sign (*oute kryptei oute legei alla sēmainei*)."[7] And that is exactly what the oracle is doing in our passage. The entire sentence delivered by Creon is full of ambiguities. The opening words, *toutou thanontos,* at first appear to be a genitive absolute ("now that he is dead"). But after we hear *tous autoentas* in the next line, the genitive phrase seems to be dependent on these words ("the murderers of the dead man"). Similarly, the dative *cheiri* is ambiguous: is it a dative of means dependent on *autoentas* ("those who struck with their hand") or on *timōrein* ("the god commands us to punish them by force")? These ambiguities are deliberate, of course, and Sophocles intends for us to hear all of the possibilities.[8]

The most ambiguous element in the sentence is the term "murderers," *autoentas.* Save for a variant reading in Soph. *El.* 272, this expanded form of the normal *authentēs* is a *hapax legomenon.*[9] The word is unusual and mysterious, appropriate to the oracular mode of expression. This mysteriousness is emphasized by the final word of the line, *tinas:* "Punish the *autoentas,* whoever they are." What we should ask ourselves at this point is, "Who are they?" The most common meaning of the noun *authentēs*, and the one which we are intended to hear, is "murderer." Specifically, as a compound in *auto-* (especially noticeable in Sophocles' expanded form), it indicates a murderer of a member of one's own family.[10] Oedipus the parricide is certainly an *authentēs* in this specific sense, but we in the audience know that Oedipus is the *only* murderer of Laius. Why the plural form? Is the oracle, like the witness, not telling the truth about the number of the culprits? Further investigation into the meaning of the word reveals that the oracle is not lying at all. For *authentēs* has a second meaning: as a compound in *auto-* it is also used to designate someone who turns his hand against himself, i.e., a suicide.[11] At first glance, this meaning has no significance here. But if we realize that oracles speak with timeless knowledge of past, present, and future and that, before the day is out, Jocasta will fulfill the oracle by hanging herself inside the palace, the noun's second meaning does have a place here: Jocasta will be an *authentēs*.[12] The word has yet a third meaning, "ruler, master," which is also appropriate.[13] For the present rulers of Thebes are the royal couple themselves, Oedipus and Jocasta. The queen "holds equal sway" (579) with Oedipus and, as his partner in the incestuous marriage, is as much a source of the city's pollution as is Oedipus himself.[14] By the end of the play we realize that the oracle has been fulfilled when, in the *exodos*, the messenger announces, 1280–81: "These troubles have broken forth not upon a single head but upon the heads of two, the commingled troubles of husband and wife." In 107 the oracle, with typical ambiguity, is saying many things at once: punish the past murderer (Oedipus), the future suicide (Jocasta), and the present polluted rulers (Oedipus and Jocasta). But the oracle does not explain itself clearly. It merely gives a sign, speaking in veiled terms which Oedipus' intelligence cannot penetrate.

Oedipus' suspicion that there are several murderers to be found, therefore, has a dual origin: the lie of the witness and the ambiguity of the oracle. As regards the issue of human knowledge, Sophocles is using the numbers problem to comment on the very foundations of our knowledge. What Oedipus knows about the murder of Laius is based, on the one hand, on a lie and, on the other, on a natural but erroneous interpretation of the oracle. Through the dual origin of the numbers problem Sophocles is saying that the foundations of human knowledge are false and unreliable; furthermore, even if the truth is divinely revealed (as it will be also by Tiresias in the first episode), the human cognitive capacity is so limited that it cannot understand the truth if it is at all ambiguous. The god may speak with ambiguity, confusing past, present, and future, but the human mind must distinguish and categorize and, when confronted by such a term as *autoentai,* must pick and choose the most obvious meaning.[15] Oedipus cannot hold two or three meanings in his head at the same time, since the human mind cannot function like the divine.

NOTES

1. Greek shifts easily from singular to plural and *vice versa,* and I am indebted to Professor Robert Renehan of Boston College for pointing out to me several examples of these shifts: Pl. *Gorg.* 478B–C, *Prot.* 324A, *Legg.* 870D; Ar. *Vesp.* 704–5, *Eq.* 730–33; Eur. *Hec.* 1187–89. In the *OT* it appears that Sophocles is taking advantage of this feature of the language, using it as a key element in the construction of his plot.

2. Voltaire is highly critical of Sophocles for allowing this discrepancy: Oedipus should have summoned the witness from the very beginning; see the excerpt from his third letter in Michael J. O'Brien, ed., *Twentieth Century Interpretations of Oedipus Rex* (Englewood Cliffs, NJ: Prentice-Hall, 1968), 99–100. Also critical is Louis Roussel, "L'épisode de Créon dans Sophocle *(OT),*" *Mélanges offerts à A.M. Desrousseaux* (Paris: Hachette, 1937), 423–27: according to Roussel the discrepancy only draws out the action, padding what would otherwise have been an only 600-line drama. On the other side, William Chase Greene, "The Murderers of Laius," *Transactions of the American Philological Association* 60 (1929): 75–86 [reprinted in this volume], claims that Sophocles "has made a virtue of necessity": the ambiguity "delay(s) the *anagnōrisis* and make(s) it coincide with the *peripeteia.*" Also favorable is J. C. Kamerbeek, *Commentaries on the Plays of Sophocles,* vol. 4 (Leiden: Brill, 1967), 51.

3. Marjorie W. Champlin, "*Oedipus Tyrannus* and the Problem of Knowledge," *Classical Journal* 64 (1969): 337–45, for example, sees in the numbers problem a reference to the Parmenidean doctrine of the one and the many. Bernard Knox, *Oedipus at Thebes* (New Haven: Yale University Press, 1957), 147–58, also studies the problem and the mathematical imagery in the play. For the limitation of human knowledge see Karl Reinhardt, *Sophokles* (Frankfurt am Main: V. Klostermann, 1933), 104–44 and, more generally, Hans Diller, *Göttliches und menschliches Wissen bei Sophokles* (Kiel: Lipsius & Tischer, 1950).

4. For the witness' motive in lying, see Greene, "The Murderers of Laius," 85: "He can . . . have had no reason for his falsehood except the natural temptation to veil his cowardice by exaggerating the force from which he fled."

5. I accept the MSS *tinas* in 107 over Pearson's printing of the singular *tina,* which he accepts from the Suda's entry under *epistellō.*

6. I believe that the plural *autoentas* is what the oracle said, not that it is a mistake on Creon's part (that the oracle said singular "murderer" but Creon carelessly reports the message in the plural). In 106 he says that the oracle "explicitly commands" *(epistellei saphōs):* cf. *anōgen . . . emphanōs,* 96. Later, Creon swears that he reported the oracle accurately, 603–4: "Go to Delphi yourself and ask if I reported accurately *(saphōs).*"

7. Cf. Vergil's description of the prophetic Sibyl in *Aen.* VI. 99–100: *horrendas canit ambages . . . / obscuris vera involvens.* For a study of the oracular mode of expression in the *OT* and of the differences between divine and human knowledge implied therein, see Steven Lattimore, "Oedipus and Tiresias," *California Studies in Classical Antiquity* 8 (1975): 105–11.

8. These ambiguities have been observed by Kamerbeek, *Commentaries, ad loc.*, and Thomas Gould, *Oedipus the King: A Translation with Commentary* (Englewood Cliffs, NJ: Prentice-Hall, 1970), 29.

9. See P. Chantraine, "Encore *Authentēs*," *Aphierōma stē mnēmē tou Manolē Triantaphyllide* (Salonica [not Athens, as in Kamerbeek's citation] 1960), 89–93, for a study of the word in each of its occurrences. For its unique Sophoclean form here, cf. F. R. Earp's list in *The Style of Sophocles* (Cambridge: Cambridge University Press, 1944), 41.

10. Cf. Hdt. I. 117; Thuc. III. 58. 5; Eur. *Rh.* 873, *Andr.* 172, 614, *HF* 1359, *IA* 1190. In Eur. *Tr.* 660 Andromache laments that she must be a slave to Neoptolemus, in the house of those who killed her husband. For the force of *auto-* compounds meaning action affecting one's own kin, cf. Aesch. *Sept.* 681, 734, 735, 810, 850, H. D. Cameron, *Studies on the Seven Against Thebes of Aeschylus* (The Hague: Mouton, 1971), 47–48, and Gerald F. Else, *The Madness of Antigone* (Heidelberg: Winter, 1976), 27–28.

11. Cf. Antiphon's second tetralogy, 3. 4, 4. 9, 4. 10. Chantraine, "Encore *Authentēs*," contests the definition "suicide" in *LSJ.* The original meaning of the word, he claims, is "a responsible agent": a suicide is an *authentēs* only in an extended sense, as the person responsible for his own death.

12. As a would-be murderer of her own son years ago, she is also an *authentēs* in the first sense. The anonymous referee of this paper also suggests the possibility that the audience may know the version of the myth in which Jocasta gets Laius drunk in order to seduce him and thus have a child in spite of the oracle's warning: in this way Jocasta is responsible for the murder of her husband.

13. Cf. Eur. *Supp.* 442. Cf. also the two meanings of the cognate verb *authenteō:* (1) to have full power, and (2) to commit a murder. In modern Greek the noun survives in the form *aphentēs* and means "boss, master."

14. According to Greek tradition, the basic acts which incurred ritual pollution were homicide, contact with a dead body, childbirth, and unnatural sex. See Louis Moulinier, *Le pur et l'impur dans la pensée des Grecs d'Homère à Aristote* (Paris: Klincksieck, 1952), 199–202, and Brian Vickers, *Towards Greek Tragedy: Drama, Myth, Society* (London: Longman, 1973), 140.

15. The ambiguities are definitely present in the Greek. Whether or not the Athenian audience during the performance would have understood the many subtleties of the sentence is an unanswerable question. They were, of course, much more aurally acute than we are today, who read more plays than we see produced. But certainly Sophocles is writing for the reader of the play as well as for the spectator: his dramatic irony is too dense to be fully appreciated merely upon one's initial exposure.

Who Killed Laius?

Karl Harshbarger

There are two versions of Laius's murder in *Oedipus Rex.*[1] First, there is the version that is current in Thebes and is expressed by Creon, Jocasta, the Chorus, and presumably the Shepherd if he were to talk about it. Second, there is Oedipus's version.

The first version is essentially this: one day, not too long before the Sphinx came to terrorize Thebes, Laius set out—so he said—to Delphi. He did not travel as a king generally might with a great many soldiers, but with only four of his men, one of whom was a herald. Laius himself rode in a chariot. At a place where three roads meet, Laius was met by a group of robbers.

> ... the robbers they encountered
> were many and the hands that did the murder
> were many; it was no man's single power. (122–23)

These robbers killed everyone except one man, the Shepherd, who returned to Thebes to tell his story.

The second version, Oedipus's version, is similar to the first in many

First published in *Tulane Drama Review* 9, no. 4 (1965).

respects and different in some particulars. According to Oedipus, the event happened about the same time and near the very same place as the murder in the first version. An old man and his party, closely resembling Laius and his party (although it is not clear whether it contained the same number of travelers), passed Oedipus. They behaved in an insulting manner, and in a fit of anger Oedipus killed them *all*.

Although there are striking similarities in the two stories, there are important differences. The differences concern the number of murderers and the number of survivors. According to the first version, there were a number of murderers and one survivor. According to the second version, there were no survivors and one murderer.[2]

Certainly, in any interpretation of *Oedipus Rex*, the *fact* of who killed Laius is central. Most discussions on the meaning of the play—especially those dealing with the problems of the fulfillment of fate—rest on the facts that Oedipus killed his father and slept with his mother; and he put out his eyes in a just and correct realization of these horrifying deeds.

Certainly, then, there is a very understandable tendency to overlook the differences in the murder stories. Even after discovering these discrepancies, it is easy to dismiss them either as unimportant or as small errors which Sophocles unwittingly committed. However, it is safer, when working with a genius of Sophocles' magnitude, to first inspect and think about what he has given us. I think it can be shown that these differences in the murder story are, in every sense, intentional. Furthermore, I believe this disparity is at the crux of any interpretation of the play.

The clearest evidence that Sophocles was aware of the differences in the murder stories is that he has Oedipus, himself, bring them up and comment on them (pushing them to the center of our attention) about half-way through the play. After all, although for most of the characters the evidence is lost in the distant past, and although it seems as if the truth will never be known, we must remember that there is presumably still an eyewitness, the Shepherd. He can tell what *really* happened. Oedipus, in the midst of his troubles, realizes this:

> CHORUS: Sir, we too fear these things. But until you see this man face to face and hear his story, hope.

OEDIPUS: Yes, I have just this much of hope—to wait until the herdsman comes.

JOCASTA: And when he comes, what do you want with him?

OEDIPUS: I'll tell you; if I find that his story is the same as yours, I at least will be clear of this guilt.

JOCASTA: Why what so particularly did you learn from my story?

OEDIPUS: You said that he spoke of highway *robbers* who killed Laius. Now if he uses the same number, it was not I who killed him. One man cannot be the same as many. But if he speaks of a man traveling alone, then clearly the burden of the guilt inclines towards me.

JOCASTA: Be sure, at least, that this was how he told the story. He cannot unsay it now, for every one in the city has heard it—not I alone.

(834–50. Italics Grene's. Jebb does not use the italics here.)

This makes it clear, I think, that these discrepancies are not accidents due to careless writing. The contradictions are deliberately established for us by Sophocles.

Granting this, it is still easy to dismiss the disparity as meaningless. Would Oedipus put out his eyes if he had not done the deed? Has not Teiresias, who reads the signs of the birds, said that Oedipus was guilty? Has not Apollo condemned Oedipus to kill his father? Is there not a bulk of other evidence to show that this is true? Yet, admitting that as a master craftsman Sophocles has led us to *suppose* Oedipus is guilty of the deed, even admitting that he may, in fact, have done it, as a matter of cold examination of the evidence, we cannot be sure that Oedipus killed Laius.

When the Shepherd arrives, when the one man who can save Oedipus confronts him, when the eye-witness is there, when we have our best opportunity to know what really happened, *Oedipus does not ask the Shepherd about the murder.* Certainly, considering the shocking, terrifying revelations presented to Oedipus by the Messenger, it is easy to understand that Oedipus completely forgets why he summoned the Shepherd.[3] But we must admit that the differences between the two murder stories are not resolved.[4]

It seems to me that this unresolved problem is a clue which Sophocles throws out to us to let us see that the interpretation he lets appear most obvious is not the only interpretation that is textually justified; and, in fact, may not even be a sound interpretation. At least, we are invited to investigate the question further. Because, as soon as one begins to speculate that Oedipus did not murder Laius, a host of other questions descends upon us. If this vital fact has been purposely left unresolved, might not other seeming facts about the play be called into question as well? If the play is built upon ironies, cannot there be irony in this, too? If the usually accepted form of the play rests on double grounds, could there be other forms and structures in the play? Could there not be other screens behind screens, masks behind masks, and horrors behind horrors?

If it is possible that Oedipus did not murder Laius, can we determine from the play if there is anyone else who might have done it? I think so. I have chosen a suspect that might appear the least likely: the Chorus. I am not urging the certainty of the Chorus's guilt. I am only arguing the possibility of the Chorus's guilt.[5]

To begin with, we must note the character of the Chorus. The Chorus vacillates a great deal in its opinions, but its actions are always to seek the safe and secure position. It often changes its opinion to rationalize some new way of seeking safety. At the end of the play it proclaims:

> Look upon that last day always. Count no mortal happy till
> he has passed the final limit of his life secure from pain. (1529–1530)

And it asks:

> May destiny ever find me pious in word and deed
> prescribed by the laws that live on high . . . (864–66)

It berates Oedipus for his pride and for his attempts to find ways to control the gods.

> When such things are done, what man shall contrive
> to shield his soul from the shafts of the God? (892–93)

If a man despises the ways of the gods and "walks with haughtiness" (884) he will fall to his ruin:

may an evil doom
smite him for his ill-starred pride of heart! (887–88)

However, we should not make the mistake of thinking that these words counseling moderation represent Sophocles' view or even the view of the Chorus. It is the view of the Chorus at this time in the play. By contrast, at the beginning the Chorus is quite happy—one could say deliriously happy— that Oedipus is a man who has wanted to know too much. It comes to him exactly because it thinks of him as:

the first of men
in all the chances of this life and when
we mortals have to do with more than man. (32–34)

He has saved the city. Somehow, he understood mysteries "in virtue of no knowledge we could give you" (37). And although the Chorus makes it clear it does not consider Oedipus a god, still it believes that "it was God / that aided you" (38). The Chorus needs Oedipus, it comes as a supplicant to Oedipus, and asks for those very talents it despises at the end of the play.

The Chorus does not remain a supplicant. As soon as the tide swings against Oedipus, it begins to stop believing him, trusting him, and supporting him. One of the reasons the Chorus is able to shift allegiances so quickly is that it can find nothing absolute to believe in. It desperately needs and seeks solid, almost physical evidence to support a faith which resists the seas of doubt. Oracles and signs are not enough. It must see "the word / proved right beyond doubt" (506–7). Up until now,

The augur has spread confusion, terrible confusion. (483–84)

Undoubtedly the gods are wise, and the Chorus hopes to follow the will of the gods. But how can one really know what Zeus and Apollo want?

Truly Zeus and Apollo are wise
and in human things all knowing;
but amongst men there is no

distinct judgment, between the prophet
and me—which of us is right. (496–502)

And is it even possible to communicate with the gods? Perhaps not. "Apollo is nowhere clear in honor; God's service perishes" (910).

It is too appalling for the Chorus to have its beliefs uncertain. If one does not know how to act, it is too easy to do the wrong thing and start the avalanche of inexplicable divine disaster. So it must believe those things which do not disturb the stone that starts the avalanche. Therefore, its religion is more political than spiritual. It seeks to prevent all dangerous actions, all violence, all suddenness, to protect the *status quo* and prevent change. This is the safe course.

The Chorus seeks to conciliate all differences. The Chorus's advice to those who quarrel in the play is to "lay the quarrel that now stirs you" (634), or, "I think it best, in the interests of the country, to leave it where it ended" (685–86). It is particularly frightened of all actions taken in anger or which happen suddenly. "Those who are quick of temper are not safe" (617). When Oedipus complains to the Chorus that in urging moderation by "softening my anger" (688) it has destroyed his chances to save the country, the Chorus replies that it is all for his saving the country, but that he must do it slowly, without anger, and in such a way as not to harm or anger any human or god.

The safe religious life also means seeking political protection from those public or divine personages who seem most powerful to the Chorus at any given moment. At the end of the play, when Oedipus has been reduced to powerlessness, the Chorus is quick to defer to the new ruler.

Here Creon comes in fit time to perform
or give advice in what you ask of us.
Creon is left sole ruler in your stead. (1416–18)

But when the Chorus is not so certain where the power is, its actions are less sure. In the middle of the play it wavers when Creon, hearing that Oedipus has charged him with high treason, comes thundering back to the palace to confront him. The Chorus, in its confusion about which way to turn or who is right, takes the middle, noncommittal ground in answering Creon.

> I do not know; I have no eyes to see
> what princes do. (530–31)

The Chorus has begun to sense that Oedipus may no longer be able to protect them.

As Creon continues to represent the force of moderation, the *status quo,* and safety, *the Chorus deserts Oedipus.* Oedipus is amazed. He loves his people and expects love and loyalty from them. Rightly or wrongly, he feels Creon is the taint Apollo spoke of. He feels he has a mandate from Delphi to banish or kill Creon. He is convinced that if he lets Creon live, Creon will murder him. He feels he must "quickly counterplot." Supporting Creon at this moment, especially urging Creon's reinstatement in the royal house, is tantamount to asking for Oedipus's life. Overwhelmed, Oedipus demands, "Do you know what you ask?" (653), and the Chorus replies, "Yes" (654). Oedipus says:

> I would have you know that this request of yours
> really requests my death or banishment. (658–59)

There is another reason why the Chorus turns against Oedipus. If the Chorus is guilty of the murder—if it bribed robbers to do it—then the Chorus itself is the taint, the corruption, the disease in Thebes. It must be purged. When it comes to Oedipus at the beginning of the play, not understanding the cause of the plague, it comes as a supplicant. When, however, it discovers that the murderers of Laius are going to be punished, that *it* is the corruption, the Chorus must turn against Oedipus or be found out. After all, when Oedipus asks Creon where the murderers are, Creon replies, "The clue is in this land" (110). If the Chorus was innocent, we would expect it to be overjoyed upon hearing Creon's news from Delphi, "the sweet spoken word of God from the shrine of Pytho" (151). But the contrary is true.

> I am stretched on the rack of doubt, and terror and trembling hold
> my heart, O Delian Healer, and I worship full of fears
> for what doom you will bring to pass, new or renewed
> in the revolving years. (153–55)

Apollo is a healer. He will make sick things well by driving out the sickness or extinguishing it. Why should the Chorus fear healing? Why should terror and trembling hold its heart? What if the Chorus is the sickness? Will it be found out?

The fear of being found out may explain another rather extraordinary fact: after Laius was murdered there was no attempt to find his murderers. Oedipus, upon learning this from Creon, is incredulous.

> How could a robber dare a deed like this
> were he not helped with money from the city,
> money and treachery? (123–25)

Oedipus suggest that an anti-Laius party bribed a robber to kill the king. Creon replies:

> That indeed was thought.
> But Laius was dead and in our trouble
> there was none to help. (126–27)

Oedipus, upon hearing this, grows even more incredulous:

> What trouble was so great to hinder you
> inquiring out the murder of your king? (128–29)

Creon replies that the sudden evil brought on by the Sphinx prevented them from seeking the truth.[6] It is at this moment that Oedipus begins to suspect trickery. How could he think otherwise? Surely justice and honor and revenge demanded that Thebes find Laius's murderers. Creon offers the defense that the terror of the Sphinx stopped them. Perhaps—but the Sphinx could have been an additional spur to find the murderers. One day Thebes' king is murdered; shortly after that a Sphinx comes to terrorize the city. Certainly the Thebans would consider the possibility that the Sphinx came to plague them because of the murder of the king. And surely the wise thing to do, above and beyond the natural call of justice, would be to hunt the murderers down in order to appease the Sphinx. It stands, then, as incredible that Thebes did not do anything. We cannot blame Oedipus for his amazement.

We can understand his suspicion of Creon. Perhaps Creon instigated no investigation because it would have revealed that he was the guilty party. And, looking further than Oedipus, we can also include the possibility that perhaps there was no investigation because the Chorus blocked it.

At this point, it is necessary to say something more about the basic character of the Chorus than that it is vacillating and seeks security and protection from those in power. From such an over-simplified explanation, and assuming that it is guilty, we would expect to see the Chorus slyly maneuvering, subtly suggesting actions to Oedipus, and behaving entirely in a protective, defensive way. Although there is more of this than one might first imagine, the Chorus's actions don't fit neatly into this pattern. The Chorus obviously has its city's interests at heart and it wants the current plague to end for reasons much stronger than personal ones. We cannot doubt the Chorus's grief when it laments

> But my
> spirit is broken by my unhappiness for my wasting country (664–65)

or

> There are no growing children in this famous land;
> there are no women bearing the pangs of childbirth.
> You may see them one with another, like birds swift on the wing,
> quicker than fire unmastered,
> speeding away to the coast of the Western God. (171–77)

Nor would a selfish, sly, maneuvering Chorus be motivated to search as hard as it does into the meaning of the eternal powers. There can be no doubt that it earnestly wants the murderer(s) brought to justice. They call upon Zeus, Apollo, Artemis, and Bacchus to assist them in their quest. How can we explain the fact that the guilty one is calling upon the gods for assistance in punishing the guilty?

The key to this and other related contradictions is: the Chorus is us. Or, rather, it is made up of people very much like us. All the contradictions which are inherent in the Chorus are inherent in almost any intelligent, sensitive person. It is the person who can act only to protect himself and at the same time care passionately for the sorrows of others; it is the person who must subscribe to the beliefs set up by others and yet knows that these beliefs are valueless; it is the guilty person who wants to escape punishment but leads others to punish him.

At one point in the play Oedipus says to the Chorus about the killer:

> The man who in the doing did not shrink
> will fear no word. (296–97)

He means that a man who is not afraid to kill will not be bothered or worried by his conscience for having murdered. And yet police files are full of records of people who killed, or committed lesser crimes, or no crime at all, and go out of their way to confess. Literature has many examples of this. According to psychoanalytic theory, people often commit crimes *in order to be punished.* The man to whom Oedipus refers is a very rare man.

If the Chorus killed Laius, it must still suffer from its guilt. It is the Chorus's guilt which has ripened inside the Chorus until it symbolically falls upon the city as a plague.[7] After all, the current plague has much of the same effect as the plague of the Sphinx. The Sphinx visited Thebes directly after the murder of Laius, and Thebes was saved from this scourge only by the actions of a new king who resembled the old king, was from the same place as the old king, married the old king's wife, and, in general, took the place of the old king. This assuaged the Chorus's fears for a number of years by replacing the old king with a replica—as if the murder were undone. But now these fears have re-grown into an infection, a disease, a taint, but most of all, a *desire to kill the king again.*

If the Chorus is guilty, and if that guilt is made more painful by a renewed desire to kill again, then the Chorus's action in the play is to find a way to relieve itself. It is faced with a dual problem. On the one hand, the Chorus is afraid of being discovered. It wishes to avoid the punishment that would follow; it wishes to avoid murder. On the other hand, if it is not discovered, if it is not punished, the Chorus can never get relief from its pain; it can never kill.

The solution—which perhaps Oedipus senses and lends himself to—is a sacrifice.

NOTES

1. Citations from the play in my text are to Sophocles, *Oedipus the King*, trans. David Grene (Chicago: University of Chicago Press, 1954).

2. There is a suggestion of a third version of the murder, also. The Chorus recalls an "old faint story." The interchange is intriguing:

   CHORUS: It was said
        that he was killed by certain wayfarers.
   OEDIPUS: I heard that, too, but no one saw the killer. (293–94)

   Here again we have the contradiction between a number of killers and one killer. Jebb translates Oedipus' reply as: "I, too, have heard it, but none sees him who saw it." This problem is related to the contradictions of the sequence of the Shepherd's actions (see footnote number 3).

3. It is not certain anyway that the Shepherd was an eye-witness to the murder. Jebb has noted this "mistake." Jocasta's story about the Shepherd doesn't make sense: "No, when he came home again and saw you king and Laius was dead . . ." (758–59). If the Shepherd returned directly to Thebes after the murder, Oedipus should not yet have been king. Nor would he have discovered that Laius was dead since he saw Laius murdered. How could the Shepherd return after Oedipus took the throne, since it was through the Shepherd that the Thebans found they needed a new king? Either this is a mistake as Jebb believes, or it is one of the many (I believe) deliberate paradoxes Sophocles sets out before us. As in the case of the murder of Laius, if we think for a moment that the Shepherd didn't see the killing, we must look with fresh insight into his confrontation with Oedipus.

4. It is interesting to note how Oedipus on purpose misinterprets the information about Laius's murder given to him by Creon. Creon is quite clear that it was a number of robbers who did the deed. Almost without exception, Oedipus changes this to murder*er*. It is only when he is confronted by Teiresias that he tells the story correctly using the plural.

5. The certainty of this guilt, like so much of the rest of the structure of the play, has to be understood to rest on a paradox. I would not want anyone to think that in this section of the essay I am making a definitive interpretation of the play. After all, there are other suspects, and the guilt or innocence of all of them remains in question. Here I am suggesting only one of *many* contradictory sides of the play.

6. Creon contradicts himself later.

   OEDIPUS: You never made a search for the dead man?
   CREON: We searched, indeed, but never learned of anything. (566–67)

   Again we must ask ourselves whether this is a mistake or a deliberate piece of writing.

7. An analysis of the text shows that the plague is more than a simple physical disease.

Lêistas Ephaske: Oedipus and Laius' Many Murderers

Sandor Goodhart

The problem of the value of truth came before us—or was it we who came before the problem? Who of us is Oedipus here? Who the Sphinx? It is a rendezvous, it seems, of questions and question marks.

—F. Nietzsche

Numberless are the pains I bear; and the whole of my people is sick, and they have no weapon devised by thought, with which a man can defend himself.... one person after another you may see, like a swift-winged bird, speeding faster than irresistible fire towards the shore of the western god.

Numberless in these, our city is being destroyed.

—Sophocles

We are accustomed to believing that we understand Sophocles' treatment of the Oedipus myth. The Priest of Zeus appeals to Oedipus for help against the deadly pestilence which is emptying the Theban *polis*. Learning from the Delphic oracle that the pollution will end when

First published in *diacritics* 8, no. 1 (1978).

the murderer of the former Theban monarch is found and banished, Oedipus champions Laius "as if he had been my father" and undertakes an investigation on his behalf. He consults the prophet Teiresias, his kinsman Creon, his wife Jocasta, and summons the lone surviving witness of the Phocal massacre, a man who turns out to be a servant of the house of Laius. And when Oedipus discovers at last not only that he is "the murderer of the man whose murderer [he is] seeking," but that the slain man was his father and the woman with whom he is living (and with whom he has borne children) his mother, that he is, in short, guilty of parricide and incest as the Delphic oracle predicted long ago he would be, he gouges out his eyes, he prophesies disaster for his children, and he demands to be exiled in accordance with his own decree to a beggarly existence on the slopes of the Cithaeronian mountains.[1]

We feel, that is, that Sophocles' presentation is purely expository, simply an elaboration of the mythic material which is in outline as old, at least, as Homer. Moreover, we seem to agree in general on how the story is to be understood. Elaborating upon Aristotle's notion of *hamartia* in the *Poetics*, we take Sophocles' play as the classic example of the tragedy of destiny. Emphasizing the wonderful divergence between intention and consequence, the fact, in particular, that it is ironically Oedipus' efforts to avoid fulfillment of the myth that bring it about, we see in the drama the powers of the gods in human affairs. If we point out, on one hand, its instruction and, on the other, its terrible price in human suffering, we recognize commonly in the play the relentless force of "Greek necessity."

But the situation may be more complicated than it appears. After Teiresias has accused Oedipus of the most baleful crimes and after Oedipus, in response to the tale by Jocasta of Laius' death has confessed his adventures on the Phocal highway and begun to fear that "the prophet can see," a curious series of events occurs. Oedipus suggests that there is a technical disparity between the account that Jocasta has related and his own recollection and that in view of this disparity he might yet be innocent. His one slight hope, he asserts, is that the man who alone escaped from the Phocal massacre (and whom he has summoned to testify on the matter) will confirm in all of its particulars the circulating account—that the murderers of Laius were many and not one. If the Herdsman indicates a single murderer, then culpability for the crime would seem to incline uniquely towards Oedipus. But if the Herdsman speaks of many murderers, then it would seem just as clear—since

Oedipus has acted alone—that Oedipus is innocent of the Phocal guilt. The one and the many cannot be the same (οὐ γὰρ γένοιτ᾽ ἂν εἷς γε τοῖς λολλοῖς ἴσος, 845).

Jocasta assures Oedipus that if in fact the Herdsman does now alter his previous story, he will face the censure of everyone since all the city heard him and not just she alone. Moreover, the Chorus of Theban Elders who are as eager as anyone to find the solution to the Phocal enigma—and thereby to end the Theban plague—caution as well that such hope as is possible be maintained until the full truth of the matter is revealed.

If we were in the genre of detective story we might expect at this point that the witness would now be brought on, questioned on the matter for which he was summoned, and the full truth made plain. But when the Herds-man in Sophocles' play arrives, rather than confirm either the circumstantial version that Oedipus fears or the empirical version on which his salvation hinges, he is completely silent on the matter of the Phocal slaughter. In the interim between his summoning and his arrival, the Corinthian messenger has appeared and shifted the action to the question of Oedipus' origin, to the linking of the history of Oedipus with the house of Laius. And it is to this issue exclusively that the Herdsman's remarks are addressed. It is not that the Herdsman skirts the issue of the Phocal murder but that it never comes up. On the issue for which he was summoned, the issue on which the solution of the play's mystery depends, he is simply never questioned. We know no more after he appears than we knew before. Oedipus may have been right all along. His hope has gone unchallenged. Oedipus may not have killed Laius.[2]

If we find such a possibility rather curious, it may be less that the tex-tual evidence is equivocal than that we have taken our cue from the best of sources, from the one figure in the play who has the most to gain, it would seem, from registering clearly any equivocation the Herdsman has to offer. For Oedipus himself makes no less of a gesture of mythic appropriation than we do. When the Herdsman dissolves the last bit of doubt on the origin of Oedipus in the house of Laius, Oedipus declares the truth he has learned.

> Alas, alas! All fulfilled, all true! O light, let me now look on you for the last time, I who have been revealed as born from whom I ought not [to have been born], associating with whom I ought not, and having killed whom I should not. (1182–85)

He responds, that is, as if the Herdsman had implicated him in the Phocal murder. He declares himself guilty of parricide and incest and anticipates
his removal from the Theban populace even according to his own decrees.
What is more, the Chorus of Theban Elders who have maintained throughout the play their independence from both the accusations of Teiresias and
the portents of Oedipus' confession, now join Oedipus in denouncing his
catastrophic fortune, and proclaim in a pious Herodotean morality the
exemplary pattern, the *paradeigma*, that his life, henceforth, will constitute
(1193–94).

What could be Sophocles' interest in constructing his play in such a
fashion? What could be his purpose in undermining the mythic pattern to
such an extent that if we follow the play at close range, it is Oedipus' gesture
of appropriation of the myth that comes into focus rather than the myth
itself, that it is only if we proceed like Oedipus to read the myth *a priori*,
to substitute what we do not see for what we do, that the mythic pattern is
revealed?

Sophocles could have resolved the matter simply. Oedipus could have
questioned the Herdsman on the Phocal murder and the old servant, under
threat of reprisal for his continued silence, could have uttered the truth. "You
yourself would best know the course of these events, sire, for you yourself are
the unique murderer."[3]

Shall we allow ourselves the luxury of believing that the Herdsman's
testimony has been irretrievably lost and that we might reasonably supply
it ourselves? It suffices, of course, to consult the edition of Richard Jebb to
recognize the remoteness of the Byzantine manuscripts which found most
texts from anything like an original Sophoclean copy (lii–lxii).

Or, is there another way of viewing what appears to be an anti-mythic
gesture on Sophocles' part, a positive reading of the play on the basis of such
a gesture which brings to light aspects of the drama that we have simply never
read before, which raises serious questions concerning the means by which
we have read the play, means that may have inhibited us from reading such a
gesture all along?

The response of critics to this scene is instructive. Gilbert Norwood, in *Greek
Tragedy*, finds the part played by "the aged Theban" in Sophocles' drama
"especially pointed."

The *Oedipus Tyrannus* has been universally admired as a masterpiece, ever since the time of Aristotle, who in his *Poetic* [*sic*] takes this play as a model of tragedy. The lyrics are simple, beautiful, and even passionately vigorous; the dialogue in language and rhythm is beyond praise; and the tragic irony, for which this poet is famous, is here at its height. But the chief splendour of the work is its construction, its strictly dramatic strength and sincerity. The events grow out of one another with the ease of actual life yet with the accuracy and the power of art. We should note the two great stages: first, the king fears that he has slain Laius; second, that he has slain *his father Laius*. This distinction, so vital to the growing horror, is kept admirably clear and is especially pointed by the part of the aged Theban. When he is summoned, it is to settle whether Laius was slain by one man or by a company; by the time he arrives, this is forgotten, and all wait to know from whom he received the outcast infant.[4]

Certainly, if we assume with Norwood the myth, then Sophocles' constructive skill is masterful. The issue of regicide for which the Herdsman was summoned becomes significantly less interesting once the Corinthian appears, the concern of the inquiry is shifted to the birth and history of Oedipus in the house of Laius, and the singular gravity of the Herdsman's truth becomes evident.

But what if we do not presume the myth? What if we allow the story to unfold as Sophocles has presented it to us? Then Norwood's argument may beg the very question it raises and what Norwood assures us is "forgotten" may become, in fact, curiously conspicuous. In the Sophoclean context in which the Herdsman appears—precisely, as the means by which the issue of the many or one is to be resolved, as the only independent means available for determining whether Oedipus killed Laius at all—what may remain "admirably clear" is the distinction between the mythic pattern we expect and the muddled and equivocal sequence that occurs, between the absolute judgment that Oedipus, with Norwood's approval, makes of his situation and the empirical obscurities to which we ourselves through Oedipus have been made witness.

Is the absence of the Herdsman's reference to Phocis an isolated issue in the play? Are there other means for determining Oedipus' Phocal guilt or, perhaps, is the issue of Phocis less important than it would first appear?

Far from isolated, the Herdsman's silence on Phocis is part of a critical pattern. The oracle in Creon's report, upon which so much depends, speaks distinctly of a multiplicity of murderers. "Apollo now clearly commands us to punish with [heavy] hand his murderers, whoever they may be" (τοὺς αὐτοέντας χειρὶ τιμωρεῖν τινας, 107).

Oedipus questions Creon immediately about the death of Laius at Phocis and his kinsman relates that the lone surviving witness of the Phocal massacre said with certainty one thing alone, that the murderers of Laius were many and not one. "He said that bandits fell in with them and killed them, not with a single strength, but with a large number of hands" (λῃστὰς ἔφασκε συντυχόντας οὐ μιᾷ ῥώμῃ κτανεῖν νιν, ἀλλὰ σὺν πλήθει χερῶν, 122–23).

Oedipus presses the Chorus for further information on the ancient crime and the Theban Elders confirm an "obscure" story that Laius was said to have met his death at the hands of "certain travelers" (πρός τινων ὁδοιπόρων, 292), a report that, Oedipus confirms straightaway, he too has heard. When Teiresias arrives, Oedipus questions the aged seer on the matter and, in the course of elaborating the details of the crisis, repeats the report that the oracle commanded that we punish Laius' murderers. "Phoebus . . . in answer to our question sent a message that deliverance from this plague could only come if we discovered those who killed Laius and either killed them or sent them out of the land to exile" (304–9).

Diverted for a time by the curious accusations of the blind prophet and by his own concern that Teiresias and Creon did the deed and have now conspired against him, Oedipus learns, when he turns to question Jocasta on the death of her late husband, the same information to which he has been privy at least three times before. Using the same word that Creon used in reporting the account of the witness (λῃσταί), Jocasta relates that Laius was said to have been killed by "foreign bandits" (ξένοι . . . λῃσταί, 715–16).

The point is critical at this moment in the play for although Oedipus fears from the circumstances surrounding Laius' death (as Jocasta has explained them) that Teiresias may have been right, it is upon this issue of the number of murderers that he will base his one "hope" that the witness he has summoned will confirm Jocasta's report in all of its particulars, indeed, the report of the oracle itself, that the murderers of Laius were many and not one. "You were saying that he told you that bandits (λῃστὰς) killed Laius. So, if he still says the same number, I was not the killer; for one cannot be equal to many" (842–45).

Jocasta confirms again that this account precisely is the accepted one and that the whole city heard it, not just she alone.

The Chorus joins Jocasta to counsel that however "fearful" these things now seem, hope should be maintained until Oedipus learns fully from the witness what happened.

And when the "man who was present" appears, of course, the full story remains hidden. It is never even requested. If Oedipus assumes he has killed Laius (and if we assume so with him), that assumption is made, it would seem, not on the basis of what he has learned from the Herdsman or what he has heard previously from Jocasta, from the Chorus, or from Creon, but in spite of it.

Moreover, far from secondary, the ambiguity surrounding Oedipus' role in the Phocal massacre would seem critical. The pattern in which the Herdsman's silence is caught is the dramatic center of the play. Whatever Oedipus' fascination with the accusations of Teiresias or with the confirmation of Teiresias' charges by Creon, whatever inadvertent support Jocasta lends to the prophet's words, whatever gravity the Corinthian's information adds to the testimony that the Herdsman will offer, it is in positive terms around the resolution to the Phocal enigma—whatever the mythic discoveries we expect—that the play is demonstrably built. It is from these moments that its very detective story quality springs.

In the overall dramatic context then, what is striking is not only that Oedipus may not be the murderer of Laius, but that there is a curious insistence in the play that the murderers of Laius may be many. The oracle, the witness as related by Creon and Jocasta, the Chorus (if we are to believe its information originates elsewhere), all the sources, that is, which are independent of Oedipus' own account, agree on at least one crucial detail. The multiplicity of murderers was the "one thing" (ἕν) about which the witness in Creon's report was "certain" and the witness's testimony is corroborated independently, if we are to believe Creon, by the words of Apollo himself.

Perhaps we are being a bit hasty in our judgements of the situation? Perhaps we are forgetting the traditional indications in the play on which the myth is founded? What, for example, of Oedipus' repeatedly singular references in his speech to the Chorus championing Laius to the monarch's murderer? Or, what, again, of the riddling language of Teiresias in his antagonistic exchange with Oedipus which we have always taken as a veiled reference to parricide and incest? Or, what, finally, are we to make of Oedipus' own account? Does not Oedipus' confession of his murderous adventure on the Phocal highway constitute—even by our very demonstration—the only first-hand testimony that we have on the matter?

These matters may not be as unproblematic as they first appear. Far from a challenge to the circulating account, Oedipus' speech to the Chorus, in the first place, may lend that account additional support. If Oedipus reduces Creon's account from a plurality to a singularity, it may be less that Oedipus implicates himself unconsciously in the guilt than that much more consciously he implicates Creon. If Oedipus wonders how the bandit (ὁ λῃστής) could have succeeded without help from the city, or why an inquiry was never held (although the oracle in Creon's own words said not to neglect mysteries), or if he pledges to expose the culprit and bring "these things" to light even if the culprit lodges in his own household, it may be that Oedipus already imagines the conspiratorial design with which he will momentarily charge his kinsman, a design which it appears now threatens him (being possessed as he is of Laius' throne and his bed) as much as it once did Laius. The scholiast, Bernard Knox points out, suggests as much.[5] Whatever the number in Oedipus' reference here, it is to the plurality of murderers that he refers later in his discussion with the Chorus, and in his address to Teiresias, and of course, the same plurality that he will depend upon with Jocasta. Moreover, we note that a reference to a multiplicity is already present in this very speech, a reference which would, indeed, be odd if his singular references were to be taken as an unconscious mythic support. He condemns the culprit whether he be one alone or with others (246–47) and in his rhetorical enthusiasm includes within his condemnation even those who would shield the murderer from prosecution, a shrewd inclusion indeed if the specific terms of his proclamation were designed to catch those who planned the deed in his view (e.g., Teiresias and Creon) as well as those who would execute it (e.g., the Herdsman). If we have been accustomed to regarding Oedipus' conspiratorial accusations as an illusion, it may be that we delude ourselves with regard to their real plausibility and that we dissolve the complicity of Teiresias and Creon only by reading ourselves through the very myth their conspiracy would establish. Even if the mythic account remains convincing, Oedipus' suspicions of capital tyranny, when viewed against the background of fifth century Athens, Bernard Knox assures us, are fully understandable.[6]

Nor may Teiresias's authority in the play be necessarily disinterested or guaranteed. Unless we privilege Teiresias *a priori* as spokesman for the mythic pattern, we may have no confidence that the knowledge of the practicing mantic is other than professional. What Teiresias knows can be deduced from what is public knowledge if we assume with him *a priori* and apodictically the empirical truth of Apollo's words. If we assume instead Oedipus' conspiratorial design, then we might expect the prophet to respond dramatically to Oedipus' taunts as he does. The forensic tone of an outraged seer, Knox points out, is entirely appropriate.[7] Antagonistically he returns Oedipus' charges verbal blow for verbal blow. It may be such generic and political considerations, for example, that the Chorus depends upon when they initially hail Teiresias as the one man "in whom alone of men truth is innate" (298–99) only to dismiss his charges against Oedipus after he appears as no more valid than their own prophetic skill. It is, of course, the Elders who intervene in the agonistic battle between Oedipus and Teiresias to declare that both men have spoken in anger; and when Creon and Oedipus have fought their battle, Creon has departed, and Jocasta has appeared to question Oedipus on this family conflict, the Chorus once again will simply affirm the purely suppository character of their mutual accusations, the origin of both positions in the "sting" of injustice.

Finally, Oedipus' confession may be less condemning than we have traditionally suspected. The details of Jocasta's account and his own account are strangely incongruent. She identifies the place specifically, he returns only a general affirmation of her words. She lists five members in Laius' entourage, he agrees with her account and then lists only three. She speaks of one who escaped, he says he killed them "all." The accounts are so noticeably distinct, in fact, that Richard Jebb sees need to clarify what he calls Sophocles' "neglected clearness" on this point and to introduce in his annotation of the speech what "we must understand" by it.[8] But more importantly, perhaps, whatever the seeming correspondence between Oedipus' Phocal adventure, the old seer's accusations, and Jocasta's tale, Oedipus finds it no hindrance to believing that the truth depends exclusively upon the testimony of the Herdsman himself. Even if the Herdsman identifies a unique murderer at Phocis, the guilt, in Oedipus' mind, only "inclines" toward him. But the

Herdsman's testimony is the *sine qua non* of further investigative progress. Oedipus may yet be innocent. Oedipus may not have killed Laius.

The situation begins to become more complicated than it initially appeared. What began as a lacuna in the pattern of a traditional reading threatens now, it would seem, to tear apart the entire fabric. Not only may Oedipus not have killed Laius, not only does the empirical situation insist that the means by which we have traditionally condemned Oedipus are themselves questionable and that the murderers of Laius may be many, but the political interactions of Oedipus with Teiresias and Creon begin to suggest that others in the play may be no less guilty than we have traditionally assumed Oedipus to be, that the mythic adoption and the guilt that it determines may, in short, be thoroughly arbitrary. We restore the myth, it would seem, only from the outside and only at the expense of the play Sophocles has given us. The best case we can make for the mythic version is circumstantial, and a case that, short of the Herdsman's appearance, no one in the play is willing to make.

And yet we feel that the mythic version must be founded. The alternatives are unthinkable. It is not simply the tradition of Sophoclean or even classical scholarship and criticism that is here at stake. The power of Freud's suggestion that we continue to find ourselves at the level of desire in Oedipus' position resides less in its novelty than in its appeal to a critical predicament that lies somehow at the heart of Western experience.[9] Parricide and incest, in Lévi-Strauss's words, "express an ancient and lasting dream."[10] To suggest that Oedipus may not have killed Laius is to play havoc with a legend that for twenty-eight hundred years has remained curiously intact. It is to raise serious questions about those for whom the myth has remained constant whether in Sophocles' world or our own.

———

Is it possible that Norwood's criticism is idiosyncratic? Surely, we feel, Jebb's interpretative annotations cannot be substituted in quality for his philological erudition and the achievement of his textual presentation, neither can Norwood's criticism, which depends so demonstrably upon Jebb's, be regarded as the model.[11] Other critics, no doubt, more sensitive to the literary value of Sophocles' text and to the rigors of a sound literary criticism, must have taken these matters into account.

The conventional view of Greek tragedy and of Sophocles' play in particular is well known. *Oedipus* is a tragedy of destiny. It is an example of the genus that Aristotle identifies as a "reversal of fortune," the passage of a great man from prosperity to atrocious misfortune. It is particularly "beautiful" (καλός) because both the commission of the actions that ruin the hero and the development of the discovery or "recognition" (ἀναγνώρισις) of those actions are brought about through naturalistic character. And it is particularly "tragic" because the disaster that follows such prosperity, the fate or destiny that is revealed to have been determined for the hero all along, revolves around a fundamental irony. It comes not simply on the heels or as the result of the hero's actions but as the result of those very actions he has undertaken to avoid such a fate.

The panorama of critical interpretations which have remained constant to this conceptual framework is vast. Maurice Bowra finds emphatic the play's religious machinery and takes the conclusion to which Oedipus comes as instructional, as indicative of the poet's "theological intention," as a "salutary lesson" in humility before divine omnipotence.[12] William Chase Greene, on the other hand, takes that same omnipotent force as a function of the ironies of the poet's dramatic technique, as constitutive of the "triumph" of his "artistic manipulation."[13]

But the lesson man learns need not be viewed as positive. Against both Bowra's "piety" and Greene's artistic "triumph," Cedric Whitman, for example, argues the "bitterness" of Oedipus' discovery, the pessimism encouraged by the undeserved fall of such a "keenly intelligent moral conscience."[14] Still other critics, like Jan Kott, remain dissatisfied with even the credit that Whitman reserves for the gods and have taken the "evil lot of man" that Whitman unearths less as a discovery than as the allegorical staple of an absurd universe. "All that is left of tragedy is the concept of unmerited guilt, the inevitable defeat and unavoidable mistake. But the absolute has ceased to exist. It has been replaced by the absurdity of the human situation."[15]

The difficulties of this approach are clear. The price in human suffering endured far exceeds whatever religious or technical wisdom is gained. Philip Vellacott, sensitive to these problems, suggests an alternative view designed both to dissolve the difficulties of the tragedy of destiny approach and preserve its insights. In the criticism of Bowra, Whitman, and most of the older critics, Oedipus' innocence is presumed. The worst of which he is usually accused is a hasty temper. The crucial events are said to derive from an accident, an instance of *hamartia*, a mistake, a missing of the mark, an error that cannot be discerned as an error except in retrospect. But we can "find what we are looking for," Vellacott assures us, namely, "some sin, some fault in Oedipus' character which would justify to men the seemingly cruel and immoral ways of Zeus or of Apollo or of Fate" if we imagine Oedipus' "state of mind when he left the Delphic oracle": "'To avoid heinous pollution, he must make for himself two unbreakable rules: never to kill an older man; and never to marry an older woman. The incident at the banquet makes it clear that these two rules, and not the resolve to keep away from Corinth, would be the probable occupation of Oedipus' thoughts as he left Delphi.'"[16] Yet as soon as he meets Laius, he slays him and all his party and his fate is sown. "Oedipus has, at the first opportunity, ignored a divine warning. That this man could be his father would be a coincidence so incredible as to be impossible; but this was the risk he ought not to have taken. He is guilty."[17]

We may resist Vellacott's assumptions. We may question whether indeed "what we are looking for" in Greek tragedy is an Oedipal *hybris* and wonder whether Vellacott has not imported to classical study an approach more commonly and more profitably associated with A. C. Bradley's reading of Shakespeare. But we would be hard put to deny that Vellacott believes in the firmity of some mythic structure—even if that structure has been enlarged now to include "the probable preoccupation of Oedipus' thoughts as he left Delphi"—any less than the most traditional of critics. And therein lies for us its difficulty.

The erudition of all of these critics is not for a moment in question. Our debt to them—and to many others whose work we have not mentioned—is irreparable. No one who reads Sophocles with any care remains unaided by their patience and research.[18]

But their adherence to the primacy of mythic expectations is another matter entirely. Whether we consider the scene of Sophocles' morality as theological or dramaturgical, its lesson as optimistic, pessimistic, or absurd, Oedipus' participation in the drama as innocent or guilty, the integrity of the moral standard by which we have measured such results remains fundamentally and consistently intact. In each case, we have premised our consideration of the play on the viability of the mythic pattern and the moral universe it implies and precluded *a priori* the kinds of equivocation suggested in the present essay. To set aside such questions, to found critical discussion of the play upon their displacement, is to lose more than the increased complexity that the play acquires from their consideration. It is to reproduce the response of Oedipus himself and to become, ironically, subject to whatever examination Sophocles undertakes on the basis of such equivocation.

Can we not develop a more independent stance with regard to the play, one which reads with Sophocles rather than one which is read by Sophocles, an approach which reads neither with Oedipus' conspiratorial suspicions nor with the expulsion of those suspicions from the insight of his mantic blindness, but juxtaposing one perspective with (and against) the other, register the processes by which Oedipus' exclusion from Thebes (personally and socially) is systematically determined? Can we not accept Sophocles' equivocation at its face value and consider the very polysemy that we say we prize as the basis for a new positive reading? Can we not, finally, question the presence of such seemingly anti-mythic elements without invoking in order to explain them the very mythic structures they challenge?

Voltaire's reading of Sophocles, contained in the famous "Lettres sur *Œdipe*" that he prefaces to his own dramatic reworking of the Theban legend, would seem to address the problem of the number of the murderers of Laius more directly and more promisingly than any of the critics we have met so far.[19] After enumerating rather disdainfully Sophocles' imperfections in other regards, and after considering the many "contradictions" and breaches of "common sense" in the matter of the number of murderers ("How can it be," Voltaire wonders, "that a witness to the death of Laius can say that his master has been overcome by a large number when it remains true, moreover, that it is one man who has killed Laius and all his following?"), Voltaire relates the Herdsman's appearance.[20]

Finally, Phorbas arrives in the fourth act. Those who have no familiarity with Sophocles doubtless imagine that Oedipus, impatient to know the murderer of Laius and to give life to the Thebans, is going to question him straightaway on the death of the late king. No, indeed. Sophocles forgets that vengeance for the death of Laius is the subject of his play. No one speaks a word to Phorbas concerning his adventure and the tragedy finished without Phorbas having even opened his mouth on the death of the king his master.[21]

Clearly, Voltaire objects to the same forgetfulness that Norwood found so marvelous. But "it remains true" for him, nonetheless, "that it is one man who has killed Laius and all his following." If Voltaire raises problems which the tradition dismisses, his reading of the play is no less mythic, finally, than any of the others. He recognizes the presence of such elements only to toss them out with the play itself. If *we* do not "forget" why the Herdsman was summoned, as Norwood suggests, *Sophocles* in Voltaire's view does. No less than the others, it is the myth that Voltaire wants—another myth, to be sure, a rhetorical myth which prizes "common sense" and "verisimilitude" as the proper decorum for tragic discourse—but, nonetheless, a structure of differences which defines its own system of valuation. And not finding this structure, his response will be even more radical than the response of classical philologists. He will dismiss the play because of it. He will reestablish the myth elsewhere, in his own dramatic reworkings of the Greek legend, or in other critical literature.

All of our forays into Sophocles' text and into the history of response to that text have led us back only to the questions with which we began. Why does Sophocles undermine the clarity of the empirical situation on which the myth is built? Why does Oedipus adopt the myth in the face of evidence which is inconclusive, which is at best circumstantial and at worst arbitrary? Why does the Chorus, while able to recognize throughout the arbitrariness of Teiresias's accusations, straightaway adopt the same myth once Oedipus adopts it and take Oedipus' culpability as necessary and operative all along? Why, finally, have twenty-four hundred years of critical tradition continued that retrospective view, reading the play from the perspective of the Chorus, or of Oedipus, or of Teiresias, less in spite of Sophocles' presentation, it begins to seem, than because of it?

Our registry of Sophocles' mythic equivocation seems to have led us to an interpretive impasse. We cannot do without such questions. Sophocles has thrust them critically upon us. And yet there seems to be little that we can do with them. No sooner do we register the existence of these problems than we face the oblivion to which criticism has in one fashion or another consigned them. We seem condemned if we are to read the play at all to choose among a series of equally inadequate alternatives, either to dismiss the problems with the mainstream, or to dissolve them within some larger neo-mythic framework, or to recognize their existence only to dismiss the play on their basis and reconstruct the traditional myths elsewhere.

Nor may our difficulty be a new one. The gesture of critical exclusion which "forgets" the kind of numerical and technical play that, we have suggested, is at stake in Sophocles seems always to have been part of our critical response in the West, whether we have chosen with Plato to repudiate the mimetic plague of tragedy and institute new structures or with Aristotle to transcendentalize the cathartic perfections of tragic art and identify what is disconcerting with the misunderstandings of critics like Voltaire. Is there no way out of this representational crisis in which Sophocles himself, who played all his life with the prophetic language of pity and fears, may have been embroiled?

There may be a way out of our dilemma. A positive reading of Sophocles' equivocation with the myth may be possible—indeed, much closer than we think—and the prolonged consideration we have given thus far to traditional difficulties may itself provide the key. If we follow a bit longer and observe a little more closely the manner in which criticism fails us, in which it insures that the ambiguities of Sophocles' text be forgotten, in which it reveals at its origins an idolatry of the Oedipal perspective and at its conclusion a certain self-destructive violence, we may begin to understand both the play to which it is a response and the particular relation between them. Moreover, it may be that we need only turn to the criticism of Gilbert Norwood—the work that proved initially such a stumbling block to the positive reading that we wanted—to glimpse in the interstices of his reading, in the expulsive gestures by which he founds that reading, the kinds of genealogical movements that will offer a cornerstone to a new view of Sophocles.

We recall, in the first place, that the kinds of critical issues that we have been considering are not at all absent from Norwood's account. It is, indeed, Norwood who suggested that the part of the "aged Theban" is "especially pointed," that the distinction between the mythic account of Phocis and the account circulating in the city is "vital" to the growing horror, and Norwood, again, who highlighted the disparity between what is expected of the Herdsman when he is summoned ("to settle whether Laius was slain by one man or by a company") and what is demanded of him when he arrives ("from whom he received the outcast infant"). If Norwood raises these issues only to resituate them retrospectively as functions of Sophocles' ironic style, his fascination with them, particularly in conjunction with what follows, may begin to suggest a concern on his part which significantly exceeds the demands of the myth of Sophocles' constructive splendor.

Just below his consideration of the Herdsman, he stumbles upon a "flaw" in dramatic construction. The arrival of the Corinthian does not appear as "the direct result of something said or done by Oedipus."

> The arrival of the Corinthian messenger at this moment is purely acciden-
> tal. Without it, the witness of the old retainer would have fastened upon
> Oedipus the slaying of Laius (not known to be the king's father) and he
> would have gone forth from the city but not as a parricide; moreover,
> the relation between him and the queen would have remained unknown.
> Judged by the standard of the whole play, this fact constitutes a flaw in
> construction.[22]

What is curious in this passage is less that Norwood is able to identify a lapse in Sophocles' technique (although such a discovery is remarkable enough given his lavish praise of Sophocles' achievement) than the fact that the particular blemish he identifies threatens to introduce into the play the very mythic confusions that we would suggest are built-in already, that without the Corinthian's information, Oedipus "would have gone forth from the city but not as a parricide" and the "relation between him and the queen would have remained unknown," that what is "accidental" in the drama is less the manner in which the mythic crimes are committed (which is the view Norwood has just so carefully elaborated) than the attribution to Oedipus of the crimes at all.

Such an observation on Norwood's part would seem, perhaps, less remarkable if the logical context in which it were raised prompted its inclusion. But we note that Norwood feels the need to elaborate at length a hypothetical tangent that has very little to do with the "flaw" he would presumably describe. Rather than discuss how the Corinthian's appearance might have been more effectively motivated, or how else the essential information he holds might be introduced, Norwood ponders the consequences of not introducing the information at all, namely, that parricide and incest would have remained undiscovered, that in some uncanny way the discovery of Oedipus' mythic guilt, in the play we have before us, is arbitrary.

Clearly, Norwood does not suggest that the discovery of the contingent qualities of the attribution of parricide and incest is in any way a function of the Herdsman's silence on Phocis. He does not read the "accident" in function of the Herdsman's appearance at all, only as derivative of the appearance of the Corinthian. Moreover, he does not imagine the notion of "accident" as useful for interpreting the play Sophocles has given us, but rather as a problem Sophocles would have to have faced if the Corinthian were not to appear. He never fears for a moment that even under such circumstances Oedipus would not be guilty of parricide and incest, only that the manifestation of this relation would not, perhaps, have taken place.

But the curious incongruence of the suggestion to the immediate context in which it occurs and its ironic juxtaposition with Norwood's discussion of issues which, if pushed far enough, would yield the kind of questions we have suggested in this essay, is already clear enough. Does this brief moment of crisis in Norwood's text unveil the origin of his own mythopoesis? Does such reflection upon the potential arbitrariness of the charge of parricide and incest (and consequently responsibility for the Theban plague)—even circumscribed as it is within Norwood's strictly mythic coordinates—specify for us the dangers that Norwood finds in Sophocles and to which his tally of flaws and perfections is already itself a systematic response?

No sooner does Norwood raise this hypothetical consideration than he dismisses it as if it had not existed. He subsumes it within the representational structure whose breach he introduced it to elaborate. He identifies for it a naturalistic function curiously not unlike the naturalistic function he found for the Herdsman just a moment before.

> Why did the poet not contrive that the news of Polybus' death should arrive and arrive now as the direct result of something said or done by Oedipus, just as the arrival of the old Theban with his crushing testimony, is due to the king's own summons? No doubt this occurrence is meant to mirror the facts of life, which include accidents as well as events plainly traceable to character.[23]

Norwood's erasure of the questions he has raised may prove decisive both to their establishment and to the critical myth whose limits they highlight. The critical oblivion to which the tradition has consigned Sophocles' equivocation now appears by Norwood's example more systematic—and the intertextual relation between Norwood's work and Sophocles' more intimate—than we have suspected. Norwood repeats Oedipus' response not simply in spite of it—not merely ironically or coincidentally as if criticism just happens to reproduce the figure it questions—but because of it, in response to it, as part of the definitional and organizing structure of the critical undertaking itself. At the heart of Norwood's text is the rejection of Sophocles'. Norwood articulates the myth of Sophocles' constructive splendor in order to displace categorically and generically the possibility that the tragic discovery is "accidental," to undo the damage that Sophocles' mythic equivocation in the tradition's view has done, an anti-mythic violence that has accidentally surfaced in the very process of being expelled.

But there is another consequence of Norwood's reconstructive gesture. His move parallels closely another case of such forgetfulness to which Norwood himself has drawn our attention. If Norwood manages to raise such anti-mythic possibilities with the myth intact, in a slightly different non-critical context, and with regard to a play Sophocles never wrote, does he not in fact respond to the demonstrably ambiguous situation confronting him as critic precisely as Oedipus responds to the crisis he faces both at Delphi and, finally, at Thebes?

Have we not, that is, in Norwood's hypothetical deconstruction and reconstruction of the Oedipus myth, the Oedipal response in its entirety? If Norwood assumes, in order to read the Herdsman's appearance in the play, the very myth he is brought on to reveal, if in the face of evidence that Norwood himself can uncover—evidence that would, curiously enough, free him (or prohibit him) from articulating the critical myth of Sophocles' constructive splendor—he "forgets" to measure "new things by old," is transfixed by the Sophoclean speaker "when he speaks of fear and terror," and renders the Herdsman's silence ironically as an indication of the foundation of the myth and of that splendor, if, in short, Norwood substitutes what the Herdsman does not say for what he does, is Norwood's critical *hamartia* not like Oedipus's own mythopoetic gesture before the crisis he faces in Thebes and, perhaps, that Sophocles faced himself in Athens?

As the mantic Oedipal position is reproduced definitionally in criticism, that is, as criticism with Oedipus would systematically "forget" the equivocation which has brought it to this moment of critical decision, we may begin to gain some insight on the nature of the literary text to which it is a response.

If Norwood's position is Oedipal, then it is Norwood's position, and the critical tradition which appropriates that position, that is itself already at stake in Sophocles' drama. If we can remember what Oedipus would "forget," and juxtapose that memory with the moment of its amnesia, if we can read Oedipus against himself even as Norwood reads the Herdsman, and we in turn read Norwood, and uncover behind all of these retrospective transfigurations the displacements which have made them possible, then we recognize in the parallel that it has been a Sophoclean reading of Oedipus that has made possible these very disclosures. Rather than a critique of Oedipus via the myth, Sophocles' play is a critique via Oedipus of us. Norwood reenacts the drama to which the play itself is already a response. It is not Sophocles' text which is the origin of Norwood's, but, to the contrary, Norwood's criticism, in the figure of Oedipus, which is already the origin of Sophocles'.

Secondly, we can begin to read Sophocles' play the moment we give up the "Oedipalization" of Sophocles' text (the retrospective reading that Oedipus himself makes from within his mantic blindness and violence) and join Sophocles in his critique via Oedipus of such a position and such a process, the moment we acknowledge the idolatry and, in the extreme, the blindness and self-destructive violence which has made it possible and which Sophocles has exposed. If Sophocles' play is already about criticism, then it has been our critical posture which has created the difficulty, our assumption of independence, our assumed innocence of an Oedipal reading, that has constituted for us (even as it has for Oedipus) the Oedipal position itself. The play raises all the questions we would ask; it has already undertaken the "deconstruction" we would now "innocently" begin.[24] Translating these questions into a context in which answers are defined, we have preempted Sophocles' interrogation for our own. We can begin to read Sophocles' play the moment we recognize that we have never not been doing that, the moment we give up the distinction between literature and criticism by which we have "decriticalized" Sophocles' play in order to render the poet inspired but mute and the critic parasitic but alone fully articulate, the moment we recognize, in short, that our critical position has always already been Oedipal.[25]

The way out of the interpretive crisis in which we found ourselves, then, is to recognize such a crisis as the subject matter of the play itself, to give up trying to explain Sophocles' drama, or to answer the questions that the play poses for us, and to turn our attention instead to the arbitrary and potentially destructive premises of such an explanatory posture both within the play and without. Rather than participate in the play's crisis—in the crisis imagined by the play and the crisis that is the play—we might follow instead Sophocles' investigation of the enabling conditions of any Oedipal reading: of Oedipus manifesting the idolatrous and self-destructive limits of such critical blindness, of the Chorus instituting that paradigmatic blindness in traditional morality, and of the classical critical tradition which for twenty-four hundred years has perpetuated that critical Oedipal institution and for which in our day such blindness and violence continues to assume the status of insight itself.

Suddenly, a new reading of Sophocles' play opens up to us. Sophocles has shifted our traditional focus entirely. Rather than an illustration of the myth, the play is a critique of mythogenesis, an examination of the process by which one arbitrary fiction comes to assume the value of truth. Suspending the empirical foundation on which the myth is built, suggesting as arbitrary the political determination that Oedipus alone is responsible for the "numberless" plague that is depopulating the Theban city, Sophocles undertakes an examination of the logic that assumes he is the unique culprit. Oedipus discovers he is guilty of parricide and incest—he translates what the Herdsman does tell him into the mythic fulfillment—less by uncovering certain hitherto obscure empirical facts than by voluntarily appropriating an oracular logic which assumes he has always already been guilty. At the genesis of his Teiresian wisdom is an oracular idolatry which has guided his progress throughout and which he will now inscribe in his head forever. Oedipus becomes "Oedipus" by assuming the myth *a priori,* by assuming he has been so all along. Unable to measure new things by old, transfixed by the speaker when he speaks of pity and fear (whether at Delphi or at Thebes), Oedipus invests prophetic language with the power of truth. The truth, Teiresias told him, has power. Apollo is sufficient. The seer, Oedipus tells Jocasta as she trembles, had eyes. The son will kill the father. I am the son. *Ergo*, by mythic definition, I have killed the father. It is the terrible price of this critical wisdom that Sophocles' play weighs in the balance.

To take seriously the suggestion that Oedipus may not have killed Laius, then, is, in the last analysis, to give up Oedipus for Sophocles, to recognize the double of the Oedipal position in ourselves and to follow Sophocles in his critique, via Oedipus, of us. Have we registered Sophocles' equivocation only to develop a new myth of Oedipus, to suggest, for example, that Oedipus did not kill Laius or more cleverly that someone else did? Or would our examination lead us to decide that the empirical situation is hopelessly mired in obscurity and prompt us either to reject Sophocles' play on the basis of its undecidability or to take our pleasure from the text in an act of unbridled critical indulgence? Or, rather, does Sophocles not compel us to give up our privileging of the empirical question entirely, to view the empirical issue as less important than the universal matrix of scapegoat politics (in which all are identically "murderers of Laius") in terms of which it functions and for which it comes metonymically (and in retrospective relation to the arbitrary determination of a unique culprit for the plague) to substitute? Shall we not begin, Sophocles demands of us, to examine the limits of our myths, the status of our mythic appropriations in context of the real social relations in which they exist, in context, that is, of the blindness and self-destructive violence that plagues identically Oedipus' world, Sophocles' world and our own?

To read Sophocles, or, more precisely, to read with Sophocles, is to give up at the extreme the Oedipus myth and the structure of morality that it implies for an examination of its genealogy. If Plato can denounce the imitative violence of tragedy and Aristotle in turn applaud the cathartic virtues of the same sacrificial ode, this language of pity and fear, this λέγειν φόβους, and if we in turn can alternately model either Plato's rejection or Aristotle's formal approbation (even as Sophocles, we must assume, modeled Oedipus in his own ambivalent fascination with prophetic language), then, by virtue of the same appropriative freedom, can we not, Sophocles asks of us, give up that Oedipal reading? At the moment of Oedipus' blindness, at the moment when Oedipus' mythic self-definition and self-justification becomes self-destructive, and our critical insight collapses in the face of its truth, we may continue, Sophocles suggests, the Oedipal response that Oedipus himself would forget. We can retrieve the crisis of "emulous desire" or "imitative rivalry" (πολύζηλος) that Oedipus himself denounces in his encounter with the prophet and join Sophocles in taking his play, finally, as an autocriticism of all of us.[26]

The stakes of such an investigation are high. Oedipus is part of our language in the West. From Homer to Aristotle to Freud, it is the same old story. Oedipus is synonymous with parricidal and incestuous desire. If Oedipus becomes "Man" in the course of the tragedy, if, as Bernard Knox so astutely points out, Oedipus becomes himself the answer to the riddle he solved, *anthropos tyrannos*, even as he becomes in the Chorus's view "equal to nothing" (ἴσα . . . τὸ μηδὲν), then what is at stake in Oedipus—as the answer to an oracle that has become a riddle, as the insistent confusion between the many and the one, as the *paradeigma* or model whose expulsion will end the "numberless" plague which is the source of the city's woes—is Western humanism at large.[27]

We understand, now, the singular silence of the mainstream of critical tradition on the issues we have tried here to suggest. Substituting the myth for such anti-mythic indications, reading in Sophocles' mythic equivocation ironically the myth itself, repeating Oedipus' mythopoetic gesture—the very Oedipal *méconnaissance* that Sophocles' play already "deconstructs"—criticism succeeds in subduing the profoundly critical nature that it found in literature to begin with, a literature whose very monstrosity—its super-imposition of its own mythic conventions upon their arbitrariness—was the source of its uncanny attraction in the first place.[28] If we would raise Sophocles' work with Norwood to the status of a "masterpiece," even as the Greeks themselves sought to elevate this semi-heroic playwright to the sacred place of "first-prize," we do so less as a way of valuing its beauties than as a way of checking its violence, a beauty which is itself already nothing other than this limitlessness or violence read from a transcendental distance.

But perhaps more importantly, we understand the way in which Freud's appropriation of the "Sophoclean legend" as the program for a scientific institution carries this blindness to a dangerous new level. What is critical in Freud's handling of the Oedipus myth is less that he borrows a Greek myth to describe a psychology of human behavior or that he identifies himself with the most conservative of classical critics, than that he introduces a dramatic fiction within the set of cultural fictions by which we govern our everyday lives.

In the famous passage of *The Interpretation of Dreams* in which Freud links psychoanalysis with the Oedipus myth, Freud is astonishingly clear about the relation that he finds between the two. "The action of the play consists in nothing other than the process of revealing with ever mounting delays and ever mounting excitement—a process that can be likened to the work of psychoanalysis—that Oedipus is himself the murderer of Laius, but further that he is the son of the murdered man and of Jocasta.[29] What is startling enough in the present context is the exclusivity with which Freud collates the play with the myth, the fact that Sophocles' play for the founder of psychoanalysis consists in "nothing other than" the traditional material, that the play, like a detective story "with ever mounting delays and ever mounting excitement," leads to one exclusive truth which will in retrospect make everything fit.

But what is even more troublesome is that Freud in turn has appropriated this classical myth as the program for psychoanalytic therapy. It is the work of psychoanalysis which can be "likened" to this detective fiction and whose truths can be read from the end. If Freud admits, on the one hand, that the play reveals an unanticipated identity between the investigator and the investigated, psychoanalysis, in his view, should be modeled not on this identity but on the replaying of the differential illusions of its drama. The outcome of therapy, for Freud, which we might assume to be open-ended, is thoroughly determined in advance. The difference between the patient and the doctor, the denial of any fundamental identity between them, conditions the very possibility of the therapeutic encounter. The patient for Freud must discover himself Oedipus and must confess his crimes at the level of desire to the doctor who knew that truth in advance and who, with his wise silence and prophetic eyes, has assumed throughout the position of Teiresias.

To be sure, the doctor has not always been free of Oedipal sins himself. But the doctor has always already confessed his sins in the Freudian schema. The doctor always is where the patient was. He has gone through psychoanalysis. If Freud can recognize the arbitrariness of this distinction in other arenas, if he can write in "Dostoevsky and Parricide" concerning Dmitri's trial for the murder of his father in *The Brothers Karamazov* that "it is a matter of indifference who actually committed the crime" and that "all the brothers . . . are equally guilty," it is the temporal mythic distinction between Teiresias and Oedipus or between the doctor and the patient that Freud insists upon when he reads Sophocles or comes to imagine the psychoanalytic encounter.[30] The confession of Oedipus is more than a theme of psychoanalysis. The production of an "Oedipus complex," the "Oedipalization" of the patient, is an enabling condition for the psychoanalytic cure.[31]

If we could dismiss psychoanalysis as just another traditionalist reading, we might accept Freud's view of the play as idiosyncratic. We might follow with Sophocles the blindness and dangers of Freud's Oedipal investments as the key to the enigma of Freud's own prophetic concerns.[32] But psychoanalysis has emerged within psychiatric medical practice as the program for a scientific institution.[33] The Oedipus myth in Freud's hands has assumed the status of scientific truth. The imperative to confess one's Oedipal guilt—and the consequences of not confessing to a guilt which is given in advance—are now political. A refusal to confess can result in a declaration of madness and a sentence of imprisonment. This is literary criticism with a vengeance.

Fleeing the myth, Oedipus discovers that he has brought it about. Answering the riddle of the Sphinx, he discovers he has committed parricide and incest. Constructing a theory of tragic irony, we discover that we have reproduced the position of Oedipus himself. Confessing our sins, we discover our Oedipal guilt and unconscious desire. The foregoing analysis and the examination to which it is but a prelude may lead us to a new understanding of Sophocles. It will demand of us that we read Sophocles' text more carefully and that we rethink the theoretical considerations on which our analyses of the past have been based, the notion of an "author" or "writer," of a literary "text" (especially one that we qualify as a "masterpiece"), and the relation of both to the real world in which they function.[34]

But at the most profound level, perhaps, it will demand that we rethink the relation of "tragic irony" to violence, that we admit the possibility that the assumption of a position outside of the circle of mythic violence (as sons, critics, or patients) is already the gesture that insures that we are in, and that the "ironic" conclusions to which we come reflect only the non-ironic relation—the identical violence—in which we have always already taken part and which such distancing gesture itself perpetuates.

To pay attention, however, to Oedipus' status as *paradeigma* or sacrificial model and to the logic of number of *arithmos* (itself, we will suggest, a logic of sacrificial genesis) as the vocabulary in which this oracular crisis is presented is already to reflect the research of the critic who, more fully than anyone else in the contemporary context, has thought out the relation of violence to human communities.

In his essays on Sophocles and Euripides (principally "Symétrie et dis-symétrie dans le mythe d'Œdipe"[35] and "Dionysus and the Violent Genesis of the Sacred"),[36] and in his study of the role of sacrifice in primitive culture,[37] René Girard argues the ability of certain works in the Western tradition (principally those that we have called "tragic") to uncover behind the mythic structures from which they are born the violence of their own genesis, a reciprocal violence of "enemy twins" which the conventional distinctions of the work once held in check but now can no longer efficaciously dispel, the same sacrificial violence that once gave rise to the myth itself and is, in fact, the foundative mechanism in the primitive universe of all cultural order.

> The genesis of *myth* can be read in the filigree of *tragedy*. The ritual expulsion demanded by Oedipus at the end of the play echoes the collective violence which constitutes the true mainspring of mythological creation. . . . The instinct which carries the interpreter to the tragic texts is not false. The poet is the only real ally of the truest and most radical reading, a reading which reassembles the scattered fragments of the defunct reciprocity, which restores the falsified symmetries, which brings together all that the myth arbitrarily separates. . . . The tragic interpretation of the myth, like all truly critical readings, is the child of a fundamental crisis.[38]

We have tried to suggest that these insights, and the conceptualization on which they are based, allow us to recognize in *Oedipus Tyrannus* the pervasiveness of mythogenetic violence. Sophocles' equivocation with the mythic determinants has introduced a crisis not simply at the level of the reciprocal antagonisms of Oedipus, Teiresias and Creon, but in the very heart of the mythic fabric, in the very empirical structure of Oedipus' relation to Laius that we have taken for so long as a cultural given and that has begun to assume the status of scientific verity in our time.

These same insights will also allow us—and here is the area in which their value in our view is decisive—to understand not only the problem but the domain of its solution, to recognize the possibilities for survival in a "post-sacrificial" universe, a universe in which the expulsion of scapegoats no longer works and in which sacrifice has become confused irretrievably with violence itself, to imagine, that is, if only hypothetically, the possibilities for an anti-sacrificial position.

They will allow us to understand, perhaps for the first time, a Sophocles who, in a profoundly critical situation that is not unlike our own, is able to ask in the face of its violence what the Chorus asks in the play's dramatic center, the question of the χορός or of χορεύειν, the question of the efficacy of the dance, of the play, of religious worship itself: if the murderers of Laius are many, if an idolatrous dishonor for Apollo is being substituted for honor itself, if "things do not fit (ἁρμόσει) so that men can point at them with the hand (χειρόδειχτα)," if, in short, the numberless (ἀνάριθμος) plague cannot end because a *paradeigma* (an example, an oracular model, a one who can stand for many) cannot be found and any attempt at sacrifice (at the establishment of a difference between the one and the many—the principle of number itself) leads only to more violence, then τί δεῖ με χορεύειν; "Why must I dance?"

NOTES

1. The Greek text upon which I have relied throughout this essay is Richard Jebb's in *Sophocles: The Plays and Fragments, Part I: The Oedipus Tyrannus* (Cambridge: Cambridge University Press, 1893) as reprinted by the Scholarly Press, Inc. (New York, 1972). All extended English quotations and most shorter quotations from the play are cited from Philip Vellacott's "literal" translation in *Sophocles and Oedipus* (Ann Arbor: University of Michigan Press, 1971). On occasion I have paraphrased Vellacott's rendering or translated the Greek myself.

2. Our interest in the paradox of number in Sophocles' play is not new. Both William Chase Greene, in "The Murderers of Laius," *Transactions of the American Philological Association* 60 (1929): 75–86 [reprinted in this volume], and more recently Karl Harshbarger, in "Who Killed Laius?" *Tulane Drama Review* 9 (summer, 1965): 120–31 [also reprinted in this volume], take up the problem. Moreover, both see the issue as heightening our awareness of Sophocles' "ironies," Harshbarger suggesting in fact that "this [numerical] disparity is at the crux of any interpretation of the play" (121). But both critics understand that irony in traditional terms. Greene is convinced, finally, that these paradoxes support the myth itself offering us yet another example of the poet's skill at naturalistic characterization. And for Harshbarger "the fact of who killed Laius is central." If Harshbarger pursues the question, up to a certain point, with unparalleled clarity (the differences between the two versions of the Phocal massacre, he notes, "are not resolved"), and if in the course of his examination he is able to raise some remarkable questions concerning Creon's role in the Theban intrigue and concerning the Chorus' sacrificial substitution of Oedipus for its own complicity in the affair (and, by extension, ours), what concerns him principally about the murder is "whether there is anyone else who might have done it." We will argue in the present essay that it is the traditional theory of "tragic irony" that is already at stake in the play, and that the play uncovers systematically the arbitrariness of the determination of any unique culprit, that the empirical issue (whether we decide Oedipus killed Laius or not) is less important, finally, than the plague of scapegoat violence for which it comes to substitute.

3. Compare, for example, the Shepherd's words in Jean Cocteau's *The Infernal Machine*, trans. Albert Bermel (New York: New Directions, 1967), 91: "You are the son of Jocasta, your wife, and of

Laius, your father, killed by you at the crossing of three roads. Incest and parricide. May the gods forgive you!" I thank Edgar Rosenberg of Cornell University for this reference.

4. Gilbert Norwood, *Greek Tragedy* (New York: Hill and Wang, 1960), 148–49.

5. Bernard Knox, *Oedipus at Thebes* (New York: Norton, 1957), 26.

6. Ibid., 81–90.

7. Ibid., 85.

8. Jebb, *Sophocles,* 104–5.

9. Freud's remarks on the Oedipus myth appear in *The Interpretation of Dreams*, trans. James Strachey (New York: Avon, 1965), 294–98, and in *A General Introduction to Psychoanalysis*, trans. Joan Riviere (New York: Washington Square Press, 1952), 339–41.

10. Claude Lévi-Strauss, *The Elementary Structures of Kinship*, trans. Rodney Needham et al. (Boston: Beacon Press, 1969), 491.

11. Cf. Jebb, *Sophocles,* xi–li.

12. Maurice Bowra, *Sophoclean Tragedy* (Oxford: Oxford University Press, 1944), 175.

13. William Chase Greene, *Moira: Fate, Good, and Evil in Greek Thought* (Cambridge, MA: Harvard University Press, 1944), 154.

14. Cedric Whitman, *Sophocles: A Study of Heroic Humanism* (Cambridge, MA: Harvard University Press, 1951), 124.

15. Jan Kott, *Shakespeare Our Contemporary*, trans. Boleslaw Taborski (New York: Anchor Books, 1966), 137.

16. Philip Vellacott, "The Guilt of Oedipus," in *Sophocles' Oedipus Tyrannus*, ed. Luci Berkowitz and Theodore F. Brunner (New York: Norton, 1970), 209–10.

17. Ibid., 210.

18. For a useful bibliographical survey of modern Sophoclean criticism and scholarship see Holger Friis Johansen, "Sophocles 1939–1959," *Lustrum* 7 (1962–63): 94–288.

19. Voltaire, *Oeuvres Complètes*, II, ed. A. Beuchot (Paris: Garnier Frères, 1877), 1–58.

20. Ibid., 20.

21. Ibid., 20–21, my translation.

22. Norwood, *Greek Tragedy*, 149–50.

23. Ibid., 150.

24. Cf. Jacques Derrida, "La Double séance," in *La Dissémination* (Paris: Seuil, 1972), 207–20.

25. "The axiom of criticism must be," Northrop Frye remarks, in *Anatomy of Criticism* (Princeton, NJ: Princeton University Press, 1966), 5, "not that the poet does not know what he is talking about, but that he cannot talk about what he knows." We are moving in this essay towards a reversal of this characterization, towards suggesting that literature is already a form of criticism (which is why criticism subverts it and takes its name) and criticism already a form of literature (in the way that criticism would like to think of it).

26. Cf. Murray Krieger, *The Tragic Vision* (Chicago: University of Chicago Press, 1960), 1–21.

27. Bernard Knox, "Sophocles' Oedipus," in *Tragic Themes in Western Literature,* ed. Cleanth Brooks (New Haven: Yale University Press, 1955), 21.

28. Cf. Neil Hertz's discussion of the relations in Freud between the uncanny, the compulsion to repeat, and literature in "Freud and the Sandman," forthcoming in *Textual Strategies: Criticism in the Wake of Structuralism,* ed. Josué Harari (Ithaca, NY: Cornell University Press [published in 1979 with the subtitle *Perspectives in Post-Structuralist Criticism*]).

29. Freud, *The Interpretation of Dreams,* 295.

30. Sigmund Freud, *Character and Culture,* ed. Philip Rieff (New York: Collier Books, 1963), 288.

31. Cf. Gilles Deleuze and Félix Guattari, *L'Anti-Œdipe* (Paris: Minuit, 1972).

32. Cf. Ernest Jones, *The Life and Work of Sigmund Freud* (New York: Anchor Books, 1963), 5–6.

33. Cf. Michel Foucault, *Histoire de la folie à l'âge classique* (Paris: Plon, 1961).

34. "The type of literary study which structuralism helps one to envisage," Jonathan Culler notes (in *Structuralist Poetics* [Ithaca, NY: Cornell University Press, 1975], viii), "would not be primarily interpretive: it would not offer a method which, when applied to literary works, produced new and hitherto unexpected meanings. Rather than a criticism which discovers or assigns meanings, it would be a poetics which strives to define the conditions of meaning."

35. René Girard, "Symétrie et dissymétrie dans le mythe d'Œdipe," *Critique* 249 (February 1968): 99–135 [this essay has since been translated as "Symmetry and Dissymmetry in the Myth of Oedipus" in René Girard, *Oedipus Unbound: Selected Writings on Rivalry and Desire* (Stanford: Stanford University Press, 2004), 59–94].

36. René Girard, "Dionysus and the Violent Genesis of the Sacred," trans. Sandor Goodhart, *boundary 2,* vol. 5, no. 2 (Winter 1977): 487–505.

37. René Girard, *Violence and the Sacred,* trans. Patrick Gregory (Baltimore: Johns Hopkins University Press, 1977).

38. Girard, "Dionysus and the Violent Genesis of the Sacred," 487–502.

An Anonymous Namer

The Corinthian's Testimony

Frederick Ahl

I'm from Corinth

Oedipus is easily distracted. He errs and loses the initiative not only when cross-questioning obviously "formidable," potentially threatening opponents such as Teiresias and Creon but also when examining socially "insignificant persons" who are not, by virtue of their power and status, in the least intimidating. Indeed, they are better able to play on Oedipus' innermost fears precisely because they are not themselves objects of fear. Thus it is not surprising that Oedipus' name and identity should be defined for him in this play not by an oracle or by Teiresias, but by two men who are given only the most imprecise identity themselves. One of them is the newcomer whose arrival robs the chorus of the chance to respond to Jocasta's appearance as suppliant. The newcomer is usually presented in translations as a messenger—though "free-lance reporter" would convey a better idea of his role. For the term messenger suggests someone commissioned and *sent* by one person to another. As we will see, the newcomer seems to be operating on his own. He lacks

From chapter 6 of Sophocles' *Oedipus: Evidence and Self-Conviction* (Ithaca, NY: Cornell University Press, 1991). The subtitle has been added for the present publication.

even the most characteristic mark of the messenger in Greek tragedy: a messenger speech. So we will call him simply "the Corinthian," since that is how he identifies himself.

The Corinthian asks the chorus where he can find Oedipus' palace and Oedipus himself. Here are his opening words, in Bernard Knox's translation, with the Greek phrases transliterated to illustrate the points Knox wishes to establish (924–26):

> Strangers, from you might I *learn where* (*mathOIm' hoPOU*)
> is the palace of the *tyrannos* OIDiPOUS,
> best of all, where he himself is, if you *know where* (*katOIsth' oPOU*)

"These" as Knox comments, are "violent puns, suggesting a fantastic conjugation of the verb 'to know where' formed from the name of the hero who, as Teiresias told him, does not know where he is."[1]

OIDa in Greek means "I know," and *POU* means "where." The echo of the syllable *POU* at the end of each of the messenger's first three lines emphasizes a play on OIDiPOUs' name. And how fascinating it is that the Corinthian should be the one to produce it here as he enters; for he will convince Oedipus not only that he knows *where* Oedipus comes from but that he can interpret Oedipus' name on the basis of another etymology: that of *OIDI*, "swollen," and *POUS*, "foot," which appears here for the first time in surviving Greek literature.

This is an important issue. Simon Goldhill points out:

> It was Oedipus who could solve the riddling language of the sphinx, the answer to whose question was the nature of the questioned (man Oedipus)—as will be the answer to the investigative process here instigated in order to free the city from this trouble. Indeed as his name *Oidipous* [*dipous* = two-foot] echoes the riddle, it was an answer that he found for himself.[2]

The reader who relies on a translation, of course, will have no idea that such wordplay is in progress. To illustrate my point, I cite these lines in Bernard Knox's own, earlier translation of the play:

CORINTHIAN: Stranger, can one of you tell me—where is the palace of King
    Oedipus? Better still, if you know, where is the king himself?[3]

The reader in English (or other modern languages) is deprived of this
crucial wordplay even by those who think it fundamental to the play's meaning for two reasons. First, the translator would have to devise a comparable
wordplay to encompass the various possibilities in Oedipus' name: to change
his name or at least append to it an epithet containing the wordplays. Second, modern scholars associate puns and wordplays with comedy not with
tragedy, and someone who substituted a punning name or epithet for Oedipus would immediately be accused of "ruining" the tragic grandeur of the
original. Shelley's parody, "Swellfoot the Tyrant," is a powerful deterrent. But
if we are to get the idea of how language itself functions in this play, we *must*
find at least an approximation. For Sophocles is here exploring and uncovering the forces of the irrational and demonstrating how those forces operate
through language—including puns and other wordplays.

I therefore adopt a compromise course. Instead of giving Oedipus a different name from which the wordplays may develop, I provide him, from
this point on, epithets in which at least some of the many Greek wordplays
may be imitated: Oedipus, "Undefeated," "Nowhere defeated," and so forth.
Thus the Corinthian's opening words and the chorus' response might appear
as follows (924–28):

CORINTHIAN: Could I ask, friends, if you know where Oedipus
    your nowhere defeated tyrant lives?
    And better, say where *he* is if you know.
CHORUS: Here is his home, my friend, and he's inside.
    This is his children's mother and his wife.

The wordplaying Corinthian is, from the outset, both courteous and
considerate. When the chorus introduces him to Jocasta, he prays for a blessing upon her and says how lucky her husband must be (929–30):

Then may she prosper, may she always live
amid prosperity, a perfect wife for him.

His blessing, Dawe notes, "is a *captatio benevolentiae* from a lower member of society to his betters."[4] There is no reason, however, to apply elitist overtones. The Corinthian is courteous and flattering as even a gentleman can be if he needs to establish himself in someone else's graces. Jocasta clearly appreciates his compliments, as her charming (and charmed) reply shows. Yet although she returns the compliment, she apparently detects from his tone that he may be after something for himself (931–33):

> Greetings in kind, my friend. So you deserve
> for all your courtesy. But tell me why
> you've come. What do you need, or want to say?

She asks him what he needs (*chrêizei*) or what he wants to say. Jocasta's use of this word shows her awareness that the newcomer may be using flattery as an overture to a request for some help or benefit. He is not *obviously* a messenger.

The newcomer ignores the first part of Jocasta's instructions. He says nothing about what he needs but immediately indicates that he has news good for both Jocasta and her husband (934): "Good news, my lady, for your home and spouse." Jocasta now, unwisely, floats two questions at the same moment (935): "What sort of news? And who have you come from?" Her second question is a good one, and one not generally posed to messengers in Greek tragedy. For it is usually assumed that the bearer of news is qualified to make the report. But Jocasta seems not sure that he *is* a messenger, and she tends to be an alert and quick-minded person, a keen observer of things and people. The Corinthian responds to her second question first (935–36):

> From Corinth. And the word you soon will learn
> could please—how not?—perhaps upset you too.

His answer is not entirely satisfactory on two counts.

First: Jocasta is asking *who* has sent him, not *where* he is from. Translators deal with the problem in some curious ways. Luci Berkowitz and Theodore Brunner, and Robert Fagles dispose of it before it reaches us. Here are, respectively, their versions of 935–36. First Berkowitz and Brunner:

> JOCASTA: Where do you come from?
> MESSENGER: From Corinth . . . [5]

Now Fagles:

> JOCASTA: Who sent you?
> MESSENGER: Corinth . . . [6]

Berkowitz and Brunner adapt Jocasta's question to the answer she receives. Fagles implies that the Corinthian has been sent by the city of Corinth. Nor is this the only instance in this scene where translators glide over major problems in the text.

Second: although the Corinthian introduces himself as the bearer of good tidings, he has gone on to suggest that his news is more ambiguous: it could be pleasing or upsetting. This is precisely the same approach taken by Creon when reporting the oracle to Oedipus (85–88):

> OEDIPUS: My lord and kinsman, Menoeceus' son,
>   what statement (*phêmên*) do you bring us from the god?
> CREON: A good one. For I say things that are hard
>   to bear could all turn out quite happily
>   if they ultimately turn out straight.

It is worth reminding ourselves that in the original production of *Oedipus*, the same actor, the tritagonist, played Creon and the Corinthian. Such an approach, then, might be Sophocles' way of using a dramatic stage convention to rhetorical advantage: the same voice introducing itself with similar words.

Let us look again at 936–37:

> CORINTHIAN: From Corinth. And the word you soon will learn
>   could please—how not?—perhaps upset you too.

Jocasta fails to pursue, or perhaps even notice, the imprecise—or is it evasive?—reply to her question about who sent the Corinthian. Why, if she is normally so quick-witted? Perhaps because the newcomer immediately focuses on her first question in a rather disturbing way. Although he introduced himself as bearer of good news, he now stresses the ambiguous nature of what he has to report: it could be pleasing or upsetting. Predictably, the clarification Jocasta now seeks is about the ambiguous tone of what he says, not about his unclear identity (938): "What is it? And what is its double force?" Here is the Corinthian's reply (939–44):

> CORINTHIAN: He'll be the tyrant. The Corinthians
>   will give him power. So it is rumored there.
> JOCASTA: How so? Does not old Polybus still rule?
> CORINTHIAN: No more. For death now has him in the grave.
> JOCASTA: Are you then saying Polybus is dead?
> CORINTHIAN: If I don't speak the truth, *I* risk dying.

Jocasta is so distracted (and apparently delighted) by the news of Polybus' death that she fails to notice how odd the first part of the report is. The newcomer does not say Oedipus *has been* appointed tyrant of Corinth, but that Oedipus *will be* appointed tyrant, if *rumor* is correct.[7]

Several translators nonetheless confer official status on man and message. Kenneth Cavander has the messenger say:

> The people of Corinth—it was already announced
> there—will make Oedipus their king.[8]

Berkowitz and Brunner render the passage as:

> Your husband now is ruler of the Isthmus![9]

These translators' changes prevent us from grasping that we are dealing not with fact but with hearsay, and hearsay that is at least doubly removed, since the evasive Corinthian is reporting rumor. Dawe comments on line 940 that it shows he is "not an official representative, but one hoping to earn a reward on his own account by enterprisingly informing Oedipus of local gossip."[10] His comment about Oedipus' rumored, pending appointment as tyrant of Corinth does, then, provide a negative clue about the newcomer's identity. He is not an official ambassador from Corinth. He seems to have picked up some rumors that were circulating and hurried to Thebes with them.

Readers are often no more interested in the identity of the Corinthian and his credentials than is Jocasta or, for that matter, Oedipus. We often approach Sophocles' play on the assumption that everyone is speaking the truth—which, as we have already seen, cannot possibly be the case. So we attribute the Corinthian's evasiveness and obliqueness to sloppy writing rather than authorial intent. We have been careless in our listening, as Jocasta has been in her questioning. We are hearing what we expect to hear. She is hearing what she wants to hear.

Jocasta is not always so incautious. When she asks Oedipus, for instance, on what basis Creon is accusing Oedipus of murdering Laios, she knows how important it is to distinguish between knowing something oneself and picking it up from someone else (704):

He really knows this for himself? Or has he just
learned about it all from someone else?

Ironically, Jocasta is fully aware of the difference between knowledge and hearsay. But her concern for that distinction seems to obtrude only when she is deeply interested in the issue under discussion. And Jocasta is not interested in what the Corinthian thinks is his good news. Her delight is in his *bad* news (945–49):

Maid! won't you go as quickly as you can
and tell your master?
Where are you, prophecies
from heaven? This is the man that Oedipus
has long been running from, fearing he might
kill him. But now this man (*hode*) has been destroyed
by Luck's (*Tychê*) hand, not by this man (*toud'*) who's now here.[11]

Jocasta gloats over the failure of divine prophecy. But now her skepticism appears more blasphemous, since she approached the gods only moments before as a suppliant with prayers and incense. Further, she is not justified in assuming that Polybus was simply the victim of Luck or Fortune, the divine name attributed to the nonevident causal forces operating within the world. The Corinthian has not yet explained how Polybus died.

Oedipus' entrance during Jocasta's final sentence intensifies the dramatic irony by endowing her words with a multiplicity of reference that probably lies beyond her intent. In conventional tragic diction, the demonstrative *hode* (genitive *toude*) may mean: "this person just mentioned," "this person here," or "this person speaking, that is, myself." Because of the distinction in gender, the last possibility does not really apply in this instance, since the speaker is a woman. But two meanings do emerge here. There is the meaning intended by Jocasta: Polybus was not killed by Oedipus; and another: "*hode* (this man, Oedipus) has been destroyed by Luck's (*Tychê*) hand, not by *toud'* (this man, the Corinthian) who's now here." The second meaning has an ironic ring. For the Corinthian will destroy Oedipus.

Given Jocasta's preamble about Oedipus' psychological condition at the opening of this scene, we might expect Oedipus, as he reenters, to show some immediate sign of stress. His conversation offstage with Jocasta seems certainly to have disturbed her profoundly. But he does not show any public signs of anxiety. He addresses Jocasta with great courtesy in the following exchange (950–54):

> OEDIPUS: Wise, dearest head of Jocasta, my wife,
> 　　Why have you sent for me to come outside?
> JOCASTA: Hear this man (*toude*)! Think, while you listen, where
> 　　the holy prophecies from heaven have gone.
> OEDIPUS: Who is this person? What's his news for me?

Oedipus not only reverses the order of Jocasta's two questions to the Corinthian but directs them to his wife, not to the newcomer. For a second time, the question arises as to the newcomer's identity, and there is absolutely no doubt that the questioner wants to know *who* he is, not just *where* he is from.

We also notice that Oedipus seems eager to acquire information second-hand, even when he could obtain it directly by his own questioning. Nor is this approach unusual for him in the play. He did, after all, send Creon to Delphi and did not go himself. Such reliance on indirect questioning seems characteristic of monarchic behavior in ancient writers.

Jocasta, instead of saying "Ask him yourself," answers (955–56):

> From Corinth. He'll announce that your father
> lives no longer. Polybus is dead!

She simply echoes verbatim the newcomer's vague statement that he is from Corinth, and reports his "bad" news. She omits the "good" news altogether. Oedipus is never told about the rumor that he will be tyrant of Corinth. The Corinthian is piqued by the lack of interest in his "good" news (957–59):

> OEDIPUS: What's your word, stranger? Tell me this yourself!
> MESSENGER: If I must first say this part of my news,
>   know well that he has passed on through death's door.

Had the Corinthian tyranny interested Jocasta (or Oedipus himself), more acute questioning about the newcomer's credentials and certainty of information might have arisen. As it is, we are still no closer to knowing the trustworthiness of his news or the details of his identity. And we will learn no more. News of Polybus' death so preoccupies Oedipus and Jocasta that neither pursues the reporter's identity, much less asks when Oedipus will become tyrant of Corinth. Further, there emerges later another, more aristocratic reason why Oedipus is not deeply concerned about who the newcomer is: Oedipus' opinion that this is a person of no consequence. Yet this mysterious nobody will explain Oedipus' name to *Oedipus'* satisfaction and establish *Oedipus'* identity even though he remains tight-lipped about his own.

How Polybus Died

Oedipus, who still fears he may be responsible for his father's death, asks the Corinthian how Polybus died (960): "Was it conspiracy or some sickness (*nosou*)?" Here, surely, is the moment for the classical messenger speech of Greek tragedy. But we get nothing of the kind. The Corinthian simply replies in one line (961): "A small scale stroke (*rhopē*) tips old bodies to sleep." Dawe calls this "the most beautiful line in Sophocles."[12] He may be right. But the Corinthian's use of the present tense makes his statement a generalization about the tendency of old men to die easily rather than an explanation of how this particular old man actually died. The Greek *rhopē* indicates a medical "turn" for the better or worse (Hippocrates, *Epidemics* I.26). Bernard Knox observes: "the Corinthian messenger answers like a Hippocratic physician: 'A small impulse brings aged bodies to their rest.'"[13] Yet Plato (*Republic* 8.556E–557A) uses that medical image as a simile of the state's vulnerability to radical political change: as the diseased body needs only a small stroke (*rhopês*) to tip the balance, so forces within the sick state need only a slight pretext to spawn factionalism and revolution. I translate *rhopê* as "stroke" (rather than, say, "turn") to catch the ambiguity, not to suggest that the ancients understood what we now call "strokes." The Corinthian rules out *neither* conspiracy *nor* medical ailment as the cause of death. His response, then, is not an adequate answer to Oedipus' question, much less an adequate explanation of how Polybus died.

Oedipus tentatively interprets the old man's expression in a medical sense. He does not ask any further details; he fills in the blanks himself (962): "The poor man succumbed to sickness (*nosois*) then, it seems." The Corinthian adds a further touch of the self-evident with noncommittal helpfulness (963): "And he had measured out so many years." Having said that, he falls silent for the next twenty-five lines. Again some translators fall short. Fitts and Fitzgerald render the Corinthian's words and Oedipus' response thus:

> MESSENGER: A little thing brings old men to their rest.
> OEDIPUS: It was sickness then?[14]

Kenneth Cavander does much the same and even adds a touch of filial sympathy from Oedipus which is not in the original:

> MESSENGER: A small
>   Touch on the balance sends old lives to sleep.
> OEDIPUS: So, my poor father, sickness murdered you.[15]

The medical imagery in the Corinthian's words is lost, leaving Oedipus' reaction incomprehensible.

Since neither Oedipus nor Jocasta appears particularly interested in the details of Polybus' death, we are left to speculate not only about the Corinthian's knowledge but about the reasons for Oedipus' disinterest and lack of sympathy. Not a word of grief escapes him when he hears of Polybus' death,

only a sense of triumph over the oracle and a curious realization that Polybus
might have died of grief and longing for him, a fleeting pang of anxiety that
he is responsible in a remote sort of way for the old man's death (964–72):

> Well, well, dear wife! Who now would give a glance
> at Pythian prophecy or ominous birds
> cawing above our heads? Allegedly
> they showed that I'd kill my father. Now he's dead,
> buried beneath the earth. And I, this man (*hode*),
> am here and did not touch my sword. Unless—
> unless he died because he missed me so,
> so in that way I could have caused his death.
> But still the prophecies in their strictest sense
> have come to nothing. Polybus is dead
> and took them to the underworld with him.

For an instant even Oedipus sees the possibility that he fulfilled the oracle
in a figurative, Herodotean way: that he is the killer of *Polybus*. Oedipus also
gives us a glimpse of how much Polybus cared for him and of his own curious combination of guilt and self-centeredness. But since he never presses
the issue about how Polybus dies, neither he nor we ever learn whether this
beautifully Delphic *ambages* provides a solution to the problem of the oracle.
Suffice it to say that a child who reacts so callously and, later, joyously, to
his father's death, when there is no suggestion of ill-feeling between them,
should perhaps excite a little more severe comment than Oedipus has earned
from critics, and remind us that there are more ways of killing one's father
than striking him down at a crossroads. To Oedipus, Polybus' death means
only his personal escape from fear—or so he thinks.

Speaking to Oedipus' Fears

Several issues and questions, I suggest, should now be in our minds about
the taciturn and anonymous Corinthian and his news. Why has he come to
Thebes, as it appears, on his own initiative? Was Jocasta's first instinct right,
that he needed something? Is it possible that he does not actually know how

Polybus died—that he simply gathered from gossip that the king was dead,
just as he apparently gathered from gossip that Oedipus would be appointed
tyrant of Corinth? This newcomer himself is, we have suggested, an anomaly
in Greek tragedy; a "messenger" without a speech who sidesteps questions.
But he has an ear for gossip and uses what he learns. After his vague mention
of Polybus' death, he leaves the talking to Jocasta and Oedipus, and listens.

He may also have been listening as he entered. For as he comes in, and
before he first speaks, Jocasta makes the remark we have mentioned earlier:
that her husband belongs to the person speaking to him, if that person voices
fears (914–17). And fear, we have suggested, is the leitmotif of this scene. Let
us now look at it in detail, beginning with Jocasta's reassurance to Oedipus
that his fears of the oracle have proved groundless (973–88):

JOCASTA: Wasn't *I* predicting this to you for years (*palai*)?
OEDIPUS: You said so. I was drawn off track by fear (*phobôi*).
JOCASTA: Don't let it go on gnawing at your heart.
OEDIPUS: How can I *not* shrink (*oknein*) from my mother's bed?
JOCASTA: What should man be afraid of (*phoboit'*)? Luck (*Tychê*) controls
    his life, and no one has proven foresight.
    The most effective course is, I should think,
    to live to the very fullest of one's powers.
    Don't fear (*phobou*) this marriage with your own mother.
    Many a mortal before you has slept
    with mother in dream fantasies as well.
    He who sees no significance in them
    endures his life most easily, and best.
OEDIPUS: You'd be correct in all of what you say
    if she who gave me birth were not alive.
    But since she is alive, I am compelled
    To shrink (*oknein*) from this, although you are correct.
JOCASTA: At least your father's death brightens your eye.
OEDIPUS: A lot. I know. But she lives. I fear (*phobos*) her.

The sexual imagery of this famous passage has elicited much comment,
notably that of Sigmund Freud in *The Interpretation of Dreams* which, "with
its first public association between the names of Freud and Oedipus, marks

the beginning of psychoanalysis."[16] Oedipus not only delights in his father's death but seems worried that his mother is not also dead, for fear he will fulfill what he thinks is his incestuous, oracular destiny. Yet, curiously, the Sophoclean Oedipus does not react as strongly as Seneca's at this point. To Seneca's Oedipus, his mother is now a widow (*vidua*) and thus available for marriage.[17]

Sophocles' Jocasta, interestingly enough, identifies Oedipus' fears of incest and parricide based on the oracle with incestuous dream fantasies. She recognizes that there is more than just a Delphic prophecy underlying the intensity of Oedipus' irrational behavior. For fears are, in Aristotelian terms, based on a disturbing fantasy: "Let fear (*phobos*) be some pain or disorder stemming from fantasy (*phantasia*) about a future evil which will cause pain or death" (*Rhetoric* 2.I382A). And Jocasta indicates that she and Oedipus have discussed his fears repeatedly over a long period (*palai*). Their dialogue on stage, then, is at least in part the reenactment of a familiar family scene. Hence, perhaps, Jocasta's earlier and puzzling calm. What was said was not as new to her as we may have thought.

Jocasta contends that what we now call Oedipal dreams are nothing unusual. Such dreams are commonly reported in ancient writers and discussed in detail by Artemidorus of Daldi in his own *Interpretation of Dreams* (*Oneirocritica* I.79). . . . Freud was familiar with Artemidorus from Theodor Gomperz's *Traumdeutung und Zauberei*.[18] Freud in a sense was rediscovering an idea well known in antiquity but later ignored (or repressed!), rather than formulating an idea hitherto unknown.

Oedipal dreams in antiquity are generally mentioned in connection with the powerful, with Plato's "tyrannical" types: Julius Caesar (Plutarch, *Caesar* 32.6), and Hippias (Herodotus 6.107). Plato, to recap briefly, argues that man is brutalized by the dominance of the irrational, despotic elements of the soul over the rational and thus rendered tyrannical and unsuitable for the proper government of the state (*Republic* 9.571C–D).[19] The passage merits another glance here:

"Those that awaken when we sleep," I said, "when one part of our soul is at rest—the part that approaches things reasonably and verbally, with gentle clarity, the part that rules the other element of the soul. That other element is like a wild and ferocious animal, gorged on food and drink. It leaps up,

pushes sleep away from it, and goes off on a lively search to satisfy the call
of its particular nature. You know it is bold and stops at nothing at these
times, for it is freed from—and unburdened by—morality and thought.
Its lust, people think, does not shrink at intercourse with its mother or
anything human, divine, or animal."

According to Jocasta, then, Oedipus allows his irrational dreams to
superimpose themselves on reality. That, presumably, is why she told the chorus that Oedipus was no longer a capable helmsman of that state. Oedipus
has abandoned reason for irrational fears, thus making "real" for himself grotesque desires and incestuous fantasies. Whereas other tyrannic dreamers,
like Caesar or Hippias, apply the reasoning, verbal faculty to the incestuous
dream, as they do to other dreams, when they wake up, Oedipus does not. He
takes the fantasy literally; he fears the incestuous image, whereas they take it
as a good sign. Oedipus assumes, as Sophocles' readers generally do, that the
prophecy (which coincides with what Jocasta regards as common, incestuous
dreams) has a literal force. In that sense he is both more "modern" and more
primitive than the other characters of the play. For in his response to Jocasta,
Oedipus admits that she is right but then instantly discounts his own recognition of her rightness. Logic cannot triumph over his fears. And standing
by him, attentively listening to the dialogue, is our wordplaying Corinthian
who will offer him an alternative way of interpreting his fears.

The Interpreter of Fears

When Alexander the Great, at the siege of Tyre, dreamed that a satyr was
cavorting on his shield, his associate Antander interpreted the satyr as signifying his impending capture of Tyre. He did so by means of a wordplay:
SATYROS = SA TYROS: "Tyre is yours" (*Oneirocritica* 4.26). "Dream
activity," Musatti comments, "plays with words . . . wordplay is a great part
of dream activity"—as Freud was equally well aware.[20] We should add, as
the Alexander anecdote reveals, that wordplay is also a major part of dream
interpretation, as it is of the interpretation of oracles. And it may be worth
recalling that in one version of the Oedipus myth, Oedipus learns the solution to the (verbal) enigma of the Sphinx in a dream (Pausanias 9.26.4).

Like a dream interpreter or modern psychologist, the Corinthian inquires about Oedipus' object of fear (989–1003):

CORINTHIAN: Who is this woman you so greatly fear (*ekphobeisth'*)?
OEDIPUS: Merope. Polybus lived with her, old sir.
CORINTHIAN: What is it about her you both so fear (*phobon*)?
OEDIPUS: A formidable (*deinon*) prophecy of god, my friend.
CORINTHIAN: Can you say what it is, or is it wrong,
    a sacrilege if someone else should know?
OEDIPUS: Of course. Apollo Loxias once said
    fate had determined I'd have intercourse
    with my own mother, and then said I
    would shed my father's blood with my own hands.
Hence Corinth, my home, has long been kept
    away from me. Happily so, although
    it is pleasure supreme to look into
    the eyes of those who brought us into life.
CORINTHIAN: You shrank (*oknôn*) from this? This kept you from Corinth?
OEDIPUS: I was determined not to kill father.
CORINTHIAN: Since I came in all good will, my lord,
    why have I not yet freed you from this fear (*phobou*)?

It is curious that Oedipus so readily accepts the anonymous stranger as confessor here. It is no less curious that when he says he cannot return to Corinth he reiterates not his fear of marrying his mother, but that of killing his father (who has just been reported dead). The Corinthian, of course, has already heard a lot. He arrives on stage as—or right after—Jocasta mentions Oedipus' fears to the chorus; he remains on stage to hear Oedipus' public conversation with Jocasta about his fears. He hears Oedipus and Jocasta ridicule oracles, and he hears Jocasta's famous comment that all men dream of sleeping with their mothers (980–83). He now rejoins the dialogue and addresses to Oedipus a series of precise questions, all of which deal with fear: Who is this woman you fear (*ekPHOBeisth'* [989])? What is your fear (*phobon*) about her (991)? Can you tell what the oracle said (993)? Is it your shrinking (*oknôn*) from this that kept you away from Corinth (1000)? He learns, that is, exactly which fears to address. Oedipus will be putty in his hands.

The Corinthian's own knowledge appears to be minimal. He is aware that Oedipus' father is dead, but either does not know or will not say precisely how Polybus died. He knows there is speculation Oedipus will gain the throne, but evades the question as to who, if anyone, sent him to announce that possibility. His questions are so designed that he himself can give the appropriate answer: the answer he thinks Oedipus wants. It is here the Corinthian makes one crucial mistake: he offers to release Oedipus from his fears. What he does not understand, but we are beginning to understand, is that Oedipus really wants his fears confirmed, not set to rest. Like the Sphinx, Oedipus is challenging people to destroy him.

Again we must ask why this anonymous man has come to Thebes and why he is so eager to play Oedipus to the Sphinx of Oedipus' fears. He gives us and Oedipus a clear answer (1002–6):

> CORINTHIAN: Since I came in all good will, my prince,
>   why have I not yet freed you from this fear (*phobou*)?
> OEDIPUS: And I'd (*kai mên*) reward you well if you still could.
> CORINTHIAN: And I (*kai mên*) came here primarily for this:
>   the hope that I'd do well when you came home.

The Corinthian echoes Oedipus' words to show that a reward is exactly what he had in mind.

We might again compare some translations that subtly redirect the text of the last two lines. Dudley Fitts and Robert Fitzgerald make the messenger more courteously self-concerned:

> I had that in mind, I will confess: I thought
> I could count on you when you returned to Corinth.[21]

Kenneth Cavander also mutes the Corinthian's motivation:

> I had hoped for reward
> When you returned as king of your palace at Corinth.[22]

H. D. F. Kitto, Peter Arnott, and Robert Fagles all stay closer to the Greek. Here is Kitto's version:

> It was the chief cause of my coming here
> That your return might bring me some advantage.[23]

Jocasta's instinct that the newcomer wanted something was, it seems, correct. But in the excitement following his announcement, he and his "good" news about Oedipus' possible appointment as tyrant of Corinth are simply forgotten. Since Jocasta and Oedipus, after the initial announcement of Polybus' death, have continued as if he did not even exist, the Corinthian must wonder whether he has lost his opportunity for getting the expected reward for his good news. He presumed—and possibly still hopes—that Oedipus might return to Corinth. But he has assessed the situation wrongly. What he thought was his "bad" news is what interests Oedipus and Jocasta. His "good" news, as we have seen, never reaches Oedipus at all. When Jocasta passes on his words to Oedipus, she does not mention that "rumor has it he will be made tyrant" at Corinth. Perhaps she does not consider this important information. Perhaps she does not want to leave Thebes for Corinth. The Corinthian, we noted, seems irritated when Oedipus demands the news about Polybus' death. Here is Oedipus' question and his response in lines 957–59:

> OEDIPUS: What's your word, stranger? Tell me this yourself!
> CORINTHIAN: If I must first say this part of my news,
>   Know well that he has passed on through death's door.

Knox also catches the mood in his translation:

> If that's what you want to hear first, here it is,
> a plain statement: Polybus is dead and gone.[24]

"What would the messenger have mentioned second?" Dawe asks. He, and we, can only speculate. A reasonable assumption is that it would pertain to Oedipus' possible future as tyrant of Corinth: what the Corinthian thought was his "good" news. "In any event," Dawe adds, "he seems nettled at the insistence of his betters that he give priority to the less attractive side of his message."[25]

The Corinthian must get Oedipus' attention again. He must persuade

Oedipus if not to return to Corinth, at least to provide some tangible token of gratitude. He has given his news, and no one has even thanked him for it. What other resources has he?

Instead of slinking away, then, the Corinthian waits for an opportunity to draw attention to himself again. As he listens to the conversation between Oedipus and Jocasta, he finds such a moment. And he carefully pursues his questions so he can determine precisely what news he must deliver to achieve the results he wants. He gathers, as he listens, that to persuade Oedipus, he must first dispel Oedipus' fear of marrying his mother, who lives at Corinth. He is possibly aware of the old accusation of the drunk at the banquet suggesting that Oedipus is a suppositious child. Hence his eagerness to establish which woman Oedipus fears, even though he seems to know Merope is Polybus' wife. But he also faces a rather deeper problem: that Jocasta seems uninterested in going to Corinth, and Oedipus never asks the logical question: "Do I become tyrant of Corinth now that Polybus is dead?"

The Corinthian therefore does not raise the matter of the tyranny again. It is irrelevant until other obstacles are removed. He has heard Jocasta fail to convince Oedipus that fears of marrying his mother are irrational. The only viable alternative he has is to persuade Oedipus that Merope is not his mother. He will thereby neutralize Oedipus' fear of returning to Corinth. But more is needed. To gain his reward he must induce Oedipus to leave Thebes—a thought that does not seem to have crossed Oedipus' mind. The obvious means is to reverse the magnetic poles of Oedipus' fear: to establish a Theban identity for Oedipus that will drive him, in fear, from Theban parents. The strategy may not work. But as he develops it, he may find a way of putting Oedipus in his debt.

Oedipus becomes, in the Corinthian's dialectic, a foundling child, and he that child's savior, who discovers the foundling and gives him to Polybus, ruler of Corinth, and a royal destiny. Oedipus' fears make the Corinthian's prospects on getting home rosier than he could have hoped when he set out. The self-seeking Corinthian and the inquisitive Oedipus are moving down different pathways to their tragic intersection. As Oedipus is trying to establish his birth, his interlocutor is trying to establish his own position as Oedipus' savior—and indeed surrogate father (whom Oedipus would want to protect from harm).

The scene proceeds (1007–26):

OEDIPUS: I'll never go where my begetters live.

CORINTHIAN: My child, you clearly don't know what you do . . .

OEDIPUS: (*interrupting*)

What, old man? Then, by the gods, teach me.

CORINTHIAN: . . . if they are why you run from coming home.

OEDIPUS: Phoebus. His words scare me. They may come true.

CORINTHIAN: Worried you'll violate those who gave you life?

OEDIPUS: You're wise, old man. It's my eternal fear.

CORINTHIAN: So you don't know there's no just cause for fright?

OEDIPUS: Why not, if I was really born their child?

CORINTHIAN: Polybus was nothing to you by birth.

OEDIPUS: Polybus did not father me, you say?

CORINTHIAN: No more, no less, than this man standing here.

OEDIPUS: You're nothing to me. How could he equal you?

CORINTHIAN: Well, he did not beget you, nor did I.

OEDIPUS: Why did he legally name (*ônomazeto*) me as his child?

CORINTHIAN: You were a gift. He took you from my hands.

OEDIPUS: Got me from other hands, yet loved me so?

CORINTHIAN: His previous childlessness persuaded him.

OEDIPUS: You gave me to him? You bought me, got me by chance?

CORINTHIAN: I found you in the vales of Cithaeron.

The Corinthian begins by telling Oedipus that Polybus was his father "no more, no less, than this man standing here" (1018). He thus establishes two themes. First, and most obvious, he denies Polybus' paternity. He negates the importance, if you will, of the news he has just brought and in so doing reestablishes the fear he has just abolished. Oedipus, if he believes the Corinthian, must once again fear he may kill his father. Second, by saying Polybus was Oedipus' father "no more, no less, than this man standing here," he establishes himself on a curious, if negative, par with Polybus. It may seem just casual cheekiness, but it is a theme to which he returns shortly, as we will see. And it is (as usual) the second part of the double statement that catches Oedipus' attention.

Oedipus takes the restoration of fear with amazing calm. His calm, I submit, arises from his long-standing fear that Polybus was not his father. The Corinthian simply confirms what Oedipus already fears. What is, however,

particularly odd is that Oedipus registers no verbal reaction to the place in
which the Corinthian claims he found Oedipus: Cithaeron, the mountain
wilderness around Thebes. For this assertion establishes an ominous connection between Oedipus and Thebes and ought, one would think, to make him
worry about the possibility that Jocasta is his mother. But if that thought
does arise in his mind, it finds no immediate overt expression. For here is his
reaction (1027–29):

> OEDIPUS: Might I know why you traveled to this place?
> CORINTHIAN: I used to watch my flocks there on the hills.
> OEDIPUS: You were a shepherd, a migrant, hired hand?

Again we see Oedipus' contempt for the Corinthian's lowly status, and
with it the beginnings of a new fear that seems to sting Oedipus—or rather
a fear he has not hitherto voiced: that he himself may be of ignoble origin.
His fears cannot be lightened by the paternal tone the Corinthian now
adopts toward him, as he claims to have been, more or less, his surrogate
father (1030): "My son, I was your savior at that time." Oedipus' fear of being
baseborn makes him later insist to Jocasta, with some bitterness, that he must
investigate his birth, even though he may turn out to be of humble stock and
thus socially "beneath" her (1062ff.).

Oedipus' immediate response to the Corinthian's disclosure is not, as
we and the Corinthian might expect, renewed fear of marrying his mother
or even of killing his father, but fear that his father may prove no more than
the social equal of a peasant like the Corinthian. Oedipus asks haughtily:
"You're (a) nothing (*mêdeni*) to me. How could he equal you?" (1019). The
anonymous messenger neither takes offense at the insult nor backs off from
the albeit negative parity he has ventured: "Well, he did not beget you, nor
did I" (1020). Oedipus retorts: "Why did he legally name (*ônomazeto*) me as
his child?" (1021).

Oedipus poses a good rhetorical counter-question. As Sophocles' audience no doubt knew, to name a child is to accept it as your legitimate offspring
under Athenian law. . . . How does the Corinthian respond to Oedipus'
objection? To cite Dawe, "The messenger does not answer Oedipus' question
precisely in the terms in which it is put."[26] In fact he does not answer it at all.
He declares (1022): "You were a gift. He took you from my hands." Oedipus

might well protest this statement for several reasons. It suggests the unlikely scenario that Polybus was the principal family member involved in accepting a foundling as his son, and further that *both* Polybus *and* Merope were lying when they insisted they were Oedipus' parents. A woman may be able to dupe her husband into thinking that he is the biological father of a suppositious child. But a woman can hardly be duped into thinking she has given birth to a child that someone had just presented to her husband. Further, as Harrison notes: "The finder of an exposed child might at his discretion treat it as slave or free, but he acquired no rights over it and he could not even adopt it, since adoption of a minor was a reciprocal transaction between the adopter and the adopted child's father or his representative."[27] It would have been very hard, certainly by Athenian law, to make a foundling one's heir. Pericles found it hard enough to get citizenship for his illegitimate son by Aspasia, as Plutarch points out (*Pericles* 32).

Yet Oedipus does not for a moment question the substance or plausibility of what the Corinthian says. Nor does he take further note of his increasingly personal and paternal pose. When the Corinthian said Polybus was no more Oedipus' father than he was, he used an almost conventional cliché of distancing. But now he is suggesting equality of *closeness* as well as equality of distance: *he* gave Oedipus to Polybus. Oedipus' shocked reaction, however, has already been spent on the first suggested parallel between Polybus and the Corinthian stranger. He already appears absolutely convinced he is not Polybus' child, although not a shred of evidence or even hearsay has been adduced to support the contention. An unknown man simply announces that he gave Oedipus to Polybus when Oedipus was a baby.

Oedipus does no more than venture a question about Polybus' motivation, addressed more to himself than to the Corinthian: "Got me from other hands, yet loved me so?" (1023). The Corinthian supplies the logical answer: Polybus had no children of his own (1024). But Oedipus' reaffirmation of the intensity of Polybus' love should remind us that he may well have died because he so missed his son, as Oedipus imagined, for a fleeting moment, at lines 969–70.

A Baby Found or Given?

The ease with which the anonymous newcomer convinces Oedipus that he is not Polybus' child and insinuates himself into a quasi-paternal role is explicable in terms of what Oedipus has already told Jocasta—and thus the audience—of his old, lingering doubts about his legitimacy. A similarly anonymous drunk once declared at a banquet that Oedipus was a supposititious child passed off on his father, a *plastos . . . patri* (780). We see immediately, however, that the Corinthian does not confirm at all what the drunk at the banquet said. For the messenger says he gave the child to *Polybus*, not to Merope, with his own hands, whereas the drunk apparently told Oedipus he was a child his mother had passed off on his father. There is, then, a fundamental, but curiously unnoticed, contradiction between the two stories.

Oedipus, still governed by fear, not by reason, ignores the inconsistency and more readily believes an anonymous Corinthian than Jocasta, just as he more readily believed an anonymous drunk than Polybus and Merope. In both cases, he proves the correctness of Jocasta's observation that he believes the person who frightens him. He accepts, then, that he is a foundling with astonishing lack of resistance. He seeks no further assurance as to the Corinthian's identity or any corroboration of his claims. He simply asks how he obtained the child to give to Polybus (1025): "You gave me to him? You bought me, got me by chance?" This is a critical moment for both men. The Corinthian, no matter how keen to advance his own situation, cannot claim to be Oedipus' father since he has already said that Polybus is not Oedipus' father "any more than I." He also sees Oedipus' horror that he might be ignobly born and knows that in the event Oedipus accepted such an identity, he would not return to Corinth for fear of killing his newly discovered father. So he says (1026): "I found (*heurôn*) you in the vales of Cithaeron."

We must not be so distracted by this decisive location of the infant Oedipus in Theban territory that we overlook the Corinthian's claim to have *found* the child. A few lines later he will say the child was *given* to him (1038–40):

> CORINTHIAN: I don't know. But he who gave you to me will.
> OEDIPUS: You got me from someone, you didn't find me?
> CORINTHIAN: No, a nomad shepherd gave you to me.

To find something and to be given something are not the same thing. Sophocles' translators have recognized this. But some of their responses have been amazing and rob the reader of the chance to see the first step in a vital contradiction. Cavander shifts the lie away from the Corinthian by not having him actually say he found the child and by attributing the verb of "finding" to Oedipus:

> OEDIPUS: So you gave me to . . . Had you bought me for your slave
>   Where did you find me?
> MESSENGER: You were lying beneath the trees
>   In a glade upon Cithaeron.

Fitts and Fitzgerald use "came upon" instead of "found" in their version, giving the impression the Corinthian is avoiding saying that he found the child. Again the verb of "finding" is given to Oedipus.

> OEDIPUS: What of you? Did you buy me? Did you find me by chance?
> MESSENGER: I came upon you in the crooked pass of Kithairon.[28]

Robert Fagles, instead of "found," uses "stumbled upon":

> OEDIPUS: And you, did you . . .
>   buy me? find me by accident?
> MESSENGER: I stumbled on you.
>   Down by the woody flanks of Mount Cithaeron.[29]

Dawe notes the problem and comments: "The messenger is not as forthcoming as he might be, especially with *empôlesas* ["did you buy me?"] in the line before, with its suggestion of things changing hands from one person to another."[30] Dawe is understanding the problem. The Corinthian is lying either now when he says he found the child, or later, when he says he was given the child. He may also be lying when he identifies Oedipus as that foundling.

Etymologizing an Identity

It is not hard to suggest the Corinthian's motive for stressing his own role in saving the infant: the more he does to save the child, the more, he might suppose, he builds a debt of gratitude in Oedipus. So let us examine the interchanges preceding the change in the Corinthian's role from one who found the child to one who was given the child (1031–37):

> OEDIPUS: What ails me as you take me in your hands?
> CORINTHIAN: The ankles of your feet should witness that!
> OEDIPUS: Dear me, why mention that old pain of mine?
> CORINTHIAN: I know where the feet are pierced, untie the knot.
> OEDIPUS: Since childhood I've been cursed by that course scourge.
> CORINTHIAN: Hence your name, recording what occurred.
> OEDIPUS: By the gods!
>   By mother? father? Speak!

The messenger claims responsibility for unfastening Oedipus' feet, which, he says, were pinned together (1034)—something he is more likely to have done if he found the child than if the child was given him. More important, he etymologizes Oedipus' name as OIDiPOUS, "swollen foot" (1036), to substantiate his claim and to establish his own connection with the *naming* of the child. Oedipus replies, as Pietro Pucci has noted, with an anagram: *DEINOn g'ONEIDOs* (1035)—"a formidable slander," or, to catch the anagram, "a COURSE SCOURgE," as I translate it here.[31] . . .

The Corinthian's etymology of Oedipus' name, however, is uniquely his. The play on *OIDein*, "swell," and *POUS*, "foot," now taken for granted, first occurs here. Jocasta in Euripides' *Phoenician Women* 21 reuses the "swollen foot" etymology for Oedipus' name, as does Apollodorus (3.5.7). So does Seneca's Corinthian messenger, who reproduces the name Oedipus from a Latin anagram (which my translation can only crudely approximate) as well as a translation of the Greek etymology (Seneca, *Oedipus* 811–13):

> OEDIPUS: Now say what distinguishing marks were on my body.
> OLD MAN: The trace of footprints pierced with steel:
>   From the swelling you got your name and from your
>   PITEOUS feet (*vitIO PEDUM*).

Similarly, modern commentators, almost without exception, also detect play on *OIDa*, "know," and *POUS*, "foot," in *OIDipous*.[32] Although it may still seem ridiculous to many of us that a man's fate is in his name, the idea of the *omen* within the *nomen* ("name")—or, as the Greeks put it, *onoma* ("name") is an *ornis* ("bird of omen")—is commonplace in antiquity.[33] . . . However, Oedipus seems not to have given any previous thought to the possibility that his "true" etymological name might be "swollen foot." For all the previous etymological plays on Oedipus' name up to this point in the play have been based on taking the *OID* element in his name as "know," not "swollen." For the first time Oedipus is confronted with an etymology of his name that explains something about him that would have been evident at his birth. The "knowing the feet" etymology, which encapsulates his verbal victory over the Sphinx, is an etymology suited to his *adult* life, not his existence as a child.

Oedipus' concern for the proper way in which the child was *named* (*ônomazeto*) by his parents we, and presumably the Corinthian, have already noted (1021). To accept the definition that a name gives is to accept the definition and indeed the destiny imposed by the namer. To name someone, then, is to set limits on, to define—even destroy—that person, not simply to accept him officially as one's child at the Amphidromia. But in *Oedipus* there is a still further significance in the notions of "name" and "naming," as we will see more plainly if we adduce Socrates' observations in *Cratylus* 421A: "The word *onoma* ("name") seems to be put together from a phrase, as if saying 'the *onoma* is the being for which the search occurs.' You could recognize it more clearly in the form *onomaston*, which clearly means *on hou masma estin*: 'the being for which the search is.'" In Sophocles' play, that being is Oedipus.

By this point the Corinthian who provides the definition for the name, the identity for which Oedipus has been searching, has, as we have noted, begun to assume a fatherly tone toward Oedipus: "My son, I was your savior at that time" (1030). Appropriately so, for he is in the process of fathering Oedipus' sense of his identity. Paradoxically, of course, he is also, albeit unwittingly, about to become Oedipus' destroyer. Yet this in itself should be no surprise. The notion that the definer is also the destroyer is commonplace in both Greek and Latin literature. In Statius' *Thebaid* (8.91–93), for example, the prophet Amphiaraus describes the god of death as both the great *finitor rerum*, "limiter, definer of things," and the great *sator*, "creator."[34]

In this connection it is worth nothing another passage from Plato's *Cratylus* (428D) in which Socrates makes the following remark to Cratylus, after the latter has suggested, on the basis of Socrates' etymologizing skill, that he is inspired and able to give oracles (*chresmôidein*): "Even I myself have been overawed by my wisdom for a long time now—and I am distrustful of it. It seems proper to me, then, to take another look at what I am saying. For being the victim of self-deception is the roughest lot of all. In such circumstances the person who is going to deceive us is never even a tiny distance away, but always with us. How can this not be formidable (*deinon*)?"

We can be carried away, Socrates warns, by our apparent etymologizing skill, which enables us to make language mean anything we want it to mean. So Socrates, after having a wonderful and witty etymological romp, stops to question and reexamine. But Oedipus does not. He accepts the Corinthian's etymological explanation of his name as "swollen foot" without a quibble, even though it is by no means the only available "etymology" of his name. In fact, he reacts with anger directed against the mother and father who subjected him to the cruelty of exposure—and, perhaps, the ironic indignity of the name (1037–38):

> OEDIPUS: By the gods!
>   By mother? father? Speak!
> CORINTHIAN: I don't know (*oid'*). He who (*ho dous*) gave you to me will.

The first part of the messenger's reply is consistent with his claims so far and with the wordplay: "I don't know." He knows only the "where," not the "who," in Oedipus' identity. The second part is more than just inconsistent; it is a bombshell: "he who gave you to me will" (1038). But it does, curiously, echo the *OIDa POU* sound-plays from the beginning of the Corinthian's first entrance: *ouk OID' ho DOUS*.

Why does the Corinthian abruptly change his story? He no longer is the man who *found* the child; he is the man who was *given* the child. His child-finding, like his news, comes at second hand. Oedipus, for once, spots the inconsistency (1039–40):

> OEDIPUS: You got me from someone, you didn't find me?
> CORINTHIAN: No, a nomad shepherd gave you to me.

But Oedipus does not pursue the issue. He is keener to track down the supposed other person than to find out why the Corinthian misled him before.

The Corinthian's admission that he did not find the child weakens, but does not delete the memory of, his claim to have been the child's immediate savior. It is a tactical, rhetorical withdrawal which may be prompted by his heightened awareness of Oedipus' fear that he is ignobly born. Oedipus is unlikely to reward an informant who finds him as a monarch's son and leaves him the child of an unknown individual, possibly a commoner. By changing his role from discoverer of the foundling to its receiver, the Corinthian reopens the inquiry his previous claim, "I found," cut off. He also readmits a chance of the foundling's nobility, and thus of Oedipus' thanks, by connecting the donor with royalty. The problem is, of course, the lowly identity of the supposed donor, as we will see. And Oedipus now wants to know the identity of this donor (1041–42):

> OEDIPUS: Who? Could you describe who this man was?
> CORINTHIAN: He'd a post with Laios (*LaiOUDÊPOUtis*). Yes, that was his name (*ônomazeto*).

Again, the Corinthian is evasive. This is not, of course, the first time we have seen him respond so indirectly. We have only to recall his answer to Jocasta's question: "who do you come from?" Here, however, he is yet more clearly playing a strategic verbal game. The verb *ônomazeto* suggests he is identifying the person who gave him the child. But he does nothing of the sort. In this line containing a verb of naming, the only name mentioned is that of Laios. Yet the verb of naming, *ônomazeto*, has already been used twice in this scene with the sense of a name that assigns identity.

The identity the Corinthian is insinuating is that of Laios, not that of the donor. He is perhaps even including a hint of Oedipus' own name. Just as ODYSseus plays on the similarity of his name to *OUTIS*, "Noman," the Corinthian seems here to be playing on *laiOUDÊPOUtis* and OIDIPOUs, syllabically including Oedipus' name between LAIOS and Noman.[35] The best I could come up with was "He'd a post with Laios," which carries a slight echo of the name, Oedipus, but which does not contain the critical ligature of Oedipus' name and Laios'.

The Corinthian gives Oedipus the fatal chance to link himself with

Theban royalty instead of nameless peasantry. Again we may compare Euripides' *Ion*, where Ion worries about how he will be treated in Athens as the son of an alien father and an unknown mother (593–94): "I'll have this terrible curse (*oneidos*), I'll be weak, and I'll be called . . . the child of nobodies (*oudenôn*)."

We have already seen that the Corinthian is a master of verbal skills, recalling "these violent puns," as Knox describes them, with which he made his entrance, puns "suggesting a fantastic conjugation of the verb 'to know where' formed from the name of the hero who, as Teiresias told him, does not know where he is."[36] The echo of the syllable *POU* at the end of each of his first three lines emphasizes an alternative etymologizing play on Oedipus' name. And how fascinating it is that the *Corinthian* should be the one to produce it; for he will convince Oedipus not only of his name's swollen-foot etymology but of *where* he was born. The nameless man who enters not knowing where Oedipus is ends up persuading Oedipus that he *knows where* Oedipus was born.

It is not only Oedipus, then, who can play the interpreter of riddling language and scramble our perceptions. In this scene Oedipus has met his verbal match in the Corinthian, as the Sphinx met hers in Oedipus. Oedipus destroys the Sphinx by solving the riddle of the feet, even though he does not know the riddle of his own identity. The Corinthian "solves" another riddle of feet while guarding the secret of his own name. He can even match Oedipus' skill in anagrams. For it is worth noting that the Corinthian claims he found the swollen-footed child on KITHAIRON (1206)—an exact anagram in the fifth-century alphabet for the land Oedipus thought he was from: KORINTHIA (794).[37]

The Corinthian's vagueness about the name of the man who he says gave him the foundling child is odd, since he later testifies that he and this other anonymous individual spent six months a year for three years running their herds together on Mount Cithaeron (1133–39). It is not as if they had chanced on one another once and briefly. No less odd is Oedipus' own lack of curiosity about the donor's name. He lets the Corinthian's vague "someone or other from the house of Laios" suffice as a response. Perhaps the explanation lies in the fact that Oedipus considers, and the Corinthian realizes that he considers, this donor to be a "nobody." The name of Laios, an important and fearful name for Oedipus, will more obviously rivet his attention.

Two conflicting fears must now wage war in Oedipus: his fear of being lowly born, of being *Outis*, a "Nobody," himself and his fear of patricide and incest. Ironically, the former fear leads him inexorably to the conclusion that he has fulfilled the latter. Further, this tyrant who fears being lowly born lets his birth and his identity be determined and defined by two nameless herdsmen and an anonymous drunk.

Oedipus fixes on Laios' clearly stated name, not only the murky donor (1043–53):

> OEDIPUS: You mean, then, the late tyrant of this land?
> CORINTHIAN: Yes. He was a shepherd for this man.
> OEDIPUS: And is he still alive? Could I see him?
> CORINTHIAN: You local residents would know that best.
> OEDIPUS: Does anyone of you bystanders know
>   the shepherd he refers to? Have you seen
>   him in the countryside or in the town?
>   Give me a clue. It's time this came to light.
> CHORUS: I think he is no other than the one
>   you sent for from the country recently.
>   Jocasta here could tell you that quite well.

The anonymous donor was allegedly a shepherd in Laios' employ; but the Corinthian cannot say whether he is still alive. The locals, he claims, might be better able to answer (1046). So Oedipus throws the issue about the unnamed employee of Laios raised by the nameless Corinthian to the collective anonymity of the chorus. The chorus identifies the donor as the man Oedipus has recently sent for: a man who was allegedly the sole survivor of a murderous attack upon Laios, Oedipus' predecessor as ruler of Thebes. This man had made a public statement that Laios was killed by a band of robbers (*lêistai*)—a statement that must be false if Oedipus really is Laios' killer.

In sum: the Corinthian is the only "messenger" in Greek tragedy who does not have a messenger speech. He is most likely an old man who has chanced upon the news of Polybus' death, but really knows little or nothing about the circumstances or causes of his death, and has come to Thebes in the hopes of being rewarded for bringing the good news that Oedipus will probably be invited to come back to rule his homeland. He is an opportunist determined to make what he can of the rumors and gossip he has heard. When he discovers that Oedipus is not interested in returning, he seeks to manipulate him into going back by finding out what he is afraid of and reversing the magnetic poles of his fears, and by insinuating himself into a paternal role with the anxious tyrant. The consequences of his rhetorical shrewdness will be disastrous for Oedipus and ultimately for his own hopes of reward.

NOTES

1. Bernard Knox, *Oedipus at Thebes* (New Haven: Yale University Press, 1957), 184. See also Thomas Gould, *Oedipus the King: A Translation with Commentary* (Englewood Cliffs, NJ: Prentice-Hall, 1970), 63.

2. Simon Goldhill, "Exegesis: *Oedipus (R)ex*," *Arethusa* 17 (1984): 182–83.

3. Bernard Knox, *Sophocles, Oedipus the King* (New York: Washington Square Press, 1959), 62.

4. R. D. Dawe, ed., *Sophocles: Oedipus Rex* (Cambridge: Cambridge University Press, 1982), 190.

5. *Oedipus Tyrannus*, trans. and ed. Luci Berkowitz and Theodore F. Brunner (New York: Norton, 1970), 21.

6. *Sophocles: The Three Theban Plays*, trans. Robert Fagles, with introduction and notes by Bernard Knox (New York: Penguin, 1982), 212.

7. Forms of the verb *audao* generally express the idea of not necessarily well-informed talk in the *Oedipus*. In line 731, Jocasta, commenting on the report that Laios was killed at a place where three roads meet, says: "Such was the rumor (êudato) that has not yet stopped." Similarly, in line 527, the chorus, talking to Creon about accusations that he "set up" Teiresias to accuse Oedipus, comments: *êudato men tade, oida d'ou gnômêi tini* ("words were uttered to that effect. But I / don't know what reason they were based upon").

8. *Sophocles: Oedipus the King*, trans. Kenneth Cavander with an introduction by Tom Driver (San Francisco: Chandler, 1961), 29.

9. Berkowitz and Brunner, *Oedipus Tyrannus*, 21.

10. Dawe, *Oedipus*, 192.

11. The forms of the Greek demonstrative *hode* ("this," "this person") are marked in the translation to alert the reader to its double use: as a reference by the speaker to himself and as a reference by the speaker to someone standing beside him onstage. Sophocles exploits this ambiguity at a crucial juncture.

12. Dawe, *Oedipus*, 194.

13. Knox, *Oedipus at Thebes*, 143 and n. 15 (on p. 247) with the ancient sources cited there, notably Hippocrates, *Epidemics* I.26: *rhopas* ("turns") for the better or the worse; Aristotle, *Problems* I.861A uses the same expression as Sophocles' messenger in reference to the aged: *mikra . . . rhopê*; Aretaeus 3.12: "old men . . . need only a short turn (*bracheias rhopês*) for the sleep of death."

14. *Sophocles: The Oedipus Cycle*, trans. Dudley Fitts and Robert Fitzgerald (New York: Harcourt, Brace, 1965), 48.

15. Cavander, *Sophocles: Oedipus the King*, 30.

16. Peter L. Rudnytsky, *Freud and Oedipus* (New York: Columbia University Press, 1987), 6–14. For the text of Freud, see *The Standard Edition of the Complete Psychological Works of Sigmund Freud*, ed. and trans. James Strachey, 24 vols. (London: Hogarth Press, 1953–74), 4:262–63. For the sexual aspects of the eye and seeing, see Pietro Pucci's excellent "On the 'Eye' and the 'Phallos' and Other Permutabilities, in *Oedipus Rex*," in *Arktouros: Hellenic Studies Presented to Bernard M. W. Knox on the Occasion of His 65th Birthday*, ed. G. W. Bowersock, W. Burkert, and M. C. J. Putnam (New York: de Gruyter, 1979). With his observations we might compare Bronislaw Malinowski in *The Sexual Life of Savages in Northwestern Melanesia* (New York: H. Liveright, 1929), 166: "The kidneys are considered the main or middle part or trunk (*tapwana*) of that system. From them, other ducts (*wotuna*) lead to the male organ. This is the tip or point (*matala*, literally eye) of the whole system. Thus, when the eyes see an object of desire, they 'wake up,' communicate the impulse to the kidneys, which transmit it to the penis and cause an erection. Hence the eyes are the primary motive of all sexual excitement: they are 'the things of copulation.'"

17. Seneca, *Oedipus*, 797.

18. Cesare Musatti, *Artemidoro di Daldi: Dell'interpretazione de' Sogni* (Milan, 1976), 19 and n. 34; Theodor Gomperz, *Traumdeutung und Zauberei* (Vienna: Gerold, 1866). [Ellipses between sentences indicate parts of Ahl's text not reprinted here.]

19. See also my *Metaformations: Soundplay and Wordplay in Ovid and Other Classical Poets* (Ithaca, NY: Cornell University Press, 1985), chap. 1.

20. Musatti, *Artemidoro di Daldi*, 7, 19–20.

21. Fitts and Fitzgerald, *Oedipus Cycle*, 50.

22. Cavander, *Sophocles: Oedipus the King*, 31.

23. *Sophocles: Three Tragedies*, trans. H. D. F. Kitto (Oxford: Oxford University Press, 1956), 80.

24. Knox, *Oedipus the King*, 66.

25. Dawe, *Oedipus*, 193.

26. Dawe, *Oedipus*, 198, on line 1021.

27. A. R. W. Harrison, *The Law of Athens: The Family and Property* (Oxford: Clarendon Press, 1968), 71.

28. Fitts and Fitzgerald, *Oedipus Cycle*, 51.

29. *Sophocles*, trans. Robert Fagles, 219.

30. Dawe, *Oedipus*, 199, on line 1026.

31. Pucci, "On the 'Eye,'" 130; cf. Gould, *Oedipus the King*, 175.

32. See, for example, J.-P. Vernant, "Ambiguity and Reversal: On the Enigmatic Structure of *Oedipus Rex*" [reprinted in this volume], in *Sophocles' Oedipus Rex*, ed. Harold Bloom (New York: Chelsea House, 1988), 112–131; John Hay, *Oedipus Tyrannus: Lame Knowledge and the Homosporic Womb* (Washington, DC: University Press of America, 1984), 27–33.

33. See Max Sulzberger, "'Onoma Epônymon': Les noms propres chez Homère et dans la mythologie grecque," *Revue des Études Grecques* 39 (1926): 381–447.

34. In Sophocles, *Electra*, 836–41, the chorus hails Amphiaraus himself as king of the dead.

35. *Odyssey* 9.365, 408, 455, 460; for more on the echoes of Odysseus, *outis*, and Oedipus, see the next chapter [not included in this volume].

36. Knox, *Oedipus at Thebes*, 184.

37. The etymologizing plays in Plato's *Cratylus* are similarly based on the old Attic alphabet: see, for example, *Cratylus* 398C–D.

Index